THE HAMMONDS OF REDCLIFFE

James Henry Hammond at age forty-two
in portrait by William Harrison Scarborough (1849)

THE
HAMMONDS
OF
REDCLIFFE

edited by

CAROL BLESER

New York   Oxford
OXFORD UNIVERSITY PRESS
1981

Copyright © 1981 by Oxford University Press, Inc.

Library of Congress Cataloging in Publication Data
Main entry under title:

The Hammonds of Redcliffe.

Includes index.
1. Hammond family.   2. Hammond, James Henry,
1807–1864.   3. Redcliffe, S.C.   4. South Carolina
—History—Sources.   5. Family—South Carolina—
History—Sources.   I. Bleser, Carol K. Rothrock.
F273.R33   975.7′04′0922 [B]   80-26962
ISBN 0-19-502920-8   AACR1

For

Florence and Charles
Lillian and Ted
Caroline and Louise

Preface

This is the story of the Hammond family of South Carolina and of their attachment to a place, Redcliffe, their plantation home at Beech Island, South Carolina. Built by the flamboyant pre–Civil War governor and United States senator, James Henry Hammond, Redcliffe was named for the red bluff in front of the house that led steeply down to the Savannah River. For twelve decades this attractive plantation home was the emotional anchor and physical magnet for Hammond and his descendants. Four generations of Hammonds were held together by their love of Redcliffe; fortunately many of them left behind a store of candid and compelling letters.

I have selected nearly two hundred letters from three large collections of personal correspondence—over seven thousand manuscripts—to tell a continuous story of Southern life as experienced by one prominent family from the decade prior to the Civil War through that of the New Deal. Although the letters contained in this volume begin with the purchase of Redcliffe Plantation in 1855 and end with its restoration in 1938, the Introduction takes the story back to the beginning of the nineteenth century with the coming of the first Hammond to South Carolina, and the Epilogue carries the narrative forward to 1975.

James Henry Hammond (1807–1864) was one of the most successful planters in ante-bellum South Carolina. He owned over fourteen thousand acres and could ride all day on horseback without seeing another man's land. At a time when only thirty-eight families in all of Maryland, Virginia, North Carolina, and South Carolina owned more than three hundred slaves,[1] Hammond owned more than three hundred thirty. Not only one of the richest but also one of the most influential personalities in the ante-bellum South, Hammond is the central figure of the early letters. However, in 1859 a new generation comes to the fore with the courtship by the senator's eldest son, Harry, of Emily Cumming. The Cumming family of Augusta, Georgia, composed of wealthy professionals, mostly lawyers and bankers, was joined to the Hammond family on November 22, 1859, when the well-bred and highly social Emily Cumming married the scholarly Harry Hammond. It is on Emily and Harry and their descendants that the story centers after the death of James Henry Hammond.

The family letters of the Civil War and Reconstruction era provide fascinating insights into the reactions of the participants to disaster on both the battlefield and the home front; however, the special significance of this collection rests on its abundance of personal correspondence in the post-Reconstruction era. These late nineteenth-century letters, many of them by and to women, paint a vivid picture of the everyday activities of an eminent plantation family that had to adjust as best it could to a new social order. Although James Henry Hammond's descendants are revealed by their letters to be thoughtful and intelligent, they foundered in the hard conditions of the postwar South. The family correspondence suggests, however, that the hard condition of being the sons and daughters of James Henry had as much to do with their fate as did the defeat of the Confederacy.

The story gains another dimension when, in 1897, Katharine Hammond, daughter of Emily and Harry, marries Dr. John Sedgwick Billings of New York, whose versatile father, Dr. John Shaw Billings, was the designer of Johns Hopkins Hospital and the first Director of the New York Public Library. The extensive correspondence around the turn of the century between the Billings family in New York City and the Hammond family at Redcliffe is a study of contrasting life styles. The final installment records the attraction of Redcliffe for the son of Katharine Hammond and John Sedgwick Billings, John Shaw Billings II, who became the second in command in Henry Luce's Time-Life empire, but could not escape the lure of Beech Island.

John Shaw Billings II devoted much of his life to collecting his fam-

---

1. Elizabeth Merritt, *James Henry Hammond 1807–1864* (Baltimore: The Johns Hopkins Press, 1923), p. 116.

ily's voluminous correspondence, and on his death the collection was deposited in the South Caroliniana Library in Columbia. These personal papers, spanning nearly a century and a half, offer the historian a remarkable supply of raw data in the field of family history—and the history of the family has of late become a field of remarkable vitality. A new generation of social historians, influenced by the concepts and techniques of social scientists, has produced a number of seminal works. These historians are seeking to deal not just with "great men and great events" but with the whole fabric of society—how all people worked and wept, married and mourned, lived and died. The study of the family is integral to this work, for domestic concerns weigh far more heavily on most individuals than the problems of state. Thus to understand a society one must seek to understand what concerned most of its people most of the time.

In exploring the influence that the family played in shaping the character, values, and institutions of society, modern scholars have done studies that surveyed hundreds of years of family history. One example is the pioneering work of Philippe Ariés on childhood, originally published in France in 1960 and translated into English as *Centuries of Childhood* in 1962. Others include Peter Laslett, author of *The World We Have Lost*, Edward Shorter, *The Making of the Modern Family*, and Lawrence Stone's monumental study, *The Family, Sex and Marriage in England 1500–1800*. Laslett's study, which sought to reconstruct through the quantification of data from parish records the lives of seventeenth-century English people of all classes, stimulated other historians with a similar purpose to computerize census records, church membership lists, tax records, deeds, wills, and inventories. In the United States, Philip Greven used town and church records to reconstitute several generations of families in the community of Andover, Massachusetts. His book, *Four Generations*, has become a model for the use of historical demography to arrive at perspectives of the American family under changing social conditions.[2]

Another approach to the study of family history has been to concentrate as Ariés did on specific parts of the life cycle—on infancy, childhood, youth, and old age. For example, Greven's *The Protestant Tem-*

2. Most of the work in American historical demography, however, has been published as journal-length articles. A recent book that seeks to bring together a number of these essays is *Studies in American Historical Demography*, edited by Maris A. Vinovskis.

perament, is a study of child-rearing practices in early America; and
Lewis Perry's *Childhood, Marriage and Reform: Henry Clarke Wright
1797–1870* explores the relationship between child-rearing and the rise
of a nineteenth-century radical reformer. Two other valuable works of
this genre are Joseph F. Kett's *Rites of Passage: Adolescence in America
1790 to the Present;* and David Hackett Fischer's *Growing Old in
America.* [3]

The present work, benefiting from this remarkably large collection
of family letters, traces in detail the history of just one family over four
generations. It has been possible to present a dramatic and coherent
story, bringing out the intra-family dynamics, the ties between husbands
and wives, brothers and sisters, and parents and children, as well as the
especially strong bonds between mothers and daughters, all following a
fluent, natural, narrative line. While the Hammonds alone cannot represent broad trends in the American past, they can give a clear picture of
family relationships, friendships, and customs, thus illuminating the
culture and society of which they were a part. The Hammond family
history, while on the one hand unique, on the other hand is more than
the story of one family, for it casts in high relief the social history of a
whole class over an entire century. The letters of the Hammonds enable
the reader to recapture a way of life that is now gone forever.

The criterion for the selection of letters to be included in this work
has been the relevance of the correspondence to the Hammond family
narrative. Although I have let the letters, and their occasionally irregular spellings of words and names, stand much as they are to preserve
their textual integrity, I have in some instances adjusted the punctuation
to modern usage. To prevent misunderstanding, I have without notice
to the reader introduced a pronoun, or a conjunction, or an article.
Omissions, though kept to a minimum, are sometimes made necessary
by extraneous or overly repetitious material, and are indicated in the
text by ellipsis points.

3. See also *Transitions,* a volume edited by Tamara K. Hareven which contains ten essays on the
family and the life course including patterns of timing of marriages, children's education, women's
participation in the working force, and the transition into old age as it is related to family structure.

Acknowledgments

It is a pleasure to acknowledge the kind assistance of many people who made this book possible. I especially wish to thank the Hammond-Bryan-Cumming family for writing and for safekeeping a long series of warm and intimate letters, since these communications provided the fabric from which a narrative could be cut. John Shaw Billings was an invaluable resource. Without the information contained in scrapbooks, letters, diaries, and genealogies amassed by him, my study of the Hammonds at Redcliffe would have required twice the number of years in pursuit of the more obscure persons, places, and events mentioned in the exchange of letters, North and South. As it is, I have spent four years on the people in this book and now at the conclusion of this association I feel bereft.

I am indebted to Allen Stokes, Manuscript Director of the South Caroliniana Library at the University of South Carolina for bringing the Hammond-Bryan-Cumming Family Papers to my attention, and for making my stay at the Library pleasurable as well as fruitful. His sustained interest and valuable assistance cannot be exaggerated, and I owe him more gratitude than can be expressed here. Mr. Les Inabinet, Director of the South Caroliniana Library, supported the project from its inception, cooperated in facilitating the gathering of the research materials, and encouraged me when the collection, so vast in size, threatened to overwhelm me. I am most appreciative too for the aid of Mrs. Marlene Sipes, and, indeed, for the support of the entire staff of the South Caroliniana Library. I wish also to thank the staff of the

South Carolina Historical Society, especially the director, Gene Waddell, and the archivist, David Moltke-Hansen, and the staff of the South Carolina Department of Archives and History, in particular, the director, Charles Lee, the associate director, Charles Lesser, and the reference archivist, Wylma Wates. In addition, I would like to thank the staffs of the Augusta (Georgia) Public Library, the Augusta College Library, the University of South Carolina Library, the Duke University Library, the University of North Carolina Library at Chapel Hill, the Columbia University Library, the New York Public Library, the Library of Congress, the National Archives, the Colgate University Library, and the Bellport (New York) Memorial Library.

Four colleagues, Eugene Genovese of the University of Rochester, Frederick Heath of Winthrop College, Kenneth Stampp of the University of California, Berkeley, and Wylma Wates, Reference Archivist at the South Carolina Department of History and Archives, invested much time in reading the manuscript, and this study benefited from their keen criticism and graceful recommendations. Moreover, Professor Genovese for fifteen years has been a source of strength. My debt to him is extraordinarily large.

I should like to express appreciation to Professor Drew Gilpin Faust of the University of Pennsylvania who shared with me an all-consuming interest in the Hammonds and with whom I have exchanged ideas and information. Her wisdom has been of inestimable value.

Two students, Ann Marcus of Colgate University and Harriet Thogorsen of the University of South Carolina, helped enormously by editing school letters of Julia and Katharine Hammond at, respectively, Harvard Annex and Johns Hopkins Training School of Nursing. Their work was made better by having been overseen by Professor George Rogers of the University of South Carolina, an esteemed historian, a highly acclaimed editor, and my dear friend. Thirteen Colgate students accompanied me to the South Caroliniana Library for the January term of 1979, expecting that South Carolina would be a warm haven from the snowbelt of upstate New York. Though the climate was less than balmy, they did successfully identify formerly unfathomable persons and events, and now they expect to find their names cited here; in this, they shall not be disappointed: David Balmuth, Elizabeth Bensinger, Robert Bickford, John Fockler, Jr., Patrick Geraghty, Joseph Goldstein, Philip Henson, Susan Holme, Arthur Marshall, Jr., Michael Stevens, Edward Streeter, Peter Thomas, and Michael Wilder.

My gratitude goes also to Michael Foley and his associates at the South Carolina Department of Parks, Recreation and Tourism for permitting me to visit Redcliffe whenever the need arose, even on Saturdays.

A special note of thanks to my friend, John G. Sproat, Chairman of the University of South Carolina History Department, who believed in this book long before anyone else and who demonstrated his faith in me and in it by inviting me to be the department's visiting professor in American history in the fall of 1976.

My personal thanks go to Virginia Sperl, Assitant Director of the Dowling College Library, Oakdale, New York, for generously expending time and expertise on proofreading and copyediting text and annotations, far beyond the call of friendship. Frederick Heath deserves additional recognition for his willingness on endless occasions to read letters and to check footnotes.

I owe a very special acknowledgment to James Henry Billings. A great-grandson of James Henry Hammond, he wholeheartedly endorsed that I write only the truth about his family, and spent numerous hours sharing his recollections with me even when these memories brought him pain or cast unflattering light upon the past.

Many other persons liberally gave of their time for interviews. They are all acknowledged in the footnotes, but I should like to add here a special word of appreciation to Mrs. Leslie Helm of Augusta and Mrs. Katharine Suber of Jackson, South Carolina.

I wish to extend a personal note of thanks to Kenneth Stampp for his special wisdom which goes much beyond the reading of this manuscript, and to Professors Willie Lee Rose and Anne Firor Scott, who have been a great source of encouragement to all women in the field of Southern history.

My thanks also to Sheldon Meyer for thinking this study worthy of an Oxford University Press imprimatur, to Curtis Church for imparting sharp editorial wisdom, and to Margaret Joyner for her fine book design. I had only one typist, Pat Ryan, and she rendered important assistance by typing and retyping the manuscript. To Rosalie Hiam, departmental secretary, I am indebted for favors too numerous to mention, and to Elisabeth M. Christian, a Colgate student who proofread both text and notes through all drafts and proof stages, goes my deepest gratitude.

No list of acknowledgments could be complete without my citing the following persons: Richard Shapiro, Noah Levin, Martin Colman, and Lionel Cohen, to whom I am most grateful for support at crucial times.

I am grateful for a Newberry Library fellowship in 1978, a sabbatical leave from Colgate in 1977–1978, and a Colgate Research Council grant.

Illustrations and maps have been provided by the South Caroliniana Library, with the exception of the frontispiece, which is used through the courtesy of the University Archives, University of South Carolina.

Finally I should like to acknowledge the efforts of my husband, Edward. In my first book I credited him with listening critically, drawing maps, and forbearance. This time he did much more, lavishing his attention on the Hammonds and their correspondence and seemingly never tiring of them or of Redcliffe. Our son, Gerald, who wanted to be declared co-author, must settle for finding his name on this page. To them go my love and appreciation.

With all this assistance, the errors should be few. If some do remain, I suppose I must reluctantly assume full responsibility.

Bellport, New York   C.B.
September 1980

Contents

Cast of Characters

The brother of James Henry Hammond,
Marcus Claudius Marcellus Hammond (the "Major") (1814–1876),
    married (1842)
Harriet Pamela Davies (1821–1880).
    They had seven children, among whom were two daughters:
        Katherine Spann (Kate) (b. 1843) and
        Anne Sarah (1846–1927).

The father of Emily Cumming (Hammond),
Henry Harford Cumming (1799–1866), married (1824)
Julia Ann Bryan (Julia A. Cumming) (1803–1879).
    They had eight children:
        Annie Maria Cumming (Hall) (1826–1855),
        Alfred (1829–1910),
        Julien (1830–1864),
        Thomas William (1831–1889),
        Emily Cumming (Hammond) (1834–1911),
        Joseph Bryan (1836–1922),
        Harford Montgomery (1838–1872), and
        Maria Bryan Cumming (Lamar) (1844–1873).

The Second Generation
    James Henry (Harry) Hammond (1832–1916) married (1859)
    Emily Cumming (Emily C. Hammond) (1834–1911).
        They had five children:
            Julia Bryan (1860–1935),
            Katharine Fitzsimons (1867–1925),
            Henry Cumming (1868–1961),
            Christopher Cashel Fitzsimons (Kit) (1870–1946), and
            Alfred Cumming (Alf) (1873–1962).

The brother of Harry Hammond,
Edward Spann Hammond (1834–1921), married (1861)
Marcella Morris (d. 1878), and married (1882)
Laura Hanson Dunbar Brown (d. 1928).

The brother of Harry Hammond,
Paul Fitzsimons Hammond (1838–1887), married (1858)
Loula Comer (1838–1914).

The sister of Harry Hammond,
Katherine (Catty, Cattie) Hammond (1840–1882), married (1861)
James Gregg (d. 1876), and married (1878)
William E. McCoy.
  They had no children.

The sister of Harry Hammond,
Elizabeth (Betty) Hammond (1849–1941), married (1871)
William Raiford Eve (d. 1916)
  They had twelve children.

The brother of Emily C. Hammond,
Joseph Bryan Cumming (1836–1922), married (1860)
Katharine Jane Hubbell (1838–1921).

The sister of Emily C. Hammond,
Maria Bryan Cumming (1844–1873), married (1863)
DeRosset Lamar (1842–1886).

The Third Generation
  Katharine Hammond (1867–1925) married (1897)
  John Sedgwick Billings (1869–1928).
    They had three children:
      John Shaw Billings (1898–1975),
      James Henry Hammond Billings (1901–   ), and
      Julian Cumming Billings (1904–1906).
  John Sedgwick Billings after Katharine's death married (1925)
  Josephine Long Toering.

  The sister of Katharine Hammond,
  Julia Bryan Hammond (1860–1935), married (1911)
  James Richards (d. 1934).
    They had no children.

The brother of Katharine Hammond,
Henry Cumming Hammond (1868–1961), did not marry.

A cousin of Katharine Hammond,
Maria Lamar (1869–1957), married (1890)
Frank Miller, and married (1902)
William Penn Duvall.

The Fourth Generation
   John Shaw Billings II (1898–1975) married (1924)
   Frederica Washburn Wade (1901–1963).
      They had one child:
         Frederica Wade Billings II (1926–1929).
   He later married (1963)
   Elise Lake Chase (1893–   ).

The brother of John Shaw Billings,
James Henry Hammond Billings, married (1928)
Gladys Rice Saltonstall, married (1946)
Augusta Poe Agnew, and married (1958)
Carly Beaumiller.

KEY TO THE CORRESPONDENCE

The superscript character at the end of each letter's title line indicates the collection and the depository in which it may be found.

b Hammond-Bryan-Cumming Family Papers, South Caroliniana Library, Columbia, South Carolina

c James Henry Hammond Papers, The Library of Congress, Washington, D.C.

f The William Hawkins Ferris Manuscripts, Rare Book and Manuscript Library, Columbia University, New York, New York

g Governors' Papers, South Carolina Department of Archives and History, Columbia, South Carolina

h James Henry Hammond Papers, South Caroliniana Library, Columbia, South Carolina

j John Shaw Billings and Frederica Wade Billings Papers, South Caroliniana Library, Columbia, South Carolina

s *The Letters of William Gilmore Simms*, edited by Oliphant, Odell, and Eaves, University of South Carolina Press

LIST OF ABBREVIATIONS USED IN THE FOOTNOTES AND BIBLIOGRAPHY

CU Rare Book and Manuscript Library, Columbia University, New York, New York

Duke Duke University Library, Durham, North Carolina

ECH Emily C. Hammond

ESH	Edward Spann Hammond
HBC	Hammond-Bryan-Cumming
HH	Harry Hammond
JBH	Julia B. Hammond
JHH	James Henry Hammond
LC	The Manuscript Division, The Library of Congress, Washington, D.C.
LCH	Loula Comer Hammond
MCMH	Marcus Claudius Marcellus Hammond
NYPL	The New York Public Library, New York, New York
SCDAH	South Carolina Department of Archives and History, Columbia, South Carolina
SCHS	South Carolina Historical Society, Charleston, South Carolina
SCL	South Caroliniana Library, University of South Carolina, Columbia, South Carolina
SHC	Southern Historical Collection, University of North Carolina, Chapel Hill, North Carolina

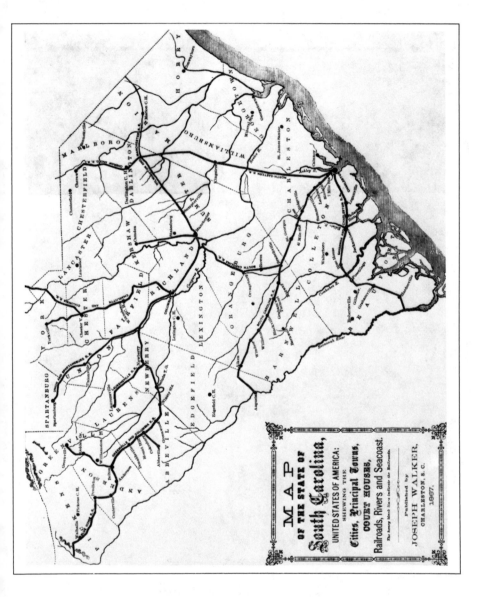

Map of the State of South Carolina, 1867

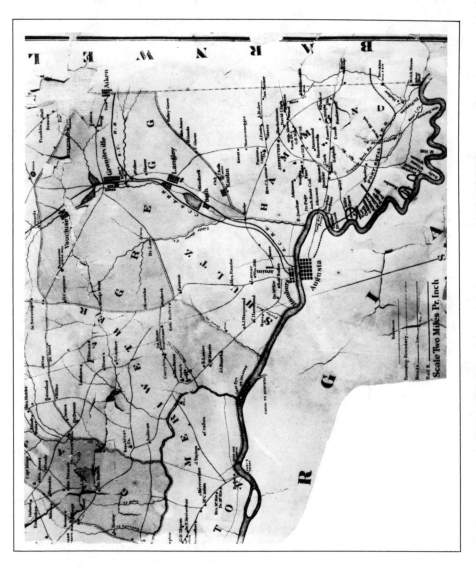

From a map of Edgefield County, South Carolina, surveyed by Isaac Boles, 1871

THE HAMMONDS OF REDCLIFFE

PART I

The Founder
James Henry Hammond

James Henry Hammond, prototypical Southern planter and fire-brand, was the descendant of a family that settled in Massachusetts in 1634. His father, Elisha, who molded the values and career of his son, migrated to Charleston, South Carolina, in 1802, landing "sick and a stranger to everybody," with "few clothes and but one single quarter of a dollar" in his pocket.[1] A graduate of Dartmouth College, Elisha became a teacher at the Methodist academy of Mt. Bethel near Newberry, South Carolina. Always restless, he was during the next twenty years a teacher at South Carolina College in Columbia, a farmer, a merchant, a school principal at Mt. Bethel, a food steward for South Carolina College, and a barge operator carrying cotton down the Savannah River. In 1828, he moved to Macon, Georgia, to head its local academy but died there suddenly on July 9, 1829, apparently of yellow fever.[2]

1. Elisha Hammond to JHH, April 12, 1827, HBC Family Papers, SCL; John Shaw Billings, comp., "History of the Hammond, Fox and Spann Families, with special attention to James Henry Hammond and information on Silver Bluff, Cowden, and Redcliffe Plantations," ibid., cited hereafter as Billings, "The Hammond Family"; Maximilian La Borde, *History of the South Carolina College from Its Incorporation, December 19, 1801 to December 19, 1865*, 2nd ed. (Charleston: Walker, Evans and Cogswell, 1874), p. 436; Chalmers Gaston Davidson, *The Last Foray: The South Carolina Planters of 1860: A Sociological Study* (Columbia: University of South Carolina Press, 1971), pp. 11 and 46; Daniel W. Hollis, *University of South Carolina*, vol. I: *South Carolina College* (Columbia: University of South Carolina Press, 1951), pp. 36–37, 64–68; Thomas H. Pope, *The History of Newberry County South Carolina*, vol. I: 1749–1860 (Columbia: University of South Carolina Press, 1973), p. 214.

2. Ibid., Joseph Earle Steadman, *A History of the Spann Family with Attached Hammond Connections, Compiled by Edward Spann Hammond from the Notes of James H. Hammond* (n.p., 1967), pp. 65–67.

All his life he regretted not having become a lawyer. Law, he thought, was the path to wealth, and he lamented that there had been no one to advise him.[3] As a young man he had thought fleetingly of becoming a Methodist preacher, but he never regretted not having done so, and thereafter orthodox religion plays no significant part in the Hammond family story.

In 1806, Elisha married Catherine Fox Spann whom he had met in Columbia, and on November 15, 1807, their first son, James Henry, was born at Stoney Battery, near Newberry. There were four children in all—James Henry, Caroline Augusta, Marcus Claudius Marcellus, and John Fox. Though the Hammonds had little money, James was well prepared for college at home by his father and when sixteen years old entered the junior class at South Carolina College. He graduated fourth in a class of thirty-three in December 1825. While a student, Hammond was active in and eventually president of the Euphradian Society, a debating club. On his last evening in office, he prophetically made a speech on the negative side of the question "Should seduction be punished by death?"[4]

After finishing college at eighteen, James Henry taught school while reading law. When he grew impatient with his own progress, his father reminded him that Daniel Webster, who had been at Dartmouth with Elisha, also had taught school to pay for his legal studies.[5] In 1828 at the age of twenty-one Hammond became a lawyer, achieving his father's ambition. Although he was an instant success in his practice at the state capital in Columbia, Hammond professed to hate the law. He gravitated to politics, becoming in 1830 the editor of a newspaper, *The Southern Times*, in which he strongly advocated states' rights and nullification of the tariff of 1828, positions popular with South Carolina voters.

In 1830 Hammond met Catherine Elizabeth Fitzsimons, a homely sixteen-year-old Charleston heiress, whose father Christopher Fitzsi-

3. Elisha Hammond to JHH, March 4 and April 12, 1827, HBC Family Papers, SCL.
4. John Shaw Billings, comp., *Descendants of James Henry Hammond of South Carolina* (New York: by the author, 1934), p. i; Billings, "The Hammond Family," SCL; Pope, *Newberry County*, p. 159; Hollis, *University of South Carolina*, pp. 230–54. See also biographies of JHH: Elizabeth Merritt, *James Henry Hammond 1807–1864* (Baltimore: Johns Hopkins Press, 1923); Robert C. Tucker, "James Henry Hammond, South Carolinian" (Ph.D. diss., University of North Carolina, 1958).
5. Elisha Hammond to JHH, April 12, 1827, HBC Family Papers, SCL.

mons, shipowner, merchant, and planter, had died five years before. Early in 1831, when James proposed marriage, her family objected on the grounds that Catherine was too young and that Hammond was obviously a fortune hunter. In an attempt to end the relationship, Catherine's family asked Hammond to renounce her dower. Outraged, he refused to do so, and continued to press his suit ardently with Catherine, who in turn pressured her family to allow her to marry him. Her mother finally consented, and the wedding took place in June 1831.

Catherine's family had been right. To be sure, Hammond claimed that "a finer, more high-minded and devoted woman never lived," and as the mother of his children and mistress of his household, he found her irreplaceable. But James Henry's actions and his views on marriage and women make one doubt that he had any deep feelings for her, or that he had the capacity to develop a loving relationship with a member of the opposite sex. To his eldest son, Harry, he wrote bluntly that he expected large dowers for his sons, "not only in virtues but in palpabilities: Somehow—God forgive me—I never could bear poor girls [even] when pretty and pure spirited . . . [I] avoided them. Even the sweetest pill of that kind should be gilded." He continued, "as to Matrimony, cast it behind you for the present and forever if you can." In his view, "women were made to breed—men to do the work of this world. As a toy for recreation, and one soon tires of any given one for this, or as bringing wealth and position, men are *tempted* to marry them and thus the world is kept peopled."[6] James Henry, through his marriage to Catherine, received a plantation of about 7500 acres in Barnwell District at Silver Bluff on the Savannah River, one hundred forty-seven slaves, and much farm equipment. Hammond also gained connections with the prominent Hampton family, for Catherine's older sister Ann was the wife of Wade Hampton II.

The bride was seventeen and the groom twenty-four when they moved to Silver Bluff Plantation, James to become a planter and Catherine to bear five sons in five years—James Henry (always known as Harry), Christopher Fitzsimons, Edward Spann, William Cashel, and Charles Julius. According to Harry, in James Henry's early days as a planter, his father had lived in isolation with only a semi-weekly mail, devoting his time to surveying the land and overseeing the clearing and

6. JHH to HH, Dec. 20, 1852, ibid.

draining of the fields. Eventually, he succeeded in bringing several thousand acres under cultivation "including large bodies of swamp never before penetrated by the foot of man." Hammond claimed that when he married Catherine, her property had been so badly managed that it had produced an annual income of only $600, and that he had increased it to $21,000.[7]

Despite his move from the capital after his marriage, James Henry's political ambitions and interests continued. Still an ardent advocate of states' rights, he sought a seat as a delegate from Barnwell to the nullification convention of November 1832. Although a relative newcomer to the area, Hammond lost by only a few votes. After the South Carolina convention met and nullified within its borders the tariffs of 1828 and 1832, President Andrew Jackson proclaimed to the citizens of South Carolina that the federal laws would be enforced. South Carolina officials made it known that they would resist enforcement, and Hammond offered his services to Governor Robert Hayne. Hayne signed a commission making Hammond one of his aides-de-camp and placing him in charge of military preparedness in his home district. James Henry found the job discouraging, for he could not find many volunteers ready to join a military organization that might have to fight. When the war danger passed in the spring of 1833, Hammond went home to his family, his planting, and his books at Silver Bluff. A year later he ran for Congress and won. By now he had become an advocate of the death penalty for abolitionists, since he considered slavery the cornerstone of the Republic and abolitionists reckless incendiaries.[8]

Before the close of the first session of Congress, Hammond's ulcerous stomach, which he complained of throughout his adult life, began to trouble him, and, blaming it on life in Washington, he resigned. Physicians advised him to travel, and he decided upon an extended tour abroad.[9] A family member wrote that he called to his older sons Harry, aged four, and Christopher, aged three: "First one to me goes to Eu-

7. HH, "Sketch of James Henry Hammond," ibid.; JHH to HH, July 16, 1859, ibid. See also: JHH to MCMH, Aug. 25, 1858, JHH Papers, LC.

8. JHH, "Speech on the Justice of Receiving Petitions for the Abolition of Slavery in the District of Columbia," in *Selections from the Letters and Speeches of the Hon. James Henry Hammond of South Carolina* (New York: John F. Trow and Co., 1866; reprint ed., Clyde N. Wilson, comp., Spartanburg, S.C.: The Reprint Co., 1978), pp. 15–50.

9. JHH to Catherine Hammond, April 14, 1836; JHH to MCMH, April 25, 1836, JHH Papers, SCL; JHH to Catherine Hammond, April 17, 1836, JHH Papers, SHC.

rope."[10] Harry won. In late July 1836, James Henry, Catherine, and Harry sailed for Europe, where they spent most of their time in England, France, and Italy. During their travels Hammond purchased many art works—sculptures as well as paintings—including works by Mouton, de La Tour, Gilbert Stuart, and Sir Thomas Lawrence.[11]

The Hammonds returned to Silver Bluff in August 1837, and James Henry threw himself vigorously into the workaday world of the plantation. He claimed that planting was "the only independent and really honorable occupation" and compared planters in the South to the nobility in Europe: "both stand at the head of society and politics." Nevertheless, he soon grew impatient with his thin Barnwell land and the low cotton prices of 1837. In the spring of 1838, he took a month's journey on horseback to Georgia and Florida in search of cheap and fertile land but found that "good land was high and cheap land poor."[12] He rode home to Silver Bluff and began to drain and ditch in an effort to improve what he already had. In February 1840, he estimated his properties, which by then consisted of 580 acres at Green Valley plantation and 8005 acres at Silver Bluff, to be worth $70,000 in the best of times, and "in the worst of times (and none can be worse than these with cotton at 6 to 8 cents) $44,650." Most likely, $50,000 "may be realized for them."[13]

Cotton planting had been a bonanza in South Carolina until 1820, but afterward the vast expansion of production in states to the south and west forced down the price and took away Carolina's preeminent position. From 1820 to 1850 prices fluctuated, generally being between bad and poor, and only in the ten years before the Civil War were prices regarded as satisfactory. Thus, James Henry scored his success at a time when low prices compelled planters greatly to increase production to make a profit.

Hammond's success can be attributed equally to his personality and to opportunity. He can best be described as a tough son of a bitch. Having wed his wife for her wealth, he proceeded to exploit her property to the fullest—hauling enormous amounts of muck up from the Savan-

10. Billings, "The Hammond Family," SCL.
11. JHH Account Diary, Aug. 6, 1836–April 7, 1837, with specimens of bills paid while traveling in Europe, passim; JHH, Diary of European Trip 1836–1837, passim, JHH Papers, SCL.
12. Merritt, Hammond, p. 44.
13. John Shaw Billings, comp., "Compilation of Silver Bluff, Cowden and Redcliffe Land Papers," Album C, JHH Papers, SCL.

nah River to enrich the land he was cultivating, and clearing and draining swamps to bring into production new land as rich as any in the South. Although this grueling, dangerous, and unhealthy work was carried out by slaves, Hammond always took credit for supervising the work himself rather than employing overseers.

The Beech Island region, where his plantations were located, was one of the naturally most productive regions of South Carolina. In addition, his lands lay within a dozen miles of Augusta, the second largest city in Georgia, an industrial and cotton-shipping center with access via the Savannah River to Georgia's largest city, Savannah, one of the principal ports in the United States. Hammond shipped his cotton through Augusta to his factor in Savannah for sale either locally or in Liverpool. He was fortunate enough to have an alternate outlet, which he could threaten to use but apparently rarely did, for in 1833 the Charleston to Hamburg railway, one of the very first railroads in the United States, started operation. Hamburg, South Carolina, was if anything closer to Hammond's plantation than Augusta. With all these advantages, Hammond, a stern and demanding master, as well as an intelligent and searching student of agriculture, prospered.[14]

In 1839 he had let his friends in the state legislature know that he was available for governor. In anticipation of his election, Hammond built a fine town house in Columbia, for South Carolina had no official executive mansion until after the Civil War. Ostensibly the house was to be a residence for his young sons while they attended school there. As a candidate in 1840 he lost the election in the state legislature, which chose the governor, by a vote of 104 to 47. Supposedly "lonely and beaten in spirit," he returned to his plantation house, Silverton, at

14. JHH to MCMH, Aug. 25, 1858, JHH Papers, LC; JHH to William Hodgson, Oct. 18, 1849, JHH to HH, Jan. 15, 1855, HBC Family Papers; JHH Business Papers, 1848–1862, passim, SCL; Florence Corley, "The Canals and Railroads in the Development of Ante-Bellum Augusta, Georgia" (Independent Study Program Paper, Agnes Scott College), pp. 6, 15–20, 22, 24, 26–29; Randolph Werner, "Hegemony and Conflict: The Political Economy of a Southern Region, Augusta, Georgia, 1865–1895" (Ph.D. diss., University of Virginia, 1977), pp. 44, 188; Kenneth Coleman, gen. ed., A History of Georgia (Athens: University of Georgia Press, 1977), p. 172; J.T. Derry, Georgia: A Guide to Its Cities, Towns, Scenery, and Resources (Philadelphia: J.B. Lippincott and Co., 1878), pp. 58–68, 90–92; Milton Heath, Constructive Liberalism: The Role of the State in Economic Development in Georgia to 1860 (Cambridge: Harvard University Press, 1954), pp. 256–57, 278–79; Charles C. Jones, Jr. and Salem Dutcher, Memorial History of Augusta, Georgia (Syracuse: D. Mason and Co. Publishers, 1890; reprint ed., Spartanburg, S.C.: The Reprint Company, 1966), passim; Alfred Glaze Smith, Jr., Economic Readjustment of an Old Cotton State: South Carolina, 1820–1860 (Columbia: University of South Carolina Press, 1958), passim; George White, Statistics of the State of Georgia (Savannah: W. Thorne Williams, 1849), p. 159.

Silver Bluff, but in fact he still had abundant political influence. In 1841 he was elected brigadier general of the South Carolina militia, named a director of the Columbia branch of the Bank of the State of South Carolina, and chosen as a trustee of South Carolina College, his alma mater. Finally, in December 1842, he was elected governor, defeating R.F.W. Allston, one of the foremost rice planters in the state, by the close vote of 83 to 76.

Hammond's governorship was neither historically significant nor innovative. His principal contributions were the reorganization of the state militia and the overseeing of the establishment of the Citadel at Charleston as the state's military academy. He did remain firm for states' rights, telling the South Carolina legislature in his annual message: "I cannot doubt that you will be justified by God and future generations in adopting any measures, however startling they may appear, that will place your rights and property exclusively under your own control, and enable you to repel all interference with them, whatever shape it may assume."[15]

Hammond's political career, nevertheless, came to an abrupt halt in 1846 just after friends brought his name before the legislature as a candidate for the United States Senate. His candidacy was blocked by the virulent opposition of his wife's brother-in-law, Wade Hampton II, at that time the "kingmaker" of South Carolina politics. Hampton, the father of the famous Civil War cavalry general, Wade Hampton III, was also the father of several daughters, and since his wife, Ann, had long since died, his daughters as teenagers were frequent visitors to their aunt and surrogate mother, Catherine Hammond, the wife of James Henry. That James Henry had a roving eye is well documented; that it should rove over his four nieces ranging in age from thirteen to seventeen is surprising but also documented. The girls apparently did not object to frolicking with their uncle, the governor, but the frolics soon went quite beyond the innocent, for Hammond later wrote of all four simultaneously covering him with kisses while he enjoyed with them every intimacy, but the ultimate. After two years, the oldest girl, at long last outraged by something James Henry had done, ran to her aunt and the tale was out. It is not clear that Wade Hampton ever knew the full story, and other than in Hammond's own writings there are only elliptic

15. JHH, "Message to the Senate and House of Representatives of the State of South Carolina, Nov. 26, 1844," in *Speeches of James Henry Hammond*, p. 102; Billings, "Hammond Family."

references to the scandal. In 1844 Hammond left Columbia following his term as governor, purportedly because of private threats by the sons of Wade Hampton to horsewhip him if they ever found him in Columbia. Finally in 1846, when James Henry was being considered for the Senate, Wade Hampton, who had kept the matter a private family affair until this time, stopped Hammond's candidacy with the threat of unleashing a scandal.[16]

In the voting of the legislature, "the odium which, in spite of his ability attach[ed] to Genl. Hammond," resulted in the election of Andrew Pickens Butler by a substantial majority.[17] Back at Silver Bluff James Henry inveighed against the Hamptons and the "injustice" they had done him. He wrote that "others" got away with far worse than he had done and that he did not deserve the "infamy which the state has wantonly landed on me and my children." At one point he wished that "South Carolina stood upon the Cliff of Hell and I had the power to cast her in the flaming gulf below. I would do it before you could cross a 't.' "[18]

Catherine Hammond had stood by her husband, at least publicly, during the revelations of his conduct with her deceased sister's daughters, and, in 1849, after a nine-year interval, presented him with a daughter, Elizabeth, their eighth and last child.[19] She did leave him, however, in December 1850 because of his affair with a slave, Louisa, whom he refused to give up. A year and a half later Mrs. Hammond and the children, who had gone to stay with her family, still had not returned home, and Hammond wrote dejectedly, "My mother never comes to see me; my wife never even sends a message unless it is something to annoy." Even the servants shunned him. He asked, "What have I done or omitted to do to deserve this fate?" The blame of course was not his. "I trace it all to the horrible connection which Satan seduced me into forming with the vulgar Fitzsimons family whose low-Irish deceit and hypocrisy can only be compared with their low-Irish pride, selfishness and utter want of refinement and tone." What would become of his children, he wondered, so deeply tainted with this Fitzsi-

16. Billings, "The Hammond Family." For a fuller description of the scandal see letter of August 13, 1857, footnote 4.

17. R.F.W. Allston to Adele Allston, Dec. 10, 1846, Robert F.W. Allston Papers, SCHS.

18. JHH to WGS, Dec. 10, 1852, JHH Papers, LC.

19. JHH to William Hodgson, Oct. 18, 1849, HBC Family Papers, SCL; Billings, *Descendants of Hammond*, p. i.

mons "blood." His only hope was that his own "blood" and "precepts" might overcome those of his wife's side of the family. [20]

Catherine remained adamant; she would not come home until he sent Louisa away. He thought that was "too much. I can't." Unwilling to have his own behavior limited by the wishes and needs of others, he complained that "nothing will satisfy [Catherine] but that I shall surrender captive and be a *hardened* convict. Slave and prisoner *day* and *night* and execute her vengeance on my accomplices." James Henry finally agreed to send Louisa away, but not until first frost when all danger of sickness in Charleston was over, "and I will not send her at all, if she is, *as before* to be put in the backyard among the negroes—in other words turned loose in the town." She must, he insisted, be taken on as his sister-in-law's own personal maid. Louisa arrived at Mrs. Fitzsimons's house in Charleston on November 17, 1852. Concern for Louisa's health, however, caused Hammond to write that if cholera became epidemic in Charleston he would send for her "and the others" to return home. He continued, "I will risk no life there. . . . These people shall remain mine everyone of them while there is breath in my body. . . . A fly should not suffer *on my account* if I can help it." [21] Following Louisa's departure, Catherine and the children returned home after an absence of two years, but a few months later Louisa was logged in Hammond's journal as having returned to Silver Bluff. [22]

We know very little of Catherine Fitzsimons Hammond's emotional life on other than the two occasions when she asserted herself by marrying against her family's wishes and by leaving home over Louisa. We know that Hammond made great demands upon her, most of which she met. When Hammond in 1836 thought that a European trip might be a panacea for his ill health, Catherine, pregnant with her fifth child in five years, dutifully went abroad with James and their eldest son, Harry. She gave birth to a son in Rome in January 1837, at a time when she was among strangers and had as her primary support only a maid who spoke no English. Meanwhile, Hammond seemed preoccupied with collecting art. She wrote home a month after the birth of

20. JHH Diary, Dec. 15, 1850, Sept. 7, 1851, June 7, 1852, JHH Papers, SCL.
21. JHH to MCMH, Aug. 11, Sept. 25, Nov. 1852 and Jan. 7, 1853; Christopher Fitzsimons to JHH, Nov. 17, 1852; JHH Plantation Journal, May 1, 3, 9, and 31, June 8, 15, and 17, Oct. 15, 21, and 25, 1851, March 4, 1852, Nov. 16, 1852, JHH Papers, SCL.
22. JHH Plantation Journal, March 5, 1853, ibid.

Charles Julius that her family probably pitied her, for she was extremely lonely in her confinement, lacked the comforts of home, and missed dreadfully "her little ones" back in South Carolina. Moreover, James Henry, who had grown bored with Rome, intended to take Catherine, the infant, and Harry to Naples "earlier than I wished," and in spite of a reported cholera outbreak. A few months later the infant died in France. Throughout their thirty-three years of marriage, it is apparent that Catherine accepted Hammond's domination of her life with all its daily stresses and strains, and even five years after his death Catherine wrote that she had devoted her married life to her husband and her "remaining years to his memory."[23]

During his long political inactivity, estranged from his wife, restive and unable to assume responsibility for his troubles, Hammond's sense of persecution and isolation increased. In the depths of self-pity, he wrote, "Friends I have none."[24] Yet, throughout his hardships, he wrote long and frequent letters to his friend, the novelist William Gilmore Simms. In their deep and mutually supportive friendship, Simms and Hammond exchanged ideas, fears, family news, complaints, and triumphs with one another.[25] An even closer bond existed between James Henry and his brother, Marcus Claudius Marcellus Hammond. Marcellus, or the "Major," was seven years younger than James, but throughout their lives they remained affectionate brothers, close and confiding friends, and spiritual kin in self-indulgence.

Marcellus's weaknesses proved more socially acceptable than those of his brother. His worst failing, according to James Henry, was his excessive drinking. James complained that "When you get three or four glasses of brandy and water, you don't know what you say or do. . . . I never knew or heard of any man who forgot all proprieties and abandoned all decent and sacred reservations to the extent you do under the influence of liquor and I am sure you have no conception of the pain you give all who see or hear you." Marcellus drank, thought James Henry, to make himself more agreeable. "Beware of this delusion,"

23. Catherine Fitzsimons Hammond to Catherine Fox Hammond, Feb. 26, 1837; Catherine Fitzsimons Hammond to MCMH, July 29, 1859, JHH Papers, SCL; Catherine Fitzsimons Hammond to WGS, Dec. 19, 1869, William Hawkins Ferris Manuscripts, Rare Book and Manuscript Library, CU.
24. Merritt, *Hammond*, citing JHH Diary, June 7, 1852, JHH Papers, SCL.
25. Drew Faust, *A Sacred Circle: The Dilemma of the Intellectual in the Old South, 1840–1860* (Baltimore: Johns Hopkins University Press, 1977), passim.

wrote the elder brother.[26] At least in his youth, Marcellus apparently lacked also the "purity of conduct" which was commonly ascribed to ante-bellum planters in their obituaries.[27]

Marcellus, after graduating from West Point in 1836, served in the West as a first lieutenant in the 4th U.S. Infantry Regiment. He took part in the removal of the Cherokees from Georgia and Tennessee to Fort Gibson, Arkansas, and resided among them with his regiment for almost three years. He resigned his army commission on December 31, 1842, because of ill health and went into cotton planting in Georgia.[28] Apparently, while stationed at Fort Gibson he established a close relationship with a Cherokee Indian woman whose family had gone west at the time of removal. She had at least one child by him, whom he referred to in his letters as "Redbird." Before he left Fort Gibson, Marcellus bought her a place and occasionally thereafter sent letters and once some money. In the 1870s, he located her again and wrote to ask "how many children have you had? how many died? how many girls? what are the living doing now, and what are you doing for a living? are you getting gray yet? do you remember bathing in the branch?" He confessed, "I remember keenly those years of 1838–9–40–41." He told her of himself: he was once very rich but the war had ruined him; he had married Harriet Pamela Davies in 1842; they had seven children— five boys and two girls, but a son named for him died in 1852. He boasted that his youngest daughter Kate had married James Randall, the author of the song "My Maryland," and he wondered had she heard it sung in the Cherokee nation. In his last known letter to her he wrote, "good-bye—it may be forever. Whatever may happen I have had some good times."[29] Though these "good times" produced no scandal, Indian agents knew of "Redbird" Hammond and commented matter-of-factly on his family connection with the Hammonds of South Carolina.[30]

If Marcellus lacked the brilliance of his more famous brother, his letters reveal him to be a more relaxed and less defensive man, always

26. JHH to MCMH, Nov. 13, 1857, JHH Papers, SCL.

27. Davidson, The Last Foray, p. 5.

28. Brigadier General Benjamin Alvord, Biographical Sketch from the Life of M.C.M. Hammond, pp. 5–7, Pamphlet Collection, SCL.

29. MCMH to Postmaster, Fort Gibson, Arkansas, June 18, 1871; MCMH to Rachel Huey, March 16 and April 5, 1874, July 16, 1875, copies, MCMH Folder, SCL.

30. Interview with Wylma Wates, Research Archivist, South Carolina Department of Archives and History, Columbia, South Carolina, Aug. 8, 1979.

willing and usually able to provide his brother, his sister-in-law, and his nephews with calm and sensible advice. His drinking and his devotion to an Indian woman, like James Henry's relationship with a female slave, were within the limits of trespass for Southern white males. Indeed, even James Henry's misconduct with his nieces would be conveniently overlooked eventually.

In forced retirement, James Henry Hammond, the "Master of Silver Bluff," continued his program, begun in the early 1830s, of acquiring the land of as many neighbors as he and the sheriff could persuade to sell.[31] Hammond's achievements with his wife's property, part of which he renamed Cathwood after her, and his success with Cowden Plantation, which he put together between 1848 and 1853 to total almost 2,800 acres, are memorialized on his tombstone: "As a planter, the impenetrable swamps of Cowden and Cathwood turned into fruitful fields bear witness to his creative skill." Hammond's landed estate at his death in 1864 exceeded 14,000 acres—almost 22 square miles.[32]

Since their marriage in 1831, Catherine and James Henry—and their five remaining children, Harry, Spann, Paul, Katherine, and Elizabeth—had lived at Silverton. This home, comparable in design to the other rough-hewn houses in the vicinity, was convenient to the operation of the Hammond plantations of Silver Bluff and Cowden, but it was in a remote, low, swampy, malarial area and hardly a suitable dwelling to display Hammond's phenomenal economic success as a member of the cotton aristocracy.

As early as 1853, after completing his Cowden transactions, Hammond began to search for a new home site. In the spring of 1855, he found what he wanted and purchased a house and some 400 acres at Beech Island, a community in Edgefield District on the South Carolina bank of the Savannah River. The house faced west toward Augusta, Georgia, seven miles away, and stood on ground close to the edge of a bank or cliff of reddish clay and sand that sloped sharply away in front of it—thus the name Redcliffe. From Silverton to Redcliffe was eight miles, and there the family moved in August 1855. About a quarter of

31. Faust, A *Sacred Circle*, p. 38.
32. Billings, "The Hammond Family"; gravestone of JHH, Beech Island Cemetery, Beech Island, South Carolina.

a mile east of the house, Hammond selected a site upon which he would build a larger and more imposing home in keeping with his social position. When the house was completed in 1859, the name Redcliffe came to designate this new residence as well as the land, and the original house was thereafter called the "Old Yard." [33] Conceived of as the family estate by Hammond, Redcliffe Plantation was intended to be the seat of a grand manor house surrounded by 400 acres set aside for experiments with fruit trees and vineyards. Planting for market was carried on elsewhere. The acquisition of the new property and the completion of the new house demonstrate that Hammond, no matter how often he might pessimistically claim that his ambitions and his productive life were over, had not lost the self-assurance and egotism that had caused him so many problems and had helped him to survive them. Redcliffe became the seat of both the hopes and the tensions that Hammond would bequeath to his descendants.

The house, when completed in 1859, was a white, wood-frame, two-story building with four rooms that opened off center halls on each floor. It looked more like a large farmhouse than the traditional planter's mansion famed more in Old South myth than in reality. The ceilings were fourteen feet high, there were double-decked porches on all sides, and both front and back porches had steps to the ground. The outbuildings included four slave houses that accommodated eight families, a separate building for the kitchen, and a carriage house and stable. Redcliffe, perhaps because it came to represent comfort and security more than the status its builder intended it to symbolize, became the warm and cherished home of Hammond's descendants for the next century.

Hammond probably had given up all thought of holding high political office when, in May 1857, Senator Andrew Pickens Butler died. James Henry told Simms that he did not want the office, for South Carolina had "committed a *great* and *wanton* outrage upon me." He went so far as to declare, in a letter in the leading Charleston newspaper, that he would not serve if elected. [34] Probably because he had been an outsider for more than thirteen years and was neither a leader nor a member of a faction in the party battles of the 1850s, Hammond was

33. Billings, "The Hammond Family."
34. JHH to WGS, Aug. 13, 1857, JHH Papers, LC; JHH to *The Charleston Mercury*, Oct. 2, 1857, JHH Papers, SCL.

the most acceptable candidate. On the third ballot the legislature elected him to the Senate.[35] He accepted.

The "outsider," once in the Senate, made a speech on March 4, 1858, for which he is still remembered. It contained his thesis about the "mudsills of society" and the phrase "cotton is king." He defended slavery by observing that all civilizations had a class of servants to do the menial duties. The North had its working class, the South its slaves; these workers, who performed "the drudgery of life," provided the foundations, or mudsills, upon which great societies developed. And there could be no civil war, for "you dare not make war on cotton. No power on earth dares to make war upon it. Cotton *is* king."[36]

His experience in Washington led him to modify somewhat his views. Although he never wavered in his support of slavery, he did assert that the South was not sufficiently united to withdraw from the Union, and even if it could unite, it would serve Southern interests better to remain within the Union and take a firm stand against Northern violations of Southern rights. He expressed these views in speeches at two banquets in his honor held after the adjournment of Congress in 1858. The first, on July 22 at Beech Island, received only passing notice, but the second, on October 29, 1858, at Barnwell Court House, received national coverage and was very well received in Northern newspapers.[37] However, Hammond's letters convey a sense that neither he nor anyone else could do anything to halt the rush of events leading to disunion. With the election of Abraham Lincoln in November 1860, Hammond resigned from the Senate. In December 1860, South Carolina seceded, and Hammond returned to Redcliffe.

James Henry at home remained ever the patriarch. He considered the members of his family of great importance, but he viewed them primarily as extensions of himself. He owned them as he owned his more than three hundred slaves, and as he viewed his black servants, so he viewed his family. He considered them not mature adults but dependents who required constant supervision, material support, and manipulation. At one point he lumped them all together as "pensioners."

35. John Cunningham to JHH, June 20, 1857, JHH to John Cunningham, June 26, 1857, JHH Papers, LC; Merritt, *Hammond*, pp. 113–15.

36. U.S., Congress, Senate, *Congressional Globe*, 35th Congress, 1st sess., March 4, 1858, pp. 959–62.

37. JHH, "Speech Delivered at Barnwell Court House, S.C., October 29, 1858," in *Speeches of James Henry Hammond*, pp. 323–57; Merritt, *Hammond*, p. 126.

There is no evidence in any of Hammond's letters or journals that he ever felt guilt about owning slaves or that he ever had pangs of conscience over his assumption that his wife and children were also a principal part of his possessions. Yet he determined to train his sons to become masters themselves on his landed estates. Hammond had held great expectations "of establishing, a rich, educated, well-bred and prominent family . . . of our name," but he became convinced that the endeavor would end with him, for he felt that his sons, whom he had set up as planters, had squandered his money, loafed about, and disobeyed his agricultural instructions.[38]

Busy with his plans for the new house, his vineyards, and his fruit trees, Hammond left his plantations at Silver Bluff and Cowden to be operated by overseers and by his sons Harry, Spann, and Paul. His letters of the late 1850s complain continually of his dilettante sons who were running his planting operations into the ground. During this period he nevertheless netted a profit, after feeding and housing over 300 slaves, of between $30,000 and $35,000 a year.[39] Simms, whom he did treat more or less as an equal, put his finger on the real problem when he told Hammond to "beware of yourself." He wrote, "You overawe your boys, overwhelm them, and make them halt and hesitate, if not fear, so that they become distrustful of themselves."[40]

Hammond had achieved much in his life—carving flourishing plantations out of undeveloped land, winning the governorship, and going to Washington as a United States Senator. His political success had as a prerequisite economic success, based not only on the labor of his numerous slaves, his personal industry, his study of agricultural science, and his marriage to a rich woman, but also on the opportunities offered by the expanding cotton economy. In the first part of the century cotton was truly king—at least in the South—and Hammond made the most of it. After the war the cotton economy declined because of foreign competition, domestic overproduction, low prices in world markets, and the depleted soil of the Old South. His sons, whether overawed by

---

38. The correspondence of the 1850s relentlessly pursues the theme of the inadequacies of the Hammond sons as seen by their father. See: HBC Family Papers, 1851–1862, passim; JHH Papers, 1851–1862, passim, SCL; JHH Papers, 1851–1862, passim, LC.

39. JHH to WGS, July 29, 1860, JHH Papers, LC; Davidson, The Last Foray, p. 207.

40. WGS to JHH, Nov. 10, 1857, cited in Mary C. Oliphant, Alfred Taylor Odell, and T.C. Eaves, eds., The Letters of William Gilmore Simms, 5 vols. (Columbia: University of South Carolina Press, 1952–1956), 3:513.

Hammond or overwhelmed by events, failed to match his achievements.

Dedicated to the defense of slavery, Hammond, when the war came in April 1861, gave the Confederacy his full financial support. By 1864 half of his estate consisted of Confederate bonds.[41] Yet he remained ever the critic, lashing out at what he considered the ruinous policies of "unprincipled" Southern leaders. "Our hope," he wrote, was that the enemy was even "more demoralized than our Leaders." Especially sharp was his criticism of Jefferson Davis, whom he had known in the Senate. Davis was, wrote Hammond, "the most irascible man I ever saw. Quick tempered, arbitrary, overbearing, he is lost when excited and he is easily excited. He has no breadth of political views or solid judgment in them."[42]

Two of Hammond's sons—Paul and Harry—fought for the Confederacy. Hammond strongly disapproved of his son Spann's sending substitutes after serving briefly in the Confederate army. Deeply troubled by the fall of Atlanta on September 1, 1864, and expecting Sherman's march across Georgia to the sea, Hammond, according to Spann, willed himself to die. "This war," Hammond told his son, "will terminate suddenly within six months. I do not care to look behind the veil. Enough that everything I have worked for, the labors of my life will all be upset."[43] On the day before his death, while lying on a couch in the library at Redcliffe, he called Spann to his side and told him that he wished to be buried in the woods on the highest ground, where there would be a view of Augusta and the Sand Hills. "But mind . . . if we are subjugated, run a plow over my grave."[44] On November 13, 1864, Hammond died, two days before his fifty-seventh birthday.

41. List of Confederate Bonds, July 21, 1864, JHH Business Papers, SCL; Merritt, *Hammond*, p. 145.
42. JHH to J.N. Hayne, April 21, 1861, JHH Papers, LC; JHH Plantation Journal, July 27, 1863, JHH Papers, SCL.
43. ESH, "Last Moments of James Henry Hammond," Nov. 13, 1864, JHH Papers, SCL.
44. Ibid.

JAMES HENRY HAMMOND DIARY[h]

May 12 [1855]

I purchased not long ago Dr. Milledge Galphin's residence in Beech Island[1] and named it Redcliffe for the red bluff in front of it. I came down there day before yesterday with some furniture, and yesterday Mrs. H. came there with more and tomorrow I propose to join her there and take up my residence there. It is a beautiful situation susceptible of magnificent improvements and has the finest view in the middle country. I wish I had purchased it before I went to Columbia and put up my Columbia house there.[2] How would my career differ from what it has been!!!

If I live and prosper I will improve the place—Lay my bones there and leave it for a family mansion. But I am now too old—too infirm—too heart broken to do anything with spirit or look forward to any earthly enjoyments.

JAMES HENRY HAMMOND TO HARRY HAMMOND[h]

Redcliffe, December 28, 1856

My Dear Harry:[1]

Your mother answered your last letter immediately. She gave you, no doubt, all the domestic news and as nothing occurs now-a-days so

1. Dr. Milledge Galphin (1794–1857) was educated at the University of Pennsylvania Medical School. By 1818 he had built himself a spacious house at Beech Island, South Carolina. In 1855 James Henry Hammond purchased the house and 366 acres of surrounding land from Galphin, who died near Redcliffe two years later. Edgefield County, South Carolina Record of Deeds, 1853–1855, SCDAH; Billings, "The Hammond Family"; JHH Plantation Journal, April 14, 1857, JHH Papers, SCL.

2. Just prior to his defeat for the governorship in 1840, Hammond had finished constructing a fine townhouse at the corner of Blanding and Bull Streets in Columbia. "Outstanding for its elegance and beauty, the house had three story columns running around all four sides and was ornamented with the finest wood carvings obtainable." When the state legislature did not choose Hammond as governor he returned to his plantation home at Silverton. With his election as governor in 1842, Hammond returned to Columbia and took up residence in the townhouse. In 1846 Hammond sold it to Thomas Clarkson, and in February 1865 it was destroyed by fire during Sherman's occupation of Columbia. Billings, "The Hammond Family."

1. Harry, the first child of Catherine Fitzsimons and James Henry Hammond, was named James Henry for his father, but was called Harry and is so listed in the family genealogy. He was born

agreeable to me that I care to think of it again, much less repeat it, I shall not go over it. Aldrich[2] and the Major[3] were with us on Christmas day and we had a pleasant party. Aldrich says the Major restrained himself and made the best impression of any new member of the Legislature. They wanted to run him for Governor and but that a majority were already pledged to Allston[4] he ought to have been elected. He and

---

March 30, 1832, received his A.B. degree from the University of South Carolina in 1852, studied medicine briefly in Charleston, and acquired a medical degree from the University of Pennsylvania in 1855. After the completion of his education, Harry traveled in Europe for eighteen months, returning home in 1857. At the time of this letter he was in Paris. Robert C. Tucker, "James Henry Hammond, South Carolinian" (Ph.D. diss., University of North Carolina at Chapel Hill, 1958), p. 111 n.; Roland Hammond, A History and Genealogy of the Descendants of William Hammond (Boston: Clapp and Sons, 1894), p. 270; Andrew Charles Moore, comp., Alumni Records, 7 vols. (Columbia: University of South Carolina, 1905), 4:n.p.

2. Alfred Proctor Aldrich (1814–1897), born in Charleston and educated at the College of Charleston, was admitted to the bar in 1835. Aldrich settled in Barnwell, where he later became a judge. Aldrich was a personal and political friend of James Henry Hammond and his brother, Marcellus. Yates Snowden, History of South Carolina, 2 vols. (New York: The Lewis Publishing Company, 1920), 2:965 n.

3. Marcus Claudius Marcellus Hammond (1814–1876), referred to as the Major or Marcellus, was James Henry Hammond's younger brother, born in Newberry, South Carolina. After graduating from West Point in 1836 he served in Florida in the 4th Regiment of Infantry, which participated in several campaigns against the Seminole Indians. Later he served in the regiment that removed the Cherokee Indians to the West. In 1840 he was stationed at Fort Gibson, Arkansas among the Cherokees.

In July 1842 Marcellus married Harriet Pamela Davies of Augusta, Georgia. On December 31 of the same year he resigned his commission on account of ill health. Between 1842 and 1846 he was a cotton planter in Georgia, but with the coming of the Mexican War he sought to regain his commission. In June 1846 he was appointed Paymaster of the United States Army, but again ill health plagued him and he resigned on April 15, 1847.

With the end of his military career, Marcellus returned to planting, this time at Hamburg, South Carolina. Between 1849 and 1853 he wrote a series of articles on California and the battles of the Mexican War for the Southern Quarterly Review. In 1856 he was elected to the South Carolina legislature from Edgefield District and served one term. In 1860 he moved to Georgia, where he was appointed Major-General of the Third Division of the Georgia Militia. In this capacity he raised thirty companies for the Confederacy, although he himself saw no action. Joan Reynolds Faunt, Robert E. Rector with David K. Bowdens, eds., Biographical Directory of the South Carolina House of Representatives, vol. 1: Sessions Lists 1692–1973 (Columbia: University of South Carolina Press, 1974), pp. 374–75; Benjamin Alvord to MCMH, Jan. 24, 1853, JHH Papers; MCMH to Postmaster, Fort Gibson, Arkansas, June 18, 1871, MCMH Papers, SCL; Alvord, "Biographical Sketch from the Life of M.C.M. Hammond"; Roland Hammond, Genealogy, p. 272; Merritt, Hammond, p. 147.

4. Robert F.W. Allston (1801–1864) was one of the foremost rice planters in ante-bellum South Carolina. After serving in the lower house of the General Assembly, Allston was elected to the State Senate and between 1847 and 1856 he served as president of this body. In 1856 he was elected governor for a two-year term. Cyclopedia of Eminent and Representative Men of the Carolinas of the Nineteenth Century, vol. 1 (Madison, Wisconsin: Brant and Fuller, 1892), p. 642; Emily B. Reynolds and Joan Reynolds Faunt, eds., Biographical Directory of the Senate of the State of South Carolina, 1776–1964 (Columbia: South Carolina Archives Department, 1964), pp. 171–72.

Tom Davies[5] have purchased a plantation in Miss. and are sending off negroes. Tom left today. The Major is buying, but gangs of negroes are worth $700 round. Prime hands any price. I bid in some for the Major the other day at cash price and among them 3 fellows from 21 to 25 years old—not superior to Robert, Arthur and Levin at $1275–1165 and 1060 and except the first they were considered very low. Girls like Leah[6] bring $900.

Spann[7] goes to Silverton[8] in a few days to take charge of Cowden[9] next year. He has been made a perfect "farniente" by his 15 months engagement and does not read, think or do. He looks badly also. I suppose your Mother wrote you that I broke off his engagement.[10] I

5. Thomas Jones Davies, M. C. M. Hammond's brother-in-law, was referred to by James Henry Hammond as "one of my near neighbors and best friends." Davies moved to Beech Island to mine white clay from chalk beds "and grew rich on it." JHH to Hon. Lawrence Keitt, July 31, 1860, Thomas Jones Davies Papers; MS vol. bd., 1927–n.d. "Myself and Family," John Shaw Billings Scrapbook Collection, SCL.

6. Robert's name first appears on the Silver Bluff slave list in 1842. Arthur, born in 1833 at Silver Bluff, appears on the 1863 slave inventory. Levin, also listed as a slave at Silver Bluff, died on May 23, 1857, at the age of thirty-five. Leah is listed by Hammond as a house servant. The names of all four slaves appear also on Silver Bluff's October 5, 1845 slave list. Silver Bluff Plantation Slave Lists, June 1843 and Oct. 5, 1853, JHH Plantation Journal, 1831–1855; JHH Plantation Journal, 1856–1887, pp. 470–72, 476, JHH Papers, SCL; Billings, "The Hammond Family."

7. Edward Spann Hammond, the third son of Catherine Fitzsimons and James Henry Hammond, was born June 26, 1834. After graduating from the University of Georgia in 1853, Spann attended medical school at Charleston, and graduated from the University of Pennsylvania Medical School in 1855. JHH Diary, April 19, 1855, JHH Papers, SCL; Billings, Descendants of Hammond, p. i.

8. Silverton Plantation, located in Barnwell district, was an addition to the Silver Bluff tract. Bought by Hammond in 1832, it became the site of the family home. The plantation house which stood on a slight rise in an oak grove "was handy for the operation of the Hammond plantations, but . . . was in a low malarial area, remote from town and neighbors and incapable of ever reflecting accurately its owner's rise to an important position in the Cotton Aristocracy." By the 1850s Hammond began looking for a new and better site, a search that led him to Redcliffe in 1855. Billings, "The Hammond Family."

9. James Henry Hammond began putting Cowden Plantation together in 1848. The area, literally a cow den in the wild swamps of the Savannah River just below Silver Bluff, encompassed almost 2800 acres by the time Hammond had completed his land purchases in 1853. He cleared the land, drained the swampy areas, and put the fields to intensive cultivation. Hammond's crop yields were reported to be phenomenal because of the rich virgin land. Today, much of Cowden plantation is included in the Savannah River Government Reservation. Ibid.; Smith, Jr., Economic Readjustment of an Old Cotton State, p. 85; Interview with Katharine Suber, Kathwood Plantation, Jackson, South Carolina, July 31, 1979.

10. Spann Hammond became engaged to his second cousin Clara Kilpatrick in September 1855. Although James Henry in this December 1856 letter feels that he has succeeded in having the engagement terminated, Spann was slow to acquiesce and the matter dragged on for six months. On January 20, 1857, James Henry wrote to his friend William Gilmore Simms that "I have taken it on myself to break up Spann's matrimonial engagements and given him Cowden in charge. There are troubles. Not so much with him and her, but elsewhere and among kith and kin."

never liked it, became at last disgruntled, but did not interfere until I found they were going to make Clara deprive herself of her property in part—the secret of the postponement—which was a fraud that Spann could not resent but which I did for him beforehand. He seems satisfied.[11]

I do not care much for the French or any foreign vines.[12] Hundreds of experiments have established the fact that for wine they are of *no value* here and for the table *inferior*. Only curiosity would induce me to cultivate any. I have had 6 olive trees sent me from Beaufort and can get more there. . . .

My wine does not improve. It did not ferment fully at first and at every warm spell it ferments now and will not clear up. It will sour in Spring. We must have the right sort of cellar to make wine here, if we can at all. If you can, find out all about the wine cellars in Italy and ascertain whether they can, in warm climates, make wine to keep with-

Simms in his letter of reply on January 23 urged Hammond not to act rashly. "Let your wife decide, without trying to influence her." According to Spann the engagement was broken off on March 26, 1857, eighteen months after he became engaged to Clara. The untangling went on throughout the spring, for Spann records on May 20, 1857, "On Saturday 16th inst. Mr. Lorton [Clara's stepfather] called at the Bank of Augusta taking Clara's letters and leaving a box for me." More pain is recorded on May 22, "Am astonished and aggrieved that Clara has retained a number of my letters after proposals from her side that all should be returned." Finally on June 13 he "received an order from Mr. Lorton today for Clara's likeness." ESH Diary 1857–1858, ESH Papers, SCL; JHH to WGS, Jan. 20, 1857, JHH Papers, LC; WGS to JHH, Jan. 23, 1857, cited in Oliphant, *Simms*, 3:493; R.W. Simpson, *History of Old Pendleton District* (Anderson, South Carolina: Oulla Printing and Binding Company, 1913), p. 79.

11. Spann met Clara for the first time in 1847 when he was thirteen and she eleven. In 1909 when he was seventy-five he wrote on learning of her death that it was a shock such as he had "never felt but once before—one relating to her, that blasted the whole course of my life." He went on to describe their first meeting: "something caused me to look back. At that moment Clara, nearly a year and a half my junior, in white short dress, stepped to the piazza and looked toward me. I gazed for some moments, strangely spell-bound, with a feeling that my destiny was there. The picture is vividly before me now, and has been for all these years." James Henry, eventually growing indignant over the prospect of Spann's losing some of Clara's inheritance, wrote Clara's family without consulting Spann, to have her break off the engagement. She did so, giving Spann a sickening, crushing blow with the result that "ambition or personal gain [was] no longer a stimulus—I have since led a wandering, almost, at times, a vagabond life, imbued largely with misanthropy and void of settled purpose or aspiration. The blow that struck me left an anguish in which a life-time is comprised." ESH to Annie H. Walker, Aug. 14, 1909, ESH Letterpress Book, ESH Papers, SCL.

12. By the 1850s Hammond was able to devote much of his time to tending his vineyards. He planted 500 Catawba vines and, though critical of "the French or any foreign vines," he asked for thousands of cuttings from French vineyards. He even sought unsuccessfully a vineyardist from France to aid him. He was proud of his wine, at one time boasting that "the still Catawba in green glasses, well iced, would pass for Rhenish in Dresden and very good Rhenish too." Billings, "The Hammond Family" HBC Family Papers, SCL.

out 25 p^ct of brandy as in Madeira. I don't think the Italian wines keep
or bear transportation. I am trenching 5 more acres (7 in all) and shall
rest there.

We are all well. I am getting better of an inflammation of the bowels. . . . Dan[13] doing well at Nashville—Catty[14] quit school in
Charleston—won't learn or submit to any other rule than her own will.
She can read and write and when I make her learn arithmetic to rule of
three I shall bother no more with *her* education.

Yours affectionately,

J.H. Hammond

JAMES HENRY HAMMOND TO WILLIAM GILMORE SIMMS[c]

Redcliffe, January 31, 1857

My Dear Simms:[1]

I have just learned tonight that Brooks[2] is dead but none of the
particulars. It is a shock for nothing so tragical could have been more
unexpected. He must have been a better, that is more religious i.e.

---

13. Dan is the nickname of Paul Fitzsimons Hammond. Paul, the youngest son of Catherine
Fitzsimons and James Henry Hammond, was born on March 27, 1838. ESH Diary, March 27,
1852, ESH Papers, SCL; Billings, *Descendants of Hammond*, p. i.

14. Katherine, the seventh child and first daughter of James Henry Hammond, was born on
September 26, 1840. She married James Gregg, son of William Gregg, owner of Graniteville
Mills, on October 10, 1861. On April 19, 1876, Gregg was murdered for no apparent reason, and,
still interesting one hundred years later, this crime was the subject of a television play on the Public
Broadcasting System entitled "The Gardener's Son." Katherine's second marriage was to another
textile mill owner, William E. McCoy, on April 13, 1878. She died childless on November 20,
1882. Billings, *Descendants of Hammond*, pp. i, 9; Broadus Mitchell, *William Gregg: Factory
Master of the Old South* (Chapel Hill: University of North Carolina Press, 1928), pp. 327–28.

---

1. William Gilmore Simms (1806–1870) was a nationally known South Carolina novelist and
man of letters. Simms and James Henry Hammond's brother Marcellus were the only persons
close to Hammond. Describing his friendship with Hammond to one of Hammond's sons following the Senator's death, Simms wrote, "Your father was my most confidential friend for near
twenty-five years. Never were thoughts more intimate than his and mine. We had few or no secrets
from each other, we took few steps in life without mutual consultation. We had,—I am sure I
had—perfect confidence in him. I believe he had in me. I felt there was something kindred in our
intellectual nature. Certainly, there was much, very much in common between us." Merritt,
Hammond, p. 147; WGS to ESH, Nov. 20, 1864, cited in Oliphant, *Simms*, 4:469–70; Faust, *A
Sacred Circle*, passim.

2. Preston Smith Brooks (1819–1857), Congressman from South Carolina, attacked Senator
Charles Sumner of Massachusetts on May 22, 1856, and beat him with a cane in the chamber of
the U.S. Senate because of Sumner's speech, "Crime against Kansas," delivered in the Senate on

more Spiritual man than any of us gave him credit for. He dies just at his culminating point. The decadence to you and I was clear, but not to the world while his family and many friends have every reason to believe that higher and perhaps the highest honors were in store for him. For him, for them, in every way he is removed at the happy moment judging by the practical standard of this world, with the keenest and most spiritual judgement. This happens to few. He must have found favour with the Deity for it to happen at all. Moreover, it is a proof that his achievement was a true mission which I never thought before. What then? God is with us to use of brute force! I have been curiously watching the denouement of this matter. I have been looking for Sumner's return, for Burlingame's[3] demonstration. The solution is Brooks' death. The North will call it a judgement. To me, looking all round, it is clearly a reward for an act approved of God. Am I deluded? This will find you in a land of Mediums.[4] Consult Brooks, learn how he fares. I thought like you that I should be dreadfully shocked by communicating with the Dead. The only time I ever did it—if I did it then—I had no such feeling whatever. I think all this is pre-arranged and that the Power that permits the communication pre-arranges every

May 20, 1856. In this speech Sumner insulted Andrew Pickens Butler, Senator from South Carolina and a relative of Brooks. The House of Representatives censured Brooks for the incident. He resigned his seat on July 15 only to be re-elected to fill the vacancy caused by his own resignation. He died suddenly in Washington on January 27, 1857. Inscription on commemorative tablet in lobby of South Caroliniana Library; Oliphant, Simms, 3:442 n. The fullest account of the Brooks-Sumner affair is in David Donald, Charles Sumner and the Coming of the Civil War (New York: Alfred A. Knopf, 1960).

3. Charles Sumner (1811–1874) did not return to the Senate until December 1859, more than three years after Brooks's attack on him. Anson Burlingame (1820–1870), Congressman and diplomat, was born in New Berlin, New York. After studying law at Harvard, he became a lawyer in Boston. He was elected to the Massachusetts senate in 1852, and in 1855 was elected to Congress where he served three terms. He spoke out in a speech against Preston Brooks's assault on Charles Sumner and was challenged by Brooks to a duel. Burlingame formally accepted and named the Canadian side of Niagara Falls as the site of the duel. Brooks declined to go to Canada and the duel was averted. Burlingame's ostensible acceptance and Brooks's refusal, which was touted by Burlingame, gained the latter great popularity in the Northern states. His fame, though, rests on his diplomatic career in China.

4. At the time of this letter Simms had just departed from Charleston on a lecture tour which would take him to Washington (where Brooks had recently died), Baltimore, Norfolk, Petersburg, Richmond, Raleigh, and Greensboro, returning home on March 15 or 16.

James Henry Hammond after his political disgrace attempted partially to fill the vacuum caused by the absence of high office with a personal theology—Unitarianism mixed with Spiritualism, and Simms shared his interest in Spiritualism. Simms had even consulted mediums for them in New York City on a tour in 1856. Billings, "The Hammond Family," HBC Family Papers, SCL; JHH to WGS, May 13, 1855, JHH Papers, LC; WGS to JHH Dec. 30, 1856, cited in Oliphant, Simms 3:475–84.

thing according to our needs. I wish I could have constant communications. I am sure they would do me good. But they are not for me. I never even dream. The night my mill burnt I slept like a top. I never had a pre-monition, but from my own wide awake intellect. I am out of the pale. Isolated. Left to do my worst or best without sign or help and bound to all the Consequences. I know that with you the battle of this life has been a fierce one and that all you are you are to your own powers. As to me, except those grand creatures in human form, who towered above humanity so high that human aid, or sympathy could never reach them, nor human intellect comprehend—such as Alexander and Napoleon, it seems to me that no man ever lived less comprehended, sympathised with or helped than myself. Ordinarily I feel as much alone in my world as Adam did before Eve came—more so—for Adam had God for his Companion who taught him right and wrong. If I could know what was right and what wrong I think I could work *alone* and ask no Companionship. I have my own standards of course. I don't, I know, come up to them. It is because I am not sure they are the true ones. I want some spirit to tell me what is true as far as I can comprehend Truth. Pilate asked Christ "What is Truth?" A fair question. But Christ gave no answer. I want an answer: so do you. I wish to ask "The Spirits" for one. They will no more than Christ give one. What then? "Do what your hands find to do." That is all, as far as I can see.

But this you think all nonsense.

Then, as to your question whether your course in regard to your Northern Literary Tour was right.[5] To be explicit: so far as I can learn, it is thought that your attempt to take the North by the nose, in its state of highest excitement and utmost exasperation, and to subdue it to your will by rhetoric and argument and even odd fact, was a little Quixotic—rather beyond Shakespeare and Petruchio; but that your retreat after finding it was "no go" was if not equal to that of the "Ten Thousand" masterly enough:[6] and so the case stands. You have lost nothing

---

5. The Northern Literary Tour by Simms was through New York State from October 25 to December 1, 1856. Simms cancelled his two remaining lectures in New York City because of audience hostility to and newspaper censure of his attacks on Charles Sumner and his assertions of the preeminence of South Carolina. Oliphant, *Simms* 3:424, 454–69; John Hope Franklin, *A Southern Odyssey: Travelers in the Antebellum North* (Baton Rouge: Louisiana State University, 1976), pp. 234–43.

6. Petruchio was successful in *The Taming of the Shrew*. The description by Xenophon (427–355 B.C.) in the *Anabasis* of the retreat of his ten-thousand-man Greek mercenary army across the Persian Empire established that retreat as one of the most masterful accomplishments in military history.

South—perhaps gained little for we always expect Self-sacrifice and hardly praise—never pay it. Have you lost nothing North?

Ever Yours,

J.H. Hammond

JAMES HENRY HAMMOND TO MARCUS C.M. HAMMOND[h]

Redcliffe, June 20, 1857

My Dear Major:

All are well far and near as well as I can know in this dreadful cold weather which keeps me in the house. But Catherine and Betty[1] went down this morning to stay all night at Silverton. Catty and Kate[2] went—Spann, Mrs. H. and Betty escorting them—to Orangeburg over a week ago. We have not heard from them since.

I got a long—2 sheet—letter from Col. Whitner by the last mail. It is an elaborate defence of himself and his sneering at Spann, insinuating all the scandal afloat about me as offensive as possible. They are cut deep. I could riddle his sophistry or recriminate fatally to him, but I shall make no reply. No good could come of it. The split is final. It is apparent from his letter that this donation of Clara's is a much cherished thing and he says—what after Lorton's letter surprises me—that he, Lorton and his wife talked it over last summer. It appears that the reason why Clara should not marry until of age was that *she* do this *herself exclusively* and the reason is also given. Her father made a "disgraceful will" towards her Mother.[3] They want revenge. They have

1. Catherine Elizabeth Fitzsimons married James Henry Hammond in 1831 when she was 17 years old. For more on her see the letter of July 29, 1859, and note 1; see also the Introduction to Part I. Betty Hammond, youngest child of Catherine and James Henry Hammond, was born on October 4, 1849. She married William Raiford Eve on December 7, 1871, and bore twelve children in eighteen years. Billings, *Descendants of Hammond*, pp. i, 11.

2. Catty and Kate were first cousins. Catty was Katherine Hammond, the eldest daughter of Catherine and James Henry Hammond, born on September 26, 1840. Kate was Katherine Spann Hammond, the eldest child of Harriet and M.C.M. Hammond, born on June 25, 1843. Both young women were attending boarding school in Orangeburg. Ibid., p. i; Roland Hammond, *Genealogy*, pp. 270, 272; receipt for tuition, piano, music and French for both Katherines at Dr. Legaré's Orangeburg School, Jan. 11, 1857, JHH Business Papers, SCL.

3. Spann, writing in 1909, said that "Clara's father [J.C. Kilpatrick], by his will, had left all of his property to her and her brother and had made no provision whatever for her mother [Amanda Whitner Kilpatrick Lorton, first cousin of James Henry Hammond]: that he [Colonel Whitner, Clara's grandfather and the husband of James Henry Hammond's aunt, Elizabeth Ann Spann] had bound Clara by a promise, while a girl, to rectify and avenge this oversight or neglect of her

trained the girl up to hate him and this act is to be a stigma on his memory, and their malice is such that they will allow no one to share with his own daughter in striking this blow. Is not this horrible? Yet it is just what I expect myself. My children have all been tampered with. Spann has evidently been disparaging me with Whitner and Co. It was also, as appears from the letter, their scheme to divide the Estate without Spann having a word and doubtless so to divide it as to tie him to them and break him off, by tales which he is evidently willing to believe, from us. It appears from this letter that Whitner said to Spann that he stood in the relation of pensioner to me, that it was insupportable, that he would advise him to save enough to buy some spot secret "his own Castle," but that his marriage would settle all that and give him a home and employment. You will see through this. I doubt if Spann ever told him or any of them that the whole and sole reason why I did not settle him was this uncertain marriage engagement. But I can't write half I could say. The long and short is that—as for me—every body wishes to use me for their benefit or gratification and not one appears to think that I have any sort of right to desire to benefit or gratify myself. Very well. All this makes me miserable enough, but we shall see whether "the rest of mankind" will gain by violating the rule of "live and let live."

Lebby wrote me he would put me up a Saw Mill out and out and furnish a 8 horse Steam Engine for $1750. I wrote for specifications. Among them was $650 for a *Portable* Saw Mill. I wrote him I intended to erect 3 or 4 saw mills, gins, grist mills, sugar mills and threshers all to suit me and did not care for any thing "portable" but the Power and asked to know how and at what extra cost it could be applied to each and all of these. Yesterday he wrote me that he wanted the 8 horse engine (which he had before promised me in a month) for himself, that as soon as he finished the work now in his shop he should sell out and quit etc., etc. You see, no man will deal with me if he can't put his finger in my eye. I immediately changed foot. Started 5 hands today and will start 7 more tomorrow to getting out timber for a Water works

father's from her portion and to do it alone upon coming of age, without the risk of being thwarted by a husband." Spann had never given a thought to her property and was interested only in "herself, and only herself. . . . Had she been pennyless, it would not have concerned me." ESH to Annie H. Walker, Aug. 14, 1909, ESH Letterpress Book, ESH Papers, SCL; Simpson, *History of Old Pendleton District*, pp. 79–80, 170; Billings, "The Hammond Family."

on the Canal. I was misgiving before. I should never have had an easy moment with a Steam Engine about a Cotton gin. It is a great power— must be mastered for Plantation purposes. I leave it to the next generation.

You can easily be the Next Gov. if you will not allow any man to see you noticeably in liquor between now and then. If you want to serve me and mine, yourself and yours and ours do this. It would gratify and benefit me ten times more for you to be elected Gov. than that I should receive the compliment of an election to the U.S. Senate. I say this in entire sincerity and earnestness.

Whooping cough will have its course. Drosera[4] etc. will mitigate and shorten. Nothing can do more. With my affectionate regards to Harriet and all.

Yours,

H.

JAMES HENRY HAMMOND TO WILLIAM GILMORE SIMMS[c]

Redcliffe, August 13, 1857

My Dear Simms:

I rec'd. your kind and considerate letter of the 9th today. I thank you for it. You have said all that can be said against the position I have taken up, and said it more clearly and more forcibly than any other can do it. I confess your letter stirred my feelings, but it did not alter my convictions. My labours—mental and physical—are such now that I feel always weary and exhausted and to write a line is an effort, but I will try to lay before you as clearly as I can my views of this matter. I don't expect to be understood by many or appreciated by but very few. But being sure of your appreciation I will try to make myself understood and as your friendship led you to travel so carefully over all the ground—I hope to succeed.

I do not seek office from the State. She has committed a *great* and *wanton* outrage upon me. I don't even ask reparation for that I can do without it. Before I will under these circumstances humble myself and

4. Drosera is a large family of insectivorous plants, including the sundews. A popular herbal remedy concocted from these plants was thought to have medicinal properties and was used as a diuretic and antispasmodic as well as a general cure-all.

go upon my knees to beg of her either office or reparation, I will lay my head upon the block. She has given the example—the first in history—of ostracising a man for (*imputed*) want of chastity, but she can offer me no bribe nor inflict on me any punishment that shall force me to sanction her sentence or succumb to it. She must spontaneously and with large unanimity expunge the stain she has fixed on me, before I will lift a finger in obedience to her beyond what the law compels everyone to do. I ask nothing. I have need of nothing at her hand. I am content to live and die as I am and expect to do it. If she needs me, I have a right to demand of her as the price of my services that she shall of her own motion repair the injustice she has done me. I don't, I will not demand it. I am indifferent about it. But my head and my hand are my own, and by all the Gods, she shall have no aid from either until she puts herself nechius in curia [*sic*] before me. Here I rest. High and Haughty you may say "Stuck up" says the Rabble called the "People." Very well. Let the Rabble and their more Rabble Representatives go on to apply the bowstring to every public man who gets his head above his fellows, the moment he does so. Time will show them what must come. Talent is not often linked with baseness and few that have been stricken will sneak back to lick the hand that strikes. I have made my statement. Let me look into the facts that support it.

I had a private quarrel. It was with a member of my own family. His position and mine were such as to make it notorious. All the State knew it. They knew also that it involved matters so delicate that while he spoke vaguely I refused all explanation even to my most confidential friends. Nay, rather than explain, I, as soon as possible, withdrew from Society, thereby confessing myself in the wrong. Three years later I am involved—by no motive of my own, in an election for the highest office of the State [U.S. Senate]. This quarrel is brought up. My Enemy is weak enough to seek from the Legislature revenge that he dared not achieve for himself. His charges and insinuations amount in substance to this, that I had attempted the virtue of a respectable female. No such charge was ever before made before a Legislature or other body politic. No such attempt, even if successful, had ever before affected a man's political position and more than slightly his social status. It would have been scoffed out of any other political assembly that ever sat in the world. Of course I refused to make any explanations. I was not to be arraigned by such a body for my peccadilloes and to open the secrets of my life to any Rabble, not even if it assumed to be a Legislature. Yet the stupid Blackguards assumed jurisdiction, condemned me to gratify the Vengeance of another private citizen, and affixed on me the brand of infamy so far as they could do it. Since that time eleven years have elapsed, fourteen since the quarrel. Now a similar election comes up.[1] My name—for it has survived all this—is again brought forward: and now again I am asked to come up for arraignment to plead guilty or not guilty, and sustain my plea. What an absurdity. I refused to do this 11 years ago. These 11 years have consumed the very prime of my manhood. By course of nature they should have cooled my political aspirations; passed in solitude ignoring politics, they have extinguished every spark of ambition. And to do now; what principle and sentiment forbade my doing then, for a bribe which having no attraction then, I look upon with loathing now, would be the most ridiculous thing that I can conceive of. I do not put a high value on political consistency—but moral consistency is all in all—the very essence of character. How is it possible for me to do now, what for 14 years, I have maintained I could not do as a man of honor and principle? "Penance." If this were a question of private and personal arrangement between Hampton and me I might plead penance and ask absolution. But I owed the State no penance, she has no power to absolve me. She can only undo her own wrongs, and I confess I am too proud to ask her to do that, much less to plead long sufferance before her. I repudiate her jurisdiction in this matter in toto. I spurn all her bribes that involve the slightest concession from me to her. I stand on my manhood against the State and the world and I will not yield an inch, save to brute force.

I am aware that another question has arisen out of all this, which is now the *main* question, apparently, though essentially a different one. It is said I have bound myself not to go to Columbia. What if this was as true as it is false? What bearing has that on my political status? But it is added that I am afraid to go there. I admit that a coward is not fit to be a public man. I never heard that Hampton had said that I had either bound myself not to go to Columbia or that I was afraid to do it. I am sure he never did. But thinking it barely possible that he might

1. U.S. Senator A. P. Butler died in office in May 1857 and the South Carolina legislature had to choose another senator. Hammond was available because he had been out of politics for over fourteen years and was involved neither in the explosive issues of reopening the slave trade and the Kansas-Nebraska Act, nor in the intraparty political battles of South Carolina in the 1850s. John Cunningham to JHH, June 20, 1857, JHH Papers, LC; Merritt, *Hammond*, pp. 113–15.

have done so, I embraced an opportunity soon after this report reached me to go there and deliver an Oration in the College Chapel.[2] My advent was heralded for 7 months before. Every body knew it. I staid there nearly a week. By God, shall I repeat that to gratify the asses of So. Ca.? I did it once—rather ashamed to do it at all. I won't do it again, unless to gratify myself. It had no effect!!!

It had no effect. In 6 months I heard that the same report was rife and you give great prominence to it in your letter. I am too old now to risk life or take life to prove my courage. I have passed all that. I don't care a farthing what the world thinks of me in respect to which they call courage. The State has known me long. If from my antecedents they think I lack the firmness requisite for a senator, they ought not to talk of me at all. A man wanting that wants all. They may throw me aside and welcome. But certainly I shall not run a tilt to gratify them; especially when I rate my services so high that I would cheerfully double the pay of a substitute in the Senate should they draft me for it.

However the *State* may doubt my courage and demand "proof." I question if there is a man in So. Ca. who would wantonly put himself in the way of any purpose he knew I seriously entertained. At least my experience is that no one ever yet did, who did not speedily withdraw. Am I a child to be twitted with such as this? Does the State of So. Ca. gravely propose to me the "chip" ordeal of School days?

But you say and all say I must go to Columbia electioneering and fight for an office I detest, for the sake of my children. I have taught my children to take care of themselves and have aimed to supply them with the "sinews of war." Depend on it they can do it. I want them to do it. I believe that the State will make to them the "amends" due to me, which she will never make to me and I am sure there is not a Hampton or any of that clique who will dare to do to them, what they have not dared to do even to me—look them in the eye. This is all fudge.

You draw a splendid programme for me with the Presidency in the vista. Do you know I would not turn on my heel to be President of the U.S. on my own terms. Come, I will not be modest. I believe I could

2. On December 4, 1849, Hammond delivered "An Oration before the Two Societies of the South Carolina College." The two societies were the Clariosophic and Euphradian societies, student organizations whose primary function was to train students in debate and oratory. Hammond had been president of the Euphradian Society in 1825. *Speeches of James Henry Hammond*, pp. 199–230, 376.

make a better President than any we have had lately. I think I could so right the ship of state as to put her on her true line and preserve Union and Unity to the point of Supremacy over all the Powers of the Earth. It is in us—we of the U.S. I think that with Presidential Power for a few years I could make it certain. I do not doubt that somebody will accomplish this. But shall I for a moment fancy that God has given me that mission? No! No!! If he had, he would have given me not only *sana mens*, but *sanus corpus*, and he would not have permitted that a little dalliance with the other sex should have kept me in idleness for 14 of the primest years of life.

My conviction is that my mission is to be a Bridge for Victors—perhaps, I should say a Beacon to warn the Voyager of the shoals of life's broad ocean. Ignoble mission! Yet I accept it, as of God, and on my soul I will not attempt to escape it by ignoring or combatting *Truth*.

I could go on much longer but to conclude by coming back to the practical; it is obvious that there is not even among the populace any particular wish for me as Senator. Tom, Dick and Harry—Everybody has been nominated for the office. There will be a squabble for it and probably a very dirty one. My friends persuaded themselves that there was a general wish for me. The contrary is now proved.[3] I hope they will not blame me, if I embrace the first suitable opportunity of saying that I am entirely out of the scrap. I shall do it any how.

There is no room for other topics.

Yours faithfully,

J.H. Hammond

P.S. Do you know that I believe the majority of those who clamor for my going to Columbia only wish to get at the bottom of the mystery and gratify their gossiping curiosity?[4] They say I have done sufficient

3. The scandal was brought up in the South Carolina legislature again, and according to Francis W. Pickens, a leading candidate for the senatorship, "the line was drawn distinctly between virtue and honor on one side, and open vulgar blagardism [sic] on the other." He described the attempt of the aristocratic families of the state to put down a man "who had no family of distinction, but was the son of a Massachusetts adventurer," and who had committed "*crimes* of the deepest die" against Colonel Hampton. Pickens lamented that he was told that he himself might have been elected "if public considerations were to guide, but it was necessary to put down aristocracy in the state, and raise a persecuted man up." Francis W. Pickens to Lucy Holcombe, Dec. 6, 1857, Francis Wilkinson Pickens Collection, SCL.

4. The facts behind the mystery are hard to come by, but they are of some interest since the mystery kept Hammond out of politics for fourteen years and he returned only as Wade Hampton II

"penance" to entitle me to do—what? Why to expose the whole matter to the public! They do not consider that I was entitled to this from the very first if I wished, or that I have done "penance" chiefly to avoid this which was and still would be to me the most painful of all penances. If my long suffering entitles me to any thing it is to be saved from this very thing which it is now demanded I shall do. If they really think I have been punished enough, what they—the Legislators should say is this "We have severely punished you for daring to give offence to Col. Hampton—altho' we do not know what the offence exactly was and can't get the facts out and upon the whole we think you have paid the full penalty. We will therefore take our hands off you of our own motion and leave you and Hampton both where we found you without asking explanation any further." But what is really the case is "We condemned you and made you infamous for offending Hampton in some unknown way. If you will come forward now cap in hand, confess this 14 yr old sin, tell us all about it and fight it through, we will pardon you if you petition for it."

---

was about to die (1858). Hammond's writings are the only major source and they often seem to cast him in a heroic light. He makes reference to a letter to Wade Hampton in which he sought to set the record straight on his "great indiscretion" by pointing out that he did not attempt to seduce Hampton's nineteen-year-old daughter but rather that he had been carrying on a dalliance with four of Hampton's daughters for a long period of time.

The dalliance is elsewhere described as going on for two years beginning when the youngest girl was thirteen and the oldest seventeen, as taking place in Hammond's home in Columbia while he was governor, and that their meetings with him were never less than once a week and usually more frequent. He claimed that they came voluntarily to his house, rushing into his arms, covering him with kisses, sitting in his lap, pressing their bodies to his and allowing him to touch them everywhere, but that his intimacy with them stopped short of actual sexual intercourse. It was only after two years that the eldest Hampton girl took offense at something he did and ran off to tell her Aunt Catherine (his wife).

After Hampton used this incident to prevent Hammond's election to the Senate in 1846, James Henry came to think of himself as the protector of the Hampton girls' reputations against their unchivalrous father who through his publicity of their indiscretions inflicted permanent disgrace upon his children for his own political gain. None of Hampton's daughters ever married. Hammond summed up: "Alas, how much I must endure, without a crime: nay, all things considered, after a more virtuous and honorable course than one in a hundred would have been capable of pursuing." R. F. W. Allston to Adele Allston, Dec. 10, 1846, R. F. W. Allston Papers, SCHS; F. W. Pickens to Lucy Holcombe, Dec. 6, 1857, Francis Wilkinson Pickens Papers, SCL; JHH to WGS Oct. 6, 1846, JHH Papers, LC; JHH to John Fox Hammond, March 6, 1842, JHH, Memorandum, Sept. 6, 1847, HBC Family Papers, SCL; Faust, A Sacred Circle, pp. 41–42, citing JHH Diary, July 3, 1845, Dec. 9, 1846, JHH Papers, SCL; JHH to WGS, July 8, 1848, JHH Papers, LC; JHH Diary, Dec. 4, 1846, Jan. 23, 1847, JHH Papers, SCL; Billings, "The Hammond Family"; Oliphant, Simms 2:218–19, 234–37, 314–19, 321–24, 343–48.

WILLIAM GILMORE SIMMS TO JAMES HENRY HAMMOND[s]

Charleston, [August 23, 1857][1]

My dear Hammond:

In writing to you as I did, I had for my object simply to place the case before you as it appears to people about the country. I knew that neither they nor I could possibly enter into its merits so sufficiently as to grasp all the details. I was fully aware also, that, to your mind, the game of office, *per se*, would be held hardly worth the candle. Nor did I overlook the fact that were you to be sent to the Senate, you would peril a great deal of previous reputation. You would have great leeway, in point of practice and current information, to make up; and several disadvantages to overcome, in consequence of so long an absence from all the fields of legislation. Still, I felt sure that you would surmount all this, and add to your reputation; because of your native good sense, your large powers of generalization, and (an unusual combination) your capacity for the grasp of infinite detail. I desire, therefore, in spite of all the peril to reputation, & even health, that you should go to the Senate, assured, that, with your resolute will, you would bring all your endowments into play, at the proper season, overcoming all disabilities. And, believing all this, I wish you in the Senate just as much *pro bono publico*, as with regard to your single satisfaction and distinction. And I was, & am, indignant, *pro bono publico*, that a damnable piece of bullying—for it is nothing less—should perpetually be resorted to, to baffle your performances & the public good. I suffered some temper to enter into the operations of my judgment, in much that I said; and was quite willing that the vulgar public should be deprived of a pretext—your enemies & opponents rather—through the very processes which they had assumed as the only tests. I would, therefore, go to Columbia— avowedly for any issue that your enemies would force upon you; not that I believe that there would, or could be, any demonstration of a personal character; but simply to kill off the miserable pretext upon which they have worked successfully so long. I desired it for other reasons which I did not express in my previous letter, but which I owe it

1. The date was supplied in Oliphant, *Simms* 3:505 n. 68.

equally to you & to myself to deliver now—to you, as showing you all
of the facts in the externals of this game, & to myself in part justification
of that counsel which I rather insinuated than gave. For years, your
friends—and you will, I take for granted, believe that I was not the
silentest among them—have been compelled to deny, almost daily, a
variety of scandals & slanders at your expense, which, through the
winds, as it were (for there could be found no more responsible authority) have been put & kept in circulation. There are two, in particular,
which, combatted with scorn & denial a thousand times before, have
been recently suffered to start up in amazing activity. These slanders
represent you as a sot, utterly lost to society, & for this reason not fit to
appear in the world; and this is assigned as a new reason why you are
no longer willing to be seen. The next is like unto it. That you have
brutally abused your wife, nay, beaten her, and that she neither lives
with you, nor will appear in your society.[2] I need not tell you that I
have opposed my own knowledge and testimony to all these stories, and
have put the denial wholly upon my individual testimony. But as this
is necessarily limited to my own social walks—a narrow province,—and
as there is no mode of giving my evidence more publicity—there remained but one course for you, & your friends, by which to silence this
fresh scandal; and that was to show yourself in Charleston and Columbia with your family, on certain occasions, and for a time sufficiently
long, to render the impression certain. One great secret of the successful
progress of slander in your case and at your expense, has been in your
reserve in respect to society, and your almost total withdrawal from that
of your own State. In your present precinct, besides, your quarrels with
Augusta, have made you enemies, who are very willing to help forward
a lie at your expense. Now, a week every season in Columbia and another week in Charleston, where your friends may gather around you,—
where you may make new friends—and where your personal appearance
alone will suffice to set at rest all slanders of your habits; where the
presence of your family will silence all those in respect to your brutality;
would seem to be only a proper concession to your friends, a proper
demonstration on behalf of your family; and this might be done regularly at successive seasons, wholly irrespective of any selfish or official
object. Nay, were you to make a visit to Columbia now, and spend a

2. See the Introduction to Part I for the story of Catherine F. Hammond's long separation from
her husband, James Henry Hammond.

week, even avowedly to prevent your friends running you, that alone would seem a desirable object, though I should be the last to desire that. A man may carry his notions of independence too far, and certainly does so, when his indifference encourages such slanders as mortify the pride of his family, and the feelings of his friends. But I wish you to understand that I counsel nothing; I simply mean to show you how the case appears to stand in the eyes of the vulgar world we live in. I can add nothing more to what I have said, except in mere dilation and this, to you, would be needless. —I am now writing from Sullivan's island, whither I have brought my wife and one of my children—which is teething and needing change of air. I have two who are puny and to a degree sufficient to occasion all our anxieties. A few weeks ago, I had to carry another to Summerville for 2 weeks. Thus, you see, I am kept fettered by cares and burdened with expenditures which I find it difficult to encounter. And the worst is that these cares are of a sort to retard and enfeeble the operations of my mind, upon which I depend for the means of meeting exigencies. You must take this scrawl with allowances. I am headachy, and listless, wanting repose, yet with no prospect of getting it for a long season. How does your wife relish Harry's letters in print.[3] Were they correct? I revised them in M.S. but did not read the proofs. Pray make my regards to her, Kate and the Boys.

Yours Ever truly,
W.G.S.

JAMES HENRY HAMMOND TO *THE CHARLESTON MERCURY*[h]

Redcliffe, October 2, 1857

Messrs. Editors:

My name has been mentioned in the newspapers in connection with the approaching election of U.S. Senator, and I have myself re-

---

3. Simms is referring to Harry Hammond's letters from Europe to his mother and father. Simms persuaded James Henry Hammond to allow him to publish Harry's letters with some editing by Simms. Harry's letters were published as "European Correspondence" in *Russell's Magazine*. "European Correspondence," *Russell's Magazine*, 1 (Aug. and Sept. 1857), 428–38, 510–20; 2 (Oct. and Nov. 1857, March 1858), 37–46, 129–32, 493–99, cited in Oliphant, *Simms*, 3:508, 4:40–41. The first issue of *Russell's Magazine* (Charleston) is dated April 1857 with the last issue dated March 1860. Most of the contributions were unsigned, but poems and articles published in this magazine by Simms did carry his name.

ceived many communications on the subject. It is, perhaps, proper that I should make public my determination not to be a candidate. I have never had much practical experience of public service, and for the last thirteen years—which have comprised the prime of my life—I have lived in complete retirement, devoted to agricultural pursuits, and wholly neglectful of political studies and current affairs. To commence, as it would be, a political career at fifty years of age is impossible. It is, at least, quite impossible to me. I have never, at any time, desired a seat in the Senate; but to consent to go there now, if elected, would be to agree to do a great injustice to the State, and the greatest violence to my own inclinations, as well as injury to all my interests.

I am, very respectfully, your obedient servant,

J.H. Hammond

Ballots [1]	1st	2nd	3rd		
Date	27 Nov.	28 Nov.	30 Nov.	[Scattering]	
Hammond	65	71	85	Dargan	3
Pickens	39	50	59	Barnwell	2
Chesnut	24	—	—	Memminger	1
Preston, J.S.	18	—	—	Allston	2
Rhett	6	—	—	De Freville	1
Scattering	some	some	14	Chesnut	1
				Blank	4

KATHERINE HAMMOND[1] TO JAMES HENRY HAMMOND[h]

Orangeburg, South Carolina, December 3, 1857

My Dear Father:

I cannot express the pleasure I experienced when I heard of the high compliment which has been paid you. It is indeed very delightful to

1. Hammond inked in on the bottom of his copy of this letter the tally of the Senatorial vote. The cloud of the Hampton scandal had faded enough that Hammond was chosen for the U. S. Senate as a compromise candidate after his long absence from politics. On the first ballot he received 65 votes and on the third ballot he was elected with 85 votes.

1. This unsigned letter is definitely from Katherine to her father congratulating him on his election. William Gilmore Simms wrote to James Henry Hammond, "I have just got back from

find that you have so many friends and that they have insisted upon your occupying the position which you should. Not only I but my friends here congratulate you. I heard this evening that you were expected in Columbia yesterday. I did not think that you would go so soon, and as Mr. Legaré was going to the depot, I went down with him thinking it possible that you would pass today.

Mother's letter though gives me no little pleasure. I am surprised and delighted to hear that you will not go to Washington until Jan. and that you intend taking us with you. Mother need not be afraid of my carrying my head any higher now, I feel far from doing so when I think of myself as a poor awkward boarding school girl among all those grand people at Washington. I shall *endeavor* to be graceful and not disgrace myself though.

I looked both yesterday and today for brother Harry. I shall be much disappointed if [he] does not come to the concert. So many of the girls want to see him. Any how he must stop to see me.

We are having delightful weather now. I hope it will not be cold again before I get home. Mr. Legaré is having gas carried all through the house. The workmen seem to be getting on quite rapidly, they commenced work on Tuesday and say they will have it in the chapel by the concert. We are to have a grand concert. I wish you could come to it, the Marseilles Hymn is to be sung which you so much admire.

A young friend sitting next to me has just said that I must show her how to do her sums, so I had better close my letter.

With much love to Mother and all,

I am your affectionate daughter.

JAMES HENRY HAMMOND TO WILLIAM GILMORE SIMMS[c]

Washington, January 20, 1858

My Dear Simms:

I am so overwhelmed here by thousands of things that I must just give up—for the present, I hope not for long—any letter writing except the most practical and sententious.

Orangeburg, where I have been delivering a course of Lectures, and where I had the pleasure of having among my auditors, your daughter Kate." WGS to JHH, Jan. 23, 1857, cited in Oliphant, *Simms*, 3:491. See also: receipt of payment to Dr. Legaré at Orangeburg school for Katherine Hammond's tuition, January 11, 1857, JHH Business Papers, SCL.

Well then I want your direct and distinct advice for myself. The South here is utterly unorganised and I fear demoralized. I have been sent here with such a name that I cannot attempt except in the most cautious and modest manner to suggest anything. Every would be Southern leader looks on me as a Rival and is shy. They are all so small that I don't think it wanting to say that if my present health continues I could in time put them all in my breeches pocket. But it requires *time*—years for the weeks that pressing questions allow.[1] I must therefore move soon and take the consequences. We have no concert, nobody proposes any or seems to think of it. Each one is striking out for himself—running off on any rabbit trail that occurs.

I have seen enough to convince me that it is out of the question that the Southern members will agree to present as an ultimatum Kansas or Disunion and unless it is done, Kansas will not be admitted with the L. Con.[2]

What then?

If it comes to this I propose to say that I vote with indifference for the L. Cons. etc. and repudiate the question as a test on Slavery.

1. By the time Hammond was elected to the Senate, the North and South were polarized over the issue of the expansion of slavery into the territories. The Compromise of 1850 had temporarily settled the slavery question, but the Act had been undermined by the passage of Stephen Douglas's Kansas-Nebraska Act of 1854 which raised again the general question and particularly the status of slavery in Kansas. The outcome was a civil war in Kansas. President James Buchanan and Senator Stephen Douglas of Illinois became embroiled on opposite sides of this controversy. Their confrontation over Kansas was splitting the Democratic party. At this point, Hammond entered the Senate.

2. In the struggle over Kansas statehood the Lecompton Constitution was a slavery constitution drafted at Lecompton, Kansas. The proslavery delegates decided not to submit the whole constitution to the people; instead the voters were permitted merely to vote for the "constitution with slavery," or for the "constitution with no slavery." If the latter option was chosen, slavery would cease to exist "except that the right of property in slaves now in this Territory shall in no measure be interfered with." Free State people refused to vote in so rigged an election; therefore the proslavery advocates, who were a minority of the territorial population, succeeded in approving the Lecompton Constitution in December 1857. President Buchanan, who wished an end to the crisis in Kansas, submitted it to Congress on February 2, 1858, and recommended the admission of Kansas as a slave state. Senator Stephen Douglas condemned the Lecompton Constitution as a violation of "popular sovereignty"—local determination of the territorial population on the status of slavery—and led the Democratic party's opposition. On March 23, 1858, however, the Senate voted to admit Kansas under the Lecompton Constitution, 33–25. It failed in the House in its original form. An amendment to resubmit the whole constitution to popular vote in Kansas was attached and passed. After more Congressional compromise, the constitution was resubmitted to Kansas voters who rejected it overwhelmingly on August 2, 1858, preferring territorial status to becoming a slave state. Kansas did not enter the union until it was admitted as a free state on January 29, 1861. Michael F. Holt, *The Political Crisis of the 1850's* (New York: John Wiley and Sons, 1978), pp. 203–7; James G. Randall and David H. Donald, *The Civil War and Reconstruction*, 2nd ed. (Boston: D.C. Heath, 1961), pp. 114–17.

I propose also to say that I am not in favor of any further extension of Slave Territory: that our 850,000 sq. miles are enough for us: that with our soil, climate, coasts, rivers and staples, we have ample ground to make ourselves the Ruling Power of the World without one foot more of soil: that our vocation should be to develop our resources and consolidate the South, that we should adopt this policy, whether to rule the Union or to discard it: admitting fully that we have not slavery to colonize new territory: that all that may be acquired will be colonized by Yankees and Foreigners and come in as free States from our inability to compete in that line: that therefore we want no more territory, no more States, but stand on what we have and defy the world.

Tell me what you think? The fire eaters will probably denounce me as a traitor. I shall not mind that if I am right. I can't elaborate the argument. If you will survey the *facts* for a moment, you can readily do it yourself. Damn all high falluting. Let us accept *realities* and start a policy on *facts*. Let us consolidate our Great Empire, develope it, ignore all asides and stand ready to rule the Union or send it to the devil on a moment's notice.

Yours faithfully,
J.H. Hammond

P.S. All uncommonly well, myself among the number. Delightful weather so far.

JAMES HENRY HAMMOND TO MARCUS C.M. HAMMOND[c]

Washington, March 9, 1858

My Dear Major:

I wrote you a short letter on the 4th informing you that I had made a speech.[1] I have sent you 2 copies and send you a third. At first I

---

1. On March 4, 1858, James Henry Hammond made a speech in the U.S. Senate in which he advocated the granting of statehood to Kansas under the Lecompton Constitution. Hammond made two major points—Cotton is King, and the Mudsill thesis. Though the occasion was the defense of the Lecompton Constitution, Hammond used his speech to compare the resources of the North and the South. He concluded that "no power on earth dares to make war upon it. Cotton *is* King." Secondly, he said, "in all social systems there must be a class to do the menial duties, to perform the drudgery of life. That is, a class requiring but a low order of intellect and but little skill. Its requisites are vigor, docility, fidelity. Such a class you must have, or you would not have that other class which leads progress, civilization, and refinement. It constitutes the very mud-sill of society and of political government; and you might as well attempt to build a house in

thought I was bound to make none but verbal alterations, then I heard that I could make them more extensively, and finally that I could write it out as I chose. This has made 3 editions and I regret I did not write all over for it is full of loose and slipshod sentences as I spoke it, but I will stop at this in this speech.

Paul[2] says, I spoke too slow and destroyed the effect. This [is] true, I did it partly because I was embarrassed, partly that I wished to appear calm and unexcited and may have carried it too far. My reputation as an Orator—ala Preston[3] is gone. I shall take no pains to recover it. The Tribune says I fell below expectation, but proved myself superior to any So. Sen. save Hunter[4] who is a long ways ahead. *This last I don't believe*, on a fair field I do not fear *him* and after my speech I doubt if he speaks on Kansas at all. I hope he will. Look for it. The Union and administration are all out. Cass immediately invited me a second time to dinner. He thinks I squint towards "Squatter Sov"[5] while denouncing it. The *prudent* men N. & S. think me indiscreet. But for Seward's

---

the air, as to build either the one or the other, except on this mud-sill. Fortunately for the South, she found a race adapted to that purpose to her hand. . . . We use them for our purpose, and call them slaves." "Speech on the Admission of Kansas under the Lecompton Constitution. Delivered in the Senate of the United States, March 4, 1858," cited in *Speeches of James Henry Hammond*, pp. 301–22.

2. All of the Hammond family except Harry and Spann went to Washington with Senator and Mrs. Hammond in January 1858. Paul and Katherine returned to Redcliffe in late April or May. Spann joined his parents and his sister Betty that spring and stayed with them until they returned home to Redcliffe on June 24, 1858. JHH Plantation Journal, Jan. 4, 1858, and June 24, 1858, JHH Papers, SCL.

3. John Smith Preston (1809–1881), born in Virginia, married Caroline Hampton, sister of Wade Hampton II, in 1830 and moved to Columbia, South Carolina in 1840. He served in the South Carolina legislature (1848–1852, 1854–1858), and rose to prominence as a champion of states' rights. Reynolds and Faunt, *Biographical Directory of the Senate of South Carolina*, pp. 293–94.

4. Robert Mercer Taliaferro Hunter (1809–1887) was a prominent Virginia politician who served in the House of Representatives (1837–1843, 1845–1847), and in the U. S. Senate (1847–1861). He declined the position of Secretary of State under Presidents Franklin Pierce and James Buchanan. During the war he served briefly as the Confederate Secretary of State and then sat in the Confederate States Senate (1862–1865). Robert M. Myers, ed., *The Children of Pride: A True Story of Georgia and the Civil War* (New Haven: Yale University Press, 1972), p. 1558; *Biographical Directory of the American Congress 1774—1961* (Washington: Government Printing Office, 1961), p. 1099.

5. Lewis Cass (1782–1866) was elected to the United States Senate in 1845 from Michigan. In 1847 he was one of the earliest advocates of the doctrine of "squatter sovereignty" or "popular sovereignty." This policy would have allowed the settlers of the territories to decide whether or not to accept slavery. Although Cass was the Democratic nominee for president in 1848 and was a sponsor of "popular sovereignty," the doctrine was not incorporated into the Democratic platform in an attempt to maintain party unity North and South. Lewis Cass was defeated by Zachary Taylor, the Whig nominee who was a national hero of the Mexican War and who had been noncommittal on the question of slavery in the territories up to that time. Holt, *The Political Crisis*, pp. 57–66; *Biographical Directory of the American Congress 1774—1961*, p. 672.

speech,[6] which I will send you, I could have been. But that demanded the exposé I made. The rank and file of So. men are delighted with my speech and over 25,000 copies have been subscribed. But So. Leaders are cold in their congratulations. I have changed the programme. The Northernmen who have spoken since have quit Kansas and latched on to me. Douglas[7] told me today that he did not know whether he should say any more. Kansas is dead. The real question is the relations of the North and South. Seward brought it up and I made the issue at once—Kansas collateral. As we agreed in Caucus to sit that out on Monday next. I shall not answer them now, but by and by.

It is the etiquette here for foreign members to call on Senators. None but the Austrian have left a card for me. But today Ld Napier[8] came into the Senate—asked Seward to get my Speech and to introduce him to me. We had 15 min. pleasant conversation—result: Seward was right if his conviction was true that the Union was a fixed fact, otherwise I was, and he did not see what the South had to lose. He was very keen in his inquiries and I was plain and open. Now all this is more egotistical than I could write to any body but you. In return criticize my speech—the last edition to the very bone and tell me how to improve. All well.

Yours,

Hammond

6. William Henry Seward (1801–1872), U. S. Senator from New York (1849–1861), was one of the most prominent candidates for the Republican presidential nomination in 1860. In a speech given on March 3, 1858, the day before Hammond spoke, Seward supported Stephen Douglas's commitment to popular sovereignty in the Kansas territory. He too opposed the Lecompton Constitution. Later, in a speech at Rochester, New York, on October 25, 1858, Seward declared that the slavery struggle was "an irrepressible conflict." "Freedom in Kansas Speech of William H. Seward in the Senate of the United States, March 3, 1858" (Washington: Buell and Blanchard Printers, 1858).

7. Stephen Arnold Douglas, born in 1813 in Vermont, was a leading Democratic contender for the presidency in the 1850s. He was a member of the House of Representatives (1843–1847) and U. S. Senator from Illinois from 1847 until his death in 1861. He was an unsuccessful candidate for the presidential nomination in 1852 and in 1856, and though chosen to lead the Democratic ticket in 1860, his party split over the issue of the extension of slavery into the territories. In a four-way race for the presidency, Douglas received only 12 electoral votes, but he did come in second to the victorious Lincoln in the popular count, with Breckenridge and Bell trailing far behind.

As early as December 8, 1857, Douglas had denounced the Lecompton Constitution in the Senate. He continued to lead the opposition to this constitution, despite what he told Hammond. After the Lecompton Constitution passed the Senate at the end of March 1858, he carried the fight against it to the House. U. S., Congress, Senate, *Congressional Globe*, 35th Cong. 1st sess., Dec. 8 and 9, 1857, pp. 5, 14–18; Holt, *The Political Crisis*, pp. 1–217, passim.

8. Sir Francis Napier (1819–1898) was the British Minister to the United States, 1857–1859.

EDWARD SPANN HAMMOND TO MARCUS C.M. HAMMOND[h]

Washington City, D.C., June 16, 1858

Dear Uncle:

Both Houses of Congress adjourned Monday at 6 P.M. The Senate continues, however, attending to executive business. I have not heard yet when they adjourn. From the accounts of yesterday's proceedings the doors must have been open the greater part of the time. Mr. Douglas occupied over an hour discussing Ill. politics.

The war spirit, so strong the early part of last week, seems to have evaporated.[1] Several accounts may be offered for its subsidence, but no doubt the main one has been suggested no where, that I have seen, in print, or heard in conversation. The current was strong for war. War speeches were made in the Senate, the House and throughout the land. The papers here and in many other places were re-echoing the cry. Mr. Toombs,[2] with his usual vehemence, was clamorous for it. There was no one who would venture to resist the current until Father did so in the Senate. Mr. Crittenden[3] immediately concurred and others came

1. The war talk referred to by Spann was not about a war between the North and the South but rather about a war between the United States and Great Britain over British harassment of American shipping in the Gulf of Mexico; Britain claiming the right of stopping and searching in her efforts to suppress the illegal slave trade. Spann no doubt made rather much of the war spirit. The matter before the Senate was a motion by Senator James Murray Mason of Virginia to empower the President to send naval forces to the Caribbean to defend our ships. Hammond played a role in defeating this proposal by pointing out that the Navy was too weak to carry out this mission and in its present condition could not win against the Royal Navy. U.S., Congress, Senate, *Congressional Globe*, 35th Congress, 1st sess., May 31, June 1, and June 7, 1858, pp. 2529–30, 2735–36; Dexter Perkins, *The Monroe Doctrine 1826–1867* (Baltimore: Johns Hopkins Press, 1933; reprint ed., Gloucester, Mass.: Peter Smith, 1965), pp. 208–52.

2. Robert Toombs (1810–1885) was a member of the Georgia legislature (1837–1840, 1841–1844), a member of Congress (1845–1853), and a U.S. Senator from Georgia (1853–1861). He became the Confederate government's first Secretary of State, and resigned in July 1861 to enter the Confederate army as a brigadier general. William Y. Thompson, *Robert Toombs of Georgia* (Baton Rouge: Louisiana State University Press, 1966), pp. 16–174, passim.

3. John Jordan Crittenden (1787–1863) rose to prominence in Kentucky as a lawyer and as a member of the Kentucky legislature from 1811 to 1817. He became a U.S. Senator (1817–1819, 1835–1841), Attorney General of the United States under Presidents William H. Harrison and John Tyler (from March to September 1841), U.S. Senator (1842–1848), Governor of Kentucky (1848–1850), and again Attorney General of the United States (1850–1853 under President Millard Fillmore). As a strong advocate of the Union during his last term in the Senate (1855–1861), he sought to bring about a reconciliation between the North and South. In December 1860, he proposed a compromise—the Crittenden Compromise—to save the Union through constitutional amendments on the slavery issue, the most important amendment being the restoration of the Missouri Compromise line. His plan was defeated. After the Civil War broke out, he was elected

to the same view. Mr. Toombs never even attempted a reply and there the fever was allayed. It was certainly at imminent risk that Father expressed the views he did, and there appeared to be a disposition with no one else to incur it. How such a thing would have been blazoned had Douglas or Davis,[4] or Hunter, or Toombs, or Seward, or any Senator or Rep. who controlls a correspondent or a newspaper done it. In the long run it will accrue more to Father's reputation that every movement he originates is not pressed before the public, for he will not to such an extent arouse the jealousies and envy of those men whose very food seems to require the flavor of a paragraphist's praise. They will act with him the more readily when he does not compete for such every day praise, and in time will acknowledge, what they will the more feel, the soundness of his views.

Last week we were all invited to a party at Lord Napier's. An amusing thing happened to Father. Just after he entered the house he had occasion to use his handkerchief, when putting his hand in his pocket for it he pulled out a pair of half-hose, one falling on the floor full length, and the other he held in his hand by the toe, exclaiming "Good God, What is this?" The joke is going the rounds. Judge Butler[5] once wiped his mouth with a woman's stocking at a dinner at the President's.

Miss Carrie came from New York Saturday seems home-sick. We expect to get off next Monday.

What do you think of the Senatorial contest?[6] Keitt and Adams and

to the House of Representatives in June 1861. Crittenden introduced in the House a series of resolutions that defined the sole purpose of the war as the preservation of the Union. He died in the midst of the war on July 26, 1863, at Frankfort, Kentucky. Albert D. Kirwan, *John J. Crittenden: The Struggle for the Union* (Lexington: University of Kentucky Press, 1962), passim; Myers, *The Children of Pride*, p. 1497.

4. Jefferson Davis (1808–1889) was a member of Congress (1845–1846), a U.S. Senator from Mississippi (1847–1851, 1857–1861), and Secretary of War under President Pierce (1853–1857). At the outbreak of the Civil War, Davis hoped to become commander-in-chief of the Southern forces, but instead he was elected President of the Confederacy.

5. Senator A.P. Butler (1796–1857) was born in Edgefield District, South Carolina. Admitted to the South Carolina bar in 1818, Butler served in the South Carolina house of representatives (1824–1832), the South Carolina senate (1832–1833), and was judge of the Circuit Court from 1833 to 1846. Elected to the U.S. Senate in 1846, he remained in that office until his death in 1857. James Henry Hammond was his replacement in the Senate. *Cyclopedia of Eminent and Representative Men of the Carolinas*, 1:240; Reynolds and Faunt, *Biographical Directory of the Senate of South Carolina*, pp. 190—91; *Biographical Directory of the American Congress 1774–1961*, p. 638.

6. As in the Senatorial election of 1857, South Carolina in 1858 was split among National Democrats, States' Rights Democrats, and moderates not committed to either polarized position. The leading candidates of the National Democrats were C.G. Memminger and John Laurence

Chesnut out and eager. Boyce, declining but also eager. Dargan, Rhett, Orr, Simms, etc., etc., spoken of.

I send some celery seed to Aunt Harriet.[7] Love to all. Remember me always to Miss Barnes.

Yrs aff.

E.S. Hammond

JAMES HENRY HAMMOND TO WILLIAM GILMORE SIMMS[c]

Redcliffe, June 30, 1858

My Dear Simms:

Although you are my only correspondent saving business ones, I have in vain endeavoured for 3 or 4 mails past to write to you. I never had so much work on hand. A good deal of desk work various and important, besides my Plantations—Canals and Mills—fixing up here and running to Augusta. Every week some one comes to see my crop etc. which compels a drive of 25 to 30 miles which is now required to go my rounds complete from this place, while a day rarely passes without several visitors at this idle season. I believe I am better for all this labour, but I do not do things as thorough as they should be done and cannot commune as much as I wish with the absent. Every body in this section has a fine crop. Mine it is agreed is the finest of all, but as corn has its critical month and cotton its critical 3 months yet to go through there is "ample scope and verge enough" still for a half crop, which has been my lot so long that I dare not give in to the idea of anything better. I am rejoiced to learn that you too have a fine crop at last, and I do hope it is the beginning of a new era in your Agriculture. You

Manning. The candidates of the States' Rights Democrats were Lawrence Keitt, Robert Barnwell Rhett, Sr., James Hopkins Adams, and John McQueen. As with James Henry Hammond's election in 1857, the uncommitted candidate, James Chesnut, Jr., was chosen by the South Carolina legislature. Chesnut was the husband of Mary Boykin Chesnut, the famous Confederate diarist who wrote A *Diary from Dixie*. Harold S. Schultz, *Nationalism and Sectionalism in South Carolina 1852–1860: A Study of the Movement for Southern Independence* (Durham: Duke University Press, 1950), pp. 172–77; Ben Ames Williams, ed., A *Diary from Dixie* (New York: Houghton Mifflin Company, 1949); the most recent edition is C. Vann Woodward, ed., *Mary Chestnut's Civil War* (New Haven: Yale University Press, 1981).

7. Harriet Pamela Davies of Augusta, Georgia, was born on July 11, 1821, and died on October 31, 1880. She married Marcellus Hammond on July 12, 1842, and they were the parents of seven children. Roland Hammond, *Genealogy*, p. 272.

ought to give as much of the credit of it to the Overseer as you can judiciously and thus induce Mr. Roach to trust more and meddle less. Perhaps, the idea may be in his own mind now and if so requires delicate fostering—though the truth is the Seasons more than all the rest have made the crop.

I am working hard at my improvements—i.e.—the Plans for them, and find alteration and remodelling entirely constantly recurring. I shall do nothing until you come and I never make a plan that I will not change in a moment to embrace a good suggestion. But don't speculate too grandly. I am not going to have a Palace, Garden and Park here that no one of my children can keep up and Mixer or some one will turn into a Hotel after I am gone. A Hotel here would in fact lay Aiken out. My house will be large—65 by 40 feet out to out besides a Tower 21x27 ft and 4 stories high—the house 3 stories including basement of 10 ft. Piazzas all round etc., etc. I want to build it out of "concrete" or "gravel wall." That is of lime, sand and our iron sand-rock here. Do make what inquiry you can for me about such walls and bring me some information.

I shall expect you any day after this time. Little can be done by writing and sounding the up country villages as to your Lectures. The plan will be to choose your route and appoint a time—not much over a week ahead, and to write your friends in each village that you will be there and willing to Lecture if any audience can be got. Let them go to work and you will arrive while the heat is on. Nothing of that sort— scarcely of any sort—can be arranged and cut and dried any length of time before hand among our people. It gets stale and there's an end. The major has been quite ill—better now—but must give up drinking and smoking—is trying hard.

Ever Yours,
J.H. Hammond

JAMES HENRY HAMMOND TO MARCUS C.M. HAMMOND[c]

Redcliffe, August 10, 1858

. . . Paul is just back. Cathie looked for tomorrow night. Harry here. I don't know what he is at. Playing Grandee of crown and I expect every day a demand for money which I shall refuse. He shall no longer have out of me one dollar over his share of what I make *clear*—say one tenth. The present crops have been reduced one half by the intense heat (3 days 100° *here*, and for 10 days 93° and over). I anticipate no better hereafter, for us. The boys do not propose to save me any trouble or Labour [and] *really are not of the least use to me,*[1] but rather a bother because they won't help me the way I want it, and any other help is hindrance—I shall not work any more for them, but take all plantation affairs as easy as an old shoe. I know I shall get enough to live on myself and shall try to save enough for Catherine and the girls[2] to be comfortable on and the boys may scuffle for themselves. These are my plans. All hope of establishing a rich, educated, well bred and predominant family, here or any where of our name, is over with me though it has been all I have devoted my life to. Your removal and now the incompetency of the boys put an end to it. My heart drops. I have no object now in life. I have no desire for further fame, no spirit to achieve it. "Life is a sad confinement." Do not be surprised if I give up the Senate at any moment and employing overseers leave every occupation alone but my vineyard and orchard. . . .

P.S. Harry has spoken to me about going to Cambridge.[3] I told him at once I had no money to give him. He said he had money (how?) I said go, but I was against it. May you never know what I have suffered about all this. I feel as if he had died. How I had looked forward to his society,

1. James Henry Hammond was referring to his three sons, Harry, Spann, and Paul. As early as 1851 he had expressed the same hard sentiments about Harry and Spann: "My boys in college have proved prodigals and expended sums which inconvenient in themselves lead me to believe that they will squander all I can accumulate for them." However, he was frequently ambivalent toward his sons, for he wrote of Harry and Spann in most glowing terms upon their obtaining medical degrees from the University of Pennsylvania. "They possess now acquirements well beyond the average of young men and their minds are well disciplined. They have fine talents, both I think very superior. As far as I can judge their sentiments are as pure and elevated as I could wish, and their dispositions excellent. . . . I thank God that I am able to give them property that with proper management will enable them to live in a manner so independent that they can pursue truth and cultivate their affections and sentiments without fear and without reproach." Such complimentary remarks, however, were rare. JHH Diary, Sept. 7, 1851, April 19, 1855, JHH Papers; see also: HBC Family Papers, 1851–1862, passim, SCL.
2. A full biographical note on Catherine Fitzsimons Hammond, James Henry Hammond's wife, is contained in a footnote for the letter of July 29, 1859, as well as in the Introduction to Part I. "The girls" are his daughters Katherine and Elizabeth.
3. Harry Hammond spent a semester (1858–1859) studying chemistry under Professor Eben Horsford at Harvard University's Lawrence Scientific School to prepare himself for a professorshp at the University of Georgia. *Harvard College Catalogues 1858–59, Lawrence Scientific School* (Cambridge: Harvard University, 1858), pp. 67, 70.

of all of them, to repay me in my latter days for these long years of solitude I have passed in these woods laboring solely for my children. For nothing else as you know. But I cannot leave all destitute for one and besides an Epicurean philosopher devouring the substances of all around is not the son I loved so and hoped for in old age. . . .

Yours,

Hammond

JAMES HENRY HAMMOND TO MARCUS C.M. HAMMOND[c]

Redcliffe, August 25, 1858

Dear Major:

Harry forgot to say any thing of the goats but I will send them up soon. I believe also that kid is better than lamb. Harry is off. He spoke about going some days before. I told him I had no money. I refused it for the first time I believe I ever did to one of my children. It was very painful. He said he had money. What amount or where from no one knows. He left here last Monday week to go to town in a buggy without a servant. He took leave of no one. I did not know when he went. Next day Catherine went to town and found that the horse had been left at a stable and a note with Tom Bones[1] saying he was off. No one else saw him. What do you think of that? He says he has gone to Cambridge to prepare for this Professorship.

You must not suppose that I do not understand and appreciate the boys. I know well their capacity. But what I fear is that they will not *perform*. They are great to prepare, like their Uncle Paul,[2] but accomplish nothing, save to empty their pockets. Nor can I help it. They are

---

1. In the 1860 census there is a listing for a Thomas A. Bones, a 34-year-old merchant in Augusta. He sold hardware, guns, and agricultural implements. U.S. Census Records, State of Georgia, 1860, Population Schedules, Richmond County, Microfilm Publications, p. 776; Bill of John and Thomas Bones, to JHH, March 16, 1857, JHH Business Papers, SCL.

2. Paul Fitzsimons (1800–1840), Catherine Fitzsimons Hammond's older brother, strenuously opposed her marriage to James Henry Hammond whom he considered a fortune hunter. Paul was the executor of his father's will and Hammond later accused him of everything just short of misappropriating funds from the estate. Robert F. Poe, an Augusta lawyer and the administrator of Paul Fitzsimons's estate, wrote Hammond in reply to Hammond's accusations of mismanagement that though there may have been some financial "carelessness," it was due to Fitzsimons's lack of a system in keeping accounts, not to fraudulent intent. John Shaw Billings, comp., "Notes on Christopher Fitzsimons (1762–1825)," John Shaw Billings Papers, SCL.

always wanting to do any thing else than what is required to be done *then*: and to do every thing in a different way from mine, so that they do not help me a particle, but waste and embarrass. They are under the greatest delusion about their wealth, and nothing I fear, but the loss of most of it will ever convince any one of them that he *must* deny himself, *must* do something—must do mostly *what he does not like to do*. It is very distressing to me to anticipate these things—nay to see their present modes of thought and plans of action in regard to their future. Harry will let all he has slip through his fingers. Spann will piddle his away. Paul will lose his in a grand stroke to make a fortune at once.

You think it hard for them to be buried here and compelled to oversee. Well, I have done it for 27 years *alone* while they are three of them and the rest of us right here. I have worked like ten overseers and made every sacrifice to make my sons well educated and well bred *independent* So. Carolina *Country Gentlemen* the nearest to noblemen of any possible in America. And they wish to be—any thing else, because it involves labor, care and self denial, as if a man could possibly escape these, or be a gentleman without them. But if they won't oversee these plantations who is to do it? Must I go back to Silverton and consume the balance of my days in trying to provide the means for their indulgences? Have they a right to ask or expect that of me? Oh no they would say. But how else can we keep above water? Actions are louder than words. This is what they do expect—that is that some how I am to provide the money and they to spend it. I did expect when I reached this period of life after such long and faithful services, with three such sons as you esteem them and every body does, I should have been relieved of every care of real business and allowed to repose for the rest of my days. And when I had this Senate thrown upon me, I thought they would have rallied around me and left my mind at least free of every thought that could interfere with my meeting my great responsibility. And how is [it]? Harry after squandering $2100 in six months in addition to $4000 the previous 6 mos. goes off to Cambridge without saying farewell. Spann sets up for the Legislature[3] and is riding all over the

3. James Henry Hammond, in the following months, wrote bitterly that Spann had gone campaigning for five weeks without writing home once. "It is said he will not return until after the election. A fine manager of Cowden!" Spann was elected to the 43rd General Assembly of South Carolina (Nov. 22, 1858–Dec. 22, 1859) from Barnwell District. JHH to MCMH, Sept. 22, 1858, JHH Papers, SCL; Faunt, *Biographical Directory of the South Carolina House of Representatives*, 1:378.

country on my plantation horse leaving his two at home, always amiss. And Paul is about to marry as you say and I fear truly a "fast woman."[4] So here I am fairly broken down by public labour and requirements— able to think of nothing else unless it is to give them up—always unwell, and as usual a ruined crop. I took a look at Snowfield[5] the other day. It is destroyed. I expected 400 bales and 40,000 bushels [of corn]. Any one may have my crop for 250 bales and 35,000 bushels. When am I to get into the New House at that?[6] And why go into it all? I had better repair Silverton and go back there. I wish I had never left it.

My health is better—had no fever for a week. All well here. Mother down—Love to all.

Yours,
Hammond

JAMES HENRY HAMMOND TO MARCUS C.M. HAMMOND[h]

Redcliffe, October 11, 1858

My Dear Major:

I knew nothing of Harry's pamphlet[1] until today and then from your letter. I have had some put up and franked them to you, which

---

4. Hammond apparently is referring here to Loula Comer of Macon, Georgia. Miss Comer was actually from a very good family. She went to Washington with her distant cousin, Mrs. Clement Clay, as a debutante in the 1857–1858 season where she met Paul Hammond. Virginia Clay was the wife of U.S. Senator Clement Clay of Alabama and the sister-in-law of Celeste Comer Clay, Loula's sister. In September 1858 Paul traveled to Macon to see Loula, and according to the Senator he "is really a riddance: he mopes about in the most gloomy silence and puts on such an unhappy look when I ask him to do the least thing that I have ceased to make the slightest requisition." Paul won out over his father's objections and he and Loula were married on November 9, 1858. JHH to MCMH, Sept. 13, 1858, JHH Papers, SCL; Ada Sterling, ed., *A Belle of the Fifties: Memoirs of Mrs. Clay of Alabama, Covering Social and Political Life in Washington and the South 1853–66* (New York: Doubleday, Page and Company, 1904), pp. ix–x.

5. Snowfield was one of Hammond's tracts of land at Silver Bluff Plantation. JHH Plantation Journal, July 9, 1856, JHH Papers, SCL.

6. The family lived in the Galphin house, later called the "Old Yard," until they moved into the new house on June 14, 1859. Hammond had drawn up the plans for the new house and William H. Goodrich, the contractor, provided the technical expertise and skilled artisans to carry out the plans. He received $22,000—a low figure because Hammond provided both slave labor for the heavy work and lumber cut from his own land. See the letter of June 30, 1858; Billings, "The Hammond Family"; JHH Plantation Journal, June 14, 1859; JHH to MCMH, June 24, 1859, JHH Papers, SCL.

---

1. Harry's twenty-one page pamphlet was published in 1858. Harry Hammond, "Notes on Wine and Vine Culture in France," Agricultural Pamphlets, SCL.

Paul will carry up tomorrow with this. Listlessness, indolence, and selfishness are personified in this family. Except myself not one will do
the very hard thing for another or even speak of it to me. All are Epicurean philosophers. And all look to me to do every thing and provide
means. For you know that without means, your Epicurean philosophers
female, drop right down to the wash tub, and male to billiard markers
or porters. This is the result of the philosophy and can only be staved
off by some one *else* doing the work, and I have it to do for seven of
them. Even the thinking. What will become of them when I die? In
twenty years not a vestige. I am building and improving here for some
Tom Foster or Trowbridge,[2] and have no heart for it, since I see how
the children are turning out. I am in for $25,000 for this place (500
acres including John Galphin's which I have bought). Which of them
can support that on Epicurean principles?

I am to speak at Barnwell on the 29th if I live and can.[3] I shall read
a speech. I wish you could see it before hand. I never missed you so
much before. I would go up but can't. Sick and deserted all around
except by lovesick Paul who mopes like a Robin choked with a berry
and is more useless than Tucker. I have done working—no Overseer
employed yet. This Barnwell affair has been a millstone on my neck for
I have expected a summons every mail since sale day in August and
never had a line to the contrary until the last mail appointing the 29.
Then the elections will all be over—everybody on the *qui vive* for the
future, and all possible influence or eclat from a speech out of the

2. Tom Foster, who was in Hammond's employ, appears in the Edgefield District census of
1850 as a 44-year-old wheelwright. Two Trowbridges—John and William—are recorded in the
Augusta census for 1860. Both are listed as carpenters. It is possible that one or both worked on
building Redcliffe. U.S. Census Records, State of Georgia, 1860 Population Schedules, Richmond
County, National Archives Microfilm Publications, pp. 125, 970; JHH Plantation Journal, Agree-
ments, March 1849, JHH Papers, SCL.

3. At a political gathering at Barnwell Court House on October 29, 1858, James Henry Hammond gave a speech which was interpreted in the North as being pro-Union. This interpretation,
however, was a simplification of his views; he had given up on disunion as a working policy
because he did not think the South was sufficiently united to embark on such a course. This led
him to advocate that South Carolina remain in the Union unless driven into a corner by the
abolitionists. Hammond's comments on his Barnwell speech were, "On Friday 29—much rain
and much warmer—attempted to make a long looked for speech to the people, but after nearly an
hour became exhausted and gave over. Yet under stimulants, went to the barbecue—dined with
Aldrich, supped at Ryan's, made a speech and sat up until 1 o'clock. Next day, yesterday, returned
home more dead than alive and went to bed where I remained until 3 o'clock today—better now
but bad. Barnwell people very kind and forbearing—speech a failure—turned it over to young
Rhett, Editor of Mercury, who with his Uncle Edmund were the only strangers present." JHH
Plantation Records 1856–1887, Oct. 31, 1858, JHH Papers, SCL.

question. My *friends* have done this. I don't think my *enemies* could have devised anything so killing. Love to all.

Yours,

H

P.S.   Let Harry get the professorship or anything. Nay let him be defeated. It will do him great good. Bring him to his feet. You don't know how he over rode all my plans here. "Young America"[4] over "old fogy" and put me in for—among other things—a miserably built house at double cost—Goodrich[5] wheedling him into all responsibility against old fogy me.

HARRY HAMMOND TO JAMES HENRY HAMMOND[b]

Cambridge,[1] Oct. 1858

Dear Father:

I have deferred writing to you till you had gotten through with your speech. I did not wish to add to your annoyance while you were engaged with it. I beg you will let me tell you now why it was that I left home.

I have put off writing to you till now because I did not wish to disturb you while you were engaged with the preparation of your speech for Barnwell. You know of the causes which induced me to leave home, but you may not be aware either that they were the *causes*, or that I appreciated as you must appreciate them. I beg you will let me state them. I have for nearly 27 years enjoyed every advantage that a man can be surrounded with—wealth, education, the love, counsel, indulgence and support of parents,—and health—And what has resulted from all this? I have dreamt of doing a great many things, I have tried faithfully to do some, and I have accomplished nothing—not one single

4. "Young America" was a popular figure of speech used in the 1840s and 1850s to designate anything that exhibited the youthful spirit of energy and enterprise characteristic of the times. Historically it was a concept related to ideas of romantic individualism.

5. Hammond later disputed Goodrich's bill, but he finally paid the contractor an additional $2,000 which, he wrote, "I paid though I should not have paid a cent." JHH Plantation Journal, Oct. 12, 1859, JHH Papers, SCL.

1. This letter was written from Harvard, since Harry was a student there in the fall term of 1858. See also letters of Aug. 10 and Aug. 25, 1858.

undertaking has resulted in success. The last of my efforts was made this year. I did my best. The negroes in the yard and on the plantation will tell you that *I failed. They, everyone of them,* can tell you that too. The neighbors, William Eve, every body who knew what I did can bear witness to both these facts. I was not aware of this until you came home—a few words from you opened my eyes and I saw how wretchedly incompetent I had been to trusts which ordinary men, overseers, and even negroes may execute successfully. Nor was this view confined to a single glance. If I walked through the yard, if I looked at the vineyard, or the garden, or the orchard, if I went to the Plantation— everywhere and every moment I saw the marks of it too clearly to be excused or mistaken once my eyes were opened. If I spoke to a negro I saw he knew it, and pitied me, for they liked me. I had let them fool me and was amiable. The overseer knew it and would have snobbed me if he had dared. You knew it—and you tried to make me think that you did not by conversing on other subjects. I could think of nothing else.

Some men have cut their throats when they were disappointed in love, others because they have failed in business—I had failed in everything. I was the living, walking realization of utter incompetency, patent to every eye. It is fearful for a man to know and feel this, and he can't do so long and remain in his right mind. There is no help for it but to blow your brains out—or forget it. I wouldn't do the former because that would only have changed the circumstances and taken away my body. Now the circumstances had been as favorable to me in this world as they could be in any. And my body has no weakness, nor vices to which I can attribute my failures. I can in no degree justify my faults and failings, nor lay any, even the smallest of them, to any person or thing. Forget them I could not so long as I remained at Redcliffe, or in its vicinity. And I quitted it.

The abruptness of my leaving is unexplained. I had determined upon going; but I did not think of leaving the day or the way in which I did two hours before I set off. My doing so was simply one of those almost involuntary efforts which men make to relieve themselves of suffering which they think passes their endurance.

Since I have been here I have forgotten all this, and myself too, in certain studies. I have felt it my duty to tell you of it, and I hope I have alluded to it for the last time.

HARRY HAMMOND TO EMILY CUMMING[b]

Athens,[1] April 7, 1859

My Dear Miss Cumming:[2]

Ever since I came back from Augusta, I have been taking all the holiday I could to think over and congratulate myself upon the pleasant hours which your charity allowed me to spend in your company while I was there. I have been eating your candy. And I have been reading the novel (Kingsley's)[3] you lent me. Besides this nothing but work and ennui have filled up the last ten days. You will pardon me then for expressing the overflowingness of my gratitude to you. Indeed so much has this feeling taken possession of me, that I have more than once had a mind to turn down this page of my heart keeping there what was already written on it, and filling the other side with altogether new characters. So that some day, when I looked back in review, I might find one which contained nothing but what was pleasant. However, I could not keep my resolution, for when I had read the novel, and when I found the candy was going fast, and when I discovered that my recollections instead of settling themselves down quietly in the pleasant past, were continually fluttering up and weaving themselves in the future, I was obliged to yield to the necessity of again approaching you to seek for alms, which I now most ungratefully but humbly do. And perhaps I would be more successful in my petition if I were to stop here, but I cannot help making a show of the desire to say something that may interest you. But that I will not say it is certain, for interest and myself,

1. Harry was appointed a professor of Natural Sciences at the University of Georgia to begin teaching in January 1859. He was the successor to Joseph LeConte, a distinguished geologist and leading American scientist. In the letter of appointment Harry was notified that he would also be required to teach French. Asbury Hull to Dr. Harry Hammond, Nov. 8, 1858, HBC Family Papers, SCL; Minutes of the Proceedings of the Board of Trustees of the University of Georgia, Nov. 8, 1858, University of Georgia Archives, Athens, Georgia; E. Merton Coulter, *College Life in the Old South* (New York: The Macmillan Company, 1928), p. 255.

2. Emily Cumming (1834–1911), second daughter and fourth child of Julia Bryan and Henry Harford Cumming, was born at Mt. Zion, Hancock County, Georgia, on November 16, 1834. In April 1859 she was living at home in Augusta. On November 22 of that year she and Harry Hammond were married at her home. W. Kirk Wood, ed., *A Northern Daughter and a Southern Wife: The Civil War Reminiscences and Letters of Katharine H. Cumming 1860–1865* (Augusta: Richmond County Historical Society, 1976), p. 107.

3. Charles Kingsley (1819–1875) was an English novelist whose best known novels in the 1850s were *Alton Locke* (1850), *Yeast* (1851), *Hypatia* (1853), and *Westward Ho!* (1855).

and all I do and say are contradictory terms. I wonder how you would do if you were living here—as I am, alone? I have had so ungrateful an imagination as to picture you here in my stead, and I did so (let me confess) that I might maliciously enjoy the ennui with which you would be devoured. But my imaginings were unsuccessful. For I at once saw you forcing (unconsciously) every one to take an interest in you, and then charitably allowing yourself to mingle in their interests till the whole of Athens grew cheerful around you. When I got here I found that Judge Black had declined owing to his health, but that the letter had been detained. So the boys were right, and the thing is settled. I have written to Joe [Emily's brother], and sent him several speeches, but have heard nothing from him. In fact I have scarcely had a letter since I came back tho' I am even with my correspondents. I have however one notable exception to mention, my cousin Mary of Dublin wrote a long eight paged letter on pink paper (what taste, please notice what good paper I am writing to you on. It is some I brought from Europe. I have laid aside what I have left in the hope that I may be allowed to use it in writing to you. By the by I have just sent for a ream, will you allow me to share it with you?) Her letter was as kind as that of a good Roman Catholic ought to be. She always gives me a solemn paragraph about my lack of religion, and I am amused at the utter impossibility of her conceiving me to be anything else than a man without hope and faith in the world. Do you entertain a similar opinion of me? I have been very frank with you, and perhaps I have said some things on this subject, which it might have placed me in better light before you, if I had left unsaid. You never allow yourself to be talked seriously to on this matter—don't fear, I'm not a propagandist—but if I have laughed at some of the passion, believe me I am always ready to sacrifice a cock to Esculapius, and I do so habitually and without murmur or refusal.

Our term [at the University of Georgia] has just finished here; the examinations are now going on. I have just been packing away all my geological books for next fall, and looking over and arranging my works on Botany, a few days more and the campaign will commence. I have had proposals to lecture to the female institute, but I shall decline for this season at least. Indeed I had much rather hear women talk than undertake to talk to them. And this reminds me of a small party I was at the other night. We had an excellent supper, and after it I found myself seated by the most interesting young lady present and perhaps in Athens. I utterly disgraced myself by not being able to maintain a conversation with her. I struggled to do so for an hour, she talking most frequently all the while until at last somebody took her off to the Piano, and I was allowed to slip away into a magnificent old arm chair in the corner where I sat happy and silent for an hour and a half till the company dispersed.

I have been making some very great improvements in the furniture of my room. In especial a sofa of colossal dimensions. I believe the whole Faculty might stretch out on it at one time. Dear Miss Cumming, let me ask you if you have not observed two sorts of people in the world, among the three hundred and sixty five thousand seven hundred and twenty four other sorts that are there. The one sort are amiable, intelligent, agreeable, interesting, sympathetic, popular . . . but whenever you saw them and talked with them, however slow you were to leave at last, when you did leave them you felt heavy and stupid. The other sort—no matter to describe them—are such, that, when you leave them, a buoyancy and cheerfulness seems to have been infused into you from their converse. Not a mere matter of temperament, for not only is your blood warmer, and your eye brighter, you also feel and think more and better than before you saw them. Is this so?

. . . If there is anything I can do which will induce you to write me a long letter, and right soon, please mention it to me at once that I may hasten to do it.

Very Sincerely and Respectfully,
Harry Hammond

PAUL FITZSIMONS HAMMOND TO MARCUS C.M. HAMMOND[h]

Beech Island, June 19, 1859

My dear Uncle Marcellus:

I should like very much to know whether you have any desire to sell your Mississippi plantation, and if so what you will take for it. Father says it's impossible for him to divide his lands, but that he will give any of us who wish division of negros at $600 a head to the amount of $20,000. I am determined to take it and strike out for myself. Father complains of this and seems to think it very ungrateful on our part. I cannot look upon it in his light: for whatever a man may owe to his parents he owes more to his wife and children, for they are helpless and entirely dependent on him. The prospect which Father lays out to us is to stay with him and attend to his business as long as he and Mother live, and at their death inherit $50,000: and with this he thinks we ought to be satisfied. This I cannot be content to do. $50,000 to a man with a family of growing children is nothing, and I do not see how Father can think of it when he has $350,000 bearing at least 7 per cent and the year before last 10 per cent per annum, and with economical habits daily complains of a want of money. Besides I believe it is best for our family to separate. All of the blood that I ever knew are people of high and strong passions, and desire to govern whatever and whoever they come in contact with. It is the dictate of prudence for such people not to be too intimately associated. But still I am very loath to leave Father alone to the troubles and harassments of his complicated business. For this reason I offered, if he would give me a separate interest in the plantation, to stay here and attend to his business as well as I did to my own for nothing; and I proposed a plan not impossible nor do I think inconvenient to any great extent, but which would be greatly to the advantage of both. This he first appeared to view with favor, but has since refused, making the offer of $20,000 worth of negros. *He does not think that any of us will venture into the world with that.*

Under these circumstances I do not and cannot honestly think it ungrateful or unfilial in me to take my $20,000, and seek to make not only a present support but a future competency for my family. I would like to have your view of this. In addition to this $20,000 I expect to receive about $10,000 from Maj. Comer,[1] and with this $30,000 and health, and no great unavoidable misfortunes in 20 years I ought to be worth more than $50,000 or even $100,000.

You have had considerable troubles in the Mississippi bottoms and may be tired of your adventure there.[2] I intend to plant and must have

1. Major Anderson Comer (1797–1867), a planter from Macon, Georgia, was Paul's father-in-law. Donald Comer, Chairman of the Board of Avondale Mills, Birmingham, Alabama, to John Shaw Billings, Sept. 11, 1946, Genealogy folder, Miscellaneous Collection, John Shaw Billings Papers, SCL; Billings, *Descendants of Hammond*, p. 5; Ruth K. Nuermberger, *The Clays of Alabama: A Planter-Lawyer-Politician Family* (Lexington: University of Kentucky Press, 1958), p. 79.
2. In Hammond's letter to his son Harry on December 28, 1856, he referred to M.C.M. Hammond as having bought into a Mississippi plantation with his brother-in-law Tom Davies.

a plantation some where by January next. Whether I will go to Georgia or Mississippi, I am as yet undetermined. If I can buy your place on reasonable terms and get time, it may be my best interest to do so. Though if you want a good deal of cash I could sell most of my negros. You have had some heavy losses there in negros besides the freshets. It has been a very bad time but the negros may die and the freshets may come again next year. Now I will ask you this question—I do not make it as a proposition for I do not know enough of the facts—If your money was refunded you and time made up and 8 per cent per annum paid on the whole investment from the time you made it, would you take it? If you answer no: then let me ask Will you sell? and at what price?[3]

I am very sorry I did not see you when you were here. I would visit you in Athens this summer with great pleasure but Loula is not in a proper health to do so.[4] Love to Aunt Harriet and all the family.

Yrs very aff.

P.F. Hammond

JAMES HENRY HAMMOND TO MARCUS C.M. HAMMOND[h]

Redcliffe, June 24, 1859

My Dear Major:

We tumbled into the new house [at Redcliffe] on the 14th. I find the air better and sleep better and altogether am better. Could do something, if I was not so utterly entangled by non-doers and expectants that I do nothing. I am at a point which you have not reached. My children and myself differ so as to what I am to do for them and they for me that an abyss separates us and there is no ground on which we can meet. Each requires to be set up in precise conformity with his imagination and in the mean time will only pretend and play at work, mope and piddle. I have to use servants—and you know how stupid mine are, but

3. Apparently Paul did not purchase his uncle's Mississippi plantation, for James Henry Hammond wrote his brother less than a week after Paul's letter that he was in agreement with Marcellus's decision not to sell the Mississippi plantation at that time. Moreover, by the following summer, Paul was running all of his father's plantations. See letter of June 24, 1859; JHH Plantation Journal, Aug. 8, 1860, JHH Papers, SCL.

4. At the time of this letter Loula was pregnant with their first child, Marcus Claude Hammond, who was born on August 5, 1859. Billings, *Descendants of Hammond*, p. 5.

it is the most satisfactory—to transmit all my business. There is no way but for me to sell all I can sell, divide and let them go. They will do nothing for, with or about me. It is degrading—overseeing, as if I have not been 35 years overseeing for them. All my lands and houses below, the marled and the drained, in short all the labour of my life I must sacrifice and see go to waste and ruin before my eyes. Gangs of negroes in the West have been sold at $1000. If any one will give me $800 for 250 he shall have them and with the rest I will anchor here and surrender myself to the vine and to mere farming. I can't do more any longer. Send me a purchaser—credit unlimited with *good* security. I can't stand this. I will cut the knot. Every one must know what they stand on little or much. For myself I demand and mean to keep an income of $10,000. I have earned that. The rest, more than as much if we could pull together, half as much otherwise, they can share among them and be *independent*. Glorious Young America with whom *independence* is all and all, if it is also starvation: or rather if it is the most ridiculous fallacy that ever entered the human brain. Who ever was, who ever can be independent? Of all the bubbles name another to compare with this.

The rot has stopped and my vineyard looks fine. Axt was here the other day with Redmond. He is very anxious to have a finger in it. He told R. that he had never seen any thing to compare with it in Europe or America. I always knew this was the spot for vines—Tom's [Davies] as good. Cultivation will make the wine. I would not give my 9 acres for Green Branch!!¹

You are right not to sell in the West *now*. Things can scarcely ever be so bad as now. It was very liberal in Tom to offer to let you out without loss. You could not expect as much from any one else *now*. Here after it may be better. A man who has it should keep it for the present, but one who has it not, would be simply a fool to give cost and charges for any Miss. plantation that has been doomed these two years.

---

1. Charles Axt, a winegrower from Crawfordsville, Georgia, won a cup for the "best half dozen bottles Catawba still wine, vintage 1858." Hammond had such confidence in Axt's winegrowing talent that he bound over a favored slave, Henderson, to Axt for a four-year apprenticeship "to learn vine cultivation etc." Dennis Redmond, a horticulturist, was editor in Augusta of the agricultural journal, *The Southern Cultivator*. Both men came frequently to Redcliffe. Green Branch was one section of Hammond's Silver Bluff plantation. JHH Plantation Journal, May 2 and July 9, 1856, June 3, July 13, Aug. 25 and 26, Oct. 18, 1859; JHH Orchard Diary, p. 90, JHH Papers, SCL; U.S. Census Records, State of Georgia, 1860 Population Schedules, Richmond County, National Archives Microfilm Publications, p. 1026; *The Southern Cultivator*, Oct. 1859.

Wise is about as fit to be President as Jeff Jennings, and [Stephen] Douglas is a sort of Jack Foster.[2] I will give them both a certificate that neither *ever will be* under any deal of the cards.

I think we both eat too much as well as drink. It is indigestion after all.

Mother[3] is down. I am expecting Eve[4] and family tonight. All pretty well. Paul and Loula (the last has an excuse) look like robins with berries in their throats—Catty ditto—Spann flits about like a night hawk. Love to all.

Yrs.,

H

HARRY HAMMOND TO JAMES HENRY HAMMOND[b]

Athens, June 29 & 30, 1859

Dear Father:

I was much obliged to you for your kind letter which I received this morning. I wish to tell you that my wishes coincide entirely with what you desire in reference to your plantation. Nothing would be more painful to me than to see you sell a single negro, or an acre of land. I

2. Henry Alexander Wise (1806–1876) was a member of Congress (1833–1844), minister to Brazil (1844—1847), and at the time of Hammond's letter, governor of Virginia (1856–1860). Jeff Jennings was a grocer in Augusta. Jack Foster was a thirty-two-year-old farmer living at Beech Island in 1860. Receipt from Jennings to Hammond, Dec. 27, 1855, JHH Business Papers, SCL; *Biographical Directory of the American Congress 1774–1961*, p. 1838; U.S. Census Records, State of South Carolina, 1860 Population Schedules, Edgefield County, National Archives Microfilm Publications, p. 100.

3. Catherine Fox Spann (1785–1864) married Elisha Hammond in 1806. She bore four children, James Henry, Caroline Augusta, M.C. Marcellus, and John Fox Hammond. Widowed in 1829 at the age of forty-four, Mrs. Hammond lived with or near her son James Henry and saw him achieve wealth and fame. In 1856 she moved to a house on the Edgefield Court House Road where she died on June 1, 1864. JHH Plantation Journal, June 1, 1864, JHH Papers, SCL; Billings, "The Hammond Family."

4. James Henry Hammond probably was referring to William Joseph Eve (1804–1863), the son of Aphra Ann Pritchard and Oswell Eve. Aphra was the sister of Mrs. Catherine Fitzsimons. William Joseph Eve and Catherine Fitzsimons Hammond were first cousins. He married Philoclea Edgeworth Casey on October 27, 1840, and they had three children. For many years the family lived in Richmond County, Georgia, where Eve was a large slaveholder and planter. In 1857 he settled in Augusta. In 1860 the value of his real estate was listed as $25,000 and the value of his personal property was cited as $86,000. U.S. Census Records, State of Georgia, 1860 Population Schedules, Richmond County, National Archives Microfilm Publications, p. 768; JHH Plantation Journal, May 15, 1857, July 11, 1857, and Aug. 16, 1860, JHH Papers, SCL; Myers, *The Children of Pride*, p. 1517.

want to see them all go down with your name to your grandchildren, and there is no sacrifice—if one were necessary—which I would not make to secure this. With reference to who shall manage your plantations under your direction—I think that Spann is prepared to continue at Cowden on the same terms as before—at least for the present—if he should get married he might desire some other arrangement—And he has worked faithfully and industriously—and so far as the general result is concerned I think successfully; for himself, without any definite plans of his own devising, or any particular ambition, he has done as well perhaps as one in a thousand would. I wish Dan[1] could realize the necessities of his position and do the same. You must not think we are so very Young America. Dan and Spann are men, and before you reached my age you had entirely revolutionized the management of the Plantation, and were a leading man in National Politics. I think that we may all hope and endeavor to keep your Plantation together and in good condition. But no mortal power can keep it going on in the very manner in which it now does. If you were to take the direction of it yourself, I have no doubt but you would develope as many new improvements in reference to it, in the next ten years as you have in the past ten, and I have no doubt that they would be as successful. The development of your own thoughts and their execution in the face of obstacles, and against the opinions of others, was the source of all the interest you took in Planting. Spann and Dan inherit this same necessity for like impulses to their interest. They do not merit perhaps nor does the case perhaps permit them such liberty as you enjoyed in these respects. And the only difficulty in the case is to adjust the balance between the conservative influence of your great experience, and the progressive tendency of their new ideas. I don't think that you can say that Spann and Dan belong to "Young America" on account of their having such desires. It seems to be Native. If you will read Schiller's *Don Carlos* you will see where Carlos asks Philip for the command in the Netherlands. Philip hesitates and says he is too young and will destroy everything. Carlos answers "Give me then to destroy." God gives man to destroy and *man* demands that much from the world. Carlos would have died for his father, but he could not have answered otherwise without giving the lie to his

1. Dan is Paul Fitzsimons Hammond. On January 4, 1857, Spann and Paul together took possession of Cowden. ESH Diary, March 27, 1852, ESH Papers; JHH Plantation Records 1856–1887, Jan. 4, 1857, JHH Papers, SCL.

whole Nature. To put the proper brakes to this nature is the delicate task. I hope that Spann and Dan will acknowledge the justice of the ones you propose.

As for me, I am doing my poor best here, if my good fortune will float me over the changes which the Trustees must make in August, or November, I shall feel safe. The probabilities fare very much in favor of that. I don't ever care about being rich. I only ask for work and the strength to perform it. I have tried being a rich man, and enjoying Luxuries. They would be just so sweet as they were, but not a wit more satisfactory. My judgment is satisfied, and my determination is fully taken to give up all notion of Eden, and to accept the usual human life of labor and self denial. As for my children, if I have any, I shall be satisfied if I teach them to work, and give them work to do, and in this way I think they will be more worthy to be your descendants than if they were millionaires. And after all I can't help feeling that I am one of the happiest and most fortunate men that ever lived. Whether I think of you and Mother or of my two brothers and two sisters, or of the excellent person [Emily Cumming] who has consented to share with me what there is for me to do here and to hope in the future. Such are the sources of my pride and enjoyment. They are above position, or wealth or fortune, they are in God's hands as they were his gifts.

I believe I will write to M. Guestier[2] to send me some cuttings of table grapes of all the varieties, and also some seeds of each sort. I would like to ask him too for some of the famous Lorraine plum trees, but I will merely inquire of him where the best varieties can be obtained. If you have any documents such as Geological Surveys which you can spare, I wish very much that you would send them to O.M. Lieber,[3] Columbia So. Ca. Boyce doesn't remember him, and he really ought to get them from the position he occupies. Spann promised to interest himself in Lieber's re-election [as state geologist]. I wish very much that he would sound the Governor on the subject, for if he [Governor Gist] is favorable, Lieber will write to him at once, and he may be induced to speak of the Survey in his [annual] message. The scien-

2. Monsieur Guestier was the famous winegrower in France with whom James Henry Hammond and later Harry Hammond corresponded. JHH Papers, passim; HBC Family Papers, passim, SCL.

3. Oscar Montgomery Lieber, son of Francis Lieber, the internationally known political philosopher, was the state geologist of South Carolina. He died from wounds received while fighting in the Confederate army. Myers, *The Children of Pride*, p. 1595.

tific branches of the colleges throughout the State are going to petition for its continuance.[4] Please mention this to Spann. Lieber has done a great deal for me, he can do a great deal more, and has the will to do all he can.

All are well at Uncle Marcellus'. He himself seems to be in better temper and spirits than I have seen him in a long time. I think of going over to see Mr. Stephens Saturday week, if I do so I will run down to Augusta Sunday evening after and I can bring Catty up. I know of no one coming up now with whom she could make the trip. My going down is uncertain too.

Give my love to all.

Very affectionately,
Harry Hammond

HARRY HAMMOND TO EMILY CUMMING[b]

[July 5, 1859]

O Emmy, Emmy if ever man's present love for woman, if ever faith in God and truth, could make a man worthy of the great love you bear me, I am worthy of it. But when I think of the great responsibility I have accepted, I tremble for *you*. Do not try to love me less, but for my sake strengthen your old affections, and do not, do not depend so much upon one chance of happiness. Your letter makes me inexpressibly happy, so do all your letters. Happier than man was made to be here. But we do not love to be happy, but for love's own sake, it is not the pain of disappointment that we fear, there is no pain, no disappointment, except when the object of our love proves other than we thought it. For me there is no possibility of a chance that such a thing should happen. But for you my dear, dear Emmy. The world before this has done me injustice, those nearest and dearest to me have most thoroughly misjudged me. I pity them for what their narrow prejudice has

---

4. The state legislature voted to extend the position of the state geologist for another year and Lieber was again appointed to the office. Lieber, however, wrote that he was forced to resign because he had not received his salary for 1858, and though he desired to continue the geological survey, his personal finances compelled him to find a paying position. Oscar Montgomery Lieber to Governor Gist, letter of resignation published in the Geonostic Map of Abbeville District, South Carolina, 1860, SCDAH.

made them feel. But you—if they whisper their judgments, belief is involuntary—No more of this now, and I hope forever, not for my sake but for yours. But do what I ask you, it is only right you should.

I would be delighted to hear you speak of my Father as you do, if you do not at the same time make me a little jealous. I shall obey your commands and you may count on seeing me Sunday, if not Saturday. Your political criticism does you credit I agree with you fully. Read *Paradise Lost* if you have nothing to do, and mark the best passages. I will get them by heart for you. It is a source of great gratification to me that our Fathers have met and spoken. I have received your Father's letter giving his consent. I shall do my utmost to justify his determination in this matter, by every thing I do.

Harry Hammond

JAMES HENRY HAMMOND TO MARCUS C.M. HAMMOND[h]

Redcliffe, July 15, 1859

My Dear Major:

I sent you yesterday a 5 gallon keg of the Bourbon Whiskey. It is yet a little sick from its long journey but is very fine. Don't judge until it has had 2 weeks rest.

Cattie has, I suppose, posted you up as to all our doings here. For me I do nothing except follow up affairs at Redcliffe. I think and feel much. It is on the decay of my places below, the demoralization of my labor there and the utter incapacity of my boys to put 2 and 2 together *practically* and *profitably*, or to manage more than a turnip patch which *must be all (every turnip) their own exclusively.* They cannot work with any body for fear they may be working for them. They want to get all they can out of me clear, and leave me and the rest to our fates— knowing that I have exhausted myself to accumulate for them, and must, they failing me, depend altogether upon the miserable hireling overseers we can get. What is that to them, or who sinks, if they can be bolstered up to swim?

Family ties are abolished in this Mobocracy and what is even worse, *faith* has vanished forever. No one trusts another, fate or God. All now-a-days work for daily pay—Saturday night at best. In this age of credit, there is no real trust—no faith I say in God or man—no love either. Paul would not turn on his heel to be assured by every human and divine guarantee of a million 20 years hence. He prefers $50,000 *now* and wants that without the trouble of even turning on his heel. He and Loula left yesterday,—for the Summer I suppose—I did not ask him about returning. He has since my return shown such an utter indifference to all my affairs, my wishes and even my conversation that I have long ceased to call on him for any thing or to converse with him except yea and nay. Tucker has been more useful and agreeable to me. Loula is a sweet nobody that one does not miss, and the absence of Paul's stolid scowl and gloom is really a relief. My children are so utterly unlike or so wholly like me—I can't say which—that we are nobody to one another and I have got to look upon them in no other light than as persons with whom I must divide my property. My trouble is how to do it with justice to all and get rid of the loafers. Such is my prospect—but as I can't live long I will try to be consoled by that. As to aid, comfort, or pleasure from them, all idea of that I discard forever. The amount fairly stated of what I owe them and the means of paying it promptly are my pressing trouble. After that comes the management of the remainder. I foresee clearly that my estate will vanish speedily unless Cattie or Betty marry some one who will save a portion. The name will be extinct here in 20 years. Jack Foster or some Dutchman grown rich by trading with negroes or such like will succeed to this place, the Bluff and Cowden, and all that I have created in my 30 years of hard and solitary labor and self denial. These are the views which lead me to think of selling everything I have that will sell and abandoning the remainder: secure something for myself, my wife and the girls and give what is left to the boys. What does it matter whether it is $5 or $50,000. Paul's share will go in the first speculation for twenty of which he is now in full feather. Spann's will leak out while he is sky larking around in perfect ignorance and innocence of the fact. Harry's will melt like ice in eating, drinking, and leaving pockets and store house open to every one who may choose to help themselves. The earlier in life the crisis overtakes each the better for him. So $5 is really better than $50,000. . . .

Yrs,
Hammond

JAMES HENRY HAMMOND TO HARRY HAMMOND[b]

Redcliffe, July 16, 1859

My Dear Harry:

I placed a full copy of the P.R.R. [Port Royal Railroad?] Survey at your option and you gave it to a man who did not thank you, though I asked you before hand, knowing its value and what men are, if he was a proper person for such a favor. I will send you the last vol. to complete his sett when you see fit. Now I will send to your friend Oscar Lieber another full sett if you desire it—I have nothing else in his line—you may write to offer it and let me know your conclusion.

I met Col. Cumming[1] at the Stephens' dinner[2] and offered him my hand and in all respects acted as if there had never been a breach.[3]

1. Henry Harford Cumming (1799–1866), father of Emily Cumming, was the son of Ann Clay and Thomas Cumming. The family was one of the leading families of Augusta. Thomas, Augusta's first mayor following the city's incorporation in 1798, was also president of the Bank of Augusta from 1810 until his death in 1834. His son Henry was considered to be one of the ablest lawyers in Georgia. In 1845 he conceived of and promoted with others the construction of the Augusta Canal, which, when completed in 1847, provided Augusta with the water power for the establishment of numerous textile mills and other factories. Augusta, especially after the completion of the canal, became a thriving manufacturing and commercial center. As lawyer, banker, and industrial entrepreneur Henry Cumming prospered, and on the eve of the war he had declared assets of over half a million dollars. U.S. Census Records, State of Georgia, 1860 Population Schedules, Richmond County, National Archives Microfilm Publications, p. 923; Jones and Dutcher, *Memorial History of Augusta, Georgia*, pp. 387–512, passim; Wood, *A Northern Daughter*, pp. xiii–xiv, 103–6; Myers, *The Children of Pride*, p. 1498.

2. Alexander Stephens of Georgia (1812–1883), who was elected Vice President of the Confederacy in 1861, had been a member of the U.S. Congress from 1843 to 1859. At a dinner on July 2, 1859, in Augusta, he announced his resignation from Congress stating that the crisis was over—"My race has been run." After reviewing his political career he said that he, too, believed in a higher law and warned that on the question of slavery it was folly "to attempt to make things equal which God in his wisdom has made unequal." Hammond, who attended the dinner, wrote Marcellus that Stephens's speech "entre nous was a poor affair and the whole thing a dead failure." Henry Cleveland, ed., *Alexander H. Stephens in Public and Private with Letters and Speeches Before, During, and Since the War* (Philadelphia: National Publishing Company, 1866), pp. 649–50; *Biographical Directory of the American Congress 1774–1961*, p. 1650; JHH to MCMH, July 8, 1859, JHH Papers, SCL.

3. The animosity between James Henry Hammond and Henry Cumming arose over the will of John Fox. Hammond, whose mother was a niece of John Fox, served as lawyer for the nieces and nephew, who sought to break Fox's will. Henry Cumming, an executor of the will, defended it in court. Hammond succeeded in breaking the will and gaining legacies for his clients, but in the process he earned the enmity of Cumming. This animosity between Cumming and Hammond lasted for nearly twenty years until they became nominal friends in 1859 when Hammond's son Harry married Cumming's daughter Emily. Billings, "The Hammond Family."

He was a little awkward about it but for the nonce played the gentleman. How he may do so hereafter I can't tell. He may think he sacrificed dignity. These proud, hypochondriacal people have such strange impulses that there is no dependence on them. I can't go further. I detest scenes and all dramatic and sensational things and will go straight on as I have begun unless checked. I am as proud as any body if it comes to that, but think it ridiculous to be always showing it. I am prepared henceforth to meet Col. Cumming as I would John Bones—but not a whit—*more so.*

None of you boys comprehended me, my views, or my position. I am not at all like the King you name, who could indulge his son in what was unreasonable. I am like Charles V, wishing and resolving *to abdicate.* I do not propose to spend my time henceforth in mending watches and saying masses or any thing like that. Perchance I may continue Senator, certainly I shall grow vines which I think will shortly be the staple of this section and experiment with them for the benefit of those around. But like him I must have means and leisure. At the age of 21 I had a profession and about $1000, and from that time forward such a stomach that I wished always to die and nothing but *faith in God* prevented suicide. At 23½ I married your mother who had a large property, but whose nett income from the death of her father had been under $600. per an. Perhaps such an amount of nominal property had never before been so badly invested. Now after 28 years of the severest toil and self denial, with the *same* health to contend with all the time, I have made on the same spot a property which, besides the place and 10 hands additional which I might require for it henceforth, will yield on the average $21,000 per an. or $3,000 nett for each of us. But this Estate like that of Charles V requires *Management* and without it is *nothing.* I wish to resign it, but I must secure 1—payment of my debts.[4]

4. He still owed over $2500 on the construction of Redcliffe, which he settled by a payment of $2000 in the fall of 1859, and there was the $10,000 Latimer debt, which was to become a tremendous burden for the Hammonds in the postwar years. Augusta Spann Latimer, Hammond's cousin, inherited between $15,000 and $20,000 in the 1840s from her parents' estates. Hammond, then governor of South Carolina, was executor of the will and he convinced her to allow him to invest over $10,000 of her inheritance in his plantations. In return, Hammond paid her interest on the money and gave her a mortgage on his Cedar Grove plantation. He made little effort to pay off the principal during his lifetime, so that, at the end of the war, the Hammonds were still saddled with the debt. For years they were unable to pay the full interest much less any of the principal. JHH to MCMH, Oct. 22, 1858, July 8, 1859; JHH Plantation Journal, Oct. 12, 1859; JHH Papers; MS vol. bd., 1927–n.d., "Myself and Family," John Shaw Billings Scrapbook Collection; Billings, "The Hammond Family," SCL.

2—The equal portion of the girls. 3—The support of your Mother and myself. All these can be established by a management that will give an income of $21,000 per an. and also give each of you boys your share. But I can't manage—won't manage any longer—never wish to crop 7 Springs branch [plantation] again. And unless you boys can arrange the matter among you to allow me to abdicate on a sufficiency as indicated for myself, your Mother and the girls, I have but one alternative. That is to sell all I can sell, let the rest—that is to say all my lands below perish, secure what I need and the girls' shares in 7 p.c. stocks and divide the rest among you which will be very little if anything. Now I do not wish to withdraw you from your career in which you have already established for yourself $2000 a year. By no means. Go on. But here are Spann and Paul on my hands—dead weights. They growl, grumble, sulk and *do nothing*. They may fool you and others, but not *me*. I *feel* their heft and weight daily. Their presence or absence is of no sort of consequence in my affairs. The way they go on does not relieve me of the slightest care or anxiety. It is not the way. It is all sham, fudge, gammon and every *negro* knows it to be so. They account them nothing though I have not interfered for 2 crops. It is a year since I have even visited Cowden and almost as long since I have done more than ride through the Bluff place. But these boys are accounted nothing but obstacles by both negroes and overseers. They don't pull off their coats and go at it. They shoot birds, buy fish, and gerrymander the County. All the negroes see they are mere dilettanti—theatrical planters though they can't give the names. There must be a blow up if this is continued and negroes, overseers, and neighbors see that as plainly as I do.

Now then on this statement which is true and accurate in every particular what is to be done? Shall I sell out at half value and leave you boys nothing or what? It is for you and them to decide. The girls, your Mother, and myself I mean to take care of *first and amply*. And as for myself I do not mean to work any more, save for my own amusement. I have earned that and claim it as the reward of near 35 years of hard labor, in solitude and self denial. By this I have achieved for all of you position and independence. My task is finished. I retire, but not to poverty and dependence, to whomsoever that may fall.

Yours affectionately,

J.H. Hammond

CATHERINE F. HAMMOND[1] TO MARCUS C.M. HAMMOND[h]

Redcliffe, July 29, 1859

My dear Brother:

I read your letter to Mr. H. yesterday rec[d]., I always read your letters, when he permits me to do so, with much interest and pleasure. You praise the Genl., you urge most kindly the decisions of our boys and you admire Cattie—but you have for a long time entirely ignored me. Now as I do not intend to be forgotten by one I so much esteem, I take the liberty of presenting myself to you, and so, the necessary consequence of my acquaintance, I come with a request. I am much concerned at what you say about Paul, the more so that it strengthens my own fears. I regretted the long stay at Macon this summer, and I was in hopes some determination as to his future settlement would have been arrived at before he left us, that he might at least have had something to think of. Paul was very unhappy at the uncertainty—he is different from either of the boys in disposition and seeing how they have failed to give satisfaction to their Father, he is unwilling to incur any responsibility for him. And he wants to be independent.

I cannot in a letter tell you all the little things which interfere with their cooperating, and which I feel for the boys, I regret that they cannot overcome the difficulties, and entirely act in accordance with their Father's wishes, which I have no doubt would be a great pecuniary advantage, and give them for a few years the benefit of his experience. Paul would I think prefer living here and Loula is quite satisfied to do so. Mr. H. has made innumerable plans and he says offers to the boys, but he speaks so violently of what I don't think he has any intention of doing—for instance, selling his negroes, abandoning his lands, quitting congress—taking his share etc. that I hardly know when he is in earnest and what is to be depended on. He is too liberal to the children with his income—but I fear it will not be so easy to divide the principal.

1. On June 23, 1831, James Henry Hammond married Catherine Elizabeth Fitzsimons (1814–1896) of Charleston, South Carolina. Catherine bore seven children in eight years. Of a total of eight children, five lived to maturity. Marriage to Hammond was not easy, as can be perceived in this letter to her brother-in-law Marcellus. Somehow, though, she suffered through his alliances with other women—slave and free—and his disgruntlement with their sons, neighbors, and the world in general. For full details see Introduction to Part I.

And it is not singular that men arriving at years of maturity—taking the heads of their own families—should desire something independent and in their own right. I do not know how far you may be acquainted with Paul's habits, or to what extent he may indulge them, but I feel it a kindness in you to give us any information that may assist us to take steps to prevent an evil so much to be dreaded, and I am sure you will do what you can in writing to Paul and Mr. H. to bring about an amicable arrangement. I am myself utterly useless—helpless in my family—I don't know how to advise the boys, and to open my mouth is only to bring a storm on my own head that I often wish I could be dumb whenever the subject is mentioned. Spann has one of the most affectionate and obliging dispositions—he is industrious and attentive to his business. He does not manage as his Father would—that is not to be expected and he probably never will. His home is a very lonely one—[at Silverton] it is very different from what it was when we lived there, and it is no vacation for him to come here for his reports always raise dissatisfaction. I can't help thinking tho' I fear to say what I think best. I am very anxious about the boys. We have been quietly blessed in this thus far and what is the use of all our means if it cannot bring us peace.

I hope yet you will get Millers Mill and I shall be glad to see you begin operations there. Come and live in one of our houses while you carry it on. I observe what you say about our giving a blow-out in our new house. You don't know in what an unfinished and unfurnished state our house is. I am packed away in trunks and boxes, scarcely knowing where to find a thing. I could not set a table without making considerable additions and furniture—these I am unwilling to get by piece meal but want them in neat sets. If you will come down I will do my best to give you an entertainment and when I am fixed I hope to do better.

It seems an endless undertaking to bring things into order. Cattie has been enjoying her visit to you very much. It is a great vacation for her to get off occasionally, for here there is no young society. I shall be very glad to have Kate and Cassie here with her and you must let them stay some time. Bettie is a nice little scholar and improving very much. Mr. H. in his frequent letters will give you all interesting information about himself. I wish I could see him better satisfied and more at ease, and I tell him only to decide on what he knows to be right and adhere to it, and there will not be much difficulty in getting us all to approve. But what is the use of our wanting things one way or another. We remain in his hands and we all feel much more confidence in his decisions than in our own. I was at Mother's last week she was cheerful and well except the heat which was very much broken out on her. With love to Harriet and all.

I am yours very affectionately,

C.E.H.

HARRY HAMMOND TO EMILY CUMMING[b]

Athens, September 26, 1859

My Dear Emmy:

. . . The bells are ringing this bright fresh Sunday morning for the Sunday schools. They are institutions of great importance in Athens, old and young, black and white crowd to them, and the lights of society, and the elders of the Church, and even the professors deliver lectures and hear recitations. There may be no rest for the wicked, but at least in this community the righteous have more the advantage of them in that respect on the Sabbath, and the weariest man I ever see is my poor presbyterian friend Mr. Wash on Sunday night, after he has attended two Sunday schools, three sermons and an indefinite number of prayer meetings—it's well for him that it is only one day in seven. I did nothing yesterday that I expected to do, and yet my time was so fully occupied with company and affairs of no importance, that I did not even take a walk. I called on one of the Trustees in the afternoon to hear what changes were proposed in consequence of Easter's resignation,[1] but I found everything indefinite. I have devised more plans about this matter than would have sufficed to the settlement of the European difficulties, and with no result whatever. In fact I believe the reformers themselves begin to think that they are at sea, for they say now, that the whole scheme is doubtful.[2] I am only afraid if it fails before the Board, that its supporters will despair and lose interest in the

1. John D. Easter in 1856 became the first doctor of philosophy appointed by the University of Georgia. He resigned in 1859 presumably over the reorganization changes proposed for the University. Coulter, *College Life in the Old South*, p. 258.

2. Harry was referring to the plan to reorganize the University of Georgia. In 1859 a committee formulated a program by which freshmen and sophomores would be transferred to an institute

College. The great error that prevents all the reasonings in this matter is the love of display, that same magnificent feeling which prompts our citizens to raise the mighty structures of their wooden palaces throughout the country. We too, Emmy, will have to live in a wooden house, and an old one, next year—but it is modestly constructed, with eight small rooms—a piazza in the rear looks towards sunrise, across the deep valley of the river, and along an extensive range of hills covered with pine woods. The view is a broad one but the landscape is not improved by the naked red hills in which the Depot stands, and some old fields in the distance with their dead pines, whose white stems and painfully twisted branches remind me of skeletons. There is no house behind us, but over the street there is a grave yard, and the hill slopes rapidly down through a pine thicket to the Factory on the river, and the sound of the water falling over the dam with its peculiar vibrations almost like the beat of the old fashioned clock, is heard all the time when the river is full. In front a white paling encloses a little flower garden that is not bad considering how little the present proprietors seem to care for it. There is a porch too in front covered in with a large rose vine on one side that is joining hands with a wood vine on the other. Here I shall propose to eat our breakfast in Spring and Summer. There is a straight walk not more than twenty feet long from the steps of the porch to the gate in front. I wish it was a circle with some thick evergreen shrubs in the centre, so that the door might be concealed from the campus. The president's house stands at right angles on the left, and in front some forty yards off is a professor's house, in a line with the last about eighty yards from us is Col. Johnston's,[3] and the college buildings, obscured by trees, are more than a hundred yards away to the right and shut out the view of the town. There are about two acres of good garden land attached to the house, and a number of fine peach trees. The rent is low, too, something under two hundred dollars [per year], which makes

---

which "might be ranked as a gymnasium." The college proper would consist only of the junior and senior classes. Also to be established were professional schools of law, medicine, agriculture, engineering, and applied mathematics. The trustees did accept this plan in 1859. Moreover, in 1860 the title of the president was changed to that of chancellor. Minutes of the Proceedings of the Board of Trustees of the University of Georgia, August 1, 2, 1860, University of Georgia Archives, Athens, Georgia; Coulter, *College Life in the Old South*, pp. 260–62.

3. Georgia-born Richard Malcolm Johnston (1822–1898) was a lawyer, educator, author, and lecturer. From 1857 to 1861 he was a professor of rhetoric and belles lettres at the University of Georgia. Coulter, *College Life in the Old South*, p. 258; Myers, *The Children of Pride*, p. 1565; Minutes of the Proceedings of the Board of Trustees of the University of Georgia, August 1, 1860.

it the cheapest house in the Campus. Does all this description tire you? I will add tho', that while the ceilings and walls look well enough, the plaster had the reputation of being insecure. And now Emmy as romantic as you may take it to be, I want to set you thinking in a quiet way about what furniture you will want. Your Mother once told you that she moved into her house already furnished, but nobody is going to do this for us, and I think you, as well as myself, would prefer this, as it is, and so a little thought as to what is necessary, and suitable, will not be thrown away, and may add materially to our comfort; and attention too must be paid to cost. I will tell you why when I come back from church. I believe I will go to the Methodists—

There was no preaching except at the Episcopal church—and I met all the Athenians there. I do not like a large congregation, and I think our protestant churches might be very properly and very severely criticized in reference to all their arrangements and conduct in these matters. But to continue what I was saying about cost. We ought to live within, or very nearly within, the salary the College gives me, in order to lay up something which after certain years may of itself yield as an independency. I do not know what your views of life may mark out for their ultimatum, you should tell me tho', and I will set you the example—I look forward to no grand career—and much less to the enjoyment of any distinguished position whatever. In a word neither my abilities, nor my taste, induce me to hope for anything but the most ordinary of lives. But there is one thing I do desire, and that is, that before we celebrate our golden wedding, we may possess in some corner of the earth, a house and lands all our own. No grand and showy building, but one constructed of such solid material, and so firmly put together that our descendants in the tenth generation may think it the work of their immediate parents, and their children may sit there and recall the scenes of their childhood just as you did the other day in the Burnt lot.[4] It will be surrounded by none of the marks of wealth, but by all those comfortable & agreeable indications which good management and good taste give of their influence & continual presence. This is my castle in the air, and our circumstances are such, that with no

---

4. "The Burnt Lot" was a lot owned by the Cumming family across the street from their home in the Sand Hills. In 1879 when Emily's mother, Julia Bryan Cumming, died, the stables, carriage house, barn, and other "out buildings" were located on it. Will of Julia Cumming, February 1, 1879, Richmond County Court House, Augusta, Georgia.

unusual disaster, we may one day, after having made our struggle with the world, realize it, provided you think it worth the thought and trouble. If you may not understand what I have said, I will illustrate it by adding that I consider what your Father has done for your home out there on the Sand Hills[5] as in the highest degree worthy of imitation, it is almost the touchstone of good citizenship besides being a great deal more in other respects. The only obstacle that may naturally present itself to you as regards all this, is my reputation for extravagance with money. I deserve it, but I assure you I never should have believed it nor would you, or any one who saw my mode of life, but for the manner in which my accounts balance. It is a deficiency—whether natural or acquired, of which I am very much ashamed. One thing tho' you must recollect, that no economy of yours can remedy my carelessness, and if you do not choose to inspire me with some of your prudence, I can only hope that a more systematic life, and the greater importance of the consequences will make me more careful and provident. . . .

I am going to walk with Col Johnston.

EMILY CUMMING TO HARRY HAMMOND[b]

September 30, 1859

. . . If I can't send it [my letter] this afternoon, you will not get it until Monday, and that I would be selfish enough to regret. I say selfish for my letters have two meanings to me and I can connect no other with them, first I write them because it is delightful to feel that the words which I am one day scratching away here, are the next to bring to you, if not much meaning, and interest, at least a faint idea of how constantly I think of you, and love you, but most of all they mean that you will with this idea fresh in your mind, after reading them, sit down and with a few touches of that magic pen of yours, make me the most

5. Sand Hills was the term applied to the ridge of hills (elevation about 350 feet) lying three to five miles west of Augusta and running in a north-south direction. More specifically it refers to the village of Summerville, incorporated in 1861, where many people from Augusta had established summer homes before the war, because they thought the climate there to be safer from the fever. Emily's father's house was located at the southwest corner of Milledge and Cumming Road facing east and was about three miles from the center of Augusta. Wood, *A Northern Daughter*, p. 105; Edward J. Cashin, "Summerville Retreat of the Old South," *Richmond County History* 5, No. 2 (Summer 1973):46–49.

elated of little women. Therefore it is that I regret the possibility of your failing to get this tomorrow, and not that I can begin to realize, that it will make any very special difference to you. You see how carefully I have studied the Calendar, I time my letters so that they will come upon your comparatively leisure days. I am afraid of being mixed up with recitations the other days. I have been quite dissipated this week. I have been out three evenings in succession only visiting not to parties, and coming home at very moderate hours. Last night I was at Mrs. Adams. I met little Mary Gardner there. I fancied she looked at me quite spitefully. I always suspected her of designs upon you Harry, especially after I told her of your calling her "that pretty little Miss Gardner." Well! she has my sincere pity, if that is any consolation to her! Your Sister paid me a short little call Wednesday afternoon, and Mother and I were going down to Mrs. Edgar's last night, but Joe,[1] who was to have been our escort, did not come out of town until after nine o'c. I shall not ask your sister to come and stay with me, because I am persuaded that she would find it irksome and yet might feel obliged to accept my invitation and I do not wish her to have any unpleasant association with me, as we are someday to be very good friends I trust. Joe's gloom arises entirely I think from his professional prospects. No— if you considered yourself half as fortunate a man, as Joe regards himself when he thinks of Kate,[2] I should be—well perhaps too happy and elevated! He is in rather better spirits tho' for the last few days, for Father is to turn over to him some cases of his at the next session of the Superior court. This cheers him, and gives him too the means of going

1. Joseph Bryan Cumming, brother of Emily, was born in Augusta on February 2, 1836. Graduating from the University of Georgia with honors in 1854, he traveled through Europe for three years before returning to Augusta to read law. On his European travels he met Harry Hammond whom he introduced to his sister Emily after Harry returned home. Joseph, admitted to the bar in 1859, was practicing law and living at home in 1860. Wood, A *Northern Daughter*, pp. xiii–xiv; U.S. Census Records, State of Georgia, 1860 Population Schedules, Richmond County, National Archives Microfilm Publications, p. 923.

2. Kate was Katharine Jane Hubbell of Bridgeport, Connecticut. While traveling in Europe with her parents in 1857 she met Joseph B. Cumming whom she married on October 10, 1860, in New York. The bride was twenty-two years old, the groom twenty-four. After the wedding the couple took up residence in Augusta. When the war came six months later, Katharine was in a very awkward situation "surrounded by Southerners and separated from her family, she had few friends who cared for her or for whom she cared." (Wood, A *Northern Daughter*, pp. xii, xiv–xvi.) In her loneliness and isolation she wrote many letters North. In 1894–1895, she compiled a scrapbook of her reminiscences of the war years and the letters she received from her Northern family as well as letters from her husband in Confederate service which W. Kirk Wood edited and published in 1976.

to New York in December. I agree with you perfectly as to releasing one from an engagement. When people truly love each other it must be merely an idle form, the only effect of which is to wound the woman, by the sort of want of confidence it implies, if not in her love, at least in her endurance for love's sake. I told Joe, that tho' it might be some notion of high honor which would impel him to such a course, I thought that if Miss Hubbell was the true loving woman that I hoped she was, it was a proof of consideration for which he must not expect very warm or genuine gratitude from her. However I hadn't the slightest idea that he would ever have done any such thing and I only mentioned his saying it to show how disturbed he felt that he could even talk of such a thing. Julien is engaged heart and soul in his canvass, speaking, going to barbecues, dancing at Dutch balls, looking up his constituents in out of the way corners, and in a word perfectly absorbed. He says he does not expect success, but of course I suppose he desires it. So far we have been greatly relieved that it has led to none of those bad results which we apprehended.[3] He comes home every night in a perfectly good state. His two brothers Joe and Tom are very good to him often putting themselves out considerably to go about with him and drive him home at night, he can't see at night, and in various ways to serve him. You are quite right, I shall never feel inclined to make acquaintance with early morning beauties, until a stern necessity forces me to it, then of course so well regulated am I, I shall rise with the alacrity of the lark, tho' probably my morning carol will be a few groans over my hard fate. Talking of larks, of course I don't want *ten* mocking birds. I told you so before. In the first place, you know I told you, I never fancied pets in my life indeed never voluntarily had one, and then why I should be taking care of Cousin Mary's birds for whom I have suspected you cherished a tenderness, I can't see. Reserve for yourself, dear, self-denying, generous Harry, the feathered songsters. I meanwhile am much better pleased with the crows which are cawing incessantly these bright fall

3. Julien Cumming (1830–1864) was the brother of Emily and the son of Julia Bryan and Henry Cumming. At the age of sixteen he entered Georgetown College in Washington, D.C., but was expelled before graduating because of his "wild and lawless conduct." He settled down enough to study law at Judge William T. Gould's law school in Augusta. Admitted to the bar, he practiced law in partnership with his brother Joseph, and, in 1859, ran for the Georgia legislature. Emily's apprehension about Julien concerned his drinking problem, a matter commented upon frequently in family letters. HBC Family Papers, 1858–1861, passim, SCL; U.S. Census Records, State of Georgia, 1860 Population Schedules, Richmond County, National Archives Microfilm Publications, p. 923; Wood, A *Northern Daughter*, p. 106.

days. It didn't rain last night, and today it is as hot and bright as August. The leaves are falling tho', and last night as the wind moved the trees, the acorns pelted down like shot on the shed. Today is the last day of September. Can you imagine it? This quick passing away of the month reminds me of one of those poems of George Herbert that I was tell[ing] you of. *Jacula Prudentum* is the name of the collection. "The year doth nothing [else] but open and shut." [4] I am glad that you are not utterly shocked at my mode of passing my time. Today tho' I have been more industrious and have really accomplished something. When you read this account of myself I have given you here, forget it, and only think how happy your letter has made me. How you boast of two long letters! When you generally write the merest little notes.

E.C.

EMILY CUMMING TO HARRY HAMMOND[b]

[October 1859]

Harry, you were really put out and annoyed with the flippancy of my unlucky letter. You have never before written me a letter so curt and uncongenial, and that resembled reproach. I am sorry. Tomorrow morning tho' you will get *my* "confession," and perhaps you will forgive what grated upon you in my other letter. I never thought of your taking me so seriously. You know I have often told you that I was quite aware of a bad habit of talking lightly when I felt most, and jesting about what was to me very earnest thought or emotion. Perhaps the unhappy mood to which I have already pleaded guilty, gave a tinge of bitterness, to what was after all only intended to be playful. Your sister [Katherine] spent the evening with me. I am afraid she found the time hang rather heavily. She impressed me most agreeably, so quiet, and ladylike, and then so *very* pretty. I never saw her look so well. She is not like you, I think. Goodnight dear Harry.
Saturday morning. I know just what a little sneer you are going to get up, dear Mephistopheles, over that last line of mine, last night, in

---

4. George Herbert (1593–1633), English clergyman and metaphysical poet, edited the *Jacula Prudentum, or, Outlandish Proverbs* which was published posthumously in 1640. A second edition considerably enlarged was published in 1651. George Herbert, *Works in Prose and Verse*, ed. by Robert Aris Wilmott (New York: D. Appleton, 1857), pp. 301–40.

which I tell you, I think your sister very pretty, and not at all like you, vain creature! You know I think you handsome, quite handsome enough to dispense with vanity in those about you. I wonder if Miss Hammond will like me. We got on very nicely last night, and once when we were alone for half an hour, she talked on as I had never heard her before. We have never yet made the slightest allusion to you tho' she mentions you incidentally sometimes. She is so pretty and so graceful. She said your Father was very busy about his vineyard, trenching, and loaming, if that is the way you designate the process of throwing in bones about the roots of the vines, which she said he was doing. I am sorry you have been disappointed about yours, but these will be so much more of the process for me to see, and I should like to watch it all, and you say you can wait until winter.

Sunday Afternoon. I hope you are having the same relief from the heat and dust, which you seem to feel so much, in the shape of the rain and cool wind that we are now enjoying. It is settling I think into a regular drizzling fall day. The Hills, from the plank road, look as distant, and misty as possible and tho' the leaves have not changed much on the trees, yet every little gust of wind brings down quite a shower of them. It is, has been, very warm here too, tho' we do not suffer from the dust much, but they say in town it has been intolerable. I have not been in except Sundays for a long time. Oh yes, you know I told you the other day I was going in. I went in to see Harker but he could not keep his appointment, as his wife, my sole superior, was ill. So now I have again to get up my resolution, for in spite of the astonishment you expressed that such should be the case, I do dread going. I have been again to the Episcopal church. There were merely "two or three gathered together." I do not think I shall go again until next December. I ought to go with Mother, and my strong preference for going to the Episcopal church, all the more convinces me, that it is right to put this constraint upon my inclination for a little while. After church we went for a moment to see Dr. Steiner,[1] who reached home yesterday. He told me he had heard of me and "of the gentleman from Athens." It seemed so strange to hear any one speak of it in that way, all that sort of mention, seemed so long past, that for a moment I was quite bewildered. He went on to

---

1. Dr. H.H. Steiner was a well-known physician in Augusta who looked after the Hammonds and their slaves. Wood, A Northern Daughter, p. 120; H.H. Steiner, M.D., to JHH, Jan. 1, 1856, a bill of medical services for servants and family for 1855, JHH Business Papers, SCL.

say that he did not know whether it was true or not, but that he had always liked you very much and thought it would be a very good arrangement. We sometimes have the same idea too, haven't we Harry? I have been amusing myself this afternoon burning some of the incense you brought me, on a little pastille burner Father gave me a long time ago. Any one coming in here might suppose I had been celebrating high mass for my own private satisfaction.

Maria[2] and I walked down to the Spring yesterday morning. The young woman is quite in the doleful, pitiful dumps, on the subject of a new adoration of hers, who after spending some weeks of his vacation here, and quite turning the heads of the young ladies, has gone back to college. She had been walking down there two or three times lately, with a party of young people of whom he was one, and the associations of the place were so overpowering that she steadily resisted all my efforts to brighten her "endarkened" soul. It occurred to me, once or twice, that I had perhaps as much reason as she to regret the absence of a former companion at that place, but still I exerted myself manfully, and at last I got her to singing—sentimental tender ditties, which suited her case, if they did not mine. We sat on the bench between the pine trees where we sat the last time we were down there, she leaning against one pine tree, and I against the other and as she sat there, with the shadows playing on her face, and her eyes uplifted, and dewy with emotion, she really looked very pretty. The day too, was lovely, but not with the beauty of Autumn. The sun had the fevered glow of June, instead of an October day, and the trees look almost as green and fresh as in the "leafy month." Only two more Sundays in Athens, and then you will be down here, Harry. Is not the time you have fixed for going down to Charleston, and on the rice plantations rather imprudently early? I almost hope you will not go. What are you going for anyhow, you do not expect to attempt the culture of rice in Athens do you? I did not get any letter from you last night. However, I scarcely expected it, after perceiving how unpleasantly impressed you were with my last letter. I don't know what you will think of the one I have since written you, Harry. It is perhaps not worth while to trouble you with the details of my change of mood, but when I sit down here to write, it seems so natural to tell you all that I have done and felt since the last time of writing that I

2. Maria Bryan Cumming (1844–1873), younger sister of Emily, was the third daughter and eighth child of Julia Bryan and Henry Cumming. Wood, A *Northern Daughter*, pp. 107, 113.

know that I am apt to grow tedious and egotistical. Again, Harry, perhaps you will not think it so strange, that I am sometimes beset by these alterations of feeling. You are prepared, I hope, dear Harry, for the display of ever so much womanish weakness from me. You were *right cross* to me, Harry. I can say it now two days after, and reproach you with it too, tho' at first I was only netted, and you know I am not prepared to make any sort of allowance for any such weakness from *you*. That is all as it should be, isn't it? Shan't we have a marble slab to our side board, with mirror at the back to display our plate? Let's furnish our dining room with oak, and green morocco.[3] Do you know, if I am extravagant in anything it is furniture. But that would not be expensive. I suppose you would perhaps think me hard and cold if I were to tell you how little sympathy I have with events like griefs, and distresses. I am sorry tho' for yr. poor friend. I wonder that such devotion does not melt even her hard heart. . . .

You don't care to be down here tho' do you Harry? You don't love me even a "little bit" now these last three days do you Harry? Never mind. Pauvre enfant. You can't help it, and *I* will make up the deficiency. Did you succeed in forgetting me *entirely* these days? Tell me dear, dear Harry, do you love me a little bit?

E.C.

HARRY HAMMOND TO EMILY CUMMING[b]

Tuesday night, [October 1859]

It is more than three days, dear Emmy, that I have not heard from you—have you been unwell?—has something happened to prevent you from writing? It is useless for me to argue to myself that it is not probable that these things are so—they are possible and their possibility involves so much that I can not satisfy myself, that you have been engaged, or lost the opportunity to send your letter, or that some such thing causes your silence. I never desired more anxiously earnestly to hear from you than I do now. It seems to me an age since I wrote to you myself, tho' it was only yesterday morning.

---

3. Harry replied that he agreed with her about the oak and green morocco, "but sideboards, are they not out of fashion?" HH to ECH, Oct. 1859, HBC Family Papers, SCL.

Wednesday morning

My own dearest Emmy, my life and my soul—tell me what can I say to you to thank you for your two letters I have just read—what can I do to excuse myself in your eyes for weakness for which you are not prepared to make allowance—you do not know, you can not, how I have lived, selfishly drawn up into myself for years, how I have driven from me any thought of, or hope of, such deep unalloyed enjoyment of such moments, hours, days of exquisite happiness as you have given to me. I have been a stone, a block, and now that you have told this stone to live and move can you be surprised, (or at least will you not in some way forgive it)—if it rather trembles in its gait—it is not that it does not live, that it isn't full of hope and strength, but what shall I say? Let me keep it a secret how restless, how juvenile I have been this week past. These books, these occupations, these men and scenes, I can not put my head and mind out to them as I used to, my life has passed away from them, it is with you, it is in the scenes you describe, it is looking at you watching every expression and movement, admiring, loving you Emmy. Don't be ashamed of me Emmy—I will write no more now— Tonight I will write you a long letter.

Thursday night

Mother says in a note I got from her this morning—"come home and do use a little forbearance—don't be running about all the time"— now forbearance means that I shall not be making pop visits at Red Cliffe, and more or less unsettling the people at your house by my continual presence, not to speak of the vast crowds on the way side who will be kept on the quiver by my buggy wheels. I have both selfishness and unselfishness enough to appreciate the great virtue there would be in the exercise of forbearance under these circumstances—but I know much better than Mother does, and as well as you do, how little I am capable of pursuing so laudable a course—and feeling this weakness, I have determined to forbear—only when I am forced to. There is only one remedy, Emmy, and that rests with you. We have already been engaged a long time, why should we postpone any longer? I have deferred speaking to you on this subject until I felt that I could see all the facts that might influence our plans. I do so now, and if you will be patient I will tell them to you. When I begged you, Emmy, to let me give not only the next afternoon, but all the afternoons and days of my life to add what I could to your pleasure, I thought that there was not a question but that I occupied a secure and independent position where I could make a living for us both. Very soon after, however, they commenced with their schemes about the college, and I began to see that there was some uncertainty in my future. I thought tho' that all that would be definitely settled by the meeting of the board in August—but this only increased the uncertainties. I then looked forward to the meeting the 15th November as the time when everything would be settled. But from all I can hear, I foresee that it is very probable that such will not be the case—the matter will be adjourned, in part at least, to an extra meeting after the session of the Legislature, or until next August. It is therefore to postpone our marriage indefinitely to await the final decision of the Trustees, and I don't feel inclined myself to defer a day for them. But we must look as fully as we can to what may happen, and I feel I am bound to tell you how the results will affect me. Suppose then that I leave here—what am I to do? The only feasible opening I see, is to commence the study of medicine again in Philadelphia,[1] in a year by hard work on the practical branches, I could fit myself very well to enter the practice. I could make two thousand dollars in Beech Island, and do nearly as well after a while in Augusta. Besides this I would have all the chances (say few—I think) which come to young men who are strong and willing to work. Now, Emmy, if I were perfectly sure that I would be thrown upon my resources in this manner— I would not do otherwise than ask you as I now do, to marry me at the earliest day you could fix in November. Had I never spoken to you I should keep silent under such circumstances—but at the point where I now am, I can only say that I could not resist the impulse I feel to ask you to share my fate even if it were as little hopeful as the one I have stated—Things are not there yet however. I have the assurances of all parties, that the college must continue to exist—and that in all events, whatever else happens (I use their words) the Trustees will need me here. This ought to be decisive. The Trustees are satisfied with what I have done, if I may believe what they and everybody says—and whether they are or not, I *am* and they ought to be. But I have no personal friends on the Board, and if they determine upon a reorganization, I

---

1. Harry had already received a medical degree from the University of Pennsylvania in April 1855. Both Harry and Spann received medical training from the University of Pennsylvania, but neither ever practiced medicine. JHH Diary, April 19, 1855, JHH Papers, SCL; Steadman, *History of the Spann Family*, pp. 78–79.

would be capsized if I am counter to any of the crotchets in which their vanity was interested—if such a collision is possible I am unable to see it at present. And to sum all the chances up, I think there is not ten in a hundred that in any way oppose the belief that I will be as comfortably and continually established here next year as I am now. This makes me as well off as the majority of men, and when I hand my resignation to Mr. Jenkins to be presented to the board should any thing arise to call for such a course, I will count pretty surely on his keeping it in his pocket. Such is the whole extent to which I foresee the future, and there is nothing then which for a moment checks the earnest and ardent desire I feel to call you mine by the dearest and most sacred tie that heaven sanctions, as soon as I can. The whole matter rests then, dear Emmy, with your pleasure and convenience. I earnestly beg you to fix the day at once,[2] and to make the date as early as will suit any plans of yours. As to what we will do afterwards—I confess that provided I am with you I can not give myself much uneasiness as to how the time will pass. If we go to Washington—and you have written nothing about Bryan—why not go early in November? Or if you do not wish to do that, we can travel somewhere if you desire it, or at the worst they are all ready and anxious to receive us at Red Cliffe.

I have already written enough for one letter, but I will add a line more to say that you do not answer my letters while here goes the third since I have heard from you—but my paper is out and I don't see how I will manage now to write you. At home there you have a whole housefull to say goodnight. I speak only to one person and she is a hundred miles off. Goodnight then my dearest Emmy—dream a dream that foretells and favors the success of the request which this letter will convey to you.

Friday morning— xxxxxxxxxxxxxxxxxxxxxxxxxxxxxxxxxxxxxxxxxxxxxxxx xxxxxxxxxxxxxxxxxxxxxxxxxxxxxxxxxxxxxxxx00000000000000000000000000 0000000000000000000000000000000000000000000000000000000000000000 0000000000000000000000000000000000000000000000000000000000000000 0000000000000000000000000000000000000000000000000000000000000000 0000000000000000000Y—Please answer this letter as soon as you can after you receive it, Emmy.

HH

2. The marriage date of Emily Cumming and Harry Hammond was November 22, 1859. From Redcliffe, James Henry Hammond wrote, "Harry was married last night and off to Florida on tour after." JHH to WGS, Nov. 23, 1859, JHH Papers, LC; Wood, A Northern Daughter, p. 107.

JAMES HENRY HAMMOND TO WILLIAM GILMORE SIMMS[c]

Redcliffe, July 29, 1860

My Dear Simms:

I never felt less like writing a letter *or doing anything* than I do now. This infernal heat has at least neutralized all the good effects on me of a change of air and occupation, and really I am competent to do nothing but to lie on a sofa and read or talk and both the last are fatiguing and to little purpose. But you are off so soon and have written me all at once so much for which I thank you that I must at once make my response. And to business first. As soon as the river rises so that I can get up my baggage from Washington I will read over and note all the errors in the appendix to your Hist of So. Ca. and send you the mem. to N. York. . . .

[The family is] as self-willed as I am, some of them have my tastes, so that I am, and now shall ever be, *minus* a congenial household, confidential companions and assistants. Betty our youngest is still the brightest creature in the world. Nothing passing escapes her and I always look to her for information as to current affairs (domestic). She is also a Captain, and here and at Washington, where we have had a new neighborhood each session, she very soon collects and commands a troop of little folks of both sexes, white and black, whom she trains to run over me and the household. Yet she is gentleness itself when by herself, loyal, loving and pure.

Cattie has grown up to be a woman. She is not deficient in beauty, and the most modest and purest creature in the world with at the same time will and spirit enough and high sentiment. But apparently purposeless and indifferent to mundane affairs.

Paul is Napoleonic. He got married in Nov. 1858 and in less than 9 months presented us with a fine grandson. He won his wife against Mrs. Clay who carried her to Washington in 1857–8 to marry a kinsman. She is a Georgian—was a Miss Comer of Macon. This year I have given him this place and Silver Bluff to manage on shares, and the negroes at the Bluff have given him the Soubriquet of "Break o' day." He gets there—6 to 8 miles off—before they get fairly to work. He has the energy, the will, the tenacity, and the capability to logic of

Old Nap. But his health is not good and he has been so much in Geo. that he thinks here is nothing worthwhile but *cotton and corn*. Vineyards, orchards, lawns, fish ponds, gardens all wither up under him. But he is logical and if we both live I will bring him out of that. He lives here and his wife is one of the sweetest, most amiable, most accomplished yet most no account person for practical matters you ever saw. Still Paul learned her to shoot. She killed a partridge on the wing and bid fair to rival Dr. Steiner until Claude was born and then an end to all that.

My next son above Paul in age, tho' one intervened who is no more, is Spann whom you have seen lately. He is the best fellow in the world with much desultory attainment and ample intellect, but wanting in purpose and tenacity, while really more ambitious than any other. He represents "Young America" perfectly, save that he has too much sense to run with. But he wants to achieve high position without any drudgery or other trouble, and to get rich without work or economy. I put him at Cowden Jan. 1857. I had just got the place in order and his share of the crop that year was over $3,000 besides servants, horse feed, lodging etc., every dollar of which he spent and had nothing to show. The next year (a better crop year) his income was about $1600. The last year it was under $1200 though a still better year. The fact was that to do something himself and for novelty he had brought in against my wishes some 100 acres of new land and allowed all the ditches on the other land to fill up. Well last fall seeing this I kicked up: and "Break o' day" coming into my views he was compelled to open his ditches and with all the backsets I suppose he will realize $2500 this crop. But "Young America" has heard of the West where dollars are to be picked up and he resigns his position.

My oldest son Harry after he graduated went to Europe. He is the only one who would accept my offer to give them that trip. He spent for me there $4,000 a year and returned just before I was elected Senator. I put him in charge of this place [Redcliffe] and Silverton with an allowance of $2,000 a year, when I got back at the end of 6 months I found everything in anarchy and revolution—Harry had set up for a grand Reformer and he had also compounded on his own individual account over $2,000 in his six months and had nothing to show for it but his horse and buggy. I took him to account and spoke very sharply I suppose. The result was he sold his horse and buggy. Without even taking leave of me went off to Cambridge, Mass. The next I heard of him was that through what influence I never knew, he was elected a *Professor* in the Geo. Unis't at Athens with a salary of $2000 a year. All that was very well, yet, as I thought, very foolish. He however has borne himself well and made a sort of reputation. Last Nov. he married a daughter of Col. H. Cumming of Augusta, who seems to be esteemed a first rate woman. This is commencement week at Athens and at the end of it they will come down—she to remain for a certain purpose[1] and he to settle whether he shall quit the college to make his home at Silverton henceforth in Spann's place.[2] I think that will be done and 2 yrs. business residence *in Geo.*, a wife etc. give the promise of a new man. If he and Paul will only do as well as Paul has done this year, they can each with the advantages I offer them make ordinarily $5,000 a year and for me $30 to 40,000 for the rest of us.

Since I began this letter I have made a complete search for Dr. Porcher's paper. I have them not. He was *very queer* if he sent me any paper he could not duplicate. I get a bushel a week and it is impossible for me to keep any but strictly business and personal letters pertaining to my private affairs on hand. I consider all public communications as duplicates merely. This continued heat has finally broken me down. I am exhausted.

Yours ever,

J.H. Hammond

HARRY HAMMOND TO JULIA BRYAN HAMMOND[b]

Athens, September 19, 1860

My Dear Daughter:[1]

I have been thinking for some time past that I would allow myself the pleasure of writing you a short letter, and your dear Mother's ac-

---

1. Emily Hammond was eight months pregnant. Julia Bryan Hammond, the first child of Emily Cumming and Harry Hammond, was born August 20, 1860, and was christened at the home of Emily's parents on November 19, 1860. Billings, *Descendants of Hammond*, p. 1; JHH Plantation Journal, Nov. 19, 1860, JHH Papers, SCL.

2. Soon thereafter Harry Hammond made his decision to leave the University of Georgia, and Harry, Emily, and their baby daughter took up residence at Silverton plantation. ECH to Katharine J. Hubbell, Aug. 21, 1860, cited in Wood, *A Northern Daughter*, pp. 96–97. See also the letter of Sept. 19, 1860.

---

1. At the time of Harry's letter to his daughter Julia she was only one month old.

counts of your greater wakefulness and daily increasing participation in the things of this life have determined me at length to do so. It seems to me a very long time since I have seen you, but I believe to day is only the tenth, since I rocked you to sleep in your cradle and left you quietly dozing, as it was your wont to do the greater part of those days. Still ten days is an important period in your little life, and I hear that you have grown a good deal and are much plumper. They tell me too that some one has traced the first glimpses of a resemblance to me just "across your eyes." I hardly think this can be so, for when I was with you I could see that you looked like no one but your Grandfather Cumming, if it were not that now and then some expression like your Mother's played over your little features. This is the likeness, my Baby, that I shall most love to watch as it develops in you. There is one thing that you will certainly inherit from me, and which of itself will compensate and more than compensate for all I may fail to give you. It is the love of the dearest and best of Mothers. This will be the first feeling that will wake up in your little heart, and it will grow and strengthen as you grow older, and that which now alone makes your Father a happy man, will not only be your stay and comfort, but will give you the best of all your pleasures. I envy you Julia, and anyone might do it—that for years to come you will be with your Mother every day. You see how I have been obliged already to leave her and you. The occasion tho' for this will I trust become rarer, when we move away from this place and are settled at Silverton. I shall be fixed then, and we will always live together except when you and she run off to take a holiday at your Grandmother's.

When I left it was my intention to have remained here until Saturday, and I was in that mind until this morning as I was going to prayers, when Mr Rutherford told me that I had already had my share of the recitations with the Senior Class, and that he was anxious to take them in Astronomy at once. I consented to let him have them on Friday morning, and then I found out that by making a little change in my hours I could get away tomorrow. This I determined to do and unless your Grandfather sends this letter out to you tomorrow morning, which I will write and ask him to do, I shall be with you before it reaches you. I enclose a letter to your Mother which I had commenced. I have been glad to hear that you were bearing the disagreeable cold you have had so patiently. In this world we must pray for the strength to bear Evil, and leave it to God's goodness to grant us in his own time and at his own pleasure relief from our pains. God Bless you my dear child.

Your affectionate father,

Harry Hammond

JAMES HENRY HAMMOND TO MARCUS C.M. HAMMOND[c]

Redcliffe, November 12, 1860

My Dear Major:

"C'est fini." I have resigned.[1] I heard yesterday that Chesnut and Toombs had resigned. Why I know not. But in half an hour Tom was on his way to Augusta with my resignation. I resigned because Chesnut and Toombs resigned and not a little because of finding a good pretext to get out of a position I have wanted to get out of ever since I held it and more now than ever. I thought Magrath[2] and all those fellows were great asses for resigning and have done it myself. It is an epidemic and very foolish. It reminds me of the Japanese who when insulted rip open their own bowels.

On a call from Porter, Simons, Lessenne, Aldrich, Buist, and others for my view of affairs I sent over my article, somewhat improved since you saw it. But it was so far behind the times that they concluded not to publish it. . . . (At least *Gist* and *Jones* to whom A. read and Porter to whom he told it, so concluded.) People are wild. The scenes of the French Revolution are being enacted already. Law and Constitution are equally and utterly disregarded. See Brown's infamous message.[3] He is a down right fool, but a fair type of both states. God knows the end. This State will certainly secede by 1 Jan.[4]

1. Upon learning of Lincoln's presidential victory, James Henry Hammond resigned from the United States Senate.

2. Andrew Gordon Magrath (1813–1893), appointed judge of the U.S. District Court in 1856, resigned from the bench upon learning of Lincoln's election. From 1861 to 1864 he was judge of the Confederacy's circuit court for the district of South Carolina. In December 1864 he resigned to become governor of the state. Oliphant, *Simms*, 1:cxxiv; Myers, *Children of Pride*, p. 1612.

3. In his general address to the Georgia legislature in November 1860, Governor Joseph Brown recommended military preparedness and the use of volunteers for the defense of the South. He said, "We should not only arm our people, but we should educate them in the use of arms, and the whole science of war. We know not how soon we may be driven to the necessity of defending our rights and our honor, by military force." Cited in Herbert Fielder, *A Sketch of the Life and Times and Speeches of Joseph E. Brown* (Springfield, Mass.: Springfield Printing Company, 1883), p. 166.

4. South Carolina seceded on December 20, 1860.

I had no hand in blighting Spann's matrimonial views. I did save him from marrying a silly coquette who cared not a copper for him.[5] He however assented or I could not have done it and I have never heard of his repenting it. . . . All pretty well but me. I can't recuperate. Intense thinking for a purpose if continued any length of time thoroughly prostrates me. I have not yet got over my Barnwell Speech. Thank God I am free once more. Grapes, Grapes.

Yrs
H[ammond]

JAMES HENRY HAMMOND TO HON. R.F. SIMPSON[c]

Redcliffe, November 22, 1860

Dear Sir:[1]

Your invitation to the mass meeting at Pendleton tomorrow comes too late for my acceptance if my health permitted. I have, however, no hesitation about giving you my views of the present state of affairs. I regard it, now, as a settled matter, that South Carolina will, by her Convention which is to meet on the 17 Dec next, secede from the present Union, with or without Co-operation from other Southern States. There can be no doubt that she intends to make a full and resolute trial of the extreme remedy—not of Revolution, but of the Constitution, for she will be doing nothing more than exercising a right expressly reserved to her in the bond of Union. It will be a great *change*, but not a *revolution* according to the political definition of that word usually recognized.

I will say, frankly, that ever since the era of Nullification I have entertained great doubts whether a single state could successfully and prosperously exercise this great right, without the support of one or more adjoining States equally aggrieved with herself, and possessing the same social and industrial institutions. I have thought moreover that in

---

5. See letters of Dec. 28, 1856, and June 20, 1857.

1. Richard Franklin Simpson (1798–1882), after briefly practicing law in Pendleton, returned to Laurens District, his birthplace, to establish himself as a major planter. He served in the South Carolina senate (1834–1838) and in the U.S. House of Representatives (1843–1849). Following his Congressional career, Simpson returned to Pendleton to resume planting and cotton manufacturing. In 1858 he became president of the Pendleton Railroad. As a delegate to the Secession Convention in 1860 he signed the Ordinance of Secession. Reynolds and Faunt, *Biographical Directory of the Senate of South Carolina*, p. 308.

breaking up the Federal Government, it was all important that the seceding States should at once adopt the present Federal Constitution without any modification, and re-organize in conformity with it, for I foresee the most terrible results from any attempt, in these days, to improve on that. I trust that when the Convention withdraws our State from the Union, it will make all those changes in our present State Government which may be necessary to meet the new condition of affairs, provisional, in view of the probable early secession of other Southern States, when the Federal Constitution can be adopted *without change*. As Georgia and Alabama have both called Conventions, I entertain the most sanguine expectation that we can do this before the 4th March next. It seems to me scarcely possible, now the people are fully aroused to an indignant sense of the exactions and insults of the non-slaveholding States and the danger of a longer connexion with them under a common Government that these Conventions will hesitate. I only regret that they do not assemble before ours and set us an example to follow.

Whatever happens the die is cast with us. South Carolina does not wish to create a Republican Nationality for herself independent of her Southern Sister States. What she desires is a Southern Slaveholding Confederacy and to exemplify to the world the perfection of our civilization, the immensity of our resources and that the wonderful progress of these United States is mainly due to us. She will by no means presume to attempt to force any other State into any measures which it does not entirely approve. She knows she cannot do it. Yet come what may, for herself, she is resolved to make the effort, staking all she is and has upon it, to free her people from alliance with those, who not content with reaping the better half of the harvest produced by her lands and labour are now instigating servile Insurrections, and seeking our destruction with knives, torches and poison. I do not see myself, how we can now take any "step backwards" or stop at any half way house. No faith can be placed in such people. Yet having with us the right, the law and the Constitution, let us be scrupulously careful to move, however sternly and decisively, calmly and wholly within the limits of the Constitution and the Law. Such a course will insure the respect and sympathy of the world and the blessing of Providence.

I have the honor to be with great respect,

Your Obt Servt

J. H. Hammond

JULIA A. CUMMING[1] TO EMILY C. HAMMOND[b]

Augusta, April 12, 1861

My dear Emmy:

It seems as if you had been gone a month, and yet this is only the third morning since you left. I was glad to hear of your pleasant ride down, and of the indications that the Doctor had not given himself up to *solitary* repinings for your prolonged absence. I can't *blame* him certainly, for wishing to have you back, for here where so many are left, to cheer and enliven each other, you and the baby are most painfully missed when you leave us.

I am glad to find you can both go to Mount Zion probably. In thinking of it, as it regards the time of going, it occurred to me that as it could not be decided until Mr. Hammond comes up next Tuesday, it would then be too late to wish for the carriage to meet us either on Friday or Saturday, so that we had best postpone it until the Monday following. That will give the chances of hearing from us or Mount Zion by two mails. I wrote to Mrs. Bryan[2] the day after you went away informing her that we were mediating a visit, tho' I could not then fix the precise time. I suppose Mr. Hammond will scarcely feel willing to remain an entire week there, and I am quite willing that he should decide the length of the visit.

Alfred and Sarah[3] came in yesterday afternoon and remained after nine. Kate [Hubbell Cumming] spent the day, the day before, so that I was reminded of your assertion that I would have visiting enough from my daughters-in-law. . . . Alfred seems very impatient at the state of things with him, as he says, while there is the constant nurturing of forces with every indication of speedy collision at several points: he should have to remain "on this contemptible service at the Augusta Armory," "he is disgusted intensely disgusted,"[4] and he has written to

---

1. Julia Ann Bryan Cumming (1803–1879), mother of Emily, was the daughter of Joseph Bryan, a Mt. Zion planter. She married Henry Harford Cumming on February 24, 1824. Wood, *A Northern Daughter*, p. 106.

2. The reference is to Mrs. Joseph Bryan, the second wife of Julia A. Cumming's father.

3. Alfred Cumming (1829–1910), first son of Julia A. Bryan and Henry Harford Cumming, married his first cousin Sarah Matilda Davis (1830–1910) on February 14, 1861. Wood, *A Northern Daughter*, pp. 108, 122; Myers, *The Children of Pride*, p. 1499.

4. Alfred Cumming, who had been a career officer in the United States Army, resigned his captaincy in January 1861 to enter Confederate service. At first, he commanded the Georgia Ar-

Col. Cooper requesting to be assigned to some active duty, the result of which he thinks will be that in a short time from this he will be in Pensacola. Every thing seems upturned and there is distressful apprehension in all minds. Tom[5] is constantly wishing he had the place of the lowest commissioned officer in the Artillery Company, which is under orders and will leave here tomorrow for Pensacola. He will not go he says as a private. Your Father seems annoyed at this and tells him he must not be impatient to go before honour calls him, as there will probably be fighting enough to wait patiently until his time comes. I do not know that he has determined *certainly,* to go to Silverton this week, but I have several times heard him say he thought he would do so. . . .

We are all as when you left us. I have not seen Julien since, tho' your Father says he saw him several times yesterday passing down the streets. Harford is better.[6] I shall probably write again before you come up. Shall send this to Mr. Boris to send to Redcliffe. I suppose Catty will give up her visit to Charleston just now.[7] Eva Eve says she is not going at present. Give my love to Mr. Hammond and a kiss to my little darling.

Ever yrs.,
Julia A. Cumming

JULIA A. CUMMING TO EMILY C. HAMMOND[b]

Augusta, May 31, 1861

My dear Emmy:

It has been so long since I have heard from you that I was much pleased when your Father handed me a letter from you, which he

---

senal at Augusta. Jon L. Wakelyn, *Biographical Dictionary of the Confederacy* (Westport, Connecticut: Greenwood Press, 1976), p. 155.

5. Thomas William Cumming (1831–1889), third son of Julia A. Bryan and Henry Harford Cumming, was listed in 1860 as a merchant in Augusta. In the summer of 1861 he entered Confederate service and was sent to Virginia as a lieutenant of the 16th Georgia Regiment (Infantry). U.S. Census Records, State of Georgia, 1860 Population Schedules, Richmond County, National Archives Microfilm Publications, p. 923; Wood, *A Northern Daughter,* p. 106.

6. Harford Montgomery Cumming (1838–1872), the fifth son of Julia A. Bryan and Henry Harford Cumming, received a medical education. Although he entered the Confederate army as a member of the Clinch Rifles, he was soon honorably discharged from infantry duty and commissioned as an assistant surgeon. Ibid.

7. On April 11, 1861, General Beauregard had demanded that Major Anderson surrender Fort Sumter in Charleston Harbor. Anderson at first refused, but then agreed to evacuate the fort on April 15 unless contrary instructions or additional supplies arrived. Beauregard's aides ordered an attack on the fort on the morning of April 12 and Anderson evacuated the fort on April 14, 1861.

brought in from the Post office this morning. My disappointment was great when on opening it, I found it had been written before your two last visits here, or in other words, it bore the date the 3rd May.

I hope you have before this received one I wrote you on Monday last. If I had known then what would have occurred, I think you would have been here before this. I mentioned that Tom and Joe would set off to Pensacola on Tuesday, but there has been an unexpected delay in their movements, and they have remained at home so much longer, that you might have seen them, which they have both desired entirely. Thomas, is not yet fairly off, but expects to leave on the two o'clock train today. He determined for some reason or other, that it would be very much to his interest to go down with Henry Allen, 1st Lieut. of the Ogelthorpe, who has been here on short leave, and he has deferred his departure from day to day since last Tuesday. Joe went away on Wednesday, having had repeated messages, from Col. Jackson [of the 5th Georgia Regiment] to come without delay. We have determined to send Lucius[1] down that he may be an attendant upon all three of the Boys, and if he could be spirited up a little, he might be very useful. I have always found him tho' so very unpleasant a servant, for my bidding, that I am not very sanguine, as to the help he may be to them. I told Tom and Joe they were perfectly welcome to him if they wished to take him, and after some address as to the inconvenience to which it might subject me, they accepted the offer declaring it would promote their comfort very essentially to have a servant, and so he goes, not for one especially, but all three of them. I find it is considered desirable on many accounts that there should be a good many coloured servants about these Military Camps. Lucius was leary to go.

The last news from Alfred was two days ago. He has had another change in his position—now fills the office of Assistant Adg't Gen'l to Gen'l Arthur of Alabama and "Chief of Staff." He was in Norfolk hourly expecting, as he said, an engagement. The last accounts from Harf was in a short letter from Jimmy Moore, written at his request, as he had been called off on some special service just as he was about writing home. Jimmy says, he is very well indeed, and very much en-

---

1. Lucius Rakeshaw was one of the Cumming family's slaves. After the war he continued in the employ of the Cumming family. He accompanied Harford Cumming on a trip to Florida and returned to Augusta following Harford's death in October 1872. According to Mrs. Joseph B. Cumming, Lucius died in 1901. Cumming, "A Sketch of Descendants of David Cumming," p. 31; Wood, A Northern Daughter, p. 108.

joys his soldier life. Julien is as usual—I have not seen him since Sunday tho' he was in the yard yesterday, and Charlotte told me he was looking better than he has been of late.[2] I heard from Joe, that he had spent two nights this week on the Hill at Joe Wilkes' room, that he had gone over to see him there, and had told him goodbye. Tom was saying last night that he was afraid he should not see him before he left.

We have had no public news of any importance for two or three days, not even in Telegrams. Your Father thinks it is designed for some purpose even in the offices on our side, but everything is in confusion, and we know not what may befall at any moment.

Large numbers of Troops are passing thro' here every day on their way to Virginia. Sometimes there are as many as three companies and scarcely a day without one at least. I have been going around to the Depot very often. Your Father and Maria and myself are feeling a sad sort of interest in seeing the poor fellows go off. Day before yesterday we went there and there was an immense crowd assembled to see Mrs. Davis,[3] who it was understood would pass thro' on her way to Virginia. After waiting some time a carriage came dashing up escorted as the papers said the next morning "by our Town son Col. De Martin" with the Lady President and her family, escorted by Col. Cooper. She passed immediately into the cars, and stood up at her seat very graciously receiving the salutations of the crowd who went out to see her. I have a letter from Mrs. Bryan two days ago in which she says your Grandfather is better again. We hear not a word from your Uncle Joe.[4] Your Father has again written to him. We had to again defer our move to the Hill. After the boys determined to go, I have been so busy making flannel shirts etc. for them that I had not taken time to think scarcely of going.[5]

2. Evidently Julien had continued drinking, for his mother had written Emily that "Julien is in the same deplorable condition he has been in for so long a time." She reported that he "sat at the table with us yesterday, for the first time, since October last, but it was any thing but pleasant to have him there. He was in that state in which he fancies he conceals his degree of inebriation, and is inclined to flourishing talk and gestures. Oh it was too sad to see such a woeful deterioration, since he had last occupied that seat." Julia A. Cumming to ECH, May 13, 1861, HBC Family Papers, SCL.
3. Varina Howell Davis (1826–1906) was the first lady of the Confederacy.
4. Joseph Cumming, brother of Henry H. Cumming and the second son of Ann Clay and Thomas Cumming, resided for most of his adult life in Savannah "where he was engaged in commercial pursuits in which he seemed not to have been ultimately prosperous." Cumming, "A Sketch of Descendants of David Cumming," p. 7.
5. The Cumming family at this time maintained two residences, one in Augusta at 242 Broad Street, and the other a summer home in Summerville. K. Woodward, ed., *The Augusta Directory and City Advertiser for 1841* (Augusta, Georgia: Browne and McCaffey, 1841); *Augusta Yesterday*

It is probable we may go on Monday or Tuesday next. I sent to Kate to come in until we should be ready to go, but she preferred remaining on there and she has been invited by Sarah and Joe Brown to stay with them. She told me yesterday (she was in for a little while) that Sally MacWhorter[6] was very sick. She seems to have no idea what was the matter with her. Your mammy has been very sick. The poor old soul looks most wretchedly but you cannot induce her to lie down or eschew action. Her cough is perfectly awful. Are these not dismal times in every way. Your Father . . . seems perfectly well. Tom sends a great deal of love to you, says he had hoped very much to have seen you. . . .

Yours,

JAC

EDWARD SPANN HAMMOND TO JAMES HENRY HAMMOND[h]

Richmond, Virginia, June 10, 1861

Dear Father:

Your letter of 3rd reached me the evening before leaving the Junction[1] for this place. I came down yesterday. I am truly grateful for the $500 you sent me. I shall use it carefully, as my demands for money will soon be heavy, and my resources slim. There must be great miscarriages in the mails. I wrote frequently while in Richmond (acknowledged caps, saddle etc.) but have been so occupied in the office and moving since reaching the Junction that I have been unable to write often.

Gen. Beauregard arrived at the Junction a few days ago, and took command of the Dept. Gen. Bonham was sent forward to command the advance posts, moving first to Bull Run creek, 4 miles, and was

---

and Today, 2nd ed. (The Arts Committee of the Junior League of Augusta, Georgia, 1951), pp. 34–35, 39–41; Wood, A Northern Daughter, p. 105. See also letter of Sept. 26, 1859, n. 5.

6. Sarah (Sally) Adams married Major George MacWhorter, who died soon after the beginning of the war. To support herself she ran a private school in her home in Augusta. Wood, A Northern Daughter, p. 113; The Adams Family of Augusta, Loose Papers, John Shaw Billings Papers, SCL.

---

1. Manassas Junction was the point at which the Orange and Alexandria Railroad joined a rail line from the Shenandoah Valley. The first major engagement of the war, the first Battle of Manassas (or first Battle of Bull Run), was fought here on July 21, 1861.

yesterday to move to Centerville, 4 miles further. Col. Kershaw had his Regt. at Bull Run, and Col Gregg's at Centerville. Both have fortified their camps with breastworks. The ground was favorable at each, if the enemy do not come in overwhelming numbers. Manassas was too level and open unless the numbers were near equal. Breastworks are going up there rapidly. We think we can hold our own and drive back a force not exceeding three times ours. The spirit and confidence of our men are at the highest notch. Their numbers, military equipment and drill are daily improving. There are three S. C. Regts. here now to go up there. One thousand mounted men, I hear, are going there tomorrow.

I have seen none of the public men since reaching here, to speak to, except Mr. Memminger. I saw Mr. Davis[2] reviewing the troops this afternoon. He looks many years older than when I last saw him and very care worn. There has been a fight going on all day, we hear, on York R. at Newport News, 10 miles from Old Point. We hear the enemy are driven back. Our side attacked, under Col. Magruder.[3] Yet many believe the war feeling North is abating.

I am right in the ss (Morriss). It is a small family—but few of the name. Marcella's[4] Father has been a prominent man in his section for many years. In 1820, when he entered the H^{se} of Delegates, he took an extreme States Rights position, so much so as to be ahead, as he has been ever since, of the sentiment of the State. He is not however a politician, but a tobacco and grain planter near Lynchburg. He has made a large fortune, has always been highly respected, and his family is equal to almost any in Va. He had but one brother, who left but one child—widow of Thos. Davis of Sumpter District, lives now in Charleston, and owns one of the largest plantations in Miss. Mrs. Morriss was a Yancey—related to Wm L.[5] and has but few near relatives. This is

2. Christopher G. Memminger (1803–1888) was born in Germany, but came to Charleston when still a child. He served as the first Secretary of the Treasury of the Confederacy until June 1864. Jefferson Davis by this time was provisional President of the Confederate States of America. *Cyclopedia of Eminent and Representative Men of the Carolinas*, 1:174–75.

3. Colonel John Bankhead Magruder (1810–1871), a Virginian and a U.S. Army career officer, resigned his commission on March 16, 1861, to enter the service of the Confederacy. On June 17, 1861, he was promoted from the rank of Colonel to brigadier general following his victory at Big Bethel, Virginia. Wakelyn, *Biographical Dictionary of the Confederacy*, pp. 305–6.

4. Marcella Christiana Morriss of Lynchburg, Virginia, was the fiancée of E. Spann Hammond. They were married on June 20, 1861. Billings, *Descendants of Hammond*, p. 3.

5. William Lowndes Yancey (1814–1863) was an Alabama lawyer, cotton planter, newspaper editor, member of Congress (1844–1846), and a delegate to the Democratic National Conventions at Baltimore (1848), Cincinnati (1856), and Charleston (1860). At the Charleston convention Yan-

almost all I know of the family. I find none are more hospitable, or more highly respected in Richmond than they. Marcella has two brothers, accomplished gentlemen, and very successful in their affairs here in every respect, and one sister.

The time for our marriage is left to me to appoint. If I survive the chances of war and one month I can almost say confidently I shall be married. I see no gain from delay. I think Marcella a prize perhaps better than I am worthy of, and you will find in her one who will be an affectionate daughter to you—and an accomplished, sensible, sweet-tempered woman.[6] I can not fix the time with the enemy in front. A leave of more than three days might subject me to mortification and stigma. But I hope Cattie will come on that one member of our family may be here.

Gen. Bonham[7] is indefatigable in discharging the duties of his position, and has the highest confidence and respect of all the military. His friends are turning every stone to get him Senator next election— Aldrich particularly. They seem to think you have retired for good although they speak of it with deep regret. Withers is also head and tail up for the place—also Manning and Preston, who are Vol.[r] Aids to Gen. Beauregard at Manassas.—It is a very great gratification to me to hear from you, and I hope you will write again to me. Love to all.

Yours affectionately,
Ed. Spann Hammond

---

cey was a leader of the "Southern fire-eaters," and it was his Alabama delegation which first withdrew from the Democratic Convention on April 30, 1860. *Biographical Directory of the American Congress 1774–1961*, p. 1855; Oliphant, *Simms*, 4:234.

6. Spann later wrote that his father-in-law, with whom he owned land from 1861 to 1865, took all the profits from the land each year, leaving Spann with the debts and the expense of his wife who cost him "for her support, and to gratify her wishes over $2500—this year—all out of my pocket." His father-in-law had promised to make it right by his will, but Spann learned that Morriss did not intend to leave him "an iota of his estate," but that he left trust deeds for his grandchildren and an income for his daughter to be handled by a trustee "for her individual use." After the war Spann wished to sell Marcella's property and take his family to live in South Carolina. He wrote her in hopes that she would "acquiesce cheerfully in this arrangement," but she refused. ESH to Catherine F. Hammond, Dec. 21, 1866, ESH to Marcella Morriss Hammond, Dec. 22, 1866, ESH Letterpress Book, ESH Papers, SCL.

7. Milledge L. Bonham (1813–1890), who was first elected to Congress in 1856, withdrew with the other members of the South Carolina delegation upon South Carolina's secession in December 1860. He became a brigadier general with the coming of the war. Early in 1862 Bonham resigned his commission and served South Carolina as a representative to the Confederate Congress, and in December he was elected governor of South Carolina for a two-year term. He returned to Confederate service in 1865 as a brigadier general. General Clement A. Evans, ed., *Confederate Military History*, vol. 5 (Atlanta: Confederate Publishing Co., 1899), pp. 377–78; *Cyclopedia of Eminent and Representative Men of the Carolinas*, 1:88–89; Oliphant, *Simms*, 1:xcii–xciii.

P.S.   I have seen Marcella again—will be married the 25 (my birthday) if Providence spares me. Wish Cattie would be here or some one. Go to Junction in morning and return 18 or sooner. Write to me here, care of Richd G. Morriss. We'll return home. I hope Mother will send her letter to Marcella now. I had reason for delaying, but regret now that I requested it.

E.S.H.

EMILY C. HAMMOND TO JULIA A. CUMMING[b]

Silverton, June 29, 1861

I can but think dear Mother that you have miscalculated the time since I have written to you. I know that in the three weeks that Jule [Julien Cumming] has been down here, I have written home, *at least four* times, and only twice to Father. However that may be, I am so gratefull for your letters that I am sure I never mean to be remiss on my part, tho' conscious that writing as I do from Silverton, my letters cannot be much more, than a bulletin of health, and an acknowledgment of the receipt of your most agreeable and acceptable letters. The reason that I did not write once or twice when Jule has written, was that I knew how pleasant it would be to you, to have a letter from himself, as an assurance of his present good state, and I knew too, he would not write, if I did. I wrote a very hurried little note to Sarah, Thursday from Redcliffe. Mr. Hammond and the Baby and I went up to spend the day with Spann and his wife. Jule was invited to go too, but he did not seem inclined to do so. I might almost have staid at Silverton, for anything that I saw of the Bride. We got to Redcliffe about half past ten o'c, and she came down stairs a few minutes before 1 o'c, after having been sent for repeatedly, to see some of the neighbors who had called to see her. When she finally appeared, she entered the room, led by the "Proud husband," gave us all a sweeping bow, and curtsy, said a very fashionable, clipped off "good morning," took her seat, next to Dr. Cook,[1] and began with much manner, and emphasis to apologize for

---

1. Dr. H.R. Cook, a good friend of James Hammond, was listed in 1860 as a 40-year-old physician in Beech Island. Although he was born in New York, his wife, Helena, was a South Carolinian. U.S. Census Records, State of South Carolina, 1860 Population Schedules, Edgefield County, National Archives Microfilm Publications, p. 162.

her delay in coming down, being at the moment when he called in the act of "disrobing." This form of expression, which I heard, without exaggeration, three times afterwards, seemed the only appropriate one, for the removal of such fine clothes as those she had on then, and as I heard had worn since she came. She was dressed in a white swiss muslin flounced, with a low neck and short sleeves, and a cape of the same, trimmed with the richest valenciennes three or four inches wide. She had on too the handsomest diamonds I think I ever saw and a belt which I am sure was solid gold with gold and enamelled knobs in front, added to this a crimson and gold net on her hair, and a crimson silk fan. She looked extremely stylish, but as you may suppose, utterly out of place and keeping with the time and place and people around her. She was perfectly easy and self-possessed, and has evidently lived in a certain gay fashionable watering-place society, in which they say she was a belle. I was agreeably surprised in her appearance, for except that she has bad teeth, I think she is decidedly fine looking. Gen. and Mrs Hammond seem very much pleased with her, and Mrs. Paul [Loula Comer Hammond] is perfectly carried away. Catty is by no means so enthusiastic. For myself, she did not impress me as having the right style or finish. Indeed she seemed to me rather a "flash article." This opinion however is to be received with allowance, as Mr Hammond intimates with a degree of earnestness which mortifies me not a little that I am envious of the notice and attention she received, and you know that I am unfortunately not superior to that weakness. I think tho' that I felt more, the superb indifference with which she treated me thro' the day. I am rather afraid, that she must have mistaken me for the Baby's nurse.

I have consumed much more time and paper than I intended, with Mrs. Spann, but you know we have so little excitement at Silverton that we make the most of it.

Jule and Mr. Hammond have gone off on an all day fishing excursion. Jule is perfectly well, and giving at least as much as he receives in the way of interest and enjoyment. He and Mr. Hammond seem never to tire of their endless talks and games of Bragg. Indeed they suffice so well for each other, in the way of society, that I cannot resist the temptation of accepting your offer to send the carriage for me. I am afraid tho', that my letter will reach you too late, for the week beginning tomorrow. In this extremely hot weather, I should think it would be more prudent not to attempt to return the same day that the carriage came down. You probably will not get this letter at the earliest before Tuesday night, and then even if it were convenient for you to send the next day, I could not reach the Hill until Thursday, and then to make my visit worth while, I would want to stay over Sunday. Sunday, the first in July, is however the regular time for the visit of the Methodist preacher, and as he is to stay at our house by invitation, I had better be here. Any day tho' the week after, that it will be convenient for you to send, I will come up most gladly. I would not be deterred even by the reason I have mentioned from coming next week, if it were not that the Baby has been so well for some days past that I do not think the change so necessary to her as it was. She is not nearly so fat as she was but she seems pretty well again, and is generally very bright and merry, tho' by no means the wonderfully good little Baby of last winter. Jule seems perfectly well in all respects, conforms exactly to our habits and hours, and mode of life, and is altogether a most agreeable inmate. I have had two notes from Sarah in the last two days, one of them written however ten days ago. She seems to feel very much her separation from Alf. I sincerely hope it may be only a short one. Spann Hammond gave me a rather vague confused idea that Alf had been preferred as the Colonel of his regiment, but that Mr. McLaw as his senior had to rank him. I should think tho' that what he has would be considered quite a desirable appointment. I wish very much that Tom might think it right and proper for him to remain at home, but I suppose he thinks that if his two married brothers have gone, he ought not to stay. Mr. Hammond says he will go, if Spann does not return to the army, about which his friends seem to entertain some doubt.[2] By the way please don't mention what I have said about Mrs. Spann. They are all very particular people, and would look upon such freely expressed opinions as mine almost as treacherous.

Poor Sally! [McWhorter] I hope she is better by this time and quite out of danger. Do give her my love when you see her. I was scarcely

2. In 1861 at Manassas, Spann was a major on General Bonham's staff, but late in that year he clearly was out of the army and had bought a plantation in Mississippi. His father wrote in December 1861 that Spann had "left here on Monday with negros to work it." By 1862 James Henry Hammond confided to William Gilmore Simms that Spann had sent substitutes to the war. In 1863–1864 Spann edited the *Richmond Whig* in that city. JHH to WGS, Dec. 12, 1861, Nov. 2, 1862, JHH Papers, LC; ESH Scrapbook, ESH Papers, SCL; Steadman, *A History of the Spann Family*, p. 79; *The Aiken Journal and Review*, June 21, 1921.

surprised at the results of your visit to Mount Zion. I am afraid that life has become only a sad burden to my dear old Grandfather, tho' I hope for him a peaceful and happy end.[3] Give much love for me to my absent brothers when you write, tell them I think of them a great deal and very often. Give my love to Father and thank him for the crackers which were very nice and fresh, and for the cannister which, tell him, I mean to assume he has made over to me, and which is a very usefull thing in housekeeping. Thank him too for the note sent me by Joe Wilkes and tell him we very gladly accept Joe's services with the understanding mentioned by him. Give my love to Maria and tell her I should be very glad to hear from her sometimes. Tell Sarah I will come soon. Dearest Mother I want to see you very much.

Yours,

E.

JAMES HENRY HAMMOND TO WILLIAM GILMORE SIMMS[c]

Redcliffe, July 17, 1861

My Dear Simms:

Through the Major I learn with grief that the insatiate archer has again sped a fatal arrow at your family.[1] Such repeated visitation of Providence must have an important purpose. Let your sorrow subside in faith.

I cannot but think you allow too much use of medicine in your family. I owe all my sufferings to horse dosing in my childhood. My observation, sad and bad, and experience lead me to throw all physic to the dogs. Every drug in the apothecary shop *is poison*. Some stand them better than others but all suffer. I have seen hundreds die of Doctors and scarcely a week passes that I do not hear of a case.[2] Throw, as I did

---

3. Emily Hammond's grandfather, Joseph Bryan, died on December 31, 1861, at the age of ninety-three. Joseph Bryan gravestone, Mt. Zion Cemetery, Sparta, Georgia.

---

1. In a letter to a close friend, William Gilmore Simms wrote that "we have lost our youngest son, the boy Sydney Hammond, two years old, teething,—and, I think, with a spinal infection." WGS to James Lawson, July 4, 1861, cited in Oliphant, *Simms*, 4:369.

2. A medical historian noted that the period from the 1780s to the 1850s frequently has been called "the age of heroic medicine." Massive blood-letting was the standard cure for virtually all ailments, and physicians, in addition, administered "huge doses of calomel and other dangerous mineral drugs, as well as purgatives and emetics to cleanse the system of all irritants." Martin

seven years ago, all medicine into the River. Get Pulte's Family Physician, Hull, Jahr[3] and a box of Homeopathic pellets not tinctures, nor
powders. Treat every case symptomatically ignoring the name of the
disease. When you hit right you make a speedy cure. If you miss, you
do no harm. I have not taken of or given in all my family white or
black any Doctor's stuff for over 7 years. The statistical result is wonderful.

I trust your health has improved. Strange to say the warm weather
has improved mine and sometimes I feel well and ready to work. But I
know that the torpor of the lower bowel, which I remember to have had
as long as I remember doses of Calomel[4] and oil, is becoming paralysis.

What of the times? It would take a political athlete who gives to it
every hour to answer. I feel quite easy as to the ultimate, but like [Hor-
ace] Greeley I want a "short, sharp and decise war." This we can accomplish successfully before Christmas if the Congress will put an absolute embargo on cotton and tobacco without regard to any other
result, but Independence and Peace.

Kaufman, *Homeopathy in America: The Rise and Fall of a Medical Heresy* (Baltimore: Johns
Hopkins University Press, 1971), p. 1.

   3. Hammond, who was frequently in a good deal of physical pain and often concerned over the
health of his slaves, developed a deep interest in medicine. He had contracts with local doctors to
treat the illnesses of his slaves, but when these treatments failed to effect frequent cures, he grew
impatient with orthodox medicine and turned to homeopathy which had gained popularity in the
ante-bellum period. Homeopathy was the method of treating disease by those drugs given in minute doses which would produce symptoms most similar to the disease being treated. Hammond
bought and read homeopathy textbooks, learned the technical jargon and in his letters strongly
endorsed homeopathy, referring to it by the abbreviation HOM. He scoffed at orthodox medicine
and its practitioners, yet he sent his sons Harry and Spann to the University of Pennsylvania
Medical School. He wrote Harry to learn all he could of orthodox medical practice, "true or false
and you must not flag. I will teach you HOM when you come home."
   Joseph Hippolyt Pulte (1811–1884) was a well-known homeopathic physician in Cincinnati. His
Homeopathic Domestic Physician, a popular treatise for the layman, went through thirteen editions
between 1850 and 1880.
   Gottlieb Heinrich Georg Jahr (1800–1875) wrote extensively on homeopathic therapeutics and
materia medica. His *Manual of Homeopathic Medicine,* originally published in German in 1834,
was first translated into English in 1836. It was revised and re-edited several times, and became
best known in the versions issued as *Hull's Jahr; A New Manual of Homeopathic Practice,* edited
by Amos Gerald Hull (1810–1859). JHH to HH, Jan. 15, 1855, HBC Family Papers, SCL; Billings, "The Hammond Family"; William G. Rothstein, *American Physicians in the Nineteenth
Century: From Sects to Science* (Baltimore: Johns Hopkins University Press, 1972), pp. 154–55.
   4. Calomel is mercurous chloride, a white, tasteless, insoluble powder. In this period mercury
and its salts were a favorite disease-fighting drug used by planters as purgatives and as "anti-syphil-
litics, intestinal antiseptics, disinfectants, and astringents." Todd L. Savitt, *Medicine and Slavery:
The Diseases and Health Care of Blacks in Antebellum Virginia* (Urbana: University of Illinois
Press, 1978), p. 155; W.A. Newman Dorland, *The American Illustrated Medical Dictionary,* 20th
ed. (Philadelphia: W.B. Saunders Company, 1947), pp. 878–79.

But if a "War" President is not required, the political chances of Jeff Davis and his special friends will be much diminished.[5] The Merchants, Bankers etc. etc. are also unwilling that business and percentages would stand still for six months, when they have so many cunning devices to bring in goods, forward cotton, and supply currency—in their own bills. Leave things to them and we could have a nice war of many years with blockades which they would—for *pay*—circumvent and with our chivalry perishing on the frontiers and the whole cost ultimately to fall on the planters. No. Do not let us play at push pin,[6] when we have pikes that the enemy cannot meet or ward off.

No cotton, no tobacco, no naval stores except at *our* option. That's the issue to make *at once*.

Yours faithfully,

J.H. Hammond

JAMES HENRY HAMMOND TO HARRY HAMMOND[b]

Redcliffe, November 17, 1861

Dear Harry:

I started Bush Howard[1] from Silverton House on Tuesday about 3 o'clock and told him to make Pocataligo and you or the Q. M. by Thursday night.[2] If no accident happened he must have done so. I gave him no permission to go any where else unless to carry the horses to you. As he had on the uniform of the Edgefield Rangers etc., no one would be likely to press his horses. Your letter was dated Friday night. It must have been written Thursday night for surely on Friday you got the horses.

I am very sorry to hear your account of the conduct of the low

5. In the Confederacy's general elections in November 1861, Jefferson Davis, the provisional President since February, was elected President for a six-year term.
6. Push pin is a children's game in which the player pushes or fillips his pin with the object of crossing that of another player. The game is referred to in literature as early as 1588. Frequently "play at push pin" referred to a trivial or insignificant occupation—child's play.

1. Bush Howard was employed by James Henry Hammond and was the son of Henry Howard, Hammond's overseer. He succeeded his father as overseer in 1863. JHH Plantation Journal, Oct. 18, 1856, Oct. 1857, June 22, 1858, Dec. 22, 1863, JHH Papers; receipts from Henry Howard to JHH, Jan. 4 and Dec. 19, 1857, Dec. 4, 1858, JHH Business Papers, SCL.
2. At this time Harry Hammond held the rank of assistant commissary in General David Rumph Jones's brigade. Oliphant, *Simms*, 4:386.

country people. You must make great allowances for people who have just fallen in a day from affluence to poverty.[3] It is a terrible collapse and slackens every nerve moral and physical. Genius and imbecility, Chivalry and poltroonery and meanness were always strangely mixed up among the Salt water people—not in each one,—but in classes. There were old families undecayed—decaying and decayed and new families founded by successful overseers and factors and then an unusual amount of loafing fishermen, hunters etc. The Chivalry has mostly gone to the wars and the sense probably also. What was to be expected of the rest? Save Paul, whom I have held back, there is scarcely a man of any spirit left from Hamburg to the River. Fifty armed men could sack every plantation. This miserable scheme of carrying on a war by Volunteers is utterly suicidal. The Chivalry go at the tap of the first drum and get badly cut up and physicked out the first campaign. Little remains for a second. Draft and *force* off your Boyds and John Lottys, or hire them off, if the lot of a common soldier is drawn by you or Paul and any gentleman. They will make just as good common soldiers as you would. Volunteers are only good for a 30 days' campaign—that is, cannot be properly called on for a longer period on any large scale. I doubt not we shall have to review our past decision against a Standing Army to see if we cannot invent checks and balances that will enable us to keep on hand a tolerably respectable one even in times of peace— if we are ever to have such times again.

Pickens had good sense enough to disband the Regt. so summarily called together at White Pond the other day and all have returned save Woodward. Paul expects him. It is however agreed to form a volunteer company and 33 have joined from Pen Corner Company—Tom Beggs among them. I think it will fall through because every man wants to be Captain.

Howard thinks he will finish corn this week at Cowden. I suppose he has some 25,000 bushels housed. I am saving the shucks which loses time. Last week he had to kill a hog to save his life for he was so fat he could not get up. The little fellow weighed 280 lbs.

3. On November 7, 1861, the Union navy seized the Confederate fort on Hilton Head Island and by November 10, 1861, Union forces occupied Beaufort and Port Royal, gaining a base for the naval blockading squadrons. In the process they occupied the plantations abandoned by the Sea Island planters who fled to the interior, leaving behind approximately ten thousand slaves. Willie Lee Rose, *Rehearsal for Reconstruction: The Port Royal Experiment* (New York: Bobbs-Merrill Co., 1964), p. 15.

No sickness worth mentioning. Dr. Davies was down and preached on Friday the best sermon I ever heard from him and I have been hearing him for over 40 years. Loula left yesterday for Macon.

Yours affectionately,

J.H. Hammond

EMILY C. HAMMOND TO HARRY HAMMOND[b]

Monday morning, December 23, 1861

Hard as it always is, to part from you dearest Harry, it seemed to me, that I had never felt our separation so bitter as when I bade goodbye Saturday night and sadly turned to come up the steps, and heard you drive away, and poor little Julia fretting in the parlor. I felt indeed forlorn. She had rather a better night than she has had lately, and yesterday, tho' she had some occasional returns of those paroxysms of crying, she was on the whole quieter and more contented. I went into town directly after breakfast yesterday, and staid until dinner-time, and after dinner I took care of the Baby, and by the time I had put her to bed, and gotten her quiet for the night I was so sleepy that instead of writing I threw myself on the rug, and slept until bedtime. Two nights before, my Harry slept there with his head in my lap, does he remember? This morning the wind is very high, and I find myself hoping all the time that it is knocking many a yankee ship to pieces. I am going to try and get to town this afternoon to inquire after the sick ones. I hear they are both better this morning, tho' Mother had a very sick night, I found her in bed yesterday. I am going to mail this letter too, and then I am going a little way out of town to bring out the nurse we are to have here. I got your note this morning. Edmond did get out safely, tho' I conjectured from his looks the next morning, that he had been on a spree the night before. I do not think you need feel any uneasiness about his driving. I shall seldom or never drive with him after dark, and he knows Father has his eye on him all the time. Do you want to know all that I have been doing this morning? I have undertaken one sad task, that is, folding up and putting away the clothes you wore while you were here. I even had the heart to burn up a pair of your stockings. Those had passed even my powers of darning. I have been showing Julia pictures, and many times seeing her kiss supposed "Pa." Kate and

I have had several little squabbles about the Yankee, and I have made her grow pale and nasty by asserting many times that I thought she was the warmest adherent of Linkum to be found the world over. It is mean in me to tease her so, isn't it?[1]

Mrs. Flournoy has been here this morning and used up all the time I meant to use in writing to my darling, and now I must hurry and tell him goodbye, and tell him that I love him dearly. I could not begin to tell you Harry how I have missed you. How dreary and desolate every place looked without you. But I would stand this over again to have again the almost unalloyed happiness that your visit gave me. Tell me my own dear Harry when you write again, that you saw and felt how happy you made me every minute of the time. Write every day.

Yours Ever

EH

EMILY C. HAMMOND TO HARRY HAMMOND[b]

Sand Hills, Thursday night [January 1862][1]

Much as I desire that you should miss me, my dear darling, I could hope that you had not felt the blank dreariness which has more than once taken possession of me, since we parted. Great as was my pleasure at seeing again my dear little Baby, after our first separation, it could not make me forget that I had that same day said good-bye to you, my Harry. You who give color and tone to my life, you who are its chief interest, and delight. I have, in view of the great pain of parting from you, almost at times doubted the wisdom of my having gone to you. But I have only to pause, and think again of those days so short and few, but so crowded with happiness, and enjoyment, to be sure, that I

1. In November 1861 the Cumming family moved back, as usual, to the town house in Augusta, but "it was arranged that your Aunt Emmie, with Julia (now fifteen months old), and myself [Katharine Hubbell Cumming] should remain out at the Hill, and keep house together in a very simple way, only occupying the rooms on the parlor floor." Cited in Wood, A *Northern Daughter*, p. 7. See also letter of Sept. 30, 1859, n. 2.

1. The date of this letter, supplied by an unknown hand, is probably inaccurate; it should be dated February 1862. On January 28, 1862, Harry Hammond received permission from Brigadier General Pemberton to visit Charleston to arrange "his money and Commissary accounts." Also on the same date Harry wrote Emily arranging to meet her in Charleston in a few days. Brig. Gen. Pemberton to HH, Jan. 28, 1862, Special Order No. 36; HH to ECH, Jan. 28, 1862, HBC Family Papers, SCL.

have done, not only well, but wisely in taking the pleasure, even when the pain must certainly follow. This journey was dull, and uneventful. After we left the station, I dozed for a few miles, and waked up, feeling as tho' my neck were dislocated, by the jerks I had given it. Then I read every line in the two papers we had, except Gen. Beauregard's report which was in such fine print, that I could not read it, while the cars were in motion. Gen. Johnston's I read. And then I dozed again, and waked up, and looked out upon the poor barren landscape, and thought of you, and how you had enlarged and diversified my life. I read too, some of the translations of Heine's poems in the book, you remember, I bought at Russel's. Some of them were quite pretty, but most impassioned effusions. Let me not forget to tell you that about 12 o'c. I was so moved with the pangs of hunger, that at once I had to request Father to purchase me a few ginger cakes, of these I partook at intervals, until I believe I disposed of them, but they were not very large. My bruised and wounded member hurt me more or less all day. Today it is better, tho' still stiff and sore. The carriage was waiting for us at the station and to my surprise *Lucius* was on the box. He told us tho' that Joe had not yet gone, and that he and Kate, and the Baby[2] were all spending the day in town. I do not exactly understand how it is, that Joe has deferred his leaving but it is for some good reason. He thinks of going in a day or two. When I went into the house they were at the dinner table, Julia and all. I did not think to speak to a soul at the table but went directly to her, to see if she would know me. As soon as she saw me, she began to laugh in the most excited fashion, but gave no other sign of recognition. When I spoke to her, she laughed only the more, and showed every little rice grain of a tooth in her head. Whether or not she was at first certain of my identity I could not determine, but in a little while, she was hanging about me, just as ever. She is looking remarkably well, and has I think grown in every way since I left her. She was very much delighted with the toys, but I think the picture books please her still more. Strange to say, she was at first quite alarmed at the barking dog, and would not touch it. Jule and Joe appreciate the magnetic swan better than she does. They were trying it with great interest, in my basin this afternoon.

I staid in town [the Cumming house in Augusta] last night, partly

2. Bryan Cumming, the first child of Katharine Hubbell and Joseph Cumming, was born on January 4, 1862. Wood, A *Northern Daughter*, p. 110.

on my own account, as a little relief to the intolerable depression I felt at parting from you, and partly on your account. The man who made your shoes says he will early next week make you another and larger pair. He says he cannot possibly do it this week. I have engaged two stools, for you at Platt's. He says they are the best he ever makes. Edgar says you would rather give up smoking than smoke his thirty dollar cigars but that he has some for thirty five, which he thinks you will endure, of these I am to take two hundred. These little matters attended to I came out to the Hill, in time for dinner. Jule is still here, apparently quiet and contented. Kate's nurse left her last night, and she feels quite bowed down with care and responsibility. And now my beloved, having told you all these things, with as much of tiresome detail as ever you will endure, I know you will think I might stop. I know from your many and repeated criticisms on my letters, that these facts of my every day life should constitute if not all, at least a large proportion of my letter, but this time Harry may I not tell you, how much I love you, how deeply and constantly I miss you, and how I long for the time when you will come home to me again? Have you written to me yet? I am afraid you will not get this for a long time. Let me know as soon as you hear from Mr. Chesnut, and tell me, all he says. It is raining terribly tonight. I should almost fear another freshet. The roads are in a dreadful state. Do you know I never heard anything more about my tea, after we left the store. Do you think there is any chance of my receiving it? And your Mother's bucket. . . .

Yours Ever,
Emily Hammond

JAMES HENRY HAMMOND TO WILLIAM GILMORE SIMMS[c]

Redcliffe, November 2, 1862

My Dear Simms:

 I am very sorry to learn [of] the illness of your Son[1] and your other anxieties. The fact is you have more sickness in your family than any I ever knew, except Dr. Bradford's. He is a Dr. of the old school and gives Calomel with a spoon and has lost Child after Child and most of

---

 1. William Gilmore Simms, Jr. (1843–1912) was the eldest son of William Gilmore Simms. Oliphant, *Simms*, 1:cxlix.

his Grandchildren though always living in healthy locations. I am persuaded you use entirely too much physic and that you had better use
none. Eight years ago I threw *all* mine to the dogs or rather fishes in
the river. I had occasion a few days ago to examine my Register of
births and deaths on my plantations and I made out a Statement of
them for these last 8 years and also one of the 8 preceding. From 1
Oct. 1846 to 1 Oct. 1854, the births exceeded the deaths 12 only. From
1 Oct. 1854 to 1 Oct. 1862 the excess of births was 84. About the same
time however (1853) I quit in a great measure the use of Molasses and
rice for the Children, and gave them instead skim and butter milk, and
these things doubtless contributed some thing to this large increase of
more than 3 p. ct. against 1/2 of 1 p. ct. before. I shall be very glad to
see you at all times, and when your son is well able to move—not
before, for collapses are the dangers of such attacks—bring him up with
you for change of air.

Paul who joined Kirby Smith's staff near Barbourville, Ky., and was
with it in all Smith's marching and fighting, but from whom I have
heard no account since taking Lexington in Sept. has reached his wife
at Macon. He will be here on Wednesday bringing all with him and
Lawson Clay and wife also (nee Comer). The men will soon return to
the army and leave the women—Loula for her accouchement and her
sister [Celeste Clay] for nurse.[2]

Harry is about going to Mobile as Q.M. on Gen. Alfred Cumming's
staff (a new Brigadier and his Brother in Law).[3] Either Aldrich's resignation has never reached Gregg or he has wholly overlooked all Harry's
letters (a little of both) so that he has been kept here all summer in the
status of a man on a R.R. Platform waiting for the Cars.[4]

Spann, whose Wife and her Parents have taken full possession of

2. Celeste Clay Hammond, the third child of Loula and Paul Hammond, was born on November 25, 1862. Billings, *Descendants of Hammond*, p. 5.

3. Promoted to the rank of colonel in 1861, Alfred Cumming, Emily's brother, was twice
wounded while commanding an Alabama brigade during the battles at Malvern Hill and Sharps-
burg. He was promoted to the rank of brigadier general on October 29, 1862. Wakelyn, *Biographical Dictionary of the Confederacy*, p. 155.

4. James Henry Hammond wrote his brother Marcellus in September 1862 that Harry was still
at Redcliffe, but that General Maxcey Gregg had agreed to give Harry the quartermaster's job once
Aldrich, the current holder of the post, resigned because of a permanently disabled shoulder.
Aldrich however had delayed "and has kept Harry on the anxious bench for over a month."
In November 1862 Harry Hammond did receive the position of quartermaster of Gregg's Brigade
and with it the rank of major. He served in that position until the end of the war. JHH to MCMH,
September 5, 1862, JHH Papers, LC; HH Petition to President Andrew Johnson [1865], JHH
Papers, SCL.

him, and sent substitutes etc. will be here soon and leave his wife, to
go himself to Miss. and look after the 30 negroes he has there—lost I
fear.

I have no clues whatever to public affairs save what the newspapers
convey. You and the Major are my only correspondents. Things seem
to be approaching a finality. Some of the parties to the War including
in such the European Powers can hold out much longer. We I think
best off of all. If my views, rejected and ridiculed as I was told 15 mos.
ago by Davis, Memminger and Barnwell etc—though I went to Richmond to expound them and did expound as Miles[5] can tell—had been
adopted then, we should have been on the flood tide above all now. I
proposed to buy the entire cotton crop at 10¢ for Confed. Notes and
hold it to Bank or Negotiate on, and to sell as much as necessary. I
subscribed 200 bales and 10,000 bushels to the produce loan. I sent
about 1 May $12,500 for the Corn and offered my Cotton to Memmin-
ger at 8¢ and 300 bales in Con. Bonds. He refused. I sold my crop last
for 17¼¢ and have taken for the whole of it (442 bales) Conf. Bonds at
20 years. So I am over a $40,000 creditor. But I fear that the Gov.ᵗ
with its hand to mouth financial schemes is sadly in want of means.
And its Military conduct has been so feeble and fitful that I fear it wants
Soldiers and can't get them. This section is *drained,* could not defend
its firesides against any force. The *Bon Dieu* must save Charleston, Savannah, Mobile, and our Coast. The Abolitionists can only do wanton
cruelties inflicting horrid suffering on us *to no purpose,* for Cotton *is*
King and the African *must be* a slave, or there's an end of all things,
and soon. We have, South, North, and Europe, committed great sins
of late years. Grown to be Titans in our own estimations, we have been
defying Heaven—some denouncing it so, (and most) swindling it and
others arming to scale the walls. We deserve a thorough scourging all,
and the War will end only when we have all got as we will all get it
before the ides of March.

My large family here over 60 black and white are doing well enough
and in good health enough. For myself, the Vulture is still at my liver

5. Hammond went to Richmond in July 1861 to argue for the establishment of cotton as a basis for
credit. Probably he is referring to Robert Woodward Barnwell, a Confederate senator from South
Carolina. William Porcher Miles, a member of the U.S. House of Representatives from South
Carolina (1857–1860), was also a member of the Confederate Congress in 1862. *Biographical Directory of the American Congress 1774–1961,* p. 1328; Oliphant, *Simms,* 4:398.

and I am not [well], except for such occasional moments when, being gorged, he sleeps.

Yours faithfully,
J.H. Hammond

JULIEN CUMMING TO HENRY HARFORD CUMMING[b]

Camp near Guinea Station, Va, March 17, 1863
My Dear Father:

The mail last evening brought me your letter of March 8th, continued on the 9th, and postmarked 10th inst. I have sent you in the last three days two hurriedly written notes, by members of the Regiment[1] going home on furlough, both of which I hope have ere this come safely to hand. I am glad you are not affected as I was, and to some extent, am still by the passage of the wholesale Act of Conscription by the Federal Congress. If I mistake not however, you overlook, at least in your remarks to me upon the subject, that immediate effect of the Law which gave and gives me most solicitude. I will take the army to which we of the "Army of Northern Virginia" are now opposed on the North Side of the Rappahannock. Here is a body of men, who, though signally defeated in the memorable struggle at Fredericksburg, [in December 1862] certainly exhibited, in the face of a most appalling fire, which made rank after rank bite the dust, a gallantry, and reckless determination, which has been surpassed by no soldiers, on either side, in this terribly sanguinary struggle. I doubt if even the Charge of the "Old Guard" at Waterloo, was more desperately impetuous there, than the fierce onset of Meagher's Brigade at the Mayre Hill—and though there was unquestionably disaffection or cowardice, or both, plainly exhibited in some parts of the field, yet it cannot be denied, that the men generally fought well. Those who were in the thickest of the fight speak in glowing terms of the beautiful precision, and steady onward movement of the Yankee line of battle, as they moved through a storm of deadly missiles to the unsuccessful charge upon our batteries. By far the greater portion of this army, thus animated and disciplined, would in a short

---

1. Julien Cumming served as Adjutant of the 48th Georgia Regiment of Infantry until he was wounded and captured at the Battle of Gettysburg. Wood, *A Northern Daughter*, p. 106.

time have returned to their homes, their terms of enlistment expired, not many of them soon to enlist again, if ever. By one stroke of the pen, these veterans are retained in the service, and into their well trained and formidable ranks, are to be incorporated the fresh, untrained levies to be made throughout the North. I fear that to this case the scriptural maxim that "a little leaven leaveneth the whole lump," is not applicable, but believe rather that the influx of raw recruits will soon assimilate itself and move harmoniously into the body into which it is to flow. We have tried the same Experiment in our Army, and while in seeking analogies, I do not for a moment lose sight of the wide difference between the two instances, in the spirit and temper of the two contending parties, nor under value the immense advantage, which the conviction, that right and justice are on our side, gives to every Confederate soldier, whatever may be his status as a citizen—still there is a sufficient resemblance of situation and policy to invite us to a careful examination of the makings of the system with our own men, with a view to arrive at a satisfactory conclusion as to the probable effect on the prospects of our enemies, of the adoption of a similar course. All those volunteers who were enlisted originally for the period of twelve (12) months, have been, as you are aware, retained in the Confederate Service, and are held by the same uniform tenure of service "for three years or the war"—with the rest of the Army. To this legislation, not only in my judgment but in that of those, whose opinions must carry the greatest weight, is to be ascribed the present efficiency of our Army. We had too a "Conscript Act," and under its operations, the raw recruits brought from the farm and the Counting Room—the plough and the pen—have been distributed into the ranks of those who, well-drilled in "The School of the Soldier," have been yet more thoroughly trained in the "School" of battle fields. The result is a body of men, that any people might be proud to have in its Armies—a result, attained not without grumbling complaints from those whose term of service has thus been arbitrarily extended; but unattended by any of the slightest outbreak or mutinous conduct. And such, with perhaps less equivocal signs of disgust and indignation, readily suppressed by a stern, military law, will, I fear be the history of the workings of the Yankee Conscript Act in their armies.

I need not say how fervently I trust I am mistaken, my supposed analogies dissimilar, and my entire reasonings incorrect.

We (our Regiment and Brigade)[2] are living quietly and in a comfort, unknown to us, since the winter set in, in our log shanties. My Report this morning shows four hundred and eighty three men for duty, and but Thirty one, sick, and according to the Surgeon, but two of these *seriously*. The other Regiments of the Brigade are in about the same state. Col Carswell,[3] upon taking command of the Regiment made the boys a short speech, in which he referred to the domestic affliction which had detained him so long at home—I believe he has satisfied all whose opinions are much worth considering, that his absence from the Regiment was unavoidable. He has inaugurated a system of strict discipline, which is greatly adding to the efficiency of the Regiment, and at the same time promotes the comfort of officers and men alike.

I have received the trunk sent by Sergeant Robbe—and am very much obliged for its contents—especially the cakes, novels and candy. Dr. Swinney's boxes have at last come to hand, and I have the pantaloons and hat. He says, the socks and shoes were not sent to him, and that the parcel, containing the two first mentioned articles, comprised all that he was entrusted with for me. I am in no immediate want of either, but mention the fact of their non-arrival, in order that there may be some investigation to determine whether they were sent by the Doctor—or overlooked, when the other articles were sent. I forgot to mention that in the folds of the pantaloons I found a supply of paper and envelopes.

Col. Gibson,[4] I think, expects to leave for Georgia next week, or early in the week succeeding—I take it for granted, it is not for nothing—he and his Brigadier are to meet on Georgia soil. It is said that our Colonel, not finding room enough for the force of all exercise of his shining military qualities in the command of a Regiment—is anxious to elevate his friend the General to the Gubernatorial Chair, and

---

2. The brigade, a part of Anderson's Division of Lee's Army of Northern Virginia, consisted of the 3rd, 22nd, 46th, and 48th Georgia Regiments and the 2nd Georgia Battalion. It was commanded by Brigadier General A.R. Wright. Charles E. Jones, Jr., *A Confederate Roster of General Officers* (Richmond: Southern Historical Society, 1876), pp. 66, 74.

3. Carswell was Lt. Col. Reuben W. Carswell. Ibid., p. 82; Claud Estes, *List of Field Officers Regiments and Battalions in the Confederate States Army 1861–1865* (Macon, Georgia: The J.W. Burke Co., 1912), p. 24.

4. Colonel William Gibson served in the 48th Georgia Infantry Regiment. Estes, *List of Field Officers*, p. 48.

then step into the vacant Brigadiership.[5] However this may be—it is certain there has been a great deal of "wire pulling" already, and will be still more, in a few days at Milledgeville. My opposition to might will be confirmed and deepened, if our Colonel's promotion is dependent on the contingency of the General's being elected Governor.

I am very grateful for your long letters to me, and hope you will continue to write whenever you can command the necessary leisure for the task.

Give my love to all at home, and let me be affectionately remembered to the absent members of the family—May the time soon come, when we "shall all be gathered round our family board once more."

Very affectionately, Yr son,

Julien Cumming

P. S.   I open my letter to say that late this evening, we heard heavy cannonading, in the direction of the U.S. Ford—and now, at nine o'clock in the night we have received orders to get everything in readiness for a move at 5 o'clock in the morning. I shall endeavour to write to you on the march but must prepare you for a gap in my correspondence, as it is quite likely, I may have no means of writing or dispatching letters.[6]

SALLIE HALL[1] TO JULIA A. CUMMING[b]

August 2, 1863

My dear Mrs. Cumming:

Returning from a ride on Saturday afternoon I found upon my bureau an invitation to Maria's wedding.[2] Though aware for some time of

5. Presumably nothing came of these plans.
6. On March 17, Union cavalry under Brigadier General W.W. Averell raided across the Rappahannock upstream at Kelly's Ford, and returned by early evening. The cannonading and march referred to here were perhaps a belated response to this raid. Shelby Foote, *The Civil War: A Narrative*, 3 vols. (New York: Random House, 1958–1974), 2:245–46, 274.

1. Sallie Hall was the unmarried sister of Charles Henry Hall, an Episcopal minister originally from Augusta. At the time of this letter he had a church in Washington, D.C. Reverend Hall was the former husband of Annie Maria Cumming Hall, eldest child of Julia A. Bryan and Henry Cumming who died in 1855 from severe burns. Cumming, "A Sketch of Descendants of David Cumming," p. 24.
2. Maria Bryan Cumming married DeRosset Lamar on August 6, 1863. Lamar (1842–1886) was the son of Gazaway Bugg Lamar and his second wife Harriet Cazenove Lamar. Gazaway

the engagement between Mr. Lamar and herself I was hardly prepared for the announcement "Little Ria"—as one used to call the "youngest daughter of your house"—is actually going to begin life for herself—I cannot congratulate you upon her marriage for you will miss her so much in the home circle. The bright face and affectionate heart will I know often return to the old homestead but then there will be a difference. It makes me sad to see a very young girl assuming the responsibilities of married life and I think you will understand why instead of congratulations I tender you only my sympathy. I am glad that you are so well pleased with her choice. Will you please tell Ria that I tender her my heartfelt wishes for her future happiness and trust that Our Father has many blessings in store for her. I have always felt a deep interest in her ever since she was a little child and to me she has ever been kind and affectionate. I regret that my mourning precludes my being present at the Ceremony. I thank you very much for your kindness in remembering me on the occasion—tis only one of the many evidences of your thoughtfulness. I congratulate you upon the safe return of your son Alfred and hope you are feeling quite happy now so many of your causes of anxiety are removed. Have you heard anything of Julien?[3] I saw by the papers that there were some letters "in transit" from the Gettysburg prisoners and hope you might be one of the fortunate recipients. Though tis not a subject of jest—I would like to be an invisible witness of Julien's experiences while in a foreign land. That fund of humour for which he is distinguished will certainly evince itself even under the most trying circumstances. However I trust he will soon be exchanged. Is Joe quite well and Harf? I had an opportunity not long since of sending a letter to Washington by a certain opportunity. Miss Clarke a sister of our Rector—went on via Nashville—and was not searched. In my letter I mentioned several facts of interest about the different members of your household, so that brother might inform Judge Bryan concerning you. I would have mentioned it to you but have not seen you for several weeks. I am just now suffering a little

---

Lamar was a prominent banker and businessman in Augusta, Savannah, and New York City. The Cummings considered his son DeRosset a very acceptable husband for their youngest daughter, Maria. Mrs. R.M. Johnston to Colonel and Mrs. Henry H. Cumming, August 5, 1863, HBC Family Papers, SCL; Wood, A *Northern Daughter*, p. 113.

3. Julien Cumming was captured at Gettysburg. He died a prisoner of war at the United States Military Prison, Johnson's Island, Ohio, on March 8, 1864. HBC Family Papers, August 1863 through March 1864, passim, SCL; Wood, A *Northern Daughter*, p. 106.

inconvenience from a sprained wrist which makes my writing somewhat illegible. Remember me very kindly to Mr. Cumming and as ever I am

Yours most affectionately,

Sallie Hall

HARRY HAMMOND TO EMILY C. HAMMOND[b]

Camp near Montpellier, April 27, 1864

My Dear Wife:

I have been on the point of commencing a letter to you several times during the last day or two, but in addition to other interruptions, and a good deal of occupation I have written so much officially, that my hand has become weary, and it pains me to hold a pen. You may have experienced the same feeling when you commenced practicing on the piano, while you can hardly call the sensation pain it is sufficient to divert the attention, and to be very annoying. I have my business pretty well reglé but there are many changes, and a great deal of activity in this Department at this time—forming ordnance and commissary trains, turning in winter equipments and comforts, and touching up generally for the campaign. There is activity and cheerfulness everywhere and I never knew the feeling in the Army more buoyant or confident than it is now. This is owing in part to the series of successes our arms have met with recently, some what to the long rest the troops have enjoyed here and to the assurance which the largely increased strength of the Army gives the men. Perhaps too the coming on of spring, which seems to have fallen upon us almost unawares in the last few days, has a natural tendency to elate the spirits of men. For myself I rejoice at this general feeling, and have much hope myself, but I feel full of anxiety as I seem to realize that a great crisis is rapidly approaching. To day Atkinson tells me that Genl. Lee has ordered every thing not absolutely necessary to be sent back from Hd. Qs. The baggage has been shipped some days since, and we may now hold ourselves in readiness for a move. To all appearances however the move may be deferred for weeks, a thing not to be taken as an indication or wondered at since it is the purpose of the Generals to keep as secret as possible their intentions at this time—This they succeed perfectly in doing, if not from the country at large and from each other, at least from the troops they command. You must know my dear Emily that I have had no letter but one from you since I left home, which will be two weeks tomorrow, two weeks! How rapidly those days go by when they are passed. Is it this life I lead or is it age and do the latter years hurry themselves like the waters that pass over the rapids where they plunge into the abyss? Although I eat and sleep entirely apart from the rest of the camp, I have a ride out every day, and somebody is always lounging in—the General for one, nearly every day—so that I have no more solitude than is good for one. Capt. Haskell has received a telegram from Mr. Chesnut saying that he has the appointment of Lt. Col. of Cav.[1] I am glad he has it and I think he will make a good officer, but I consider especially on Capt. Trenholm who expected to have had the place. Trenholm had in some part raised the Battalion. I understand he furnished three hundred horses for it, arms, accoutrements and clothing for the men, commanded them for more than a year, led them gallantly and skillfully in a very creditable fight, and has the reputation of being an excellent officer. Haskell has two wounds—has been a very efficient officer, a good soldier, and has lost two brothers, good men, in the war. I have an idea that the latter motives must have had much influence in the matter, as I think indeed it ought to have. I have no idea who will succeed him. I don't feel that I can ask the General for the appointment, he knows I want it well enough, but I am sure he has other views, i.e. that he would refuse any request should I make it.

I send you my steam signal paper with Genl. Lee's endorsement. Please keep it, like many a sick man's dream it may turn up as a curiosity some day, when some one else has made the invention over again, and used it.[2]—28th. I was so tired last night my dear Emily that I could not finish my letter to you, nor answer yours of the 22nd which I received some time after dark. I had been out on a long ride after grazing-ground for my stock. I am glad you are to be in funds, please write

1. In the spring of 1864 Captain A.C. Haskell, assistant adjutant general of McGowan's South Carolina Brigade, was promoted to lieutenant colonel in the South Carolina cavalry. It was reported that "Capt. A.C. Haskell received the most flattering farewell from the brigade. I have heard that men wept over his parting address." J.F.J. Caldwell, *The History of a Brigade of South Carolinians Known First As "Gregg's" and Subsequently As "McGowan's Brigade"* (Philadelphia: King and Baird Printers, 1866), pp. 123–24.

2. Apparently no one heeded Harry's request, for the family papers were thoroughly searched without success.

those bills as soon as you can. . . . Kiss my little Julia and remember
me to all.

Goodbye my dear Wife.

HH

HARRY HAMMOND TO EMILY C. HAMMOND[b]

On the Plank Road to Fredericksburg
16 miles from Orange C[ourt] H[ouse], May 7, 1864

My Dear Emily:

I commenced a letter to you yesterday in pencil, but as I was not
able to finish it I have concluded to throw it aside and begin another.
This morning I had a letter from you dated the 30th of last month. I
was very glad to get it, but I wish my dear Emily you had told me in it
that you loved me. I hear from you so seldom now that you must never
fail to tell me this when you write, that is to say I always want you to
think when you do write that I ought to know just how much you love
me at that very time.

We left camp on the fourth very suddenly in consequence of the
movement on the part of the enemy.[1] They had thrown themselves
across the rapids and formed a line of battle perpendicular to that
stream, their center resting on the Plank road about 20 miles East of
Orange, their left on the Catharpin road several miles south of the plank
road, and their right on the river road. Genl. Lee advanced to meet
them on these three roads. A.P. Hill on the plank road in the centre,
Longstreet on the Catharpin road on the right and Ewell on the river
road (called also the Black or Black House road) on the left. The wagons
following their respective corps. About noon on the 5th our right and
left engaged the enemy about the same time. Our centre did not touch
their lines until several hours later and was consequently a good deal
advanced. So that at one time the firing was in the rear of my train on
both the right and left. Ewell and Longstreet however pressed the flanks
of the enemy back and straightened out our line, making it nearly perpendicular to the Plank. That evening our centre engaged the enemy
heavily—in our Brigade Col. Miller and Lt. Col. Bookter were mortally

1. Early on the morning of May 4, 1864, the Army of the Potomac, generally inactive since
Gettysburg, started to move across the Rapidan River.

wounded, but the loss so far has been slighter than in any other fight, and the wounds generally not of a severe character. This country is called the Wilderness,[2] and I had no idea there was so desolate a country in Viriginia. The plank road runs through a tolerably level country, which is thickly wooded with a low growth of scrubby oaks and hickories. There seem to be no inhabitants, and you meet with no houses for miles and miles, and then only small and mean ones and generally deserted. This makes it very difficult for either side to use artillery, and I never heard so little cannon firing in a battle. The movement of troops too in line of battle is very much interfered with from the same cause— the country is intersected with white oak flats which are wet and marshy making it altogether a place unfit for the maneuvering of troops. On the 6th the sun had not risen when the battle was opened with great vigor by the enemy on our left and extended rapidly to the centre. Ewell had built breastworks on the night of the 5th and repelled a series of assaults inflicting severe loss on the enemy. In the centre our corps was driven back by the enemy and for a few moments affairs seemed in a critical condition,[3] all the wagons were ordered back, but before the movement commenced, Longstreet came in on the right centre, recovered the lost ground and advanced our line of battle north of the plank road, and two miles further than it was before. Genl. Lee elected an excellent line of battle and the artillery was moved in to position during the afternoon. Such was the state of affairs last night, we had established the line we wished, had driven the enemy back every where, captured 4,000 prisoners, and suffered as far as I can learn very little loss ourselves.[4] Our loss has been very heavy however in officers which is due to the difficulty of moving men over such ground. This morning except a few cannon that are on Ewell's line, all is quiet. The enemy are said to be in some strong works which we can not assault without great loss, but they are so surrounded by woods that they can not use

2. After crossing the Rapidan River, Grant had hoped to get through the tangled and wooded area near Fredericksburg before engaging in battle, but instead the two armies met on May 5 and 6 in the Battle of the Wilderness, the first engagement of the forty-day Wilderness Campaign. Randall and Donald, *The Civil War*, pp. 418–19.

3. "Lee saw a whole brigade in full retreat. Moreover, this was not just any brigade; it was Brigadier General Samuel McGowan's brigade of South Carolinians, Wilcox's best and one of the finest in the army." Shelby Foote, *The Civil War: A Narrative*, 3:168. See also letter of Aug. 19, 1864, n. 3.

4. Union casualties were 18,000, with over 2000 killed. The Confederate casualties probably exceeded 10,000. Randall and Donald, *The Civil War*, p. 419.

their artillery, while there is an open space in front of our guns which gives us a fair sweep at them in case they make an attack on our line. Such is the general outline of the operations thus far, we have causes to feel thankful for our success but it is doubtful whether the battle is over yet. The weather is intensely warm and dusty and the scorching power of the sun seems greater to me as its rays pierce through the leafless branches of the trees that seemed to have been caught napping. Last Monday we had a terrible gale of wind and the mountains were white with snow the next morning, during the wind a tree was blown down on my tent tearing one of my flies to pieces and scattering things generally. Henry was in the tent but at the opposite end from that on which the tree fell and was uninjured. I had to leave him at Montpellier when we marched, and he cried piteously on quitting me. I told him to try and make his way to Spann in Richmond in case I should not return. . . . . Write to me dearest, kiss my little Julia and give my love to all. I hope your Mother is better before this.

HH

HARRY HAMMOND TO EMILY C. HAMMOND[b]

Camp near Model Farm,
Petersburg,[1] June 30, 1864

My Dear Emmy:

Communication of all sorts has been so completely cut off for many days past that I have not thought it worth while to write to you. There was too previous to this an interval when I did not write to you because sometimes we were moving, sometimes the heat and dust had me paralyzed, and all the time I was in one of those spells of hopeless weariness which I am ashamed to make confession of. They made me, you know, a most unhappy person before I knew you, and when I am so far separated from you I find myself still subject to their influence. I have had less trouble than usual and any personal discomfort, heat and dust aside, has not been more than average during that time. I thank you

1. Unable to defeat General Lee during the forty-day Wilderness Campaign, General Grant altered his strategy. He moved his army south of the James River for the purpose of taking Richmond, the Confederate capital, from the rear. To defend Richmond meant to hold Petersburg, the gateway to Richmond. Ibid., pp. 422–23.

very much my dear Wife for the letters you have written and especially for one of the 9th June. They have come to me very irregularly. The earlier dates reaching me last. I trust however that now our cavalry are on the right, that is the road south of us, our communications will be resumed and rendered secure, tho' from the damage done the roads I suppose some days, perhaps many, must elapse before trains come through, and I only commence this letter in the hope that I may be able to send it by hand to the other side of Stony Creek or to some point where it can be mailed, letters it is true are carried daily to the P.O. in Petersburg but none have gone from there yet, and there is no telling when they will. I am glad to hear your Father has returned and is well again. I was quite uneasy on his account when I heard how much he was exposing himself. My first information of Grandmother's death[2] was given me by Gregg[3] who merely stated the fact, and I did not hear from you for nearly two weeks afterwards that she had passed away with so little of that struggle mental and physical which generally renders the aged so unhappy as death approaches, and which I had especially apprehended in her case. I have received a letter from Mother in the last day or two which I propose to answer as soon as I finish this one. The two boxes she sent me reached me safely, and have been of great service to me in furnishing the first necessaries of life. I am very much obliged to her for them and to every body for the pains they took in sending them to me, but I shall not send home for any thing more, I know it puts them out of their way to attend to such matters and they think that I am taxing them too heavily by my requisitions. Under the new orders allowing the sale of one ration to officers I can feed my servant, and for the rest I can take my chances with that part of the Army who get nothing from home and who are not only more desiring of such things than I am, but in a much worse position as regards to such supplies as are to be had here. I am sorry to have given you so much trouble about my servant. I did not count upon the chances of servants being thrown out of employment here by the casualties among their masters, which I might have anticipated. In this manner I have gotten a tolerably good boy who with the exception of being very wasteful serves me well enough for $20 a month. Henry I have not heard

2. Harry Hammond's grandmother, Catherine Fox Spann Hammond, died on June 1, 1864. JHH Plantation Journal, June 1 and 2, 1864, JHH Papers; Billings, "The Hammond Family," SCL.

3. James Gregg was Harry Hammond's brother-in-law. See letter of Dec. 28, 1856, n. 14.

from for six weeks nor can I conjecture what has become of him. The enemy have not been in his immediate neighborhood at least not in heavy force as far as I have heard. Without an accident he should have rejoined me before this time, but nothing can be counted on in such times and I may never see the poor fellow again. . . . By the way I have never heard if my bills at Mr. Winkle's and Henry's and Shacklefords for my last suit of clothes was settled. It will be very awkward to pay so large an amount some day in good currency if the currency was to get good. Meanwhile these men are entitled to their money to speculate on. They only earn their subsistence by cash payment which enables them to buy low and sell out before the proceeds of the first sales become mere paper.

I had a note from Gregg this morning telling me he was slightly wounded and at Col. Baynes', Easy St between 4 & 5 Richmond. I hope Catty has not made the attempt to come on to him as the interruptions to travel at this time would have exposed her not only to great inconveniences but to great risks also. If his wound is sufficiently serious I make no doubt he will go home as soon as the roads allow the trip to be made.

As for the situation of affairs they remain about the same. The two lines of breastworks are still there between the two armies just as they have been for some two months past,[4] the proposition is enunciated, the *onus probandis* lies with Grant. Our supplies are holding out so far, the men have never yet missed their daily bread, there is a little corn still left for our horses, and some grazing, not to speak of oats and clover fields which will keep them alive for a week or so of themselves. It looks now as if with good fortune we might for a while at least expect to keep the raiders absent. The enemy throw a number of shells daily into Petersburg but they do little damage, the people (women and children) seem not to mind them at all—on one street yesterday where such a number of shells burst that I would have considered it a warm place in the field, women were passing about with little concern, dodging around a corner when they heard a shell coming, or putting their heads out of their windows to see the damage they had done when they struck

---

4. The "two months past" encompassed the forty-day Wilderness Campaign during which the armies had marched nearly 100 miles, fought five major battles, usually with Union troops attacking entrenched Confederates, and suffered 60,000 Union casualties and 30,000 Confederate casualties. Clarence C. Buel and Robert U. Johnson, eds., *Battles and Leaders of the Civil War,* 4 vols. (New York: The Century Company, 1884), 4:182.

near their houses. I have moved into a good camp under a few trees in an open field within a few feet of a cool well. We are just on the outskirts of the town and there are some houses quite near us—a lady yesterday sent Wardlaw and myself some ice cream and cakes, and took us in the evening to visit Mrs. Wright, widow of the unfortunate Dr. Wright of Norfolk, who is a very nice old lady and has quite a pleasant family.

Chaffin's Farm 6th July—At last I hear my dear Emily that there is some possibility of a letter going by mail this rather a rumor however than any definite information—in this respect being like almost everything I learn now, simply conjecture—I have had a long ride today and I am very tired. I will finish my letter at another time. I love you always my Emily.

HH

HARRY HAMMOND TO EMILY C. HAMMOND[b]

Chaffin's Bluff,[1] August 19, 1864

My Dear Emily:

I have to thank you for two letters—both of them unusually interesting to me—since I last wrote, one came yesterday, and the other I have just received. Why is it my dear Wife that it gives me pleasure of some sort to have you tell me how worried you are, how bad tempered indeed so bad tempered that you hate almost everything and even our poor little Julia, and that you are not going visiting, and that you feel there is a great gap between you and almost everybody else. This is a confidence I know you would not make any one else, and even if it does you no good to tell me of it my poor dear child it is a proof of your love for me that I value highly, and however little I may be able to help you in this trouble, the intention and the strong desire to do so that I have is pleasant. Perhaps I feel too that if I were with you it might be that you would not have these things so much to heart. And it does me good too my Emily while I may not say that all this evil was not true of you—to know that it is exceptional, and that not only I but all who know her know that nothing is more foreign to the nature of my

1. Chaffin's Bluff, just below Richmond, was a fortification on the James River near Malvern Hill. Caldwell, *A History of a Brigade of South Carolinians,* p. 168.

darling wife than these same wrong feelings—your confession to them is only a shadow that makes the light of your clear patience and cheerful christian trustfulness and faith more clear to me. I cannot feel tho' any pleasure in hearing you say that you wish you were not a woman. The only solution of this country is in the hands of women not only now in all that they inspire men to do and bear and to believe in, or in the present help and aid they render to the country—but if ever this war does end it will be their part to restore order and to reform society. It would not be easy to estimate the influence that the first generation of women after this struggle will exert upon the whole future history of this country. Nor do I sympathize with you at all when you make it a matter of regret that you are not beautiful. I do not understand why this should trouble you at all while I am not there with you—Why do you want other people to think you beautiful—I am sure that I desire nothing less than this, no one can for a moment deny that my Emily is in appearance everything *comme il faut* for a lady, beyond this why do you desire attractiveness. Isn't it enough for you that you satisfy entirely the man who loves you more than any one else ever can and that to him your person is in every way the sweetest, dearest, and most agreeable that the whole earth can furnish, or that he can conceive of. How can you account for such wishes under such circumstances and how is it that they make you unhappy.

I received the [Augusta] Constitutionalist yesterday. I do feel very much obliged to your Father for his kindness in sending me this paper, it is only *his* way of doing things. It would surprise me from any one else. I suppose the stories I see advertised in it are by Col. Johnston.[2]

I stopped at Mr Morriss' when I was in Richmond last, and the servant at the door told me they were all well. I can not believe Spann is seriously ill. I suppose Gregg only takes Spann's own statement of his case. I dare say the poor fellow does suffer a good deal and is far from enjoying good health. I hardly know tho' how his affairs are. I don't like the Morriss's and feel no disposition to have anything to do with them.

We have had a good deal of heavy fighting here, and the other evening when I wrote the last lines in my letter to you I thought the enemy would perhaps break in upon us here, our troops having been sent off to another part of the line and only a picket line being inter-

2. Richard Malcolm Johnston and Harry Hammond had been colleagues at the University of Georgia. See letter of Sept. 26, 1859, n. 3.

posed between us and a heavy force of the enemy. Genl. Lee has been here superintending the fighting himself. It is said the enemy are re-crossing the River, tho' I do not think it certain yet. Conner was only slightly wounded, he is now in command of Lane's Brigade, Genl. M\(^c\)Gowan having assumed command yesterday.[3] Hunt was only slightly wounded. Poor Girardey was killed, it does seem fatal to promote a man now a days to be Brig-Genl, the casualties among that class this summer have been remarkably numerous. Girardey's line was necessar-ily very much drawn out and it was broken by a heavy force of the enemy. Lane's and M\(^c\)Gowan's Brigades were called in to recapture the works thus lost, and whipped the enemy back with great slaughter[4] —It is the first time we fought negroes and I am sorry to say no quarter was shown them. Everything is unsettled here now—but I expect we will see our way out today or tomorrow. The weather is somewhat cooler owing to recent rains, there is too the promise of an easterly storm. I wish it would come and drive the enemy out of these bottoms. Kiss my dear little Julia and don't strike her more than is good (not for her) for you. Good by my dear Wife.

HH

HARRY HAMMOND TO JULIA B. HAMMOND[b]

Camp near Petersburg, November 7, 1864

My Dear Julia:

I don't know whether you remember how I drove you down to my camp one day last winter, when you were at Montpellier with your dear

3. General Samuel McGowan (1819–1897) was born in Laurens County, South Carolina, to which his parents had emigrated from Ireland. He graduated from South Carolina College in 1841 and was admitted to the bar in Abbeville, South Carolina in 1842. He became an eminent lawyer and served in the South Carolina legislature for twelve years. When South Carolina seceded he joined the state brigade and was promoted to brigadier general on April 23, 1863. McGowan displayed extraordinary bravery when wounded for a third time during the Battle of Chancellors-ville. In 1864 he fought in the Battle of the Wilderness and at the "Bloody Angle" of Spotsylvania, where he was wounded on May 11, 1864. The command was taken over by Colonel J.N. Brown until his capture when it passed to Lt. Col. J.F. Hunt. In August 1864 McGowan returned to duty and resumed the command of his brigade. After Appomattox he returned to law practice in Abbe-ville and eventually became an associate justice of the state supreme court (1879–1893). Wakelyn, *Biographical Dictionary of the Confederacy*, pp. 297–98; General Marcus J. Wright, *General Of-ficers of the Confederate Army* (New York: The Neale Publishing Company, 1911), p. 102; Cald-well, *A History of a Brigade of South Carolinians*, pp. 148, 155, 156, 180.

4. "The battle was called by a variety of names, but with us it was commonly known as the battle of Fussel's Mill." Caldwell, *A History of a Brigade of South Carolinians*, p. 178.

Mother. You know you got some long curls at the carpenter's and Genl. McGowan gave you a cake when you went to his tent to see him. Well if you did remember that, and how sober and solemn the pines looked all dripping with the rain as they were, and how quiet everything was except the Blacksmiths at work, and the soldiers cutting wood to warm themselves with, you would remember a scene very much like that in which I am this evening writing to you. The pines are not so tall and instead of the hills, this is a flat swampy place, but there are the same tents not altogether so comfortable perhaps, and the same noises. So that if you had gone to sleep there that day, and were waked up here this evening you would at first believe you were in the same place. But there has been many a sad story for the people you saw that day, and many weary anxious hours for all of us since then. I wish you and your Mother were here with me and maybe after a while I will find a house here where you can stay and I will write to your Mamma to come here, and bring you with her. But now the Yankees keep shooting so, every day and every night, that no body knows what they are going to do from one day to another. I think tho' that Lee's Army have killed so many of them whenever they come up close to them, that they will go away to a place between two rivers called City Point, and build houses and stay there until the winter with all the rain and mud passes over. They will leave a few here, and we will have to drive them away too. And when that is done I will write for you and your Mother to come here. Tell your Mother I have been very busy, and that is the reason I have not written to her. I went down the other day to see your Aunt Catty who is living in a house a good ways from here, farther than from the Sand Hills to Redcliffe—right close to a cavalry camp. A week before last the Yankees tried to get to that house and your aunt got left behind, and at last got an ambulance, and just ran away as the Yankees came up the road she was going, and our soldiers met them there and killed a great many of them. There is a young lady staying at the same house and she has just come from Paris, she was a very pretty young lady, and had so much pretty hair on her head that I was astonished at it—but your Aunt Catty told me that they had tied it on for her, to make her look pretty. You must ask your Mother to get you a slate and pencil and learn how to make letters. I have heard of little girls who could write even before they could read. And you must learn too how to make horses and houses on the slate. I dare say you and little Bryan are just having your tea in the Basement and your Mamma is in the parlor knitting, and talking to your Gran'ma. I wish very much I was there with you now. Tell your Gran'ma I brought the cake she gave me all the way to camp without cutting any of it, but I have eaten it since and given some other people some of it, and we all thought it very nice. Don't you remember the dogs you saw at Genl. McGowan's the day I carried you there—Well one of them is here now and has followed us all about ever since we left Montpellier until he has grown to be a great big dog and keeps everybody away from Blue Harry's fire. Tell your Mother that I love her and you better than any body, and you must love her and take good care of her until I come back, and tell her to write to me for I have had no letter from her yet. And you must go with her over to Redcliffe when you can. God bless you my little Daughter and keep you safe.

Harry Hammond

HARRY HAMMOND TO EMILY C. HAMMOND[b]

Camp near Petersburg, November 8, 1864

I had the great pleasure today my beloved wife of receiving your letter of Tuesday the 1st, being the first you wrote me since I left. I was glad to know I had not waked every one in going away that morning for I tried very carefully not to do so and I am also very glad to hear that they had all hoped I had not gone. I did not receive the telegrams your Father sent me, altho' the last thing I did on Monday afternoon before walking to the Depot was to call at the Telegraph office—it was the second time I had been there that day. I am only sorry that so much money should have been spent for a paper of so little use to me tho' if it had reached me I think I should have risked a few days longer on it. It is very well however in view of the intentions of certain people here that I did not do so. As for this matter I don't know what will come of it. The Div. Adgt. addressed me a note asking for an explanation or rather report of the circumstances. Genl. McGowan told me today he rather thought that my statement would be satisfactory on the subject, at least that the Maj. Genl. seemed "mollified" when he last spoke to him of it. Suber[1] told me however that he heard the Adj't say that he

---

1. Christian H. Suber, born September 4, 1828, in Newberry District, served briefly with Harry in Gregg's Brigade. J.F.J. Caldwell, *A Memorial of Christian H. Suber* (Charleston, S.C.: Walker, Evans and Cogswell Co. Printers, 1892), p. 5.

has requested it of his Genl. as a personal favor, to be allowed to prefer charges against me,[2] if he does of course that will be a first for the court. I am very much relieved to hear that Father was so much better. Atkinson was here this morning, and he told me that his Mother had been to Redcliffe and that she said Father was better. I was able too this morning to send Catty word of this. Catty said she was having a very pleasant time of it. She like Maria had her successes at Reviews. Genl. Hampton claimed his kinship with her[3] and introduced her to Maj. Genl. Lee who invited them all to drive to his quarters. You and I Emily somehow we never manage to get among great Folks. You would tho' if it was not for me.

The jacket you speak of is a flannel summer jacket I suppose and is too light for winter wear. Henry can have it next summer. You can send on the handkerchief and gloves whenever you get them ready. I shall not go to Richmond until next month unless I should hear from the letter Father has sent to Maj. Genl. Smith sooner than that. . . . I feel some how brighter and more cheerful today my darling than I have done since I left you. People here don't think I am crosser as you my dear love sometimes think I am but I feel I have been a very doleful man for the past ten days. I trust my Emily that those days when we lived together and loved each other so entirely there in Athens may yet be matched by days as bright. It is all of earthly good and happiness I ask of Heaven. And if heaven permits me once more to live with you and you will only love me as you did then I know I shall be happier than ever I was and I will only ask then that I may deserve that love. . . .

Everything remains pretty much as when I left, our infantry is a little more drawn out to the right, and the enemy have gained no advantage since they took the Welder road in August. I have still several days work on hand and then I will never have too much to do again in

2. John Shaw Billings reported that when he was a boy he was told that his grandfather had been court-martialed during the war. Harry Hammond, as quartermaster, was responsible for the personal baggage of his brigade's officers. During a sudden enemy attack he was ordered to move everything to the rear. Because of a shortage of wagons he decided to destroy much of the personal baggage. Later the brigade's officers brought charges against him for burning their belongings. He was tried, found guilty, and fined a small sum. According to Billings, this "curdled him [Harry Hammond] completely on army life." John Shaw Billings, MS vol. bd. 1927-n.d., "Myself and Family," John Shaw Billings Scrapbook Collection, SCL.

3. General Wade Hampton, son of Wade Hampton II, was Katherine Hammond Gregg's first cousin.

the Q.M. Dept. So much is simplified by the changes that have been made.

I love you always my own and only love. Kiss my little Julia for me.

Harry Hammond

EDWARD SPANN HAMMOND TO HARRY HAMMOND, LAST MOMENTS OF J.H. HAMMOND[h]

Nov. 13, 1864

. . . He passed away about 10 minutes before 10 A.M. (13 Nov. 1864). Mother simply exclaimed "What! Dead? Dead?" but seemed incapable of realizing it. Seeing her stand bewildered, scarcely a tear on any eye, so sudden and unexpected was the scene while all were busy in getting remedies, or in attendance, I led Mother to the other room, but she soon returned. Just after our return Mrs. Fitzsimons[1] threw herself by Father's side and exclaiming with a flood of tears, "my best friend, you have left us," closed his eyes.

Father was deeply affected by war reverses of the year (1864). He seemed to succumb at the fall of Atlanta, and Hood's movement to Tenn., leaving the way clear to the coast to Sherman. He apprehended a vandal march that would desolate everything on its line,[2] and that in S.C. to annihilate or desecrate broadcast would be the order of the move. He seemed not simply desirous, but determined, not to be witness to what he was powerless to mitigate or prevent; and, as if he sought and hastened his death, not by any act, but by force of will. "It is time for me to die," he said; "death will be relief. I can no longer enjoy life, or be of any service whatever." Yet he never lost confidence in the high qualities of the people, and the resources of the South. In October he remarked, "this war will terminate suddenly within six months: I do not care to look behind the veil. Enough, that every thing I have worked for, the labors of my life, will all be upset. I would be powerless, and so for a time will be all those true and faithful to the

---

1. Probably this reference is to Christopher Fitzsimons's widow, Elizabeth Stoney Fitzsimons. She was a sister-in-law of Catherine Fitzsimons Hammond and visited Redcliffe frequently. John Shaw Billings, comp., "Notes on Christopher Fitzsimons (1762–1825)," John Shaw Billings Papers, SCL.

2. Sherman's march to the sea began on November 16, 1864, only three days after James Henry Hammond's death.

South. Were I all, and more, the most partial attribute to me, I could do nothing for the State for at least fifteen years. It will be a terrible ordeal you have to go through. I wish to escape it. You boys can bear it, and then the South and So. Ca. will enter upon a career of prosperity and power grander than anything they have yet known. The South will rule this country. I will be too old and crushed, should I survive, to realize it."

HARRY HAMMOND TO EMILY C. HAMMOND[b]

Petersburg, Va., February 18, 1864 [1865][1]

My Dear Emily:

I have borrowed this sheet from Maj. Wardlaw[2] to write to you. I came into his quarters a few moments since and find a man who is just leaving on furlough for Aiken. He is waiting for this letter which he has promised to take charge of. We have just had the news of the fall of Columbia and of course we have no news further west than that point. All the intelligence that we have had here before, seems however to indicate that the enemy are not moving at present toward Augusta, and I have strong hopes that our Army is being concentrated from that point to pursue Sherman. I still feel hopeful of affairs in South Carolina, we have men there in sufficient numbers to fight the enemy and I am waiting anxiously for Beauregard to concentrate his forces and make his attack.

Here we enjoy the usual winter quiet, today is a beautiful warm clear day after a great deal of very cold and wet weather. I have heard nothing from Richmond yet of my own affairs but I expect a letter every day. I am quite well and as comfortable as one can expect to be in camp. The spirit of our men is very much improved with the improvement in rations and on the whole the situation here seems to be satisfactory and encouraging at present.

I still hope to see you my dear wife before very long and I think of you and love you always. Please inquire at the Provost Marshall's or

1. This letter is incorrectly dated as is indicated by internal evidence. General Sherman and his troops entered Columbia on February 17, 1865.
2. Major A.B. Wardlaw was listed as commissary of McGowan's Brigade. Caldwell, A *History of a Brigade of South Carolinians*, p. 199.

Trans Off. for soldiers coming this way by whom you can write to me.
Give my love to Mother and all, and kiss my dear Little Julia for me.

Ever yours,

H. H.

HARRY HAMMOND TO EMILY C. HAMMOND[b]

Petersburg, March 10, 1865

My Dear Emily:

A retired soldier is to leave the hospital tomorrow morning for Abbeville and I will send this letter by him. They are granting no furloughs
now not even to the sick to go beyond Charlotte, N.C., so that it is
comparatively a rare occurrence to hear of any one who is going within
reach of the mail lines to Augusta. . . .

Except to say that I am well and comfortable and that all is quiet
there is little to say. It has never been quieter on these lines than for a
week past, there are days when not a cannon is fired. Notwithstanding
there are constant rumors that we are to move. This however will be
impossible until the weather changes and the roads have a chance to
dry, it has been raining nearly every day since my return. The weather
has grown quite warm and the approach of spring was very disagreeably
announced to me the other morning by the croaking of some frogs in a
little wet weather pond in my camp. About daylight they set up the
loudest and most lugubrious sound I ever heard. I did not know that
even a frog could utter anything so direful, and it was so loud that I
started in my sleep thinking it came from under my pillow. Such an
announcement of Spring is in harmony I fear with a very general feeling
just now. For myself tho' I can not somehow share this and I feel more
cheerful than usual and am not without good hope that fortune will be
on our side this summer.

Yesterday the first military execution occurred in our Brigade, four
men were shot under the charge of desertion. We have had some sixty
or seventy desertions recently from the Brigade most of them going over
to the enemy at night while on picket. These men had started home
with their guns and were taken scarcely a mile from their quarters, they
avowed that they were merely going out foraging, but the evidence I
suppose showed their intention to desert. The desertion has been a sort

of mania with us, men went off in squads and there was a good deal of excitement about it.[1] But it has passed over, none have left us I believe for more than a week past, and I hope and believe that they have ceased entirely. Our supplies continue sufficient and the Army is much recruited I learn, by the amnesty that has been granted to those absent without leave.

They are hurrying me to finish my letter. You are right to purchase whatever you need or may need for a year to come, these heavy infantry raids must reach Augusta before long and that is now almost our only market. I am waiting and watching for my [transfer] paper, and still hoping that it may be approved tho' there is it seems to me a general disinclination to help QMS in almost any matter. I shall not under any circumstance start sooner than the 1st April as I will have to close my accounts here before I leave. If I don't come, I will send Julia her stories as soon as the mails are opened again. Thank you for the present you have for me, I have one for you too. I love you always my dear Wife. Kiss my little Julia and remember me affectionately to all.

                                                        Harry Hammond

HARRY HAMMOND TO EMILY C. HAMMOND[b]

                                          Petersburg, March 27, 1865
My Dear Emily:

I shall write you at least a letter a week and let it take its chances until there is more certainty in transmitting them. I had thought of writing some thing to you every day and sending it whenever opportu-

---

1. A fuller account of desertions in the brigade follows: "The first desertion I remember was that of a soldier in the First Regiment, who was soon followed by another of that regiment. Then nine men of Orr's regiment of rifles left us. Then one or two men of the Twelfth regiment deserted, one of them, one of those two deserters who were convicted at Orange Court House and pardoned. Three or four deserted from the Fourteenth regiment. Finally twenty-six men of the Thirteenth regiment marched from their post on the picket-line, at a signal. All of these went to the enemy. The last party were fired upon by their comrades, but I do not know whether with any effect. Eleven men of the First regiment quitted the corps in the early part of March, and started for home. But five of them were captured next morning and brought back to us. They were tried before the corps court-martial, sentenced, and four of them shot on the following day. The fifth was respited, on account of his youth and the temptation supposed to have been offered him by the rest. It was a sad spectacle, and its sadness was increased by the fact that one of these four had been an excellent soldier, and bore that day the scars of three wounds received in battle. The whole number of deserters in the brigade reached a hundred and four." Ibid., p. 198.

nity offered, but there has been such quiet with such *expectancy* that it hardly seemed worth while to pen such a diary; but I should have done it had I not fell upon another expedient which, as it may turn out as fruitless a labor as the diary, I will notify you of now. I have been keeping my hands and thoughts busy about you by making first a cedar work box for you, and then a cedar case for Julia into which I have put five whole and two parts of stories from Anderson, laboriously printed, illuminated, and illustrated. I have two cedar cups too—a large for you and a small one for Julia. Now I did not intend to let you know of all this but to make a surprise of it some day. But it is all so uncertain that I tell you, so that you may know how my prison work has been for you and Julia. It is indeed a prison life we had here, or rather a sort of exile for we have fresh air enough. I have little or nothing to do, and it seems that day by day my duties become lighter. Col. Corley told me this evening that he had approved my application for a transfer and that it was gone forward. I hardly think that much will come of it, tho' I have just taken the pains to write to Melton to look the matter up for me. I have received five out of the seven letters which you had written to me up to the 13th of this month. The others I presume were mailed at some point short of Richmond and will be an indefinite time on the road. Maj. Wardlaw has heard from home the Yankee stragglers were at his place for seven whole days and destroyed everything, poor Mrs. Wardlaw did not have a change of clothes left for herself, or her child, and for ten days she and the ladies and children were all huddled together in the parlor and never once undressed. The high water in the Catawba detained a corps there. 29th March. I had the pleasure dear Emmy dreaming about you all through last night. You seemed to have gone to strange lands and I was following you and Julia from place to place catching glimpses of you now and then, but only getting up with you once when the hotel asked us a £100 for a night's lodging and we had to turn out.

You have probably heard of the attack Genl. Lee made here last Saturday on the enemy's lines Southeast of Petersburg.[1] Our troops behaved admirably, swept over two lines of works and were eager to go on

---

1. On March 25, General John B. Gordon attacked Fort Stedman in the Union lines but was repulsed with the loss of nearly 5000 men. Following this defeat Lee abandoned Richmond and tried to escape to the west but was trapped at Appomattox. Foote, *The Civil War: A Narrative,* 3:840–44.

when they were ordered to retire, which they did very reluctantly and with heavy loss. Whether this order was caused by the unexpected obstacles that Genl. Gordon saw before him or by the failure of the supports to come up I do not know. The enemy grew ornery at this point and made demonstrations all along the line which continued for a day or two. All is quiet again however and I am preparing a garden. Our supplies are holding out very well, and officers who have been sent out to look report large quantities of corn and bacon on the railroads in N.C. Write to me Emily as often as you can find any way to send the letters. If it were not for the little hope I still entertain that I may be relieved and sent South[2] I should feel very desolate out here without your letters. I love you always.

H.H.

2. Harry Hammond's long sought after reassignment never came, and he surrendered with the Army of Northern Virginia at Appomattox Court House on April 9, 1865. HBC Family Papers, 1864–March 1865, passim; HH Petition to President Andrew Johnson [1865], JHH Papers, SCL.

PART II

The Preserver
Harry Hammond

Southern planter families, including the survivors of James Henry Hammond, saw and remembered Reconstruction after the Civil War as a dismal period in Southern history as well as in their personal lives. The heirs of James Henry, having been born to comfort, ease, and luxury and with every reasonable expectation that this life style would continue, found themselves after the war poor, their field of action narrowed, and their only comfort that their lot was a common one. Most Southern planters reacted to military defeat, the abolition of slavery, and their loss of political and social control with uncertainty, discouragement, and with moods often close to self-pity. Their discontent further lowered their morale and increased their sense of despair.[1]

Looking backward in 1897, just before his sixty-fifth birthday, Harry Hammond recalled that when he returned home in 1865 following the surrender at Appomattox, he owned "a pipe, some tobacco, and literally nothing else." An Augusta merchant with whom his family had traded for many years refused him credit. The only bright moments he remembered were when his mother gave him a twenty-dollar gold piece and his brother Paul turned over to him some $60 which had been his share of the silver coins belonging to his father.[2] He did of course inherit land

1. Henry Hammond to HH, May 29, 1897, HBC Family Papers, SCL. A dramatic account of Southern planters in the Civil War and Reconstruction is James L. Roark's book *Masters Without Slaves*. The best survey of Reconstruction remains Kenneth Stampp, *The Era of Reconstruction 1865—1877*, but also see Michael Les Benedict, *A Compromise of Principle*. Reconstruction in South Carolina can best be studied in Joel Williamson, *After Slavery*, Willie Lee Rose, *Rehearsal for Reconstruction*, Thomas Holt, *Black Over White*, and Carol Bleser, *The Promised Land*. The best comprehensive study of the newly freed slaves is Leon Litwack's *Been in the Storm So Long*.
2. HH, Speculative Notes, No. 1, 1873–1900, HBC Family Papers, SCL.

from his father, but when, in 1866 as executor of his father's will, he put up for sale most of the fourteen thousand acres possessed by James Henry, he found that no one was buying land at that time. Harry withdrew the land from the market and undertook to farm it with his brother Paul.

The transition from a slave labor to a free labor system seems to have gone uncommonly well for Harry and Paul, who leased most of the estate from their mother and planted crops. Their success with free labor doubtless was made easier because most of their over three hundred former slaves, unlike those on some other plantations, remained on the home place.[3] Mary Boykin Chesnut, the famous Confederate diarist, commented in 1866 upon the same phenomenon. "The colored ones hang on. . . . We will have to run away from their persistent devotion. We are free to desert them now I hope. In point of fact their conduct to us has been beyond all praise."[4] The freedmen, who chose in 1865 to remain on their former masters' plantations, appear to have been greater in number than indicated in some earlier studies. The Hammonds drew up contracts which gave each worker $15 cash at the end of the crop year, a house, water, firewood, three pounds of bacon, and a peck of meal weekly, every other Saturday off, and the loan of a mule and a plow to work their own crops.[5]

Once Harry started working the land, his goal became the maintenance of his father's holdings in the hands of the family. However, James Henry had invested heavily in the Confederacy and was able to leave his family little else but his land, which had to be sold to settle his estate. In October 1869 Marcellus went to Redcliffe to "witness the dispersion of my brother's broad lands which he hoped his descendants for generations would occupy."[6] However, Harry had worked out a

3. Catherine Hammond to MCMH, Sept. 3, 1865; JHH Plantation Journal, April 1, 1866, March 5, 1867, JHH Papers, SCL; Paul Hammond to WGS, March 8, 1869, Ferris Collection, CU.

4. Mary Boykin Chesnut to Virginia Caroline Tunstall Clay, April 1866, Clement Claiborne Clay Papers, Duke University Library, Durham.

5. JHH Plantation Journal, 1866–1867, passim, JHH Papers; MS vol. bd., 1955, "Some More Small Family Facts," John Shaw Billings Scrapbook Collection, SCL; MCMH to WGS, Dec. 3, 1869, Ferris Collection, CU. Contracts with laborers, of course, changed over time. See: HH Account Books (13), 1865–1914; Account Book of Paul F. Hammond and His Son Claude, 1882–1884, HBC Family Papers, SCL; Hammond Family Account Book, 1883–1885, Hammond Family Collection, SCL; Farmer's Club Records, Beech Island, Aiken County, vol. 2, Dec. 2, 1899, SCL.

6. MCMH to WGS, Oct. 19, 1869, Ferris Collection, CU.

complicated plan whereby most of the estate, though divided up and sold in pieces by sealed bids, would remain in the hands of the family. The house at Redcliffe and nearly 400 acres surrounding the house were sold to the widow of James Henry for $8,000. Paul and Harry took large sections of Silver Bluff, Harry purchasing Cedar Grove plantation, Paul acquiring the upper section of Silver Bluff, and the widow buying the remainder of the tract. Later in the year the two brothers bought Cathwood, and still later Cowden went to the youngest of the Senator's children, Elizabeth Hammond Eve.[7]

Eventually, as James Henry's children went their separate ways, so did his land holdings slide away from the family. Harry's brother Spann, their sister Katherine Hammond, and her husband James Gregg, Superintendent of the Graniteville cotton mill, made no purchases, apparently taking their shares in cash. Spann, who was living in Virginia, had argued vehemently against Harry's plan for disposing of the estate which Spann referred to as Harry's "highhandedness." He favored waiting until prices rose and then selling the whole estate to a single bidder. In letter after letter he vented his anger at his brother's willingness "to sacrifice *all* my ultimate expectations to escape the immediate embarrassments" to family pride which would result from selling the land to outsiders.[8] Although Spann returned to South Carolina in 1870 and bought a place in Beech Island, the brothers were never again close. Spann practiced law and was elected a magistrate. In 1882, four years after his first wife Marcella died, he married a Barnwell, South Carolina, woman, and they had two children. He died at Blackville, South Carolina, in 1921 and is buried at the Beech Island cemetery near his father.[9]

Though the Hammond plantations had been reorganized, prosperity remained elusive. Ironically, Harry in 1875 told the Beech Island Farmers Club, "Cotton will never be called King again." He recommended

7. Ibid.; MCMH to WGS, Nov. 15 and Dec. 3, 1869, ibid.; Catherine F. Hammond to WGS, Oct. 22, 1869, ibid.; Catherine F. Hammond, signed affidavit, Nov. 1869, Edgefield County, South Carolina; Paul F. Hammond, signed affidavit, Jan. 6, 1870, Edgefield County, South Carolina, JHH Business Papers; Billings, "The Hammond Family"; Catherine Hammond to her children, June 3, 1883, HBC Family Papers, SCL.

8. ESH to HH, Nov. 28 and Dec. 30, 1868; ESH to MCMH, Dec. 16 and 17, 1869, ESH Letterpress Book, ESH Papers, SCL; HBC Family Papers, 1866–1877, passim, SCL.

9. MCMH to WGS, Dec. 30, 1869, Jan. 24, 1870, Ferris Collection, CU; South Carolina Governors Papers 1877–1890, passim, SCDAH; Steadman, *History of the Spann Family*, pp. 79–81; *The Aiken Journal and Review*, June 21, 1921.

that they resort to a diversified agriculture, for the eight-year-long depression was "becoming chronic," and "we have no reason to look for brighter times."[10] Paul Hammond, without any outside sources of income and unsuccessful at planting, was compelled to sell back some of his lands to his mother. He died in 1887 at the age of forty-nine, a self-confessed morphine addict. Paul's widow, Loula Comer Hammond, disposed of his remaining land holdings. Elizabeth Hammond Eve and her husband William Raiford Eve also found it hard to make farming a success, and they eventually sold Cowden out of the family. Elizabeth, the Senator's youngest child, lived to be ninety-two years old, dying in 1941.[11]

Harry and Emily settled down to farming and raising a family. In addition to their daughter Julia, born in 1860, they had another daughter, Katharine, born in 1867, and three sons: Henry, born in 1868; Christopher, called Kit, born in 1870; and Alfred or Alf, born in 1873. To support his family Harry had as his share of his father's estate $20,000, but Cedar Grove plantation cost him $22,500 and came burdened with a prewar debt of $8,500 at eight per cent interest. To buy it, he had to borrow five thousand dollars from his mother-in-law, Mrs. Henry Cumming.[12] In 1873, Harry's mother turned over Redcliffe to him and his family, and she moved into "Old Yard," the original house at Redcliffe. Harry paid his mother $3,000 in cash and $5,000 was charged against his inheritance.[13] Prices, indeed, were depressed, for in 1859 his father had paid $22,000 for Redcliffe and in addition benefited from the low cost of slave labor and from the free lumber cut on his own land. But even at those depressed prices the costs of Redcliffe and Cedar Grove brought Harry dangerously close to insolvency. Time and again he would be saved by an infusion of Cumming capital.

Henry Harford Cumming, Emily's father, a prominent banker, lawyer, and industrial entrepreneur in Augusta, Georgia, had listed his assets at around $400,000 on the eve of the war.[14] He had not given it

10. Minutes, April 3, 1875, Farmer's Club Records, Beech Island, Aiken County, SCL.
11. John Fox Hammond to Catherine F. Hammond, June 12, 1886, JHH Papers, SCL; Letter to the Editors of The Charleston News and Courier, Sept. 1885, Legal Size Papers, HBC Family Papers, SCL; Elizabeth Hammond Eve, "Notes," arranged by John Shaw Billings, John Shaw Billings Papers; Billings, "The Hammond Family," SCL.
12. Julia Cumming to HH, Aug. 17, 1869, HBC Family Papers, SCL.
13. Catherine F. Hammond to her children, June 3, 1883, HBC Family Papers; HH to Paul F. Hammond, Feb. 21, 1887, JHH Papers; Billings, "The Hammond Family," SCL.
14. U.S. Census Records, State of Georgia, 1860, Population Schedules, Richmond County, National Archives Microfilm Publications, pp. 923–24.

all to the Confederacy, and, after the war, his large holdings in an Augusta cotton mill, later known as the Augusta Factory, began paying substantial dividends.[15] Henry Cumming, suffering from depression, committed suicide in 1866, but his widow Julia used her legacy in the hard times of Reconstruction for the support of her remaining children, and Harry and Emily were among those who benefited most from her generosity. At Mrs. Cumming's death in 1879, she left an estate of over $140,000. Emily received approximately $28,000.[16]

The Augusta and Port Royal Railroad also augmented the income of the Hammonds in the 1870s and 1880s. The railroad bought a right of way through Cedar Grove, Cathwood, and Cowden plantations. However, the family claimed that the railway embankments damaged the drainage and hence the agricultural value of the land. This led to lawsuits with the railroad which ended in a small windfall in the 1880s.[17]

In the 1890s, the spinster aunt of Emily Hammond died and left her niece $40,000. That inheritance enabled the family in 1896 to build a cottonseed oil mill at a cost of $21,000. Harry's sons, Alf and Kit, ran the family oil mill until 1901 when, squeezed by the big companies, they sold it for $30,000.[18] Both Alf and Kit received jobs with the oil trust which had bought them out.

Despite these inheritances, windfalls, and investments, the Hammonds did not grow rich. Droughts and heat, rains and floods, and the continued decline of cotton prices, which reached their nineteenth-century low of less than five cents per pound in 1894,[19] conspired to keep Harry Hammond toiling unceasingly just to hold his own.

Unlike his father, he was not ambitious for elective office. It is clear from his letters that Harry, weary of war, had quickly taken the oath of allegiance and sought to settle down to operate his plantations without slaves. He wrote but few letters on Reconstruction, and though scornful

15. Jones and Dutcher, *Memorial History of Augusta, Georgia*, pp. 418–19.
16. Will of Henry H. Cumming, July 13, 1863, Will of Julia A. Cumming, Feb. 1, 1879, Inventory of Estate of Mrs. Julia A. Cumming, Oct. 1, 1880, Richmond County Court House, Augusta, Georgia; HBC Family Papers 1869–1879, passim, SCL.
17. HH to ECH, June 11, 1882, HH, Speculative Notes, No. 1, 1873–1900, p. 2, John Shaw Billings, comp., "Random Recollections of Henry C. Hammond," HBC Family Papers, SCL.
18. HH to ECH, Aug. 4 and 15, 1901, JBH to Kit Hammond, July 28, 1901, HH to ECH, July 30, Aug. 2, 1901, HBC Family Papers, SCL; James Dawson to C.C.F. Hammond, June 6, 1904, Kathwood Manufacturing Company Papers, SCL.
19. *The Statistical History of the United States from Colonial Times to the Present* (Stamford, Conn.: Fairfield Publishers, Inc., 1965), p. 301; Minutes, Oct. 6, 1894, Farmer's Club Records, Beech Island, Aiken County, SCL.

of the "rabble" making up the Republican regime, he took no active part in the restoration of conservative rule in 1877.

Harry Hammond's occasional attempts to gain funds, self-esteem, and status from government appointments ended in frustration and disappointment. He had been nominated and had expected to be confirmed as Superintendent of the 1880 United States Census, but Senator M.C. Butler wrote Harry from Washington that "yesterday this miserable creature in the White House [Rutherford B. Hayes] withdrew your name. Why I cannot comprehend. It is however of a piece with his character and is simply outrageous."[20] He accepted the lesser position of Director of the National Census for South Carolina.[21] The year 1883 brought more controversy and another partial failure. The South Carolina Department of Agriculture published a 726-page handbook entitled *South Carolina Resources and Population, Institutions and Industries.* The title page bore the names of the Governor and the Commissioner of Agriculture. Neither title page nor preface revealed that Harry had been the originator of the idea of a handbook, the editor of the volume, and the author of most of the chapters. Hammond deeply resented this "theft," for the Handbook was the major scholarly achievement of his life. Posterity has been kinder to him than were the state officials, since the book is commonly known as the "Hammond Handbook" and is recognized for its significant contribution to the economic history of the state. Hammond listed his earnings for the Census and the Handbook at $7,100.[22] Harry's attempts to revive the family fortunes and status were at best half successful. The responsibility for maintaining Redcliffe and the family's position fell, as it often did among the late nineteenth-century Southern elite, at least in part on the female Hammonds.

The patriarchal omnipotence which James Henry had so aggressively asserted became impracticable, even as a goal, for his son, who had to depend on his mother and mother-in-law for funds. His wife Emily, who has been described as sweet-tempered, frail, and bent-looking but with a will of iron, took charge of daily affairs at Redcliffe. Her strong personality had particular influence upon her three eldest children. Henry, a successful lawyer, politician, and judge, never married,

20. Senator M.C. Butler to HH, Jan. 22, 1880, HBC Family Papers, SCL.
21. Francis A. Walker, Superintendent of the Tenth Census of the United States, to HH, March 23, 1880, ibid.
22. HH, Speculative Notes, No. 1, 1873–1900, p. 2, ibid.

perhaps because of his profound attachment to his mother. Julia declined to marry the man she loved because of her devotion to Emily; she married only at the age of fifty-one, three weeks after her mother died. Katharine, at the age of twenty-six, wrote home from nurses' training school at Johns Hopkins that "I must remember I have lost my place in your regard, that I have left you, and so don't deserve even what I get."[23] It was Emily more than her husband who made Redcliffe a center of social activity. Henry recalled that guests came to Redcliffe because they recognized his parents' home as a place of culture, "rare in these parts."[24]

Redcliffe was not an unhappy place for the five children. All retained positive views of their father, whom they thought would have been a more famous man than their grandfather if the South had not lost the war.[25] The three sons adjusted to the New South with varying degrees of success. A popular bachelor, Henry pursued his legal, political, judicial, and social career in nearby Augusta; Kit, after he left the cottonseed oil business, returned to farming at Beech Island; Alf became a corporate man, retiring as superintendent of Swift and Company in Columbia in 1938.[26] There is no evidence that the parents attempted to send any of the three to college. Perhaps Harry needed them to help work the land. He, in fact, thought it "a bad and unhealthy outlook" that a majority of the younger men and boys were deserting the farms for employment in cities and towns "or devoting themselves to professional studies."[27] Henry did attend Richmond Academy in Augusta but prepared for the law by reading in the office of his mother's brother, Joseph Cumming. It was, however, the Hammond daughters, Julia and Katharine, who were encouraged to pursue advanced formal education. Evidently Harry thought his daughters had minds at least as good as his sons, and he hoped that both would use them. He encouraged them to become doctors, an extraordinarily advanced idea for the parent of nineteenth-century Southern daughters.

Julia, benefiting from the settlement of her grandmother Cumming's

23. W. W. Woolsey to JBH, Sept. 3, 1890, Katharine Hammond to ECH, April 15, 1893, HBC Family Papers, SCL; Interview with Henry Billings, Sag Harbor, New York, June 21, 1979.
24. Billings, "Random Recollections of Henry C. Hammond," HBC Family Papers, SCL.
25. Katharine Hammond to ECH, July 5, 1893, Henry Hammond to HH, March 29, 1897, HBC Family Papers, SCL.
26. HBC Family Papers, 1886–1935, passim, SCL; Columbia, S.C., *The State*, May 3, 1962.
27. Minutes, January 3, 1885, Farmer's Club Records, Beech Island, Aiken County, SCL.

estate, was taken by her father in 1881 to Cambridge, Harry having spent a semester at Harvard in 1858. There she enrolled at Harvard Annex, later to become Radcliffe College, which had been recently established for women. Julia clearly found life in Cambridge stimulating and broadening. She was struck by the women she met, "not," she assured her sister Katharine, "that I mean to say the people are any better than we are, but they have other thoughts in life than getting married." [28] After three months, however, lonely for Redcliffe and for her mother, she returned home, never to leave again except for brief intervals. She rejected a marriage proposal from William Woolsey, an Aiken banker and planter, whom she continued to love long after she had turned him down, and remained single until 1911 when she married the owner of an Augusta livery stable and brought him to Redcliffe.

There is no evidence that Julia ever regretted her decision to return home. In 1889 she described a summer day at Redcliffe: she rose early, worked with the servants at household tasks, and supervised the cook until "everything was all straight . . . so that I felt easy to leave Mother." After putting on her bathing clothes and packing food, she rode over to the plantation about ten miles away where her father and brother were working in the fields. To cool off she took a dip in the creek, had a nap, and then read while her father and brother fished. After eating their midday meal, her brother suggested another swim, "so I got into my bathing clothes again." After a long swim, she rode home and made some ice cream for the guests expected that evening. [29] It had been a "delightful day."

Julia's father, Harry, was less content. Disappointed and frustrated by his failure to do more than maintain the remnants of his patrimony, he became in his last years increasingly detached, crotchety, and cynical. In fact, as his planting ventures became less and less profitable, he began to require a bottle of claret with his midday meal and several brandies thereafter to anesthetize himself for the remainder of the day. [30] Driven by the memory of his father whom he both admired and resented, Harry was unable to adjust to the practical realities of a lesser world than that in which his aspirations and ambitions had been formed. However, through the difficult times of the Reconstruction and

28. JBH to Katharine Hammond, March 13, 1881, HBC Family Papers, SCL.
29. JBH to Katharine Hammond, Aug. 11, 1889, ibid.
30. Interview with Henry Billings, Sag Harbor, N.Y., July 19, 1979.

post-Reconstruction periods, Harry did play a key role in his family's affairs and in the Beech Island community. He helped sustain the local farmers' club, and he maintained one of the few interests that he shared with his father, agricultural experiments; he supported also the local school, and he opened the Hammond family cemetery to the Beech Island residents. Meanwhile, if only for a time, he kept the bulk of his father's lands in family hands, and, most importantly, he preserved Redcliffe—the home and its surrounding land—making it a legacy to be transmitted to succeeding generations of Hammonds.

This section opens with a letter from Catherine Fitzsimons Hammond to her brother-in-law Marcellus in September 1865. An air of easy domesticity pervades the letter. Catherine was able to accept the new order better than either her husband, James Henry, or her son, Harry, perhaps, because the lot of the Southern woman did not change nearly as much as that of the once dominant Southern planter. However, until 1881 when Julia went off to Cambridge, the post–Civil War letters in general reflect the parochial concerns of a defeated and depressed society.

CATHERINE F. HAMMOND TO MARCUS C.M. HAMMOND[h]

Redcliffe, September 3, [1865]

My dear Brother:

I was much gratified to receive your kind letter and Harriet's, and hear from you all. What can give the boys fever on that hill—fishing perhaps or exposure to night air.

I cannot compare troubles and cares with you. I often can scarce restrain a burst of complaint at my change of circumstances—but as I compare my lot with many others, I see only cause for thankfulness. As to the future, if I could, I would scarce lift the curtain. We are in God's hands who alone has brought about this wonderful state of affairs and who only can unravel it. The boys are hopeful and very attentive to business. The crop promises well. We have not lost many negroes. I wish we could get rid of many of the useless ones. 300 mouths to feed is no small charge[1]—meat and corn both low, but the new crop coming in. They have been engaged at boat building, but so far have realized nothing from it.

Cattie admired John, Wife, and children very much,[2] John looks

1. According to Virginia Tunstall Clay, the wife of Senator Clement Clay of Alabama (for more on Mrs. Clay see letter of August 25, 1858, footnote 4), who took refuge at Redcliffe in the late fall of 1864, many slaves had remained at Redcliffe. She reported that at James Henry Hammond's funeral in November 1864 she was much impressed "by the procession of two hundred of the older slaves, who marched, two by two, into the baronial parlors to look for the last time upon their master's face." Save for this retinue, "Redcliffe was now practically without a defender." Cited in Sterling, *A Belle of the Fifties*, pp. ix–x, 213, 232. Elizabeth Hammond Eve mentioned, while compiling her family notes, that their slaves took no notice of Lincoln's Emancipation Proclamation until after the war ended and even then "very few of them left us." Elizabeth Hammond Eve, "Notes," arranged by John Shaw Billings, Loose Papers, John Shaw Billings Papers, SCL.

It is difficult to move beyond this impressionistic evidence for there is no Hammond plantation journal for 1865, but what little evidence there is confirms Mrs. Hammond's estimate of the number of freedmen remaining on the Hammond lands in 1865. The October 1864 tax returns for Barnwell District list 259 slaves held by Hammond at Silver Bluff. These slaves plus 21 Redcliffe servants listed in the Edgefield District tax returns account for 280 slaves remaining on those two plantations alone in October 1864. Barnwell District Tax Returns, October 1864, SCDAH; Edgefield District Tax Returns, October 1864, SCDAH.

2. John Fox Hammond (1820–1886), the youngest brother of James Henry Hammond, graduated from the University of Virginia, then studied medicine at the University of Pennsylvania. He received his medical degree and in 1847 entered the United States Army as an assistant surgeon. When the war came, John Hammond remained in the Union Army. In 1862, under General McClellan, Major Hammond served as Medical Director of the 2nd Corps, Army of the Potomac, throughout the entire Peninsular Campaign. On March 13, 1865, he was brevetted a lieutenant colonel and in 1876 he received the grade permanently. John Hammond married Caroline E.

happy. They live in a comfortable rented house [in New York] and Cattie says she never saw a better served dinner than she had there. I don't know what course Cousin should adopt to draw her money. At present there is none in the Estate—but we have had to go in debt for the expenses of the plantation. Whatever is just and right will be done— but it comes very hard on us to pay money[3] that never was any benefit to us or to my dear Husband and at a time when it is so hard to raise money. I have no right to act in the matter and indeed [k]now little about it that I fear to speak of it at all. I hope Alfred will come on and see it attended to and I think he ought to do it.

I hope you will save all Mr. Hammond's letters. We sent on some of the pamphlets he corrected and arranged for publication to England by James.[4] But he writes that upon inquiry it could be published on better terms at the North. Spann advises that we defer it as this is not the time to do it. He is deeply interested in it and will probably give it more attention than Paul or Harry as his tastes are more in that line. I can't trust myself with the past. Thank God I find more to do every day than I can accomplish and I am able to interest myself in it. My children are very kind and my household cheerful and satisfied. My servants behave pretty well. Robert has left. I have a very good boy to drive. The grounds around here are sadly neglected—but we keep but one man and there is too much. I do not know if I can keep this place—but enough trouble for the present—we need not anticipate. Cattie's health is not so good as when she left here. Her London Dr. hopes to cure her.[5] Her last the 18th of Augt. she was going to Scotland. James said he would not return until our affairs were more settled. I fear the work

Lawrence, of New York City, on April 15, 1863. This marriage produced two daughters, Katharine Betts Hammond, born March 24, 1864, and Elizabeth Percy Hammond, born March 17, 1865. Poughkeepsie, New York, became their permanent home. Billings, "The Hammond Family," HBC Family Papers, SCL; Roland Hammond, *Genealogy*, pp. 273–74.

3. Mrs. Hammond is referring again to the Latimer debt. For the background on this debt which "cast its black shadow across the Redcliffe family . . . and blotted out any hopeful gleam of prosperity" in the post-Reconstruction era. See letter of July 16, 1859, n. 4.

4. James Gregg, Katherine Hammond's husband, had accompanied his father, William Gregg, to England in the summer of 1865 to buy new machinery for the Graniteville cotton mills. On this trip he carried some of his father-in-law's pamphlets to London for publishers' consideration. Broadus Mitchell, *William Gregg: Factory Master of the Old South* (Chapel Hill: University of North Carolina Press, 1928), pp. 235–40.

5. Katherine Hammond Gregg, in search of medical treatment, had accompanied her husband and father-in-law to Europe in 1865. Ibid.; LCH to Celeste Comer Clay, Sept. 17, 1865, Clement Claiborne Clay Papers, Duke; Elizabeth Hammond Eve, "Notes," arranged by John Shaw Billings, p. 3, Loose papers, John Shaw Billings Papers, SCL.

of the Convention touching Slavery[6]—it is dead and I for one don't want it back.

Dear Brother, I would be very glad to see you here. I never leave home but to go to church and generally walk there. I have not been to Augusta since Cattie left. The girls have been intending to go to see you for some time. I was a good while without a driver, and there has been a protracted meeting at the Baptist church for three weeks. They went almost every night, most of the time borrowing a driver. The meeting is resumed again but I hope it will not continue long. They have baptized upwards of 20. I wish Annie[7] would come down. Can't she come in to Carrie's? I will send for her any day there. I will write to Harriet soon.

With love to all I am yours affectionately,

CEH

JAMES GREGG TO CATHERINE F. HAMMOND[h]

Paris, France, October 17, 1865

Dear Mother:

We have determined to sail for America on the 18th of November and I have written to Wm to get us a good furnished house in Philadelphia where I propose to reside until every thing gets settled at the south. I particularly desire and will be much pleased for yourself, Betty, Miss Mary,[1] and Kate[2] to come on and stay with us as I know you

---

6. Southern legislatures in the fall of 1865 adopted detailed "Black Codes," ostensibly to protect the freedmen and the states from any problems that could arise as a result of the sudden black emancipation. In reality, though, the codes were a body of vagrancy and apprenticeship laws which in effect channeled the blacks back to the plantations where labor could then be coerced from them. South Carolina's codes, which were particularly severe, prohibited blacks from working outside agriculture or domestic service without a permit, and made the violation of a labor contract a criminal act. These codes were viewed outside the South as the initial step to re-enslavement. D.L. Wardlaw and Armistead Burt, "Report of the Committee on the Freedmen of South Carolina, October 25, 1865," pamphlet, SCL.

7. Anne Sarah Hammond, daughter of M.C.M. Hammond, born on October 1, 1846, was a frequent visitor at Redcliffe.

---

1. Miss Mary Wimberly, 35 years old in 1860, lived as a companion to Catherine Fox Spann Hammond, James Henry Hammond's mother, until the elder woman's death in 1864. In her will Mrs. Hammond left Miss Wimberly $500. After the death of Emily Cumming Hammond's father in 1866, Miss Wimberly went to live in Augusta with his widow, Julia Bryan Cumming. U.S. Census Records, State of South Carolina, 1860, Population Schedules, Edgefield County, National Archives Microfilm Publications, p. 160; Edgefield County Wills, Book E, 1852–1866, p.

must be terribly harassed at home, and Kate's health requires that she
be kept perfectly quiet. Dr. Bennett says that she can be cured by constant treatment, *very* regular hours and quiet. Neither of which except
the first can she have if travelling or keeping house. Betty in Phil[a] can
get the best of Masters and go far toward perfecting her Education. I
will insist on all of you coming—for you will be less harassed by the
Yank in Phil[a] than at home. Miss Mary and Kate's Expenses I will pay
so tell them to feel no uneasiness on that score, but to make up their
minds at once. I have bought a set of china here and will get my glass
in England, will also buy blankets. I wrote Wm to write you as soon as
he procured a house and state what was in it so that you could ship us
from home our silver and such things not in the house which we would
need. The silver had better be sent by Express and insured. We will if
not detained by accident or otherwise arrive on the 29th and I shall take
the first steamer home—spend a week there and hope to carry all of you
back with me. You must not think of refusing to come on and stay with
us, for it is absolutely necessary that Kate be where she can get the best
of treatment and she will never be quiet and satisfied whilst you are at
the South.

She has been in a regular stew. Can't speak a word of french and
everybody is cheating her. She buys a dress and a day or two after finds
that she can get one exactly the same for half the money. Is terribly out
with all the dressmakers who have all made her terrible misfits, she has
I believe now concluded to carry the stuff and have her other dresses
made by Miss Mary.

Father is here and is hugely pleased, is getting to be as good a loafer
as myself, if he stays here a few months longer will be ruined.[3] Kate

525, SCDAH; MS vol. bd., 1927–n.d. "Myself and Family," John Shaw Billings Scrapbook Collection, SCL.

2. Catherine Spann Hyde (1846–1900), better known as Kate, became the ward of her uncle,
James Henry Hammond, at the age of one and one-half years when her mother, Caroline Augusta
Hammond Hyde, died. She was three years older than Hammond's youngest daughter, Betty. In
1860 she was living with her grandmother, Catherine Fox Hammond. When James Henry Ham-
mond died in 1864, Kate Hyde went to live as companion-housekeeper to his widow, her aunt by
marriage, Mrs. Catherine Fitzsimons Hammond. She died on March 18, 1900, four years after
Mrs. Hammond's death. Catherine Spann Hyde's gravestone, Magnolia Cemetry, Augusta, Georgia; Billings, "The Hammond Family," HBC Family Papers, SCL; U.S. Census Records, State of
South Carolina, 1860, Population Schedules, Edgefield County, National Archives Microfilm
Publications, p. 160.

3. According to William Gregg's biographer, Broadus Mitchell, Gregg repeatedly delayed his
return to America, ostensibly so he could purchase additional machinery in order to diversify

has met many Washington acquaintances, Mr. Cochran, Mrs. Gwyn, and family, Mr. and Mrs. Jacob Thompson—all are kind, willing to show attention. I recᵈ Harry's letter am glad to hear that the carriage is sold, have recᵈ notification of the rect of amt $400 by bank of Liverpool. As I will be at home so soon he had better let the horses remain until I come. I will then make some disposition of them. Give my love to all and believe me

Your affect Son,

James

HARRY HAMMOND TO CATHERINE F. HAMMOND[h]

Redcliffe, February 24, 1865 [1866] [1]

Dear Mother:

I have just received your letter saying that you would not sail until the 7th of next month.[2] As soon as I heard that you were not going to Europe as you had expected I wrote and I would have written again but I waited to hear something more definite of your movements. I wish very much you would all give out the trip and settle down somewhere. I do not say come back to this distressed country but even that, I think, might and would be better for Catty, who is the one chiefly considered in your movements, than going about rough at adventure as you seem to be. Please put Catty on her guard against European physicians for me. I know something about them. I saw a good deal of them, and tried

---

production at his Graniteville cotton mills, but more likely so that he could enjoy life in London and on the continent. He went to Europe in the summer of 1865 and returned to America on May 1, 1866.

James Gregg and his wife, Cattie (whom he alone called Kate), returned to New York in December 1865. If anything, Cattie's health had deteriorated on the overseas trip. It was decided, however, that they would return to Europe so that she could consult a well-known physician in Paris. On this trip her mother and younger sister were to accompany them. Elizabeth Hammond Eve, "Notes," arranged by John Shaw Billings, p. 3, John Shaw Billings Papers, SCL; Mitchell, *William Gregg*, pp. 235–40.

1. The letter is misdated. Catherine Hammond, with her daughter Betty, left South Carolina in early January 1866 for New York City. In New York they joined James and Cattie Gregg.

2. Their trip to Europe had to be delayed because Mrs. Gregg became seriously ill the day before their scheduled departure. Mrs. Eve wrote that they set sail for Europe on March 12, 1866. Elizabeth Hammond Eve, "Notes," arranged by John Shaw Billings, p. 4, John Shaw Billings Papers, SCL; LCH to Celeste Comer Clay, Feb. 13, 1866, Clement Claiborne Clay Papers, Duke.

them myself and for my friends, and my experience taught me that they were not trustworthy and I did what I found all other English and Americans did who had lived much on the continent viz., send for an English or American physician whenever they could be had. I except English physicians. I think they are nearly as good and as honorable as our men. I mean individuals, I do not think they are as a class. In France, Germany, and Italy medicine is not held as a liberal profession, the medical fraternity rank there as our dentists and drug store people do here. There is no schedule of prices and they extract just what they can from their patients. I can prove the delusions that men world renowned in the profession have practiced upon their patients. They understand scientific matters there far better than we do, because every one selects some speciality and devotes himself to it, but their treatment isn't half so successful as ours. They attain success either by some scientific discovery that has nothing to do with the treatment of disease, by amassing wealth in an irregular practice like our patent medicine people, or by being court physicians; the latter may kill a score of common people provided they can relieve some lord or prince of a colic and lose no reputation. I assure you I have seen others suffer and suffered much myself from European practice. Nothing I think is worse, and I may say I know it from experience, than to be ill in a strange country, and to call a physician upon whom you can not rely. I could state cases, and nearly every case in my experience would illustrate what I am saying but it would make my letter too long. As for climate Italy may be very well for people from England, but our own climate is infinitely superior to it, and every variety can be found on this continent and the adjacent islands. For people who are not really unwell, for those sick of mind, or to whom movement is the thing necessary, European travel is excellent, to all others it is a Humbug and one that not infrequently proves fatal. I believe Catty can be more successfully treated in this country than anywhere. She will certainly find more high-toned honorable physicians who are more generally successful in their practice than she can anywhere. I am at the same time sure that neither here nor elsewhere will she find out any specific remedy, any wonderful or unaccountable one. It is natural to hope for this and no doubt it is human nature to think that there is somewhere an air, or fountain, or some hidden charm that can restore health and strength—it is a general superstition but only a superstition—all treatment is simple, and she ought to understand hers.[3] If I were her I should study out my own case in the standard authorities, at least so far as to preserve myself from the ignorance or impositions of Doctors.[4]

Mr. Walker and Miller speak of building a brick wall around the grave here and making it a neighborhood burying place. This would cost about $1200 and I should prefer it to any monument. There would be more permanence and stability in it.[5] The finest and most costly monument could not induce the preservation of the spot and the memorial. I do not like those costly monuments. I would rather have something severely simple and above all durable—not durable as stone and masonry may make a thing—but durable from the sacredness that the sentiment of our friends and neighbors and their children and children's children attached to the spot. I would rather have a very simple stone[6] and let those who knew Father look forward, for themselves and those that were to come after them, to the time when they should lie down beside him whom they loved and respected. We are not able to do much, our means are limited, but what ever can be spared I hope will be devoted to making a neighborhood burying place, and to enclosing and improving the grounds. I do not know of the grave of a single distinguished man that has any striking monument to mark it—such things are reserved for the rich—I do not think it would have been Father's taste. I shall let you know as soon as I get the neighbours to take part with me in this matter.

I believe I have written pretty fully to Gregg about our arrangement of the Plantations—$3000 for Cowden and $3500 for Cathwood. I am planting up here with 4 hands and I hope to be able to keep the place

3. Evidently Cattie had a gynecological problem because in Paris she was under the care of Dr. James Marion Sims, the renowned gynecologist, who was originally from South Carolina. Sims, the founder of Women's Hospital in New York City in 1855, had practiced in Paris from 1862 to 1866, and had attended the French empress Eugenie, "who was affected like my sister." Elizabeth Hammond Eve, "Notes," arranged by John Shaw Billings, p. 5, John Shaw Billings Papers, SCL.

4. Harry Hammond's skepticism of physicians is reminiscent of his father's comments to WGS. See the letter from JHH to WGS, July 17, 1861.

5. Harry Hammond eventually did build a brick wall around his father's grave and "to give it permanence we made it [the enclosure] large enough to be used by the neighborhood." Catherine F. Hammond to WGS, Oct. 22, 1869, Jan. 16, 1870, Ferris Collection, CU.

6. Harry's desire for a simple marker for his father's grave was disregarded and the family erected a seventeen-foot spire ornamented with an oversized bust of Hammond draped in a Roman toga. Billings, "The Hammond Family," HBC Family Papers, SCL; Catherine F. Hammond to WGS, Oct. 22, 1869, Ferris Collection, CU; JHH gravestone, Beech Island Cemetry, Beech Island, South Carolina.

up and pay expenses and rent. Paul's prospects are very good. All are
well here now tho' I am afraid that Aunt Jane is about to be stricken
with dropsy. Give my love to Catty and all.

Very affectionately,

Harry Hammond

HARRY HAMMOND TO CATHERINE F. HAMMOND[h]

Redcliffe, May 14, 1865[1866][1]

My Dear Mother:

You doubtless account for the fact that you have not heard from me
since you crossed the water by the well known deficiency in the qualities
of a good correspondent. I do not believe however that even at this late
date I have any letter to answer of yours, but I send this in the hope of
bringing one from you. You will have doubtless heard before this of
Mr. Cumming's death. I had gone up to town for the purposing of
arranging to take him off to the north or Europe for we had all become
so uneasy about him that I had made up my mind to sacrifice everything in order to make the only effort that seemed to promise anything.
He had gone to his office in the morning and was absent at dinner time
and was supposed to be out at the hill, as I was leaving town late in the
afternoon Mr. Walton stopped me and told me that Mr. Cumming had
been found dead in a little room close to his office by young Lamar;[2]
he shot himself as was proved by the evidence of persons in the P.O.
below (who heard the report of the pistol but paid no attention to it)
about ten o'clock that morning. It had happened only a very few moments after he had gone into his office, and, as he walked there with
Joe[3] and spoke to Mr. M[c] Whorter just as he entered his office, I think
that he performed the act without premeditation. The windows and
doors were all open. I have no doubt that death as relief from his suffering had presented itself to his mind daily for months past, but he had
repelled it—the dark thought—and had declared in response to the expressed uneasiness of his family that they need fear nothing of that sort.

1. Clearly this letter is misdated based on the internal evidence. Henry Harford Cumming's
death occurred on April 14, 1866.
2. Lamar was DeRosset Lamar (1842–1886), the husband of Maria Bryan Cumming Lamar,
and Henry Harford Cumming's young son-in-law.
3. Joseph Bryan Cumming, Henry Harford Cumming's son, practiced law in Augusta.

I daresay that being seized with one of the sudden and overwhelming attacks of despair to which he was subject he found his burden so much heavier than he could bear that he thus threw it violently from him. He spent a night with me a few days before, and, but for his deep depression and gloom which made his whole manner strange, you would not have noticed from what he said when roused briefly that his mind was affected. Mrs. Cumming has recovered her composure and has made a great effort to resume the active routine of her life. Emmy has been home now some thing better than a week. I do not know of a sadder home now than Mrs. Cumming's, which I used to think the pleasantest and most cheerful that I ever knew. All her children are gone except Maria and her husband. Mr. Cumming's will was quite short leaving everything to Mrs. Cumming.

I suppose Miss Mary [Wimberly] and Kate [Hyde] keep you well acquainted with our condition here. The wet weather has been greatly against our gardens and crops. I have however about 30 acres of pretty fine cotton here and a garden that would do very well if I had somebody to work it. By the way I would like you to get some asparagus roots for the garden at the proper season for transplanting, the London and Paris asparagus you know is far superior to any in the world.

I have sent the cotton to N.Y. to Geo. Broome to be sold. I wish it had been sold last winter in Augusta. I am also sending the Governor a list of the lands to see if they can be sold and at what prices.[4] There is about 11,000 acres on which 600 hands might be employed who ought to produce 2400 Bales of cotton besides provision. I give you this in round figures so that you may offer it to any capitalist in search of a speculation in cotton lands. Paul is doing, I believe, as well as he could expect with bad seasons and bad seed.[5]

4. George Broome advertised himself as a commission merchant at 62 Broadway, New York City. Broome placed the following ad: "For sale—the magnificent estate of the late governor Hammond of South Carolina—1,200 acres of Savannah River Swamp, thoroughly reclaimed and reduced to cultivation. . . . 2,500 acres of superior upland adjoining. . . . 8,000 acres in forest, and convenient to two large markets where wood and timber are of great value. There are three settlements, two elegant mansion houses, extensive barns, gin houses, carriage houses, stables, saw and grist mill, extensive orchards and vineyard, with comfortable quarters for a large force of laborers." Billings, "The Hammond Family," HBC Family Papers, SCL. From this figure of 11,700 acres for sale it is clear that only Silver Bluff and Cowden were being offered. Not included were the Marsh Place with 2000 acres and Redcliffe with 400 acres of land. Ibid. This particular offer did not result in the sale of the Hammond plantations.

5. Paul Hammond lived with his family at Glen Loula (originally a part of Redcliffe) and rented from his father's estate the upper section of the Silver Bluff tract. In 1869 he purchased this land which consisted of the Sand Hills, Green Pond, and Long Branch tracts. Ibid.; LCH to Virginia C.T. Clay, Aug. 22, 1869, Aug. 11, 1871, Clement Claiborne Clay Papers, Duke.

I wish you had carried over a copy of Father's writings, as one ought to be sent to my friend Professor K.F. Neumann of Munich, who is writing a German history of the U.S.A. He begged me to send him all such publications.

I wish I was in Paris[6] a little while with a pocket full of money. I would like to lay in a supply of new scientific works especially on fish and fishing, but I have to satisfy myself with what I have and in the particular line referred to I have my own investigations and experiments as my only amusement. Give my love to Catty.

Very affectionately,

Harry Hammond

E. SPANN HAMMOND TO CATHERINE F. HAMMOND[h]

Lynchburg,[1] November 13, 1866

My Dear Mother:

My thoughts have been with you throughout this day. Two years have rolled around since the most eventful occurrence common to every member of our household. Day after tomorrow is the anniversary of a day that from my earliest recollection was observed by a family reunion, a quiet domestic festival, when every member of the family within reach, embracing three generations, and once or twice four, assembled around our family table.[2] But that is past: it lives only as a family tradition, and the cloud of today[3] casts its shadow over the 15th too.

Today too was a beautiful autumn day. The dew glistened like myriads of diamonds, just as you once pointed it out to me, and said Father so much admired. And as each moment rolled on I but live over that

---

6. Katherine Hammond Gregg, accompanied by her family, was in Paris being treated by Dr. Sims. They—Cattie, James Gregg, Betty, and Mrs. Hammond—had arrived in Europe on April 1, 1866. Dr. Sims recommended a trip to the seacoast and they went to Dieppe, but Cattie was too weak to go into the ocean. Her health did not improve; they went to Manchester, England, for a short period, and then sailed for home in September 1866. Elizabeth Hammond Eve, "Notes," arranged by John Shaw Billings, p. 5, John Shaw Billings Papers, SCL.

---

1. After the war Spann and his wife, Marcella, resided in Lynchburg, Virginia. Marcella, on August 1, 1866, gave birth to a daughter, Elizabeth Delaware Hammond. Steadman, *A History of the Spann Family*, pp. 79, 81; Roland Hammond, *Genealogy*, pp. 270–71; Elizabeth Hammond Eve, "Notes," arranged by John Shaw Billings, p. 5, John Shaw Billings Papers, SCL.

2. November 15 was his father's birth date.

3. November 13, 1866, was the second anniversary of James Henry Hammond's death.

day, so freshly is every successive incident recalled to me. At the moment I now write, I crept gently to his couch and pressed my last kiss on his forehead.

I am entirely alone—my family in Richmond. Marcella is by the couch of her Father, who I fear will not be spared many days longer. I have just heard from her, and she expresses but little hope for him. She has always been the pet of her parents, and it goes very hard with her. The children are well.[4] My affairs here would not permit my going with her.

There are odd moments between the heats of labor every day, on my lounge and by the road-side, I indulge in varied meditation, wide apart from the plodding practicalities that more actively engage me. In the quiet and loneliness of my home at this time, these long evenings, no romping with Willie, or the usual busy bustle of the household, I find only a book, or my thoughts to give occupation. But today I have been present only in form at any of the operations going on around me. My thoughts have been with you. I know that you also have been meditating as I have been. I felt it this morning, just as if, seated by you, you had reminded me of it. I have accompanied you over the path, through the field, the pine grove and the little gate to the sacred spot; have witnessed your brushing away the fallen leaves and attending the plants, have joined you in reflections upon incidents in the past and how fleeting are all things here: and have looked with you over little cherished relics, mementoes hallowed by a thousand cherished associations.

While we should constantly bear it in mind to erect a suitable monument as soon as our means will admit of it, I think it far more important that some steps should be taken toward establishing Father's reputation before the world. The public mind was never at any period in

---

4. Only one child, Elizabeth (Bessie) Delaware Hammond, is cited in the family genealogies. Among some miscellaneous papers of John Shaw Billings there are several pages of material on a Willy Hammond. It seems that Marcella had lost a baby in Richmond in 1863 or 1864 and that Spann, to comfort his wife, had taken home an infant from the poorhouse. He was given the name Willy and raised as their son. Billings describes Willy as "a wild attractive bird . . . who ended up in a Virginia jail serving a sentence for bigamy." Willy tried to claim a share of Marcella Morriss Hammond's estate on the ground that legally he was her son. Spann fought the claim and allegedly Willy disappeared for good. John Shaw Billings, comp., "File on Willy Hammond," Miscellaneous Collection, John Shaw Billings Papers, SCL. See also reference to Spann's "adopted boy" in a letter of Celeste Comer Clay to Virginia C. T. Clay, Dec. 31, 1866, Clement Claiborne Clay Papers, Duke.

our country more grasping for knowledge than at this time. While the great mass catch only at floating paragraphs in daily papers, there are great minds in their closets eager for the original and profound. These are the men that must soon be brought conspicuously before our people. It is these who would welcome a publication of Father's works, and would set store upon them if they possess the merit which he and we have always thought they possessed, and which has been accorded to them universally when an opinion upon them has been expressed. I would therefore suggest that steps be taken to have a carefully corrected edition, of considerable size, with picture and a brief biographical sketch, published at an early day.[5] I have but little doubt that so far from its costing any thing, that several of the first publishing houses of the country would readily undertake it and pay to the family a percentage on every copy sold, or a handsome sum for the edition, for the privilege of making the publication. The publisher in the North can arrange with the press there, I can do something with the press in this State, and with Randall[6] in the leading paper in Geo. and almost in all the Cotton States, it would receive such wide notices as at once to place it conspicuously before the whole country. I would suggest that Uncle M[arcellus] and Mr. Simms be consulted before doing any thing.

Yours affectionately,

E.S. Hammond

E. SPANN HAMMOND TO MARCUS C.M. HAMMOND[f]

[Virginia], March 2, 1868

Dear Uncle M:

Yours of 25 Feb. came yesterday. I am glad to hear your farming prospects promise so favorably this year. Is there no trap in the late rise in cotton—just at the season when the crop is to be pitched? I regard large gangs of negroes as unprofitable and white overseers ruinous. The latter, since the war, are all consummate scoundrels and, as such characters are, lazy except at their villainies. The reason is patent. Land is

---

5. *Selections from the Letters and Speeches of the Hon. James Henry Hammond of South Carolina* appeared in 1866. Printed by John F. Trow of New York, it contained an introduction by Harry Hammond. (The work was reprinted in 1978 with an introduction and notes by Clyde N. Wilson.)

6. James Ryder Randall was a journalist and Marcellus Hammond's son-in-law.

dirt cheap to buy or rent, and all are on a footing as to laborers. The skilled manager can make more than honest wages farming on his own hook. Those who are employed are simply adventurers—sharks; smirking around their employers, busy to keep up appearances and more busy at plundering. I have just discharged the last I expect ever to employ, and find myself robbed of all my finest tob°—several hundred dollars worth probably—corn and meat in proportion and no telling what else and the loss of two mules by almost criminal carelessness.

I wd rather employ negro head men and hold the keys myself. Although I have almost the choicest land the length of the James R. I am terribly in debt. I regard it more prudent to let four-fifths of it lie idle than to go beyond ten hands—the utmost limit I regard of profitable labor on any one farm. With good management and fair seasons I can produce $10,000 worth of produce—did produce over $8,000 worth last year. The year before with 13 hands, I did not pay expenses.

By curious coincidence, I found some time back a copy of Father's Speeches, *etc.* which I had intended sending Mr. Simms in July 1866— his name and that date in it. He has probably just about got it by this time as I mailed it a week ago. I never had the letters Mr. Simms returned, though I asked Harry for them. He declined. I think Mr. Simms' Rev. article [1] will be the very thing if he is not too flattering nor says too much. A short article, one that will be entertaining and excite a little curiosity and interest, one which the papers could take a pointed extract or so from might resurrect Father's name. The time is inopportune to do more. Hero worship now is only of someone living who has patronage, or at best a party leader. Bacon and Napoleon are no more than myths just now; this is a period of action, the contrary of Tacitus' idea of the happy nation—with annals barren of events. In this country a new spirit seems to have sprung up—discarding all imitation of the careers of men and nations, to strike out something original. It will not be long, when entanglements thicken, before old land marks will be looked for, and then the words of the pure and wise will be like watch-

---

1. Apparently William Gilmore Simms intended to write a review essay on Hammond, for he thanks M.C.M. Hammond for his and the family's cooperation in sending correspondence and papers which he was to retain until "I shall be able to undertake the article on J. H. H. For the present that must be delayed." A bit later Simms again wrote Marcellus and apologized for doing nothing on the review, "but it will not lose in value by being brooded over." WGS to MCMH, March 28, 1868, May 2, 1868, cited in Oliphant, *Simms*, 5:121, 126. Simms died in 1870 and

words. It will be only to just gently keep in memory that Father made utterances of this kind that I think such an article at this time called for. It should aim at nothing more. Among Father's writings I must confess I fail to find the merit I hoped for in the first article in the book.[2] A sentence here and there might be saved but the bulk of it seems to me dross to his other writings. There are some fine short passages in Anti-Debt and the Institute Speech. The last paragraph of the College Address is perhaps the finest he ever wrote. The last 10 lines of the Kansas speech nearly equal it in its prophetic solemnity. The exhortation in the Calhoun and Barnwell addresses are very fine—classic and polished—while the character in the former is intense in its vigor and thoroughness—I hope to see Mr. Simms' article when it comes out, and may have it noticed in some papers here. I have thought of getting an invitation sent to Mr. Simms to deliver a lecture here, but it would not pay him unless he had other invitations on the route.

I fear things are not coming to a head soon in Washington. They are a black-guard set from the President to Forney. I am content to remain curbside of any responsibility for their proceedings and hope the South will not clamor any more for representation. I had hoped the President would have been ousted last week,[3] the Radicals had it all to themselves. They would inevitably have "busted up" before the Fall election. As it is, it is hard to say how things will go: but I rather think the Rads will hold the power and we fare no better for two years more at any rate.

We are all ailing—bad colds. Marcella sends love to you and joins me in love to the rest of your family.

Very affectionately,
E. S. Hammond

his editors state, "we can find no evidence that Simms wrote this article on James Henry Hammond." Ibid., p. 121.

2. Spann's reference is to the 1866 publication of selected letters and speeches of James Henry Hammond. The first article is Hammond's report of a meeting of the States' Rights and Free Trade Party of Barnwell District held on July 7, 1834.

3. The reference is to President Andrew Johnson's impeachment, the resolution for which was passed by the House on February 24, 1868; the trial before the Senate opened on March 5. John Wien Forney (1817–1881), a Philadelphia journalist, was in 1868 editor of the Washington *Chronicle* (a newspaper very critical of Andrew Johnson), and Secretary of the United States Senate.

PAUL HAMMOND TO WILLIAM GILMORE SIMMS[f]

Beech Island, March 8, 1869

My dear Sir:

. . . You very kindly inquired about myself, Harry and Spann and Mother and Bet. While of course our circumstances are very different from what they once were, we have little cause to complain in comparison with many of our relatives, old friends, and acquaintances. My new success has hardly been so great as I have sometimes heard that it was represented. But with the exception of '67 I have every year since the War made enough by planting to keep my wife and five children comfortable,[1] and the last year some money. I divide my time chiefly between my business and studying the writings of Swedenborg.[2] I could hardly express to you the satisfaction I have derived for three years from these works, or the controlling influence which the truths that I have got from them exercise over all my views of life. Plenty of work in the fields, a study like this ever broadening as I pursue it. My wife and five children to love and provide for, a little poetry, a stray novel now and then, the newspapers and occasional sports are powerful weapons with which to battle against the Demon of Discontent, who however not infrequently makes himself felt and I fear even at times gets the mastery.[3]

1. Paul and Loula Hammond, married in November 1858, by March 1869 had five living children; one child had died in infancy. Loula would give birth to another child in May 1869. As noted earlier, Paul and his family lived at Glen Loula, a plantation given to them before the war by James Henry Hammond. After the war, Paul planted the upper section of Silver Bluff and Cathwood plantations, which he purchased in October 1869 from his father's estate. Roland Hammond, *Genealogy*, p. 271; Billings, "The Hammond Family," HBC Family Papers, SCL; State of South Carolina, Edgefield County, Cathwood Plantation, affidavit signed by Paul Hammond, Jan. 6, 1870, JHH Business Papers, JHH Papers, SCL.

2. Emanuel Swedenborg (1688–1772), the Swedish philosopher and religious writer, claimed to have direct contact with the spiritual world. Paul's wife wrote that her husband had read Swedenborg until his mind was "entirely colored by religious thoughts" and from an "*infidel*" he has become a Christian." LCH to Celeste Comer Clay, Feb. 13, 1866, Clement Claiborne Clay Papers, Duke.

3. In 1885, Paul wrote a long unsigned article to the editor of *The Charleston News and Courier* in which he confessed to having been addicted to opium for many years, "taking morphine daily by hypodermic injections chiefly; in quantities ranging from the 60th of a grain at a time and the 20th of a grain a day to 18 grains in a single dose and 40 grains within the day." "The Opium Habit; plans of treatment; a new remedy and a certain cure," submitted to *The Charleston News and Courier*, Sept. 1885, Legal Size Folder, HBC Family Papers, SCL; see also: John Fox Hammond to Catherine F. Hammond, June 12, 1886, JHH Papers, SCL.

Mother is about as she was when you last saw her, having a moderate competency from the rent of the plantations. Bet is what we always knew she would be, a sweet, cheerful, unselfish, and sensible young lady. At present she is on a visit to her relatives in Georgetown.[4] Harry plants like myself a part of the plantation. He has become thoroughly interested, studies it scientifically, and is in fact a good planter, while he amuses himself as before with many novel theories. Of Spann I cannot speak advisedly. I only know that he is in Virginia and from time to time projects to move either here or to Florida.[5]

We would all be very glad to see you whenever you can spare the time to make us a visit.

                              Yours Respectfully and Sincerely,
                              Paul F. Hammond

JULIA A. CUMMING TO HARRY HAMMOND[b]

                              Sand Hills, August 17, 1869
My dear Mr. Hammond:

Mr. Joe Cumming's driver leaves early in the morning, and by him I send a few lines. I address them to you, instead of Emmy, as an answer to your note brought by him last night. Fortunately, I have not much to say, for it is a painful effort to me to sit up this evening—so to come to the point, I desire only to reassure you of my desire and purpose to give to you and Emily such pecuniary aid as will carry out your purpose of obtaining a comfortable and desirable home for your family, that this can be done I think, without inconvenience to me, and that I

4. Elizabeth Hammond was on a visit to her Aunt Elizabeth Stoney Fitzsimons, the widow of Christopher Fitzsimons, Jr., and sister-in-law of Catherine Fitzsimons Hammond. Also living in Georgetown were Elizabeth's cousins Paul and Martha Fitzsimons, son and daughter-in-law of Elizabeth Stoney Fitzsimons, and their five children. U.S. Census Records, 1870, Georgetown County, Pee Dee Township, National Archives Microfilm Publications, p. 11; Elizabeth Hammond Eve, "Notes," arranged by John Shaw Billings, p. 6, John Shaw Billings Papers, SCL.

5. Spann did come back to South Carolina. M.C.M. Hammond wrote William Gilmore Simms that Spann had bought a small place within a mile of the Cedar Grove Plantation, which was owned by Harry Hammond. At that time Marcellus was uncertain when Spann and his family would make the move from Virginia. Spann returned to South Carolina in 1870 and became both a planter and an attorney. His wife, Marcella, concluded after living in South Carolina for six weeks that she could not stand it, "and Spann took her to the depot and she never returned." She died in Virginia in 1878. MCMH to WGS, Dec. 30, 1869, Jan. 24, 1870, Ferris Collection, CU; LCH to Virginia C.T. Clay, Aug. 11, 1871, LCH to Celeste Comer Clay, Sept. 8, 1878, Clement Claiborne Clay Papers, Duke; Roland Hammond, *Genealogy*, p. 270.

am sufficiently persuaded of the extent of hers and your grateful feeling, for the little I can do for you. As for Emmy, she has from her early childhood been only a comfort and a blessing to me, an affectionate, considerate child, always delighting in her Father and Mother, and doing everything in her power for our happiness. And for yourself Mr. Hammond, I have long felt, and often have given expression to the feeling, that your kindness and consideration for me, especially in the times of the direful calamities which have come to me, since you became a member of the family, could not, and were not surpassed by any son of this house; and you will excuse me for what you may consider an unnecessary repetition of the same thing when I again assert that I have as entire confidence in your kind and considerate concern for me, as in either of my own sons—Dear old Tom[1] always excepted as being the most affectionate, without disparagement to the others—

As to the Inscriptions, I fully approve the addition you suggest for Mr. Cumming's [gravestone] and have felt since I first read them that just that thing was lacking in as much as it was so prominent a part of his character. I fear however it is too late to make the change, as the sculptor had been waiting for them for some time, and went to work, immediately, on their being handed to him. I have sent today however to beg he will suspend the work, until I can see him.

I have not been quite well since I left Redcliffe and yesterday, I had a very sick day. This morning I felt better, but this evening, I am again so weak and suffering, so conscious that "every thing" physically is out of joint, and equally conscious that no cunning skill of the Physician can "put it right," that Life is a right hard thing just now, calling more earnestly for those beautiful graces or virtues, whatever they may be called, fortitude and submission, than I can fully respond to.

Give much love to Emily. Tell Kate everything in and about her household has seemed very quiet, not to say dreary looking, since she went away.

A large party of our neighbors and friends left for the North this morning—Mrs. Adams, and Mrs. McWhorter and two children, Judge Gould's family, Mrs. Frank Miller, and Mr. Branch, etc.

If this intolerable heat soon subsides, and still more, if I ever have the consciousness of more than a kitten's strength, I will surprise you by

1. Thomas William Cumming (1831–1889) was the third son of Julia Ann Bryan and Henry Harford Cumming. After the death in 1870 of his wife, Mary Morgan Hazen, he lived with his mother at her home in Summerville. After his mother's death he resided with the Hammonds at Redcliffe. Cumming, "A Sketch of Descendants of David Cumming," p. 28.

riding over fast (one of these mornings) and spending the day. Maria is not well and has [not] been for some days.[2] . . . All the rest well.
Very Truly Yours,
Julia A. Cumming

MARCUS C.M. HAMMOND TO WILLIAM GILMORE SIMMS[f]

Beech Island, December 3, 1869

Dear Doctor:

Not having heard from you for some time I write again and this time to inquire how you are. Has your ailment yielded to treatment? Has your stomach recovered its tone? And are your spirits cheerful? I trust you are yourself again. That diet—exercise—good company and a very little of the drugs have brought you up to your own "age standard." How comes Gilmore? Does he plant next year and has he the prospect of a full supply of hands? These labor conventions suggested by Carpetbaggers or Scalawags are but a repetition in varied form of the old cry of "40 acres and a mule." The poor negro is just relieved of that delusion and was beginning to rely on his own industry for maintenance when to him comes the strike for higher wages—the demand for him of $2.00 a day or $18.00 a month for farmwork. And this on land indiscriminately whether it can [produce] $5.00 a month or not. Why both employers and employees would soon break down. The farmer in a year and the latter in ten years at most. I have worked hard for 4 years here. Have done my "level best" and have never made the ends meet. . . . I fear there will be suffering. God help us all of both races. And may he d—n the reckless in the meddling in this vital question. Some have engaged hands, but the engagements may be broken or, worse, the hands may work so badly as to impoverish the employer.

The folks out our way are in turmoil. Harry and Paul have now taken the Cathwood place intermediate between the two places purchased by them and divided it. Thus the best and the bulk of the lands are in the hands of 2 of the heirs.[1] Spann is here. Has not settled, but probably will do so shortly.

2. Maria Bryan Cumming Lamar, the youngest child of Julia Cumming, was eight months pregnant at the time of this letter. In September she gave birth to a daughter. Ibid., p. 31.

1. James Henry Hammond's estate was sold at public auction on October 20, 1869. His widow purchased Redcliffe and the surrounding 400 acres. Four years later she transferred the house and

I am picking the last of my crop. It turns out half only of what I expected in August. I don't know what to do. Have advertized to rent some land or for a partner. I can't follow up the darkies as I have done. Physically impossible.

I was offered the agency for S.C. and Geo. at urge of the Piedmont and Arlington Life Insurance Co. Have an idea of making a short trial any how. I won't go into new section. I will not interfere with Atkinson who has been there. What do you suggest about the whole thing? [2]

Randall you know lost his baby—a boy. He and Kate in great distress. [3] Annie [Marcellus's daughter] happens to be at home. She and Mrs. H. send love to Mrs. Roach and Miss Mary L., offer my best regards to them, to Gilmore, etc. [4]

Cordially,
M.C.M.

JULIA A. CUMMING TO EMILY C. HAMMOND [b]

Sand Hills, June 13, 1871

My Dear Emmy:

It seems a very long time since I have heard from you. Why did you not write by Bettie [Hammond] who, Miss Mary [1] tells me, was in

---

this property to Harry and Emily. Paul and Harry took more of Silver Bluff and what was left was kept by the widow and planted by Harry. Harry paid her rent for this land and this was her only cash income in the years following the Civil War. The brothers, later in the year, bought Cathwood; Cowden went to Elizabeth Hammond and Dr. William Raiford Eve, following their marriage in 1871. Eve, unsuccessful at farming, ultimately sold Cowden out of the family. When old Mrs. Hammond died in 1896, she bequeathed what was left of her share of Silver Bluff to her daughter, Elizabeth Eve. The Eves in turn sold this land to Emily Hammond for $4500. Harry continued to plant there though now it belonged to his wife instead of his mother. When Emily Hammond died in 1911, her estate sold what was left of Silver Bluff—2000 acres—to her son Kit for $11,000. Soon after, Kit sold the remnants of his grandfather's estate out of the family for $25,000. Only Redcliffe remained and after 1916 it was owned jointly by Harry and Emily's children, Julia and Henry. Catherine F. Hammond to WGS, Oct. 22, Dec. 19, 1869; MCMH to WGS, Oct. 19, 1869, Nov. 15, 1869, Ferris Collection, CU; Catherine Hammond, signed affidavit, South Carolina, Edgefield County, Redcliffe, Nov. 1869, JHH Business Papers; Billings, "The Hammond Family," HBC Family Papers, SCL.

2. Marcellus had considered accepting the life insurance agency because, as he wrote Simms, his financial situation was so bad that he would "do anything about for a decent salary. This farm is poor—but with capital, I could do well here. As it is I have not near enough a support." MCMH to WGS, April 7, 1869, Ferris Collection, CU.

3. The reference is to the death of his grandson, the child of Katherine and James Randall.

4. Mrs. Augusta Simms Roach, Miss Mary Lawson Simms, and William Gilmore Simms, Jr. were the three eldest living children of William Gilmore Simms. Oliphant, Simms, 1:cxlviii-cl.

---

1. This is the same "Miss Mary" Wimberly who had lived with James Henry Hammond's mother, Catherine Spann Fox Hammond.

Town the latter part of last week? I almost every evening inquire of
Tom or Derry or Joe, should he happen to come over, have you seen
anyone from Redcliffe today? Last Friday I think it was, making this
customary enquiry, Derry replied, I saw Spann Hammond today, and
he told me Harry had been quite sick for a day or two with Dysentery,
but was then much better, and since then, I have heard not a word. I
do not think you are much concerned to find opportunities for sending
a letter and I am often so long without news from you that I become
extremely anxious.

I cannot write you much of a letter this evening, for I have been
feeling quite unwell today, and for the first time in some weeks, felt
unable to sit up. My general health, has been better of late, than for
two years, tho' this evening, I am painfully conscious of the familiar
malaise of the last two years from which I have been comparatively free
of late.

Poor Tom,[2] this is a sad day to him, and this morning, when he
said goodbye to us I could scarcely endure the *witness* even, of his
desolate melancholy face. He supposed it was the anniversary of his
marriage, which I think was yesterday,[3] but he went down into Harf's
room, and said, Harf do you remember this day five years ago? He laid
his face on the bed, and Harf says he cried and sobbed like a beaten
child. I say when he told us goodbye, this morning—he expects to leave
in the early morning Train, for Knoxville, and consequently determined
to spend tonight in town, but a wretched night I fear it will be to him,
for he has had a Despatch from Mr. Hazen to say his little boy Marion,
is very ill. Poor, poor Tom, I fear he will feel his afflictions are greater
than he can bear. I have a most irresistible presentiment the child will
die.[4] God grant he may not for his poor Father's sake.

We are all as usual here, leading a *very* monotonous life, not to say

2. "Poor Tom" is the same person as "Dear old Tom" of the August 17, 1869 letter, note 1.
Thomas William Cumming, an engineer by profession, built railroads in the South before the
war. In the summer of 1861 he entered the Confederate service. He was seriously wounded once
and captured on three separate occasions. After the war, he was appointed city engineer of Augusta.
In 1866 he married Mary Morgan Hazen of Knoxville, Tennessee, who died four years later,
leaving two children. Tom Cumming traveled extensively after her death to the West Coast, Europe, and the Near East. On September 11, 1889, he died at Redcliffe. Cumming, "A Sketch of
Descendants of David Cumming," pp. 26–28.
3. Mrs. Cumming is correct; the anniversary date was June 12. Wood, A *Northern Daughter*,
p. 106.
4. Julia Cumming wrote soon after to tell Emily of "poor Tom's added affliction. His little boy
Marion died today at noon, as he informed us by Telegram." Julia Cumming to ECH, June 16,
1871, HBC Family Papers, SCL.

dull one. Maria works assiduously, at her machine, all the fore noon. I sit in my accustomed seat, near the sofa, sewing, or knitting—the children are out in the Lot, noisy and merry as possible, their merriment sometimes varied by a pretty fierce quarrel, and high words, Julia rather the noisiest of the three[5] and the loudest singer. How often I find myself longing to have you and yours with us. I need you very much dear Emmy to cheer and comfort me, for you can do it, more than any other person in this wide world. I bless God, that the pretty uniform tenor of my life is tranquil, remarkably free from nervous agitation so called. Yet I often think how much it would add to the sum of my happiness if I could be with you more, and feel that at stated times at least I might feel that I would see you. I wonder if in "the changes and chances of this mortal life," it may not come about that we shall be more together than now.

Harford has been much better of late than I for some time thought he would ever be again.[6] The greater part of last week he seemed very comfortable, took his one meal a day with relish, and looked better than for a long time, before he went to Florida. He sat up in a big rocking chair fully dressed a part of the day for some days, and everything about him was more promising. Yesterday however he had a slight return of Diarrhea which made him weak and depressed all day, but this evening he is much better again, and has just sent to me for something to read, a sure indication of his feeling pretty well. Miss Mary was here this afternoon, says your Aunt had a little tea drinking again last night, her guests three only, Mrs. Gardner, Mrs. Foster and Mrs. Montgomery. She and I seldom if ever honoured with an invitation. Your Uncle Alfred[7] has been very ailing lately and Miss Mary's sympathy for him is

5. The three children of Maria and DeRosset Lamar were Henry Cumming born October 4, 1865, Paul Cazenove born June 16, 1867, and Julia born September 14, 1869. After Mrs. Lamar's death in childbirth in 1873, Julia's name was changed to Maria in honor of her mother. Interiew with Mrs. Leslie Helm, Augusta, Georgia, July 30, 1979; Wood, *A Northern Daughter*, p. 107.

6. Harford Montgomery Cumming (1838–1872) was the seventh child and fifth son of Julia Ann Bryan and Henry Harford Cumming. Appointed a surgeon during the war, he contracted pneumonia while attending the sick and wounded during General Hood's winter campaign of 1864–1865. At the war's end he went home to convalesce. He became a "beloved country doctor" in Beech Island. He died in October 1872 in Florida, where he had gone in hopes of recovering his health after he had suffered a relapse of pneumonia. Cumming, "A Sketch of Descendants of David Cumming," pp. 30–31; Wood, *A Northern Daughter*, p. 107.

7. Alfred Cumming (1802–1873), born in Augusta, was the son of Ann Clay and Thomas Cumming and brother of Henry Harford Cumming. He was Augusta's mayor in 1839 during an exceptionally severe yellow-fever epidemic. He became nationally known when he was required, during his term of office as territorial governor of Utah, to deal with the Mormon War, 1857–1858. He resigned his position upon Lincoln's inauguration and returned to Georgia, where he lived in retirement until his death in 1873.

constantly expressed. She says he is becoming very helpless and yet will not have a servant. Even Lucius, whom he has thought so much of, never comes to do anything about his room or person. Give much love to Harry, who I hope is quite well again, to Mrs. H. and to Julia.

Ever yours my dear precious child.

Julia A. Cumming

JULIA A. CUMMING TO EMILY C. HAMMOND[b]

Augusta, February 18, 1873

My dear Emmy:

I have been trying since last Saturday to send you a written communication, but have entirely failed in all my efforts. At that time, I sent to Mrs. Gregg's [Catty Hammond Gregg] to ask Bettie [Hammond Eve] to take a letter to you, but found she had gone home the day before; and last night, I intended at my usual time for writing, to send you an amount of epistolary stuff that would have tired you to go thro' with. Unfortunately however I was so unwell that I could not write, and tonight, after a day of great pain in my back, it has become all-pervading, and I am sitting up in bed with a large mustard plaster on my spine and with just enough fever to give me a little artificial strength. It has been one of those days of bustle and unrest, which not infrequently happens here, and having been quite sick last night, I have not had my usual strength to resist the worries of it. Miss Mary came just as I had taken up my formidable looking key (to a larder meager enough to require one by no means so imposing) and she looked so depressed and anxious that I forgot all about my dinner, tho' I had planned to have one a touch above our daily slim ones (having invited Alf and Sarah, Julia, your Aunt Sophia, etc., etc.) so sorry was I to see her look so badly. She soon told me, as I suppose she has you also, that she "had taken the liberty" to make an appointment with Dr. Steiner to see her here, and he was to come at 12. So that when I went to see after my bill of fare for the day, I found everything so behind hand that I went vigorously to work myself, in our miserable cold pantry, so that by the time "The lights were fled, the garlands dead, and all my guests—departed,"[1] I felt very much like taking my own departure for good.

---

1. Mrs. Cumming misquotes Thomas Moore's "The Light of Other Days." The correct lines are "Whose lights are fled,/Whose garlands dead,/And all but he departed!"

Really, speaking seriously, I have felt very sick, and nothing but an unusually strong purpose to do just what I am doing sustains me under the great malaise I am now suffering. I presume the cause of it all is severe cold, taken the day of the Firemen's Celebration. I stood from about eleven o'clock until the gas was lighted, with the exception of an hour for dinner on the balcony, and you will recollect it was intensely cold. But I could not resist it, for really I think I have never seen a pageant on our streets, taking into view the number of persons, the beauty and show of the engines, the enthusiasm of the firemen, and the wonderful feats of activity and skill displayed in the competition of the various companies, to equal it.

I was quite touched by your last note when you spoke of the restraints mental and bodily you had borne to save Maria and myself from a feeling of "disgust" or whatever word of this meaning you used which I do not now recollect. My dear Emmy, how can you feel so, and give yourself so much mindless, morbid distress? My prevailing feeling is one of consideration at the bodily suffering which characterizes, more than is common I think, your troubles of this sort, but apart from that I cannot even regret it. You are the very person to multiply your off-spring,[2] especially, if they get most of your nature (and not the slightest disparagement to the paternal one is here indicated), and besides this, the profound, intense enjoyment you have in loving and cherishing your children much more than repays whatever of disturbances they may have cost you. I hope you will have a large and happy family, and that each one, tho' occasioning some peculiar infelicity from wayward-ness of conduct, or from unavoidable ills inherent in our common humanity, may be to you and Harry loving and bright, and causing that delight and pride which it seems to me would be ingratitude to their Maker not to feel, and which I can truly say has thrilled my heart with these emotions, notwithstanding the bitter, bitter griefs which have so far fully blended with them. So cheer up my dear child and *believe* you will one day deeply feel it is all right. . . .

Love to Julia, dear little Kate and the little men. . . .[3]

Julia A. Cumming

2. Emily Cumming Hammond had given birth, the month before, to her fifth and last child, Alfred Cumming Hammond. Billings, *Descendants of Hammond*, p. 1.
3. Julia Bryan Hammond (b. Aug. 20, 1860), Katharine Fitzsimons Hammond (b. Feb. 17, 1867), Henry Cumming Hammond (b. Dec. 10, 1868), Christopher Cashel Fitzsimons Hammond

MARIA CUMMING LAMAR TO EMILY C. HAMMOND[b]

Sunday night, July 13, 1873

Dear Sister Emily:

Mother insists that I should write you a few lines to tell you of my condition tonight, thinking you may have heard through Mrs. Hammond of our sending for Dr. Campbell yesterday evening. Dr. C has just left here and after talking with him I don't think any one could tell what he thought or what to think themselves. As well as I can tell you the state of the case is this.

Julia[1] being sick with measles last week (she has entirely recovered) and having no nurse at all part of the time, I was obliged to lift her about a little and yesterday while stooping over a clothes basket taking out clothes I "ruptured the membrane" as the Dr. says, and tho' having no pain had every other symptom of immediate labor. The Dr. assured me that there was no danger about it, and *pretended* to believe that it had come to the full time and everything would be over safely in the course of the night. He even wished to wait up here but I would not hear of that. I know it is not the time and I have not the *feeling* that it will come on yet, tho' this symptom continued all through last night and today until a late hour this evening. It has however passed off now and the Dr. says the membrane may have reformed, in which case I may go on till September (a thing he told me would be impossible last night). So what is one to believe? In the meantime I am sitting up and walking about my room but not going downstairs and Derry is ready to send for Dr. C at a moment's notice, and the worse thing to me about the matter is the uncertainty as I am about as comfortable as usual, and Margaret is here with the children. We will send you word when I am *really* sick, but as I don't think it will be for a month or two yet, can't you come up and see us if only for a day? It would be so pleasant to us all. I have written much more than I intended, on this not very agreeable subject, and now I must close as it is getting very late. Will you

(b. May 24, 1870), and Alfred Cumming Hammond (b. Jan. 11, 1873) were Emily's five children. Ibid.

1. See June 13, 1871, note 5.

please hurry up my work. I literally have not one garment ready and last night was in despair. I am going to beg you to lend me a double gown or so. Any thing in fact that you can spare for a while. I am so afraid to go back to the machine again. All are pretty well, Mother about as usual. Do come up and hear all about us. Mother says she would send for you if she had any horses of her own.

Goodnight dear sister Emily. I would give anything if you were here. I am not frightened, but I wish it was all natural. Love to Mr. H and Julia. Derry and Mother send love,

Affectionately,
M.C.L.

JULIA A. CUMMING TO EMILY C. HAMMOND[b]

July 16, 1873

My Dear Emmie:

As I promised I write a line or two now quarter past 12 to let you know of Maria's condition, as according to my own judgment, and Dr. C.'s opinion. After you left she continued sleeping heavily with but little fever, but complaining of great soreness and pain when she would make the slightest movement. About 5 p.m. she became extremely nervous and agitated declaring she felt worse than ever, but this state was very soon overcome by the use of Bromide and red Lavender. The fever had abated very much, and in that respect she seemed better. Dr. C. came as usual after dark, and hearing from Mrs. Meté [midwife] how she has passed the day he immediately knelt by her and passed his hands about to ascertain if there was any tendency to Peritonitis, and when he left her he told me he apprehended the pain of which she complained was of that character. Mrs. Meté thought differently [that it] arose from the contraction which was slowly taking place in the womb. Dr. C., I thought, looked very anxious and enquired of her how Morphine affected her, when she herself asked him to try a portion, which he did, and since then, or as soon as it began to affect her, she fell off into a pleasant sleep. A full, warm perspiration soon broke out all over her, and the skin soft and natural, and when she was roused (from some apprehension she was sleeping too heavily, Mrs. Meté felt) she sent down for Dr. C. to know if she could use coffee to counteract the effect of the Morphine. She was made anxious, I think, merely because she snored a little, which habit Derry charges her with doing habitually. At any rate, the Dr. declared the treatment was having the happiest effect, "it had developed the fact that it was not inflammation," and that he was immensely [relieved] and thought better of the case than he had at any previous time. She herself says "she feels a great deal better, she is free from pain, and her sleep is delightful." I may be too hopeful, but I bless God for what I consider the favourable change.[1]

You must not fatigue yourself and run the risk of hurting your baby by coming over tomorrow. I will try very hard to send you another Bulletin tomorrow. I am certainly much relieved,[2] but I find myself startled at every sound, especially when Derry or any of the nurses come stealing down to my door and softly calling "Mrs. Cumming." I like Mrs. Meté more and more.

Much love to all your household and to Mrs. Hammond.

Ever So dear Emmie,

J. A. Cumming

P.S.   It seems like a week since you were here. . . .

CATHERINE F. HAMMOND TO JULIA A. CUMMING[b]

[1873]

Dear Mrs. Cumming:

I was sorry to hear yesterday of your serious indisposition recently, and regret that you should have had any inconvenience or anxiety about the papers which you sent me. I was in no hurry for them, and have

1. The attending doctor wrote Emily Hammond: "The tenderness has not extended and the pain has become less acute on pressure indeed I may say that the area of tenderness has much diminished—her fever has been less since you left pulse ranging from 88 to 100—most of the day—has taken nourishment and been comparatively cheerful—her skin has been however too hot and her mouth dry showing some lurking fever in her system. All the processes relating to her puerperal state have however progressed naturally and lactation is being established during the last two days—this is favorable as an indication and will be beneficial in its influence I hope. I left her last night at 11 o'clock quite cheerful and disposed to sleep." Evidently things deteriorated the next day for the doctor added to his note that symptoms had reappeared, "I hope it is hysterical in its origin but even that cannot be lightly regarded in a case like hers." Hurly H. Campbell, M.D. to ECH, July 1873, HBC Family Papers, SCL.

2. Maria Bryan Cumming Lamar died four days later on July 20, 1873, at the age of 29, while giving birth to her fourth child. The infant daughter died a few days later. Cumming, "A Sketch of Descendants of David Cumming," pp. 31–32; Letters of condolence to JBC, July—Oct. 1873, passim, HBC Family Papers, SCL.

invariably said so whenever it was mentioned, and would on no account have had you exert yourself while so feeble and suffering.

Receive my sincere acknowledgements for your kind and prompt compliance, in an arrangement which I trust will long conduce to the comfort and welfare of our children.[1] I have felt gratified at the preference which Harry and Emmie seemed to have for this place, so dearest to me by many associations, and I have thought how I could put them in possession of it [Redcliffe], without injustice to my other children.

It was a great liberty in me to ask your assistance, but I was sure you would understand my motive, and exercising a clear judgement, decide as you saw best.

My wants are few, my capacity for managing limited. I bought the place [in 1869] and have lived here only to preserve it for my children. My income is not and never will be sufficient to keep it up. As their own they can gradually make improvements without feeling the expenditure and that will increase its value. I expected to have moved this summer, but my family has been such as to prevent any change and next month everything must give way to my little Bettie,[2] but I hope to make the exchange of houses in the fall or early winter.[3] I believe Emmie gives me credit for much selfishness in choosing the most comfortable home, but it is better they should at once relieve me of the charge of this, depending as I do on my children, it is uncertain how long I may want a home here or else where.

Again I must thank you for your kindness and liberality.

I was in hopes to have seen you and talked it over, for I but poorly express myself in writing. I have missed your visit very much and regret that your feeble health has prevented you from coming.

1. It is said that much of the furniture at Redcliffe during Emily and Harry Hammond's residency was provided by Julia Cumming. Also, there is a receipt signed by Emily Hammond acknowledging that she received fifteen hundred dollars from her mother toward the purchase of Redcliffe from her mother-in-law. $1500 receipt, September 5, 1873, signed by ECH, HBC Family Papers, SCL; interview with Mrs. Leslie Helm, Augusta, Georgia, July 30, 1979; interview with Katharine Hammond Suber, Kathwood Plantation, Jackson, South Carolina, July 31, 1979.

2. Probably Mrs. Hammond is referring to her daughter Elizabeth Hammond Eve's pregnancy. Mrs. Eve gave birth to her first son, Edward Armstrong Eve, on October 27, 1873. Elizabeth Hammond Eve, "Notes," arranged by John Shaw Billings, p. 6, John Shaw Billings Papers, SCL; Billings, *Descendants of Hammond*, p. 11.

3. Catherine Fitzsimons Hammond lived at Redcliffe until November or December 1873, at which time she moved into the Galphin house (the "Old Yard"). She turned Redcliffe over to her son Harry and his family, and she continued to occupy the "Old Yard" until her death in 1896. Billings, "The Hammond Family," HBC Family Papers, SCL.

I hope Maria and Harford are better. I urge Emmie to go to you and try to persuade her there are enough of us to take care of the children.

            With the most affectionate regard, I am yours,

                                            C.E. Hammond

JULIA A. CUMMING TO EMILY C. HAMMOND[b]

                            Sand Hills, February 17, 1876

My Dear Emmie:

I have intended each evening this week to write to you, but I really have not had the energy to take a pen in hand, I have felt so *badly*.[1] For a week or more, I have suffered a great deal, from the fullness and weight, and pain in the bowels, which of all my grievances, is far the worst, so that I have been scarcely able to move about at all. I have not tho', been lying down only in the afternoons, but in a reclining position in my chair, nearly *all* the time.

You have again pained me Emmy, by your last letter. How you can so often charge me with indifference toward you, failure to go and see you, but above all the intimation that this neglect is in consequence of "as Harry says, our poverty and *insignificance*." I do think this is all wrong, and tho' you may say it is half jest, there is no very covert dash of *earnestness* too, and it disturbs and grates on me *very* much. I am so conscious, in my heart of hearts, that you fill more space, and loving, longing interest there, than any thing in the world. That when you talk or write in that way, I think *well* what is strong affection worth if so little understood and confided in. But I did not intend to say more, than to beg you never will indulge those ideas again, but *try* and entertain, a *juster* estimate of the consideration for you and yours which I earnestly say, is held by *every* member of your family. As for Harry I fear you have misled him, with the notions he takes up about us and I boldly say to him, to his teeth, they are *unworthy* of *him*.

Another sad death, and terrible (unexperienced hitherto) family bereavement in our little community occurred yesterday. Poor Rosa West,

---

1. Julia Cumming's letters to her daughter Emily in this period are full of her physical sufferings. She died on March 12, 1879 at the age of seventy-six. Julia A. Cumming to ECH, 1876–1879, passim, HBC Family Papers, SCL; A *Memorial Notice of Mrs. Julia A. Cumming*, 1879, ibid.

after a long and suffering illness, died yesterday morning and was buried in the cemetery *here* this afternoon. I never knew a case of consumption more violent or with more intense distress, until at last, the lungs failed entirely and, as (I heard) Dr. Geddings said, the feeble life she had had, for some days sustained *mainly* by the Heart. The poor heart at last gave way, and life was gone while they thought she was sleeping, or rather I should say tho' surrounded by the family, they did not see *when* she ceased to breathe. I went to the funeral in the Church, but not to the grave. Her brothers and sisters-in-law and a very large number of relatives were present. Poor Dr. West, who walked with Harford foremost in the procession, looked *lonely* and *so* sad.

I scarcely know what to tell you of Joe, I fear he has not as yet been much benefitted, tho' I have hope he will feel more so now that he is at home again. I understood at first that Dr. Loomis's opinion entirely corresponded with Dr. Steiner's, but I *now* hear of a most material difference and that is Dr. L says it is organic and not *merely* functional—his derangement about the heart; that the aortic valve is out of order, declaring however, at the same time with the German physician twenty years ago, and Dr. Steiner now, that it will not shorten his life and he would recommend or guarantee him rather as *sound* for an insurance case, etc., etc., but he must be careful of himself and while, as Joe tells me among other flattering things, he said to him, "I see you are *capable* of an immense amount of *brain* work. You must steadily avoid it, for this trouble of the heart is the reflex action of the Brain and here is the *rub.*" I am myself *persuaded* all Joe's recent troubles, his attacks I mean, now continued much longer than ever before, are the result of pecuniary difficulties and the poverty to which he is now reduced by the necessity of selling his chief sources of income when he had so large a sum for these times to raise, $1800, and *this*, with the danger to himself of doing much work, occasions a constant, unavoidable tension of feeling and anxiety. I heard him say since his return, it was not change of scene or climate he needed, for he knew nothing equal to his home surroundings, but it was the terrible apprehension that he would become unable to work, and that if Mr. Hubbell would settle $25,000 on Kate and the children there might then be some chance he could take sufficient *rest* to restore him.[2] I *think* for two days

2. Henry Wilson Hubbell (1805–1884), the father of Katharine Hubbell Cumming, established commercial firms and ties in the Far East as early as the mid-1820s. In 1856 he returned to New York after having "traveled 370,000 miles and traversed almost every sea." He became one of the

past he is looking better and he says he sleeps better,[3] but he is excessively imprudent as for instance acting as pallbearer at the funeral today. I was shocked when I saw him come in on one side of the coffin and watched him all thro' the service. . . .

When are you coming dear Emmie. I missed Julia so much.[4] Love to her and to Harry.

Ever Yrs,

J.A. Cumming

EMILY C. HAMMOND TO JULIA A. CUMMING[b]

Redcliffe, June 21, 1878

My dear Mother:

Hoping as I have done for the last week that I should see you each and every day of that time it has not seemed worth while to write. But Kate Hyde returns to town this afternoon, and tho' I hope to follow her tomorrow and perhaps see you before this note reaches you, yet so many disappointments have met all my plans lately, that I will take what I know to be a safe opportunity to send you a line to tell you how much I have been pained at the daily lengthening interval since I last saw you. I hope to go up tomorrow afternoon by the cars and will bring Katy and Henry and stay until Saturday afternoon if I can be conveniently sent to the Ferry[1] at that time.

---

founders of the Mutual Life Insurance Company and a highly respected member of the New York business community. Wood, A *Northern Daughter*, p. xiii.

3. Joseph Cumming's medical and financial worries evidently decreased after 1876. He lived until 1922, dying at the age of eighty-six. He was admitted to the bar on the eve of the war, and later became a distinguished lawyer in Augusta. In 1886 he was elected president of the Georgia State Bar Association. He served as general counsel to the Georgia Railroad and Banking Company as well as being active in state politics. Cumming, "A Sketch of Descendants of David Cumming," pp. 29–30; Wood, A *Northern Daughter*, p. xiv.

4. Through the middle seventies Julia Hammond lived with her grandmother Cumming in her home outside of Augusta. On occasion, Mrs. Cumming, in letters written to her daughter Emily at Redcliffe, reported on Julia's educational progress—her lengthy French lessons and her positive liking for geometry, etc. Julia A. Cumming to ECH, 1873–1876, passim, HBC Family Papers, SCL.

---

1. The Sand Bar Ferry connected Beech Island, South Carolina with Augusta, Georgia, across the Savannah River, from 1786 until 1922. In 1922 John Shaw Billings noted in his diary that "The Sand Bar Ferry was out of business and a huge concrete bridge was in the process of construction over the wide stream." John Shaw Billings Diary, Jan. 16–Dec. 31, 1922, p. 226; MS vol. bd., 1817–1967, "A Miscellany of Clippings and Such with Mildly Historical Overtones," John Shaw Billings Scrapbook Collection, SCL.

I scarcely suppose this will reach you in time for the carriage to meet me, but that will make no difference, as I can very well come out on the street cars.[2] I wrote twice to Tom [Thomas Cumming, her brother] last week telling him in the first note that I had changed my time of starting from Wednesday until Thursday. I wrote to him again Friday to say that I hoped I had not been expected in such stormy weather and consequently had put no one to the trouble of coming to the station for me, but I fear from what Kate Hyde tells me, that neither note was received as she says you sent twice to the station for me. Thro' Kate I have my first news of you since Tom came down. Miss Mary she says reported you not quite so well last Friday. I was truly sorry to hear this, for I had heard with delight how much better you had appeared for the last week or two. I hope it was only a passing cloud. The children were bitterly disappointed at not getting up to Cazzy's party,[3] especially Katharine. Did you ever know such a storm at this season. It has brought wide spread calamity to this community. It was, every one said, the largest crop that had been planted in the swamp since the war, and the most of it was to be laid by at the next working. All of this is destroyed and the whole work to be gone over again, fences to be repaired, seed corn procured, etc., etc. It is so really deplorable for the country at large.

Kate Hyde brings a sad account of poor Catty and her extreme depression.[4] Even the thought of change does not seem to amuse her.

2. Horse-drawn streetcars began operating in Augusta about 1866. In town proper each car ⋁ drawn by one horse, and could be stopped and boarded anywhere along the route. The car was operated by a driver and a conductor, "and the latter would gallantly dismount, tip his hat, and politely assist the ladies to the platform." The Hill cars, which Emily took to her mother's, were drawn by two horses, and at the foot of the Hill two more horses were hitched at the front. Slowly the four horses pulled the car up the long steep grade. When the conveyance arrived at the top of the hill, the two extra horses were unhitched and the car went on to the terminus, the Augusta Arsenal. The round trip from Augusta to the Sand Hills cost thirty cents. Electric trolley cars replaced the horse-drawn streetcars in 1890, W.R. Walton, "Nostalgic Nuances," clipping March 10, 1951, MS vol. bd., 1817–1967, "A Miscellany of Clippings and Such with Mildly Historical Overtones," John Shaw Billings Scrapbook Collection, SCL.

3. "Cazzy" probably is Emily's nephew, Paul Cazenove Lamar, who lived with his grandmother after the death of his mother Maria Cumming Lamar in 1873.

4. Katherine, since adulthood, had been in bad health. Her first husband, James Gregg, son of Graniteville mill owner William Gregg, took her to Europe in 1865–1866 in search of a cure for her apparent gynecological troubles (see letters of October 17, 1865, and February 12, May 14, 1866). Cattie remained unwell and unhappy. Her sister-in-law Loula commented that although Mrs. Gregg had wealth and elegant surroundings they had not brought her contentment. Two years after James Gregg's murder in 1876, Cattie married for a second time. Again, her spouse was a textile manufacturer, William E. McCoy of Augusta, who in 1881 became president of Riverside

Mrs. Hammond feels much troubled about her, but knows she can do nothing for her.

Tommorrow afternoon then dearest Mother I look forward to the great pleasure of seeing you and all your dear household. Of course if it be stormy enough to make you think I shall not come, don't send for me and if I should come I will take my chances on the street cars. With much love to all and confidently hoping to see you tomorrow.

Yours Ever,
Emily C.H.

JULIA B. HAMMOND TO EMILY C. HAMMOND[b]

[Cambridge], March 5, 1881

Dear Mother:

I did not feel well yesterday so I did not go to Cambridge, but sent for a doctor. Do not be alarmed, the doctor was Miss Helen Morton[1] Aunt Anne's[2] friend.

Cotton Mill. Evidently her health and mental state did not improve; she died at 42 years of age in 1882. Loula Comer Hammond wrote her Alabama relatives that she supposed they knew how Cattie died. She had been "a morphine eater for fifteen years and tried under the treatment of a Dr. Burchard to give it up and she had died of paralysis of the heart." James Gregg to Catherine F. Hammond, Feb. 24, 1866, May 14, 1866, JHH Papers, SCL; LCH to Virginia C.T. Clay, Aug. 22, 1869, and Aug. 4, 1885, Clement Claiborne Clay Papers, Duke; Elizabeth Hammond Eve, "Notes," arranged by John Shaw Billings, pp. 3–6, John Shaw Billings Papers; clipping of Mrs. Katherine Gregg McCoy Obituary, Thomas J. Davies Scrapbook 1849–1903, SCL; Roland Hammond, *Genealogy*, p. 271; Jones and Dutcher, *Memorial History of Augusta, Georgia*, p. 24.

---

1. Helen Morton, the daughter of Edwin Morton and Betsey T. Harlow Morton, was born in Plymouth, Massachusetts, on September 27, 1834. She received her medical degree from the New England Female Medical College in 1862. In 1873 the school was absorbed by Boston University. In 1880, Dr. Morton was one of 2432 women out of a total of 85,671 doctors in the United States. A long-time member of the New England Hospital Medical Society, she died on March 24, 1916, and is buried in Plymouth. *Boston Almanac and Business Directory* (Sampson and Davenport & Co., 1881), p. 395; *Annual Catalogue and Report of the New England Female Medical College*, 14th, 1862; Boston University Archives; Helen Morton death certificate, Office of Vital Statistics, John W. McCormick Building, Boston; U.S. Census Records, 1880, Table XXXI, "The Number of Persons in the U.S. Engaged in Twenty Selected Occupations. . . ." (Washington: Government Printing Office, 1883), p. 738.

2. Anne Elizabeth Cumming (1805–1883), Julia's great-aunt, was the daughter of Ann Clay and Thomas Cumming. She married Peter Sken Smith (1795–1858) in 1836. Anne was his second wife; they had no children. The Smiths first lived in Florida before moving to Philadelphia in 1843. Sometime before 1858 they moved to Springfield, Massachusetts, where Peter Smith died in 1858. After her husband's death, she returned to Augusta to live with her sister, Sarah Cumming, and her brother, Henry Harford Cumming. Myers, *Children of Pride*, pp. 1678–79.

Cambridge 9 P.M. I am in Cambridge at last.[3] The sun shone for the first time today since I left you a week ago. I shall turn back to Boston, and resume my account of Dr. Morton. I had the cold as you know neither much worse, nor much better than when I left you. Father, as you also know, is very anxious so he said send for Dr. Morton, as we would like to see her any how.

She came. Not at all like any of the things that rise in your mind when you think of a female doctor. But a lady, refined, highbred, and above all kind, gentle, and sympathizing, in short I can convey to you in no other way, what a great impression she made on me, than to say she was something like yourself. Her connection with Aunt Anne, and I suppose her pity for the evident pain I had in leaving you, made her more than most kind. It was not her profession, nor yet her kindness, that carried my heart away, it was herself.

Would it interest you to hear how she looked? She was wrapped in a great silk cloak lined with fur, and an old fashioned bonnet (which is all the fashion now). . . .

When she pulled off her cloak she had on a rich plain black silk, without flounce or puff of any kind, her hair in a net low down on her neck, and falling in something between curls and crimps about her face. She had dark soft eyes, and brows that had a tendency to rise, alltogether the face of one who had struggled, and endured.

She recommended me to the boarding house I am now writing in.[4]

---

3. Julia Bryan Hammond went to Cambridge, Massachusetts, to attend Harvard Annex—an institution of higher education for women taught by Harvard professors. The first classes began on September 24, 1879, with twenty-five women students. The second year (1880–81) enrollment grew to forty-seven students, one of whom was Julia. In 1882 the Annex, officially known as the "Society for Collegiate Instruction of Women," was incorporated. In 1881 the Annex offered thirteen major areas of study—Greek, Latin, English, German, French, Italian, Philosophy, Political Economy, History, Mathematics, Physics, Botany, and Astronomy. In 1894 the Annex was incorporated as Radcliffe College. Mary Gillies Carlton, "A Brief Sketch of the Life of Arthur Gilman," p. 5; "Private Collegiate Instruction for Women by Professors and Other Instructors of Harvard College, Second Year Reports of the Treasurer and Secretary," 1881, p. 3; Radcliffe College Archives, Cambridge; interview with Jane Knowles, Radcliffe College Archivist, December 18, 1978. According to Ms. Knowles, Julia was listed as a "special student," and took no entrance examination. One can surmise that Julia was seeking to fill in her rather sketchy educational background before taking the admission examination which was the same as that required for males entering Harvard.

4. There were no dormitories at the Annex. It was assumed at the beginning of the experiment that women attracted to the institution "would be of sufficient maturity to admit their safely enjoying considerable freedom from restraint . . . no restrictions are placed upon them except that they are held to lady-like behavior in all respects." After the formation of the committee on students,

It is Mrs. John Brooks, 67 Sparks St., Cambridge. *Do* don't let it be a week before a letter shall come with this address. So far I like the people of the house very well, but I have hardly seen them.[5] My room is very pleasant—looks out to the west and has a right pretty view of the outskirts of Cambridge.[6] It is not as large quite as Grandmother's room at the old yard, but it is not near as full. It is fresh, warm, and clean. There is a bath room near.

I have just finished unpacking my things. When we first got to Cambridge this morning, we lost our way and father and I took a pretty good tramp. Then we found the place, left our bags, and went to Mr. Gilman's[7] (where we take dinner tomorrow). From there we went to

---

all boarding places were to be approved by the committee, or, if other housing arrangements were made, the committee had to approve of the living arrangement. *The Society for the Collegiate Instruction of Women Commonly called "The Harvard Annex," The Story of Its Beginnings and Growth, Its Organization and Present Supporters, The Scholastic and Social Life of Its Students, Etc.* (Cambridge, Mass.: W.H. Wheeler, Printer, 1891), p. 12; Franklin B. Wiley, "All About the Annex," *The Boston Evening Transcript*, November 14, 1891; Arthur Gilman, Secretary, *The Society for Collegiate Instruction of Women by Professors and Other Instructors of Harvard College, Ninth Year*, Nov. 5, 1888, Radcliffe College Archives, Cambridge.

5. John Brooks, a Harvard graduate, was forty-five years old and a merchant. He was described as a "scowling, stern looking, tenderhearted gentleman, given to puns." His wife, Harriet, at forty years of age was depicted as being "very beautiful; tall, black eyes and hair, most exquisite, delicate features, a perfect nose and chin, and wears glasses. She dresses very plainly, but would shine in sackcloth and ashes." Their two children were Arthur, aged twelve, and Margaret, aged ten. A former student who lived in the Brooks's house remarked that the "children are handsome and interesting." Two servants also resided there—Mary Casey and Margaret Burk. There seemed to be no economic necessity for Mrs. Brooks to board students. The same student wrote, "I fancy she likes the company and some pin money." U.S. Census Records, State of Massachusetts, 1880, Population Schedules, Cambridge, Supervisors District No. 60, Enumeration District No. 426, National Archives Microfilm Publications, p. 8; Kate Eugenia Morris to a friend Nellie, Dec. 27, 1879, Radcliffe College Archives, Cambridge.

6. The Brooks's house was new in 1879, built of brick and set on a hill in the vicinity of Mt. Auburn. A graduate student at Harvard Annex, who occupied the room prior to Julia, wrote that her room was on the third story in the back of the house and that it was "large and light with a beautiful view. It is one of those rooms one never feels lonely in. There are no squeaks or rustles, or possible spook-holes in it." Kate Eugenia Morris to a friend Nellie, Dec. 27, 1879, Radcliffe College Archives, Cambridge. Julia wrote that before her the room had been occupied by a Miss Morris, whom she described as "a quiet, sedate, thoughtful, modest, intellectual woman." JBH to ECH, April 10, 1881, HBC Family Papers, SCL.

7. Arthur Gilman (1837–1909) banker, educator, and author, is best known as the founder and leader of Radcliffe College in its early years. When Radcliffe College was incorporated in 1894 Gilman went on to serve as Regent (1894–1896) and as a member of the Board of Associates until his death. Gilman's motive for first proposing an institution of higher education for women in Cambridge was that his daughter Grace was coming of age, and Gilman and his wife wanted Grace to be able to pursue her education close to home, and yet at the same time they opposed coeducation. Arthur Gilman to Charles Eliot, Oct. 23, 1879, Radcliffe College Archives, Cambridge; W.E. Byerly, "Arthur Gilman and the Harvard Annex," *Harvard Graduates Magazine*, March 1910.

the professor of Political economy[8] but he said I was not advanced enough for his class, which rather threw cold water on father and myself. Anyway father told him some thing about his own branch he did not know, father will tell you of it. Then we went to the Botanical Garden[9] but the professor was not there so I came back to my room, and got here just at one, the very hour that I had been bidding my dearest Mother goodbye. Then I had dinner, and father who had been away came back, and we rested a little while, then went again to the Botanical Garden, where I saw a very pleasant gentleman, the professor Mr. Goodale,[10] and I begin work with him on Monday.

Then we tramped around Cambridge, and Father quite broken down has just gone, and with my body nearly as tired as my heart, which is continually slipping home, I must close this letter, with almost all untold of what I am doing, and all untellable of the love and anxiety of my heart for you. Good night take good care of yourself. I will soon be back to help you in the delightful labor of doing so.

Julia

HARRY HAMMOND TO EMILY C. HAMMOND[b]

Boston, March 7, 1881

Dear Emmy:

It is half past ten and I am just in from Cambridge, it is hardly worthwhile to write as I dare say you are overrun with our news which

8. The professor of political economy, James Lawrence Laughlin (1850–1933), received his A.B. from Harvard in 1873, and his Ph.D. in 1876. He was appointed an instructor in political economy at Harvard and was promoted to assistant professor in 1883. Professor Laughlin was an early member of the Annex teaching staff. Samuel Morison, ed., *The Development of Harvard University 1869–1929* (Cambridge: Harvard University Press, 1930), pp. 156, 190.

9. The Botanical Gardens, one of Harvard's oldest scientific establishments, contained an Herbarium and a Conservatory in addition to the gardens. The Botanical Gardens functioned as a laboratory for botany classes and as a museum. Ibid., pp. 345–48.

10. George Lincoln Goodale (1839–1923) received his A.B. from Amherst College in 1860, and an M.D. from both Bowdoin and Harvard in 1863. He was university lecturer and instructor of botany at Harvard (1872–1873). In 1873 he became an assistant professor in vegetable physiology and in 1878 he was promoted to professor of botany. From 1888 to 1909 he held the Fisher Chair as professor of natural history at Harvard. Known as an excellent lecturer, Professor Goodale helped expand the number of botany courses offered at Harvard. In 1878 he became head of the Botanical Museum, and in 1879 he was appointed Director of the Botanical Gardens, a position which he held until 1909. Ibid., pp. 340, 346, 371, 374; *Historical Register of Harvard University 1636–1936* (Cambridge: Harvard University Press, 1963), p. 227.

I can assure we are not with yours. It being now well on in to the second week and only one letter so far. I hope you will do better by Julia when I leave her and I will then knock off myself as you won't care to hear of me.

To keep on with the record I rose early and found it a charming cloudless day just the right temperature and the streets dry. I went first to see after my RR. ticket and then called on Mr. Edward Atkinson[1] and introduced myself. I found him very pleasant and he gave me a card to the professors of the Tech. Inst.[2] where I went and had a very pleasant talk with old Prof. Rogers.[3] Coming back the car stopped on the Boston Common just in front of the library[4] and I got out and went in to that magnificent room, introduced myself to one of the officers and in a few moments had before me a pile of books on So. Ca. to examine and did not get through until one [torn] and then jumped on a car and [torn] to Boston to Julia.

I found she had left at 2 for Prof. Goodale's and I followed her there where I found her with a book of 1000 pages and a microscope which she was to master preparatory to the study of Botany. The Professor gave me a lot of new books on Cotton in German and Italian to look at and we did not leave until nearly six when this most pleasant mannered

1. Edward Atkinson (1827–1905) was an industrialist and an economist. In 1842 he began working at the Boston textile commission house as an apprentice; he worked his way up to become the treasuer for a group of textile manufacturing firms. During the 1880s he helped found the Boston Manufacturing Mutual Fire Insurance Company. Atkinson also published several pamphlets on cotton manufacturing, wages, and fire loss. He specifically urged the South to develop its own cotton manufacturing industry, and had corresponded with Harry Hammond on the subject. Atkinson was also a founder and a director of the Massachusetts Institute of Technology. *The New York Times*, Dec. 12, 1905.

2. Tech. Inst. refers to the Massachusetts Institute of Technology, which was incorporated in 1861, and opened its doors in 1865. Justin Winsor, ed., *The Memorial History of Boston Including Suffolk County, Massachusetts*, 4 vols. (Boston: James R. Osgood and Company, 1881), 4:274–76.

3. Professor William B. Rogers (1804–1882) was the president of M.I.T. in 1881. Rogers, a graduate of William and Mary, became Professor of Natural Philosophy and Chemistry at his alma mater in 1828. In 1835 he went to the University of Virginia as a professor of natural philosophy and geology. He also became the geologist for the State of Virginia. In 1853 he moved to Boston, where he became active in the establishment of M.I.T., and served as its president from 1861 to 1870 and 1878 to 1881. Harry Hammond remembered Professor Rogers from the days when Harry was a student at Harvard. Ibid., p. 276; *Report of the Commissioner of Education for the Year 1882–83* (Washington: Government Printing Office, 1884), p. 124.

4. The Boston Public Library, established in 1852, was located on Boylston Street across from the Boston Common. Between 1868 and 1877 the library had undergone great growth, increasing from 144,000 volumes to 320,000, and the capacity of the central building had doubled through a number of constructional changes. The library was open daily to the public. U.S. Census Records, State of Massachusetts, 1880, vol. 13, part 18 (Washington: Government Printing Office, 1885), pp. 139–40; Winsor, *The Memorial History of Boston*, 4:291.

man invited us to dine with him tomorrow afternoon at quarter before six. From there Julia and I walked through the slush to the Gilman's and then made our way back to Mrs. Brooks' where I had been invited to tea. After tea we returned to the Gilman's and went to hear a reading of Chaucer by one of the professors, and as they have discovered here how Chaucer pronounced his words it was Sanskrit to Julia and I.

I walked home with her and as I had to wait half an hour for the car to pass, she came back to the corner with me and then left me there and returned alone to her house about 125 yds. distant and in plain sight. I could not see her enter exactly but I have no doubt she is there sleeping quietly for she tells me while she has no appetite she sleeps well. Like you, trouble makes her sleepy. Her cold is better but she is very silent and is going through a bitter spell of home sickness.

She returns to prof Goodales at 9 in the morrow and then goes with Mr. Gilman to the professor of physics [Robert W. Willson] [5] where I am to meet her at 11 and stay with her till after dinner. And the next day she is to come into Boston and see me off or stay till I am nearly ready to start. Love to all.

Yrs affectionately,
Harry Hammond

JULIA B. HAMMOND TO EMILY C. HAMMOND[b]

[Cambridge], March 14, 1881

Dearest Mother:

I feel so lonely without you that I feel an irresistible desire to keep on writing to you, but now I have to study so much I will have to deny myself this luxury. Don't you think you and Kate can come on for me? I feel myself to be so dull, and to do such little credit to you, that I long to let everybody see what a Mother I have. I expect I will get quite contented to be without you, soon, but it is not quite so yet.

I got Kate's nice letter just after I had mailed a long one to her. Thank her a great deal, and tell her to keep on writing me just such letters. It will do her good, while it is a great pleasure to me.

My congratulations to Ella[1] and I hope everything was all right at last, in this vexed case. Tell Kate now it is getting warmer she should work with my laboratory. She could study my Youmans' Chemistry[2] . . . then she could write me every thing she does, I know she would be interested.

Tell Henry I am not going to let him off from my letter, but will look for it every day till it comes, and he must exercise a great deal of patience, and write a letter to his poor lonely Sister who wants to hear from him so much. I fear you are not taking good care of yourself. Are you working too much? You must not miss me for I will soon be at home. I am going to my Physics now, then I go to Boston to meet Mrs. Brooks and go to a womans club.[3] I have just been reading a book by Frances Power Cobbe[4] on the duties of women. It was very good. If you see it read it. We were shocked this morning by the news of the assassination of the Czar.[5] I am so glad cousin Kate is better. March 14th, 1½ P.M.

7½ P.M. First, I am disappointed to say my tuition was the full hundred dollars.[6] Now I will tell you of the womans club. It is near the Tremont House,[7] where father and I staid (second, father is just too good in writing to me. I believe he likes me better than any of you do, for I have just got another letter from him on his way home). It was a big room not quite as large as our hall, when I went in there were about

1. Ella Bruce, a black servant at Redcliffe, probably the cook, was born in 1859. She was the daughter of Sally and John Bruce. U.S. Census Records, State of South Carolina, 1880, Population Schedules, Aiken County, National Archives Microfilm Publications, p. 9; JBH to Katharine Hammond, March 24, 1881, HBC Family Papers, SCL.

2. Edward Youmans wrote *A Class-Book of Chemistry* in 1851 that became a standard text and underwent two revisions.

3. The New England Women's Club, one of the oldest women's clubs in America, was founded in Boston in 1868. The Club's stated purposes were to provide a meeting place for women outside of the home, to increase women's awareness of current issues, and to bring women together to do social service work. Managed completely by women, the Club held weekly meetings with guest speakers lecturing on topics as diverse as literature and women's suffrage. Incorporated in 1877, the Club was located at 5 Park Street in Boston at the time of Julia's letter. New England Women's Club, Club Histories Folder, Manuscripts, Schlesinger Library, Radcliffe College, Cambridge.

4. Frances Power Cobbe (1822–1904), an Irish author who wrote on religion and morals, published a book in 1881 entitled *The Duties of Women*.

5. Alexander II, emperor and tsar of Russia from 1855 to 1881, was assassinated in Petersburg on March 13, 1881 by a member of the terrorist group, People's Will.

6. Tuition at the Harvard Annex cost $200 a year for the full course, which was $50 more than Harvard's tuition. The fee for a single course was $75. Ellen E. Dickinson, "The Harvard Annex for Women," *Domestic Monthly*, March 1884, p. 381.

7. The Tremont House, a hotel located in Boston at the corner of Tremont and Beacon Streets, was built in 1828. Winsor, *The Memorial History of Boston*, 4:479.

a hundred women there, all handsomely dressed, and they looked like
ladies. This club is for the general advancement of women, from reformed clothes to voting. There was a woman reading an essay on the
women of Europe, or rather on the women of France and Germany.[8]
I did not think it much, strained altogether. I forgot to say there was
one old man present. The lady had inveighed against the manners of
the storemen of Paris, this old man said he had always found them very
polite. The lecturer retorted quickly with a toss of her head "Well I
suppose it was because I was poor, and plainly dressed." Women will
do very well while you praise them but we don't like the other side. To
give you more of an idea of the place I will tell you a little thing. Hung
on the walls all about were pictures, and right by me was an engraving
of a Madonna, under the picture was a card on which was printed,
"Seek truth and follow *where ever* she may lead." The mere outward
difference of the two seemed to strike me as showing the inward difference. The one pure, above earth, yet sympathizing with earth, her child
pressed to her breast, and the light from above on the lovely face. The
sordid, common card to be torn up in a few days and trampled in the
mud, would that all the sophistry it potentiates would meet with the
same fate. While the other has, it has been the highest thought of great
men, to be preserved with veneration, as part, an emblem that there is
something higher than we are.

Ah, one does not know till they leave those who on earth have filled
their every desire, how strong is the longing to have some thing in the
big world that is yours, can help you, feel for you, "When other helpers
fail, and other comforts fall Help of the helpless Lord with me abide."[9]

I think one thing added to the intolerable anguish of being separated
from you, that has added to my depression, is the feeling that I am
living such an utterly selfish life, for at home I always let you, dearest
of comforters, beguile me, with the thought that I am helping you. The
way I found this out was, I was coming out on the car, there was a
woman standing; I got up to offer my seat, and for a moment the bright-
ness of home came back, and I knew what I wanted. I hope in the end

8. Julia's reference is to the New England Women's Club meeting which was held on March
14, 1881. The speaker, Mrs. H.H. Robinson, read a paper entitled "Bohemian Sketches" in which
she discussed her foreign travel experiences. Record of Club Meetings, March 14, 1881, New
England Women's Club Papers 1868–1970, Schlesinger Library, Radcliffe College, Cambridge.

9. Two lines are incorrectly quoted from the hymn "Abide with Me." Julia should have written,
"When other helpers fail, and comforts flee,/Help of the helpless, oh, abide with me."

that the work I am now doing will be of help to many. I am not wise, I cannot look far into the future, for instance the last of June seems wrapped in the impenetrable unrealisability of an eternity, and I want some thing to do now that has some object, that is not subjective even in the present.

But I must stop writing for I have no time, as Miss Presbrey,[10] and Arthur[11] came in to see me, and I have a big pull to make tonight. Tell Kate, do, to send her picture. A kiss to my own Mother and the spirit of her little girl is even now wandering round the library longing to have its body with it that it may [w]rest those stocking[s] from out the dear little hands and place in their stead the newspaper that lies so near, and now I kiss the dear boys that lie around asleep among their pets and peep at the books Uncle Tom and Kate are reading, and with a last and first thought for Chere come back to my studying,

Julia

JULIA B. HAMMOND TO HARRY HAMMOND[b]

Cambridge, March 27, 1881

Dear Father:

I do not think that any of them at home appreciate as you who saw me here do, how much I need the comfort and sustainment of letters from home, and I cannot tell you how glad I am to get your letters. I am only going to try to show it, by making this an entirely cheerful letter.

10. Clara Briggs Presbrey (1864–1946) of Taunton, Massachusetts, attended the Harvard Annex from 1880 to 1882. During the academic year 1881–1882 she took language courses in advanced German, French, and Greek, a course in intermediate Italian, and a course in fine arts. Julia described Clara as being only 16 years old and "a very unpretending girl." After her two years at the Annex, Clara studied art for several years in Boston and New York. She became a portraitist specializing in ivory miniatures and crayon sketches. She never married and spent most of her life in Taunton. "List of Students at the Annex 1881–82," Radcliffe College Annual Reports, 1879/1880–1907/1908, Schlesinger Library, Radcliffe College, Cambridge; JBH to ECH, March 7, 1881, HBC Family Papers, SCL; Clara Briggs Presbrey death certificate, May 7, 1946, Office of Vital Statistics, John W. McCormick Building, Boston; The Taunton Daily Gazette, May 8, 1946.

11. Arthur Brooks, the twelve-year-old son of Harriet and John Brooks, was born September 29, 1868. He graduated from Harvard in 1891 and became a lawyer in the firm of Myers and Brooks. U.S. Census Records, State of Massachusetts, 1880, Population Schedules, Cambridge, National Archives Microfilm Publications, p. 8; Harvard College Class of 1856, Secretary's Report, 1899 (Cambridge: Riverside Press, 1899), pp. 11–12; The Cambridge Tribune, Feb. 13, 1915.

I am more cheerful than when you went away, but I cannot say that it was my will force that did it, but as it were an aggregate of wills, for every one tries to make me feel more at home and more cheerful.

First and best of all, Dr. Goodale has proved all and more than we thought he would. He praises my work and says I am getting on well, till I feel so delighted, that I would try to take the whole of Botany as one big pill at a gulp. As I wrote he read me one of his lectures to see if I could understand it, and in every way tries to interest and encourage me.

I begin regularly in Physics Monday though I have been going to the lessons (twice a week) all this time. Prof. Willson is going to fit up our room for a work room, where we can perform experiments for ourselves. The subject is, Light. And another thing, I am glad to say, those old smart girls in the Physics did not know what Ether was, nor any of its essential qualities.

But you must not think I am in arms against all the Annex. But the girls in the Botany class I like, especially Miss Copeland.[1] But the girls as a usual thing in the Annex do not have anything to do with each other. Dr. Goodale is giving a series of lectures in Boston to which he asked me to go, [but] it takes so long to get in and out of Boston that I don't think I will be able to go twice a week to them.

I am very much interested in the history. The time before the last I asked Dr. Young[2] about the Irish rept, and the last time almost all his lecture was taken up with telling us of it. I will send you my notes, but I fear they will give very little idea of the lecture, for he lectures as fast as he can, and the facts hurriedly jotted down will give no idea to any one who has not heard the explanations.

I have just returned from tea at Mr. Gilman's. He walked home with me. I think he means to be very polite to me and since I have

1. Ella Bradford Copeland was a student at the Annex for the 1880–1881 academic year. Shortly thereafter she married Russell Allen. Ella Copeland came from Vermont where she had helped her mother, "a widow and quite poor," maintain a boarding house. Julia wrote that Miss Copeland hoped to set up "a garden with hot houses from which she can sell plants and teach lady's horticulture and a little botany. She seems a nice steady fresh tempered girl." Elizabeth Shenton to Ann Marcus, Oct. 18, 1976; JBH to ECH, March 11 and March 17, 1881, HBC Family Papers, SCL.

2. Ernest Young received his A.B. from Harvard in 1873. As a student of Henry Adams, he was awarded one of the first Harvard Ph.D.'s. From 1874 to 1888 he taught history at Harvard. *Historical Register of Harvard University 1636–1936*, p. 477; Morison, *The Development of Harvard University*, p. 156.

heard his and his wife's history I feel sorry for him, and admiration for her. Did you hear it? How he married a girl he had known but a short while, that turned out to have insanity in her family, and afterward took to drink, neglected their children, and in the end went crazy. When she was sent to an asylum, where she dragged on a miserable existence, while Mr. Gilman was left alone, not knowing how to take care of them, with these three girls. The first Mrs. Gilman died and the present Mrs. Gilman[3] immediately stepped into her place, and rescued the whole family from the "slough of despond," and her stepdaughters are devoted to her.

Now for the history of yesterday. I went in to Boston at nine and got to Marlboro St. at ten where Henry Lamar, and Jimmy Suitor[4] have the whole of Mrs. Durant's house[5] to themselves. The boys were not down, but the servant hurried them up, and in a few minutes they came down, I laughing about their being so late. I sat down to the breakfast table with them, and took a cup of chocolate, while they ate their breakfast. Though we had any amount to say to each other, I had to hurry off to meet Mrs. Whiton[6] at the Tremont House. When I got there she was there with her little boy. She had finished every thing she had to do, but to go for a few moments to the Doctor with her little boy, and she would do whatever I wished.

3. Arthur Gilman married Stella Scott in 1876. Gilman actually had four children by his marriage to Amy Cooke Ball and three more in rapid succession by his second wife. Stella urged upon her husband the need to establish a women's college in Cambridge. She became one of the seven managers of Harvard Annex and for many years chaired the committee on students. She died on November 7, 1928. Her son Arthur wrote that his mother "maintained to the end her interest in everything pertaining to Radcliffe, and its growth, from the infancy which she sponsored, was a constant source of pleasure to her." U.S. Census Records, State of Massachusetts, 1880, Population Schedules, Cambridge, National Archives Microfilm Publications, pp. 2–3; Mary Gillies Carlton, "A Brief Sketch of Arthur Gilman," pp. 2–3; Radcliffe College Archives, Cambridge; Arthur Gilman to President Charles Eliot, Oct. 23, 1879, ibid.; Arthur Gilman to Ada Comstock, Dec. 17, 1928, ibid.

4. Julia's first cousin, Henry Lamar, was the son of Maria Cumming and DeRosset Lamar. Jimmy Soutter was Henry Lamar's first cousin. John Shaw Billings, comp., "The Lamar Family [Genealogy]," John Shaw Billings Papers, SCL.

5. Henry Fowle Durant and Pauline Durant, the founders of Wellesley College, owned a home on Marlborough Street in Boston. In the spring of 1881 they were traveling in Europe. Derry [DeRosset] Lamar to ECH March 30, 1881, HBC Family Papers, SCL; Florence Converse, The Story of Wellesley (Boston: Little, Brown and Company, 1915), p. 27.

6. Helen Whiton, the wife of Massachusetts state senator Starkes Whiton, lived in Hingham Center. Mrs. Whiton became a friend of Harry and Julia Hammond when they stayed at the Tremont Hotel. According to Julia, Mrs. Whiton was "a plain, pleasant little woman who was very kind to me and begged me to write her and tell her all about how I got on." JBH to ECH, March 7, 1881; Mrs. Whiton to JBH, June 12, 1881, HBC Family Papers, SCL; The Boston Evening Transcript, March 3, 1881.

We went to some fine dry goods stores, and do beg Mother to send to New York for clothes for the boys, for Mrs. Whiton's boys wear these clothes altogether. She can get a very good suit for six dollars, and it will save her so much work. The stores were almost as fine as in New York, but not quite. After this Mrs. Whiton took me to lunch, which was a treat, she said the whole day must be her treat, and would not even let me pay on the cars. She said she wished you were with us, as I did too. I felt more certain somehow, that you were gone, when I took my seat at table at the Gilmans', and you were not by, than I have felt since you went. The vague unreasonable idea follows me, when I am in Boston, that you must be somewhere there, in those places that I at first only knew with you.

Then to come back. We went to the Art Museum,[7] and the Natural history rooms. The Art Museum was very interesting, but I did not have much time for it. The children would have enjoyed seeing the real armour, and then the curious Tapestry, the gorgeous chinese embroidery just one mass of brilliant colour, and the curious things picked up by the men sent out to find Stanley.

I got back to Cambridge at five where I found your delightful long letter waiting for me, and while I sat by the fire and read it Mrs. Brooks did up my hair, for I went to dinner at Mrs. Greenough's[8] at six. The Miss Battie[9] was there, and after dinner there came in some of the promised students. I had been here three weeks without their putting in

7. The Boston Museum of Fine Arts opened in 1876. Its collections included Egyptian sculpture, embroideries, and carvings. By 1880, only one of the four blocks planned for the museum had been completed. Winsor, *The Memorial History of Boston*, 4:405–6, 484.

8. Mrs. Mary Battey Ketchum Greenough was one of the seven women on the Ladies Advisory Committee for the Annex. Her husband, James B. Greenough, taught at Harvard. In 1878 Arthur Gilman approached Professor and Mrs. Greenough about his plan for having Harvard professors teach women. They responded enthusiastically to his proposal and "promised their heartiest cooperation." Greenough was already giving private lessons to a Miss Abby Leach. Eventually he became chairman of the professors teaching at the Annex. In 1879–1880 he taught Sanskrit. Throughout the 1880s, Mrs. Greenough served as a member of the Corporation of the Harvard Annex and became a member of the committee on students "with charge of general discipline of students, oversight of their homes while in Cambridge, of their amusements, clubs and social life, and the consideration of questions which may arise regarding these and kindred matters." She died in 1893 at the age of fifty-seven. *The New York Times*, July 5, 1880; Arthur Gilman Private Records, Jan. 14, 1879, Radcliffe College Archives, Cambridge; Gilman, *The Society for the Collegiate Instruction of Women, Ninth Year*, Nov. 5, 1888, ibid.; *The Boston Evening Transcript*, July 20, 1893; *The Boston Globe*, Oct. 12, 1901; Gilman, *The Cambridge of Eighteen Hundred and Ninety-Six*, p. 182.

9. Miss Battie (misspelled thus by Julia), a niece of the Greenoughs, was in Boston attending Dr. Gannett's school. The Gannett School, organized in 1852 by The Reverend George Gannett, offered a full four-year course of study to women, but it was not authorized by the state to grant college degrees. Miss Battie probably is the daughter of Dr. Robert Battey (1828–1895), a promi-

an appearance. I wonder what our white headed friend would say to that. They were not so very much of young men I did not think, pleasant enough, rather rough young fellows. Afterward we had some dancing, and then ice cream. It was a pleasant bright family and the evening went off very nicely.

I have an invitation tomorrow, to Mrs. Swan's (the Mother of Miss Swan)[10] to go to hear a very fine essay on art read, then Tuesday night Miss Copeland begged me to go to her house to tea, Wednesday comes the Philological lecture, and Thursday Mr. Gilman says I must go to a lecture on American Literature which is to be very fine, but I really can not go to all.

I enclose Mrs. Gray's note asking me to tea but of course could not go, as I went to the Gilmans, but I went to see them. Dr. Gray is a very finished and entertaining man and was very polite, but I do not think he is a person from whom one could get much spiritual comfort, or aid.[11]

Miss Horsford[12] and Miss Longfellow[13] have both called on me, but I was out, you see I spend a good part of my time at the Botanic

nent physician and surgeon of Rome, Georgia. JBH to HH, March 21, 1881, HBC Family Papers, SCL; *Report of the Commissioner of Education for the Year 1879* (Washington: Government Printing Office, 1881), p. cii; *Biographical Souvenir of the States of Georgia and Florida* (Chicago: F.A. Battey and Company, 1889), p. 52; Allen D. Candler and Clement A. Evans, *Cyclopedia of Georgia*, 3 vols. (Atlanta: State Historical Association, 1906), 1:139–41.

10. Mrs. Swan presumably is Mrs. Sarah Hodges Swan (1825–1910), who lived at 16 Berkeley Street (which ran into Phillips Place where the Arthur Gilmans lived). In 1880 Sarah Swan was a fifty-five-year-old widow. U.S. Census Records, State of Massachusetts, 1880, Population Schedules, Cambridge, National Archives Microfilm Publications, p. 4; *Cambridge Directory*, 1881; death certificate for Sarah Hodges Swan, Oct. 17, 1910, Office of Vital Statistics, John W. McCormick Building, Boston.

11. Julia visited her elderly cousins, William and Sarah Gray, in Boston soon after she arrived at the Harvard Annex. Anna G. Gray to ECH, March 9, 1881, JBH to Katharine F. Hammond, March 11, 1881, HBC Family Papers, SCL; Joseph Bulloch, *A History and Genealogy of the Habersham Family* (Columbia: R.L. Bryan Company, 1901), pp. 37–38, 44, 46; U.S. Census Records, State of Massachusetts, 1880, Population Schedules, Boston, National Archives Microfilm Publications, p. 4.

12. Lillian Horsford was the daughter of Harvard Professor Eben Horsford with whom Harry Hammond had studied chemistry in 1858–59. Miss Horsford, another member of the Ladies Advisory Committee to the Annex, married Professor William Farlow of Harvard's Botany Department. She served as the treasurer of the Annex from 1891 to 1894. David McCord, *An Acre for Education: Being Notes on the History of Radcliffe College*, rev. ed. (Cambridge: Crimson Printing Company, 1958), p. 44; *The Society for the Collegiate Instruction of Women Commonly called "The Harvard Annex,"* p. 8; *Harvard College Catalogue 1858–59*, p. 67.

13. Alice Mary Longfellow (1850–1928), the eldest daughter of Henry Wadsworth Longfellow, was also a member of the Ladies Advisory Committee. She took courses as a special student at the Annex in 1879–1881 and 1884–1890. *The New York Times*, July 5, 1880; McCord, *An Acre for Education*, pp. 44, 47; Carlton, "A Brief Sketch of the Life of Arthur Gilman," p. 5; *The Society for the Collegiate Instruction of Women Commonly called "The Harvard Annex,"* p. 8.

Gardens. I think I can safely say my cold is entirely well. Today has been a wretched day, a keen piercing wind and clouds of dust. Have you forgotten the papers you promised to send me? And some of the magazines if you could, for I never see any thing of this kind here. When are you going to send on the microscope? I do not need any more books as Dr. Goodale keeps me well supplied. I have just begun a Botany by Bessey,[14] a very interesting book. Write to me often and recognize how I have not complained once in this letter. Tell them to write every day. Thank you and Mother for my watch. Kiss my Mother for me and don't let her be anything but well and happy.

With love to all and thanks for your letter

your affectionate daughter,

J.B. Hammond

JULIA B. HAMMOND TO KATHARINE F. HAMMOND[b]

Cambridge, April 7, 1881

Dear Katharine:

I went to Wellesley yesterday, meeting the boys[1] on the train and going with them. It was a dark cold day with snow, and the thermometer certainly not more than 25°. I could see that the grounds might be beautiful, but to speak of them, I will wait till I have seen them under brighter skies. The place contains three hundred acres. We first came to two great brick buildings, each as big a[s] Redcliffe, both built with towers, bay windows, steeples and etc., but the solidity of the brick kept it from looking too ornate (ask mother how to spell my word). These were not finished and as I walked through them I was struck with the thickness of the walls, they being at least eighteen inches through.

These buildings are for a scientific school and Music Hall.[2] Then we came to the main building which is so big I find nothing to compare it with. Just in front of the main entrance is a court nearly as big as our

14. Charles Edwin Bessey, professor of botany at the University of Nebraska, published *Botany for High Schools and Colleges*, which was in its second edition by 1881.

1. Henry Lamar and Jimmy Soutter were "the boys."
2. Wellesley was building a new science building to be called Stone Hall, and also a Music Hall. Converse, *The Story of Wellesley*, p. 56.

hall, in the centre of it are flowers and palms growing, and around numerous pieces of statuary, on the walls on all sides pictures.

There were three great winding stairs that you could see from the top, as at Aunt Kate's only a great deal larger. And such a kitchen, great boilers to make soup three feet in diameter and every thing else in proportion. The Matron of the kitchen carried me through this part of the house. She took me into a room where there were eighteen pans, as big as Mother's biggest, full of morning's milk. She gave me a nice glass of milk and some cake which was very acceptable, as the keen wind made me feel very hungry.

Then two young ladies from Alabama came in and took me all over the house. They have chemical and physical laboratories, and lessons in physiology and biology. And it would have been cheaper there than at the Annex,[3] as I went through I thought I ought to have come there.

But before I left I changed, for the girls did not seem as they all do here to be studying for some thing, with them it seemed only to be to get through college.

They do not see any one, they have no such friends as Miss Copeland and Miss Dabney. The teachers too seemed to me shallow, that it was all rather show than reality. And though I liked the idea of having some one to look after me, still I did not like the thought of having some strange girl thrust on me for a roommate. Already I have become attached to this plain little room, where no one comes without my permission, and that holds all that I can see and feel of home in the shape of the dear letters you have all written me, and the garments that with such care you folks at home had made for me.

Tell Miss Betty[4] when you go after Mother's dress, that I think of her often, and the three pounds I have gained since I came here makes my dresses fit nicely. I weigh 115 lbs. Before I close on Wellesley I must mention the lovely little lake that you see in the picture, but it did not look very bright yesterday.

Your last letter was written so nicely—write me often, about what

3. Tuition at Wellesley was $60 a year and with room and board the fees totaled $190. Tuition at the Annex was $200 annually and Julia paid additionally $10 a week for her room and board at Mrs. Brooks's. *Report of the Commissioner of Education for the Year 1881* (Washington: Government Printing Office, 1883), p. 566; Dickinson, "The Harvard Annex for Women," *Domestic Monthly*, March 1884, p. 381; JBH to ECH, March 6, 1881, HBC Family Papers, SCL.

4. Miss Betty, a seamstress for the Hammonds, lived in Augusta. JBH to ECH, March 2, 1881, HBC Family Papers, SCL.

you are reading and studying, it will be like taking notes and a good thing for you and help you to remember. Before this reaches you I hope Uncle Tom and Father will both be at home. Give my best love to all.

I have walked over five miles today and am tired. I go in to Boston to a lecture, then I spend the day with Henry Lamar.

I forgot to say we took dinner at Wellesley. Tell Henry he might write. My love to all; your loving and tired sister sends you and Mother a good night kiss and tumbles into bed, to dream of you all,

Julia

JULIA B. HAMMOND TO EMILY C. HAMMOND[b]

Cambridge, April 13, 1881

Dear Mother:

You will think I complain too much, but I only wish to remind you all of your duty. Since your letter of the 4th I have heard nothing from you except your postal of the 6th.

I got back from Miss Presbery's[1] this day for dinner, and ever since dinner I have been working.

The Presberys were just as kind as they could be. They have quite a nice house, but so curiously arranged according to our notions. The kitchen opens right into the dining room, and the stable right into the kitchen.

They have three horses, and had a very nice horse for me to ride. I only had one ride though as it snowed all day long Tuesday. We amused ourselves in the house. I will send you what we did. Miss Presbery had no company. I think her Mother and Father want her to come more out of herself. They wish her to have a companion, for with all her talents she is the quietest, most retiring, without being self-depreciatory, of any girl I ever saw. She has not much interest for people in general, and as she says, I believe I know more people in Cambridge than she does.

---

1. Clara Presbrey lived at 103 Weir Street in Taunton, Massachusetts, and Julia spent a few days there during her spring holidays. JBH to ECH, April 19, 1881, ibid.; U.S. Census Records, State of Massachusetts, 1880, Population Schedules, Taunton, National Archives Microfilm Publications; *The Taunton Daily Gazette*, May 8, 1946.

I never had more pressing invitations, they begged me to come home with her when ever she came, and to make up my mind to stay a month with them after the end of the term, and they would take me to Newport and all round. The children hung on my neck and would not let me go till I promised to come again. Her Father[2] is a handsome, goodhearted man, and was very pleasant but that he spoke slightly of women physicians.

He is busy all the time. I could not help noticing that with all the time he was making over his daughter's education, he did not ask me one question about the Annex, my studies, or any thing.

They had no papers, reviews or books lying about, but he is too busy to read them at any rate. His wife is a right pretty woman (deaf as I said) very proud of her daughter, indeed they both are, but perfectly absorbed in fancy work. Miss Presbery does not like her studies, she only likes drawing and painting, so when she gets home she never seems to think of them again, certainly never mentions them except as a bête noire.

This my first glimpse at real New England life. It reminds you of the stories you read. Miss P.'s Grandmother lives in a very nice house, but as they say, "keeps no help." Even at Dr. Presbery's they have no servant to wait at the table. They have but one girl who takes charge of the house, cooks, and does the washing. I will have to tell you in detail of this glimpse of New England home life when I get to my dear home.

Though they were all kind, very kind, still I am not sorry to get back to Mrs. Brooks, which is getting to have quite a home feeling to me, nor to think that tomorrow I go back to Dr. Goodale and Miss Copeland. Then tomorrow I go to experiment on light with a very nice girl Miss Albee.[3] I send you her second letter to me, added to which I have a message from her today asking me to come tomorrow.

2. Dr. Silas Presbrey was a prosperous physician in Taunton. He graduated from Harvard College in 1860 and received his medical degree in 1865. Very active in community affairs, he was a member of the school committee, served as water commissioner for over thirty-five years, was a trustee of Bristol Academy and a member of the Taunton Hospital committee. He was also active in the Massachusetts Medical Society, of which he was the president for two years. In 1881 he was 41 years old and his wife Sarah was 40 years of age. Ibid.; Marquis, *Who's Who in New England*, 1909, p. 874.

3. Helen M. Albee attended the Annex in 1881 and 1882. According to the school's records, in 1882 she took Greek II, English II, German II, and natural history. "List of Students at the Annex 1881–82," *Radcliffe College Annual Reports*, 1879/1880–1907/1908, Schlesinger Library, Radcliffe College, Cambridge.

I see in today's Times a notice of Gen. Gary's death.[4] I hope we have had our last snow storm. It has been raining all day. I hope to get my letters tomorrow. With love to all. Good night chere. Tell the rest good night for me.

J.

GEORGE LINCOLN GOODALE TO HARRY HAMMOND[b]

Cambridge, April 14, 1881

My dear Sir:

Please accept my hearty thanks for your package containing the valued cotton-seeds, and for the book by Dr. Porcher.[1] I have already glanced at the work with much interest and expect to derive pleasure and profit from its careful perusual. We shall not have any Cotton in flower until well into June, if we do then; consequently it will not be wise for me to ask you to trouble yourself about the matter till then.

Your daughter has had a little rest from her work, during the Easter Recess, but she has resumed her studies now. I have been pleased with her power of application, and by her willingness to apply herself to the task in hand. I am confident that she will acquire the methods of examining plant-structure, and gain considerable facility in the use of the microscope.

Thanking you for your kindness in remembering the seeds, I remain

Your obedient servant,

George Lincoln Goodale

---

4. General Martin Witherspoon Gary, a lawyer from Edgefield County, South Carolina, had served in the war as brigadier general in the Army of Northern Virginia. It was Gary and the more extremist Democrats in South Carolina—those willing to use force—who spearheaded the movement to overthrow the Republican Reconstruction state government in 1876. Gary, "The Bald Eagle of Edgefield," succeeded, through the combined pressure on black voters of persuasion and intimidation, in bringing about a Democratic victory with the election of Wade Hampton, the Confederate war hero and owner of large plantations in South Carolina and Mississippi. Gary died of uremia on April 9, 1881, at the age of fifty-two. *The New York Times*, April 10, 1881.

---

1. Francis P. Porcher (1825–1895), a botanist and a physician, was a professor of medicine at the Medical College of Charleston and a surgeon in the Charleston hospitals. Dr. Porcher wrote several books on the plant life of the Southern states, including *A Sketch of the Medical Botany of South Carolina* (1849) and *The Resources of the Southern Fields and Forests* (1863).

JULIA B. HAMMOND TO EMILY C. HAMMOND[b]

Cambridge, April 27, 1881

Dear Mother:

I have just come up from tea, and have slipped on my dressing gown, and am sitting here in my window, thinking of myself and you all. All day it has been cloudy and since dinner it has settled into a kind of mist. The sky looks very dark as I look out on it, but the earth is getting to look very green. Mrs. Brooks said the children must stay downstairs this evening, so we have no reading, and my room is very quiet, but you know I do not mind being alone, and how I have spent long days by myself while you have all been away, but what I do mind is the thought that not tonight and not for many nights am I to see you. I have been thinking very gravely as to whether it were worth all that it has taken for me to come on here. I felt that I must have a new beginning, that I was walking backwards and must have a push forward. *But* did not this very fact of having got so mixed up show that there was an ineradicable weakness, that should know itself enough to at least not take away that, that might serve others. Ah! Chere, a hundred times I declare to myself, I will not write you such misgivings, but you will forgive me "just this once," and I can not think how much the whole thing has cost, and how you are working and striving, and I living here in luxury making so many demands on you. I have been studying just as though I were at home only I have the time without interruption, for Dr. Goodale has not only lost his little boy, but his wife has been quite sick since the child's death, so we have not been studying with him. I hope to have a long letter from you tomorrow. As you all say I am having a very good time here, but you must remember that all the time I am putting a tremendous restraint on myself not to fly back right straight to home and mother. I inclose a paper I prepared for Dr. Goodale on Plant Tissues. Tell the children to look on the right hand side of the pond about two hundred yards from the waste way and they will see a Kalmia tree,[1] I think it blooms a little later than this. Let them get some of the flowers, and see the curious way the stamens are arranged,

1. Named after the Swedish botanist Peter Kalm (1715–1779), the kalmia is a genus of North American evergreen shrub with showy flowers.

demanding the help of insects in fertilization. Then they could read Gray's book on Insects in the economy of plant life. Miss Presbery is very kind and she is a great resource to me. Mrs. Brooks I can not say too often is very kind. I heard today of a Miss Ravenel of Charleston boarding alone in Boston, [2] and going to the art school, I am going to see her. . . .

April 28th. A bright pleasant day. Miss Copeland is going to teach and help me while Dr. Goodale is not able to do so. I am to work with the microscope in the morning and analyze flowers with her in the afternoon. Is it not good of her? She is a most thorough and patient teacher. She has just what should be called a lovely disposition. I hope you are all well. Beg Henry to follow Kate's good example, and write to me. My love to Father and Uncle Tom, Dearest take good care of yourself.   Julia

JULIA B. HAMMOND TO KATHARINE F. HAMMOND[b]

Cambridge, May 1, 1881
Dear Katharine:

It is a lovely bright day, a little cold in the house, but delightful out of doors. I am going into Boston this afternoon to Phillips Brooks' great church.[1] I am going with Miss Ravenel, a young lady from Charleston, who is studying at the Art School in Boston.[2] She is a tall dark eyed,

2. The Miss Ravenel of Charleston referred to by Julia was Rose Pringle Ravenel, the daughter of Eliza Butler Pringle and William Ravenel. She was born on February 28, 1850, and in 1881 she lived at 65 Charles Street in Boston. Henry Edmund Ravenel, *Ravenel Records* (Atlanta: Franklin Printing and Publishing Co., 1898), p. 158; Phillips Brooks to Rose P. Ravenel, Feb. 25, 1881, Arthur Ravenel Collection, SCHS.

1. Phillips Brooks, an 1855 graduate of Harvard College, was the gifted Episcopal rector of Trinity Church. Located in the Back Bay section of Boston, Trinity Church is a massive building made of granite with a large square tower. Inside, the decoration is ornate. Brooks was consecrated sixth bishop of Massachusetts in 1891. His death in 1893 at the age of fifty-seven resulted in great mourning, and an impressive memorial service was held in Boston. On January 22, 1910, a Saint-Gaudens bronze statue of him was unveiled on the grounds of Trinity Church. Winsor, *The Memorial History of Boston*, 4:479, 488; *The Boston Evening Transcript*, January 23, 1893; "Life of the Great Divine," *Boston Herald*, n.d., in Phillips Brooks folder, Harvard University Archives, Cambridge.

2. Miss Ravenel attended the School of Drawing and Painting, which was founded in 1877 and was affiliated with the Boston Museum of Fine Arts. Along with the actual drawing and painting classes, the school offered lectures on art history, the theory of colors, and anatomy. *Report of the Commissioner of Education for the Year 1880* (Washington: Government Printing Office, 1882),

dark haired, plain looking young woman (the last is a prominent characteristic of all the young women I have met, who are studying here).

She has been on here three years. When she first came on she was nearly dead with a fall from a buggy, had to go about on crutches. She had been studying in Miss Ticknor's association for home study,[3] but when she got to Boston she knew of no one but the ladies with whom she had been corresponding. Now she says like Miss Battie and Miss Rayl[4] that she likes the north better than her own home. These girls may be willing thus to give up their home, but while Redcliffe stands and you all are there willing to have me with you, to love me and to be loved by me, I could never tarry away, there is never a land as fair as our dear home.

Indeed I am just beginning to really enjoy Cambridge, now that I feel I have not a weary time to be away from you all. Miss Ravenel is staying in a dingy boarding house on Charles St. No body has such a nice boarding house as I have.

When I came out from Miss Ravenel's I found I had just missed a car, so I thought I would walk on out to Cambridge till the next car caught up with me. The road after you leave Boston follows the bank of the Charles River: on my left lay the river over a mile wide, its dark glistening water heaving incessantly under the fluctuating wind. On the opposite bank are a series of hills, which though not high have distinct valleys between, which outlines them plainly. On their sides, sloping to the water, already the green meadows show, and the varying shadows of a cloudy evening chased each other up and down the hills through the valley clear out on the river where the restless waters shook off their sport. Behind lay the great city a seeming mass of red brick, from which thousands of eye-like windows stared. Above this mass rose the numberless church steeples, some as fanciful as the pictures of Turkish

---

p. 153; Hetty S. Cunningham to Rose P. Ravenel, March 20, 1883, Arthur Ravenel Collection, SCHS; Winsor, *The Memorial History of Boston*, 4:406.

3. Anne E. Ticknor founded the Society for Encouraging Studies at Home in 1873. The Society, designed to enable women to receive higher education through correspondence courses, flourished in the 1870s and 1880s. Arthur Gilman wrote Anne Ticknor for her opinion on the possibility of establishing a college for women in Cambridge. Apparently she approved, for Gilman wrote that she "entered into my plan with cordiality." Arthur Gilman Private Records, January 6, 1879, Radcliffe College Archives, Cambridge; Winsor, *The Memorial History of Boston*, 4:346; *The New York Times*, July 5, 1880.

4. Miss Rayl, who with Miss Battie came from Rome, Georgia, seemed to like Boston, since she planned to stay for two years. Julia characterized her as a "woman of the world." JBH to ECH, March 8, 1881, HBC Family Papers, SCL.

mosques, some plain and simple pointing ever upward. And there rising conspicuous the granite bulk of the Bunker Hill Monument. All touched here and there by flitting rays of the sinking sun, all quite from here a thing that can be thought and grasped, but once within its maelstrom of human noise and life all thought is lost, but of the immediate work before you. And my work was first to pay for my sacque which tell Mother I am sorry to say cost $8.00. Next to buy a pair of shoes for my dear girl. I thought they were very nice, and I think you will find they wear well. They cost $3.75. I hope they will fit.

I hope Father lets you ride Uncle Tom's horse now. I am certain you can do it, only you must be careful and learn that the best riders do not ride the hardest. I think excursions on the dead river are much more dangerous. The children listen to your letter as though it were a story. Their lives are so repressed in a city that they know nothing of such free life as ours. . . .

Thank Mother for her letter of the 27th. I will finish with an account of the church-going.

7 P.M. I have heard Phillips Brooks. He is a tremendous man, over six feet. He has a clear cut, clean shaven face. He wore a black gown, you might almost call it a mantle as it opened all the way up the front, showing his black clothes underneath. When he began to preach he threw his head back, and for three quarters of an hour afterwards the words poured from his lips, so fast some times that the one tripped over the next proceeding. He preached not as to individuals, but to humanity. The essence of all human beings and essentially human yet never personal. He spoke with the fervor, the intense eagerness of one who, overlooking all, sees danger, *and yet* beyond, above, sees an infinite hope.

His text was from the first Psalm which you know, it was "The righteous man shall flourish like a green bay tree planted beside the stream."[5] He said—Not only, as you see, is the tree to grow, but beside the stream which brings it fresh food and precious moisture. David did not choose this illustration lightly. And here is what is the true picture of a righteous man, he is a man who has found that the greatest hap-

---

5. Julia has confused the reference. The man who "shall be like a tree planted by the rivers of water, that bringeth forth his fruit in his season," is the righteous man of Psalm 1. Ironically, it is the wicked man in Psalm 37 who was seen "in great power, and spreading himself like a green bay tree."

piness the highest good, is in casting aside the false standards of the world, and taking instead thereof the law of God. But it is not only the man that is needed, but the circumstances. Looking round you, you say were I only rich I would have leisure to be good; were I only poor, says the rich man, I would have no temptations. And every one thinks his lot is far from the stream. But all water does not lie above ground, but much is beneath the earth. The tree must send forth its roots. Ay yes you must strike your roots deep into humanity, mingle with men, and from them draw sustenance for your souls. Follow the law even though it be in darkness, and sometime somewhere your tree will bear fruit for good, not only for yourself, but for those about you.

For years you may struggle here seemingly without fruit, but quickly softly your tree will be borne away and planted beside the river of life, where each day it will bear fruit.

But I can not give you an idea even of all that he said, and you must not think that these are his words, only some few of his thoughts imperfectly expressed.

Miss Ravenel is quite a nice girl. She talks a great deal, does not care to go home, but loves Boston. She is going to be a wood carver and has already sold some of her work.[6] Her home is on the Battery next to the house where the big palmetto grew.

But I will tell you of the church. It is tremendous and in the shape of a cross, and has a great skylight in the middle. It has many frescoes on the wall. And beautiful stained glass windows, one of them having come from a church in England. I wished you could have seen, but some day you will see it. I am going in every Sunday that I can to this church.

I must thank you again for your picture. It brightens me up every time I look at it. You and Mary did well to have it taken. Now Kate you must write me a long letter soon.

With my love to you all,

Julia

6. By 1883 Rose Ravenel had returned to the family home on the East Battery in Charleston, where she lived until her death in 1943 when she was ninety-three years old. A letter sent to Miss Ravenel soon after her return confirms that she had some skill as a wood carver, for the writer commissioned her to carve a frame for a wedding present. "I should like the frame of stained oak like the one you made for me before. I do not want it to be more than $30. Of course I do not expect the frame to be as wide as mine or the carving as elaborate for that price, but I like the style very much." Hetty S. Cunningham to Rose P. Ravenel, March 20, 1883, Arthur Ravenel Collection, SCHS.

JULIA B. HAMMOND TO EMILY C. HAMMOND[b]

Cambridge, May 5, 1881

Dear Mother:

I received your letter of the second this morning. It is a lovely bright warm, you might almost call it hot, day. My windows are up and one of them open letting in a warm flood of sunshine. Seated in my big chair is Miss Presbery intoning her Latin lesson. She studies very hard when she has anything to learn, and learns very quickly, so though she is taking three things she has times in which she does no studying. While I am all the time struggling at something and accomplishing nothing. You have no idea how I miss Dr. Goodale, he was so kind and encouraged me so much and above all interested me so much.

I will certainly leave here the first of June, as it is useless to spend money staying here. I will not come home to you much more learned than when I left you. But one thing I have finally proved that such people as yourself, Father and Uncle Tom are the rare exception anywhere, even in Cambridge, that after all, in being stupid I have the mass of mankind with me, only the mass don't seem to be as conscious of it as I am.

I had no idea how dependent I was till I got off here by myself, and I don't exactly see how I who am so weak can strengthen others. . . .

These people are so wonderful to me in their perfectly quite unapproachable conceit. They think if only a little of Mass. could be carried south every thing would be all right. They criticize every thing. The other day they were talking of the prayer book. They said they thought it ought to be abolished, that [it] was old fogyish, and not at all applicable to the present (a fact). . . .

And now Chere I wish I could gather a lot of the sunshine about me and send it straight home to my best beloved Mother, she must not be unhappy about anything. Now I am going to Mount Auburn[1] with Miss P. I am very fond of her. My love to all. Could you find out if

1. Mount Auburn Cemetery was a favorite place for Harvard students to take walks. They were not alone; most of Boston strolled through the grounds. Julia described Mt. Auburn as a place full of beautiful sights with trees, flowers, and fountains. JBH to HH, June 1, 1881, HBC Family Papers, SCL; Morison, *Three Centuries of Harvard 1636–1936*, p. 207; Ann Douglas, *The Feminization of American Culture* (New York: Alfred A. Knopf, 1977), pp. 208–13.

Grandmother has a little book: *Day to day*. If not I will bring [one] to you to give to her.

May 6, 1881

Chere, if you knew how much your letters were to me it would lighten the trouble of writing them. Every time I read them or think of them I see more in them. It is a soft rainy day just the kind of day to study and read. My love to you all.

J.B.H.

JULIA B. HAMMOND TO KATHARINE F. HAMMOND[b]

Fort Adams, Newport, R.I., June 7, 1881

Dear Katharine:

I found your letter waiting for me when I got to Newport, and if any thing could make me enjoy myself more it is having such bright nice letters from you, wishing that I may enjoy myself.

Frank Gray[1] came to the train with me, where I met Mrs. Brooks, Mr. Brooks and the children. Miss Alice Longfellow and Mr. Myers[2] soon came in, and we had a large party. We had to travel about an hour and a half on the train when we reached Fall River,[3] where we got on a magnificent steamer.

We went down in to the supper room where the time slipped away so rapidly that I did not have but a half an hour on the deck, we having left Boston at six and getting to Newport at nine. But that half hour was the most beautiful I ever saw. The moon you know is about half full? And here the daylight lasts such a long time that even at nine the west-

---

1. A Boston resident, Frank Gray, son of Sarah and William Gray, was a distant cousin of Julia's. Bulloch, *A History and Genealogy of the Habersham Family*, p. 46.

2. J.J. Myers was described by Julia as a thirty-eight-year-old Boston lawyer who put himself through college by log-rafting on the Allegheny River. "His muscle is as big as Dunbar Lamar's," she commented, and wrote that he had been a devoted friend of the Brooks family for more than ten years. He had become her friend during her stay with them. "He knows a great deal," as well as being "truthful, cordial, and without one particle of morbidness, sentimentality, and [is] pretty free of weaknesses." JBH to ECH, April 22, 1881, HBC Family Papers, SCL.

3. Fall River, Massachusetts, was incorporated as a city in 1854, and was a center for cotton manufacturing from 1871 to 1929. The Fall River steamer to Newport, Rhode Island, left from the Old Colony Depot usually at 6 p.m. *Massachusetts: A Guide to Its Places and People* (Boston: Houghton, Mifflin Company, 1937), p. 229; *The Boston Evening Transcript*, March 2, 1881.

ern sky was still red. The river is not very wide here (or is it the Sound?) and we could see the lights on both shores. The boat rushed on leaving a silvery gleam on the moonlight waters in its wake, the night was lovely and soft, but from all this bewitching scene I had to tear myself and what seemed worst of all from Mrs. Brooks who has been so kind to me. It felt like I was leaving some of you all when I parted from her.

When I stepped on the Wharf there was Uncle John[4] waiting for me, as he had telegraphed me he would be. Nothing can be kinder than he is in everything. He is very tall and slender, with a long white beard. He said he knew me at once because I looked so much like Father.

When I stepped into his parlor what should be the first thing I saw but a picture of Father lying on the table. Dear Father how glad I was to see his face even a picture. Uncle John seems to be very fond of Father and says he, "I always loved Harry."

Fort Adams is just at the end of a crescent-shaped piece of land that juts itself out into the water, on the other end of the horn, some four miles by land and one and a half by water, is Newport. As I sit writing I have a beautiful view of the town, tho' the day has clouded over and turned very raw and cold which makes the furnace heated house much pleasanter than out of doors.

Uncle John is here entirely alone, and so he passes almost all his time, his wife being with their two daughters in Poughkeepsie. He, like Mr. Wickfield, has a "Motive" only this time it is two instead of one daughter that he lives for. He seems for a long time, even farther back than when Grandfather was Governor, to have had great ideas on the subject of higher education for women, and these theories he is carrying into practice with his daughters. One of them broke down from over-study last year, and is very delicate now, having come near breaking down again this year, and it is only by the devoted attention of her Mother who reads her lessons to her, and by the greatest watchfulness that they keep her going on with her school. Does not this seem strange to us? My especial interest to him is to hear all about the Harvard Annex. He has been looking up colleges here and abroad, but has not decided where he will send his daughters.

4. John Fox Hammond, the brother of James Henry Hammond, was Julia's great-uncle. A career officer in the United States Army, he was stationed as a physician in 1881 at Fort Adams, Newport, Rhode Island.

1. Catherine E. Fitzsimons (Hammond) with her mother, Catherine P. Fitzsimons, in portrait by Charles Willson Peale (about 1815)

. James Henry Hammond in Governor's uniform (1842–44)

3. (Above) James Henry Hammond, United States Senator from South Carolina (photo by Mathew Brady, 1858); 4. (Below) The "Major," Marcus Claudius Marcellus Hammond, brother of James Henry Hammond

5. Henry H. Cumming, father of Emily Cumming Hammond

6. Julia Ann Bryan Cumming, wife of Henry H. Cumming, probably a Brady photo of the 1850s

7. Emily Cumming Hammond as a bride, the picture carried by Harry during the war

8. Major Harry Hammond, C.S.A., son of James Henry Hammond

9. Emily C. Hammond and two of her children, Julia B. (twelve) and Henry C. (four), in 1872

10. Julia at age nineteen in New York City

11. The Hammond family at Redcliffe in 1889: Harry, "Lessie" (Harry's niece), her friend Mr. Thomas, Katharine F., Christopher ("Kit") and Henry C. (seated); Emily, Julia, and Alf (standing)

12. Wedding daguerreotype (1863) of the grandparents of Frederica Wade Billings (see number 30), Lt. Col. George Robison Black, C.S.A., and Georgia Ann Eliza Bryan

13 and 14. Emily Hammond and Harry Hammond in the 1890s, both about sixty years old

15. Katharine in nurses' training at Johns Hopkins Hospital, 1893

16. Katharine and her cousin, Maria Lamar Miller, in identical ballgowns, 1895

17. Katharine Mary Stevens Billings, mother of John Sedgwick; her marriage photo (1862)

18. John Shaw Billings, father of John Sedgwick Billings, in his Union officer's uniform; probably his marriage photo

19. Tintype of Katharine Hammond and John Sedgwick Billings, courting in Baltimore, 1893–94

20. The famous wedding party at Redcliffe of Katharine and John Billings on April 20, 1897

21. Beech Island Farmers' Club about 1900

22. Sharecroppers at Redcliffe in the 1890s

23. Three generations
in 1899: John Shaw,
John Sedgwick, and
John Shaw Billings II

24. Dapper John Sedgwick
Billings in Atlantic City,
1907

25. Three children of Katharine and John Billings, John, Henry, and Julian, on vacation in the Catskills, 1904

26. Katharine Hammond Billing: her father Harry, and her sons Jo (nine) and Henry (six), on the ste of Redcliffe, 1907

27. John Sedgwick Billings with his two sons, John Shaw II and James Henry Hammond Billings, about 1910

28. Katharine and her sons, in 1913

29. John Shaw Billings II in 1921, a new reporter for the *Brooklyn Eagle*

30. Frederica Wade Billings in 1928 with her only child "Skeeter," Frederica Wade Billings II (1926–29)

31. John Shaw Billings II in 1944,
editorial director of all publications at Time, Inc.

32. Redcliffe, dilapidated in 1932

33. After restoration by John Shaw Billings II

The eldest is named Cattie and the younger Purcie.[5] Cattie's picture is very delicate and refined looking. Uncle J. thinks that it looks like Aunt Cattie,[6] of whom he speaks often. I am astonished at the interest he takes in hearing all about home and everyone there. He seems devoted and admiring of his wife and daughters.

This morning we got in a sail boat and went over to Newport, where waiting for us was a stylish turnout, a single horse victoria. Into this we got and drove all round Newport. I do just wish you could see the magnificent houses and grounds here. Some of the houses are wonders in the way of ornateness being three or four different vivid, glaring colours, and with all kinds of fixings about them. They have immense green houses. But some are built of stone, with these beautiful parks covered with green grass about them.

Then we went to the telegraph office where I telegraphed to Uncle Tom asking him to come here to see me. How I do long to see some of you again.

Then we drove to a wilder part of the island, where there were few houses and wild rugged rocks on which the white surf burst, and where we could look straight out across the Atlantic, and see the sail-boats in the distance grow dimmer and dimmer till they faded out, and the soft gray sky met the dark waters uninterruptedly. As we drove along we saw some fishermen unloading their boat, and they seemed to be taking out bushels of fish. Some times the rocks ran out miles, and enclosed in their midst still, quiet bays of water. We saw the "tower that to this hour dost stand looking seaward," but only in the distance.

I am sorry to hear Lessie has grown to be stuck up. Tell Kate Gregg[7] that I have only left one of her letters unanswered and for that, as it was a short one, I sent her a card, and thought she would have written to me before. I am glad you had a chance to go in bathing. Tell Mother I yearn to be with her taking care of her while Father is away, and that

---

5. Katharine Betts (Cattie) Hammond was born in 1864, and Elizabeth Percy Hammond was born a year later. Roland Hammond, *Genealogy*, p. 264.

6. Katherine Hammond Gregg McCoy, for whom John Fox Hammond's daughter Cattie was named, was the ill-starred daughter of James Henry Hammond. She was frail and unwell throughout most of her short life. For more details about her see letter of Feb. 24, 1866, and footnote 4, June 21, 1878.

7. "Lessie" (Celeste Clay Hammond, 1862–1924) was Julia's first cousin and the third child of Loula Comer and Paul Fitzsimons Hammond. She married Matthew Calbraith Butler Lamar in 1881. Kate Gregg, Lessie's younger sister, was born in 1870. Billings, *Descendants of Hammond*, pp. 5–6.

she must truly keep well. I am so glad her tooth is better. How much you must miss Uncle Tom, but I will soon be back with you all with such oceans of saved up love as will almost drown you all.

Uncle John, as Father will tell you, has a very low voice and seems the softest of men and as yet he has not showed the cloven foot[8] but has been in every way most kind to me. Poor Maria[9] when you see her tell her I am so sorry to hear she is sick. . . . Take good care of our Mother.

Yours loving,
J.B.H.

HARRY HAMMOND TO GOVERNOR JOHNSON HAGOOD[g]

Beech Island, South Carolina, September 1, 1882

Governor Hagood
Chairman Board of Agriculture

Dear Sir:

I beg leave to submit the following statement with regard to the Hand Book of South Carolina.

The Portion referring to the Topography, Physical features, Geology, Climate, Soils and Agricultural Methods and Statistics and Water Powers is completed in so far that it can be furnished to the printers as rapidly as desired.

The List of the Flora prepared by Mr. Ravenel is also ready.

The Chapter on the Institutions, Governments and Laws of South Carolina has been prepared by G.H. Sass. Not knowing the amount of labor that would be required by this work, I offered Mr. Sass as a Min-

8. Julia's reference here to the "cloven foot" was to John Fox Hammond because of his decision to remain in the Union Army during the Civil War. He had written his sister-in-law, Catherine F. Hammond, in June of 1886 that he was sixty-five years old and that his health was frail. "I have to be careful as regards pure air, diet, clothing, rest, and exercise—mental and physical. Close application to studies and other professional duties for nearly thirty-seven years, wearied and wore me. . . . Age came to my relief and at sixty-four I was retired. . . . I am much like a sapless old tree that stands the storms for ages, and then to fall prostrate in a calm." He died less than four months later in Poughkeepsie, New York. John Fox Hammond to Catherine F. Hammond, June 12, 1886, JHH Papers, SCL; Roland Hammond, *Genealogy*, p. 273.

9. Probably the reference was to Maria Hammond Cassin, the eldest daughter of Loula and Paul Hammond. She was born in 1861, married Alphius Philip Cassin in 1878, and died in 1882 following the birth of her second child. Billings, *Descendants of Hammond*, pp. 5–6.

imum $100 with the promise to present his account when the work was completed to the Board of Agriculture. This I have done, with the recommendation that they give it favorable consideration.

Dr. Mannigault's list of the vertebrate animals of the state has been submitted to Professor Spencer Bain for additions and more complete classification. The curator of Mammals at the Smithsonian Institution, Washington, DC, has undertaken this work. Its cost will be from $25 to $75.

Prof. C.V. Riley, Entomologist, Dept. of Agr. U.S. Washington DC, has undertaken to prepare a list of the invertebrates of So. Ca.

Col. Wm. L. Trenholm of Charleston is preparing a chapter on Trade and Transportation.

Col. Hugh S. Thompson had undertaken to prepare the Chapter on Education, his nomination for Governor of the State interfering with this, he has secured the services of Prof. R. Means Davis to do the work.

My arrangement as to compensation is the same with these gentlemen as with Mr. Sass, and they are to have their work completed early in October.

I have worked up the subjects of Population, Wealth, Debt, Taxation, religion, Crime, pauperism, occupations and Manufacturers so far as the data at hand allow. They are in such a state as to be easily completed when the data on these points from the census of 1880 can be gotten. I am making every effort to obtain these from the Census Office with as little delay as possible. I think these data essential to the completion of the work. In analysing and comparing the figures of the Census for 1850, 1860, 1870, and 1880 so far obtained, I find they present four distinct, well marked and peculiarly interesting periods, viz. the period antecedent to the War, the period preparatory to the War, the period of War and Reconstruction, and the period subsequent to the War. While the latter period in So. Ca. only opens with 1876, the figures of the Census of 1880 so compared with those of 1876 and the early ones show that a new period of progress has been entered upon, whose indications should not be omitted in a Hand Book of the State.

I am now at work on a statement concerning the cities and towns; this will be the last subject touched on.

The work of printing may commence early in October if there is no great delay in obtaining the data still wanting, and if nothing unforeseen occurs should be completed so far as my work is concerned before the meeting of the Legislature.

To do this however I shall be so continuously engaged upon the Manuscript, that I respectfully ask that someone be deputed to arrange about the printing, as to who shall do it, in what manner and as to price etc. As the scope of the work cannot be stated definitely the contract had better be made at so much per 100 pages. As only 1000 copies of the map have been published and as it shows quite a number of corrections, improvements, and additions that might be cheaply and easily made now, that it can be covered by a coup d'oeil, perhaps it would be better to start the Hand Book at 1000 copies, with the privilege of a larger edition at reduced rates.

Very Respectfully,
Harry Hammond

CATHERINE F. HAMMOND TO HAMMOND CHILDREN[b]

Beech Island, June 3, 1883

My dear children:

My first and most earnest thought, wish, and effort has been to relieve and assist you all as I saw your necessities and for this reason I have shared out to you whatever I could save or spare. Much of the property I have given was such as I could not manage or make available my self and I was unwilling to burden any of you with my cares. I know too a person can do better and be more independent with their own. To Harry I gave the house [Redcliffe] because I knew he desired and would keep it up better than any of the others. I offered Spann any other part of my lands. I had nothing else to give. My income has been barely sufficient for my support with economy. His having but one child and she provided for, his need seemed less, and he wished nothing in the Estate lands. I made some presents in money to Paul—$1000 from the Marsh and $500 again, because I thought he did much in the management of the plantations before the division and I relieved him of his Bluff place, he bought it at an inflated price, his health was bad and a helpless family. To my dear Cattie I gave the expense of my European travels[1]—and as I had no right to put Bet to the expense as a return to

1. According to Elizabeth Hammond Eve, she and her mother, Catherine Fitzsimons Hammond, accompanied Katherine Hammond Gregg to Europe in 1866, so that Cattie could consult

her I gave Silverton.[2] And to Bet (as having a large family[3] and as the youngest getting less from her Father than any of the others who were educated and supported up to the time of his death) I gave the Marsh— pleased that the Dr. could make it useful, for it was only an expense to the Estate and to me before. I make these statements that though I have a very limited knowledge of business I have endeavored to be equal and just to all. My household and personal effects are old and of little value. If Bet survives me let her take all that are not mentioned in my will. I know she will do right. To Harry I give the telescope. My dear children, let there be no discord or dissentions. Be united, help each other when- ever you can. I have lived beyond the time of my Mother's life.[4] My health is better than in earlier years though I know my strength lessens. Old age is not desirable for one's comfort. I endeavor to wait in patience God's will and receive as he sends life or death, health or suffering in submission. I have received invariable kindness and respect from my children and grandchildren. How dear you have all been to me you will never know. I never forget my loved Claude.[5]

Catherine F. Hammond

HARRY HAMMOND'S PREFACE TO HANDBOOK OF SOUTH CAROLINA, 1883[b]

PREFACE

Redcliffe, Beech Island, S.C., 15th October, 1883.

I have brought together in these pages as many facts and figures as I could in the time at my disposal, touching the Resources of South Car- olina and the more obvious conditions of life in her limits. The map I

Dr. James Marion Sims. As cited earlier, the Hammond party remained in Paris from April to September 1866. Cattie died in 1882, a year before this letter was written. Elizabeth Hammond Eve, "Notes," arranged by John Shaw Billings, pp. 3–4, John Shaw Billings Papers, SCL.

2. According to Bet, her mother gave them the old home, Silverton, in 1879. In March 1880 they sold it and moved to Cowden Plantation. Ibid., p. 6.

3. Elizabeth Hammond and Willian Raiford Eve had twelve children born between September 1872 and January 1891. At the time of Catherine's letter to her children in June 1883 the Eves had seven children. Billings, *Descendants of Hammond*, p. 11.

4. Catherine Pritchard Fitzsimons (1772–1841), Mrs. Hammond's mother, was sixty-nine years old at her death.

5. Presumably this reference is to her grandson Marcus Claude Hammond (1859–1914) who at the time had been disinherited by his father, Paul Fitzsimons Hammond.

have prepared to accompany this volume will enable the reader to locate and bound each enumeration district of the 10th U.S. Census within the State. This gives for the first time the framework in which to fill all the details of the Census. These may be considered in connection with the Physical and Geological features of the State, which in so far as ascertained, are also portrayed on the map.

I return my thanks to many persons, who in response to my inquiries have contributed important data for this volume, and in especial to General Johnson Hagood, who being then Governor of the State, caused the work to be undertaken, and gave it effective furtherance.

Should this book induce others to promote or to prosecute similar work, or assist them in extending our knowledge in these regards, and in making it available for human use, I shall esteem myself fortunate.

HARRY HAMMOND

HARRY HAMMOND TO GOVERNOR HUGH S. THOMPSON[b]

Beech Island, December 18, 1883

Sir:

After waiting in vain during several weeks for a reply to the communication I made through you to the Board of Agriculture, I am informed, that, sometime since, at a full meeting of the Board, it was determined to make no acknowledgement of my labors on the Hand Book during the last summer, not to allow me the courtesy, always extended to authors and editors, of distributing a certain number of copies of my work, and also to obliterate all trace of my connection with the work by cutting out and destroying the page containing the preface and bibliography, and that in this mutilated condition the book is now being distributed by the Department of Agriculture.

It is well known to the Board of Agriculture, that I was the sole editor of the Hand Book, that its entire plan without direction or suggestion from anyone was mine, and that I was the author of sixteen out of its twenty chapters[1] (the names of the writers being in each instance prefixed to the six chapters respectively contributed by others), in fine, that, with the exceptions stated which appear in the book itself, the entire work, tables, maps, illustrations, and text, is mine.

It is also conspicuously manifest that the action of the Board above

1. Harry Hammond's anger apparently accounts for his mistakenly writing "twenty" instead of twenty-two, which was the number of chapters actually contained in the Handbook.

referred to effectually effaces all mark of my handiwork from the volume. As it stands after this manipulation the public would naturally suppose that you, or the Commissioner of Agriculture, or the Board as a body had prepared the work, whereas it is known to every member of the Board, that with the exception of Chancellor Johnson not one of them has contributed a single fact, thought or expression or the suggestion of one that is, or might have been, put in the Book. I wish to say that this action of the Board has taken me by surprise, and that I am wholly at a loss to conceive of the motive that has induced them to mutilate the property of the State and to deprive me of any little credit or benefit I may have earned by my labor. At the same time I fail to discover in my motives anything that should have provoked this hostile action on the part of the Board.

For these reasons I feel it my duty to protest against this mutilation of the Hand Book of the State:

1 As an injury done to public property by destroying with the preface statements necessary to the clear and complete understanding and use of the Book and with the Bibliography a record valuable to the State and not to be found elsewhere.

2nd As an injustice and injury to me. Eliminating my name from my work thereby depriving me of the chief consideration for which I gave my labor, to wit such satisfaction and benefit as I might naturally expect from a public acknowledgement that I had conscientiously and faithfully performed my task.

In conclusion I must request that you will direct the parties now engaged in mutilating the copies of the Hand Book to desist at once from their work of destruction, and that they be required to make reparation of the wrong already done.

I ask that you will also inform me without delay that these very natural and proper requests of mine have been complied with. I have the honor to be very respectfully,

Harry Hammond

GOVERNOR HUGH S. THOMPSON TO HARRY HAMMOND[b]

Columbia, December 21, 1883

Dear Sir:

Your letter of the 18th inst. has been received. Your letter of the 15th ult. reached me promptly and its receipt was acknowledged by my secretary. None of the matters referred to in that letter could be acted upon except by the Board of Agriculture, and the letter was therefore submitted by me to the Board at its meeting on the 6th inst. In response to your request that I direct the persons engaged in removing the preface to the Hand Book to desist from their work and make reparation to you, I have to say that I have no authority to take action in the matter. The Board of Agriculture, by a resolution adopted, at the meeting on the 6th inst. authorized and required the Commissioner to remove the preface, and it is not within my power to rescind that resolution or reverse the action of the Board. Your letter will be submitted to the Board at its next meeting.

Your allusion to the fact that as the Hand Book appears without the preface it might be supposed that I or the Commissioner or the Board of Agriculture had prepared the work, makes it proper for me to say that, so far as I am concerned, I am entitled to no credit whatever for the Hand Book and that I claim none. When, by virtue of my office, I became a member of the Board of Agriculture, I found the work far advanced towards completion and I knew nothing more of the history of its inception or of the manner of its execution than was known to the general public. I was not aware that my name appeared in the Hand Book until I saw a copy of the work.

Very respectfully,
Hugh S. Thompson

HARRY HAMMOND TO THE SOUTH CAROLINA BOARD OF AGRICULTURE[b]

Beech Island, May 26, 1884

In closing my correspondence with your honorable body regarding your mutilation of the Hand Book of the State,[1] and your suppression of my name as its author I beg to say—The contemptuous coolness with which you have responded to my respectful and not unnatural attempts to ascertain a reason for your very unusual course admonishes me of your advantage in as much as it seems you are free from compulsion in the matter "tho' reasons were as plentiful as blackberries."

1. Although in this letter Harry Hammond accuses the South Carolina state officials of "literary piracy," for not acknowledging that he was the author of *South Carolina Resources and Population, Institutions and Industries*, the book is commonly known as "Hammond's Handbook."

I was aware that popular sentiment did not strongly support a man's claim to property in the product of his brain and that the laws even of the United States encouraged literary piracy, but I had not anticipated such privateering on this occasion and perhaps my wisest course now is to admit "in hoc signo vinces." Nevertheless I must state my conviction that your honorable body has seized and appropriated property as peculiarly and wholly mine as any dollar that Scott, Moses, or Chamberlain[2] wrung from me for their private uses. If there be any value in the work I have done I can only trust that your honorable body may not be able to appropriate the interest the State has in it, as wholly as you have that which I had. Very Respectfully,

Your obt Servt,
Harry Hammond

HENRY C. HAMMOND[1] TO EMILY C. HAMMOND[b]

Beech Island, May 28, 1885

Dear Mother:

Not with a malicious intent to encroach on our friend Mr. Angus Brown's[2] private style of communication I will say. It is raining. It rained yesterday. It rained day before yesterday. The grass walked up the corn rows day before yesterday. The grass ran up the cotton rows yesterday. The grass flies up the corn rows today. Bright prospect shadowed by a prodigious cloud of grass. The garden in a state of sappy nonproductiveness. Father imbibed his usual amount of sherry today. His face did not turn red. . . . The work which Brooks and myself have this day done in our twenty five apiaries would rival any labour of

2. Robert K. Scott, Franklin J. Moses, Jr., and Daniel H. Chamberlain were the three Republican governors of South Carolina during Reconstruction (1868–1876). To understand how stinging Hammond's denunciation was one has to be aware of how harshly white South Carolinians judged Republican rule.

1. Henry was sixteen years old when he wrote this letter to his mother, while she was visiting a Mrs. Perry at Governors Island, New York. Thomas W. Cumming to HH, April 26, 1885, HBC Family Papers, SCL.

2. Angus Brown, a farmer and neighbor of the Hammonds, sold some land to James Henry Hammond in 1848. Still living in 1911, Brown wrote a letter of condolence on Emily Hammond's death. He was then living on Pendleton Street in Columbia. JHH Plantation Journal, Aug. 4, 1868, Aug. 11, 1869, JHH Papers; Angus Brown to HH, Sept. 7, 1911; Billings, "The Hammond Family," HBC Family Papers, SCL.

Hercules, and it has so far revealed my powers of endurance that to quote poor Tom I feel like Miss Horn did after the horse had dragged her, and not only do I feel like a horse had dragged me but rather to use a rough expression like I had been drug backwards through hades by my left heel. (This is not a brown sentence but a very long and black one.) Katharine has I suppose written you at length about the German at Aunt Loula's. Suffice to say it was as usual a success. A large spoke was burned out of the hub last Wednesday night. Ellen Barnes' store which constituted a third of the Beech Island commercial hub has fallen with all its contents a victim to the hungry flames. Loss one hundred dollars (100.00). I met a Miss More at the theater (the Beech Island theater) who was certainly very fascinating if not very beautiful. She gave me a most cordial invitation to come up and go with her rowing on the Christal bosom of the noble Savannah. Can you say any thing in favour of her pedigree? Father suggests that my acquaintance be limited with Miss More as he does not happen to have encountered the name of her great-grandfather in any stray scientific journal. Miss More's father was a steamboat captain. He lived on Bay street and was known as Cannada More. Father says his only recollection of Cannada M. was that he swindled grandfather out of three thousand dollars. I say confound the three thousand dollars so that Miss More can chat with me pleasantly for two hours. When Father said I had better postpone my visit, I got Hatie Ganahl [3] to write her some mendacious note saying I was sick. I enclose her answer.

My financial embarrassments passeth all understanding. I the "Nabob," the "Capitalist," the "Walking Bank" am "broke." My creditors pursue me and though I tell them you owe me twenty one and a half dollars they abate not their "Clamours." I promised to pay George Landrum seven dollars and a half for his dress coat, and when I dance in it every stitch whispers tauntingly "Seven Dollars and a Half." If you will enclose me three dollars and seventy five cents ($3.75) (not as a partial payment but as a free gratis endowment) I will feel my heart palpitate freer. I will then torture Father with unmitigating entreaties until he

---

3. Hattie Ganahl of Augusta went to New York in the 1890s to become an actress. She had no success and was "only on the fringe of the stage." She returned home and became a journalist with *The Augusta Chronicle*. MS vol. bd., 1927-n.d., "Myself and Family"; MS vol. bd., 1952–1957, "Billings move to Redcliffe from New York," John Shaw Billings Scrapbook Collection, SCL.

gives me the other $3.75. Uncle Tom is much better.[4] How did you like Miss White? I insist on your going to Cambridge with old "Mooney Myers." Please be so good as to give my most formal respects to Miss P. Tell her that even while writing the word respects I sit up as strait as though I had swalered a ram-rod. Even if Miss P. does decline my love I take it for granted that the second lady of the U.S. will not. Allow me to burden your gay thoughts with a brief account of the deplorable condition of my wardrobe. I am reduced to one pair of dress pantaloons and the far famed of old New Yorkers britches. Now the dress pantaloons won't do for a cornfield or a beehive. My occupation, as you well know, demands that my pants be washed at no great intervals. Germans are not danced in the daytime or britches washed at night. So that when I want my old New Yorkers washed, buttoned, patched, and generally renovated I have to retire and draw the draperies of my couch around me. Please make the acquaintance of a clothier before you return. Imagine my kissing you for I must say good night it is one o'clock.

HCH

4. Thomas Cumming, Emily's brother, lived at Redcliffe in the 1880s. Harry Hammond, in a letter to his wife, diagnosed Tom's illness as a "perversion of his digestion by taking spirits in lieu of bread and meat. I think he has got a good scare this time if it will only last him." HH to ECH, May 17, 1885, HBC Family Papers, SCL.

PART III

The Belle
Katharine Hammond

In the mid-1880s, Katharine Fitzsimons Hammond, second daughter of
Harry and Emily, becomes a central figure in the family correspondence. Seven years younger than Julia, she appears in her letters and
photographs as a slightly spoiled but attractive, vivacious, and flirtatious
young woman. Katharine had a steady stream of admirers, several of
whom proposed marriage. Her confidence, energy, restlessness, and numerous friendships frequently carried Katharine away from home. Her
travels helped bring a broader world once more to those at Redcliffe,
but she herself was never able to escape the magnet of home.

Katharine's first major trip took place in 1888 when she was twenty-
one years old. She accompanied Susan Merrick, a tuberculosis victim
living in Aiken,[1] to a health resort in Bethlehem, New Hampshire,
where they stayed all summer. Travel to Northern summer resorts had
been an accessory of wealthy planter life in ante-bellum times, but
times were different now and Katharine went North as an all-expenses-
paid nurse-companion for the ailing Susan. Though Katharine, through
her letters to Redcliffe, offered her family a wider view, she wrote fret-
fully of missing home and of unappealing Yankees. She repeated the
trip in 1889 and had much the same reaction. Much more to her liking
was a trip during the Christmas season of 1889–1890 to Charleston—

---

1. Aiken with its warm and dry air had been a health spa for consumptives since before the Civil
War. Amory Coffin and W.H. Geddings, *Aiken: Or Climate and Cure* (Charleston: Walker, Evans
and Cogswell Printers, 1869); Paul H. Hayne, "Aiken, South Carolina," *Appleton's Journal* (Dec.
2, 1871), pp. 623–26.

her debut, so to speak, in Charlestonian plantation society, though her place in it was always rather tenuous. She attended the exclusive and glittering St. Cecilia ball and went riding on the Battery with Charleston beaux bearing aristocratic names.[2] No serious romance came of these outings, but she loved the whirl of society. Local suitors such as Jerome Fair continued to come and go. In May 1891, Parker Jordan, a banker from Greenwood, South Carolina, declared his love for Katharine, and her stinging rebuff stirred his surprised response that he thought he was more than just a "ball-room acquaintance."[3] Jordan hung around for several years as "her friend forever," but Katharine's affections had become engaged by a Philadelphian named Arthur Earle—a tubercular young man who had come South for his health and held for a time a supervisor's job in an Augusta mill. Katharine came to care very much for this handsome, soft-spoken, easy-mannered romantic, and she probably would have married him had her family not objected so strongly. Harry Hammond, playing on his daughter's emotional commitment to Earle and on her bent for nursing, convinced her to enter Johns Hopkins nursing school early in 1893—the better to nurse Earle.

Arthur returned home to Philadelphia to establish himself in business so that he could marry Katharine, but the depression of 1893 and his continued poor health combined to wither Earle's prospects and he became a shipping clerk "in a dingy little office writing in dingy books."[4]

Katharine, now at Johns Hopkins, wrote daily letters to Redcliffe filled with doubts that she could survive her probationary period as a student nurse and describing the day-to-day routine of nurses' training. Harry dreamt of his daughter becoming a doctor and wrote her frequently in hopes of bolstering her spirits and perhaps his own. Her work, he acknowledged, might now seem dreary, but it was work that could lead to her becoming independent. "I don't mean independent as to money, but independent as to interests in life."[5]

In the early months at school, Katharine's feelings for Arthur remained intense, and in April she wrote her mother, "I don't want any-

2. HBC Family Papers, Dec. 1889–Jan. 30, 1890, passim, SCL.
3. D.W.P. Jordan to Katharine Hammond, May 30, 1891, ibid.
4. Arthur Earle to Katharine Hammond, March 9 and 10, 1893, ibid.
5. HH to Katharine Hammond, March 23, 1893, ibid.

thing but to marry Mr. Earle." By July, however, she informed her family that "Dr. Billings and I are getting extremely chummy."[6]

Dr. John Sedgwick Billings, a resident physician at Johns Hopkins and a dashing, lively, good-looking man, was attracted by Nurse Hammond on his ward rounds. His credentials and prospects were considerably more favorable than those of most of his predecessors. John Shaw Billings, John Sedgwick's father, was a surgeon in the Union army during the Civil War. In the postwar years he built up the Army's medical library and he founded the *Index Catalogue* and the *Index Medicus*. Both indexes advanced dramatically the efficiency of medical research and practice. He served also as chief consultant on the building of Johns Hopkins Hospital. After his retirement from the service in 1895, he became the first Director of the New York Public Library, a position he held until his death. When he died in 1913, he left an estate of $200,000.

His son John Sedgwick, an undergraduate at Johns Hopkins, received his medical degree at the University of Pennsylvania in 1892 when he was only twenty-two years old. Soon after he and Katharine met, he was helping her with her classwork and in her letters home she was calling him "B.B." (Beautiful Boy). From the summer of '93 to that of '94 their mutual attraction deepened, and before long Arthur was out of the picture. In spite of her growing attachment to John, Katharine was perpetually homesick for Redcliffe and her family, doubted her ability to graduate with her class, and at times found nursing in the wards of an urban hospital drudgery. It amazed everyone at home that she stuck it out as long as she did. In August 1894, after seventeen months of training and just six months short of graduation, Katharine went home, ostensibly on her annual leave, and never returned. John, asked to stay on for another year at Hopkins, declined because, he wrote, "this place will be a purgatory to me after you are gone."[7]

Back at Redcliffe Katharine filled her days with part-time nursing. In June 1895, she looked after the dying Mrs. S.H. Hardeman, wife of Judge Hardeman of Washington, Georgia. Their son Frank, a cotton factor, fell in love with his mother's nurse, broke his engagement in the

6. Katharine Hammond to ECH, April 15 and July 10, 1893, ibid.
7. John Sedgwick Billings to Katharine Hammond, July 8, 1894, ibid.

hopes of winning the charming Miss Hammond, but in the end lost her attention. By September 1895, she was in Summerville just outside of Augusta nursing Jessie Scott, daughter of Thomas K. Scott of New York, and in February 1896, she looked after a cousin, Fanny Fitzsimons, in Columbia. For over two years John wrote love letters pouring out his feelings for her, and related to her the life of a neophyte New York City doctor in search of rich patients and appointments to first-rate clinics. Katharine replied infrequently and guarded her own feelings. Their correspondence at times was stormy.[8] She suggested again and again that he forget her but never quite let him do so. In one final attempt to convince her to marry him, he came to Redcliffe in September 1896; her guard collapsed and they became engaged.

Katharine Hammond's acceptance of John Billings's proposal was in part the culmination of a selection process in which a flirtatious young woman rejected one male suitor after another until the one with the most force and financial and social prospects was permitted to save her from spinsterhood. Late nineteenth-century American society forced women to play such roles, and Katharine played hers well. She was, however, more complex than this loose-fitting stereotype suggests. The end of Julia's romance with William Woolsey in 1892, which had almost culminated in marriage, left the oldest Hammond daughter still searching for love and regretting very deeply the final negative outcome. Katharine would hardly have been unaware of her sister's regrets. Harry Hammond's dream that his daughters might somehow become part of the world he had experienced in those carefree days when he toured Europe and studied at the University of Pennsylvania and Harvard also may have helped to shape his daughter's choice. Like other intelligent women of her time, Katharine had come to sense that marriage meant the end of that independence which she had sought. Although Katharine found many satisfactions in nursing, this alternative was not enough for the young woman whose personal charms and devoted family had accustomed her to being the center of the scene, not just an adjunct to doctor or patient. The other choice, that of remaining home as the "loyal daughter," had not proven satisfactory for Julia, and, in any case, that role had already been filled by the older sister. Marriage to John, who seemed to be amusing, deeply devoted to her, and willing to accept

8. Thomas K. Scott to Katharine Hammond, Oct. 3, 1895; see also: HBC Family Papers, Sept. 1894–Sept. 1896, passim, SCL.

and even share her love of Redcliffe, must have appeared the best choice.

Yet her visit to John's parents in New York City that winter was not reassuring. Compared to her own people at Redcliffe, whom she considered warm and affectionate, the Billings family she thought cold, dull, and humorless. Nevertheless, when she went back to Redcliffe in January, their wedding date had been set for April 20, 1897. The bride would be thirty years old, the groom twenty-eight.

B.D. LAMAR[1] TO KATHARINE HAMMOND[b]

July, 1885

My Dear Miss Katharine:

After being your devoted admirer for five years, I find that your hold upon my affections strengthens and that my love for you deepens as time goes on. I feel that existence without your love and esteem would indeed be a blank to me. I love you with a love I hope is unselfish. I Offer you my *Heart* and *Hand* in marriage. If you accept my offer I will with the help of God be true to you in word and thought and deed for all time and shall make your happiness the first thought of my life and spare nothing in my power to promote your comfort and welfare. My Dear Miss Katharine, I am as you know no boy and change in my feelings seems impossible. If your heart and better judgement decline my offer, I will bear my misfortune as best I can. Promising that you shall always find a true and willing friend in me no matter what happens, My Dear Miss Katharine, hoping I shall receive a favorable reply,

I remain yours devotedly and in deep suspense,

B.D. Lamar

JEROME W. FAIR[1] TO KATHARINE F. HAMMOND[b]

Beech Island, June 7, 1887

I scarcely know how to answer your letter. I have been struggling with two conflicting emotions ever since I received it, pride and love. If I replied in accordance with the dictates of my heart I would simply say, "Darling I forgive you, because I love you better than I do myself." You perhaps feel sorry for me now, but if the above was my reply, your

---

1. Barney Dunbar Lamar of Beech Island, thirty-one years old in 1885, has the distinction of being Katharine's first documented boyfriend. Katharine, aged eighteen at this time, declined his marriage proposal. He married in 1888 and she married in 1897. John Shaw Billings, comp., "The Lamar Family [Genealogy]," John Shaw Billings Papers, SCL.

---

1. Jerome W. Fair (1864–1890), a beau of Katharine's and a planter at Beech Island, died of tuberculosis on April 4, 1890. Gravestone of Jerome W. Fair, Beech Island Cemetery, South Carolina.

pity would turn to contempt for my weakness. On the other hand if I answer as pride suggests, I would assume an air of insulted dignity and say "I did not care" and perhaps pout a while then thoroughly despise myself and be utterly miserable, and end by loving you, if possible, ten times more than I did before and then perhaps receive worse treatment than ever. Now what am I to do? What intermediate course can I pursue? After thinking of nothing else but our trouble since its occurrence, I have determined to lay my heart bare before you, confess everything, and throw myself on your kindness. First think of my love for you for the last four years. Through all the anger and vicissitudes of that time, have I wavered one fortieth in my devotion to you? Have I not been more than constant? Through all this time have you ever given me any encouragement, or one spark of hope and have I not loved you anyhow? Even more have I not worshipped you? And how must all this end? Am I to be dropped and humiliated for any passing acquaintance and then be expected like a "spaniel to fawn and lick the hand" that has administered the chastisement and is now ready to give another? Heaven forbid!

During the last three years of our acquaintance, we have had several little unpleasantnesses and often I have been very much in fault and each time I have acknowledged it and humbly sued for forgiveness. I know I have a hasty temper, that has nearly been my life's undoing, but at heart I trust I am not so very bad for no one can be utterly wicked that loves another as firmly and devotedly as I do you. I do not flatter myself that you care anything for me, fate is ever too ready to cross my path perversely for me to ever hope you do, but you know we cannot go on this way always (falling out and making up). Now I have been very candid and honest with you, don't you think it but fair for you to be equally candid with me? If you care anything for me tell me so and nothing under heaven could ever induce me to say an unpleasant word to you, but if you don't care anything for me, well we will not discuss the consequence but it will be best for you to tell me so, best for you and best for me. About our present trouble I don't think even you can blame me any. You know you always treat me in just such a way, and I know there is not one person in a hundred but what would have taken offence at your conduct, and if you know the motive that prompted me to insist on seeing you when I did (I mean before you went up stairs), I know you would think better of me, but what's done can't be undone.

It is with hesitancy I give you this letter. I know it must affect a change in our relations to each other, and I fear it may not be for the better, but anyhow read it carefully, think about it very calmly and answer according to the dictates of your heart, and I promise to be governed by your reply.

But whatever your reply may be let me come to see you Sunday evening. I have a letter that has given me lots of trouble, and I want you to dictate a reply. Please do not refuse this for it may be for the last time. And if we must part, "I will pray for courage to remember or favor to forget." In conclusion let me beg of you not to think too harshly of me, and if we see no more of each other, may I hope that in your happy future, if I am so fortunate as to be remembered, it will not be as an acquaintance with whom there is an unpleasant association.

WALTER ASHLEY[1] TO KATHARINE F. HAMMOND[b]

Aiken, October 24, 1887

My dear Miss Katharine:

Your last letter reached me just on the eve of my departure for Atlanta. Now I almost shudder when I even mention the name of the place. I arrived here Friday afternoon completely worn out and feeling as if I had been to an Irish wake. I am now convinced that no matter how well supplied a man may be with food and drink, he must have just a little sleep to sustain him. Of course I saw Grover and the Madam,[2] and was immensely disappointed in them both—He looked like a "ward politician," and she was not one-half as good looking as any picture of her I have ever seen. At the same time I felt very sorry for them while they were on exhibition, and it brought back with considerable force the time when I was on exhibition as "the living skeleton." I think my trip was well worth the money to see the many beautiful women. I did not think there were that many in the world. I did nothing but watch them in spellbound admiration, and of course saw

1. Walter Ashley, an attorney in Aiken, South Carolina, was another one of Katharine's suitors. Walter Ashley Letterhead, July 1889, HBC Family Papers, SCL.

2. President Grover Cleveland and his bride of one year, Frances Folsom Cleveland, came to Atlanta to appear at the Piedmont Exposition. *The Charleston News and Courier*, Oct. 17 and Oct. 19, 1887.

nothing else. I think now your mother's judgment was good in not letting you or Miss Julia go. The ladies had a fearful time, and the men behaved like perfect brutes. I could have blushed a thousand times for the boasted manhood and chivalry of the south. Many men from South Carolina, that I knew, forgot that they had been born and bred in the midst of civilization and gentility. Well, I don't think I shall say anything more about Atlanta, because everything that could be said has been said by the newspapers, and I do not care to rehash their correspondence. I still remain true to my resolution on the Cigarette question, and I really think I have been benefited by it. My neck is about well now from my last batch of boils, but I am unable to say how long I can hope for a cessation of hostilities. I am very glad you like Theophrastus, because the book is looked upon by many of her reviewers as her very poorest. That is, if anything George Eliot has ever written could be called poor. I am afraid that I cannot tell which one of the characters reminds me of your father. You see I have really seen very little of him to be able to judge of his peculiarities, and that would be the only ear-mark for a character in a work of that kind. Yes I think you have some friends who remind me of many of those characters. I would like very much to see the book again to see what you like in it. I am not an advocate, as you well know, of a person starving one's self for the sake of losing a few pounds. And besides I think that when you commence eating again, you register beyond the mark you began at. But I am doing something equally as inconsistent, I am giving up one of the greatest and most bewitching pleasures of my life, cigarette smoking, for the sake of gaining a few pounds of flesh. I am not at all certain that I can get up to the state ball, because I have spent most of my lucre on this last (tear) of mine, and I am now morose and melancholy over the Gala Week in Charleston and the State fair that I may have to give up in consequence. Verily I can say unto you, that the way of the transgressor is hard. I am longing to get to Beech Island again, but I very much fear that it will be quite a long time before I can have that pleasure. I have been dissipating so much of late that it is time that I remained at home some. You are mistaken, when you so strongly insinuate that I am devoted to Aiken. Personally I detest the place, but as long as I live in a town, I deem it my duty to say everything I can in its favor. We have three or four Yankee girls in Aiken now, but I have been away so much and have had so much to do while at home that I have not met them. I have an invitation to call this week but I do not know whether I shall or not. I hope that Kit is perfectly well by this time,[3] and that he did not give away all of his love affairs when he was not himself. *He must* have said something about Miss Black. I don't remember seeing any piece published in any paper on Beech Island. If you have the piece please send it to me. I would like very much to read it. There can be nothing too gushing said about B.I. I have too many pleasant recollections of the place and *some* of its inhabitants. I trust that everyone I know or take any interest in, is now well, and that your time is not taken up, in toto, in visiting sick and taking them. You certainly have had a siege of sickness to contend against. I know the young lady you allude to when you speak of the fair one who froze me, and would never, no never, respond. Do you think I really was very much smitten? I did not know my admiration ever impressed any one. I thought they all took it as you do—as a joke—Do not I pray you, when you glance at these eight closely written pages, say, with a look of sadness on your face, "poor boy, too much prohibition hath driven him mad." It is not the case—Prohibition does not prohibit. I saw your young kid of a beau "Monte" Moses in Atlanta. I did not have a chance to speak to him and ask him how you were. Give my love to your Mother and Miss Julia, and tell Miss Julia I am patiently waiting for the messages she is to send me. Please let me know as soon as you can what you conclude to do about the Columbia Ball.

Very truly yrs.,
Walter Ashley

KATHARINE F. HAMMOND TO JEROME W. FAIR[b]

Bethlehem, N.H., July 20, 1888

My dear Mr. Fair:

Do you know you have only written to me twice since I left home. It makes me feel so funny to think how you begged to write so much oftener than I thought I could answer. While here I am writing before I hear from you at all, and then making mad haste to answer your letters in hope that you may feel bound to write again. I expect I know what is the reason of it too, you have something better to occupy your

---

3. Katharine's younger brother, Christopher Cashel Fitzsimons Hammond, aged seventeen, had broken his back and was confined to bed for over a year.

time. Carrie is the only young person left at home now, is she not, and of course you don't want it to be lonely for her. Oh it is so dull up here, there is nothing in the world to do, but take your meals and sleep. Yes I forget I have a good deal to do for Miss Merrick,[1] but not even enough of that to keep me busy. I ought to get fat living in this way but at present I would do well for Cal's living skeleton. How is old Cal, do you ever see him often? I am so delighted to hear about all the fine crops, and I hear yours are especially good. What is the river doing with all of the rain you are having?[2] For Julia tells me there has been a great deal of rain, and I should think from their letters, that you had not been having any very hot weather. We had only a day or two of warm (I don't mean hot at all) weather, and now it has begun to rain again so I suppose it will be cold when it clears off. This rain is very depressing, and does not add to my cheerfulness. Do you remember the time I told you I did not believe I could cry? Well I will have to go back on my self. I think I have repressed as many tears as there have been rain drops during the night. And it is not easy work to keep them back. I would let them come if I thought they would do me any good, but I think they would only make matters worse, for it would worry Susie [Merrick] then. How egotistical people do get when they are blue, but I always did have a mean way of making you "listen to my tale of woe."

There is but one man in the house, I mean that we know or that seems nice enough to know. He is an ugly little fellow, he dances a good deal with his sister and has danced once with me, and though he is the best dancer here, we would hardly allow him to try to dance at home. How I wish you were here, the music is so good, tho' their

1. Miss Susan Merrick's family, though they were Northerners, had a place in Aiken, South Carolina, for Susan at that time had tuberculosis, and Aiken was considered to be a healthful climate. She had met Katharine in Aiken and had asked Katharine to accompany her North for the summer season where they were to spend several months visiting relatives and staying at a large hotel in the White Mountains. Katharine and Susan remained friends throughout Katharine's lifetime. Susan died August 25, 1946, and a telegram was sent to John Shaw Billings, Katharine's son. He noted that "Mother's oldest friend, Susan Heywood dies." HBC Family Papers, 1887–1890, passim; MS vol. bd., c. 1860–1951. Time Inc. data, p. 163, John Shaw Billings Scrapbook Collection, SCL.
2. Flooding of the Savannah River was a recurrent problem for the Augusta area. The year before this letter was written the Savannah overflowed its banks after ceaseless rain for four days (on July 29, 4.18 inches fell), and in September 1888, the Augusta area suffered one of the worst floods in its history. Richard Henry Lee German, "The Queen City of the Savannah: Augusta, Georgia, During the Urban Progressive Era, 1890–1917" (Ph.D. diss., University of Florida, 1971), pp. 228–29; Jones and Dutcher, Memorial History of Augusta, Georgia, p. 189; George Paterson, The Destructive Freshets and Floods of the Savannah River: Their Causes (Augusta, Georgia: Printed by J.M. Richards, 1889, p. 13.

waltzes are not like or as good as ours, still I think we could have some very good fun dancing. I don't think I am going to have any chance to play tennis or walk. You see Miss Merrick can't do either, and I am with her all the time. I am sorry about the walking, for I had hoped to see a good deal of the mountains in that way, but we will have some very nice times.

What are you reading? or haven't you time for anything of that sort now that you are so busy with your crop. I have not been able to read anything. This sounds very contradictory, when I have just said that I have nothing else to do. But my time is not my own, and I do what Miss Merrick wants to. And there is no chance for reading down stairs, there is such a noise. I am so glad you go up to Redcliffe, do keep it up. Julia told me she had had a ride with you Sunday evening. I wish I had been her. The cloud effects are perfectly beautiful this morning, some of them look as if they had dropped to the ground, and others are wreathing mountains so deeply blue that the clouds look like the thinnest gauze. Mt. Washington is completely covered by clouds this morning, and it is most of the time. These mountains are not ever so rugged as I thought they would be. They are so much bluer and softer than the mountains of N.C. I think I am beginning to like these much better than I thought I should. You don't know what a relief it is to me to write to you. I just go on complaining as much as I want to, and feeling all the time that you will understand me, and not think too much about anything I say to you. Of course I shan't show your letters to Miss Merrick. We had a long talk about you last evening and she said some very nice things about you, and gave me rather a raking. I will explain to you the next time I write. Go to see them at Redcliffe and tell me how they all are and what they are doing, and all about yourself.

Very sincerely,
Katharine Hammond

EMILY C. HAMMOND TO KATHARINE F. HAMMOND[b]

Redcliffe, July 6, 1889

My dear Katharine:

Julia wrote you of our great delight and relief in getting your telegram Thursday. I suppose you could readily realize how constantly you had been in our thoughts, all those days and nights that you were, as Kit kept saying "on the Brimy Deep," and how anxiously and constantly we watched clouds and winds. We see by the papers, that the rain and thunder storms are very severe in the North, and especially in Penn. I hope none of them will be on your line of travel[1] but that you will just have clouds enough to temper the brilliancy of all the views of sky and sea that will greet your eager eyes. Julia says if you had only said "All well" but as I told her all that is said is "I feel splendid" so I know you would not feel even "passablement" if Susie and George[2] were not "splendid" too. I have a little hope that we may hear from you today, if you wrote as I hope you did, a few lines on the ship to be posted as soon as you reached shore. Mr. Woolsey[3] was here last evening. I was sitting on the piazza, coffee cup in hand, watching the clouds and thinking of you, when I heard a buggy stop at the hitching post, and soon saw a seemly form coming up the steps and at first thought it was Jerome, but soon saw it was a more magnificent looking person and at the same moment, heard a familiar voice. "Mrs. Hammond or is it Miss Julia" and lo it was the president [William Walton Woolsey]. As usual he utterly declined our little refreshment, until Julia proposed a cup of coffee when she came out, which offer I heard with fear and trembling supposing as I did I was at the moment imbibing the only

1. In 1889, as in 1888, Katharine Hammond accompanied Susan Merrick North for the summer. They left about July 1, and again their chief residence was a hotel in Bethlehem, New Hampshire. ECH to Susan Merrick, July 12, 1889; Walter Ashley to Katharine Hammond, July 10, 1889, HBC Family Papers, SCL.

2. Susan and George Merrick were brother and sister.

3. William Walton Woolsey figures very prominently in the correspondence from this date until 1909. Woolsey, born in Cleveland, Ohio, in 1843, graduated from Yale and lived in Wisconsin, New York, and South America before moving in 1871 to Aiken, South Carolina, for his health. He was the nephew of Theodore Dwight Woolsey, President of Yale University (1846–1871). Upon Woolsey's arrival in South Carolina he purchased a plantation, Breeze Hill. In 1869 Woolsey had married Katherine Converse and fathered three sons and a daughter. After his wife's death (a possible suicide) in 1888, Woolsey attached himself to the Hammond family at Redcliffe. A romantic relationship between Julia Hammond and Woolsey developed, but when Julia repeatedly refused to leave her mother, Woolsey married Bessie Gammell in 1892. In 1889 he had become president of the Aiken County Loan and Savings Bank and head of the Aiken Board of Trade. After the bank failed in 1894, due to the pressure of low cotton prices coupled with the overexpansion of the institution, Woolsey restricted his activities to cotton production until his death in 1910. Henry C. Hammond, Katharine and Julia's brother, described Woolsey as a big handsome man, bright and witty. Also, he wrote that "he was the baldest man I ever saw, not one hair on his head." HBC Family Papers, Letters of correspondence 1889–1909, passim; John Shaw Billings, comp., "Random Recollections of Henry C. Hammond," HBC Family Papers, SCL; Cyclopedia of Eminent and Representative Men of the Carolinas, 1:375; Randolph Werner, "Hegemony and Conflict: The Political Economy of a Southern Region, Augusta, Georgia, 1865–1895" (Ph.D. diss., University of Virginia, 1977), p. 174 n.

one to be found on the premises. However Julia rustled one up somewhere, and he swallowed it down good or bad. He was equally obdurate
about having his horse put up and spending the night, as he said he
was obliged "to spare his horses by a night ride, as it was to go with the
plough Monday morning" and he only had a minute to stop and was
going to drive thro' to Breeze Hill. It was then nearly nine o'c. and he
sat an hour I suppose, telling us the most thrilling adventures of that
day, two trips to Augusta, thousands of dollars paid in notes in bank,
winning this "one from N.Y." and writing the "other one from Texas"
etc. etc., and of many years ago in Wall Street and the big world generally. Through it all, the same polished debonair gentleman with the
same fluent tongue. Suddenly he sprang up and said he must positively
go as it would even then take him until 2 A.M. to reach home. . . .

Goodbye. I've much more to tell but will keep it for next letter.

ECH

WILLIAM W. WOOLSEY TO KATHARINE F. HAMMOND[b]

Breeze Hill, July 14, 1889

My dear Miss Catherine:

I have called twice at Redcliffe since we parted and found your
Mother and indeed all your people looking very well. They told me of
your safe arrival and of your enjoyment of New York etc. You are now
I suppose on your way to Bethlehem—I think you will be as much
interested in the mountains as in New York which is as sickly and dirty
a city as our Anglo-Saxon civilization has produced. Priest-ridden, ruled
by foreigners, policed by the same—it is a disgrace to America in its
present political condition. It is however most interesting as a collection
of human beings each with his or her separate loves fears and hopes—
and is as full of surprises as a woman. One always wonders what will be
the next caprice—now it is charity and the crop of paupers is carefully
planted and grown. Then it will be style, and while we imprison the
poor we have created we grow wild over red hair or a certain look—
("chic"). Then religion comes to the front and we build a church or
two, heavily mortgaged, engage members of the choir at from thirty to
fifty dollars a Sunday to raise the song of praise for us (they are sure to
give thanks at that price). This constant change makes the city interest-

ing. We are only sure of one thing that there will be some new fancy fashion or caprice, that the old passion will be discarded and a new love installed.

The mountains however are to be trusted. We all know some people who are firm—and steadfast, always to be found where we left them, reliable, and we say of them "they are like a rock." The mountains you will love—New York affects one like brandy—we are carried away under its influence. One is apt to do and say things, at which we afterward are horrified but the mountains point upward—teach reflection: from the time of Moses religion and true patriotism have come from the hills.

Here we are having the same cool weather as when you left. We had a few days of heat and then October in July began again. The coolness suits the crops of corn—and every man you meet has the best in the County. Cotton does not look the right color yet—but is growing fast—the pastures look as green as in Kentucky.

Now I have written you as uninteresting a letter as I well could in my effort to keep it free from gossip and not be "ridiculous" myself— Do you write me one in answer and tell me all about yourself, what you are doing, where you will be, and when you will be there—and don't in the meantime forget.

Yours faithfully,
W.W. Woolsey

CHRISTOPHER CASHEL FITZSIMONS HAMMOND[1] TO KATHARINE F. HAMMOND[b]

Beech Island, July 14, 1889
Dear Katharine:

Sister has just received your letter from Holyoke, saying that you have not received any letters from home in some time. Well they write to you morning, noon, and night. I have my ink out all the time. I saw Sister writing to you at the waste way the other day. I don't think there is any thing left for me to tell, but about Cotton seed. I have been promoted, I think, in that business. You remember when you left, I

---

1. At this time Kit was nineteen years old and living at home.

was very busy building a seed house, at Cathwood.[2] Well since then, I have been putting up a pair of scales. The mill was to send me a man to do this work, but they concluded to try and see what I could do, at putting them up. I was to go to C. today, and put them up but had a slight cold, and could not go. I suppose Mother wrote you about Caz's and Frank Miller's[3] trip to the mill, and Frank M's inquiry, as to how many Cotton crops we grow in a year? The Lawyer [their brother Henry C. Hammond] left today to continue his brilliant career at the Augusta bar. He says he is a pauper now, but is going into an office, where three more of these animals live. Jerome was here last night, he has a very fine crop. Well the next thing after Cotton seed is Miss Eve,[4] she, as you know, is at Bay Point. I have not heard from her myself, but Grandmother heard that after one night in the tents, they had to get a house. They have the same house which Aunt Loula staid in down there. How did you like the bathing at Manhattan Beach? Aunt Loula and Kate[5] are to start tomorrow. Holyoke must be beautiful, did you take the drive which George was speaking of when he was here.

We had a big day of church yesterday, everybody except Brooks, and Celia, and Aunt Sallie,[6] was there. Mother and Sister have been very busy writing to you and they are almost as bad about the mail as myself. Father and Alf[7] have been to the plantation almost every day since you left.

2. Cathwood, part of Harry Hammond's land holdings, originally had been called Cedar Grove Plantation. MS vol. bd., 1927-n.d. "Myself and Family," John Shaw Billings Scrapbook Collection, SCL.

3. Caz is Paul Cazenove Lamar, Kit's first cousin, and Frank Miller is Maria Lamar's suitor whom she married in 1890. JBH to Katharine Hammond, July 12, 1889; HH to Katharine Hammond, Nov. 14, 1890; Henry C. Hammond to Katharine Hammond, Dec. 1890, HBC Family Papers, SCL.

4. Catherine Fitzsimons Eve, their first cousin, eldest child of Elizabeth Hammond and William Raiford Eve, was born September 15, 1872. Billings, Descendants of Hammond, p. 11.

5. Loula C. Hammond, the widow of Paul Fitzsimons Hammond, and Kate Gregg Hammond, her youngest child (nineteen years old at this time), went to Huntsville, Alabama to visit relatives on an extended holiday. Ibid., p. 5; LCH to JBH, Aug. 3, 1889; LCH to ECH, Sept. 2, 1889, HBC Family Papers, SCL; LCH to Virginia Clay-Clopton, Sept. 12, 1889, Clement Claiborne Clay Papers, Duke.

6. Brooks, Celia, and Aunt Sallie were servants at Redcliffe. In family letters, Brooks is referred to as Redcliffe's yard man; Celia helped inside the house and later served briefly as a baby nurse to John Shaw Billings, and Aunt Sallie was the cook and in charge of the kitchen help. Photograph Album, 1741–1955, HBC Family Papers; MP vol. bd., c. 1875–1912. Earliest pictures of John Shaw Billings; MS vol. bd., 1855–1908. Autobiographical account of "the early life of John Shaw Billings II," John Shaw Billings Scrapbook Collection; HBC Family Papers, 1890–1905, passim, SCL.

7. Alfred Cumming Hammond, Katharine's youngest brother, was sixteen years old in July 1889.

You see this letter is all little pieces, for every thing I start, I think Sister or Mother must have told you, all of this some time ago.

Let me tell you of a better way of making a living than nursing. You just find some rich fellow, and you just talk ginning to him. Now when you find this fellow you let me know, and I will send you some facts which will run everybody out of that State.

Kit's ginnery has declared a 40 per cent dividend. He is making so much, that he is thinking of stopping work. Give my love to Miss Merrick, and tell her I am so very glad to hear how well she has been.

Yours truly,
C.C.F. Hammond

KATHARINE F. HAMMOND TO JEROME W. FAIR[b]

Bethlehem, July 15, 1889

My dear Mr. Fair:

Why don't you write to me? Have you forgotten me too and gone back on me? I think if you knew how perfectly heartbroken and lonely I am you certainly would write to me every day. Do you know it is two weeks today, and only one letter from you in all that time. And for a whole week I did not get one line from home. Are you all dead, or, much more reasonable to think, have you all forgotten me? Even the one letter you did write me was rather unsatisfactory, it was so short, and you did not tell me anything about yourself or anybody else. Our stay in New York was most pleasant, but very damaging to our purses, and my ankle. But don't say anything about it, for I have not mentioned it to them at home, and am getting on very well now so it is no use to worry them about it. So you take care and don't say anything about it. Our visit to Holyoke was delightful, but short. The weather was so bad Susie could not stand it for more than two days. It was the loveliest place I ever saw, and all of her family are almost as nice as she and George. So you see I continue in my devotion to the whole Merrick family. Don't you think me foolish? Well I think I am the greatest fool I ever knew, yes just that. I have left my own delightful home so warm and bright, and all the delightful people that I love, to come up here in this frozen North where I am so lonely. Now can anything beat that for foolishness. You know I can write to you differently from the way I write to them at home. You won't care how miserable I am, and it would worry Mother and Julia. And I do want somebody to just tell everything to. You know I always did hate the mountains, and this doesn't prove the exception to the rule. I suppose these mountains are very fine, but no mountains have ever come quite up to my expectations, but I must say that these are the best I ever saw. But there is the coldest leaden sky and I don't believe the sun ever shines. When it comes over me that I will have to stay here two months and a half it almost kills me. I have not said anything about the people, for they are simply not worth thinking of. I feel as if I could never know any of them, and I am sure I don't want to. The only good thing here so far is the music, it is perfectly lovely. It plays three times a day. Not much dance music so far, but last night they played the serenade and any amount of pieces just as lovely. There are some girls trying to dance now, and such dancing I never saw, it would make you hoop. How I do wish you were here, what a lovely time we could have. We are sitting around a huge fire with our winter clothes on and even then nearly frozen. You can imagine how I am enjoying it. George left us this morning, and it has made me miserable. He was the best fellow I ever knew, and so good to me while I was sick. I weighed today, and what do you think, I had lost, my weight was only 127. I never was so thin, and never looked so hideous. I am glad you can't see me. It strikes me this letter is the most dull I ever saw, but I have been interrupted immeasurable times. I have written part in my lap and part in the dark so you will have to pardon the whole thing and I will do better next time. Now you must write to me as often as you possibly can. I am so anxious to hear from you. You won't I know say anything about my having been sick and my ankle being hurt. Tell me everything when you write.

Very sincerely,
Katharine Hammond

JEROME W. FAIR TO KATHARINE F. HAMMOND[b]

August 13, 1889

You know it is the hardest thing in the world, to say the right thing to one when any of their relatives die, unless you are a Christian, and to say the wrong thing is worse than to say nothing, so just let me say

I am very sorry for your uncle's death.[1] Will this alter your plans any in the way of coming home sooner? As you have so many pleasures to look forward to in New York, I don't see why you should not make the most of them as you have not had much amusement this summer, and it promises to be unusually dull here this winter. Doesn't this strike you as being the most unselfish advice you ever heard when I am just crazy to see you.

Let me tell you, you do me a very great injustice, and make a sad mistake when you think I am in love with Miss Black, and I beg you will be so kind as to tell me who told you, if you won't tell me please say to them, that the smart way to get to heaven is to tell the truth here below.

Miss Black[2] is very charming and nice, but I have known you too long to be in love with her or any one else. And here let me ask you, do you think it would be strange if I were to fall in love with someone? I have, as you know, been desperately and constantly in love with you since my earliest recollections, and, never, no, not once, have you given me any hope or the slightest encouragement: Does it never occur to you that such love as this might in time consume itself in air of despair? Or do you think "that the heart that truly loves, loves on to the close." I am sorely tempted to take you at your word and write you pages of local matters, and about local celebrities, but to do this would be so stupid and dull I know you would feel quite justified to take dire vengeance on me at some future time. You must not expect my letters to be specially good or interesting, as I write three times to your once. That is answer each of your letters three times, so if you will write to me oftener I will promise to do better.

Yours as ever,

J.W.F.

1. The letter must be misdated; Thomas Cumming, brother of Emily C. Hammond, died on September 11, 1889, at Redcliffe. William W. Woolsey to Katharine F. Hammond, Sept. 11, 1889, HBC Family Papers, SCL; Wood, A *Northern Daughter*, p. 106.

2. Augusta Georgeanna Kirkland Black (Gussie Black), the daughter of Georgia Bryan and George Robison Black, was born on August 9, 1865. Gussie's mother died when she was six years old, and her father married Nellie Peters. Miss Black attended Mrs. Ballard's school in Atlanta from 1881 to 1883, and "spent much time thereafter visiting around among her friends and relatives." In 1889 she met Peyton L. Wade, who was studying law. They were married on April 13, 1895, in Atlanta. Their only child, Frederica Washburn Wade, was born on September 11, 1901. Frederica married John Shaw Billings (Katharine's son) in 1924. Gussie, who lived with Frederica and John Shaw Billings for many years, died on May 5, 1938. MS vol. bd., 1908–1962. Genealogical data re the Black . . . families, John Shaw Billings Scrapbook Collection, SCL.

WILLIAM W. WOOLSEY TO JULIA B. HAMMOND[b]

Aiken, September 3, 1890

My Darling:

I have already asked you to marry me and you have refused to leave your Mother—

I shall wait and see if I cannot overcome that objection—hoping that you will become reconciled to a parting which puts so short a space between you.

In the meantime you have no more devoted friend and lover than your

W.W. Woolsey

HARRY HAMMOND TO KATHARINE F. HAMMOND[b]

Beech Island, January 6, 1891

My Dear Katharine:

I just drop you a line to say, what I thought I had said at first and what I am sure I have asked others writing to you to say at least half a dozen times, that you are to use the money for periodicals to defray your own personal expenses. These of course are greater in consequence of your prolonged stay and if the sum referred to is not enough to see you home[1] let me know and we will try to help you. As to the periodicals, Westermann writes me all the Booksellers are in a ring not to allow club rates so I will have to go back to some of the old agencies which used to send me my papers whose catalogues I have recently received offering me the same terms.

There are literally no incidents here worth jotting down. We have had a very quiet Xmas.[2] Not a glass of wine a nut or raisin or bit of

1. Katharine made a three-month visit to Dr. and Mrs. Charles Henry Hall at 157 Montague Street in Brooklyn, New York from mid-October 1890 to mid-January 1891. Charles Hall, originally from Augusta, had married in 1848 Annie Maria Cumming, Emily Hammond's older sister. Although Annie Maria died in 1855, the Cumming family remained close to Reverend Hall and his family. Dr. Hall died in 1895 at the age of seventy-four. Letters in HBC Family Papers, passim; Photograph Album, 1741–1955, HBC Family Papers, SCL.

2. Katharine Hubbell Cumming of Connecticut, as a young bride of Joseph Bryan Cumming of Augusta, Georgia, recorded that Christmas Day among the Cumming family was depressing "as

cake. Whist nearly every night and no company not even Henry Cumming until Saturday night when he, H.C.H., and Mr. Woolsey fell in
on us. The first I sent to town Sunday evening and Mr. W returned to
Aiken yesterday at the same hour I went to the Ferry to meet your
Uncle Alfred[3] who is here for a day or two and as Kate Gregg is to
come over and sing for him tonight we are very gay once more. Kit was
on the pony all day yesterday at his wood hauling at Cathwood, returned about sundown, took another horse, caught the train to Augusta,
went to the Theatre, slept in town, got here to breakfast, took horse
again, and is out looking after the wood he's hauling to the Beech Island
Depot. Alf is now sleeping for twelve o'clock. His horn blew at 6 this
morning. Peter is off and he is keeping up the stable for the week with
the help of Brooks[4] who is once more working very happily with us.
Peter is slightly crazy I believe, but he says he will come in next week
as soon as he finishes building a small methodist church (7 members)
on town creek of which he hopes and believes he is to be pastor. Milly
and John have left Mother for Mr. Davis's service. They went off in
many a wagon load with a hog, an extra bale of cotton, all the children,
and Old Ginny in the rear with a large looking glass under her arm. I
expressed the hope to her that every time she looked into it she might
look prettier and prettier and so regain the errant affections of old
Moses. Of course your Grandmother is very much broken up by this
but she is very plucky and I trust she may soon be accommodated with
other servitors. . . .

The General [Woolsey] and Julia are going to drive and I want to
send my letter by them. All are well.

Very affectionately,

Harry Hammond

---

his mother being a Presbyterian, she had never observed the day in any way, excepting by giving
it up to the servants for their pleasure and having a cold dinner." Apparently Emily Hammond
continued her mother's solemn treatment of Christmas, for her family's Christmas letters all contain comments on the lack of celebration of the day. When Katharine Hammond Billings in 1897
sent presents from her home in New York City to her family at Redcliffe she received this stern
reply: "You know we don't like Christmas presents won't give any or accept any." Wood, A Northern Daughter, p. 7; JBH to Katharine Hammond Billings, Dec. 1897, HBC Family Papers, SCL.
   3. Alfred Cumming (1829–1910), the first son of Julia Bryan and Henry Harford Cumming,
was the eldest brother of Emily C. Hammond. Wood, A Northern Daughter, p. 108.
   4. Peter was the stableman at Redcliffe and Brooks, as already cited, was the yardman.

WILLIAM W. WOOLSEY TO JULIA B. HAMMOND[b]

Aiken, August 27, 1891

Julia darling:

This will seem a very short love letter. I have written and destroyed a longer one.

You know now Darling that I love you and that my whole effort is to so arrange my affairs as to move this Fall if possible—I do not ask you to engage yourself to me in form because in case my affairs miscarry I will not injure you; but if all goes well and you will be my wife, we will marry soon and I will do my best to make you as happy as you ought to be—

You are my choice in all the world Julia and if you care for me we can be very happy together.

How I regretted not being able to see you last night—I hope tonight will make amends.

There is one social complication in my life which will I think be out of the way before Oct. That was one of the reasons that I did not mean to speak until then. But fate arranged otherwise—

Yours with love,
W.W. Woolsey

WILLIAM W. WOOLSEY TO JULIA B. HAMMOND[b]

Aiken, March 12, 1892

Dear Miss Julia:

You have been in my confidence in this matter so to you rather than to your Mother I write to announce my engagement to Miss Bessie Gammell—[1] I know that I will have the kind wishes of all my friends at Redcliffe. I only hope that life may so arrange itself that you may all

1. Evidently Woolsey failed to eliminate "the one social complication" in his life. On April 6, 1892, Bessie Gammell, daughter of Marie Ancrum and William Gammell of Charleston and Savannah, married William Walton Woolsey. They had two daughters—Marie and Elsa. Bessie Gammell Woolsey died in Florida in 1951. John Shaw Billings, comp., "Woolsey Genealogy," Loose Papers, John Shaw Billings Papers, SCL.

know her and like her. Your escape from death was most fortunate and I hope the wounds have by now healed and the lameness is gone.

I shall hope to see Ego[2] and his growing beauty soon. My hand which was badly hurt has prevented earlier letter writing—

With kindest regards to all, I remain,

Yours sincerely,
W.W. Woolsey

[Julia's notation:] How swiftly in the succession of our days the supreme crisis in our individual fortunes, or that which seemed so, drifted away as we take the next day's toil and the next and the next. How it drifts to a diminished position in the sum of things, takes at last its rightful place, holds no longer undue eminence in the milestones of our life's journey.

> "A sigh too much or a kiss too long
> A moan and a little weeping rain
> And life will never be the same again."[3]

JULIA B. HAMMOND TO WILLIAM W. WOOLSEY[b1]

Redcliffe, June 4, 1892

This morning a new phase came to me. I felt it in the night and tried to sleep through it, but when I waked it swept over me like an irresistible flood, it was remembering. One scene came back to me, do you remember one hot day as we were riding through that thickest forest, just before you get to that cool, dark, dash of water, we were going to sail over in that old boat, I got a gnat in my eye to my great discomfort, and you tried to get it out? Tried but did not succeed, until you

2. Ego was the Hammonds' collie who died in 1901. MP vol. bd., c. 1875–1912. Earliest pictures of John Shaw Billings, John Shaw Billings Scrapbook Collection, SCL.

3. Julia misquotes the Scottish author, George MacDonald (1824–1905), who wrote in *Phantastes* (1858):

> Alas, how easily things go wrong!
> A sigh too much, a kiss too long,
> And there follows a mist and a weeping rain,
> And life is never the same again.

1. This letter is one of many such letters that Julia wrote after Woolsey's marriage but never sent. HBC Family Papers, 1892–1898, passim, SCL.

fell into quite a little despair, and said, "Ah you should not have such an old lover who cannot even see how to get a gnat out of your eye!" I teased you then about being old but it caused even my hurt eye to look at the handsome fresh face before me that I loved so much and that stood for me for so much that was bright and courageous in this sad world. For weeks I have been in a very different frame of mind, each morning as I got up I looked out on the dear hills I have known always and could have shouted for joy that I was not looking over certain level fields, and at night I have hugged myself as I lay down on my bed and felt I was free. I felt I was not made for passionate love, and loved Mother, and loving the children more was able to be more patient with them. I have been very loyal to you, for Mother says, she loves you, and Father is crazy to see you. Do you remember the day we went into the depths of the swamp where the great big water-oaks stretched on every hand, no under brush but the sand palmetto, and you said then how if the events that have happened did come to pass I should never see you again? That was a right resolution on your part. Tho' I do not feel it in me for a moment to soften to anything except the past, still I would rather it should be so. My goodness, the gibes and ridicule and graver things I have heard heaped on you of late, you would get over some of your fears of being loved as an ideal if you knew this. You are happy. Bon Jour.

July 23rd. No! No!! No!!! Yes I will, sweet, once more say it not to anyone for I would as soon take out my physical heart and hand it over to be examined as to turn over these pages to anyone to read. I write them to put things that harass me out of mind, and then the inevitable human longing to justify yourself, to have the sympathy of other human beings. But I wish to record myself as not blaming you in the least. I try not to allow myself to dwell morbidly on my ridiculous folly in believing for one moment that you cared for me, as I again and again go over our years of intercourse. I do not find one place where you gave me grounds for thinking such a thing, you only accepted my devotion. There was nothing wrong in your doing this, it was perfectly honorable, I believe this, it is not sarcasm. I am glad you are out of my life and only trust I will never want you back again. I know all your faults even better than the lovable, lovely things about you. I do not want to feel bitter, if I can only make of this dead self of mine a stepping stone to higher sympathy with others.

ISABEL HAMPTON[1] TO KATHARINE F. HAMMOND[b]

Johns Hopkins Hospital
Training School for Nurses[2]
Baltimore, January 23, 1893

Dear Madam:

Your application is accepted, and your appointment to enter the School is fixed for the Spring term, the exact date sent later. It will be necessary to have two plainly made wash dresses, four large white aprons, two bags for soiled clothes, a good supply of plain under-clothing, and every article clearly marked on the bands.*

Kindly let me know if I may rely upon your coming at the above date, and oblige.

Yours truly,
I. A. Hampton, Supt.

* If teeth are in need of attention have them put in order before coming.

ISABEL HAMPTON TO KATHARINE F. HAMMOND[b]

The Johns Hopkins Hospital
Training School for Nurses
Baltimore, February 21, 1893

My dear Miss Hammond:

Your appointment is made for Tuesday March 7th. Kindly let me know if I may rely upon your being at the School that date.

Yours faithfully,
Isabel Hampton

1. Isabel Hampton, Superintendent of the Training School at Johns Hopkins, was born in Welland, Ontario, in 1860. She graduated from Bellevue Hospital School of Nursing in 1883. Before going to Johns Hopkins she served in a similar post at the Illinois Training School. Harry Hammond described her in 1893 as a woman in black silk, "almost as awkward as I am though a tall stately ladylike person of 35–40." HH to ECH, March 8, 1893, HBC Family Papers, SCL; Ethel Johns and Blanche Pfefferkorn, *The Johns Hopkins Hospital School of Nursing, 1889–1949* (Baltimore: Johns Hopkins Press, 1954), pp. 37–62.

2. Johns Hopkins, in his will in 1873, arranged for the funding of a nurses' training school in addition to the Hospital. The school opened in October 1889. Johns and Pfefferkorn, *The Johns Hopkins School of Nursing*, pp. 8–52.

KATHARINE F. HAMMOND TO EMILY C. HAMMOND[b]

Johns Hopkins Hospital
Baltimore, March 7, 1893

My own darling Mother:

Here I am at last—and with my mind and heart so full of a thousand different feelings—that I am afraid—I cannot write of one of them. But this one is perfectly clear—that I love you—that I long for you— that I shall pray night and day that when we meet all may be unchanged, and that I may not bring you any more pain!

Father left me after the first few minutes. Every thing is so grand and magnificent that it does not seem possible for me to have anything to do with it. . . . What do you think is in the center table, there is the most gorgeous and magnificent basket of flowers—roses of every kind—hyacinths—and great masses of violets. It was the first thing I heard when I came in—that there were flowers for Miss Hammond—I believe that was the reason the man let me in—so that I might get the flowers. Miss Hampton is not here. Of course you can guess who these flowers are from—just one kind line from Mr. Jordan,[1] without any name.

I am to go on duty at half past seven in the morning. Father will come to see me at dinner time from 12 to 1—and then I may have two hours in the afternoon with him. I have had a bath—the bath room is just across the hall and after the journey and excitement, I am pretty tired. So with love and good night to you and Julia and the boys.

Devotedly,
Katharine

P.S.   I should have had more time for writing if I had not had so much company.

1. D.A. Parker Jordan (1851–1901), called "DAP" or "Parker," was a Greenwood, South Carolina banker and industrialist who courted Katharine for several years. Though fifteen years her senior, Jordan proposed several times, was turned down, and finally gave up. In one of his last love letters to Katharine, Parker wrote, "I loved too well to keep a friend." D.A. Parker Jordan to Katharine Hammond, July 29, 1895, HBC Family Papers, SCL; *The Greenwood Index*, Dec. 12, 1901; J.C. Garlington, *Men of the Time: Sketches of Living Notables: A Biographical Encyclopedia of Contemporaneous South Carolina Leaders* (Spartanburg, South Carolina: Garlington Publishing Co., 1902), p. 237.

HARRY HAMMOND TO EMILY C. HAMMOND[b]

Baltimore, Md., March 7, 1893

Dear Emmy:

We got in about 12 hours late at about 6 P.M. Katharine insisted on going at once to the Hospital so we put her trunk on a hack and traveled off over the cobblestones up hill and down hill, ever so many turnings, no stores, tenement buildings, few people, quiet streets, plenty of houses, 1¼ miles the driver said, and came upon a magnificent brick building with a cupola which struck awe into Katharine's heart. Walked up several broad flights of stone steps and entered a spacious hall with a window in the center like St. Paul's[1] with several lofty galleries circling above into aerial heights with high corridors leading right and left. A space was fenced off for an office on one side. There was no one in it and the whole place looked lonely. Presently a meek looking individual came along in a great hurry and ran against a white capped young woman in a white dress who was seeking him. When she was through her business we asked for Miss [Isabel] Hampton and were informed she was out of town but that he would call Miss Bock,[2] the assistant. He flew about noiselessly over the marble floor and we waylaid him and again pressed for a sight of Miss Bock and explained our business, and asked if a telegram Katharine had made me send Miss Hampton had been received. Ah well he said I expect you are the Miss Hammond for whom some flowers were sent here this evening and perhaps you had better go at once to the Training School and pointed the way across the rotunda to the back of the building and showing us into a long low passage, well lit, directed us to a door at the far end and told us to ring a bell and ask for Miss Bock. We did so and came to another large hall where some woman directed us to a parlor. Here Katharine gave a cry of great joy at seeing on the walls the familiar engravings of Raphael's

1. Harry's reference was to St. Paul's in Augusta, an Episcopal church built in 1818. A. Ray Rowland, ed., *Historical Markers of Richmond County, Georgia*, rev. ed. (Augusta: The Richmond County Historical Society, 1971), pp. 18–19.

2. Harry Hammond thought he heard her name pronounced Bock, but in fact it was Lavinia Dock. She became Miss Hampton's assistant in 1890. Like Miss Hampton, Miss Dock graduated from the Bellevue School of Nursing. At the end of 1893 she was appointed superintendent of the Illinois Training School. Johns and Pfefferkorn, *The Johns Hopkins School of Nursing*, pp. 75–94.

loggia,[3] which she declared she could kiss they looked so homelike. After a few minutes Miss Bock came in. We bowed and were asked to be seated. Our interview was brief. She said it was all right, Katharine would stay. I then asked when I could see Katharine tomorrow. She inquired of Katharine if she were not going to work tomorrow. On her affirmative reply Miss Bock said I had better call about dinner time, say between 12 and 1—and so I left and came to this hotel, eat dinner, and am so hot and tired that I don't know if you can understand what I have written, which I believe is perhaps the gist so far of our journey. Tomorrow I will call on Mr. Miles[4] and Middleton[5] and go to see Katharine, when I will be able to advise you more fully as to how things are, and then home as quick as I can.

Yours affectionately,
Harry Hammond

EMILY C. HAMMOND TO KATHARINE F. HAMMOND[b]

Redcliffe, March 7, 1893

My darling Child:

Nothing has happened since you left us, but that we have missed you so endlessly that I need not begin to tell you of it. I hope you have forgiven me for breaking down as I did yesterday and thus making our parting harder. I thought I would have kept up better but at last my courage failed as I did not think it would. I have had such a wonderful

3. James Henry Hammond brought back from his European trip "30 large and very fine engravings," among which were presumably those referred to here. JHH, Diary of European Trip 1836–1837, vol. I., Aug. 7, 1836–April 7, 1837, Feb. 22, 1837, JHH Papers, SCL.

4. Dr. Francis T. Miles of Charleston held the chair of anatomy in the medical department at the University of Maryland. Harry Hammond sought out Miles to inquire about the nurses' training school. Harry wrote to his wife that Miles "knew nothing in the world about Johns Hopkins Training School." He supposed the reason for Miles's ignorance was that the University of Maryland also had a nurses' training program and "it is a point of professional honor to ignore all other schools." HH to ECH, March 8, 1893, HBC Family Papers, SCL.

5. John Izard Middleton, a Charlestonian, born on Feb. 16, 1834, and a classmate of Harry's at South Carolina College, had been living in Baltimore since the end of the Civil War, and had married Harriett Sterrett on April 26, 1866. Harry's hope had been to elicit information from both Miles and Middleton on Johns Hopkins nurses' training school. However, he learned from Miles that Middleton had taken his only daughter who was suffering from tuberculosis to a sanatorium at Summerville, South Carolina. Hammond's comment was, "So I have made pretty much of a water haul as usual, and except for certain usual impressions which may be deceptive, know about as much concerning the Johns Hopkins as when I left home." Ibid.; South Carolina Historical Magazine, 1 (1900), p. 250.

happiness and blessing in having my good and affectionate children in my sight and touch almost unbrokenly for more than thirty years that now the thought of separation is almost unendurable.[1] It is almost death. I know I could stand it better if it were one of the boys whose business or even pleasure led them away from home for months or years. Much as I should miss them and grieve over giving them up it would not be the pangs that sometimes almost takes my breath away, the overwhelming thought of giving you up, my beloved, beautiful child, my dear, dear little daughter. Everywhere I look I see you. "Katharine arranged this. Katharine made that. She took care of all these things and brought comfort and order to all about her." But I must not distress myself or you with these recollections but rather turn my thoughts to the good and useful work you are going to do, the help you are going to be to so many poor suffering ones and the satisfaction you must feel in such worthy efforts and my pride and pleasure in all that is so excellent and self sacrificing in you and my unspeakable joy at seeing you even for the little time allowed you. Henry very unexpectedly came in a little while ago. He has just come over to see us for an hour or so and I fear I cannot send this by him as I had hoped to do.

Evening in the Library. Henry started back on his horse a little before sunset. Of course he had nothing to tell me of you and your Father, but merely came to cheer us in our loneliness. He and Bryan[2] won their case, that is, the verdict of the Jury was an award of $250.00, instead of $1500.00 as claimed by the plaintiffs. He said the Judge and other friends complimented him on his speech and your Uncle Joe said "You did Bully old fellow" in remembrance of a similar remark made to him by your Uncle Julien, after his maiden speech. Your Uncle Joe wrote me a note today about you which brought many tears to my eyes but also comfort to my soul. You know how great is his gift in saying just the right thing to move and impress those whom he addresses. He was delighted that your Father was with you and everyone says the same thing. I know you and he have gotten on well and pleasantly with each

---

1. Katharine was twenty-six years old when she left home to attend Johns Hopkins.
2. Henry Hammond (1868–1961) and Bryan Cumming (1862–1943) were first cousins and at this time practiced law together. Both young lawyers lived in Augusta with Bryan's parents, Katharine Hubbell and Joseph Bryan Cumming. Wood, A *Northern Daughter*, p. 105; JBH to Katharine F. Hammond, July 19, 1889, HBC Family Papers; MS vol. bd., c. 1860–1951. Time Inc. data, p. 90, John Shaw Billings Scrapbook Collection, SCL.

other. I long for morning which may bring me some news of your trip. Your Grandmother has a bad cold and is a little feverish this evening but sitting up and quite cheerful. "Kit and Kitty"[3] drove to the plantation today. Kit seems much better and will go to Savannah tomorrow. Every day, Warren[4] is up here, he and Alf and Kit absorbed in high fin[ance]. Alf was much disappointed that your Father hurried him off before you started. I say goodnight only to say good morning in another letter tomorrow. Julia and Ego are my faithful guardians at night. Write me about the smallest thing in your new life and surroundings.

Your Mother

HARRY HAMMOND TO KATHARINE F. HAMMOND[b]

Baltimore, March 9, 1893

My Dear Katharine:

The office I inquired at is shut and they tell me here that I do not leave until 9:25 and that I will reach Augusta at 4:30 tomorrow. Just think how short. I don't see why you should not find something to do when you are off duty. The Peabody library I told you of is open from 9 A.M. to 10:30 P.M. That is one resource. Study the guide book and I think there is some place you can go to whenever you have time to go to. They are now changing many of the horse cars to run by a wire cable laid under the street and kept moving all the time by steam power. The driver has a clutch to catch this moving wire when he wants to go and lets go and puts on brakes when he wishes to stop. This will make smoother and faster riding. It will all be fixed by time your Mother comes. It is all nonsense about your not passing your probation[1] suc-

3. Probably "Kitty" was Kate Gregg Hammond, a first cousin of Kit's.

4. Warren, frequently mentioned in the family correspondence, was Benjamin Warren Fair (1867–1929), the younger brother of Jerome Fair. Warren was a farmer and lifetime resident of Beech Island. In 1902, he married into the Hammond family when he wed Sarah Jane Eve whose mother was the former Elizabeth Hammond, the youngest child of James Henry Hammond. *The Aiken Journal and Review*, Sept. 4, 1929; Billings, *Descendants of Hammond*, p. 12.

1. At Johns Hopkins Training School there was a month's probationary period. At the end of this period examinations in reading, penmanship, mathematics, and English dictation were given. Katharine passed the month's probation and signed a formal contract binding herself as a "Pupil Nurse" for two years to Johns Hopkins Hospital. Alfred Cumming to Katharine F. Hammond, April 19, 1893, HBC Family Papers, SCL; Johns and Pfefferkorn, *The Johns Hopkins Hospital School of Nursing*, pp. 37–62.

cessfully. If you don't I will send the Charleston earthquake up here and tumble the whole thing down. But you will, and when you get your diploma you will go into the female medical college here which will be about ready for you, and when you are through at the finest hospital and training school and medical college in the world you will go to New York or London or Paris and become a wealthy Doctoress of Medicine and support us all and pay for the negroes' mules, and sell poor old Joe Danforth a horse on credit and one to Robbin Perry also. Attend all the lectures you can, in and out of the hospital. Try to read the papers a little every day and keep up a good heart and know that all our hearts at home are with you every step you take.

Goodbye,
H.H.

HARRY HAMMOND TO KATHARINE F. HAMMOND[b]

Beech Island, So. Ca., March 23, 1893

My Dear Katharine:

If I had written you recently I would not write today, these coldish damp gray days make one feel dull, and you want some thing bright and cheerful from home. Nevertheless this is the first morning I have dressed without fire since I got back. It is a cold spring. The corn Alf planted before I went to Baltimore is not up yet. The trees are as bare as in mid winter. The rye and now and then a clump of Jessamines with some shivering blooms of peach and pear are the only foreshadowings of spring except Winfield's new straw hat, which I stumbled over just now by Milly's house.[1] Your Grandmother tells me it was pretty much the same 61 years ago the 30th of this month when your narrator was born, the trees then being all covered with snow and ice. It seems too uncommonly lonesome here. Your going has served to start a general stampede. Henry's absence we are used to, and Kit is off again to see about irregularities in his agent's accounts. Kate Hyde[2] is in Athens and Julia has staid of nights with your Grandmother as there is no one

1. Winfield and Milly were long-term servants at Redcliffe. Milly is listed in Harry Hammond's plantation journal as having worked in the fields picking both grapes and cotton. HH Plantation Journal, Dec. 1879–March 26, 1880, HBC Family Papers, SCL.

2. Kate Hyde was Catherine Spann Hyde (1846–1900), the niece of James Henry Hammond. For a fully entry on Kate Hyde see letter of Oct. 17, 1865, note 2.

else but little Betsy and Anne there. The latter is as pretty and silent as a picture but very good and efficient so quiet and self contained and doing her errands with such swiftness and directness that one could imagine she had been "trained." Then we fear we shan't even see Warren [Fair] much for he has drawn money twice on his cotton seed. The Dunbars[3] too are going to sue Kit. Frank [Dunbar] bought two cars of damaged seed from his uncle at Ellenton while Kit was sick, and $80 of his wages were knocked off in consequence. They claim the seed was not damaged, and while Kit had nothing to do with saying they were (that being Mr. Haskell's decision in Savannah) they are going to sue Kit for withholding Frank's wages to make the loss good. In spite of what Henderson[4] says, Kit's proof is all clear, and they will only lose their time and money if they push the case.

I have had poor luck in trying to help you by getting information about your hospital. You know Dr. Miles was so engaged with seriously ill patients that I went five times to see him and wasted thus my short stay in Baltimore. Middleton was away with his sick daughter and writes me she is so ill at Summerville that he can't come to see me as he hoped to do. (He will return however to Baltimore as soon as the weather is warmer.) Mrs. Byrd, you say, has met with an accident so that she can't call on you, and Woolsey, poor fellow, says he didn't write to Mrs. Gilman[5] because he had a toothache. Our world is one big hospital.[6] Lessie[7] is sick in bed (she goes to the surgeons as soon as she is able to drive up). Your Grandmother has had a severe attack and

3. The Frank Dunbar family were neighbors of the Hammonds at Beech Island. U.S. Census Records, State of South Carolina, 1880, Population Schedules, Edgefield County, National Archives Microfilm Publications; Elizabeth DeHuff, *The Family of James Dunbar Our First Dunbar Ancestor in South Carolina* (n.p., 1954), pp. 3–4, 52–53.

4. Probably the reference is to Daniel Sullivan Henderson, a prominent Aiken attorney. Reynolds and Faunt, *Biographical Directory of the Senate of the State of South Carolina*, p. 236.

5. Elizabeth Dwight Woolsey Gilman, sister of William W. Woolsey, was the second wife of Daniel Coit Gilman, first president of Johns Hopkins University (1876–1901). Johns Hopkins University, *Daniel Coit Gilman, First President of the Johns Hopkins University, 1876–1901* (Baltimore: Johns Hopkins Press, 1908), p. 59.

6. In the list of patients, Milly, little Gaspar, Robbin, Binah's Harry, Gussy and Gussy's infant, Brooks, Em, and Binah were all servants at Redcliffe. U.S. Census Records, State of South Carolina, 1880 and 1900, Population Schedules, Hammond Township, Aiken County, National Archives Microfilm Publications; MS vol. bd., 1855–1908. Autobiographical account of "the early life of John Shaw Billings II," John Shaw Billings Scrapbook Collection; Billings, "The Hammond Family"; HH to Katharine Hammond, June 4, 1893; HH Plantation Journal, Dec. 1879–March 26, 1880, HBC Family Papers, SCL.

7. "Lessie," as cited earlier, was Celeste Clay Hammond, the daughter of Loula Comer and Paul Hammond. Billings, *Descendants of Hammond*, p. 5.

looks much worse. This morning she is up and dressed and sewing and I hope will soon be as usual. There is some uneasiness about your Aunt Kate's cough but I think she will be all right with warm weather. Miss Bessie [8] is still a handsome invalid. Milly too is laid up with a bad cold, and Albert Palmer's daughter is cooking for your Grandmother. Tom Davies [9] has boils on the back of his neck so he can't turn his head, and little Gaspar is suffering from the same infliction. Jerome has just sent me a bottle for medicine for rheumatism, and old Robbin says the itch will kill him if I don't do something for him. So it goes. The rest are all well at present. The only complete recoveries are your patient Kate Gregg, [10] who came Monday and is said to weigh 160 lbs, to be delighted with Savannah and full of the best spirits, and my little patient with the dropsy, Binah's Harry. He has shrunk up to half the size he was some weeks since and has gone back to Cathwood [plantation]. How is all this for a hospital ward. I forgot to mention that Gussy's infant is well again after a week's indisposition. Brooks spent last Sunday looking up a nurse for it and came back in triumph with a funereal little person in a black straw hat and black calico who was introduced to me as James' wife's sister-in-law's daughter. So cheerfulness again pervades the Brooks family. Gussy is back in the kitchen, and Em and Binah are ministering to our reduced household. These hospital notes are perhaps not complete but they must suffice for the present. Please tell me how many nurses there are at the Johns Hopkins. How many are living in the home? How many patients are there, about how many to a ward?

Doubtless you have heard all the particulars of Miss Mary's death. [11]

8. Elizabeth (Bessie) Hubbell, the sister of Katharine Hubbell Cumming, was the daughter of Jane Bostwick and Henry Wilson Hubbell. Wood, A *Northern Daughter*, p. 110.

9. A friend of the Hammond family since the 1850s, and a brother-in-law of M.C. Marcellus Hammond, Davies came to live in Beech Island in 1865. Obituary of Thomas Jones Davies, March 29, 1902. Thomas Jones Davies Scrapbook, 1849–1903, SCL.

10. Again, the reference is to Kate Gregg Hammond, the youngest child of Loula Comer and Paul Hammond.

11. Mary Wimberly (1825–1893), originally companion to Mrs. Catherine Fox Spann Hammond (1785–1864), after the war transferred her services to Emily Hammond's mother, Mrs. Julia A. Cumming. (See letters of Oct. 17, 1865, note 1, and June 13, 1871, note 1.) She took charge of the Lamar children when their mother, Maria Cumming Lamar, died in 1873 and even accompanied them to New York. After Mrs. Cumming's death in 1879, Miss Mary returned to Beech Island to live with James Henry's widow, Catherine Fitzsimons Hammond. She had been described as a woman who always "wore black silk, did beautiful sewing and saved her money." When she died in 1893, Emily Hammond wrote that her death "brought a great sadness to us all." ECH to Katharine F. Hammond, March 20, 1893, HBC Family Papers; MS vol. bd., 1927–n.d. "Myself and Family," John Shaw Billings Scrapbook Collection, SCL.

Poor lady, she had been much disturbed during the winter, thinking where she could go in her feeble health to await her final summons, and it came suddenly but not unexpectedly. The last attack came while she was standing at her dressing table and lasted barely 20 minutes. She said to Mrs. Lockhart who came to her assistance that it was useless to do more for her. She knew she was dying, and almost while she spoke, having seated herself in a large rocking chair, she passed away. At her request she was buried by the side of your great grandmother in the Augusta Cemetery. It is the old part of the grounds, a neglected lot with a few simple headstones. Your great grandmother lies at her Mother's feet[12] beside whom rests your great-aunt Eliza, who died a young girl but a tradition of whose goodness and beauty and intelligence still lingers in the family. Besides them are three homeless waifs whom my Grandmother gave home and care to for many long years—Mrs. Jones (daughter of Governor Brunson of Georgia), Uncle Turner, and Miss Mary. When the Dead wake at the last day I trust these three to say things of my Grandmother's goodness to them as pleasing to the Judge of all as many an epitaph on the handsomest monuments in the Cemetery.

I note what you say about the dictionary and will attend to it as soon as you have finally decided to continue where you are. This I consider a matter still open to be determined, and it worries me much that I must leave it entirely to you to decide upon without any help from my judgment. I would feel easier in doing this if you were well over your homesickness. When it comes to the point of making up your mind, try and put this feeling from you, and if you think you are paying too high a price for what you are getting—that is occupation—I hope you will decide to come home and take the chances of getting something else to do. You are doing dreary work—but it is work, honorable work, the hardest thing in the world to find, and work that in the end should make you independent, a still harder thing to be. I don't mean independent as to money, but independent as to interests in life. But even these great gains may be bought at too high a price, and so nobody can tell so well as yourself what the price demanded is. You will—as

12. The widow of Elisha Hammond and mother of James Henry Hammond, Catherine Fox Spann Hammond, died in 1864. She was buried in Magnolia Cemetery in Augusta. Her mother, Elizabeth Fox Turner Spann Clarke, died in Augusta in 1827 at the age of sixty-nine. John Shaw Billings, comp., "Notes on Elizabeth Fox Turner Spann Clarke," HBC Family Papers, SCL.

every one has to in the higher concerns of their fate—have to make the decision for yourself. I don't believe you will give up for lack of pluck. I am rather afraid that you possess that quality to a dangerous degree. Nor do I believe you will give up for lack of ability. Your fears about the lectures and instruction are wholly groundless. I never could write out a lecture, never did, not one medical student in 50 ever does to any purpose, but they find no difficulty in graduating. I was specially interested in physiology when I studied medicine and I give you my word I did not understand 10 sentences of the lectures I listened to the whole winter of my first term. I don't believe the lecturer did either. You have no idea what fools the smartest people are. Go, said a very wise man to his son starting on a tour through the courts of Europe, go, and see by what fools the world is governed. Doctors, Nurses, Divines, Lawyers, Statesmen, Generals, I have known many of them, it is the same with all. Those that succeed and hold high place, primp for the public with an earnestness, a timidity, and a hypocrisy, that would make any woman who paints and pads and powders to be a representative beauty, blush for very shame.

You will never have time to read my letter, and it will, I fear, make you feel dull if you do, which is far from being my wish.

The sun is out. Rain gone. Alf says a long spring drouth. Well still low and muddy.

Yours affectionately,
Harry Hammond

HARRY HAMMOND TO KATHARINE F. HAMMOND[b]

Beech Island, So. Ca., March 25, 1893

My Dear Katharine:

We have had no letter from you today, but as I have just had a note from Mr. Woolsey enclosing a letter from Mrs. Gilman concerning the Hospital, which has given me much satisfaction, I write to tell you about it. I would have preferred to send the letter to you, but Woolsey asked me to return it to him, which I did with thanks. The letter said that the ordeal you were going through was a hard one. There was never any petting or sympathizing where you were, discipline severe and unremitting and duties arduous and often repulsive. But that you were under constant and kindly observation. Miss H. [Hampton] was a large hearted and wise woman, and would always do the right thing. The writer had known girls of your station in life to undertake this vocation, and to be happy and satisfied with it. But they were born for the work, and those not born for it would find it a burden too heavy to bear, the writer herself felt she had not the innate ability to pursue it, honorable as it was. That the only way to know whether one could stand the life, was to try it, and if you found you couldn't no discredit whatever would attach to you for relinquishing it, on the contrary it was creditable to you to have put yourself on trial, and she thought that you and all of us here would never regret your month's experience, if it went no further with you. It was a very friendly and sensible letter, and if I have made you understand its import, I hope you will look at the whole thing from that point of view.

Kit is back rather disappointed at making so little by his winter's work.[1] Maria, Frank, Mrs. Denny, and Henry are here, have had dinner, and are thrumming away on the guitar above me—what chatterers. Henry sent your Uncle Joe's new coachmen (Kelly being still in bed with his fracture) to Maria's this morning with a note. He took Henry's horse, and was thrown, dislocating his shoulder. Henry rode the horse down and will leave him, and pay for the coachman's Doctor. Alf is hauling out compost and was too highly seasoned with that valuable compound to dine with us. I have not seen your Grandmother since yesterday morning, and she was so much better then and has been since, said to be, improving so steadily that it was not necessary for me to see her. Celia Lamar was taken alarmingly ill, but the doctor said it was only Hysteria.[2] Miss Mary left Kate Hyde ⅜ of her estate.[3] The estate amounted to $2,500 and Kate will get about $1000. She returns today. Your Mother and I drove to Silver Bluff yesterday, and were

1. Kit traveled as a seed buyer for the Southern Cotton Oil Company. During the spring and summer he lived at home at Redcliffe and his father described his life as "up before the sun he gallops to Cedar Grove, mounts the Reaper and all day long these long hot days cuts grain, clipping off a short hour to the mill to bathe and swallow some eggs and hominy, back home after dark and last night out again till no one knows when at a surprise party." HH to Katharine Hammond, May 24, 1893, HBC Family Papers; MS vol. bd., 1855–1908. Autobiographical account of "the early life of John Shaw Billings II," John Shaw Billings Scrapbook Collection, SCL.

2. Celia M. Lamar, a neighbor of the Hammonds, was about thirty-five years old in 1893. U.S. Census Records, State of South Carolina, 1880, Population Schedules, Hammond Township, Aiken County, National Archives Microfilm Publications.

3. Emily Hammond had hoped that Miss Mary would leave "the most of her little savings to Kate." ECH to Katharine F. Hammond, March 20, 1893, HBC Family Papers, SCL.

caught in a heavy rain, but stopped out of it at Prince's House. The rain is putting work back.

Yours affectionately,
Harry Hammond

HARRY HAMMOND TO KATHARINE F. HAMMOND[b]

Beech Island, So. Ca., April 13, 1893

My Dear Katharine:

You must be deeply in my debt in the matter of letters, but you have been so good in writing to your Mother that I will not hold you to a strict account. We have felt much disturbed at all the trouble you have been through lately, and I sincerely trust it has passed away. As to your going to Philadelphia, if you effected any good for any one by it you were right to go, if you did no harm you were not wrong. It was however a fearful hardship imposed on you, and I feel very sorry that circumstances imposed it on you. The older I get the more I doubt people's right to act on their own responsibility, and do things out of the usual. The usual are the regulations that society imposes on all its members. We are a great Army all, coming from where we do not know and going for some unknown purpose to some place we know nothing about. But we have to keep in ranks, and preserve the elbow touch, straggling is not allowed, we had to shoot stragglers in the army, and society also is almost certain to let fly at them. Not one person in a hundred is fully conscious of the motives that impel them to do anything. There is no greater delusion than to think you understand what you are doing, and why you are doing it. Therefore it is wisest and best, unless you see things very clearly, to stick to regulations. I feel very very sorry for poor Earle[1] and it would be a great satisfaction if I could see my way to be of service to him in his trouble. Trouble, there is trouble

1. Arthur Earle may have been the only man Katharine ever really loved. Earle, whom Katharine had met when he was living in Augusta, suffered from tuberculosis. In 1893 he was a shipping clerk in Philadelphia. On April 5th Katharine received word that Earle was very ill. She rushed to Philadelphia to see him. Ten days later she wrote her mother, "I don't want anything but to marry Mr. Earle." Katharine in fact may have entered nursing school to learn how to care for him. Arthur Earle to Katharine Hammond, March 8, 9, 10, 22, 31, and April 12, 1893; Katharine Hammond to Arthur Earle, April 3, 15, 1893; two telegrams, Laura H. Earle to Katharine Hammond, April 5, 1893 and ECH to Katharine Hammond, April 10, 1893; HH to Katharine Hammond, April 17, 1893, HBC Family Papers, SCL.

every where—poor Lessie is having a much harder time than was expected—much suffering—still confined to bed, very pale and waxen, and no certainty as to when and how it will all be over, no one to visit her, nobody but Kate full of germans[2] and concerts and nonsense. She went to the Augusta Hospital with Dr. D. [oughty] to see him remove a tumor from a woman's stomach. Carrie Cumming,[3] the General's daughter, is very seriously ill. Mrs. Lamar's daughter Celia has been carried to Milledgeville and put under treatment to see whether it may or may not be necessary to put her in the Asylum. George Walker[4] is seriously ill, loss of appetite, can't sleep, weighs only 90 lb. Here is Carry[5] dropped down on Mother with her very pretty little Baby, and she is wearied to death already, and of course Mother is a little tired of it too. Everybody seems to be in the fire and all of them trying to jump into the frying pan. Kit, dead broke but restless, is hurrying me now to go to the plantation, where I am trying to make some arrangements to haul wood, for him to raise a little money on. Alf is working very hard, up at daylight and to bed tired out at dark. He has got all his cotton planted and a much better stand than usual on most of it. His corn is up to a very fine stand, and his work looks well and so does he. Henry has a case in this court, and your Mother and Julia, who went up to see Lessie yesterday, say he looks well and, what is better, well dressed. He has discovered another nice young lady, was to play tennis with her yesterday, a Miss Butler by name. Who she is, I can't even guess. Your Uncle Joe [Cumming] was sick night before last, from drinking beer too many days in succession. Your Aunt Kate [Hubbell Cumming] is reported better though they think there is much cause still for anxiety about her. Miss Merrick tried to rope Kit and Warren into carry[ing] her two young ladies to the Cosmos tonight, but as it would have cost them $10.00 I advised them to be taken ill. Kit is a curious lady killer, here is his list, Miss Heyward, poor little Emmy, and the Genl's Carrie

2. Germans were a series of round dances with many variations, or the parties at which such dances were performed.

3. Carrie Cumming was the daughter of Alfred Cumming, Emily C. Hammond's brother, and his wife, Sarah Davis Cumming. According to Alfred Cumming, his daughter had a very serious attack of the grippe. Wood, A *Northern Daughter*, p. 108; Alfred Cumming to Katharine Hammond, April 19, 1893, HBC Family Papers, SCL.

4. George O. Walker was the husband of Ann Sarah Hammond, daughter of Harriet Davies and M. C. M. Hammond. Roland Hammond, *Genealogy*, p. 273.

5. Possibly Carry was Caroline Victoria Hammond, daughter of Loula Comer and Paul Hammond. She married Henderson McCarney Dixon in 1890. "Her very pretty little Baby" would be eight-month-old Catherine Fitzsimons Dixon. Billings, *Descendants of Hammond*, pp. 5, 7.

and now Maria who is staying here. He is hurrying me again and I must go.

Very affectionately and in haste,

Harry Hammond

KATHARINE F. HAMMOND TO EMILY C. HAMMOND[b]

Nurses Home

J[ohns] H[opkins] H[ospital], April 15, 1893

My dear Mother:

Every morning awake a little after five—this morning I woke with a start and completely and without any drowsiness—for I had a most vivid dream of you and home. You and I were to have gone somewhere in the carriage—everything was ready and you were waiting for me—and I with my usual cranky temper was making difficulties. It seemed a very serious difficulty to me. I had lost some letters from Mr. Earle that I had not read—and he was still sick—so I fussed and fumed hunting for them until Julia came and quietly took my place in the carriage and drove off with you—but strange to say leaving the dogs behind for me. Has this dream any moral?—I could not even doze after it—it was so vivid. I had seen you and Redcliffe so plainly and the carriage disappearing down the road by the stable. I wonder if Miss Hampton is going to send for me today, and if this was meant to warn me—that I must remember that I have lost my place in your regard—that I have left you—and so don't deserve even what I get—that Julia ought to and does have first place—has she not gained the right to it. And I must remember too this other feeling that has come into my life—and will keep it always bitter until it is satisfied. There are a great many things I must remember when I have that interview—and I must be very cool—and not yield to any weakness. All my life I have done nothing else—I have been swayed by every passing passion—and now when I need self control—and strength—I have nothing that I can count on—and would weakly call on others for help. How can people say that they will do this or that—and then do it—you know Mother that I never can be counted upon—that I have no character. This month has taught me a lesson—a very severe lesson—but like everything else in the world this lesson has to be paid for—if the penalty is hard the lesson will last all the longer.

I wish you could understand how mixed my feelings are about this thing. Just before I went to Mr. Earle I was beginning to think that the thing might become an absorbing interest—that the two years would pass quickly—and in the work and even the life was much that I would grow to like—the work especially was much to my liking. But then I went to him—and everything is changed—and the fight is harder than ever. I don't want anything but to marry Mr. Earle—and yet that is like saying I don't want anything but the pleasant things in life. The disappointment to me has been that this work does not seem to promise what it did before his illness—that if I work at it now it will be two years lost. The end I was working for does not seem at the end of this work now. It cannot lead to my marrying Arthur—as I had hoped it would. And meanwhile life is so frail a matter—that always there is this haunting fear over me. I am almost afraid to think—and I start and tremble every time one of the little mail boys comes into the ward. Oh Mother I am so afraid for him—I cannot know any rest from this fear—it is with me night and day.

1:45—I write this this morning—and I am always sorry when I throw the burden of my troubles upon you—poor little Mother as if you did not have enough to stand any way. Please dearest recollect always who it is that is complaining to you, and that nothing can hurt me very much.

I feel so much better today than I did yesterday. I staid awake last night and saw that the windows were open—and it makes me feel like another person today.

I have not had any letter from you since Monday now and that was only a hurried note. I do hope I shall have a letter tonight. I had a note from Hal[1] yesterday. He is in Washington and wants to come over and spend tomorrow with me. I did not care particularly about it—and am afraid he saw it from my note. And now I care less than ever—for I have just found a note waiting for me from Mrs. Gilman asking me to dinner tomorrow. My hours are from ten till four and I have accepted— if Hal should come I will tell him I would have had to go to the dorm anyway—and I will stay with him until it is time to go there. So that will cut me out of going to lunch with him.

---

1. Hal Hammond, a cousin from Atlanta, was about Julia's age. He claimed to have nearly fallen in love with her several times when they were young, but that every time he almost did, she would "kill my *aspirations*." Hal Hammond to JBH, Sept. 29, 1895, HBC Family Papers, SCL.

Part of my work this week has been in the dispensary—where the people come in to be examined. I have to prepare the women for the doctors to examine them. It is the dirtiest and most uninteresting work I have done yet. They are of course a poor class of people who come in in this way—I mean they are poor people—and their clothes are fearful. You can imagine my surprise today when Miss Gilman walked in with one of the women. Someone she was being charitable to. She did not recognize me at all at first—afterward she asked if I had been sick I look so badly. She was very kind and pleasant—told me of her Mother's note that I had not received then and urged me to come. I had quite a little talk with [her].

I got several servings today from Miss Reid[2] and another head nurse—and Miss Dock came in and inspected my work—and there was anything but approval in her look. Miss Reid is very quiet when she tells you that you have no sense and no ability—and you feel as if you would work yourself to death rather than have her speak to you again. My! in what a different way these people manage their labor, from anything I have ever seen or known of before. There are no strikes here— no nonsense either—at least not loud enough for the Head to hear them. I will have to go down to town tonight. I broke my watch[3] the other day—and I am having it mended. It is perfectly indispensable in my work or I would not have had it mended—for it will cost an awful amount ($1.).

Oh I hope I shall hear from you today Mother. I need a letter from you so much to help me start the next week. After a while I shall try and train myself not to expect to hear from you very often—but just now I can't begin. Is it that you don't want to write to me and tell me that you find it impossible to do what I have asked you to Mother. I hope not—for I shall be so deeply hurt and disappointed if you cannot do it for me.

My love to Julia and the boys and Father.

Devotedly your,

Katharine H.

2. Susan C. Read graduated from Johns Hopkins Training School in 1891. She worked as a nurse at Johns Hopkins Hospital until her marriage to William Sydney Thayer, a professor of medicine at Hopkins. Johns and Pfefferkorn, *The Johns Hopkins School of Nursing*, p. 64.
3. Arthur Earle had recently given Katharine a Waterbury watch. Arthur Earle to Katharine Hammond, March 8, 1893, HBC Family Papers, SCL.

ARTHUR EARLE TO KATHARINE F. HAMMOND[b]

[Philadelphia], April 28, 1893

Katharine my Darling:

How glad I am that you asked me that question!—for I like to answer it so well—and I know well enough you did not ask, "for information." If it were possible, I love you a thousand times better than I did before I was sick, and when you came to me my Angel!—tho it did not surprise me that you should do so much—for had you not told me you loved me? Why my dearest Love I feel deep in my being the certainty that I cannot love you less—and I love you with my heart and soul—but my Katharine I am so worthless and weak!

. . . Yes Darling I have finally written to your Mother, for a week I have not been *able* to, and so it was not done until *this evening*, and I fear was not well done—no I *know* it was not. I told her Darling that if I came to Augusta as I wished to do, that I should certainly come to see them, but I could not say anything about making a stay as everything including my getting well is so indefinite. I also said (which I have not said to you my Darling) that I must get to work just as soon as I am able and must in any event lose about two months and the expense of being sick! Yes, I must think of something besides the *present* pleasure, I must work, for I must have my wife. I will tell you more about California later, now I will tell you that we had a very enthusiastic letter from a distant relative, and among other things he says California (his part) is a Heaven for mortals. Yes I do want to see you in your uniform, and with respect to everything, I want to see you out of it as soon as may be, and I just hope this California scheme may be in good working order in six months *at the very most*, and then goodbye uniform, goodbye avarice and jealousies of the east, and welcome the freedom of the soft air and the absence of a false or too exacting Public Opinion. Oh Katharine my Darling pray that California may be a "go," and *soon!*

No Darling, I never thought of a connection or comparison of the things that we may *see* with the inner eye. I knew that I could always see every "feature" of a well remembered landscape, and *very* often could not see the *face* I wished to at all. But ah it was *so good* that you came to me, *now* I can see your face again, your dear true face, my own Darling, God bless each feature and expression! Katharine, Katharine I love you *so much!* and now let me ask (as you did) did not seeing what a poor miserable wretch I am make you love me one shade less? and do you know the true distinction between love and pity?

My Katharine good night as you know I am yours,

Arthur

HARRY HAMMOND TO KATHARINE F. HAMMOND[b]

Beech Island, So. Ca., June 4, 1893

My Dear Katharine:

So you gave the wrong man the right dose, well Jupiter they say nods, and even I meet with mishaps that should not be. Here is a very serious one, the note I sent you to sign got misplaced after I got it back, and can't be found so I will have to ask you to sign a duplicate and return it to me as soon as you can. Sign opposite your initials. Your recent letters give me the idea that you are making very rapid progress— you repeat so often you "don't know" and "you can't know." The most learned people I ever meet are those who say to me most frequently "I don't know," witness the professors at Harvard. The most learned I ever heard of such as Spencer, Huxley, etc. are always talking about the "unknowable" and with cheerful humility call themselves "agnostics" or the "unable to know." How different all this is from my neighbors, black and white, in Beech Island—they know everything. They can name without hesitation a perfect remedy for any disease that affects man or beast, and direct you how to cultivate your crop under every emergency. You remember when Mr. Toombs and Mr. Stevens and your Grandfather said at the Club House that they were sorely perplexed to know what to recommend about the finances of the Confederacy, that old John Clark rose and said if there was any subject he thoroughly understood, it was finance, and told them exactly how everything ought to be arranged. I fear the happiness he experienced from his then state of mind gave him as little satisfaction as your present mood does you. You still have another step to make in nescience (or no-science), and that is to find out how very little anybody knows. When you do you will deplore your own deficiencies in a less angry and sadder way, and you will also be very sorry for everybody else. All are well. We have had a deluge, it washed up a considerable amount of cotton, but unfortunately it didn't wash away a surplus of negro women who are trying to tear each other's eyes out. Burney, Em, Kate, and Ella waylaid Gussy to beat her—there is a scream now in the kitchen—no harm done, old Celia[1] was only hectoring Em, who became slightly hysterical and retired. Nobody hurt so far, but threats as thick as hail. Gussy was just hit one lick, enough to give her a sweet relish for the sport, and she piled in on Ella, who delivered the blow, and scratched her face until she cried for mercy. It is great fun for them. It is a pity to stop it. The fierce joy that armies feel is getting to be quite a luxury in these times of peace.

Yrs.

H.H.

KATHARINE F. HAMMOND TO EMILY C. HAMMOND[b]

Johns Hopkins Hospital, July 5, 1893

Now my dearest Mother I am going to try and write you a little better letter than I have done for the last few days. I am sitting by my window and there is such a delicious cool breeze coming in—and it looks so lovely—and I have finished my work and I ought to be very happy. And I would be but for a few things—and I am trying to fight them down all the time—that is all except my longing desire to see you—that I am giving full sway to since you say you are coming so soon. You don't know how I think of it—dream of it—and never let it out of my mind for an instant. I have not had any letter from you now for what seems an age—and I want one so much—one telling me all of your plans—and everything about your dear sweet self. I have had a letter from Father today—and as are all of his letters most interesting and nice. There is more in Father than all the other men I ever knew. I believe he is a far greater man than his Father was—and he would have shown it if he had had half the chance that Grandfather had. He tells me that you had gone to the Hill. I hope you had a pleasant visit— and that the heat was not too great. He tells me also of how Julia is

1. Burney, Em, Kate, Ella, Gussy, and Celia were servants at Redcliffe. See letter of March 23, 1893, note 6.

working—you don't know how distressed I am about it. It is entirely too much for her to do, do get a servant, Mother. The idea of her going to cooking when she has so many thousand other things to do. And she need not try to fool you by saying I am working harder—for it is not so. I have done both things and I know. If only I had the hame[1] for this work it would not be hard. The other day Miss Rudolph (my new head nurse) watched me write out my report—after I had made a thousand mistakes that she had to correct—she asked in perfect despair—expecting to have me answer "yes" of course—"didn't you *ever* go to school?" Her amazement was great when I told her hardly ever.[2] She is very kind and patient of my innumerable mistakes—but I am afraid her patience will give out. If she were to report to Miss Hampton my utter ignorance I am sure she would dismiss me at once. I sent you a telegram I had yesterday from Susie [Merrick]. I assumed that I would see her as much as I possibly could. It is very kind of her to come—and I only wish I could see more of her. I am sorry to hear how hard the boys are working—but am delighted to hear with what success. I do hope and pray Father will have a more successful year than last. I am so dead drunk with sleepiness I will have to say goodbye. I don't know what will happen to me if I don't get over this spell of drowsiness—now I can hardly see the page before me I am so sleepy—I go to ride in the street cars—and I go sound asleep—if I walk I am asleep—if I stand up I work—So goodbye dearest.

Your sleepiest child you have got,

Katharine

KATHARINE F. HAMMOND TO EMILY C. HAMMOND[b]

Nurses Lawn, J.H.H., July 25, 1893

My dearest Mother:

I have not written to you for several days it *seems*—but I know it is not that long. Neither have I heard from you for a long time—and that always makes me sad. I am writing to you out of doors—it has been so

1. A hame is the part of the harness of a draft animal to which the traces are fastened.

2. Probably Katharine exaggerated the effect of her lack of formal education (her extant report cards from Summerville Academy cover only January through March 1879). HBC Family Papers, SCL. Presumably she received considerable informal instruction from her parents who customarily spent each evening with their children reading in the Redcliffe library.

cool for the last few days that it was a pleasure to be out even in the middle of the day. I thought I would come out today and get a little sun burnt—for I am the yellowest thing you ever saw. I don't get white from staying in the home—not even as white as I used to get at home— but I am frequently sallow. . . .

I am afraid to tell you all about my work—you think it is so dreadful—but it is not at all—it is only in the telling that it seems so. It will sound fearful if I tell you that I have been nursing a murderer—or a man arrested at a murder—and got so badly hurt that it cost him his life too, poor fellow. He was brought into the ward with a broken skull—and the way he has suffered and raved for the last few days and nights has been something fearful. He had to be tied in bed—and then held there—if I learn nothing else I will be an expert in tying raving lunatics in their beds. All of the patients are crazy—I had an awful struggle with a man with a broken thigh. He was raving and would not lie down—but sat up in bed tearing off his bandage. First I talked to him—then I tried to push him back—but he was too strong and grabbed at my face—so I put my knee against and my two hands on his throat and choked him till he fell back. Then the orderly sat on him—and held him by main force while I stuck a hypodermic in him. The murderer died—it is the first time I have been with a man actually at the moment of death and had to attend to them afterwards—It was not so fearful. I did not mind it so much—it was so quick—over in a minute— and he out of the room and the whole scene changed—where the restless suffering body had once been was an empty bed—and all seemed natural and quiet—and the soul. We are not allowed to think of that— and this time there seemed to be none with it. Always ever so? Here is the end of my paper and I am sleepy. Love to all—and most of all to you dearest Mother—

Your devoted,
Katharine

KATHARINE F. HAMMOND TO JULIA B. HAMMOND[b]

Nurses Home, J.H.H., August 2, 1893

Dear Julia:

I ought not to write feeling as I do—especially after the compliment you paid me in your last letter—that my letter had been cheer-ful. For

I am in a desperate humor today—and can't control my indignation and anger—and the more I think of it the more they grow and the harder it seems to stand quietly such insults—and the thinking on it makes me know more than ever I was not in the wrong. I have told you I am sure that Miss Hampton is no lady—she is coarse, high tempered—overbearing arrogant snob! Even a mild senior nurse—who is a perfect gentlewoman—says she is all of this—and if you allow her to get the best of you—she will never give you any rest. What Dr. Wells said is wrong with Miss Hampton—it makes a great deal of difference if you have influence to back you—or if you are a Miss Nobody. I think I have been particularly free from her insulting nagging—and it is all due to my social position I am sure. But for some reason this morning she forgot it—and herself, and was in an awful temper with me. It was all about things that had happened in my night work. First she stopped me just at the big door to the ward—it was a spec. of mine. I had marked in my night reports as going down—and it had not gone. This you will think on the very face of it is false, as Miss H. said. I had been told to write my reports between 3 and 4 A.M. The spec. go down at 6. I always put it down as going and send it afterwards. This time it was all ready as usual—and the orderly got it mixed—and did not tell me of it until just as I was leaving the ward. In the hurry of getting things straight, after my last night—I forgot to tell the head nurse—and this is the only place where I can be blamed. Well Miss H. gave me such a talking to about this—but I mind myself to stand it—for I had been in the wrong. She was most insulting then, accused me of telling a falsehood—and when I routed her from this position she said that I had very little mind—her words were "well you have either got very little mind—or it is not half in your work." This point I did not dispute. She left me, but only for a little while. The next matter was medicine I had borrowed from one ward for the other. She wanted to know why I had not reported to my two head nurses that these things were lacking in the wards. I had never been told to tell them—but I had told the night nurse—and as she did not tell me to do more about the matter, I usually let it rest there. Sometimes tho' I did tell—and sometimes I didn't—when I did tell—they took no notice of it and I began to think I was officious for telling what they ought to have known. I was so angry by this time that I did not have the coolness to defend myself—I did not mention the indifference of the head nurses whom I had told—and that I had never been instructed to tell—and so had ceased to do so. I

was very mad and hurt then but when after a lapse of half an hour—
she came back to me again I lost my head completely—and fairly trem-
bled and cried with indignation. Then I told her she had been most
insulting to me—and that I would not stand it—that I was willing
enough to do what I was told—and that I expected my work to be criticized amply—and as long as I was spoken to as one woman should be
spoken to by another—I would feel that it was what I must expect—but
that I would not allow her to say that I was trying to impose upon her—
and would be false to cover up an error or omission. She told me to
hush several times—and to control my temper—but I didn't, and the
only thing I am sorry for is that at the end I was in such a rage—and so
deeply hurt—that I broke down and cried. Oh she was horrible—I
loathe her! I have tried not to tell you of late how my feeling about her
has changed—and how I see at every turn that she is a cruel, insolent,
bad tempered woman and there are not a half a dozen nurses in the
school that have any better opinion of her. As she turned away from
me—she said she would expect an apology from me before the day was
over—and that I would be sorry I had spoken so. I told her I *would not*
apologize—and if I had had the composure I would have said that I had
not said half that I wanted to. If I only felt that I could control myself
I would go to her this evening and have a real square talk with her—
and I know it would be better for me all the time I am here. I become
so agitated tho' that I just can't—perhaps I will write to her. I am
ashamed to have written you all of this—for tomorrow it will be all over
and it is what we all have to go through with.

Yesterday I was so glad that I was off night duty—today I have almost wished I was back again—for then you are free of Miss Hampton.
I want to tell you all about my visit to the Middletons—but I have
hardly got time now. It was a beautiful ride out in the cars. Mr. M.
met me—and drove me to the house. Mrs. M. is the saddest woman I
ever saw—very gentle and pretty. It was very kind of them to have me—
I am the first person she has seen.[1] The house was cool and dark and
homelike—very simple. We sat in the hall. Mr. M. and I doing most
of the talking, it was very quiet and pleasant. Ice cream was brought to
us there—it was good—then we went for a long long drive in the most

---

1. Katharine is referring to the death of Harriett and John Middleton's daughter, Mary Alston
Middleton. Miss Middleton, who had just died of tuberculosis at Summerville, South Carolina,
was only twenty years old. *South Carolina Historical Magazine*, 1 (1900), p. 250.

beautiful country. It made my heart ache to look at it—think it is the first time I have been in the real country this summer. Mr. M. was a funny reckless driver—he would turn around to talk to us and the horses would go dashing down hill. Mrs. M. did not seem to mind it tho'— and I enjoyed a little walk around the grounds and garden—he pointed out his daughter's tennis court—his eyes filled and voice shook. A simple homelike tea. Mrs. M. kissed me and said in her sad sweet voice she had been glad to see me—and we drove away leaving her a lonely black figure—with a lost life seeming to hang over her. Mr. M. would bring me to town—and was altogether as kind as one could be. And I came home feeling a great longing to be back in the country, a little dreary towards this life—and a good deal of heartache. For anything outside of this life tires you more than it does.

I feel very well today—physically—but my temper is still saying be prepared to take me home with you. I am sorry to hear how bad Henry looks. Love to all.

Yours,
K. F. H.

EMILY C. HAMMOND TO KATHARINE F. HAMMOND[b]

Redcliffe, August 3, 1893

My dear Katharine:

I was right, you have been on that dreadful night duty! I do not know whether to thank you my darling, for your perfectly wonderful consideration, in refraining from telling me, or whether to feel that I can never trust any fair seeming of yours again. You know my first suspicion of this state of things, was some casual mention you made of not "sleeping well in the day" and it flashed over me "that means she is working at night and is it possible she could have told me and I have not noticed it?" And today I took your July letters, and wondered why I had not observed various little things, that with this light thrown on them plainly indicated that you were on night duty but I had never for a moment supposed, that you would not tell me the instant the announcement was made to you that your time had come for this fearful undertaking. How did you live through it my dear child? I understand well now your saying that you feel restless and excited.

One of the things I noticed too, was your saying you had watched the man with the broken leg for "twelve hours" and I knew that you did not stay in the ward in the daytime for that length of time and I wondered what you meant but still did not believe it was possible you were on this terrible duty. Tell me now will you be on again when Julia and I come to see you? You know we will get there the twenty-eighth of Aug. and return Sep. 12th. It would hardly seem worth while to go then if that were the case. Write at once about this matter and give me some details of your vigils in those dreary wards. We feel like joining in your "Hurrahs" we are all full of eagerness to hear how your visit to Mrs. Middleton passed off. I hope we will hear something about it tomorrow and some explanation of Dr. B's[1] letter at the same time. What was it, he was apologizing for? And what did he mean by saying he would follow you even into the "Gynecology Ward"? You have nothing to do there have you? Of course he could not have meant anything disrespectful. Has Miss Townsend never come back? And how does it happen that Miss Turner not Miss Shean is in your room now! Never talk about wearying me with any and all details of your work and life. Your letters are profoundly interesting to all and are eagerly looked for every morning.

My new cook Sophie [Eubanks] arrived today with a heavily loaded wagon of "Plunder." Is it not strange that a woman who had the smartness to accumulate all this gear, and a place where she was working for seven dollars a month, should be willing to come down here away from town, and a married daughter, for four dollars a month? I fear she must be a fearful cook to do such a thing. Lizzie assures me that she is as "neat as a pin." Heaven grant that she at least knows how to wash hominy and rice and to make a decent biscuit. Kate H. was a wonderfully good cook, when you consider what she is and what her mode of life has been. Her soup and fried chicken and hominy make me think of her mother's appetizing cooking but she is so perfectly erratic that it is a relief to think of having a sober quiet person about. . . .

1. "Dr. B." was John Sedgwick Billings, Katharine's latest beau and the man she would marry in 1897. Billings, the only son of Katherine Stevens and John Shaw Billings, was born on July 31, 1869, in Georgetown, D.C. Billings, who had spent a year in Aiken as a child, received an A.B. degree from Johns Hopkins University in 1889 and his M.D. from the University of Pennsylvania in 1892. He interned at Johns Hopkins Hospital and was Assistant Resident Physician when he met Katharine. MS vol. bd., 1855–1908. Autobiographical account of "the early life of John Shaw Billings II," John Shaw Billings Scrapbook Collection, SCL.

Goodnight my poor darling. How thankful I am that you are not to be in the Hospital ward tonight. It is late.

Your Mother

EMILY C. HAMMOND TO KATHARINE F. HAMMOND[b]

Redcliffe, August 6, 1893

My dear dear Child:

I have felt great concern and distress about you for the last two days and failing to hear from you yesterday it has to be endured for still another day, so I cannot hear from you until tomorrow, Monday morning. Your two letters are lying side by side: the one in which you gave vent to your so natural delight and exultation at being free from that nightmare existence and those hours of darkness spent in arduous and harrassing work of the most painful character and that you were once more at liberty to look upon the light of day and the noonday sun; the other giving an account of your most painful encounter with Miss Hampton and of the distress and mortification it had occasioned you.

My darling child my heart bleeds to think of the indignities to which you were subjected by that cruel woman whose little brief authority makes it possible to inflict such suffering upon you. I am afraid you have not told us all and that the bitterness of this thing was some slur upon your conduct in connection with the kind young fellow [John S. Billings] who seems to be doing what he can to lighten your dark hard life there. I come to this conclusion principally from his own note in which he said "he would find you in whatever ward they put you." I am sure you have not been indiscreet, but he may thoughtlessly have exposed you to remark. I have wondered and wondered how the thing would eventuate. If Miss H. should insist upon an apology I take it for granted that you will not give it. And then will you come home dear child and be satisfied here after all the adventure and excitement of the last five months? No one can judge of that as well as yourself but I confidently expected to hear from you yesterday and rather expected to hear that you would be at home shortly. And when I pause and think how useful and ornamental too my Katharine was in her own home and how we have missed her and how anxious we have often been about her, I say to myself "*of course* she will come home and every one

will feel how good it is to have her here." Your Father has written you
his advice and opinion in this matter and you know when he is not
warped by prejudice or temper he is very wise and conservative. How
good the Middletons must have been to you. It was extraordinary kindness under the circumstances and I wish I had some way of showing to
them how highly we all appreciate their attentions to you. Henry left us
Friday afternoon, he did not look very well or strong, but I thought he
was on the whole, much better. We have not heard from him since he
went up. Who do you think is here! Who but Henry Cumming who
suddenly presented himself down here, after an absence of ten months
or so. His wife and child and Annie Palmer[1] are at Highlands No. Ca.
Henry is pretty much as odd and strange as ever, but not I think quite
as talkative. Warren [Fair] too is up for the day. Poor chap he looks
quite depressed. I fear his whole summer's work is a failure. You know
my new cook, Mrs. Sophia Eubanks, has been installed in office. We
hope she will do pretty well, and she is very pleasant and seems very
desirous to please. Now if only our poor dear old Celia don't set her by
the ears against the whole community. I hope things will work on quietly for a while at least. Your Grandmother is entertaining the young
preacher Mr. Cornelson today, who preached a very stirring sermon
today on the text "Rejoice Evermore." It was partly, I suppose, the
contrast with Mr. Davis' prosy homilies and partly because the spirits of
the whole country are so lowered, that any thing that has the flavor of
optimism seems to take off the strain a little, at any rate, we were quite
moved by the discourse. I earnestly hope you have been to church today
and have heard encouraging words and soothing music. Have you been
to Mrs. Hodges?

I am sorry to hear of Mr. Earle's health and of his poor business
prospects. I am afraid he has many companions in these rare straits,
and some times I fear Kit is going to lose his place. Poor fellow, it will
be hard on him if he does.

I long for tomorrow to come so that I may know which way your
affairs turn. Be assured tho my dear Child, that we shall be with you

---

1. Henry Harford Cumming II, son of Mary Morgan and Thomas William Cumming, was the
nephew of Emily C. Hammond. He married Carolyn "Carrie" Palmer. Wood, *A Northern
Daughter*, p. 106; MS vol. bd., 1955. "Some more small family facts," John Shaw Billings Scrapbook Collection; Photograph Album, 1741–1955, HBC Family Papers, SCL.

wherever you stand. Never withhold your fears from one line or one word you have time and strength to trace. Goodbye my Beloved.

Your devoted Mother

KATHARINE F. HAMMOND TO EMILY C. HAMMOND[b]

Nurse's Home, J.H.H., August 9, 1893

Dearest Mother:

From your letter that I received last night, I am afraid you have been very anxious about me, and my difficulties. I don't know how there should have been a day's delay in my letters—they are written every day—and usually about the same time. I hope then you have gotten two together in which I tell you of the talk I had with Miss H. and tho' she dismissed me from the school at first because I would not apologize—took me back without my asking to be taken back. Sometimes I am a little sorry I did not leave her room after the first three minutes—then I would have been at home with you now—and oh so happy to be there. The more I think of it the less sorry I am that this fight took place—Miss H. will not hurt me in the same way again. I have heard since of some of the tumbles she has had with other people and she was far meaner to them—for much less cause—and they stood it much more quietly—but she has been after them many times since. No, Dr. Billings had nothing to do with this—I really am perfectly frank with you and tell you everything. I have not spoken to him for a week—and he has not followed me as he said he would—even to D— I think he would be much more prudent than I would ever think of being. But I don't mean to say that I am never going to see him—for it is pleasant, and a diversion—and I shall go out with him occasionally— and not feel that I am breaking any rules—for Miss H. has nothing to do with us outside of this building—inside I shall conform to her rules—and not speak to him or any other Doctor. . . .

I was so delighted to get your letter last night—for I did not expect to hear from you—it being Tuesday. Your letters are such a help and comfort to me—when I read them and see that you love me and are willing to take my part against anything—why it gives me strength to stand anything—except being away from you. I did not half know my love for you—or knew that you loved me ever so much until now when we are parted in this way. I feel that I must get back to you—that I am losing something of invaluable importance out of my life every minute that I am away from you. I have not had Father's letter yet. I hope it will come today. I do hope Kit won't lose his place—that would be too terrible after all the work he has done for the Co. Has he been to see Mr. Haskell,[1] yet? Oh I am sure he will have more to do than even this year—every year at this time he has felt uneasy.

My work has not satisfied me of late, surgical work is so different from medical, and mine never looks finished now. I have more too— the whole side of the ward—nine bed patients and only two empty beds. Of course these patients, and the care of them is only a small part of what I have to do. I have Miss Hampton's book—and must read it in my hours off now—so don't be surprised if I don't write so often. One more day gone—and you will be here in 27—Ah, is it not good to think on, to dwell on, to dream on. I am so afraid you won't enjoy it at all.

> With deepest love,
> Katharine

HENRY C. HAMMOND TO EMILY C. HAMMOND[b]

Augusta, August 10, 1893

My dear Lady:

Your most welcome note by Kit reached me yesterday. I was glad to have such pleasant news from you and from Redcliffe generally. . . .

I read with great interest and sorrow the several letters you enclosed me from Katharine. I don't know how you and Julia do to live through the daily receipt of such letters. I never knew of any one in such a sad and sorry plight. The wonder is even greater how she can endure all she seems to suffer. Objective misery is bad enough, but that coupled with the subjective agony she encounters is beyond anything I have ever heard of. I presume that the whole thing will end in her return with you and Julia. That evidently is what she is looking forward to doing. It almost seems idle for you and Julia to go to Baltimore if it is certain

---

1. L.W. Haskell, Kit's boss, was the manager of the Southern Cotton Oil Company of Savannah, Georgia. MS vol. bd., 1870–1946. Redcliffe after Billings Restoration, John Shaw Billings Scrapbook Collection, SCL.

before hand that things will result that way. Why not write to her to break up and come home at once? She seems to want you to make sure for yourselves that she has undergone all that she claims. I suppose you can assure her that you have no doubt on this point. My prediction as to the outcome of the undertaking has been verified in every particular. Earle is *the* cause of the whole trouble. Of course I believe every word she says about the hardships of the Hospital life and etc. But these are all subservient to the one great cause—Earle. Have him out and there would not have been more than she could well have stood. The trials of her life at the J. H. are only the straws that break the camel's back. I never felt so sorry for any one in my life and with this feeling is one of utter inability to help her.

I will be down Saturday on the three fifty train if possible.

With all my love, devotedly yours,

Henry C. Hammond

HARRY HAMMOND TO EMILY C. HAMMOND[b]

Beech Island, September 7, 1893

My Dear Emily:[1]

We have had a hot still cloudy night and fortunately no rain as we had all the peas . . . cut and not even raked up. I have had breakfast and Alf is loading cotton for the gin so I write you a line until the mail comes when I hope to hear pleasant news of you.

Mother came up yesterday evening to talk her party over with Alf and myself. She was greatly pleased especially with entrapping the parson's wife into being a witness to the dancing, and her jokes with Katharine, offering her Barrett, as there could be no harm with such a fatherly looking fellow, and the preacher's nephew too. The Hankinsons[2] were invited and did not come because they were giving a party themselves. I believe there was a third somewhere else, and I have been

1. Emily Hammond and her daughter Julia set sail from Savannah on August 28th to visit Katharine in Baltimore. They left Baltimore for home on September 12th. HH to Katharine Hammond, Aug. 28, 1893; Henry C. Hammond to Christopher C.F. Hammond, Aug. 29, 1893; HH to Christopher C.F. Hammond, Sept. 13, 1893, HBC Family Papers, SCL.

2. There were many Hankinson farm families who lived near Redcliffe. U.S. Census Records, State of South Carolina, 1880 and 1900, Population Schedules, Hammond Township, Aiken County, National Archives Microfilm Publications.

approached to subscribe to a dance the young men are to give Friday. Alf gave 50 cents so I followed his example. You see what gaieté you are missing. You and Julia had better hurry back before the height of the cotton-picking season is over and the spirit of the neighborhood again subsides. While the papers are full of the Sea Island disaster,[3] Dr. Eve reports that the trees and houses in Beaufort looked like there had been a fire, as to the casualties he saw nothing of them and did not meet a person who had seen a dead body. He only encountered one old negro who claimed to have lost a very small child. As for St. Helena and the famine, he was on that Island and a gentleman gave him a delightful breakfast, coffee and crackers, just the thing. You know he relished it very much. The negro in charge of his island had foolishly taken flight at the beginning before the storm was at its height, but his barn, not being so nervous, held its position until the waves moved it over to an adjacent island. He asserts emphatically that the sea did not go over his dwelling but only crawled up under it, doubtless seeking protection in this harbor of safety. I pause here for the mail.

The mail brings us pleasant news of you. I hope it will continue. I had an idea you may remember that you would find Katharine in better plight than you expected. Perhaps the occupation she has will prove the best sedative for the Earle affair. You do not give me your own impressions of the Hospital work. As to the crop it has suffered (the cotton) 10 or 15%. I have netted $164 on five bales short staple and I think the price will go up. My croppers were . . . hurt but very little, their cotton being later. Caterpillars everywhere up here but rather late to do great damage I hope.

A letter from Kit this morning says he is on the road but he hardly knows what his route will be. Julia's letter looks fine in print. Tell Johnston to write me an endorsement and forward it to me, just a line to the president. Senator Edmunds sends a fine endorsement.[4] Only ½ Kit Fitzsimons' rice was lost, damage to dams $500 where he had expected

3. A hurricane hit the Sea Islands on the night of August 27–28. HH to Katharine Hammond, Aug. 28, 1893, HBC Family Papers, SCL
4. George Franklin Edmunds (1828–1919) represented Vermont in the United States Senate from 1866 to 1891. Senator Edmunds resigned his seat unexpectedly giving the illness of his only daughter as his excuse. At least as early as 1888, his family was staying in Aiken, South Carolina, probably for health reasons. Aiken, apparently, is the link between the two men. Edmunds's endorsement refers, most likely, to the post Harry sought as Assistant Secretary of Agriculture in the Cleveland administration. *The Aiken Journal and Review*, March 7, 1888; Farmer's Club Records, Beech Island, Aiken County, vol. 2, Sept. 2, 1893, SCL.

$1500. I will forward Julia's letter to Kit today. If it does not rain I will go to the plantation this evening. You haven't said if you would hand my papers to Butler[5] when you went to Washington. I have a lot of them ready and they might as well go. I don't like to stop writing but I believe I have told you everything. The worst damage of the storm is the staining of the ceiling at the back door. . . .

Yours,

H. H.

JOHN SEDGWICK BILLINGS TO EMILY C. HAMMOND[b]

Johns Hopkins Hospital, November 14, 1893

My dear Mrs. Hammond:

This note is apropos of nothing—unless it be that your daughter has had some foolish ideas lately that she is not doing well, and you can now write and tell her that you have heard from 'strictly outside sources' how splendidly she *is* doing. I was so sorry to have missed seeing your son.[1] I had heard so much about him that I was really disappointed. The Doctor's banner still waves triumphantly to the fore here and the devoted nurse still grovels in the dust at his feet. They are just finishing the new Negro Ward and if you were here I would take a mild, subdued pleasure in regaling you with some of the rumours as to the Negro nurses we are to have here. At least that is what they say, and Miss [Isabel] Hampton—Imperial Juno herself—weeps tears of rage and disgust at the thought. We will hope for the best however. Please give my kindest regards to Miss Hammond and tell her Rupert[2] was very much cut up at her not wishing to see him. Come now Mrs. Hammond—is that a good name you have for me?[3]

Yours most sincerely,

John Sedgwick Billings

5. Matthew C. Butler represented South Carolina in the United States Senate from 1877 until 1895.

---

1. Henry Hammond visited his sister Katharine in Baltimore at the end of October. Katharine Hammond to ECH, Oct. 25, 1893, HBC Family Papers, SCL.
2. Rupert Norton was on the medical staff at Johns Hopkins Hospital with John Sedgwick Billings. MP vol. bd., 1862–1913. Billings family tree; pictures of family homes, John Shaw Billings Scrapbook Collection, SCL.
3. Mrs. Hammond referred to John Sedgwick Billings as "Beautiful Boy."

KATHARINE F. HAMMOND TO EMILY C. HAMMOND[b]

J.H.H., March 12, 1894

Dearest Mother:

I have only time for a postal—but will have to write a note as I am out of cards. Yesterday afternoon John and I started out as early as I could and went into the country. It was a lovely afternoon and I indulged my spring fun by sitting and enjoying it and not even thinking. I ought to have thought for I had carried my book with me to get him to help me with my lesson and lecture. But it was too delicious to do nothing but rest.

I enjoyed my work so much yesterday morning. I had the ward all to myself—and it is full—so I had to go at a run to get through—but felt all the time if I managed right I would get through.

Mother, do you know that every day I am away from you is a great effort—that there never is a day that I grow tired of wanting to come back to you. If I felt the least bit justified in doing it I would come home tomorrow. If I could only forget for a little time how much more you and home are to me than anything here. But as I often say this is an excellent training for cotton planting. It teaches you a great deal of hardship, self-denial, and self-restraint—and is teaching me to know that what I had was the best thing in the world, and that I was the most fortunate and blessed person to have had it—and it will be a return to paradise to get back. For when I ever get home I never intend to leave Redcliffe—even to go to the Hill.

I have been up since 4:45 trying to study a little. I am afraid I will go to sleep in the ward today. Write to John if you can—he is so good to me. . . . Tell me please all about Father's affairs.

Love to all—and most of all to you dearest and sweetest Mother.

Yours,
Katharine

HARRY HAMMOND TO KATHARINE F. HAMMOND[b]

Beech Island, April 18, 1894

My Dear Katharine:

There is nobody here today but your Mother and myself. I am well satisfied to be here and would be willing to pass the rest of the time in this room of mine when I get my net up. But in deference to public opinion I have acceded to an attempt to reopen the Washington matter tho I think nothing will come of it. The fact is all of you children can't keep still to such a degree that the whole world feels in motion. Kit rolled off on his wheel yesterday to Aiken just to hear what was going on at Court which is in session there this week with a big docket of criminal cases and may not be back for a day or two. Alf has been to the Island at hard work every day this week. We are trying to clear and plant some and to make a Bridge over the creek. The river rose a little yesterday, and he could not get over on the temporary structure, and today he and Julia have gone down to make some improvements, they will not be back until late tonight. We have had frost for three nights past, but it seems not to have killed the cotton which has been planted much earlier than usual this year. A great deal of the Oats was killed by the cold before this, rather less of mine than of the crops across the ferry. We are in a drought too, and this is bad on the grain.[1] [Benjamin] Tillman seems to have been more on the rampage than ever of late and has, I fear, strengthened himself very much with his party. I am sure from what he has been giving out to the press that he has been looking to the leadership of the populist party, and he is excusable for thinking that his chances to be next President are as good as his chances to be Governor of South Carolina were a few years ago. If the discontent and bankruptcy is so great throughout the country as it is here and seems to be in most places there is no telling what may or may not happen. I remain a [Grover] Cleveland man to date and as usual in a minority

1. Harry Hammond declared that 1894 was the worst year he had ever seen—the corn was killed, the fruit was killed, and cotton sold at 4.59¢ per pound. Farmer's Club Records, Beech Island, Aiken County, vol. 2, Oct. 6, 1894, SCL; *The Statistical History of the United States from Colonial Times to the Present*, p. 301.

here of one. You know there are three sorts of people or were in So.
Ca.—Slaveholders, non-Slaveholders and Slaves. The Slaveholders and
the Slaves administered the Government until Secession. Secession was
brought about by the non-Slaveholders cooperating with the abolitionists of the north. They were whipped out, and the Slaves came into
power. The old leaders and the non-Slaveholders joined forces and
overthrew the freedmen's government in 1876. Then Tillman comes,
and organizes the old non-Slaveholding element against the old Slaveholders and the negroes and gets control of the State, and is giving us
a Hamburg massacre and an Ellenton riot government.[2] If we live long
enough we will see what will come next, otherwise not unless we are
prophets. Nevertheless I am not hopeless. There are a heap of good
white folks and good negroes in Carolina and it is not improbable that
they may yet work out things to a good issue. We must always continue
hopeful. Nearly 2000 years ago the man of many sorrows proclaimed
the coming of the Kingdom of God. Magna Charta, the Bill of Rights,
and the Constitution of the United States, gas, railroads, telegraph, and
electric lights all have come, but the Kingdom has not come yet. Nevertheless for all these centuries all good people have prayed daily Thy
Kingdom come and without these prayers what would the world have

2. Benjamin Ryan Tillman (1847–1918), South Carolina's famous and controversial governor,
in the spring of 1894 was campaigning for a slate of legislators which later that year named him to
the United States Senate over incumbent Matthew C. Butler. Butler was a member of a prominent
Edgefield family, whose social position and conservative political views were much more acceptable to Harry Hammond than were those of Tillman, whom Harry deemed a populist. The references to the Hamburg and Ellenton events of 1876 demonstrated the fear of elite whites, like
Hammond, that the division among white voters (for which they held Tillman responsible) would
lead to a repetition of the failure to control the blacks, and the supposed breakdown of order with
which they associated Reconstruction in South Carolina, especially in its last year. On the evening
of July 8, 1876, and during the following day at the village of Hamburg, directly across the Savannah River from Augusta, and a few miles north of Beech Island, an attempt on the part of local
whites to disarm a black militia unit led to an armed clash during which several participants were
killed. Twenty-nine blacks were captured, several of whom were ordered to run and then were
shot. At Ellenton, a community ten miles from Redcliffe, in early September 1876, racial strife
developed from the effort of a white posse to arrest two blacks who had allegedly attempted to rob
the home of a white woman. Eventually a battle involving sizable numbers left dead two whites
and an undetermined number of blacks—estimates range from 15 to 125. Thomas Holt, *Black
Over White: Negro Political Leadership in South Carolina During Reconstruction* (Urbana: University of Illinois Press, 1977), pp. 199–200; Francis B. Simkins, *Pitchfork Ben Tillman* (Baton
Rouge: Louisiana State University Press, 1944), pp. 262–72; Francis B. Simkins and Robert H.
Woody, *South Carolina During Reconstruction* (Chapel Hill: University of North Carolina Press,
1932), pp. 486–87, 505–6; Joel Williamson, *After Slavery: The Negro in South Carolina During
Reconstruction, 1861–1877* (Chapel Hill: University of North Carolina Press, 1965), pp. 266–71.

been? Say the Lord's prayer and try to act up to it, and we will deserve and obtain the best life and immortality has to offer us.

Very affectionately yours,

Harry Hammond.

KATHARINE F. HAMMOND TO EMILY C. HAMMOND[b]

Ward B, J.H.H., April 20, 1894, 2:30 A.M.

Dearest Mother:

Did John finish my letter to you this morning? It was his fault that I didn't—for as he told you I suppose, I went out to walk with him—so that was the reason—that I didn't finish. But I feel quite sure that he did not tell you that after quite a brisk, vigorous quarrel we determined we were both wrong—and no amount of talking would make us right— so we are friends again until the same subject is reopened. He is always good to me even when he is angry with me—but I am right glad he has gotten over being angry—

I don't seem to have written you anything but the scrappiest notes of late and yet I have done nothing else either—this night duty is just ruining me. I don't do any work—and yet I don't have any rest and holiday from it. I have a letter from Kit tonight. It was mighty good of him to write—I wish he would do it oftener. I was so glad to get Father's letter a few days ago, his letters always do me good. When I first read what he said about the Washington plans—I thought he said he had accepted the place. My heart fairly stood still for joy—and it was a deep disappointment to find that he had not meant this. What has he done in the matter—and is there still a chance of his getting the place? What tremendous work Alf must have done on the Island—I hope and pray there won't be a freshet next fall. That was not the first rumor I heard through Mrs. Perry of my being engaged to poor John. I am afraid the Adams are sad gossips. A friend of his in W. told him he had heard at Mrs. Perry's lunch table that he was engaged to me. And the worst of it is that he lives there, it is his home and his friends who are hearing this painful news of him—and his Mother heard the same thing.

I haven't been busy tonight so have gotten rather sleepy. My most troublesome patient died tonight. Poor Miss Tyler—I disliked her so—

she had been such an awful patient—in every way so trying and difficult. I had thought from the first day after the operation that she was
very ill—but whenever I mention such things they always make me feel
that I have been silly and unnecessarily uneasy. At first she made the
most awful noises in every conceivable way—last night after a hypodermic of a ¼ she quieted down wonderfully—was so quiet that I felt
alarmed—and watched her pulse closely. When I turned up the light at
4 yesterday morning I saw the change then. Tonight she had a special
so I had very little to do with her. I feel so ashamed of something I said
to her yesterday evening. When I first came in I was lighting the gas
and she began ringing her bell—she did not ring and then stop but kept
the bell in her hand and rang steadily until I got there. I went in and
shook the gas lighter in her face and said "Miss Tyler if you ring your
bell like that—or make any fuss tonight—I will come in here and hit
you on the head with this stick." I did not for a moment alarm her—
for as I said it she kept on asking for the many things she wanted. She
must have weighed 160 lbs and I had to turn and lift her as if she had
been a baby—that's one thing I have learned to do since I have been in
this ward—turn over these abdominal sections and make Albumin. Father would have a fit if he saw the bottles full of good champagne I mix
with white of egg. One of these cases is not supposed to move themselves at all for three or four days after the operation—and then only a
very little. So consequently they sleep with their bells in their hands
and ring every five minutes. This ward never was on such a boom—
and I have had four and five abdominal sections in a week. The baby
we made all of the tremendous preparations for Sunday night did not
get here until Monday noon. He is a fine little fellow—but don't you
think it is very peculiar—he has not eaten a mouthful yet. There is no
doubt tho' of his lungs being good. Miss Hamilton (his nurse) has the
funniest places for keeping the little man—the first night she put him
on the linen room table—but in the morning the maid thought it was
a blanket and pillow and nearly swept him off with her broom stick. So
now he sleeps on the shelf in the linen room.

There was a great laugh at me all over the hospital among doctors
and nurses. When I got tired of making as I thought unnecessary preparations for this young man's arrival—after I had boiled kettles full of
water—and dish pans full of instruments—I remarked in a disgusted
tone before a doctor and a nurse that I had not seen such preparations

since I used to watch them kill hogs on the plantation. To my great surprise they all thought this funny—while I had only meant to express how weary and disgusted I was.

I had let my shoes and stockings get into a most deplorable condition, but I braced up and got in a fine supply the other day—it was just laziness that kept me from getting them before. But my feet have gotten so tender from wearing the old ones—that I can't enjoy the new ones. This will wear off in a day or two. I know meanwhile I can faintly realize the disadvantage under which some of these young women work with this constant trouble with their feet.

Does Julia do all of the house work? Oh won't I be glad to get back and clean up your room and sweep the hall! How much cotton is she going to plant this year? Was the cotton hurt any by the cold? I am afraid the corn must have been. . . . We have been having one or two very pretty spring days. The bells have begun to ring—and it is nearly six—so goodbye dearest, and I love you better than all the world.

Yours,
Katharine

JULIA B. HAMMOND TO KATHARINE F. HAMMOND[b]

Redcliffe, April 24, 1894

Dear Katharine:

I am in one of your own furious tempers, Father has cut down a beautiful elm growing in the old orchard. Mother and I had just been looking at it yesterday. What a beautiful tree it was, and I had just been thinking how I would show you this part of the place that Alf had fixed up so nicely, and Father has gotten into one of his vile tempers and gone out and cut the tree down to spite Mother and me. But you know what Father is, and I did not have the beefsteak ready for his dinner the minute he sat down to the table, so Mother brought out the ham, and the corn beef, and the beefsteak came in in five minutes, then there was butter and crackers, toast and loaf bread, rice, asparagus, macaroni, turnip greens, sweet potatoes, stewed fruit, but Father after eating quantities of these took Mother's distress all through as a charming relish, but enough, it is just the old, old story, without any glory. . . .

Now bye, bye, I already feel sorry for my bad temper and wish I

had accepted the inevitable for I have only made Mother feel bad, do
come home to stay and help me to take better care of her.

Your devoted and repentant,

Sis

HARRY HAMMOND TO EMILY C. HAMMOND[b]

Baltimore, May 9, 1894

My Dear Emmy:

I avail myself of a moment's pause for the train to carry me back to
Washington, to give you my whereabouts. After writing to you and to
Katharine I went to the U.S.D.A.[1] (that's how they write it and that's
about all I have learned today). I found my boss Mr. True[2]—and if
truth were always as gentle and noncommittal it would make little head-
way in the struggle for life. We talked to little purpose and looked for
Dr. Dabney[3] to no purpose. Perhaps I am wrong but they seem to be
at sea, and don't know which way to steer. I saw the programme for the
book and found my name and other names put down and scratched out
for the various chapters.[4] I was introduced to a number of employees
who with two exceptions seemed like the three wise men of Gotham,
the only people who were busy were crowds of women in little bits of
rooms sorting cards and thumming on typewriters. After much incerti-
tude we landed in a very small remote room, and got a quorum of those
who are to work on the Hand Book, and looked at each other. I foolishly opened my mouth and spoke, and the rest opened their mouths
and kept silence. Nothing came of it, and we then returned to look for
Dr. Dabney—everybody in the meanwhile but myself having taken
lunch—Dabney has grown longer and broader since I saw him in
Charleston, and was ill mannered enough to say I had grown greyer.
He asked me if I thought the work would be profitable, and I said if you
are going to write on the profits of cotton culture you can put it all in

1. U.S.D.A. stands for United States Department of Agriculture.
2. Alfred Charles True (1853–1929), directed the Office of Experiment Stations of the Agriculture Department.
3. Charles W. Dabney, Jr., Ph.D., was the Assistant Secretary of the Department of Agriculture.
4. Hammond contributed two chapters—"The Culture of Cotton" and "The Handling and Uses
of Cotton"—to the U.S.D.A. publication, *The Cotton Plant: Its History, Botany, Chemistry, Culture, Enemies and Uses* (Washington: Government Printing Office, 1896), pp. 225–78, 351–84.

one paragraph, but it is safe to try for something more, for you can't do any harm. By this time everybody had had enough of me and I was told to knock around, and come back and get any help I wanted etc., etc. I took a car to the capital to see all those interested in me and especially to see Randall[5] about getting over to Baltimore. I saw no one. Randall comes over at 11 A.M. and returns at 2½ P.M. I believe I rode up the Hill with Tom Reed[6] and quoted Latin to him about how easy it was for him or me to go to the devil, in reply to a remark of his of a personal character to me. I may have been mistaken. But I am not mistaken in believing that everybody takes me for a very old person and treats me accordingly, it is really distressing. Finding it was near 5 P.M. I boarded the train for Baltimore, and made my way out to the Hospital. It actually looked homelike. Some women in invalids' chairs were rolling about laughing and talking. I passed Miss H. but did not recognize her. The maid who answered the bell assured me Katharine would be off duty at seven, and at seven said she would be down at half past and at half past said she would be there to the last supper at 8. I then began to make a row and addressed various enquiries to head nurses and others— a very ugly head nurse had twice put me to the right about before this. Finally the maid announced that Katharine had gone out and I said now I have come 500 miles to see her, and you have let me sit here (I was awfully tired) and miss her. This remark brought a very nice young person to the front, who gave me pencil and paper to write Katharine a note, and also uncovered Miss H. who came in and apologized for not recognizing me (nobody does or has but Mr. Black), spoke very highly of Katharine, said she was looking well, and was doing well, and had exhibited unusual intelligence, and is being splendidly strong and willing. Asked after you, said she had fallen in love with you, was sorry Katharine had had an evening off and had been out since 4 P.M. Took my letter to give to her and showed me a whole parcel of letters for Katharine in her box. It was no use to wait so I came here and got dinner at 8½P.M. and will now take the train back at 10:07 as I am expected at the Dept. about 9 A.M. in the morning, and my luggage is

5. James R. Randall, Harry's cousin by marriage, was the husband of Katherine Spann Hammond, daughter of M.C. Marcellus Hammond. Randall was a newspaper writer in Baltimore. Roland Hammond, *Genealogy*, p. 272; James R. Randall to Katharine F. Hammond, 1893, HBC Family Papers, SCL.

6. "Czar" Thomas B. Reed of Maine was Speaker of the House from 1889 to 1891 and from 1895 to 1899.

at the Hotel Johnson. I was afraid that this disappointment would happen and now I can hardly see Katharine until the day after tomorrow. Give my love to all.

Yours affectionately,

Harry Hammond.

KATHARINE F. HAMMOND TO EMILY C. HAMMOND[b]

Nurses Home, J.H.H., May 17, 1894

Dearest Mother:

There is something the matter with me. (John says I have got wheels in my head). If I have they have stopped going—I can't do anything—I can't work. I can't study—I don't want to do anything but *sleep*. When I think of the difference between the work I do this year and what I did last, I can't believe that I am the same person. Now I drag around in a half dazed state never doing anything—then tho' I was tired afterwards more than I am now. I used to work for hours in a perfect rush. I don't pretend to study now—and I don't intend to even try for the next two lessons. I wish I could sleep with an easy conscience and not feel that I must get up at four. It is no use to go to bed early some nights lately. I have gone practically at 7:30 but it is all the same—I never get enough sleep. Are you sorry Mother to think where I am going to stand in my class—for it will be at the wrong end this time? Miss Hampton came down in the kitchen yesterday to ask when we wanted our holiday. I said the last of July or first Aug. When I asked how much time I was to have—just to hear her answer—at once she jerked out "a fortnight." For an instant it took away my breath—but then I recollected that it did not make any difference to me. But is not that the most unjust thing when they advertise that they will give you two weeks every year—that would only mean two weeks for the whole year [and a half].

I had a splendid mail yesterday from home—one letter from you— a fine long letter from Julia and a note from her. How is her cold—I am afraid it was a very bad one. I hope it is better now. How beautiful things must look with all the rain you are having—but how hard on the boys—they must be working very hard. How does Kit go to the plantation? I am so distressed to hear how badly Henry is looking—and I know how bad he does look some times. I hope he can stay at home and have a little rest now—it will do him more good than anything else. I was just thinking how much smarter Henry was than Dr. Billings—Henry has done so much more for himself—and there has been so much less spent on him and giving him the chances to do.[1] There must have been quite a small fortune spent on this young man—if I am not mistaken he will make it show some day too—but he is only beginning to work for himself as Henry is doing. I was going out to the country with him yesterday afternoon but it rained—so I went down town instead to see about my class notes and got a machine for a month. It was very nasty and wet—and I came back so sleepy and tired that I went right to bed. We have two more lectures and how I am ever to stay awake to take notes in them is more than I can see now. I am so sorry to hear how bad Brooks is behaving. I hope his quarreling won't lose you your cook. Does he want Gussie to have the place? I will write my next letter to Julia. Everybody admired Father and he looked splendid—so handsome and distinguished.

Love,
Katharine

KATE HAMPTON[1] TO JULIA B. HAMMOND[b]

1201 Eutaw Place, Baltimore, May 23, 1894

Dear Julia:

I am sure my letter will be welcome, for it tells you of your dear Katharine. We saw her at the Hospital, that grand and wonderful building and Monday she dined with my niece, Caroline.[2] She looks very

---

1. Henry Hammond attended the Downer School in Beech Island before being sent to study at the Richmond Academy in Augusta. His stay at the Academy was brief, just six months, and, thereafter, he was taught by his father at home in an "atmosphere of literary and scientific interest." He learned the law in the office of his uncle Joseph B. Cumming, and was admitted to the Georgia Bar when he was only twenty years old. Hency C. Hammond Memorial Resolution of the Augusta Bar Association, Jan. 15, 1962, HBC Family Papers, SCL.

---

1. Kate Hampton (1824–1916), Harry Hammond's first cousin, was the daughter of Wade Hampton II and Ann Fitzsimons Hampton, the sister of Harry's mother, Catherine Fitzsimons Hammond. Charles E. Cauthen, ed., *Family Letters of the Three Wade Hamptons*, 1782–1901 (Columbia: University of South Carolina Press, 1953), p. 166.

2. Caroline Hampton Halsted (1861–1922) was the daughter of Sally Baxter and Frank Hampton, Kate's brother. She was a cousin of Katharine F. Hammond. Caroline was head nurse in the

well, perhaps a little thinner and just as we called she was busy in the
diet kitchen, helping make all kinds of good things, for the invalids,
which looked very tempting. I think your Mother need never fear that
her child's heart will rest anywhere but at her own Home, or that any
employment will blot out the love and sweet influences of home life.
Katharine told us she had seen your Father recently and we were so
glad to hear how much improved your dear Grand Mother is. Hers is
a wonderful constitution. I hope this unseasonably cold spell has not
hurt her.

A week ago we left home, Ann and I[3] to visit our dear child—our
darling. It is delightful to us to find her so happy in her home and her
husband. I think Baltimore a lovely spot and our long drives in the
afternoon are delightful, the country so beautiful, every foot of the way
and the houses so handsome. It is very refreshing to us, who have lived
so long among ruins and rough ground. . . .

My sister Ann writes with me in dear love to her, and do give our
love and remembrances to all of our relatives who are always so kind to
us and believe me,

Yours sincerely,
Kate Hampton

MARIA LAMAR MILLER TO KATHARINE F. HAMMOND[b]

Sand Hills, June 12, [1894]

My dearest beautiful Sister:

Thank you most heartily for your letters which came this morning.
I think it was only fair that you should write to me frankly Kate, and I
do appreciate it. You need not think I am satiated yet with your egotism! Wait till I cry "enough!" I am so sorry that all these things have
happened. I do wish I could talk to you about it. I think you have two
selves Katharine—One a tall upright goddess, merciful (though perhaps
a little scornful) to the world, to her other self, stern, austere, merciless.

---

operating room at Johns Hopkins Hospital until her marriage in 1890 to the famous surgeon
William Stewart Halsted. Halsted, among other things, devised the radical mastectomy procedure
which was named for him. Ibid.

3. Ann Hampton (1826–1914) was Kate's sister and an aunt of Caroline Hampton Halsted. Ibid.
Kate and Ann Hampton were allegedly involved as young girls in the scandal concerning their
uncle, James Henry Hammond.

Please let me plead for that other self, that dear lovely lovable human woman covered with humility. Don't let the goddess be too hard on her because she is no match for fate. It is not her fault that the world and human emotions are as they are. If she could exorcise that fiend—or angel of destruction—Disillusionment from the world, doubtless she would. Don't let the inexorable goddess stand over her and condemn her to a frozen hell. Why should coldness and hardness be her position. The woman is far too sweet and precious and rare for that. It seems to me the goddess lacks a keen discernment in dealing so harshly with her tender sister. What has the erring one done willfully? Nothing. I have a great mind to express one of my Katies to you at once, so that you will have something on the spot that you must love, and cannot be cold or hard to.

There never was anyone more lovable and loving than you Kate, and all this is not your fault, and you must not be too hard on yourself about it. We have the same sort of morbidness in our Nature to struggle against, and it is surely something that one must not give up to. But I have lots more help than you. Frank is a great help. Often in the midst of a clear sky when the children are well and Frank is *almost* all I would have him[1] (and I suppose we can never get nearer than *almost* to our desire), at some sudden flash of my own temper, or some closer look into our poverty and prospects, or (loathsome thought) at the sight of Frank's disgust with a dull carver, I feel that I am certainly the most wretched and contemptible of earth's vermin. I feel that I am making Frank's life wretchedly unhappy and that I will certainly have the same effect on the children when they grow to appreciate what I am. I think that the only way in which I can alleviate the circumstance that I have lived would be for me to obliterate myself entirely, and leave Frank and the children to try and put the odious recollection of me behind them.

---

1. Maria Lamar (1869–1957), Katharine's first cousin, married Frank Miller of Augusta in 1890. He apparently remained unemployed and in debt through much of the 1890s. They had two children—Cazenove and Julien. In 1900 Maria separated from Frank and spent much time in New York City. No one knew exactly what happened between them, but Maria divorced Frank in 1901, and in 1902 she married a Colonal Duvall whom she had met in New York. The marriage appears to have been a happy one. Maria Lamar to Katharine Hammond, April 16, 1890; HH to Katharine Hammond, Nov. 14, 1890; Henry Hammond to Katharine Hammond, Dec. 1890; ECH to Katharine Hammond, Sept. 29, 1893, April 6, 1894; Katharine Billings to ECH, Jan. 7, 1900; John Sedgwick Billings to Katharine Billings, June 2, 4, 8, 9, 1900; Katharine Billings to John Sedgwick Billings, Oct. 13, 1901, July 19, 1902, HBC Family Papers; John Shaw Billings, Loose Notes, John Shaw Billings Papers, SCL; Mrs. Leslie Helm to Dr. Carol Bleser, Sept. 17, 1979.

When I get in these fits if Frank does not dispel it at once, as occasionally he omits to do in inadvertence, or just because he may be "out done" with me, I am morbidly wretched for days, and the only reason why I don't get out of this world is because I haven't the grit. Now just think of such a state of mind for a woman who is married to the only man she ever thought of marrying, and is not tired of yet? Of course in my saner moments I realize that I don't make Frank miserable except when I am most upset about it, but that does not help me at all in the next fit of "blues"—and I think it is just the same vein of morbidness that makes you punish yourself so for a fault that you have magnified way out of its natural proportions. You see I have not hesitated to talk to you of myself when my affairs are much less interesting than your own. I hope you will profit by my good example! Do be a little more lenient with yourself, a little more self-forgiving. I just know that in the privacy of your heart you are living in a sack cloth and ashes, accusing yourself, and wearing hair-jackets—would it not be wiser, and perhaps just as religious to bend to Nature's will—if you don't *bend* she is very apt to *break* you in.

I am sorry to hear that a nurse's life is really so impossible. I want to hear all about that when you come. Oh how delightful it will be to see you again! It seems wonderful to think it is really possible to see you again. And I am perfectly happy to hear that you have no thought of returning [to Johns Hopkins]. We had such a pleasant day at Redcliffe Sunday. They all seem very well, and there seems to be a sort of buoyancy in the air over them over the expectation of your advent. Miss Julia says it seems as if she could not possibly wait till the time comes. It seems rather absurd to speak of you ever spending five minutes away from Redcliffe again—but won't you promise me that whenever you can be spared, and can spare the time yourself from Redcliffe that you will make me a little visit. Just promise that you will come to me as soon as you can go anywhere—that you will make me the first visit you pay away from home. Please! Well, if you are so busy, I just know you haven't time to read all this.

Don't you let them work you to a frazzle—Everyone reports you looking magnificent, my dear Venus de Milo. Oh you dear beautiful thing the idea of you wanting to be a nurse or a sphinx!

Devotedly Your Sister,

Maria Miller

KATHARINE F. HAMMOND TO EMILY C. HAMMOND[b]

[J.H.H.], June 20, 1894

Dear Mother:

These charts will show you a few of some of the things I do for my special patients. Oh they are fiendish! Miss Macdonald made me copy this chart yesterday because of the blots in it that I had never put there either. Tho I do most of these things—I never have a chance to write down half of them—and I never fill out the remarks. I am in such a hurry.

I did not get any letter yesterday—this is two days I haven't heard from home—and I am very anxious about Julia—and very unhappy at not hearing. The letters you all write me are the only things that can keep my spirits up at all. I have been so homesick and depressed of late. Each morning it is a dreadful struggle to start out for the ward—instead of making a bolt for home. When we finish prayers I feel that I must go up and tell Miss Nutting my heart is just breaking to get home I can't stand it another day. I suppose I feel this more because I know I am never coming back and when I am so crazy to get home at this very minute—it seems cruel that I can't—just because I have been foolish enough to put off my return for six weeks. Ah, but it will have to pass— and I will certainly get home and see you dearest—and be the happiest mortal in the world. . . .

With love to all,
Katharine

ARTHUR EARLE TO KATHARINE F. HAMMOND[b]

[Philadelphia], July 26, 1894

Dear Katharine:

It would not be in keeping with the rest if I did not write you on odd paper, and I will not change now. Why did you not send that telegram collect as I said, and why, why can I not even *look* at you once more? I am deeply grieved that you are not well Katharine, what is it besides overwork? for of course it is that partly. And Katharine do not think that I have been careless and thought nothing of this, and of all things that pertained to you and your life, in this long time in which no word has passed between us. You can believe all that I say now can you not Katharine? even if I had been a liar, I could not possibly have *ever* lied to you.

And now there are many things I could say to you, save that I think perhaps it would be as well to let them rest as they have done so long.

One thing I am most glad of, there is yet something in your life, you have the will and desire to help those that love you, your own, and you have the physical strength to do it, you are as purely unselfish as you always were, whatever else you may think is gone, and you will be happy again I am sure dear, when you get back with them again, and the past will be just a dreary dark cloud that is drifting by. I am glad you are going home because I feel so *sure* that you will find it a happy change from this. Katharine dear, do not feel that your life is barren and bleak, I know it will not be so, I know it by the way you write, by the way I know you. And as it is like saying one's last words, I want to tell you now dear, that once, a few months before I left Augusta, I was told that I could see you no more, unless I would make a promise, that there should be no talk of an engagement or marriage between us for a year, you did not know of this did you Katharine? Well you know I could not go without seeing you, and I promised, thinking that everything might be in better condition in that time, and knowing that it was not possible for my love to change in any way, save to become greater. And then, so soon, everything grew so bad and from bad to worse, and tho later I felt that the promise I made had in a large degree been forced from me, still my own trials and longing for you, made me fear lest I should harness you with the same or greater, but I never gave up hope until you had told me that I must, and if I could have but died when I came so near it, it would have been so much better for everyone who ever knew me, but then I had a hope, a power.

You never told me why it was that you ceased to love me dear, and I do not wish to ask, there were reasons enough that I know of, without trying to conjure up fresh ones. And as I am talking about myself (a man's favorite occupation) I will tell you what there is to tell. I am as you will have imagined, still at the Iron Works,[1] still working at reduced

1. Arthur Earle worked at the Pennsylvania Iron Works Comapny located in Philadelphia at 50th Street and Lancaster Avenue. Arthur Earle to Katharine F. Hammond, Jan. 27, 1893, HBC Family Papers, SCL.

pay, and when the *whim* seizes me, and I have the money, *still* paying
a little of the indebtedness that my expensive sickness caused. I am not
what you would call sick, tho this pain in my heart or lungs (whichever
it is) never leaves me, but is worse or better—as it happens. . . .

Tell you goodbye Katharine? my Angel of Light, noblest and best of
women! I was away from home so much—so many years, away from
Mother and Laura [his sister], that I might have forgotten how true and
good women were if I had not known you. What is it to tell you "goodbye" Katharine? to wish you *true* happiness—that I know you will have,
for you find it in doing for others. I could say the words goodbye, dear,
but I said them before, and yet you are before my eyes, tho I cannot
see you clearly as I used to do, but maybe that's because my eyes are
growing old. Say goodbye—write and tell you that I am sorry for all the
terrible pain and loss that I brought to your life, tell you what a poor
recompense it was for what you gave me! curse myself endlessly for
everything that I have done and been to the one that I love. But I am
not writing what you would have me write, but I cannot help it, I will
give all the hours that remain of my worthless life to be with you five
minutes as we were in the past—for only five minutes of those that have
gone—goodbye? Katharine dear the goodbye that I can say, was said
before, now I can but wish and pray that you will forget what I did and
should not have done, and what I left undone and should have done
and remember what I did do, and what I left undone—but no that's too
much; I would say forget me, but I do not think that that is sense, just
remember that I meant to do what was best and if I failed it was from
two causes, incapacity and circumstance.

And it was best for me not to see you again? you say you will write
and tell me? There is no use in my saying that it would seem very good
to me—there is no justice in my pleading for it—anything I did say
would be pure selfishness and a shutting out of all regard for *your* feelings. I have no right to ask for anything for myself, only—nothing.

But you will not judge Mother and Laura and "Yankees" in general
by me. When you go home you will have seen that there are so many,
that I should be ashamed to breathe the same air that they do.

Katharine dear, do not think anything about this letter just destroy
it, and may the good God bless you, and may you find days of happiness for every second of misery that I have brought you. I shall think of
you always dear as apart from everything else—my Angel—that stooped
so low from Heaven to show me what truth and light were. There al-

ways was much I desired to say and could not, and now more than ever;
with you, I cannot *feel* "goodbye," tho I say it.

I am yours,
Arthur Earle

WILLIAM W. WOOLSEY TO KATHARINE F. HAMMOND[b]

Aiken, August 6, 1894

Dear Miss Catherine:

With all your friends I rejoice to know that you are at home enjoying your well earned vacation.

I only hope that brighter weather may soon come so that Redcliffe
will look its bravest for you, without as well as within.

We would be delighted if you could come to us at Breeze Hill before long.

It is splendid to think you are at home again.

With kindest regards to all.

I remain

Yours sincerely,
W.W. Woolsey

JOHN SEDGWICK BILLINGS TO KATHARINE F. HAMMOND[b]

J.H.H., August 23, 1894

Dear Katharine:

I did not write to you today, as I intended to, because I wanted to
see which way things were going. In your letter this morning you left
me in the most unblissful ignorance as to your plans. You told me what
Henry advised and what you feared you would do, but not a word as to
what you intended to do. I caught vague rumors about you today—that
you had not come back and that Miss Patterson had telegraphed you
last night. I had a watchful eye on the front door last night and would

not have been very much surprised to see you walk in. Miss Shearn and Miss Bean[1] are back—the former in G and the latter in H. Mary Elizabeth [Shearn] looks splendidly and has had a good time. She thinks you are not coming back, but says had she dreamed of it, she would surely have gone to Redcliffe and dragged you back. Miss Hemming (who is "specialling" in F and who I did not take off tonight at her own request, so that she may get tomorrow) agrees with her, saying that when Katharine says a thing she means it. Those are the only people I have conversed with on the subject, tho' half a dozen of the Housemen have asked me when you got back. Of course I did not know— how should I, when my state of mind was such that I even looked into No. 23 this morning half expecting to find a note there. Well my long expected trip to Washington is over and it is a boy—10½ pounds,[2] and I can vouch for the strength of his lungs, as I heard him all night long. Sister is doing finely, and all is as satisfactory as possible. I read your novel through today—it is funny in parts and interesting in sections. Do you compare the Heroine . . . to your glorious self—and if so, are you going to marry one of your Aiken County men or ABCDE *etc*. Not that each and every one of them are not better men than myself in everything which goes to make up an eligible party. I have half-a-dozen novels to send you with a little volume of Henley's Hospital verses[3]—but will hold them until I am sure that they will not chase you all over the country. Will you not please let me know what you are going to do. If you are going to stay at home, you should have written to Miss Nutting[4] to that effect—as it is, you will—but enough of that, I will keep this until tomorrow morning's mail, when I will add a line if I hear from you, as I most sincerely hope and pray that I do. I shall take three days vacation next week and go to the Snowdens—that is, if my private

1. Mary Elizabeth Shearn and Mary C. Bean were student nurses at Johns Hopkins Hospital. MP vol. bd., 1862–1913. Billings family tree; pictures of family homes, John Shaw Billings Scrapbook Collection, SCL.

2. William Billings Wilson, the son of Kate Billings Wilson, was born on August 20, 1894. MS vol. bd., 1955. "Some More Small Family Facts," John Shaw Billings Scrapbook Collection, SCL.

3. William Ernest Henley (1849–1903), English poet, critic, and editor, wrote a series of hospital poems.

4. Miss Nutting, who had been in the first graduating class of Johns Hopkins Nurses Training School in 1891, had become by 1894 Superintendent of Nurses. Johns and Pfefferkorn, *The Johns Hopkins School of Nursing*, pp. 80–81, 94, 97–98.

patients come up to tune as they are expected to. Until tomorrow. Sweetness.

John

August 24, 1894

P. S.   No letter this morning—still as I have neither seen you, nor heard of your coming, I take it for granted that you are not here. I walked around by B at 10 o'clock last night, but your window was as black as the ace of spades.

Now Katharine, if you are going to stay at Redcliffe, you must write to me as often as you can—I must have your letters and need them more every day. Are you going to regret what you have done? I knew, in spite of your denials, that what I may have said at various times, had had some slight influence upon you and—But there is one o'clock—I must fly to mail this.

Ever yours,

John

JOHN SEDGWICK BILLINGS TO KATHARINE F. HAMMOND[b]

J.H.H., August 30, 1894

My dear Child:

What on earth has upset you? The first part of your letter was nearly tigerish in its fierceness, and as I promptly forget everything I ever say in my letters, I have been racking my brains to try and remember just what I said to bring all this down upon my head. But I cannot. One thing though—your remarks about Miss Hemming are foolish, and I thought you would be the last one to misunderstand our slight intimacy—why it was only the nice things that she said about you that made me pay any attention to her at first. And as for my taking her out—what rot. But you have shown me fairly and squarely by what you say that my "so-called kindness! in going out with you, has been the cause of your giving up nursing and going to your mother." I shall never forget this nor cease to reproach myself with it. And now I am sure you will totally misunderstand a letter that I wrote you a few days ago and will say something very bitter. I am sorry for all this Katharine—very sorry and feel that I am very much to blame for many things that I have done. . . .

I must stop now and get to work as this is not my day for writing you. I had to say something in answer to your letter—I hope you are just a little sorry that you wrote it.

Yours ever and always.

John

JOHN SEDGWICK BILLINGS TO KATHARINE F. HAMMOND[b]

Montclair, N.J., November 28, 1894

Dear Katharine:

I have put off writing this until the last of ten letters that I have just finished, this in order to think over what you have told me of your idea of continuing your nursing. I am afraid I cannot help you much—however here is what I think: do not flout it too scornfully, nor say any mean things to me. I have tried to put myself out of the question entirely and look at it as an outsider. If you wish to finish your nursing and *especially* if you wish to get a diploma and use it (your nursing) outside of your own home, my advice would be to go back to the Johns Hopkins by all means. The training there is much better, the diploma is oftentimes more value, and by going to Columbia, you are not going to silence those carping fools (if there be any such) who have been saying mean things about you—not in the least. I am quite positive that you could arrange it so as to go back there next September and graduate the following June, without having any of your previous time taken off. All you would have to do, would be to study moderately hard for a month before returning, so as to pass your fall examinations. I am quite sure that you could go back, and every soul would be glad and eager to get you back there—that is Dr. J.S. Billings, Jr. giving the best advice he is capable of giving, to Miss Hammond who is thinking of returning to nursing. In the matter of John Billings the man and Katharine Hammond the woman—that is a different matter. *He* has nothing to say. Your being a trained nurse would not have any effect upon me that would be patent to you. Write to Mary Elizabeth [Shearn] about it—I shall do so myself tomorrow. Enough for tonight . . .

Yours,

John

JOHN SEDGWICK BILLINGS TO KATHARINE F. HAMMOND[b]

New York, April 3, 1895

Dear Katharine:

There is one good thing about this town—I have paid four duty calls since 8:30—expected to find the people out, they were out, and in consequence I am back at home[1] again in less than an hour. Now older and wiser heads would probably tell me that I should wish to see them—so I do—in the other place.

I have had two letters from you in eight days—not counting the flowery one which I enjoyed extremely—and both of them were studiously friendly and carefully signed "yours sincerely" and then your full name. Does it mean that because I have refused to take the hint so far, you are adopting the pile-driver method? I hope I am wrong but wait for an explanation. For my own part I think a face-to-face explanation is needed to get things straight—why if I wrote you ten Century Dictionaries, I could never clear away the wrong, crooked, misleading ideas you seem to have about me—and my thoughts, hopes, feelings—everything. But probably what I have just said has only made things worse, so I will "quit it." My absence at Montclair has been so far noticed that the Hartleys[2] are coming up to pay me a formal call on Saturday—it is a pity, for now I will have no legitimate excuse for refusing their invitations. . . .

I went to St. Vincent's[3] for the first time today—it is a dirty hole

1. In the fall of 1894, John Sedgwick Billings left Johns Hopkins Hospital and moved to New York City where he rented an apartment at 26 West 47th Street, hung out his shingle, and began his private practice in December. By time of this letter to Katharine, John had taken a job as Assistant Bacteriologist in the New York City Department of Health for $1200 a year. This position involved only four hours of work daily, enabling him at the same time to establish himself in private practice. On July 1, 1895, he moved to 44 West 48th Street where he shared a four-story brownstone house and office with another physician, Robert J. Carlisle. John Sedgwick Billings to Katharine F. Hammond, July 3, 7, 1895, HBC Family Papers; A.A. Smith to John Shaw Billings, Oct. 23, 1894, A.A. Smith to John Sedgwick Billings, Jan. 25, 1895, MS vol. bd., 1877–1959, Career Data on John Sedgwick Billings; MS vol. bd., 1855–1908. Autobiographical account of "the early life of John Shaw Billings II," John Shaw Billings Scrapbook Collection, SCL.
2. John's sister "Daisy" (Jessie Ingram Billings) was married to Bradfield Hartley. MP vol. bd. 1862–1913. Billings family tree; MS vol. bd., 1955. "Some More Small Family Facts," John Shaw Billings Scrapbook Collection, SCL.
3. Early the next year he resigned his position at St. Vincent's Hospital "as it clashed with all my other work and I did not get on at all well with the Sisters." John Sedgwick Billings to Katharine F. Hammond, Jan. 9, 1896, HBC Family Papers, SCL.

compared to *the* hospital. The Sister Superior looked at me over and, I think, gave me the marble heart—"Dispensary Physician, nit" as they say in the fourth ward. I am glad—d . . n this pen—to hear that you are perfectly and entirely satisfied with Redcliffe—perhaps not so much so to learn that nothing would induce you to leave it. Now if I could only say the same—unfortunately, I would give a great deal to get away from here—anywhere, anywhere out of "the world"—not exactly in the same sense as Thomas Hood's[4] unfortunate; however, as I really have no curiosity about the life to come—and your heaven of absolute non-existence would bore me after a while I fear. I do not dare to send my love to any one.

Yours as always,
J.S.B. Jr.

JULIA B. HAMMOND TO WILLIAM W. WOOLSEY[b]

Redcliffe, June 27, 1895

This is not a letter to go to you.[1] Katharine is just back from Mrs. H.'s death bed[2] and her simple graphic account of so much affection and such agony of parting filled me and thrilled me, and the importunate thoughts of you that I am trying all the time to quell, keep down, come in an overpowering flood. I feel strong hands clinging to me. Your beautiful eyes looking at me appealingly, and I hear you say, "You are the greatest thing in the world to me." And the pain of being separated from you becomes unbearable, a wild restlessness takes possession of me, being a woman I live it down, and I trust no one knows or even guesses the trouble, and I hold myself down with reasoning on the facts, my own unloveableness, your—Ah! I will not think it! Facts! Facts!! I grasp their iron hardness and try to grow hard, and shrink from sight.

---

4. Billings's reference is probably to "The Dream of Eugene Aram," the most widely read poem by Thomas Hood (1799–1845), the English editor, humorist, and author of several serious poems about death.

---

1. As cited earlier, although Julia Hammond and William W. Woolsey continued to correspond long after his marriage, these and many other very personal letters were never sent.

2. Mrs. Jule Hardeman was the wife of Judge S.H. Hardeman. Mrs. Hardeman, whom Katharine had nursed, died at her home in Washington, Georgia, on June 24, 1895. MS vol. bd., 1855–1908. Autobiographical account of "the early life of John Shaw Billings II," John Shaw Billings Scrapbook Collection; B. Frank Hardeman to Katharine F. Hammond, Aug. 25, 1895; S.H. Hardeman to Katharine F. Hammond, May 10, 1896, HBC Family Papers, SCL.

KATHARINE F. HAMMOND TO JOHN SEDGWICK BILLINGS[b]

Redcliffe[1]

Dear John:

How dangerous it is to jest—so you took my proposition seriously? We should understand each other fairly well, and yet see what misapprehensions have arisen. John tell me once again that your senses are not so apoplexed as to have made you regard with fulmining correctness my proposal to buy you a ticket from N.Y. to Augusta? I cannot believe it—Are you acting jest for jest? I would accept this idea as the simplest solution of the matter, but for a certain tone that pervades your letter. If you are really solemn about all of this let me imagine John if it did not occur to you—that if your burning desire to see me during this long, long time has not compelled you to go down in your own or somebody else's pocket for the price of a R.R. ticket from here to there that my offer of transportation would move you to action. Do you think that I think—or ever have thought that R.R. fare stood in the way of your visiting me? Your insufficient means have served only as a laughable excuse for your not doing so. Fearing further misunderstandings, my offer to invest in a ticket on your account with a view to bringing you to Redcliffe was a Jest—a J.E.S.T.

The above is one view of your letter the most favorable—in passing merely let me refer to your "pride" and "particularly puritanical up bringing" on the score of R.R. passes. They are most commendable. You say "I know you people think nothing of giving and receiving R.R. passes." I don't know what *you* may know of my people but I never knew one of them to ask for a pass—except upon that one occasion when I wanted a poor forlorn sick little creature to visit me and this was the only possible chance of his doing so. Now Mr. Pharisee, is not my memory correct—did you not apply for and use free passes on your trip west—two years ago? I certainly have a strong impression of some contretemps in your arrangements caused by the delay to receive these passes—thereby I gained another pleasant evening with you before your departure?

---

1. This undated latter of Katharine's was returned to her in John's letter of Oct. 17, 1895.

I fully appreciate all that you and Dr. Norton felt and said about southern women. It certainly requires all the blindness that being in love brings to make a hard headed northern man overlook the glaring imperfections of southern women.[2] The two breathe a different atmosphere of thought, sentiment and action.

I thank you for inquiring about my health—it is in its usual good condition.

John I have answered your letter, as best I could, frankly and honestly. Will you let me add a word to my direct answer. I don't like your letter—don't like the tone or manner of it. Don't I read between the lines of your letter all sorts of things? Won't I save you the disagreeable task of telling me plainly in unvarnished terms that you have enough— enough of me and everything that concerns me. I am truly fond of you, and don't want to lose any of it by receiving any more letters like your last—or having to write any more like this one. Let's stop right here— and it is not too soon I am sure—and for the future subsist in happy memories of what has been to me a charming and delightful association.

With best wishes—kindest regards—not to speak of love

Most sincerely,

[Katharine F. Hammond]

JOHN SEDGWICK BILLINGS TO KATHARINE F. HAMMOND[b]

New York, October 17, 1895

Dear Katharine:

What a fool I was to take you so seriously—and yet it was splendidly acted and played out on your part—lasting through three letters. I would hardly have thought that that sort of thing would amuse you— but as your friend A. Lincoln said "For those people that like that kind of a thing, I imagine that that is just the sort of thing that those people would like." At any rate I have the satisfaction of knowing what a pleasant joke the whole thing has been to your family, your brothers, Maria,

2. In the letter of October 9, which so upset Katharine, John not only declined Katharine's offer of a railroad ticket to South Carolina, but also offended her by writing that "these cut and dried Northern men can never understand nor appreciate Southern girls unless they happen to be in love with them." John Sedgwick Billings to Katharine F. Hammond, Oct. 9, 1895, HBC Family Papers, SCL.

Mr. Buist, Mr. Jordan,[1] et al., et al. And then the exquisite finish your remembrance of those passes must have given you—I would not disturb it for the world. Really I must congratulate you on your appearance in a new role—new at least to me.

Of course I have nothing to say about myself—anything of the sort would be superfluous and impertinent on my part, after the successful and glorious conclusion to which you have brought the 'association'— or was it "episode"? Wishing you most heartily the greatest success in whatever you may undertake, and that your journey 'down the long years' long gradient' may be the happiest of the happy, believe me

Yours as always,

John Sedgwick Billings

P.S.   Your friend Dr. J.K. Mitchell[2] is still anxious for you to come here—he thinks he has plenty of work for you.

JOHN SEDGWICK BILLINGS TO KATHARINE F. HAMMOND[b]

New York, January 3, 1896

Dear Katharine:

What do I care about Rupert and the rest of them? Have I not had a letter from you, and has it not changed everything from gray to gold— no, not everything, but the change is so marked that they have had no chance as yet to grow blacker by contrast. And what a fool I have been—I have known all these months—and weary ones they have been—that what I needed was to hear from you. Well—the chances are that you would have left any previous letter unanswered. I am heartily thankful for the gifts the Gods provide—and like Oliver ask for more. I

1. Buist was a fleeting beau of Katharine's who lacked the permanence of D.A. Parker Jordan. (See Katharine F. Hammond's letter to her mother March 7, 1893, note 1.) In one of Jordan's several long farewell letters written to Katharine in the summer of 1895 he declared, "Someday you will know that I have loved you with all the love of my life—someday you will know that I have always loved you. Then and not till then you will know how I have suffered and how my heart is touched. I can't say more. My heart is too full. Goodbye and God bless you." Parker Jordan to Katharine F. Hammond, July 16, 1895, ibid.

2. John Kearsley Mitchell, son of the famous physician Silas Wier Mitchell, and a prominent neurologist, had been to Redcliffe professionally in 1888 to attend Katharine's brother Kit. In 1894 Dr. Mitchell had written that when Katharine finished her training he could promise her "steady employment and huge emoluments" in Philadelphia. John K. Mitchell to ECH, Jan. 14, 1894, ibid.

only wish you could experience something like the fierce exultant bound of the heart into the throat that I had, on seeing your dear writing on the outside of the letter. That is impersonal *of course;* I am only wishing you a certain keen form of happiness. As to the brevity of my letter—I honestly confess I was afraid to write more, as my thoughts refused to keep on in the "Peace on Earth" groove. I cannot tell you how glad I am to hear that Mrs. [Maria Lamar] Miller is coming on to New York. Please beg her, for me, to let me know as soon as she gets here—perhaps I have not ten thousand questions to ask her? I only hope she will have endurance enough to talk on one subject every time she sees me. So you are enjoying yourself at dances and balls—that is fine. I hope you get every bit of pleasure possible. But why—on the heels of such a frivolous (by comparison) announcement—do you speak of going to Turkey?[1] It is none of my business—but positively the only good thing I can see in it, is the fact that you would have to sail from here.

Your photograph has this minute come—and any word of thanks I could send would be all too few. It is stunning—but it is not my Katharine Hammond of old days—it is Miss Hammond of Beech Island, so well known in Augusta Society. I never knew the latter at all well—and now I am afraid she has driven the girl who used to sit on the Wallrock hills with the wind and sun playing hide and seek in her brown hair—she has driven her far back into the past and bolted the door. By Jove, you are stunning though—your cousin is out of it entirely. You said something about another one—I wonder if it looks more as I knew you—I wonder. But I cannot let this one out of my hands a day—and so am at your mercy. Can I have a little bit of a photograph taken for you—just for you? I suppose the other photograph is the better one and is being kept for my alphabetical friend.[2] I have expected all along to hear the announcement of your engagement to him. That would be the finishing touch to a series of misfortunes that have be-

1. Clara Barton was planning to go to Turkey, and Katharine had toyed with the idea of making the trip with her. Later in the month, John wrote Katharine of his conversation with his father concerning Clara Barton's effectiveness as the head of the American National Red Cross. He wrote, "to my surprise he [John Shaw Billings] had no use for her—said she was a humbug and worse and that the medical profession as a whole were down on her. He said speaking as one who knows, that it would be a sheer waste of time for you to go with her. No danger but no use." John Sedgwick Billings to Katharine F. Hammond, Jan. 25, 1896, ibid.

2. "My alphabetical friend" refers to D.A. Parker Jordan, to whom John made reference in another letter as "Alpha to Omega Jordan." John Sedgwick Billings to Katharine F. Hammond, Jan. 13, 1896, ibid.

fallen me lately. If you can spare time to answer this, I am going to take heart of grace, and tell you what this poor unworthy self has experienced lately on his way through the world. It has been a rocky old road—but what care I. But don't let me write if I am going to bore you. I send no New Years wishes—none are good enough for you. And you will write to me—won't you?

Yours always,
John

JULIA B. HAMMOND TO WILLIAM W. WOOLSEY[b]

Redcliffe, March 28, 1896

How can you write me so, and then come back to me, loving me and expecting me to love you?

Some day you will go away never to come back to me, to forget me, I look for that day each time I tell you goodbye. By the side of my dear Grandmother's coffin,[1] an inspiration came to me, a hope long mine became a conviction, humbly I dedicate my life to "the struggle for others." Many Times shall I fail, be sick in despair, but this hope will find me, enable me to begin again.

How glad I was to see you yesterday no words can tell. My darling Mother and you are endless joy to me, God helping me I will never be a hurt or hindrance to either of you.

JULIA B. HAMMOND TO WILLIAM W. WOOLSEY[b]

Redcliffe, June 11, 1896

"You say, you don't believe that I love you. Well I don't know what I can do to express it for I love you better than anything in the world, and want you with me every minute of my life." You threw yourself on your knees and tried to console me. My eyes are sore with the tears I have not shed.

Someday you will leave me, but hardly while you have so much

---

1. Catherine Fitzsimons Hammond, James Henry Hammond's widow, died on March 25, 1896, at the age of eighty-two. Gravestone of Catherine Fitzsimons Hammond, Hammond Cemetery, Beech Island, South Carolina.

trouble.[1] There is nothing for me to do, and I can't say if I am disgusted with love and living, tho not with you.

JOHN SEDGWICK BILLINGS TO KATHARINE F. HAMMOND[b]

New York, August 13, 1896

Oh my dear:

You must be ill, or overworked or the heat is too much for you, to talk as you do. You told me not to talk about coming to Redcliffe—and I have not said a hundredth part of the things that I wanted to say. You know I am coming—and you ought to know that if I could not come and knew it, no subject would be more distasteful to me. Why dear—I love you with my whole heart and soul—the only reason I let four long days go by without writing was because I had told you so, and your not writing me made me think that you did not like it—and that I must not say such things—and until I knew whether you were angry with me, it was impossible for me to write about indifferent things. If you could only go somewhere where it is cool and quiet—where you would have none of this beastly work and worry—and where you would have someone with you who would not bore you—someone you loved in your strange fantastic—and yet utterly delightful way. I cannot bear the thought of your being sick and weary and nervous—*you*—while so many worthless women are enjoying life in a way they have no right to. 'Worthless' has no reference to morals. Hartley has almost consented to take the sea trip to Savannah with me—he is very fond of the water—and talks of taking his wheel and riding around Savannah for a couple of days if the roads are decent. Can you tell me anything about them from a cyclist's point of view—perhaps [Frank] Miller knows. I had a devil of a time last night—your beautiful boy was ignominiously clubbed by a policeman—but he will be fired all right. You know there was an awful crowd at the Bryan ratification meeting at the Garden.[1]

1. William Woolsey's Aiken bank had gone into receivership in 1894. ECH to Katharine Hammond, April 3, 1894, William W. Woolsey to JBH, May 10, 1894, HBC Family Papers, SCL.

1. William Jennings Bryan delivered his speech accepting the Democratic Party's presidential nomination on the evening of August 12, 1896, in 88-degree heat at Madison Square Garden. Twelve thousand people jammed inside the Garden with a crowd of fifteen thousand more outside in the streets. Louis Koenig, *Bryan: A Political Biography of William Jennings Bryan* (New York: G. P. Putnam's Sons, 1971), p. 224.

Well the police would not let anyone get within two squares of the place and clubbed everyone indiscriminately. I had two press tickets and tried to get through the lines—I was turned down and started to walk away but did not move fast enough for his majesty Mick, so he told me to "——— ———!! out of here" and at the same time hit me across the shoulders with his big long night stick. It did not hurt me at all, but the effect was as if an elephant had butted me—I went ten feet into the crowd. Of course I did not lose my temper—oh no. I started to unbutton my vest to get at my Inspector's (B.O.H.) [Board of Health] badge, and the crowd thought I had a gun and broke in all directions crying "For God's sake, don't shoot, Mister!" I showed the badge, called for the captain, and had the man sent back to the station house and his club given to one of the reserves. Then I tore up my tickets and hunted for a place to recover my equanimity in—and a long cold drink. But I don't think I have ever been so angry. And what I got was nothing. I saw one fine looking old man with private box tickets clubbed and choked until he dropped. Hurrah for the Reform Policeman. I should have shown my badge at first—it will take me anywhere in this town. It is just a little cooler today—just enough to tell the difference and that is all. The work at the Mill must be very exacting if your brother has to go back with his shoulder not well yet—he has my sympathy for being laid up in this weather. Now suppose we have an understanding—no, I won't ask it now. It must keep until I see you—but I give you fair warning—if you do not want me to say what I feel in my letters—you must tell me so—and I will *try* to obey you.

Yours ever,

John

JULIA B. HAMMOND TO WILLIAM W. WOOLSEY[b]

Redcliffe, September 18, 1896

Dearest:

John Billings is here,[1] and he delights me to the bottom of my heart by his severe virtue, his clean purity, his simple devotion to one person

---

1. John had not seen Katharine since the summer of 1894, and during their two-year separation Katharine had an array of suitors, but the undaunted Billings set sail for the South on September 5th to see if their relationship could be revitalized. He remained at Redcliffe for two weeks, and at the end of his visit Katharine and John became engaged.

whom he loves, trusts, and admires. I am looking at my love for you thro' the light he throws on it, the candid, resplendent light of truth. I see this love has terrible defects, but the singleness of that love, the full knowledge that its only return will be pain, and that yet it gives itself ungrudgedly makes me able to hold up my head unashamed tho' at times full of grief.

Oh gracious God help me thru this true repentence to work out an ability to help those I love so well. Give me patience, hope, may I not be discouraged, oh divine charity come into my heart.

JOHN SEDGWICK BILLINGS TO KATHARINE F. HAMMOND[b]

Waynesboro, [Georgia], September 23, 1896

My Darling:

It was all very well to talk of our both being so much happier than the last time we parted, and that we were actually going to be happy all the long time before we meet again—but I came very near actually breaking down in Augusta. The only thing that kept me up was your own beautiful fortitude. You are always going to be like that to me, are you not—helping, strengthening, consoling, and pointing out the right.

How the thoughts have been racing and tumbling through my mind—all nervous of this visit to Redcliffe—the nearest I have ever come to perfect earthly happiness as yet. And the feeling of the very first days is creeping over me again—that—it is all a beautiful dream and that I am going to wake up to stern reality again. But no that feeling is weak compared to what it was before and will soon be succeeded by another—that *you* are the only reality in the world for me and all the rest is "such stuff as dreams are made of"—no, again, for you are all that the happiest mortal could dream of happiness. Sweetest Sweetness—that will ring forever with your "Beautiful Boy" in my mind—S.S. and B.B.—there is the answer to the *third* question of your catechism—"who belong?" I am just beginning now—I have worked these two years and planned and been happy and miserable by turns all for you—but *now* I will do all that for and with you and everything I may do or accomplish will be done by two—in one. Although you are at home with those that love you, you must not think that I do not realize that yours is, if anything the harder part—to sit with folded hands and wait. And so realizing, be sure, be very sure my best beloved, that anything I may do to shorten the time of paralyzing inactivity will not be left undone and you must be equally sure that when it is over your "resting" is done with until—well, until we can both rest together.

There my thoughts got gloomy over "our long home" and I stopped. But now they have raced away again and have been on "Mother and Julia." How I have grown to love them—and how I wish them to love me. Not in years and years have I learned to love anyone as I have Julia—and your Mother has all that and more—a reverent awe at her gracious age, mingling with the feeling of affection. And 'tis useless to tell me that your father was ever in a bad temper in his life. For days I have prayed and hoped that you will love my people as I do yours—let that be so, and I will have no misgivings as to your being contented in New York. Why I could live at Redcliffe all the rest of my life—almost. But then I am a man and a young one—you and I may finish up there yet.[1]

This scrawl is an "unpremeditated offense," dearest—it is only the expression of those of my flying thoughts that could be caught and put on paper. When a man closes his eyes and says softly to himself for half an hour or so "Hearts dearest, I love you, love you, love you so"—his thoughts are such as are told by the eyes alone and read only by *her*, and at the mere thought of writing they fly far away. It was only as I left you precious, that our parting and what it meant, came overwhelmingly home to me—and while my life will be more happy than before, the thought of our parting will never leave me, until we see each other again—and through the second wait—ah, that will be hardest of all—it will be with me—until we are joined one unto the other by those

> "Mighty bands which no mortal strait
> Nor death himself with all prevailing hand can separate."

They "put me off at Buffalo" sure enough at Millen, [Georgia]—the conductor almost had to throw me off to make me transfer, as I knew nothing about it. My tender, beautiful foot with rose-bud blossoming toes, is behaving itself, and gives me no trouble. The rest on the steamer will finish the cure completely. This has been three hours in

---

1. Although Katharine and John Sedgwick Billings never lived together at Redcliffe, their son, John Shaw Billings, lived at Redcliffe from 1954 when he retired from Time, Inc. until his death in 1975.

the writing—and we are drawing near to Savannah—now for a rest. A heart full of love for 'Mother and Julia' and oh my darling, my whole soul goes out to you.

Ever,

John

WILLIAM W. WOOLSEY TO JULIA B. HAMMOND[b]

Breeze Hill, September 23, 1896

Dear Miss Hammond:

Your great news, I am asked about on every hand. I answer that I have no doubt of the engagement, but have never heard it officially announced.

Is that diplomatical enough to please you.

I am sitting with my feet in the sunshine to keep warm, think of that, and yesterday I was hunting the shade. We have a wonderful climate: Why try to find the North Pole at home, when it so often looks and pokes us up.

The gin is at last working well and I have taught Hampton how to run it and am happier—Last year it took me six months to recover from breathing the lint. Mrs. Woolsey talks of driving over with me to call on your Mother and all before long.

My King cotton is turning out a disappointment. I don't believe it will make ⅔ of Peterkins under the same circumstances. Every time I trust one of these loose ended Agricultural-experimental stations I suffer for it.

We have a lot of new books of which I will bring a sample when next I visit Redcliffe. Love to all,

Yours sincerely,

W.W. Woolsey

JOHN SEDGWICK BILLINGS TO KATHARINE F. HAMMOND[b]

New York, October 22, 1896

Oh my dear—my very dear:

I have so much to make me feel badly. Dot's letter from Will[1] today tells her that he has had to go to the Hospital—he must be in a very

1. William Hanna Wilson, husband of "Dot" Kate Sherman Billings, John Sedgwick Billings's sister, was in the South for his health.

bad way. But your letter in which you speak so positively of not coming, and say that the only place you want to go to, is Washington—and then what you say about Clare's letter[2] and about yourself. But I will brace up—or try to—only that thing about Frank Hardeman[3] hits me hard.

Dearest, what did Clare say, to give you such an idea—and oh how I would that I could sweep your brain clear of such foolish notions. Sweetness—it is only your love for me that makes you think such good thoughts about me and my future. I will never be anything—in the way of famous or distinguished. Never—never—and what is more I don't want to be nor do I think that such fame as is to be won—Dearest Sweetest love—*I have just gotten your telegram:*[4] Mother has just poked her nose in and handed it to me—Oh my dear, I am so happy: I am just the happiest man here in this big city—and am so sorry and ashamed of my meanness in the first of this letter—and I take back what I said about F.H.—I could tear this up and begin again only—only, dear heart, you are to know me through and through—good and bad. But I will never be able to get rid of my trait of jealousy—but I will try and fight it always. Sweetness, I have no words to thank you with—nor, luckily, have I any words to tell you of the black misery I have been fighting against for four days—it seems four weeks. Have I shown it in my letters, Sweetheart—I have set my teeth and said I would not, every time I wrote. Yesterday it was horrible—*that* was the cause of my apathy, and I feel that it took all my will power to prevent my being overcome with despair. But it is all right now—my dear, you are very good to me.

Now I am going back to my lecture—utterly useless, for I have scolded you a dozen times and it makes no impression. Anyway—as I said, I have not ambition enough to think the game worth the candle. All my ambition is to be an honest straightforward gentleman and to make you happy and be deserving of you—I will do my best in my work

2. The reference is probably to John's sister, Clare Billings Ord.

3. B. Frank Hardeman, a cotton merchant living in Athens, Georgia became acquainted with Katharine when she nursed his mother in her final illness in 1895. Frank broke his engagement to try to win Katharine's love, and there are many letters between 1895 and 1897 from Frank to Katharine. B. Frank Hardeman to Katharine Hammond, 1895–1897, passim, HBC Family Papers, SCL.

4. The telegram confirmed that Katharine would go to New York. She arrived in December and spent six weeks with John and his parents. Before she returned to Redcliffe their wedding date was set for April 20, 1897. MS vol. bd., 1855–1908. Autobiographical account of "the early life of John Shaw Billings II," John Shaw Billings Scrapbook Collection, SCL.

of course—but my work can never be anything but secondary to you—
never, never. These great men are wedded to their work—always, and
their wives and children and friends are minor considerations. This is
always so. They win fame it is true—but of true contented, peaceful
happiness, they can never know as much as the others. It is not an
enviable life to me—I would not have led my father's life for twice his
name and fame[5]—we children love him, but oh how much more we
would, if he would let us—but he cannot—he is shut off from that.
There has never been a moment when he could not put his family
troubles behind him, and do his work as well as ever. Aye—he has
done it. That is what it is to be a great man. Sweetheart, this is the
plain, unvarnished truth I am telling you—he knows it as well as the
rest of us. Now don't say I would have done likewise had I not known
you—Dear, you have saved me. I have always hated my father's life—
hated it fiercely and vindictively, for what it deprived him of, and have
often sworn to myself that never, never would I isolate myself in that
way—for you have to do it. No—I would have gone on as I started—
loose and careless and only turned to listen to the cataract as I went
over. But that is all past and gone—that was in the dark ages before I
knew you. And now I am a man—your man and yours alone—who is
going to have a great deal more happiness than he deserves. And to say
you cannot help me—why my darling, you are I, and I am you—and
what one does, the other deserves the credit of. Help me—aye that you
can, and will, and do—every moment of my life you help me, and I
do things easily or turn aside readily and willingly, somewhat of my
own strength but half of it comes from you. I am a very weak some-

5. John's father, John Shaw Billings, was born in Indiana on April 12, 1838, of poor parents.
He received an A.B. degree from Miami University in 1857, an M.D. in 1860 from the Medical
College of Ohio in Cincinnati, and served as an army surgeon during the Civil War. Remaining
in the service after the war, he was placed in charge of the Library of the Surgeon-General's Office
and founded the justly famed *Index Catalogue*, a multi-volume guide to medical literature, and
the equally important *Index Medicus* a monthly guide to the current medical periodical literature.
In addition he published a textbook on the principles of heating and ventilation, contributed to the
tenth and eleventh censuses of the United States (he purportedly suggested punched cards to Hol-
lerith), designed the buildings for Johns Hopkins Hospital, and lectured at both Johns Hopkins and
the University of Pennsylvania Medical Schools. After retiring from the Army in 1895, he became
the first Director of the New York Public Library, a post which he held until his death in 1913.
He essentially established the institution as it now exists by combining various smaller collections,
planning the design of the central library building, and raising funds to establish the branch libraries. "Dr. John Shaw Billings, Director of the New York Public Library, 1896–1913," *The
Bulletin of the New York Public Library*, April 1913, pp. 3–8; Estelle Brodman, *The Development
of Medical Bibliography* (Baltimore: Medical Library Association, 1954), pp. 106–27.

body—and I want smiles and sighs—sympathy and love—and yours and yours only—and lastly, Sweetness, it is all over—all settled. You have said that you loved me and would marry me—and all these foolish, foolish thoughts of yours, are of the past—long, long ago in the unhappy days. No use now in thinking these things my dearest—the milk is spilled, and we will just have to make the best of things. So—'put by your foolish fears, and through all the coming years, just be glad.' Oh my darling, you have made me so happy. . . .

Your,

John

PART IV

The Restorer
John Shaw Billings

The marriage of Katharine and John Sedgwick Billings was not a happy
one. Four months after her wedding day Katharine wrote home to her
mother that "I can't be happy away from him [John] any more than I
can be happy without you."[1] Katharine made many trips back to Redcliffe, leaving her husband in New York City to look after his patients
and to write her in the early years of their marriage devoted, loving
letters. For twenty years, in addition to maintaining a private practice,
John worked for the New York City Department of Health and in 1915
became its Deputy Commissioner. He retired from the Department in
1917 amid some criticism of his handling of a recent polio epidemic in
Brooklyn, and in 1918 he briefly joined the Army Medical Corps as an
epidemiologist. After the war, he became medical officer for the New
York Stock Exchange and the New York Telephone Company, and for
those businesses he pioneered preventive medicine through annual em-
ployee health examinations.[2]

The first of their three children, John Shaw Billings, born at Redcliffe in 1898, was named for his paternal grandfather. In later life John
Shaw, not awed by his grandfather's achievements, described him as a
"cold remote man, dedicated to work. . . . I am named for him but I

1. Katharine Hammond Billings to ECH, Sept. 21, 1897, HBC Family Papers, SCL.
2. MS vol. bd., 1877–1959. Career data on John Sedgwick Billings; MS vol. bd., 1855–1908.
Autobiographical account of "the early life of John Shaw Billings II," John Shaw Billings Scrapbook Collection, SCL; Interview with Henry Billings, Sag Harbor, New York, June 21, 1979; John
Duffy, A History of Public Health in New York City: 1866–1966 (New York: Russell Sage Foundation, 1974), pp. 265, 273–75, 541.

don't like his personality or his manners. He and his descendants lack the warm humanness of my mother's family."[3] Henry, named for his maternal great grandfather, James Henry Hammond, was born in 1901. Julian, named for his maternal great uncle who died in a Union prisoner-of-war camp, was born in 1904 when Katharine was thirty-seven years old. He lived only two years.

The marriage somehow went all wrong. Katharine, always homesick for Redcliffe and her own family, and often sick after 1907 as a result of thyroid and heart conditions, was made even more miserable by the steady build-up of marital tension. According to her, John, who in good years earned as much as $20,000 spent it all quickly on his clubs and society sports, leaving his family strapped for funds. Each partner was strong-willed and unaccustomed to compromise; she was "sick and temperish," and he was "selfish and fickle."[4] As their affection for each other dwindled, their marriage began to wobble dangerously. In 1912, following a five-year affair with a former patient, Josephine West, Billings was named correspondent in the West divorce suit and the scandal made the New York newspapers.[5] After 1919 Billings made no attempt to conceal his attachment for a nurse in his office, Mrs. Josephine Long Toering. Katharine, her health deteriorating steadily, died of a heart attack in 1925 at the age of fifty-eight and was buried beside her mother in the Redcliffe cemetery in "a coveted place Aunt Julia gave her."[6]

Five months after Katharine's death Billings married Mrs. Toering. In dismay his son John wrote, "how utterly ashamed I am. Mother not dead six months and father goes off and marries the woman who wrecked her life and happiness. Lord how I hate them." His father's second marriage referred to by John as "this awful union," broke "the last link" between them.[7] John's father, in ill health since his retirement from the New York City Health Department in 1918, did not long survive his second marriage. He died in April 1928 of septic arthritis. Though Henry, the younger son, had remained close to his father, the hostility John felt survived his father's death and continued to color his memories and impressions of his Billings relatives.

3. MS vol. bd., 1855–1908. Autobiographical account of "the early life of John Shaw Billings II"; MS vol. bd., c. 1860–1951. Time Inc. data, John Shaw Billings Scrapbook Collection, SCL.

4. Ibid.

5. The New York Herald, July 11, 1912; MS vol. bd., 1908–1912. Resumé of John Sedgwick family history, John Shaw Billings Scrapbook Collection, SCL.

6. John Shaw Billings Diary, July 8, 1925, John Shaw Billings Papers, SCL.

7. Ibid., Dec. 9, 1925.

The family bonds had been loosened years before in 1911 when Emily Hammond died. Her grandchildren had been as passionately devoted to the gentle but firm matriarch as her own children had been. After Emily's death, Harry Hammond, withdrawing more than ever into a semi-spartan life, lived in a basement room at Redcliffe until his death in 1916. With the deaths of Emily and Harry another chapter at Redcliffe ended. One mourner marked the passing of Harry as the closing of a simpler yet more heroic age. "To my thinking your father was the wisest man among us; knew more, thought more, lived a larger life. To a natural endowment, enriched by study and travel, there was added a love of humanity." He concluded, "We have rarely honored enough those best deserving of honor, but have given too much thought to the evanescent phases of current political and military life."[8]

Redcliffe continued to be occupied by Julia and her husband Jim Richards whom she married in the Redcliffe parlor on September 28, 1911, three weeks after her mother's funeral. Though her Hammond and Cumming kin thought at first that Julia had made a mistake, her marriage to Jim proved to be a very happy one for nearly a quarter of a century.[9] The couple's financial resources, however, dwindled away.

Richards, who had always been a poor businessman, lost most of his wife's small inheritance. His luckless ventures and the Southern agricultural depression in the 1920s reduced Julia and Jim to a meagre living selling Redcliffe milk, eggs, and vegetables. The end of the long winding road that led to absolute ruin clearly was in sight, for by now almost all the Hammond lands had been sold away. When Emily died in 1911, only 2000 acres of Silver Bluff remained, and her estate sold this property to her son Kit Hammond for $11,000. Soon thereafter, Kit sold 1500 acres of it out of the family for $25,000. All that remained of James Henry Hammond's vast holdings was Kit's 500 acres and the house at Redcliffe on 373 acres.[10] Although Redcliffe's physical deterioration grew more obvious with each passing year, the couple hung on there until Jim died in September 1934, and Julia followed him six months later. The death of Julia in March 1935 left Redcliffe's fate in doubt.

Against this backdrop, John Shaw Billings emerges. Between his

8. James Henry Rice, Jr., to Mrs. James P. Richards, Jan. 9, 1916, HBC Family Papers, SCL.
9. Interview with Katharine Hammond Suber, Kathwood Plantation, Jackson, South Carolina, July 31, 1979.
10. Ibid.; Billings, "The Hammond Family," SCL.

birth at Redcliffe in May 1898 and October 1907, John made ten visits to Beech Island. On a four-month visit in 1907, when he was nine years old, the "happiest memories" of all his childhood visits to Redcliffe would later be centered. Never again would the okra soup taste as good, the water from the silver dipper be as sweet, the fireplaces burn as bright, the beds feel as soft, or the family behave more affectionately. "Redcliffe acquired a hazy glow of perfection which it never lost through the wastes of time to come."[11]

Redcliffe meant much to John even though his trips became less frequent when he was sent off first to Repton in Tarrytown, New York, in 1910, then to St. Paul's at Concord, New Hampshire, in 1912, and from there to Harvard in 1916. He thought the atmosphere at school was privileged and unreal and he confided that he was happy to leave when the United States entered World War I. He went to France with the American Ambulance Service and learned to fly before being discharged in 1919. Back at Cambridge, Billings grew impatient with Harvard, which he wrote "was conducted like an overcrowded nursery."[12] Involved in Connecticut's gubernatorial campaign in the summer of 1920, he found reasons to stay on through the fall election and never returned to Harvard, dropping out, as his mother had, just one term short of earning his diploma.

On New Year's Day 1921, Billings went to work for *The Brooklyn Daily Eagle* at $30 a week, and in October he was sent to Washington as an assistant correspondent. After eight years with the newspaper the hard-working and ambitious Billings felt he had no future there, and just at that moment John Martin, the editor of *Time* magazine, called and asked him to come to New York to take over the magazine's national affairs section. "I stammered yes in joyous excitement. At last here was an escape from the Eagle at this most critical moment—an escape to higher realms." The *Eagle* was "a paltry thing I could now kick aside and forget," and the chance at *Time* "a step up which I did not have to go out and hunt."[13]

From the time of his grandfather's death in 1916 until his extended

---

11. MS vol. bd., 1855–1908. Autobiographical account of "the early life of John Shaw Billings II," John Shaw Billings Scrapbook Collection, SCL.

12. John Shaw Billings Diary, March 1, 1920, John Shaw Billings Papers, SCL; MS vol. bd., c. 1860–1951. Time Inc. data, John Shaw Billings Scrapbook Collection, SCL.

13. John Shaw Billings Diary, Jan. 23, 1929, John Shaw Billings Papers; MS vol. bd., c. 1860–1951. Time Inc. data, John Shaw Billings Scrapbook Collection, SCL.

visit South in the fall of 1922, Beech Island had been only a cherished memory for John. On this visit he met Frederica Washburn Wade, whose mother was the lovely Gussie Black frequently referred to in the family letters of the late 1880s. In 1889 Miss Black of Beech Island met Peyton Wade, who was studying to be a lawyer; they were married six years later in Atlanta. Frederica, their only child, was born September 11, 1901. Her father became Chief Justice of the Georgia Court of Appeals. After Judge Wade died, Frederica and her mother built a small house at Beech Island and returned there to live in May 1922. John met the beautiful but shy Miss Wade, fell in love, and married her at the Beech Island Presbyterian Church on April 19, 1924.[14] Aunt Julia gave the wedding reception at Redcliffe.

The next five years brought them a mixture of happiness and sadness. When Katharine died in July 1925, John and Frederica attended the funeral at Beech Island. John wrote in his diary, "arrived at Redcliffe and up the long front steps where Aunt Julia stood to welcome us in. Oh, this fine old house, with its great arms open impartially to life and to death."[15] In November 1926, a daughter, Frederica Wade Billings II, whom they called Skeeter, was born. When Skeeter was seventeen months old, her father recorded in his diary, "Our hearts are bursting with love for her and everything is subordinated to her welfare and comfort." That same month, April 1928, John's father died.[16] The following year, although an epidemic had struck parts of Georgia, the homesick Frederica begged John to take his vacation there so she could visit relatives and show off the baby. Skeeter became suddenly ill at Indian Springs, Georgia, and died of meningitis a few days later in an Atlanta hospital.[17] Her death, wrote Billings, was the greatest tragedy in their lives.[18] There were to be no other children.

Meanwhile Billings's career at *Time* magazine skyrocketed. Henry Luce made Billings managing editor in 1934; he recorded in his diary,

14. MS vol. bd., 1809–1962. Genealogical data re the Black, Kirkland, Robison, *et al.* families of Georgia and South Carolina, ibid.; Addendum on Billings-Wade Courtship, Loose Papers, John Shaw Billings and Frederica Wade Billings Papers, SCL, cited hereafter as Mr. and Mrs. John Shaw Billings Papers; marriage certificate of John Shaw Billings and Frederica Washburn Wade, April 19, 1924, ibid.; *Augusta Chronicle*, April 20, 1924.

15. John Shaw Billings Diary, July 8, 1925, John Shaw Billings Papers, SCL.

16. Ibid., April 1928, April 27, 1928.

17. Interview with Henry Billings, Sag Harbor, New York, July 19, 1979; MS vol. bd., c. 1860–1951. Time Inc. data, John Shaw Billings Scrapbook Collection, SCL.

18. MS vol. bd., c. 1860–1951. Time Inc. data, John Shaw Billings Scrapbook Collection, SCL.

"I have in fact made good."[19] The following year when Julia died, he was torn between duty to *Time*—he was in the middle of editing an issue—and his desire to go to Redcliffe. Though he said "he felt guilty as a dog running out like this," he was drawn to Beech Island, for one thought kept returning to his mind, the future of Redcliffe. "God knows," he wrote, "I want it more than anything else in the world." John, Frederica, and John's brother Henry attended the funeral. As soon as they arrived at Redcliffe their Uncle Henry took the brothers aside and asked them what was to become of Redcliffe now that Julia had died. He and Julia owned the place jointly; but he said he certainly did not want it. Nobody could afford it "unless John you are a damned enough fool to want to buy it." John wondered who had told Uncle Henry of his fantasy. Soon it became apparent that all the family gathered for the funeral were under the impression that Katharine's son not only wanted Redcliffe but that he could afford to buy it. His Uncle Kit and Uncle Alf also yearned for the homeplace, but neither of them had the purchase price. Frederica called John aside and told him that the idea of buying Redcliffe filled her with apprehension. How could they manage it from New York City? Uncle Henry continued to press John and offered him Redcliffe for $15,000. On the train North after the funeral, Frederica remained opposed, and John let her talk out all her reasons. "All I had to say was that I wanted Redcliffe more than anything else in the world." Henry was on his side, but John thought his brother "overplayed his hand by minimizing the risks and exaggerating the joys."

Back in their New York apartment at 1200 Fifth Avenue, Frederica, her mother Gussie Black Wade, who had lived with them since 1932, and John talked all afternoon about the restoration of Redcliffe "if" they bought it. Finally Frederica's imagination was caught, and she said she needed to see some interior decorating books of ante-bellum homes. John knew he had persuaded her, and that same afternoon he had their chauffeur, William, drive them "to Macy's where F. found two volumes with lots of pretty pictures which she wanted." Billings was convinced that these two books brought Frederica around as much as her wish for him to have an interest outside of his *Time* office.[20]

19. John Shaw Billings Diary, April 30, 1934, John Shaw Billings Papers, SCL.
20. Ibid., March 16–March 20, 1935.

Billings recalled a visit to Redcliffe in 1912 when he was fourteen years old. An old friend of his mother's seeing Redcliffe for the first time turned to John and said, "This is a most beautiful place! Someday you must make it your purpose to own and love it as your mother does."[21] Conjuring up all these old memories, he indulged his dream and bought Redcliffe. Uncle Henry now said he was a fool to do so, "but a fool must follow his natural bent." John replied, "I am a fool— but a very happy one!"[22]

All this had taken place in March 1935. By August, after renovation had begun at Redcliffe, Billings wrote, "I long to chuck my Time job and go to Redcliffe for good." Only the fact that he needed his salary for the repairs and upkeep kept him at work in Manhattan. "I hate all these lying, thieving Yankees and would gladly never see one of them again. I work for Time, but my heart really isn't in it."[23] When Henry Luce and his new bride Clare Booth Luce bought Mepkin plantation near Charleston in 1936, perhaps influenced by Billings's example but more likely by that of other rich Northerners who acquired Southern plantations for hunting preserves, Billings felt intruded upon; "I felt," he wrote, "South Carolina belonged to me."[24]

His power and responsibilities grew at Time, Inc.—he had become managing editor of *Life* magazine in October 1936[25]—but, more and more, his thoughts turned to Redcliffe. Within three years he had lovingly restored the fine old house to *his* vision of its ante-bellum greatness. At a formal dance in 1938 honoring his twenty-year-old cousin Mary Gwynn Hammond, daughter of his Uncle Kit, Billings proudly turned the floodlights on the newly completed restoration. Redcliffe by illumination, reported Billings, looked "like a great white frosted wedding cake or a spectacular movie set."[26]

The correspondence opens on Katharine and John's honeymoon. It soon became apparent that the marriage of Katharine Hammond to John Sedgwick Billings would be one of tension rather than harmony as

21. MS vol. bd., 1908–1912. Resumé of John Sedgwick family history, John Shaw Billings Scrapbook Collection, SCL.
22. Henry Hammond to John Shaw Billings, March 25, 1935, John Shaw Billings to Henry Hammond, March 27, 1935, Mr. and Mrs. John Shaw Billings Papers, SCL.
23. John Shaw Billings Diary, Aug. 17, 1935, John Shaw Billings Papers, SCL.
24. Ibid., April 6, 1936.
25. Ibid., Oct. 23, 1936.
26. Ibid., April 28, 1938.

polarities of families and geography, custom and character pulled and hauled at the participants. Redcliffe came to dominate their marriage and caused John to cry out, "I am afraid of Redcliffe—it always comes between us."[27]

27. John Sedgwick Billings to Katharine Hammond Billings, May 4, 1904, Legal Size Papers, HBC Family Papers, SCL.

KATHARINE H. BILLINGS TO EMILY C. HAMMOND[b]

Skyland, North Carolina[1] [April 25, 1897]

Dearest Mother:

Tho it is Sunday we have just gotten a large mail. Most of it letters and cards that you have forwarded to us, and then just a few precious lines from you and Julia. It is so good of you two to write me these notes when you are so busy—and must be so very tired with the long strain you have been on. Today, it is all over—and I hope you are having a quiet, easy day with the boys. My heart is right there with you all—and I am loving you and thinking of you all the day long, and it will be the same every day. John has been reading me the finest letter from an old German doctor, a friend of his Father's. It was all so grand and magnificent—written in German. Along with the letter came a beautiful embroidered handkerchief for me. I will have a splendid collection of handkerchiefs—I take them all out and look at them and gloat over them two or three times a day. I would never dream of using them. You have put away my beautifulest one of all for me—the one you gave me—take good care of please 'm. What became of my flowers that night? When you have time do tell me of the rest of that evening—and how you got rid of some of the people next day. Have any more presents come? A letter from Mr. Chaffe says he has sent me something by express. Was there any thing with these other cards you enclosed to us? I don't want to forget to thank any one, and our list is in rather a muddle as it is. John is helping me splendidly—he can answer five to my one—but I hardly feel that it is right for me to let him do it. I shall write again to some of the people after I get to New York, and have plenty of time and nothing to do. You will look upon my letters as long lists of things I want you to do. I am ashamed to have left my affairs in such a condition. Now I am going to ask if you have sent me my white corsets—the pair I wore at the wedding—and a pair of bicycle corsets I left in my wardrobe. I was foolish enough to come off here without a pair of white ones, and any where else I could not get on without them. But as I only weigh 127 I could do without any at all.

1. After their wedding on April 20, John and Katharine left Redcliffe and spent a week honeymooning in a small private cottage at Skyland, North Carolina near Asheville. MS vol. bd., 1855–1908. Autobiographical account of "the early life of John Shaw Billings II," John Shaw Billings Scrapbook Collection, SCL.

Yesterday afternoon John and I climbed to the top of a mountain—not a very high one. When we got there we might as well have stood on the ground and looked up into the sky—for any view we got. You remember how hazy the mountains looked that August we were here. I rather like the haze for then you don't see the bald scabby places on them. The ground is blue with violets but there is hardly another sign of spring. The trees are hardly in bud. This afternoon we are going to ride on horseback—we won't go very fast or very far, so you must not be anxious about me. It is warmer today, and still bright. John says he appreciates your note very very much—that he will insist upon writing to you tomorrow. He is as good to me as ever you would have him be, and we are as happy as it is possible to be.

Love to all,
your Katharine

HENRY C. HAMMOND TO HARRY HAMMOND[b]

Augusta, May 29, 1897

My dear Father:

Your letter by Will Wilson has just reached me.[1] I do not know what prompted it—it comes without preface, introduction, or explanation. I do not know what, if any, comment I should make concerning it. However, since you bring up the matter of family finance in the manner set out in your letter I will say: Accountings are always advisable, between whom it matters not. Accounts are in themselves of value regardless of their further personal feature as showing the good, or bad management of the accountant. The sole reason for your making a statement of the various ways by which the family funds have come and gone would be the natural interest we would all take in it and the valuable lessons which such a history might teach us. But once and for all let us put behind us a personal individual consideration of this matter. It is not I or me, but we and us. All have put in as much as they could, all have taken out as little as they could. Who will be heard to complain of the much they have given or the little they have received?

Often the thought is brought home to me of the hardships and the

---

1. Will Wilson, Katharine Billings's brother-in-law, was staying in the Augusta area because of his ill health.

disappointments, in a material way at least, which have befallen you
and the generation and class of which you were a member. Born to
comfort, ease and luxury; with every reasonable expectation that they
would be continued during your lifetime to suddenly become the target
of the slings and arrows of outrageous fortune was a shock the with-
standing of which required the fortitude of a hero. The poverty, the
narrowed field of action, the anxiety and the care which without warning environed you life in its prime was made tolerable, I should think,
only by these considerations: Your lot was the common lot; fairly good
health, food, clothes and a shelter; a family that promised not to disgrace you and which up to this time has kept that promise; but above
all things else together added, squared and cubed you have had the best
woman in the world for a companion, for a friend, for a coworker and
a cosufferer, for a wife. In this last regard I cannot believe you have
lived the better part of your life too near a mountain to know it was a
mountain.

Into your keeping as a matter of course Mother willingly and lovingly entrusted her all. Today she is satisfied and pleased with your
administration of the joint stock. Does she, or any one, require of you
an accounting to prove that there has been no wrongful, or negligent
misdirection of funds? Perish the thought! For the common weal with
yours and hers you have done your best, which was the best—you have
not done less, could you have done more?

Where do we stand today? Grant that we were hasty, even ill-ad-
vised, in the ventures prompted by our unexpected inheritance,[2] still
we have made better use of it certainly than the old people did of their
three wishes. A number of galling debts have been wiped out, and however hopeless a view you may take of the situation I still hope there is
considerable left to us. Considerable in a material way, but life is not

2. Sarah Wallace Cumming, the unmarried sister of Henry Harford Cumming, and aunt of
Emily Cumming Hammond, died on December 6, 1895. She left an estate of about $300,000, of
which Emily inherited between $40,000 and $50,000, including some real estate in Augusta. John
Shaw Billings referred to his grandmother's inheritance as a "lifesaver." The reference by Henry
Hammond to the "ventures prompted by our unexpected inheritance" included the building of the
Kathwood Manufacturing Company, a cotton-seed oil mill which was located at the former Cedar
Grove Plantation now known as Kathwood. MS vol. bd., 1927–n.d. "Myself and Family," John
Shaw Billings Scrapbook Collection; Bryan Cumming to ECH, June 7, 1897; List of Inheritances
of Emily Cumming Hammond, c. 1912, HBC Family Papers; Henry C. Hammond to ECH,
Dec. 10, 1896, Kathwood Manufacturing Company, Beech Island Papers, 1896–1901, 1904,
SCL.

made up wholly of material things. Freedom from disease and the major sins should bring about as much happiness as we have a right to expect. We can all of us claim so much as this. Let us have peace and good cheer. I have no care on earth but for you, Mother, Julia, Katharine, Kit and Alf. The little substance I have, or may accumulate, my best thought, my best love is yours. Nothing could possibly weigh against the delight that would come to me with the consciousness that good, friendly, cordial, loving relations existed between us all. It may not be the part of youth to counsel age, but let age beware of crystallizing into such form as will cut and wound and lacerate the hearts of those who gladly serve and freely love.

Very affectionately yours,

H.C.H.

JOHN SEDGWICK BILLINGS TO KATHARINE H. BILLINGS[b]

New York, July 21, 1897

My precious, my precious:

It is awful—my eyes were so misty on that old car that I could not be sure I saw you on the ship, waving to me [1]—but I waved back, and the lump in my throat was so big that I could only nod my head when the conductor asked if I wanted a transfer. And oh this empty house— and the dull, sickening pain in my heart to think of your being away down the coast there—possibly—nay, probably ill and no one to take care of you as your own boy could. But there—I will not talk about it any more now. But my sweetest Sweetness—mother or no mother— Redcliffe or no Redcliffe, this is the last time you leave me. Not so hard as last time—why it is a thousand times worse. I am unconsciously looking and listening for you every moment. But I *will* be brave. . . .

Thank God that by the time you get this you will be safe at home, not to stir until I come—and I also thank Him, that you have your dear mother and all the others dear to you, to soften the pain of our separation. You see, Katharine my very dearest, that I cannot keep away from

---

1. Katharine, with William Walton Woolsey as her escort, went to Redcliffe for a visit just three months after her wedding. John Sedgwick Billings followed her on August 9, and spent his two-week vacation there. On August 24 they returned to New York. MS vol. bd., 1855–1908. Autobiographical account of "the early life of John Shaw Billings II," John Shaw Billings Scrapbook Collection, SCL.

the subject—it dominates my mind entirely. Father cheered me up by remarking that you had gone out in a little storm. He misses you already—told me tonight that I was a poor substitute to sit in your place opposite to him. How do you find everyone—I hope your mother is as well as she and Julia say, and that you have struck your father at the very beginning of one of his long sunshiny moods—the only ones in which I know him. And oh how I hope you were not seasick—and that the K.C. got into Savannah on time—that Henry met you—that you wrote me a long, long, long letter on shipboard—and that you had a comfortable trip up to dear old Redcliffe—and that you are thinking of and loving your husband. My darling—my precious—I love you so: my whole being is thrilled with it and it fairly shakes my soul. Tell your mother and Julia to be as good as good can be to you—nothing anyone could do would be good enough—I send no love to anyone but my darling, sweetest, dearest wife—and my God how I love her. Katharine—dearest on Earth or in heaven—do you hear my far cry across the waters to you, dear. Oh how I will pray for your happiness tonight, my darling—and you remember me in your prayers, my wife—I need them. My wife—mine—all mine—how can fate be so cruel as to have dragged us apart in this way. I will try to be sensible tomorrow—forgive me—

Your husband,

John

JULIA B. HAMMOND TO WILLIAM W. WOOLSEY[b]

Redcliffe, August 17, 1897

Dearest:

It is raining hard. I am sitting here by the open window looking out at the dripping trees and the sodden grass, the sun ought to be up, but he certainly is invisible and this drear light that feebly filters thro' the clouds might be very second class moonlight of most inferior quality. The pools of red muddy water look vindictive and make one's heart sink for the poor swamp planters. The cotton hangs in melancholy wisps from the boles, and if the rain keeps on much longer it will topple out and bury itself in the cozy earth under it. Katharine leaves tomorrow which makes us very sad. Father is in a temper beyond words, and the servants creep around with the surliest expression, hoping you will give them a reproof and they can throw up their job and enjoy the delicious jollity and glorious gain of the cotton picking.

My mind and heart feel better after that Jeremiad. Ah but sweetest thing I have been meaning to see you. I enjoyed seeing you so much the last time you were here,[1] it seems if you were only here again all sorrows would end, but no, you would be devoting yourself to Kit. My own dear Boy. We have spent just such days together, if you were only here today we could read and talk and I could revel in seeing your enjoyment of my family. Just to think of such a treat, brings a light into my life that never was in land or sea. Now I must go and dress, and after that see about the darling Mother's coffee, and all the time think of you still, but with some of the sting gone of wanting you so bad, so bad, always prayerfully for your well being, and as a part of that the maintenance of those miles of rain between us, good morning and good bye.

KATHARINE H. BILLINGS TO EMILY C. HAMMOND[b]

New York, September 21, 1897

Dearest Mother:

I have been so cheered up by a lot of unexpected home letters (it is Tuesday and I don't usually get letters on that day) that I can write you a much better letter than I could have done an hour or two ago. The letters were from Julia, Henry and Lessie—and Lessie sent me a splendid picture of Loula Comer.[1] If you see her please tell her how glad I was to get it. I am going to write and thank her in a few days. I was mightily relieved to hear that Julia's dress would do at all. I am afraid it was only her cheerful, hopeful way of looking at it. I have been very doubtful about it myself. Privately what do you think of it?

It is bitterly cold today—I have actually suffered from it and from all the bad smells the place is reeking with. I was out for a little while this morning to do some shopping for the house and to see Mrs.

1. Woolsey had returned home to Aiken from this visit to Redcliffe on August 11. W.W. Woolsey to ECH, Aug. 12, 1897, HBC Family Papers, SCL.

1. Loula Comer was Lessie's seven-year-old niece, daughter of her brother James Henry Hammond and his wife, Georgia Black Hammond. The child was named for her paternal grandmother, Loula Comer Hammond. Billings, *Descendants of Hammond*, pp. 5, 7.

Cohen.[2] She was wonderfully better—looked like another person from the one I had seen Sunday. Poor soul she has suffered a lot! The rest of the day I have tried to work at my curtains, but have felt so wretched I could do very little. This dreadful feeling of nausea that I have suffered from so intensely for the last week—I think can mean but one thing— don't you think so dearest? John says I am very premature to think it means anything and that I ought not to speak of it even to you—there is such an uncertainty about it. But I can't help it—I must tell you—I have felt so wretched and sick and depressed and oh Mother I need your sympathy and advice so much! If only I were nearer and could talk to you and tell you everything. I am so worried about the future—and the present is such a terror to me—this terrible feeling of nausea—every smell frightens me—is it going to last a long time dearest? I want to beg and insist that you will not speak of this to any one except Julia and Father—not even the boys. You see I may be mistaken and it would be rather mortifying. I haven't been unwell since I was at Redcliffe—but after all that may have been due to the fact that I had a very bad cold at the time it was due—so you see I have nothing to make me believe that things are not as they always have been—except for the sick and unnatural way I have felt for the last ten days. This nausea sours me against all the world. I can't take any interest or pleasure in anything— so naturally I have been very trying to live with. John has been as kind as he could be—but seeing every day how much people can and do suffer—he thinks I am making an awful big fuss over my small share of it. I have felt that I must go in and fix up our apartment[3] feeling every day that I would be too sick and not able to get it ready before Mrs. Billings got back—consequently it has not all been pleasant work—and now that it is ready I have a perfect horror of the place. It is so crowded and full—we have all the bad smells of other people's cooking—even to

2. Mr. and Mrs. Henry Cohen, friends of Henry Cumming Hammond, were staying at the Fifth Avenue Hotel. Henry Cohen was an eminent lawyer and later judge in Augusta. Nora was admitted to a sanitorium for a rest-cure shortly after their arrival in New York on September 7, 1897. John Sedgwick Billings to ECH, Sept. 8, 16, 1897. HBC Family Papers; MS vol. bd., 1855–1908. Autobiographical account of "the early life of John Shaw Billings II," John Shaw Billings Scrapbook Collection, SCL.

3. On May 2, 1897, Katharine and John arrived in New York City following their honeymoon in North Carolina. At first they lived with John's parents at 32 East 31st Street where they paid $100 monthly for room and board. They quickly tired of that arrangement and moved in September to their own apartment at 162 East 31st Street. The reference to her feeling nauseated and her belief that she was in the very early stages of pregnancy proved true. John Shaw Billings, her first child, was born on May 11, 1898. MS vol. bd., 1855–1908. Autobiographical account of "the early life of John Shaw Billings II," John Shaw Billings Scrapbook Collection, SCL.

sit here and think of it makes me feel sick and suffocating. I know I will get over this when we go there day after tomorrow. Today I begged John to let me go home and see you—for with it all I have been so homesick for you and Redcliffe. Of course he would let me go—make any sacrifice to send me—but I can't leave him—I can't be happy away from him any more than I can be happy without you.

Now dearest you don't know what a relief it has been for me to tell you all of this—and feel that you sympathize with me. But already I begin to fear your tender heart will be troubled, and anxious about me—and that you will feel my troubles more deeply than I do. Please don't take me and them in this way—for then I must deny myself the comfort of speaking of them to you. And you are the only person in the world I can speak to—and tell my worries to. For John seeing how troubled and anxious I am about affairs and means and ways and every thing, thinks it will divert my mind and make it easier for me not to discuss such subjects at all. So we don't speak of all the serious things that we are both, perhaps, thinking of. This you know is a different treatment than any I have ever allowed to be pursued with me before— perhaps it is the best—I haven't taken much comfort out of it yet.

I have longed so for the country the last few days—and some fresh clean smells and air and sunshine. So John has promised to take me somewhere out of the city tomorrow. We will start out when he gets back from down town and take our lunch with us—the weather will be beautiful for a day out of doors.

You are not going to worry about me dearest—and you are not going to tell any one but Julia and Father—please don't dearest—just for a little while at any rate until I am more certain—then I won't mind.

With love to all,

Devotedly,
Katharine

HARRY HAMMOND TO KATHARINE H. BILLINGS[b]

Beech Island, October 10, 1897

My Dear Katharine:

I would have answered your letter at once but I did not have a single sheet of paper—You town people can't appreciate the delays arising from being seven miles from a sheet of paper. Of course I had to go to town. There from pure weariness I took two glasses of beer, no more I assure you. There also I asked your Uncle Joe to join me at the mill the next day, which he agreed to do coming by the 3:40 P.M. train. Well I contracted a strong weariness waiting at the mill for him, reinforced by a failure to get a bite from any fish which I had hoped to have for our dinner. I tried to mitigate this uncomfortable condition by a couple of spoonfuls of Planat Jr. Brandy, and afterwards gave Joe a little assistance with a bottle of Margaux. The sum of it all was, what with one thing and another, my right eye broke loose again until I believe my brains are softening and running out at the corner—the outer canthus.[1] I am too old to drink anything but water. Robust young people in a full tide of prosperity, may break the lingering day by a glass in moderation with impunity, and they may never know its poisonous nature until the sands in the hour glass run low, and the grasshopper is a burden. In spite of the blatant temperance movements of this age I have recently discovered that the increase in the consumption of alcoholic drinks is much greater than the increase in the population; and what surprises me to learn still more is that a very large proportion of these poisons—they are really poisons—are dealt out in patent medicine cure-alls. The fact is I am fast becoming afraid that this generation is facing fearful damage from the widespread indulgence in a multiplying list of hypnotics, whose use is rather than otherwise encouraged even by the regular profession. It gives their patients a temporary and factitious relief, and crowns the prescriber as a magical pain killer. I hear you take an occasional sip of cordial for your health. Let me warn you against it and against all other ready relief agencies. Pain and discomfort are not meant to hurt you. They are mere danger signals universal in their nature. Just like all pleasurable sensations are. And yet men and women have made good and evil and an eternal hell and an eternal heaven out of them and sat in judgment with these witnesses against God and his works, and the idols they have set up in the place of the old faith in sanctification by trials and pains are Mrs. Winslow's Soothing Syrup, the essence of Jamaican ginger (Derry), creme de menthe (Maria), etc. etc., a perfect pantheon. If I do not make my meaning clear just in your own mind go over the contrast between your Aunt Catty [an invalid most of her adult life and an opium addict] and what came to her,

1. The canthus is the angle or corner on each side of the eye which is formed by the junction of the upper and lower lids.

and your Grandmother and her years of useful life, becoming actually stronger and more cheerful as her physical frame grew weaker. She had never tampered with her physical consciousness as others blunt it with remedies—leaving the basis in which their moral and mental consciousness should rest a wreck—but it remained keen and sensitive to the last, vibrating to camphor water and bromide with an ease and smoothness that heroic doses of hypnotics failed to secure for those others.

I won't tell you how sorry I am to hear of your indisposition and discomfort. I have been through it. You won't believe it, but for 65 years I have hardly taken a step or drawn a breath without feeling that I was contending with all the hosts of nature. When the battle waxes too fierce, I take a novel, and shut the blinds and go out of myself. It would be far better if I could pull myself together and go out as I have done lately with Tom Davies[2] and your Uncle Joe [Cumming]. But I feel it bores them so that I can't do it. Your Uncle Joe says when he goes home and raises a row, he says to your Aunt Kate that he has been holding himself in all day, against the stupidity and meanness of his clients, meeting them with quiet smiles and placating arguments and now if he can't break loose in his own house which is his castle what is he to do.

Now for the news. They have ginned 800 bales. And Alf says this means that the ginning will largely overrun last year's. They have made some bad oil out of damaged seed but have some 300 tins of good seed on hand.[3] Everything is in good order and working smoothly. Oil is down to nothing and there is no money or anything else in the country except some bad debts. Pat Galphin is just bankrupted for several hundred dollars. Paying high wages to my tenants the Clarks. My little crop is the poorest I ever had. So is most everybody's, but there is so much acreage in that prices will keep down. Julia sold $12 worth of butter last week and her cows are doing well. . . . I have put up a large shed to the carriage house which is useful and disfiguring, built George Newman's house over, patched the roof here including a large space over your room where it leaked. It is thundering and we will soon see how effective this work is. Kate Hyde has sent back the Genealogy, and

---

2. Thomas Jones Davies (1830–1902), Marcellus Hammond's brother-in-law, was born in Edgefield District, and had lived at Beech Island since 1865. He was Harry's life-long friend. Obituary of Thomas Jones Davies, March 29, 1902. Thomas Jones Davies Scrapbook, 1849–1903, SCL.
3. The reference here is to the Kathwood Manufacturing Company.

I am going to draw up a chart for you as soon as I get Bryan's book on the Bryans. Loula Comer and Henry's dog are back once more, both very happy, the dog the happiest. For Loula dissolved into an hour of tears when your Mother and Julia left her by oversight and went to the post office. . . .

Remember me most kindly to Dr. Billings and also to Mrs. Billings.

Yours affectionately,

H. H.

WILLIAM W. WOOLSEY TO JULIA B. HAMMOND[b]

Aiken, October 31, 1897

Dear Friend:

We are a feeble folk just now. Mrs. W. with a bad cold—and myself again with neuralgia.

We are gathering in the remnants of our five cent cotton and are congratulating each other that it is not yet down to 3½.[1]

Aiken is waking up, a few early tourists have come and are making the streets interesting with new costumes and colors.

I was in Augusta on Tuesday for some repairs to my Engine and kept on the lookout for any of you, but alas without effect except a brief glimpse of Henry, who did not seem to have very late news from Redcliffe.

The darkies have apparently lost all desire for work since cotton got thin.

I am digging sweet potatoes and will be gathering corn next week.

I intend to put my land out on share crops the coming year, most of it. At present prices of cotton, other things pay best, unless you can get cheaper labor, by working on shares.

I have only a moment in which I can write.

Thank you for being yourself, the finest person I have ever known. With love to all

Yours Sincerely,

W. W. Woolsey

1. The average price of cotton per pound in 1897 was 6.68 cents. In 1898 it dropped to 5.73 cents. The lowest price for cotton in the nineteenth century was 4.59 cents per pound in 1894. Farmer's Club Records, Beech Island, Aiken County, vol. 2, p. 545, SCL; *The Statistical History of the United States*, p. 301.

HARRY HAMMOND TO KATHARINE H. BILLINGS[b]

Beech Island, November 23, 1897

My Dear Katharine:

What I fear for you is that you are leading too exciting and exoteric a life. What with the dinners and lunches and visits and shopping and no end of other work I hear of your doing and above all wanting to do, it really seems to me you have allowed yourself no room for the esoteric life, which is the true inwardness of individual existence. I hope these forms of expression will give you pause. That is what I wish to do. Just see what you have done within a year, indeed in less than a year. A visit to New York—a wedding—a return to New York—a trip South and another trip to New York—besides those long stairs there to climb. In fact it is all "such a gitting upstairs" that I want you to stop and think about it. Why I haven't had but one wedding in 38 years, one dining out in all that time, and in that period not a mile have I been carried by stream for fun, hardly a visitor except on business, and if I have paid any visits it was always a side issue, and not the leading motive. It is true I have rusted out, but that is better after all than wearing out and amounts in the end to the same thing. I can recommend it to you from experience. You may think it something too much like Dunbar Lamar's[1] epigrammatic characterization of a negro "owes no gratitude, bears no malice." But it isn't quite as barren as that. You must bear in mind that you are not used to the ozone so stimulating in the northern air. One cannot be exposed incautiously to it with impunity unless they are journeying like Nansen[2] through Arctic solitudes. And now you are asking for the powerful stimulus in addition to all you have had, and are craving of a visit from your Mother. It will be too much for you, don't you know she has completely filled my life for more than a generation and with your cup already running over you want to put her in too. If you are going to hold your hand in the battle of life you must keep a reserve corps that you can call on when needed. You mustn't have all your troops in action at one time. I think your Mother is just

---

1. Barney Dunbar Lamar, a Beech Island farmer, was one of Katharine's earliest recorded suitors. See letter of Barney Dunbar Lamar to Katharine Hammond, July 1885, note 1.
2. Fridtjof Nansen (1861–1930), Norwegian Arctic explorer, headed many expeditions to the ice fields of Greenland and the North Pole between 1888 and 1896.

such a reserve force, being always at your service in great or small emergencies no matter what the weather is or how the wind blows. She is your trump suit and I don't think you should lead trumps just now when you know you hold enough to control the issue of the game. Besides your Mother's company would only increase the excitement which fills the atmosphere at present about you. You would appreciate this more, if you could observe the effect she produces in Julia since they have been living here by themselves. Julia has lost her faculty of sleeping and sits up with your Mother until next day. The only quiet she has is to jump up at dawn and take rest in a round of household duties that would be a good day's work for a plow boy. She is rushing about all day just like those swift footed Yankees until I feel quite uneasy for her. Wait and see how she stands it. Meanwhile get some good novels of an elevated tone and rest yourself in the fortunes and misfortunes of ideal heroes and heroines. It is quieting and enlarging. If you want to be popular don't give people good lunches and dinners. I have made myself very unpopular by giving good [barbe]cues at the club. If you can make anyone invest in you to the extent of going to trouble to entertain you, you may be sure they will not lose the interest in you which they feel is their due, but when you invest in them the interest due to you always chafes them. Of course it is a great deal easier to entertain people than to be entertained by them. The latter imposes more burdens than I could ever endure but that was sheer weakness on my part and I hope you will prove stronger.

Now I did not mean to write you a letter and especially one so full of such excellent and unpleasant advice. I suppose you will not wish to hear from me again for a long time. Well that will only give you time to ponder well all the wisdom herein contained. If I were to write again I might contradict what I have here writ as invariably true.

Yours affectionately,
Harry Hammond

HENRY C. HAMMOND TO EMILY C. HAMMOND[b]

Augusta, December 10, 1897

My Dear Mother:

You have asked my opinion as to the best arrangement that could be made for the management of the family property—your and father's property. Julia and Kit, too, have asked for it. I give it merely as a member of the family—as one of our number—claiming for it no special weight or value, beyond that which comes with my deep and earnest wish to see all realize the greatest possible content, peace and happiness out of the little we have.

Fortune has been much harder upon you and father than it has been, or can be upon your children. You have fallen from a great height—one which we have no reasonable hope of attaining. There should be some comfort in this for us. We were born poor, and conditions beyond your and father's control have kept us so, and we are so now; but our lot today compares most favorably with what it has ever been—let us make the most of it.

The development of the plantation and the water power and the building of a Ginnery and an Oil Mill has been our dream for years. Like a clap of thunder out of a clear sky came the possibility of a realization of it—We have done so.[1] It is idle now to question the wisdom or the unwisdom of this move; or to charge responsibility or blame upon this or that person. The die has been cast and we must stand by the throw.

I would only call to mind one obvious fact, that this enterprise has been entered into largely on account of Kit and Alf, and that they were and are now looked to to make the most of it. You, father, Julia, Katharine, I—not one or all of us—would have undertaken the erecting and operating of such a concern—Kit and Alf were the "reason why." We all know the history of Redcliffe, Cedar Grove, and Silver Bluff. Like our manufacturing interests we would not choose them to-day as investments, but we have them—they are ours, a big part of ours. By lands I mean all our property except the very little personally we own.

Father has withdrawn from the immediate active management of the mill and plantations. This, together with my absence, has thrown the work and responsibility largely upon Kit and Alf; though in my poor way, I have done all that I could to assist them. Of course the title to all this property—legally and morally—is in you and father—it is yours. It would not be natural or usual, nor is there a desire on the part of any of your children that there should be a division at this time of the prop-

1. See letters of May 29, 1897, note 2, and Oct. 10, 1897, note 3, for references both to the unexpected inheritance from Emily Hammond's Aunt Sarah Cumming and to the building of the Kathwood Manufacturing Company.

erty. It being settled then that it shall be kept together, who is to manage it and how? For my part I should never have struck out here for myself had I known such an opportunity would have been afforded me as the Oil Mill and plantation now affords; but no need to talk of that, for as the oil mill and plantation are there, so am I here. Katharine has cut loose and gone a thousand miles away to try her fortune, under extremely different conditions. Julia has found her place with you at Redcliffe. Naturally and inevitably the management of the mill and plantation go to Kit and Alf.

The mill and plantation go hand in hand, for while work goes on in both the year round the busy season of one is winter and of the other summer; they dove-tail all around the line and are of great benefit, the one to the other. Kit and Alf are especially qualified to take care of them. They are trained in the work and have it at heart. My plan then is simply this: Give over the management of these properties to Kit and Alf and with the valuable help they will get from father and with whatever I may be able to do for them, they will make a success of it if that is possible.

Practically, how will this be done? We need consider only the plantation part of the arrangement, for the mill is already fixed. Kit has invested some cash in the plantation and put in some property. Let this be estimated and he be given credit for it. We will accept his own values. In the permanent improvements on the place and in the net income all would share; but in addition to that Kit and Alf should receive additional compensation, for they would be putting in all of their time and thought, while the others only a small part of theirs.

Now what should that compensation be? I am not wedded to any exact amount but only want to say; salaries are low at present in every department of business; the small amount involved does not warrant large outlays, and where the permanent improvements and net income are to be shared equally by those receiving salaries, they should be proportionately smaller. I wish to see Kit and Alf make all they can, but in view of what I have said, and in view of your, father's, Julia and Katharine's interests I think $725.00 for Kit and $525.00 for Alf per annum would be a maximum amount. As far as my salary is concerned I would cut that to one-half what it is at present, making it $250.00, and I would further agree not to demand it unless it was actually earned by the business over and above all other expenses.

So far as I know, no other views have been given. There has been some talk of Kit's renting the plantations and operating them independently. This does not meet with my approval; on the contrary, I would be unconditionally opposed to such an arrangement as much or more on Kit's account as on our own. Ye cannot serve two masters.

I am not fixed in my views on these subjects but am able to support them by fact and argument, and I am willing to elaborate them in detail and to answer any questions that may be asked in regard to them.

Very truly yours,
Henry C. Hammond

EMILY C. HAMMOND TO KATHARINE H. BILLINGS[b]

Redcliffe, December 29, 1897

My dear sweet Katinka:

. . . Thank you and John very much for yours [letters] and please dear child forgive me that I have not written you as often as I would like to have done, for I must own this is my first letter since one to John sent Thursday P.M. In the meantime Julia and Tee Wee[1] have written you each a short note. You know Julia and I have a good many little things to attend to besides entertaining company and then you know I am benumbed by the first sharp cold. Until this Tuesday afternoon I have not heard from you since Thursday either. Tho' I had a very pleasant letter from John Sunday. We did not know the mail had been delivered Saturday Xmas and when Warren [Fair] told us that it was at Mrs. C. we ventured to send for it and she graciously sent it and so I got John's letter Sunday. Last night I got a batch of very interesting literature from you. Julia told you how much we were pleased with the magazines. This P.M. I got your letter of the 24th and 26th. Dearest will you let me say that a dear little daughter of mine makes mountains of mole hills as perhaps I did myself in the same connection when I was young. I remember that I often went rather reluctantly and with no invitation but your father's to this very house and used to have my misgivings as to whether I was entirely welcome and whether my visits

---

1. Tee Wee was Ann W. Brumby, a close family friend at Beech Island who later taught at the Lucy Cobb Institute in Athens, Georgia. MS vol. bd., 1855–1908. Autobiographical account of "the early life of John Shaw Billings II," John Shaw Billings Scrapbook Collection, SCL.

were not somewhat ill timed on occasion, but the bare mention of such
a thing, would bring down on my devoted head such accusations of
unfriendliness and "morbid vanity and egotism" that I was afraid to act
much upon these prepossessions of mine and when yr Grandmother
used to tell yr Father, and he would faithfully repeat to me, that she
knew she would see more of him but for me, I could only beg that she
would believe that I never meant to do "that whereoff I was accused"
and that I might be forgiven. And then you know I lived for four years
a very insignificant member of the family of which yr G. Mother and
yr Father were the heads, and you know how often I have told you of
the respect and gratitude and affection with which her treatment of me
thro' the most of that time inspired me, afterwards it was different and
I shed many tears of bitter mortification of being forced upon her by
circumstances. Indeed as you well know I have had a generous share of
"humble pie" in my life and tho' I have sometimes rashly asserted that
it had "soured upon me" in my heart of hearts I know it to be a salutary
thing to mortify the flesh and to hold our thin skinned pride in check.
I think I understand your and John's position both in this matter and I
can but say to you that I think you ought to highly value and cherish
the affectionate pride which makes him wish to identify you with all
that he is and does. That it is yr duty and might to be your pleasure to
show him that you appreciate this even if you do not find yr taste always
gratified in the companionship he presses on you, but they are most of
them good and delightful people I am sure from what I know. . . . It
is eleven o'c and tho I am not sleepy yet this . . . letter should stop
sometime. . . .

JULIA B. HAMMOND TO WILLIAM W. WOOLSEY[b]

Augusta, January 28, 1898

I have been sorely angry with you today, but now I have thought it
all out and I no longer blame you.

It was one if not the greatest affliction God has put upon you that
women should love you as they do, and it is not your fault that God
also made you so that you should fail them, hurt them, ruin them.

With all your limitations I accept you now. My God poor Bessie
[William Woolsey's wife], poor you, my darling I am going to try to be

a good wholesome friend to you as you have begged me to be. Oh God help me. God is so far off and I long so for warm human love. And you are in so many things so far above other people. To die, not to lose you or Mother.

But I am going to bury the thought of you ever. All intercourse as you wisely said must cease between us. Good bye, and if I may never say it is comfort to write here that I have loved truly and long, and now I must let this love go to others. Oh darling! Oh dearest! Oh my own, hearts do not break.

HARRY HAMMOND TO KATHARINE H. BILLINGS[b]

Beech Island, March 1, 1898

My Dear Katharine:

An overflow of company has stopped me until now from answering your letter. Kit Fitzsimons and his son Christopher IV[1] arrived Saturday with Henry from the Mill, and there was our Kit and next day Alf. Not many after all but Christopher IV drew in Lessy and Bubba and Babie, and this gave something the air of a crowd, which was heightened and made louder by Soda and Preble, the two fox terriers that accompanied Henry. These dogs got to chasing cats on Sunday and Preble got badly scratched, so bad, that Henry left her here to get over her lameness. Julia was put in charge and undertook to keep them in her room last night, but their behavior became so bad that she had to turn them out of doors about 1 A.M., and then you should have heard them storming the house, charging and barking round the yard and Piazzas, and scratching at the doors and rattling the windows as if the Spaniards with the populations of Mexico and S. America were invading us. Then we have had an exciting time with Gussy and Brooks. She announced her intention of quitting at once, leaving Brooks and Francis and the three children to shift for themselves, and making her way to new fields and pastures green among the kitchens of the Sand Hills. Her grounds for doing this were that Brooks had appropriated her wages (making none

---

1. Christopher III (1856–1926), son of Susan Milliken Barker and Christopher Fitzsimons, was the second cousin of Harry and Emily Hammond's children. He was an executive with the Southern Oil Company of Columbia. Christopher IV was his son by Frances Motte Huger. John Shaw Billings, comp., "Notes on Christopher Fitzsimons (1762–1825)," John Shaw Billings Papers, SCL.

himself) for the two months past, that he had been driving around with other ladies in the cart she had helped to buy, and this unregenerate black nigger threatened to beat her and never opened his mouth to her without "cussing of her." I tried to explain these charges to Brooks who only met them with hilarity, until I was forced to tell him that if Gussy went, the horse would come back into my stable and he and his might seek their fortunes elsewhere. It took a full half hour's silent and solitary reflection for Brooks to appreciate the gravity of the affair, when he did the excitement with him and old Francis became very intense. There was a proposition to appeal to the law in the person of John Dunbar to restrain Gussy from upsetting the family, and its agricultural hopes. On further consideration this idea was abandoned, and the alternatives of paying court to Gussy adopted; he is to cut wood and tote water for her, to stop cussing her, and ride no other lady with the horse and cart which is and is to be joint property, and we hope that in this way there will be evolved a modus vivendi for them and for us.

Just here I was overcome with sleepiness, although I had laid down at eight the night before and kept my bed until after sunrise this morning. True I had several waking spells but I must have got in a good deal of sleep. When I waked up I found that your Mother and Julia had gone with Daisy in the cart to the Mill. They did not return until after dark reporting everything moving smoothly, an out turn of 850 gallons of oil in the last 24 hrs. This is the first night run they have made this season. Wray takes it at night and Alf in the day. They want to wind the season's work up in the next week or two, so that Wray can go to Barnwell to put the mill there in order. . . . I trust the boys will make ends meet if they have no accident.

I got a very pleasant letter from Dr. Billings. It will give me much pleasure to have him here and I trust he will find some interest in his trip as he assures me he will.[2] It is indeed very kind in him to escort you, and it relieves us of anxiety about your well doing on the road.[3]

Your Mother and Julia report that as they passed Jeems Brooks'

2. The senior Dr. Billings first came to Beech Island in 1899. After a short stay he escorted his daughter-in-law Katharine and her year-old son back to New York on May 15, 1899.

3. Henry had written his sister that he longed for Katharine to make up her mind "to come home for the great event," but had not urged it for fear that her delivery might be more hazardous in South Carolina than in New York. Katharine, however, decided to return to Redcliffe, where her first child was born. Henry C. Hammond to Katharine Hammond Billings, Jan. 15, 1898, HBC Family Papers, SCL.

house they saw his wife's bedding and clothes scattered about the yard, and pigs rooting it up. There had been a slight family fuss in this branch also of the Brooks family. Mrs. Brooks was met in the road and showed where her loving husband had knocked out her front teeth. Said she had started to the magistrates but had been persuaded by Mr. Kit to await the course of events. Anyhow if Jeems would treat her only half right she would say nothing although she had weighed 200 lbs when she married him and now look at her. She would not turn the beam at 160 lbs.

I am off to Augusta to arrange for my club Saturday.[4] Mr. Woolsey writes he and a Mr. Harrington will be here tonight.

All well,

Yours affectionately,
Harry Hammond

JOHN SEDGWICK BILLINGS TO KATHARINE H. BILLINGS[b]

New York, April 20, 1898

A year ago today—and my happy life really began. I never lived before then—and have lived three lives ever since. One in the past starting from April 20, 1897—one in the present—one in the golden future. Happy-Happier-Happiest. Ah my Sweetheart—this is the first and last anniversary of our marriage that we will be separated—one from the other. My dear, my whole life must be spent in a vain attempt to repay you for your goodness to me in taking me for your husband. . . .

My love to everyone: and you my precious, sweetest wife,

Your Husband

4. The Beech Island Agricultural Club was founded in 1846 by James Henry Hammond and eleven other farmers. From the time of its incorporation on January 5, 1856, the members had held a meeting and barbecue on the first Saturday of every month. Evidently Harry Hammond was responsible for this particular barbecue. Julia wrote that her father arrived home around nine o'clock and reported that the meal had been a great success. The bill of fare was wash pots full of hash, sausages, tongues, sauce, "fifty pounds of red snapper and bass, rice, big hominy, biscuits 9 doz., corn muffins, drop muffins, cabbage, Irish potatoes, sweet potatoes, tomatoes, potato-pone, coffee, and whiskey." Her father boasted that "everybody said it was the finest dinner ever given at the club house." *The Augusta Chronicle*, May 5, 1946; JBH to Katharine Hammond Billings, Saturday, [c. Feb.–March 1898], HBC Family Papers; Farmer's Club Records, Beech Island, Aiken County, 2 vols. *passim*, SCL.

JOHN SEDGWICK BILLINGS TO KATHARINE H. BILLINGS[b]

New York, May 11, 1898

Oh my darling—my darling—my precious sweetest wife—how can I ever deserve all the happiness you have given me.

A Boy!!!—and ten pounds!!!! And Dr. Doughty[1] said it was a small baby, and would not arrive until the 23d. Well—well—well—I simply cannot realize and take in my happiness over it all. And you are both well—Henry's telegram said so. And I am hoping that you had a comparatively short and easy time—Oh I pray to God you did. And how I thank him that you are over with it. And I wanted a boy so—oh so much—tho' I did try and make you think that it did not make much difference, it did. Oh my darling—how I want to come to you—now—right away—take the 4:30 train this afternoon. But I will abide by your decision, my own wife—I realize that I ought not to come now—that you are safely over and through with it—Flint[2] goes away for a week in two days—there are a dozen reasons that I will not trouble to go over—and they all seem as nothing by the side of my wild longing to get to you—to be with you—to hold you in my arms, and have you tell me everything—perhaps you would tell me that you wanted me with you and that I might have helped you somewhat. Oh Katie—my own Katie—I cannot even begin to tell you one half of all of the glad, happy, proud thoughts that are surging through me. And yet I am anxious—very anxious—I want to know everything about everything. Surely your Mother or Julia has written me a long, long letter today, telling me—say one millionth part—of the things I want to know. If they can do that, they did well. How long you were—did Doughty get there in time—how you are now—whether you have or have had any fever. Why that is just the merest beginning to a very few of the things I want to know. Proud—oh my dear, how proud I am, both of you and the

1. The reference was either to Dr. William H. Doughty, Sr. (1836–1905), or to his son, William H. Doughty, Jr., born in 1856. Both were prominent Augusta physicians of the period. William H. Walsh, *Walsh's Directory of the City of Augusta, Georgia for 1902* (Charleston, S.C.: W.H. Walsh Directory Co., 1902), p. 392; Jones and Dutcher, *Memorial History of Augusta*, pp. 268–69, 277.

2. John Sedgwick Billings was an assistant to the prominent physician, Austin Flint, of New York City. MS vol. bd., c. 1860–1951. Time Inc. data, John Shaw Billings Scrapbook Collection, SCL, p. 246.

baby—and a little too, of myself. A boy—and ten pounds. Katharine as you read this drop that letter, and make that nurse hand him to you— and kiss him for his father—"his father"—and that is me—John Billings—and he is John Billings IIId[3]—I will never, never take it in. Our baby—our son—who is going to be a fine splendid man some of these days—just such a man as his mother is a woman. Oh Katie, when they let you write—tell me all about him—everything—his eyes—nose— mouth—body—everything. Is he sound in mind and limb—is he a Billings or a Hammond—or both—or neither? Mother is wild with delight and after having written to you is now writing to all her friends. And I have done a little—just a little myself. I have telegraphed—first of course to you—then cabled to Clare[4]—and then telegraphed to Dot, Daisy, Aunt Emily, Rupert and Arthur Browne—and ended with one to Wm Osler IInd[5]—John S. Billings IIId sends greetings! And then— because I could not keep still, I made a round of my friends on my wheel and told them of the great event—the Rogers, Carlisles, Nortons—and Mrs. Van Dusen. All the servants are chuckling—Mammy[6] has been giving the news to the Dairy woman and the butcher—and Wesley has gone out to take Henry's telegram to father, and to get a bottle of Champagne to drink your and John Third's Health. He is tertius to Dot—and quintus to your dear, darling little Mother. I ought to stop here—and not write you a long letter to tire you. Here is Mammy "Just what I told her—she would have a boy. Tell her I wish her all luck and joy with it—that I hope she had a good time—and to kiss the boy for me." I tell you—Henry's telegram was just a ray of bright sunshine, and every one here is happy. Oh my darling—tho' I have never told you so, and you probably thought me heartless, I have worried myself terribly many a time, thinking of all the dangers you were exposed to. And you are safe through them all—Oh I can never thank God enough.

3. John Shaw Billings, born in 1898, was, in fact, John Shaw Billings II. However, to distinguish him from his grandfather, John Shaw Billings, and his father, John Sedgwick Billings, his father referred to him as John Billings III.

4. Clare Billings Ord and her husband, William Wallis Ord, were living in London, England, at 2 Queen Street. Clare Ord to Katharine Hammond Billings, Feb. 1, 1898, HBC Family Papers, SCL.

5. Dr. William Osler had supervised John Sedgwick Billings at Johns Hopkins Hospital. MS vol. bd., 1855–1908. Autobiographical account of "the early life of John Shaw Billings II," John Shaw Billings Scrapbook Collection, SCL.

6. "Mammy" was Helen Harrison, a servant in the Billings household, whom John Sedgwick Billings described as "semper fidelis." MP vol. bd., c. 1875–1912. Earliest Pictures of John Shaw Billings, ibid.

Mammy sticks her head in the door to say "Tell them to take him up on top of the house—upstairs before he goes down—this for good luck—you went on the roof Mr. John." Let his Uncle Henry do this. I am not going to put in one single word of sordid everyday news about houses—Stokes—my dinner at the Carlisles—that will all keep. To think that I was sleeping calmly at 5.30 this morning when that boy came. Oh Katie if I could only kneel at your bedside, and with my head buried in the coverlet, your hand to my lips, give thanks for my great happiness. "Ours—for we are going to be happy all the rest of our lives." Shall I send out little announcement cards, pinned to yours? Tell your mother to write me your answer. I suppose I must in decency, stop now. But oh my precious—my Sweetest Sweetheart Sweetness—I thank you—and worship you and love you—love you—love you. Did you suffer much my darling—oh I hope not—if I could only have stood it for you. The only way to stop is short.

Your Husband

HARRY HAMMOND TO KATHARINE H. BILLINGS[b]

Beech Island, March 7, 1900

My dear Katharine:

I enclose my record of the four long years of my life I sacrificed to our lost cause. I hope it will serve your purpose, it certainly served no purpose of mine.

I am glad to hear that Johnny-boy is afraid at night, it is evidence of a religious temperament, which will counterbalance his worldly love of money to which you refer.

Our severe winter has grown milder during some days past, but it is drizzling tonight and the forecast is for cold tomorrow. Today is the first day I have been able to do any work in the garden. I planted your Mother's dried peas and got the [ground] in order for early vegetables. The preparation for crops is very backward, more so than last year even. Today too I have been down with Kit and Alf giving them some bearings for the telephone line they are building from Mail's store to the Mill. I got back to dinner and your Mother & Julia left immediately after in Henry's buggy with his spirited pair to pay the boys a visit. They got back safely just before dark.

The school and the library and the Sunday School are all getting along better than was expected, but not as well as I desired. . . .

It will be a couple of months more before the outcome at the Mill will be known for certain. Kit says they have done a business aggregating $70,000 and there ought to be a profit on it but profits have so seldom come my way that I pause to prophesy one.

I sincerely trust that Dr. Billings is secure from a return of his ailment[1] and it would give me great pleasure to know that there was something which might bring him our way.

I must tell you of a sad accident that happened to me at the club last Saturday. There is desire prevailing very widely here that no drinking be allowed at our dinners. I was supporting this side with great earnestness in the debate when the stopper came out of a flask I had in my coat pocket and the liquor ran out on the floor before them all. I need not say that my temperance talk was of no avail.

All well, remember me most kindly to Dr. John. By the way I must tell you poor Kate Hyde is very unwell,[2] heart wrong, kidneys wrong, slight dropsical effusion, impairment of vision. I persuaded her to go to the hospital, Dr. Coleman advised it and Julia carried her there Monday. The Dr. says with a careful nursing she may get back to her usual precarious state of health in a week or ten days, and there was no chance for her to get this at Miss Anna's.

Yrs. affty.

H. H.

JULIA B. HAMMOND TO KATHARINE H. BILLINGS[b]

Redcliffe, February, 1901

Dear Katharine:

Mother has thought it best not to tell you, but I think it is a thing for you to know and act on. Father starts next Sunday for Washington

1. Katharine's father-in-law, John Shaw Billings, was operated on for gallstones in 1900 and again in 1906. The last two decades of his life had been fraught with health problems. He underwent five operations between 1890 and 1892 for lip cancer. The final operation for lip cancer, performed by Dr. William S. Halsted of Johns Hopkins, involved a radical neck dissection. In 1913 after another gallstone operation he developed pneumonia and died on March 11, 1913. "Surgeon-Bibliophile," MD, April 1976, p. 120.

2. Kate Hyde died on March 18, 1900, and was buried in Magnolia Cemetery in Augusta. Gravestone of Catherine Spann Hyde, Mangolia Cemetery, Augusta, Georgia.

to give the evidence before the labor commission on everything pertaining to labor in South Carolina. He is given ten cents a mile and $1.50 per day. We are crazy for him to go to see you, Johnny-boy, John and New York. I am afraid Mother's urgency has clinched the matter, and that he certainly won't go but you and John can write and urge him to do so, which will make you all right, tho' I have no doubt that nothing you can do will keep him from saying he hasn't been invited.

His reasons for not going are these—He is too old and helpless. He will cost you too much. Dr. Billings will expect him to walk round libraries and he is too lame, etc., etc. He is more lame than I ever saw him and we feel anxious for fear he will hurry and hurt himself getting off and on cars. Otherwise he is looking splendidly well, and seems delighted with this trip, just now he is not speaking to anybody for he got mad with Henry for teasing him about a book.

He has thrown away the shirts Mother bought him and now has his collars open only to his navel. He says he is going to wear his cardigan jacket instead of an over coat. But when he hasn't Mother to worry with his freaks, and feels the coercion of the big outside world, he will do pretty much what all old gentlemen do, be better out than he is in. . . .

Sarah Lamar[1] is the talk of the town for a cake walking with Margie at a great party given by the Barney Dunbars.[2] A young man said if they had had watches in their garters he could have told the time of day. They tricked old Cal into making a fool of himself, and he is deeply mortified and distressed. Yesterday was day of tremendous rain the river at one jump has gone to 26 feet. Warren [Fair], Kit, and Du Puis[3] were here, the latter the most morbid unhappy thing you ever

1. Sarah Lamar, daughter of Celeste Hammond and Matthew Calbraith ("Cal") Butler Lamar, was eighteen years old at the time of this letter. She married Ernest Morris the following year. Billings, *Descendants of Hammond*, p. 6; John Shaw Billings, comp., "The Lamar Family [Genealogy]," Loose Papers, John Shaw Billings Papers, SCL.

2. The Barney Dunbars were Sarah Lamar's aunt and uncle. John Shaw Billings, comp., "The Lamar Family [Genealogy]," Loose Papers, John Shaw Billings Papers; MS vol. bd., 1809–1962. Genealogical data re the Black, Kirkland, Robison, Reid, Bryan, Lamar, and Peters families, John Shaw Billings Scrapbook Collection, SCL.

3. S.E. DuPuis worked with Kit and Alf at the Kathwood Manufacturing Company. When the Hammonds sold this concern to the Southern Cotton Oil Company in 1901, DuPuis was hired by the new owners. By 1911, he had become manager of the Southern Oil Company's mill at Warrenton, Georgia. MS vol. bd., 1809–1962. Genealogical data re the Black, Kirkland, Robison, Reid, Bryan, Lamar, and Peters families, John Shaw Billings Scrapbook Collection; S.E. DuPuis to Judge Henry Hammond, Sept. 6, 1911, HBC Family Papers; Kathwood Manufacturing Company, Beech Island Papers 1896–1901, 1904, SCL.

saw. They are all disgusting, Lottie and Marie thrown into the bargain. It is sad Lottie[4] is getting very stout all over and has the most enormous appetite.

Warren's club dinner was a great success, and he sent us a splendid leg of mutton.

Lots of people sick everywhere, but Mother keeps wonderfully well. . . . It is a lovely day today and I have been as busy as could be trying to straighten out after the awful weather and Sunday.

With lots of love to you all,

Julia

JULIA B. HAMMOND TO KATHARINE H. BILLINGS[b]

Redcliffe, [ca. 1901]

My dear Katharine:

Your long fine letters are very nice, so glad you went to ride with that funny old "English." Don't mind about Marietta, for men must come and men must go, also women. I hope the cook difficulty is all settled by this time. When I wrote to Johnny-boy the other night, Mother seemed very well, tho' greatly worried about Father who is on one of his worst tears, wants us to furnish the Old House[1] and send Winny down there to cook for the teachers.[2] The girl from Missouri is

---

4. Lottie Chafee Hammond (1875–1967), wife of Alfred Hammond, was the niece of the murdered James Gregg, Katharine Hammond Gregg McCoy's first husband. Lottie was pregnant with their first child, Clara Chafee Hammond, who was born on May 21, 1901. Billings, *Descendants of Hammond*, p. 2; MS vol. bd., 1927-n.d. "Myself and Family," John Shaw Billings Scrapbook Collection, SCL.

---

1. The "Old House" is "Old Yard," the original home at Redcliffe.
2. The teachers referred to taught at the Downer School in Beech Island. The Downer School dated back to the 1846 will of Alexander Downer. Downer, an orphan, established a fund to be administered by the State of South Carolina, to provide free education for orphans of Richmond County, Georgia, and Edgefield District, South Carolina. The Civil War, Reconstruction, and the insolvency that continued to plague the State of South Carolina in the late 1870s ended this enterprise. When the state discontinued the funds, the local families hired teachers to educate all the children of the area and used the Downer building as their schoolhouse. It was destroyed by fire around 1887. In 1897, the legislature granted the people of Beech Island the use of the interest from the Downer Fund which had been accumulating in the state's Sinking Fund. The Fund's Board of Trustees was authorized to spend $5000 for the purchase of a site and the erection of a new schoolhouse. Harry Hammond sold a tract of land at a very low price, and a two-story frame building was built. The schoolhouse served also as the neighborhood auditorium and public library. The building was ready for occupancy in September 1899, and was used until fire destroyed it in the spring of 1924. When the school had reopened in 1899, there were only two teachers employed, but as enrollment rose the number of teachers increased to four. Harry Hammond,

even dearer to him than Miss Deane, for she complains of her food from start to finish, which you know means to Father that she has proper discrimination. She is a great big, common thing, ugly and weighs 165 lbs., and wants onions. When Father with his shoes blacked and cravat on isn't driving them around, they are in his room. He has not spoken to Mother in days, he did her just this way when I was gone, so it isn't me. To return to Mother, in the middle of the night she called me. I ran into her and found [her] in great distress for the pain was not only in right arm but in left and all thro her chest. Her mind was clear and composed, but her distress was very great, and she thought she was very sick. I ran down and told Father how bad off she was and would you believe it he hollered to me to take the lamp out, and never came near her and has not spoken to her since.

I was dreadfully anxious, but she did not want me to call Warren, and she began to get better, but she nor I did not sleep much all night, and she was very weak. She staid in bed until eleven o'clock, when to my infinite relief she got up, had a good appetite and by afternoon was going round as usual. Last night she went to bed at 10 o'clock and slept until after eight, she is dressing now, but she said she had slept splendidly. In writing to her don't mention these things I have told you for it only makes her feel bad. She is thinking seriously of taking the teachers here to try and please Father, but I am determined not. Father would make us into mincemeat and season us with onions to please that girl. . . .

Tell Johnny-boy this is what Antony Henley[3] said of our horse, "Miss Julia that's show a pretty horse you ridin'. It's the prettiest horse in Beech Island, t'aint no horse it's just a flower you ridin'."

I must run and see about Mother, I am so happy to have her well again. Kiss the boys with lots of love to you and John, and don't forget wherever you are there are trials and tribulations to loosen your soul wings.

Julia

---

actively engaged in hiring the new teachers, was accused by Julia of being overly interested in their well-being. HBC Family Papers, 1901–1902 *passim*, SCL; Arabella Sumter Dunbar, "The History of the Development of Education in Beech Island, South Carolina" (Master's Essay, University of South Carolina, 1929).

3. Antony Henley, twenty-eight years old in 1900, was a black farm laborer at Beech Island. He was married and had two sons. U.S. Census Records, State of South Carolina, 1900, Population Schedules, Aiken County, Hammond Township, National Archives Microfilm Publications, p. 25.

HENRY C. HAMMOND TO EMILY C. HAMMOND[b]

Augusta, July 18, 1901

My dearest Mother:

I have your letter of July 16th and am pleased and relieved to know that the situation at Katharine's has ere this been greatly improved by John's convalescence and Julia's arrival.[1]

I hope Katharine and the baby[2] will have no serious back-set and all from now out will go smoothly.

I sent your letter to Te Wee[3] and I am very glad indeed that you found time to write it. It of course sets everything straight.

I feel very hopeful that Mr. Cadwalader[4] may recover on his own and John's account. I realize of what vital importance the situation is to them.

There is nothing final or definite to report in the oil mill matter. Mr. Dawson went down on the 4 o'clock train and we all made a close inspection of the plant, which showed up very nicely. Dawson appeared well pleased with things and I think for various reasons is anxious that the V.C. people should buy us out.[5] While he will make a strictly accurate report on our plant and a conservative recommendation, I think it will be as favorable to us as he feels he can consistently make it. As far as the plan has developed at all, it contemplates employment for Kit, Alf and DuPuis—I lose my job.[6]

1. Emily Hammond had gone to New York City to attend Katharine at the birth of her second child. Julia went to New York about a week later.

2. James Henry Hammond Billings was born on July 13, 1901. Billings, *Descendants of Hammond*, p. 1.

3. "Tee Wee" (Ann W. Brumby) was at that time being squired about by Henry C. Hammond. HH to ECH, Aug. 9, 1901, HBC Family Papers, SCL.

4. John L. Cadwalader, a prominent New York lawyer, President of the New York Public Library, and a friend of Andrew Carnegie, J.P. Morgan, and John Shaw Billings, Sr., came down with "acute gouty bronchitis" in July 1901. Since all the leading New York physicians were off on holiday, Billings, Jr. was assigned to Cadwalader's case. Billings accompanied his patient to Bar Harbor, Maine, where he remained until mid-September. He received a $10,000 fee from Cadwalader for his services. John Sedgwick Billings to Katharine H. Billings, July 18, Aug. 21, 1901, ibid.; MS vol. bd., 1855–1908. Autobiographical account of "the early life of John Shaw Billings II," John Shaw Billings Scrapbook Collection, SCL.

5. Dawson, a representative for the Southern Oil Company, made an offer (which Henry declined) to buy the Kathwood oil mill for $27,500. Henry Hammond to C.C.F. Hammond, July 25, 1901 (copy of telegram), HBC Family Papers, SCL.

6. Harry Hammond wrote that Kit and Alf were to get positions with the Southern Oil Company which were to pay them between $2100 and $2400. "They think these positions permanent and

Dawson spent the night at Alf's and was very pleasantly entertained by Lottie. Also much to his delight, he caught a string of fish last afternoon and this morning.

We will not know before the middle of next week what offer will be made us and in the meantime we have suspended some repairs on the waste way.[7]

I took tea with Lottie, reaching Redcliffe about 11 o'clock last night.

Father seems to be getting along very well—Sidney and Winnie taking good care of him. He has invited all the flies in so that Walker can fan him to some purpose.

The work at Redcliffe about completed except for the wind mill and some odds and ends of carpenters and painters work. Little returned to Augusta this morning, but goes back on Monday—Springs, Hamlet, and Jackson on deck, the latter doing some brick work.

Father is much interested over his Farmers Institute.[8]

Please tell Julia that Ego is receiving every attention from father and Jackson, but that poor fellow appears very very weak and I fear there is scarcely any hope for his recovery.[9] He is affected exactly as was the Allens' dog which died yesterday. Preb is still with the Doctor and I hope, somewhat improved.

Tell Julia it would do her heart good to see her garden after the rain. Ask her please to send me full instructions and as soon as it is dry enough I will have it all worked over for her.

Please write me a line and let me know how all are as often as you possibly can.

With all my love, Ever yours,

Henry

---

opening to promotion." Henry Hammond, who was listed on the Kathwood letterhead as President, would lose his position. HH to ECH, July 29, 1901, ibid.

7. The company was sold for $30,000, and the Southern Oil Mill provided jobs for Alf and Kit. Harry Hammond wrote his wife, "The oil mill appears not to have been a very bad investment after all." HH to ECH, Aug. 15, 1901, HBC Family Papers, SCL. See also: JBH to Kit Hammond, July 28, 1901, Henry Hammond to ECH, July 30, Aug. 2, 1901, HH to ECH, Aug. 4, 1901, ibid.; James Dawson to C.C.F. Hammond, June 6, 1904, Kathwood Manufacturing Company Papers, SCL.

8. The Beech Island Agricultural Club sponsored a Farmer's Institute, and invited four lecturers from Clemson College to address the members. Henry Hammond to ECH, Aug. 2, 1901, HBC Family Papers, SCL.

9. Ego, the beloved collie, died sometime between July 18 and July 25, 1901. Henry Hammond to ECH, July 25, 1901, ibid.; MS vol. bd., 1870–1946. Redcliffe after Billings restoration, John Shaw Billings Scrapbook Collection, SCL.

HARRY HAMMOND TO EMILY C. HAMMOND[b]

Beech Island, July 22, 1901

My Dear Emily:

I was very glad to hear through Julia and Kit that you were all well last Thursday. Besides telling that all are well here, there is nothing to report except that there comes this morning what looks like a three days easterly storm. Kit, Warren, and DuPuis dined here yesterday and Kit afterwards went up for Miss Rena[1] to take her down to Alf's which I presume he did. This left me alone here but that has often been the case. On the 3[d] July 43 years ago I was the first of the family to sleep here [at Redcliffe]. The doors and windows were not in. I slept on a cot by the fireplace in your room and was roused by a thunder storm in the night. The ensuing 7 years were very eventful to me. Then I came back here to live and to love you and nothing else but to be loved by you. I have kept on and on, but you? I fear that you like everybody else of my acquaintance can't help feeling that the meannesses which the wear and tear of years, age, ache, and penury have brought to the surface on me were innate and were there all along. The current of my life has long since stopped leaping and rushing and bubbling and boiling, it goes more and more sluggishly along shores that grow flatter and flatter until I feel the surge at tide at the Delta is reaching me. Don't regard me objectively. Try to take a subjective view and to idealize that a little. Perhaps a sermon Masters invited me to hear him preach yesterday put me on this strain. It was on the duty of parents to children. He came out strong on the importance of making children obey and against the modern sentimentalism of sparing the rod. I am sure he preached it at his wife who hinders him from scourging those outrageous little chaps of his as he should. I have been thinking ever since what a chance preachers had from the pulpit at their wives.

Mr. Little and the painters are here at work but I cannot tell you what they are doing except that they seem to have a variety of jobs on hand which make a good deal of noise and smell.[2] Springs says he may

---

1. Miss Rena was Lottie Chafee Hammond's sister.
2. In the summer of 1901, Redcliffe underwent extensive repair and renovation. Painting, plastering, carpentry, and the installation of a new roof were all completed. In addition, the improve-

get through tomorrow. The house looks fine and so does the grass. Two parties telephoned to say they heard Cal Lamar had died here last night. I went over to see him, found him very well. Give my love to all.

Yours affectionately,

Harry Hammond

HENRY C. HAMMOND TO HARRY HAMMOND[b]

Augusta, September 19, 1901

My dear Father:

In a letter received from Mother today—written because, on account of high water, I could not get to Redcliffe—she tells me that she has discussed with you the plantation problem and that she had showed you a letter written by me making suggestions to her as to a letter it was proposed she should write Kit. It appears that you first seemed to think well of these suggestions but upon reflection you advised that they be withheld until another effort might be made to get Alf to take hold of the plantations. Later still it appears that you came to the conclusion that you would yourself take the active management of these properties into your own personal charge, using as capital to operate them your share in the funds arising from the sale of the mill. There was also in mother's letter an intimation that you felt that hitherto you had been opposed, or restrained, in your desire to continue an active exclusive control of these properties, and that for the future you meant to take them in hand and personally manage them. Now this is what, in the general way, I gather from Mother's letter, and I may be, probably am, doing her an injustice in making the above statements. Her letter was mostly a prayer for family peace and the expression of a controlling desire to conform to any wishes of yours and evincing anxiety only as to your real comfort, peace and happiness.

Let me say once and for all that, while I have earnest views in the matter I propose to discuss with you, I shall in no event oppose, beyond what I shall here say, nor shall I counsel opposition to any stand you may take in this connection.

ments included electrical wiring throughout and installation of the first indoor plumbing. HH to ECH, July 15, 22, 24, Aug. 4, 8, 9, 15, 20, 1901; C.C.F. Hammond to ECH, July 25, 1901; Henry Hammond to ECH, Aug. 20, 1901, HBC Family Papers, SCL.

Nevertheless, I will here and now speak frankly:

The operation of the plantations at all is not essential to our liveli-hood. Katharine, Kit and Alf and I are entirely independent of them. I will not undertake to discuss the revenue they yielded under your man-agement, but for the last six years certainly they have not paid one dollar, but on the contrary have cost many. Therefore you, Mother and Julia have about formed the habit of being independent of them. In view of Kit's and Alf's present employment I have several times seriously suggested the sale of all the personal property and a-renting of the land for what it would bring. I hesitate in this view only on account of the plantation's admirable equipment and the further fact that Kit has the whole business organized and systematized. The equipment today rep-resents a cost of $6,000 and it could be sold for $4,000. I would give that for it. It will require at least a capital of $5,000 to run it—that is, a person without money who had to borrow it would, before cotton reached the market, be $5,000 in debt. Therefore you see, the business is a large one financially. It means practically the control and direction of 25 plows on a plantation four miles in extent; besides the running of a mercantile business of several thousand dollars a year. Without any wish to reflect on your ability and expressly disclaiming such a purpose I do not think as a business proposition solely you could succeed. Your age, your lameness, your habits, the distance you would daily have to travel are in themselves a bar to success even granting that you were otherwise ever so capable. Dozens of times of late years I have heard you say: "I am not fit to plant. I cannot ride all over the field and I cannot walk or stand. I do not know what my niggers are doing now or where they are."

As to the great distance you would have to travel: The unhappiest recollections of my life are your toilings backwards and forwards over that 16 miles of sand under the cruel whip of necessity. (Mother's anx-iety about you on these trips alone should weigh against any reasons that might be given for your undertaking them again.) And why should you do it? For the remote possibility of making a few more dollars? As to your age: I am proud and delighted to see how splendidly you bear it. But it must be remembered that at the time you are pitching this proposed crop next March you will be seventy years old. Says the psal-mist: "The days of our years are three score and ten; and if by reason of strength they be four score years, yet is their strength labor and sorrow, for it is soon cut off and we fly away." Do not let us add to the labor and sorrow nor fly away sooner than need be. I cannot understand how one circumstanced as you are should champ the bit for "the strenuous life." It is unusual I might say unnatural. Most men are only too willing to put aside life's fierce struggle if only kindly fortune will permit them to do so. The question does not present itself to my mind in the way of money making or losing. This is scarcely to be considered, though it might become serious, by the side of the utter unnecessity of the proposed undertaking—its altogether illadvisedness—its radicalism—its turning backwardness—its undoingness. If farming is what you wish to do surely you can give your theories and plans execution at Redcliffe as well as anywhere in the world. Mere amount signifies nothing. At Redcliffe your every effort on this line is directly productive of comfort and pleasure to us all and especially to Mother and Julia, who love so much to see the place kept up, the chickens, turkeys, cows, and horses prosperous.

Another matter I deem of first importance is your constant, or supposed constant, presence at Redcliffe. I cannot think without serious apprehension of Mother and Julia being left there alone for a majority of the time and it generally known that this was true. It would mean of course that during your absence Julia could not leave the house. You are a little band and in that open country must stand together. Try and bring yourself to see this thing as I see it, as every member of the family sees it, as I believe 9 out of 10 reasonable people must see it. And after all, even if you cannot see it that way, do what all of us have to do, sacrifice your inclinations, your wishes, your interest for those who in many things have done so for you and who would willingly do so again. As God is my judge I have spoken without regard to personal interest other than that inspired by love for all and a heartfelt desire to see the family surrounded by peace, comfort and happiness and especially that your and mother's declining years may not be harrassed by an absence of these blessings.

Affectionately yours,

H.C.H.

WILLIAM W. WOOLSEY TO JULIA B. HAMMOND[b]

Aiken, September 19, 1901.

Dear Friend:

What great events have happened since my last—Poor President McKinley[1]—no man ever made a finer ending (in my time), unless, perhaps Grant's with its patient work on the history that was to provide food and support for his wife and children (after he was gone), may be really finer.[2]

I believe in [Theodore] Roosevelt as he has traditions behind him and must live up to a recognized family standard. The trouble (and sometimes the advantage) with the self made man, is that he is untrammelled and like a man with crossed eyes you never know where he is going.

Here we are all well—The crop is good, the best for three years—every crop is good, the pea crop the best of all.

We ginned a little yesterday to get things in running order again. After the usual half day struggle, we got started and emptied the gin house of its 4 bales. One bale made 37¾ per cent on field weights. I saw Kit and Henry on Saturday last both looked very well.

My 17 boarding horses are eating me up now that grain is so high.

The Gammell girls are here now and every day some new trip is planned and the old one given up.

If you were here I would go to B.I. for a rest[3]—but alas—I may not yet. Love to Miss Catherine and John.

Yours Hastily,
W.W. Woolsey

1. President William McKinley was shot by anarchist Leon Czolgosz at the Pan-American Exposition in Buffalo, New York on September 6, 1901, and died on September 14.
2. President Ulysses S. Grant published *Personal Memoirs of U.S. Grant* in 1885. The major portion of the second volume was written during his terminal illness. He died of cancer of the throat on July 23, 1885.
3. Julia had been in New York City with her sister Katharine Billings and her new nephew since July. B.I. is Beech Island.

JOHN SEDGWICK BILLINGS TO KATHARINE H. BILLINGS[b]

New York, April 20, 1902

Well, lady—here's looking back on five happy, useful, growing years, during which my admiration and love for my own splendid wife has steadily increased. I thank God for you and all you have given me—a happy home and our two splendid boys—enough of a purpose in life for any man. What if we have differed now and then—the differences left no scars and only went to show that we both have good warm blood in our veins. Am I right? When I think of those boys and the temptations and struggles before them I grow thoughtful—but with your truthfulness and honesty to form yourself, they cannot go far wrong. The loving cup I send you is brimming over with deep true love for you—as Miss Rogers said, I would throw both the boys in the river for you—much as I love them. May the candy be fresh and good—may the day be a beautiful one—the boys all right in body and mind—and may you wish at least once on April 20th [their 5th wedding anniversary] that you had with you your own loving husband—God bless you and the boys, my darling, and let me do just a small part of what I wish to do for you.

John

KATHARINE H. BILLINGS TO JOHN SEDGWICK BILLINGS[b]

Redcliffe, April 20, 1902

My dearest Husband:

How good you have been to me and I would be perfectly happy if I felt a little more worthy of all you do and feel for me. You have made this day very dear, and happy to me—with your precious letter, and beautiful gifts. Every word of that splendid letter shall sink into my heart—cheer me and comfort me, and make me strong in times of trial!

The loving cup is perfectly beautiful—so handsome and plain—and the initials are beautifully engraved. I am so glad you had them and the date put on. Indeed it is the prettiest loving cup I have ever seen. It shall grace our table on every festive occasion. It is just exactly the right size not a shade too large or small. The candy is delicious—we have all had a taste—and are saving it to spree on this afternoon. Warren brought the bundles out for me, last night, but did not bring them up here till this morning. We opened them in the nursery, both children hung over them excitedly. Henry noticed the loving cup—as much as John did—and I had to break my rule, and let John have a goodly share of candy. I slept with your letter under my pillow—and read it the first thing when I opened my eyes this morning—and have been happy ever since. I knew your letter would give Mother almost as much pleasure as it did me—I knew nothing could make her happier than to know how good you are to me—so tho' I looked upon your dear words as sacred and meant only for myself—I let her read it. Mother is growing very old and frail—her pleasures are few now—her greatest comfort is to know that her children are happy. I have been so impressed, with her delicacy since I have been here—and how soon and certain the end of every human life, that I have made an effort to be cheerful all the time. But you have given me so much to make me happy and contented it has not been much of an effort.

After the storms of yesterday afternoon and last night, today is lovely—bright and fresh with cool wind from the North. Julia and I have just been for a long drive with the two children—they must have known it was a special day for me, for they both behaved beautifully. We were two hours late for Henry's dinner—but he was patient and uncomplaining—indeed jabbered gaily. I let Mrs. Thatcher[1] have this morning off for there are always interruptions on Sunday afternoons. I was glad to see something of the children. I have seen little of them this last week. John pulled out two fish at the Mill yesterday—he was wildly excited over them. He was a restless fisherman tho' and soon gave it up for the more childish sport of throwing bricks into the creek. We had a pleasant day with Kit he is the kindest old host in the world.

We have Warren and Miss [Mary] Gwynn[2] and Kit with us today.

1. Amanda Thatcher, a widow, began working for the Billingses as cook in the fall of 1900. After the birth of Henry Billings in the summer of 1901, she became nurse to John and Henry who called her "Nana." Later she became the Billingses' housekeeper and remained with the family until 1910. MS vol. bd., 1855–1908. Autobiographical account of "the early life of John Shaw Billings II," John Shaw Billings Scrapbook Collection, SCL.
2. Mary Gwynn (1876—1962), daughter of Louise Keene and Andrew Gwynn of Baltimore, Maryland, taught at the Downer School where she met the Hammond family. She married Christopher Cashel ("Kit") Fitzsimons Hammond on September 16, 1903. Billings, *Descendants of*

Henry could not come over and Alf and his family are in Charleston. I am not seeing anything of Henry.

After supper, and I am sleepy—the dinner bell rang as I finished the above sentence. After dinner, we all went through the garden gathering the first few roses. Then I hurried off to dress John and myself— we were to have callers Mr. and Mrs. Carey Lamar, Jim Richards and Willie Eve.[3] It was seven o'clock before I could get to Henry to give him his supper. Julia has gone to church with Warren. Kit is talking to Miss Gwynn. I am going to chat [with] Mother a few minutes and then go to bed. Mrs. MacWhorter and Miss Adams[4] are coming in to see me tomorrow—it is very lovely of them, they are the only people from the Hill who have proposed to come to see me. We have all been enjoying the delicious candy so much—and the loving cup has been greatly admired.

Good night my precious Love—you have been so good to me.

Devotedly,

Katharine

HENRY C. HAMMOND TO KATHARINE H. BILLINGS[b]

Augusta, January 29, 1903

My dear Katharine:

Replying to your letter of 27th January this moment received. Your letter conveys nothing definite as to the conditions now existing in your

Hammond, p. 2; *The Augusta Chronicle,* Oct. 17, 1946; MS vol. bd., 1955. "Some more small family facts," John Shaw Billings Scrapbook Collection, SCL.

3. Carey Lamar married Anna Baker in 1888; Jim Richards, a friend of Julia's, owned a livery stable in Augusta; and Willie Eve, the twenty-three-year-old son of Elizabeth Hammond and William Raiford Eve, was Katharine'a first cousin. John Shaw Billings, comp., "The Lamar Family [Genealogy]," Loose Papers, John Shaw Billings Papers, SCL; Billings, *Descendants of Hammond,* p. 11.

4. After Mrs. MacWhorter's visit, Katharine wrote, "It made me sad to see how aged and broken Mrs. MacWhorter had become in the last year and one half." Mrs. MacWhorter was probably Sarah ("Sallie") Adams MacWhorter, the daughter of Sarah MacMurphy and John Marsh Adams. According to John Shaw Billings, Major MacWhorter, Sallie's husband, was an Augusta dandy who owned a large tract of land, but did not work it. He permitted his wife to support him by teaching school. In an earlier letter Katharine had identified Miss Adams as Annie Adams, Mrs. Mac-Whorter's unmarried sister. Katharine Billings to John Sedgwick Billings, April 2 and 20, 1902, HBC Family Papers; John Shaw Billings, comp., "The Adams Family of Augusta [Genealogy]," Loose Papers, John Shaw Billings Papers; MS vol. bd., 1927-n.d. "Myself and Family," John Shaw Billings Scrapbook Collection, SCL.

household. It does not do more than give a general impression that for some cause or causes they are most unhappy. Of course, with no facts before me I cannot undertake to advise you. However, you do not ask my advice about things there, but only about your coming here with your children.

The time to sit steady in the boat is when things seem to be at their worst. Go slow! Think well! Look ahead! Think of others—especially those you are responsible for. I am shocked and distressed by your letter—those at Redcliffe would be—your relatives and friends here would be. Do not understand that I am not most anxious to serve you nor that I am not even pleased that in the circumstances you have brought this situation to my attention. Let me advise with you and let me help you all I can. For the present at least I entreat you let this matter be between you and me—let us be frank and honest with each other, but let us two alone deal with it for the time. Let no intimation of present conditions go out to any one—last of all to those nearest to us at Redcliffe.

As to the simple financial question of you and the boys and their nurse staying long, or short at Redcliffe dismiss that from your mind as not worthy of consideration. Everything there is moving smoother than I ever knew it to do. Mother and Julia both have some little spending money in bank—no debts. Father has a little and no expenses. Kit and Alf are self supporting and on the whole doing well. I made considerable money last year, but managed to spend most of it foolishly. This year my prospects are not very bright still I may not complain. In a general way the families' condition is more comfortable than ever before. These material matters while [not] of primary importance are in good condition. Peace, happiness, dignity, self-respect, decency, these considerations for the moment are most of concern. Keep ever in your mind the example of Mother's married life—think of the relations which thro all the trying years she has been able to maintain with Father. Remember how much this has been in the end to us, remember how much the same conduct on your part will be to your two boys.

Speaking more particularly of your plans for the immediate future, I understand from Mother and Julia that you expected to come to Redcliffe some time in the early spring for two months. If the circumstances require it come at once—come on the next train, but it would seem much better and would quiet suspicion and keep your secret your own to pursue some such middle course as this. Immediately begin writing letters to Redcliffe giving simple but good reasons for your coming sooner. Then in the course of a few weeks or a month come south prepared to stay as long as your circumstances suggest.[1]

I write in great haste for the next mail and send you this under special delivery stamp. What I have said is on the moment without the reflection which the case calls for. Please write to me immediately more fully. I enclose my check for $100.00 to avoid for you any immediate embarrassment. It is a present to the boys.

Please give them my love and John my good wishes and kind regards.

With a heart full of love and sympathy for your dear self,

ever and always yours,

Henry

JOHN SEDGWICK BILLINGS TO JOHN SHAW BILLINGS II[b]

New York, February 22, 1904

Dearest of Eldest Sons:

The doctor came yesterday and brought you a little baby brother,[1] as Grandmama and Aunt Julia have already told you. And his name is to be Julian—get Grandmama to tell you all about *her* brother Julian, his namesake. You took all the cold weather away with you in that snowstorm— it is very warm and rainy and all the horrid dirty snow is being melted and washed away. So dirty old New York will be a little cleaner by the time you are ready to come back to us. Tell Grandmama that everything goes splendidly—that Mother is as well as possible, and the little baby the same. He slept without a whimper or a cry from 9

1. Katharine heeded her brother's advice, for she and her sons did not arrive at Redcliffe until March 25. They returned to New York City after a five weeks' visit, although Katharine had wished to stay longer. John wrote, "It's no use—I need you, want you and must have you and May 1st is my uttermost limit." John Sedgwick Billings to Katharine H. Billings, April 23, 1903, HBC Family Papers; MS vol. bd., 1855–1908. Autobiographical account of "the early life of John Shaw Billings II," John Shaw Billings Scrapbook Collection, SCL.

1. Julian Cumming Billings, born on February 21, 1904, was named for Julien Cumming, Emily Hammond's brother, who had died a prisoner of war in 1864. Julian Billings lived only two and a half years, and at the time of his death on August 26, 1906, "still could not crawl, much less walk, and had not made an intelligible sound." Billings, *Descendants of Hammond*, p. 1; MS vol. bd., 1855–1908. Autobiographical account of "the early life of John Shaw Billings II," John Shaw Billings Scrapbook Collection, SCL.

last night to 9 this morning. He has a folded left ear . . . but otherwise is fine.

Our own nurse came last night, and Dr. Brodhead recovered from his pain, came this morning—so that we are fairly started. I hope you had a fine trip down and were the best of boys to Mrs. Parsons and Aunt Julia. Remember—thumbs out!

Henry misses you very much—he sends his love, and says if it were not for new baby brother he would come to Redcliffe too. He says "Old Mother Hipple hop" and "the Lord is my shepherd" for the baby night and morning. I hope you say your prayers every night and that you think of us all now and then. When you get your trunk unpacked get Aunt Julia to write a letter to Mother for you. All of us send you kiss after kiss, and tell you to keep well. For the farther off you are the more we love you.

Your loving father,
John S. Billings

KATHARINE H. BILLLINGS TO EMILY C. HAMMOND[b]

New York, March 13, 1904

Dearest Mother:

Did I say I had missed you and Julia terribly when I was in bed. Well that was nothing to the way I missed you this morning when I gave the baby his first bath. And tomorrow morning I know it will be even worse—for this morning I had Miss Holmes by to hand me things—and tomorrow I will have to do it all by myself. He is such a mite of a baby, tho' he has gained half a pound this week—still he only weighs eight pounds, and you know Henry weighed more than that when he was born. They tell me I must keep this baby's band on because his navel is not quite as small as it should be and it is the most awkward thing to put on and keep tight. I don't feel as if I would ever learn.

Well this is the first time John has been with me when one of the children was born—and if it was worthwhile to say such a thing—I would say it would be the last. I think if I had staid here when Johnny-boy was born there would never have been any more. There is much to be desired in his treatment of me at such a time. To say I would choose yours and Julia's company for such an occasion would not be paying you much of a compliment. John has been selfish and thoughtless too long to change. I hope I won't be living with him when I come to die—for I would not find even death restful if John were around looking out for his own comfort and interest. He went off to Washington yesterday without a word to the nurse or myself about paying her—or her staying with me until he came back. Perhaps you and I have spoilt him always paying for my nurses, and his when he was sick. Of course Miss Holmes has been paid.

The mail has just come in, and I had letters from Bessie,[1] and Julia. Tell Julia I never expect her to let John be bad—her punishment and influence must keep him good. I mean she must punish him, and her influence will do the rest. How prosperous it sounds to have so many Windmills put up. I hope your cough is better Dearest—and Father's too. Do both of you take good care of yourselves and each other until they are perfectly well. This March weather is very treacherous. Julia writes you are having a mild spell of winds. Here we are freezing and I am afraid you will catch it later. As you have probably heard from Henry, I want John to stay at Redcliffe as long [as] possible, and you all are willing to keep him. And yet today when Bessie's letter said she would not go to Redcliffe until the 22nd, and then she wanted to make a good long visit, I couldn't help feeling an added degree of longing for John, when I knew that his return was put off another week. And yet I would not have him here for anything now. The weather is so bad, and confines them to the house so much. I am so occupied with the baby. And more than all I am still weak and irritable and cross, and I don't want John to have another dose of him. I only feel a natural longing for the child, and am perfectly satisfied and contented about him where he is. No words can tell how grateful I am to you and Julia for taking him and giving him such care. I feel he is so much better off than he would be with me. Just suppose he had been with Mrs. Billings or any of John's family. I would have gone crazy, and he couldn't have come back to me too quick.

1. Bessie Hall was the granddaughter of the Reverend Charles Hall. See letter of Jan. 6, 1891, note 1. She visited Redcliffe in the spring of 1904. Mrs. Charles Hall II to Mrs. HH, June 6, 1904, HBC Family Papers, SCL.

When I compare the difference in the way Margaret and Evelyn[2] have treated me in the last month, it makes me indignant with the whole lot of Billings! Dear Evelyn she is so kind and good! She has come in to see me, and taken care of the baby and myself every minute she could spare from her Doctor and her work. Yesterday when she was here, and heard that I was going down to lunch for the first time today, and that I would have to take this first meal down stairs alone as John was away! She said she would come to lunch with me—and Sundays are her only free day for rest and seeing her brother—she values her Sundays as only working women can. I was deeply touched, but I accepted it from her, for I was lonely. Margaret Billings was here, and knew it all, but she would have seen me dead before she would have given up a minute of one of her church services.

Henry's day in the country yesterday was most successful—he and Nana [Amanda Thatcher] both enjoying it greatly. . . . With fondest love to John and all.

Devotedly,

Katharine

JOHN SEDGWICK BILLINGS TO KATHARINE H. BILLINGS[b]

New York, May 4, 1904

Dearest:

At last I think I can write you a letter which I will not tear up—as I have done steadily since last Saturday. For things have not been well with me and my letters have been catalogues of my troubles and protests against your injustice to me. But today I have a letter—not a——— from you: even if you don't tell me you love me, you don't say that you do not. And then my knee [hurt in a bicycle accident] this morning shows signs of improvement. For a week now the wound has made no attempt to heal, just an open sore, and the stiffness and pain on bending has kept me standing in street cars, and dining at Mother's where I can have my leg on a chair. But this morning the wound looks nice and

2. Margaret Janeway Billings, thirty-two years old at the time of this letter, was the sister of John Sedgwick Billings. John Shaw Billings described his aunt as "a weak, nervous old maid . . . addicted to faints and flutters." Evelyn Hemming was Katharine's friend from student nursing days at Johns Hopkins Hospital. MS vol. bd., 1855–1908. Autobiographical account of "the early life of John Shaw Billings II," John Shaw Billings Scrapbook Collection, SCL.

pink, and it does not hurt to walk, if I do not go too fast. No, no, business has not worried me, except to get around to see every one. I have paid the rent, my club dues, annual and monthly, a big bill at Park and Tilford, and a number of small ones, and have enough money in the bank to run things, to come and get you people and bring you home, and all without sending out any bills. Had business been bad I would have come to you [at Redcliffe] as soon as the St. Louis exhibit was done, which was Monday. I am perfectly well barring my knee, weigh 5 lbs more than I did two weeks ago Sunday. But just one word. On the receipt of your father's telegram I wrote him a letter, thanking him warmly for the invitation but telling him why I could not accept. I am afraid you have been sick, Dear, I cannot account for your letters any other way. I am afraid of Redcliffe, I always get a spell of such letters, and the boys are apt to be sick. I am so sorry to hear about your catarrh, one would think that in such a dry climate you would [be] free from it. But Gilbert says half the people in Aiken are dying of catarrh. John's letter was delightful, I cannot believe that he wrote it alone from a copy—Dear Mary must have held his hand very firmly. And I am so happy to know that he is riding horseback again, don't I know he looks grandly. And old Henry-boy: he always gets what he wants. How about John's thumbs—never a word have I heard. And the photograph, have my constant prayers had no effect. I will surely get John's desk the next time I am down town, and have it stocked and ready for him. But I must send him some little toy too. So far I have heard nothing of the hunt for your wedding anniversary gift—I am glad you are sorry it was lost—you had said nothing. As to the nurse, you stated baldly and simply "Kit and Mary are paying for our nurse." The check is here waiting to be remailed to you. Mother had a relapse three days ago, fever 104° pulse 130 and great weakness.[1] I was much alarmed and feared pneumonia for some hours. Bradfield[2] seems to be having some trouble in

1. Katharine Mary Stevens Billings (1837–1912) was born in Rochester, New York. Her father, Hector Lockhart Stevens, a lawyer from Pontiac, Michigan, served one term in Congress (1853–1855). On September 3, 1862, Katharine Stevens married John Shaw Billings, then a young Army surgeon. John Shaw Billings II remembered his grandmother as being "a stout old lady, a semi-invalid in a negligee nursed by her spinster daughter, Margaret." She died in 1912 while vacationing in Sharon, Connecticut. MS vol. bd., c. 1860–1951. Time Inc. data, John Shaw Billings Scrapbook Collection, SCL.

2. Edwin Bradfield Hartley married John Sedgwick Billings' sister "Daisy" (Jessie Ingram) on September 3, 1890. There is frequent mention in the letters of Hartley's need for financial aid from his father-in-law. MS vol. bd., 1955. "Some more small family facts," ibid.

getting a place in Dayton, but so far has not asked for money. Things go fairly well here, but I am so busy that I have not touched my abstracting yet. Oh how I have missed you people, my heart has fairly ached for you. And physically I have been more uncomfortable than ever in my life—nothing constant in my thoughts but my aching knee, and all the time *you* writing me of "my jolly companions," of my spending money on a good time, telling me of my great rudeness and brutality to your family and how they scorned and despised me, or else not writing to me for three days, when I was as worried as possible about John. Do you wonder that I grew wrought up in writing to you— you were lucky that I tore the letters up. What was it, surely you did not treat your Mother the same way, and yet I was as innocent of any wrongdoing as she. I am afraid of Redcliffe, it always comes between us. How on earth could I have travelled that first week, why I did not sleep the first two nights just from the pain in my knee. And yet I don't think I complained to you, and I tried to arrange to save you any worry by telegraphing you. It was not my fault that my plans went awry. And you have treated me shabbily—I think you will admit it. I know you were worried about John. But why be unjust to me.

Enough said. If you won't write to Norton I will go down there when my knee is well enough. And as for the summer, we will settle that in June. You decline Bay Head,[3] I decline Pennsylvania and doubly decline your remaining where you are later than June first.[4] I won't do anything about a cook until you come back. I had to say all that I have said Dearest. I love you with all my heart and soul, there were times when it was a fight not to telegraph for you, and I would have broken down like a baby had you walked in the door. I had no one to wait on me—Oh rats—can't I talk of anything else. Please thank Julia for her loving little note—kiss the boys black and blue for me, and don't

3. Bay Head was a resort on the Jersey shore—"a cluster of several hundred well-weathered summer cottages and boarding houses between the ocean on the east and Sunset Lake . . . on the west." The family vacationed there in 1902 and 1903. In 1904, a compromise was worked out and Katharine and the children spent the month of July with her Billings in-laws at Onteora Park in the Catskills. From August 1 to September 19 Katharine, her three sons, and Mrs. Thatcher boarded at a place called Big Hollow which was seven or eight miles from Onteora Park. MS vol. bd., 1855–1908. Autobiographical account of "the early life of John Shaw Billings II," ibid.

4. On May 21, 1904, Dr. Billings had come to Redcliffe for a week, and on May 25, Reverend Chauncey Williams christened Julian Billings at St. Paul's in Augusta. The Billings family left Redcliffe for New York on May 29. Ibid.; see also Julian Billings's baptismal certificate, ibid.

let's do anything from now on but love each other. I will bring a trunk full of old clothes, where is the steamer trunk.

Your own loving,

John

HENRY C. HAMMOND TO EMILY C. HAMMOND[b]

Augusta, December 18, 1906

My dear mother:

You have several times spoken to me about turning Redcliffe over to Julia and myself, with the consent and approval of your other children; you and father, of course, to remain in absolute control and possession during your lives. I spoke to Julia about the matter and she said she would be glad if some such arrangement could be made. She said she had a very strong personal attachment for and sentiment about the place, but she very wisely added that she could not in justice to herself accept it as a part of her inheritance at a valuation so great as to leave her nothing to live on. This is a very proper view to take of the matter, and I of course share it with her. Redcliffe is a very charming and attractive place in many respects, and I regret that the interests of all the members of the family except you, father and Julia, require that they be away from it all or most of the time. However, in a matter of this kind not only must its beauty and charm as a home be taken into consideration, but its actual market value must be considered by those who are to dispose of it, and its actual value as an income bearing property must be considered by those who are to become its possessors. Father, I think estimates that there are about 340 acres of land, and that it has been reduced by the sale of 10 to the Downer school. Of this amount I estimate that only about 80 or 90 are cleared; of this 80 or 90 only about 40 is good land—that it is rolling—the balance being very ordinary to poor. The woodland is without marketable timber, and none of it invites to clearing or cultivation. It is true that the tremendous rent of $500.00 has been paid the past two years for this land, and that $450.00 is promised in payment for it next year. I am bound to believe that this is exceptionally high rental—being about $6.00 an acre, which is warranted only by exceptionable circumstances, and could scarcely be counted on as a permanent thing. But even this rental has to be reduced largely by the payment of heavy tax and insurance, and if the question of repairs on the property, owing to the great size of the house, were taken into consideration, even this exceptional rent falls to a very small amount; but say a net rental of $250.00 could be obtained annually, this would mean interest at the small rate of 5 per cent on an investment of $5,000.00. Now all of this is from the view point of persons who might accept the property at a certain valuation as an inheritance.

The view point of persons who were to relinquish their claim upon it is a somewhat different one. Their interest, of course, would be to get every cent the property would sell for in any market, and they should in justice to themselves inquire as to what this would be.

While the place is very attractive in many regards, and while it might be sold to some wealthy person desiring a home in the country, still I for one am bound to believe that this chance is a very long shot. What northern person has ever bought such a place, or is likely to do so? There are no instances, certainly not in this section of the country. It is true that a few wealthy northern people have spent large amounts of money at Aiken, on "The Hill," and one I believe at North Augusta. But all these people and that class of people are society people who, in my opinion, would never consider going into the remote country. For this reason I am bound to believe that the value of the place if it were sold would depend upon the condition of the local market for agricultural purposes. In this view the big house on the property would not be an attraction, but the expense of keeping and maintaining it, on the contrary, would be an objection. However, it will be for Katharine, Kit, and Alf, to say frankly and candidly what they think the property is worth, and at what price they would be willing to part with their share of it.[1]

Speaking for myself, and as far as I am authorized by the above statements of Julia, for her, I should say the property should be valued

1. As early as 1902, Harry Hammond delivered Redcliffe into Julia's care and she became totally responsible for the management of the lands and of the laborers. In 1907 an agreement was signed by all five Hammond children that Redcliffe would pass to Julia and Henry "within one year after the death of the survivor of the two life tenants, Harry Hammond and Emily C. Hammond," after the payment to Katharine, Kit, and Alfred, "of one-fifth of eight thousand dollars." HH to JBH, July 25, 1902; Agreement between K.H. Billings, C.C.F. Hammond, and A.C. Hammond with J.B. Hammond and H.C. Hammond, March 31, 1907, Legal Size Papers, HBC Family Papers, SCL.

at [an amount] certainly not to exceed $5,000.00. If you care to consider the matter further, I would of course have no objection to your showing this letter to the parties at interest.

Always affectionately,

Henry C. Hammond

JAMES P. RICHARDS[1] TO JULIA B. HAMMOND[b]

Augusta, March 17, 1907

My Dearest:

Mother just telephoned me that she heard from you and that you and Miss K. would leave Sat. for Redcliffe. Since she telephoned I read your letter written Sunday. I was so disappointed not hearing from you yesterday and this morning. So glad to hear from you. Darling I feel and pray for you God bless you. I know how you feel that your dear Mother is sick. I pray that she is not very sick and will soon be well. Oh darling, I know how you feel when your all and all is sick and you can't be with her. Darling I am yours and when you need me call and I will come to your rescue. The place of your dear Mother I will never be able to fill. But, oh darling, I will do all I can for your happiness which you deserve more than any one else I know. I will do all I can to let you know by Sidney when you get back. Send him by the stable every time he comes to town. I don't think Henry despises you, he should not. Do all you can to try and win him back I am afraid you won't be able to have both of us.[2] If he could understand us as we understand each other. Oh Darling, how will we ever win him again? He loves you I know but he is so deep. If I could only help you or

1. Jim Richards, who had been a frequent visitor at Redcliffe since 1902 and Julia's long-time friend, asked her in 1906 to marry him. Although she refused his proposal, he vowed to continue to press his suit. Jim Richards to JBH, Sept. 21, Oct. 8, 1906, HBC Family Papers, SCL.

2. Emily Hammond had objected to Jim Richards as a son-in-law. She considered him an unobtrusive, yet second-class, visitor to Redcliffe, without culture or charm. He was tolerated, but nothing more. Julia would not marry Jim over her family's objection, but she saw nothing improper in continuing to see him frequently. The Beech Island neighbors began to gossip, and Henry Hammond ordered Julia to make a choice: marry Jim at once or stop seeing him. Out of consideration for her mother's objection, Julia agreed to ban Jim from Redcliffe for several years. Though the association ceased publicly, they continued to correspond and occasionally met secretly. Richards continued to profess his love for her. HBC Family Papers, 1907–1911, passim; MS vol. bd., 1908–1912. Resumé of John Sedgwick family history, John Shaw Billings Scrapbook Collection, SCL.

advise you what to do. Darling I love you I know your goodness you are the best that ever lived. Your dear Mother and myself only know you. If others knew you as we do they could not help but love you. I am glad you wrote to Mother again she was so pleased to hear from you. Darling she loves you and will do all she can to help us along. I hope so that your suffering may be repaid in happiness. Try and hold your own with Henry and don't get mad. Do all you can to win him back. I know how happy it will make you to win him. Oh how terrible for us to lose him. He was always so good and kind to me. It is hard for us to have to give him up. I am afraid I will never be able to win him back.

Lovingly yours,

Jim

P.S. Love to Miss K.

WILLIAM W. WOOLSEY TO JULIA B. HAMMOND[b]

Aiken, October 19, 1909

Dear Miss Julia:

It was a pleasure to see your writing again and to be reminded of the fortunate result of the hunting accident which I had almost forgotten. Forgetfulness comes with old age and I was 66 my last birthday.[1]

Just now I am slowly recovering from an attack of my old back weakness which I have suffered from several times in the last three years, making me afraid to take long drives or rides and often rendering it impossible to go even to Aiken.

However I must not complain, for I enjoyed such exceptional health for so many years.

What a wonderful world we live in now man has at last conquered the air. Flying machines will be as common as autos soon and much safer.

My little girls[2] are in Charleston at a boarding school for the winter—Ashley Hall—Miss McBee is the Principal. So far they like it.

1. This is the last known letter of Woolsey to the Hammonds. He died suddenly in Charleston on April 28, 1910. *The Aiken Sentinel,* May 6, 1910; *The Aiken Journal and Review,* July 8, 1910.
2. Woolsey had two daughters by his second wife: Marie De Hertburn Woolsey, probably born in 1893, and Elsa Gammell Woolsey, born about 1896. John Shaw Billings, comp., "Woolsey Genealogy," John Shaw Billings Papers, SCL.

Mrs. [Bessie Gammell] Woolsey is in Savannah but returns on Friday. John is hunting moose in New Brunswick. Will is a sophomore at Williams College. Catherine at Englewood, and Con and his family are at home again.[3] All are well.

My love to your dear Mother and Father and to any other member of the family with you.

Yours Sincerely,
W.W. Woolsey

JOHN SHAW BILLINGS, SR. TO HARRY HAMMOND[b]

New York, November 18, 1909

My dear Major Hammond:

Permit me to offer my hearty congratulations and best wishes on the occasion of your golden wedding anniversary.[1]

For each man who is so fortunate as to have this happy experience it is an unique occasion, so there is no use in wishing you "many happy returns." You have seen a great deal of history made during your fifty years of wedded life, and while you have had some unpleasant experiences, I hope that you are still able to look at the passing show—with friendly and sympathetic interest.

I hope that you still receive our Library Bulletin regularly. One of our Trustees, Mr. John S. Kennedy, died recently and by his will gives

---

3. The reference is to the children of Woolsey's first marriage: John Munro, Converse, William Walton Jr., and Catherine. John (1877–1945), the eldest son, was educated at Philips Andover, Yale University, and Columbia University Law School. He became a lawyer in New York City and served as U.S. District Judge (1929–1943). His best known decision was rendered in 1933 when he declared that James Joyce's *Ulysses* was not obscene and hence could freely enter the United States. All that is known of the other Woolsey children is that Converse farmed at Aiken, South Carolina. Ibid.; MS vol. bd., c. 1860–1951. Time Inc. data, John Shaw Billings Scrapbook Collection, SCL; *Cyclopedia of Eminent and Representative Men of the Carolinas*, 1:375.

---

1. Emily Cumming and Harry Hammond were married at Emily's home at Sand Hills on November 22, 1859, and celebrated their fiftieth wedding anniversary at Redcliffe. Harry had written Emily two months before their marriage that, though he foresaw their lives to be most ordinary, he did desire "that before we celebrate our golden wedding, we may possess in some corner of the earth, a house and lands all our own." It was not to be museum-like nor a grand and flashy building, "but one created of such solid material, and so firmly put together that our descendants in the tenth generation may think it the labor of their immediate parents." HH to Emily Cumming, Sept. 25, 1859, HBC Family Papers; MS vol. bd., 1926–1936. Letters, snapshots, clippings, programs, invitations; MP vol. bd., c. 1875–1912. Earliest pictures of John Shaw Billings, John Shaw Billings Scrapbook Collection, SCL.

us $2,250,000.00.[2] That will enable us to enlarge one field of work, or rather to improve some portions of the field which already covers the world's work.

This is a part of the "passing show" above referred to.

"Cakes and Ale" shall be forthcoming in the years to come, as in the past—let us hope that our appetites may not fail, and our digestion remain competent to dispose of all that comes to us.[3]

Always sincerely yours,

J.S. Billings

SENATOR BENJAMIN R. TILLMAN TO HARRY HAMMOND[b]

Trenton, S.C., September 7, 1911

My dear Sir:

I read with deep sorrow of the death of your good wife[1] and I cannot refrain from expressing to you my feeling of sympathy. When a tender tie as that which binds a husband and wife together is snapped it almost breaks the heart-string and this is increased four-fold when the couple has lived together so long. I have been married forty-three years and I know what my wife is and has been to me, and judge you by myself which is the only way we can fathom the mystery and misery of such a separation. My health has been so poor for a year or more that as a sensible man I have thought of Death a great deal. Old people on the brink of the grave as I am[2] cannot enter into the emotions and feelings of the young, but we can understand each other's feelings better than the young ones can understand ours. Mrs. Tillman and I often discuss how sad will be the home-coming when the other is buried. I have

2. John Stewart Kennedy, banker, investor, and philanthropist, died on October 31, 1909. At his death his estate included seventeen million dollars' worth of stock in the Northern Pacific Railroad and the Great Northern Railroad. He contributed liberally to Columbia University, the Metropolitan Museum of Art, the American Museum of Natural History, and the New York Public Library.

3. John Shaw Billings (1838–1913), who had suffered ill health for many years, died while Director of the New York Public Library less than four years after this letter.

1. Emily Cumming Hammond died on September 4, 1911 at the age of seventy-six and was buried at Redcliffe. There are over one hundred fifty letters of condolence in the collection of family papers, HBC Family Papers, Sept. 4–Oct. 4, 1911, passim, SCL.

2. Benjamin R. Tillman, U.S. Senator from South Carolina, had suffered a stroke in 1908 and another in 1910. He died on July 3, 1918.

been spared as it were by a miracle and I must hope that in the Divine scheme of things it is for some wise purpose, though I fail to see and understand it. Broadly speaking life and death are both mysteries. We are sent into the world we know not why or whence; we go out of it willy-nilly we know not where and without being consulted. It is wisest that this should be so, and as my own time approaches I realize as never before the pathos and beauty of Tennyson's lines:

> "All things are taken from us and become
> "Portions and parcels of the dreadful past.

But again the same poet teaches us that

> "It is better to have loved and lost
> "Than never to have loved at all.

A useful life such as yours has been would have failed of its purpose in many things had you not been inspired and led upward by a beautiful and noble helpmate such as you have lost. Whether there be a hereafter or not the beauty of such lives entitle those who live them to immortality with the angels.

May you have a blessed reunion with your wife hereafter, and may we all get to Heaven, if there be a Heaven.

I trust I have not bored you and you will understand my motive, and believe me, my dear sir,

Very sincerely, your friend,

B.R. Tillman

ANNIE V. RICHARDS[1] TO JULIA B. HAMMOND[b]

September 12, 1911

Dear Miss Julia:

I have been thinking about you so much and want you to know that you will receive a warm welcome in our family.[2]

---

1. Annie Vernon Richards, of Augusta, was the forty-three-year-old sister of Jim Richards. She visited Redcliffe frequently after Julia and Jim were married. She died on August 28, 1951, at the age of eighty-three. MP vol. bd., c. 1875–1912. Earliest pictures of John Shaw Billings; MS vol. bd., 1870–1946. Redcliffe after Billings restoration, John Shaw Billings Scrapbook Collection, SCL.

2. A week after Emily Hammond's death, Jim Richards wrote to Julia and her brother Henry again requesting permission to marry Julia. They were married on September 28, 1911. Richards

If it had been left to me to select a wife for Jim you would have been my choice.

We could not be satisfied with any but the best for our dear, good, noble, unselfish Jim, therefore we are pleased.

Dixon[3] said to Jim, I am glad you are going to get such a fine lady.

I crocheted a bag for you which I send with my love.

Hoping both of you will be very happy.

I am Lovingly,
Annie V. Richards

KATHARINE H. BILLINGS TO JULIA H. RICHARDS[b]

New York, May 29, 1912

Dear Julia:

This will be a difficult letter to write you—I wish I was feeling fresher and more equal to it. Perhaps by this time you have heard of Dr. Billings' letter and mine to Henry. I wish I could tell you just exactly how this thing happened, and of the feelings that burst out, that were smothered, but so very strong and old. For so long Dr. Billings has treated Mr. Myers[1] so villainously and rudely it has been impossible for Mr. M. to come here when there was the slightest chance of his meeting Dr. Billings. Yesterday morning I was extremely busy, there

---

never attained the status of "master" of Redcliffe, as that title continued to belong to the Hammonds. As noted earlier, Jim was a poor businessman, and Julia's small inheritance was misspent on luckless ventures. Ultimately, they were reduced to living off the sale of farm products at Redcliffe. Nevertheless, the marriage was a very successful one. Jim died of a heart attack in September 1934, and Julia succumbed in March 1935. James P. Richards to Julia Hammond, Sept. 7, 1911; James P. Richards to Judge H.C. Hammond, Sept. 7, 1911, HBC Family Papers; MS vol. bd., 1908–1912. Resumé of John Sedgwick family history, John Shaw Billings Scrapbook Collection, SCL; Billings, *Descendants of Hammond*, p. 1.

3. Lucian Dixon Richards, of Augusta, was Jim's brother. MP vol. bd., c. 1875–1912. Earliest pictures of John Shaw Billings, John Shaw Billings Scrapbook Collection, SCL.

---

1. James Jefferson Myers (1842–1915), a Harvard graduate, practiced law in Boston. Katharine Billings, twenty-five years his junior, was introduced to him by her older sister Julia, who had known him since 1881 when she was a student at the Harvard Annex and boarding with Mrs. Brooks. (See letter of June 7, 1881, note 2.) Over the years a friendship developed between Myers and all the Hammonds. After her marriage, Katharine entertained Myers in her home whenever he came to New York. Her husband, John Sedgwick Billings, disliked Myers; in part, because he considered him a bore, and, in part, because he was envious of his wealth. As marital tension mounted, John became almost irrational on the subject of Myers, as is evidenced in this letter from Katharine to Julia. MS vol. bd., 1908–1912. Resumé of John Sedgwick family history, John Shaw Billings Scrapbook Collection, SCL.

was a man moving the telephone, a laundress coming in and out, hunting up clothes and money, a maid cleaning and poking into everything. Before Mr. Myers had been here fifteen minutes I had had to jump up and run out to them, giving directions and orders, at least four times, finally in desperation, I slammed the door and turned the lock without thinking, and left it so forgetting it entirely. The sitting room door by which Mr. M. had entered, and where we were sitting was unlocked. Dr. Billings hasn't been in here 3 times this year at that hour. I should never have locked the door on him, of course, and I had forgotten it was locked until he rattled it. When he came in red hot with rage, and bellowing at Mr. Myers and myself, he would listen to nothing we said. In about three quarters of an hour, he came back and was more insulting to us both. He said then, and repeated last night more in detail, that if I did not end my acquaintance with Mr. M. at once, he would not give the boys and myself one cent to live on this summer, he even went farther and said I should not have the boys with me if I did not promise to end my friendship with Mr. M. This was all said in the most insulting cruel hard way. At first I said I would not concede to one or any of his demands. But today I saw little Henry, and all day I have been thinking of them both and realize the cruel disappointment it will be to them if they don't go to Cotuit.[2] And always and every time I have felt and known I would sacrifice myself to the limit for my boys. Dr. Billings never meant to give us enough money for the summer, but I had saved most of mine that Henry had sent me, and meant to make up the deficiencies from this little reserve. Now I am afraid to use that money—I may need it soon even worse than I do now.

Every spark of feeling I ever had for Dr. Billings has long been dead. He has killed it with his cruel hard treatment, his neglect of me, his utter selfishness. Nothing would hold me for a day, to the semblance of a tie to him, but for the boys. It is for them I have suffered and put up with all I have done. And thank God they are worth it— they are the finest boys that ever lived! I have just told Dr. Billings that if he will furnish us with money for our expenses this summer, I will go to Cotuit with the boys, not see Mr. Myers at all, not let him come to see us, or ask us up to Boston. And how under the sun I will get through the summer without dear old J.J.'s help, the Lord only knows.

---

2. Cotuit was "a little oyster village on Cape Cod" where Katharine and the boys spent several summers in a rented cottage. MS vol. bd., 1927–n.d. "Myself and Family," ibid.

Not to have one ride or outing all summer, to be off in that far away corner of the earth, with not a friend near me, not even an acquaintance to have no pause from washing our clothes, fretting over expenses, mending and doing for the boys. As dear as they are I know I will get dreadfully tired of it and regret many a time the automobile and all the pleasures J.J. was constantly giving. Why the mere matter of the feeding he gave us, we will all miss that, the many trips we had to Boston and about—the actual nursing care he gave me when I was sick. I fear I won't be much better at the end of the summer than I am now! And the boys will miss him almost as much as I will, for he was endlessly good to them. Well I may break down and not be able to stand it, but I shall have tried to do my best.

I go to Betty's tomorrow,[3] and will take the boys back there after Field Day to stay until we can get in at Cotuit. When I yielded to all of Dr. Billings' demands, he hesitated about the money—he hates to pay it to us, partly because he finds it hard to make it, can't make it, and greatly because he wants it all for himself.

I have had to pay all the expenses of the moving, and I bet I will have to keep on paying for extras until all my money is gone. Try Julia to understand this letter. I don't make it clear, but I surely make it clear that I am in a great deal of trouble. That I need all of your sympathy. Don't think I am yielding to Dr. Billings in any way, except to get my boys. I would like to open suit for a divorce, and I should have liked to do it for many a long day. Got up at 4:30 A.M., and it is now 11 P.M. and I have been working every minute of that time.

Good night,
Katharine.

KATHARINE H. BILLINGS TO JULIA H. RICHARDS[b]

"Yardley"[1] Fishkill-on-Hudson, June 5, 1912

Dear Julia:

I wish I might talk to you instead of writing this letter. I think I might make you change your feelings about several matters. Last night

3. Betty is the Bessie referred to earlier. Granddaughter of the Reverend Charles Hall by his second marriage, she was Katharine's "cousin." She rented a summer place at Fishkill, New York. Ibid.

1. "Yardley" is the name of Betty Hall's summer place where Katharine and the boys were visiting. John Shaw Billings described it as "a fine old home." Ibid.

and this morning I wrote a long letter to Henry, that I felt pretty certain you would see. So I did not hurry to write you even a note by that mail. Since my letter went to Henry I have had two from you—one written Saturday the 1st and the other Monday at Henry's house. Your sympathy as far as it goes is very comforting to me. But there is much you do not seem to take in at all, and I fear I will never make you understand in letters. Your feeling towards Dr. Billings has always been to idealize him. You ought to know from your own experience—that his best qualities are not the livable, lovable qualities—that makes a woman live happily with a man. That in my life there has never been, and never can be, an easy comfortable companionable day, such as every day you spend with Jim. How can I make you see the forlorn loneliness of the life I have spent with Dr. Billings. Your life spent to "at-one-ment" with the surroundings you love, your friends of a life-time, and now the man who loves you beyond everything. Why you just could not comprehend the narrowness and meanness of my life, as spent with Dr. Billings. I have got my boys! That is the one great thing in my life—they *are* my life, and I have no thought of living without them, or but for them. And here again the influence is a bad one for them. Dr. Billings and I can never make them a home, and every time they are with us together, they see nothing but unhappiness. It is absurd for me to abuse Dr. Billings, to say that he is mean and selfish, hard and close, is of no importance whatever except that it weakens me and my case to give way to such expression. It is enough to say I shall never live with him again—tomorrow, the end of the summer, or the end of six months, or six years if I live so long. Don't you see under these circumstances how wrong it is for me "to yield—do just what Dr. Billings wants" me to. This would only lead to more insults and troubles. I have made expensive arrangements for the summer, it is too late to make others. I have got to have the money for the boys and my own board and lodging. I can only get it by sacrificing myself. I don't want to put myself in the right that is gained by Dr. Billings' abuse of me. 2nd I doubt if my life could be harder than it has been for the last ten years. If it could be harder, then it would kill me. Death could not be worse than such a life. I have answered your 3rd reason for staying with him by my first announcement that it was ruining the boys to see such a life as we lead. I have for so long felt so deeply on this point and thought so much, and as I have looked first one way and then another for the right feeling on his part for the boys. I can't see it—he will have failed them as he has failed me. And you tell me to try and forget—all this that has been making my life so miserable for so long. Either you are entirely out of sympathy with me, and I can't believe this, or you have forgotten all of the many things I have had to endure. Oh my Sister, I know it is this last, I know you can't think so lightly of me at this time!

What do you mean by saying "Everybody is glad you have given up Mr. Myers, he certainly showed little sense of discretion in getting you into so much trouble." Great Heavens, what a reward for all the kindness Mr. Myers has shown me and my boys! How it would shock him to know that you felt this way about it! Let me tell you at once—as I am sure I told you before, that I made no such promise to Dr. Billings as giving up my friendship with Mr. Myers. I only promised for this summer that if he would support the boys, I would not see Mr. Myers at Cotuit, or accept his hospitality in Boston. I made this as plain to Dr. Billings as I want to make it to you. I promised nothing beyond this summer! And because of the boys only was the promise forced out of me for that long. Mr. Myers has been nothing but kind, generous, and considerate of my boys and myself. I feel Mr. Myers has given me much help towards regaining my strength, he has done for me what you couldn't do, and Dr. Billings wouldn't do. He has brought me every bit of cheerfulness and pleasure I have had since my long wretched illness. And who was to blame for that awful illness—didn't Dr. Billings bring me almost to the grave with mortification and misery.[2] If I had had only what Dr. Billings cared to give of pleasure and interest in these last two years I feel I would never have gained even this far along the road to health. When I recall all that Mr. Myers did for the boys and myself last summer—the healthy pleasures he gave us—the good food he lavished on us—the refreshing use of his car. Why it did worlds of good to us all, and God knows how we are going to get on without it this summer. I fear the boys will miss it as much as

2. In 1907, Katharine Billings was diagnosed as having what was then called "Graves Disease," an enlarged and overactive thyroid, which affected her heart. In June 1908, she was shocked to learn of her husband's affair with one of his patients, Mrs. Josephine West. At first Katharine contemplated divorce, but ultimately she remained in the marriage for a number of compelling reasons: divorce was considered socially disgraceful; her sons loved their father dearly; her own ill health worsened and left her more and more an invalid. She wrote her mother in 1910 that "I expect I have relapsed into my old disease. It doesn't trouble me so much. I never thought I was going to get well again. . . . My heart is a little worse, I am a little more swollen and my nights are hideous." HBC Family Papers, 1907–1912, passim, SCL.

I will. Can you recall a summer or a winter, when Dr. Billings did anything beyond the barest duty towards us?

You may remember that I told you Dr. Billings was anxious for the boys and myself to come here and spend the summer with Betty. And his expressed reason for wishing us to do so was that in so doing I might save enough money for John's school.[3] Now not many men calculate on paying for their boy's schooling out of imposing their family on a lone woman, and sacrificing his wife and boys to any hardship so that money is saved. I have never for one hour ceased to be thankful I was not persuaded into making that arrangement. Do you often hear of Dr. Billings proposing to give up his tennis tournaments, or not going to Newport or Southampton, or Bay Head wherever these meetings take him?[4] But again I am betrayed into showing up his meanness and selfishness, and my own righteousness! We are none of us perfect, and more and more I feel my own weaknesses. I don't want to work—I don't want to be anxious—I don't want to be pinched and poor—I don't want to struggle, struggle always—for what others have that are no better or more deserving than I.[5] I know from your letters you are very tired from your hard work in the oats harvesting. Let Jim read this letter and explain it to you, tell you what it means. I know his explanation of me will be fair. I sometimes feel that Jim knows and understands my troubles more than you do. Forgive me if I have seemed impatient. I don't mean to be so—I am just so torn and harassed—and worried I am nearly crazy. To feel I must sit quiet and take what is meted out to me—of insults, disgrace, and hardships—from one who has given me nothing but abuse is impossible and more than I can endure! I need

3. John Shaw Billings was to begin the fall term at St. Paul's School in Concord, New Hampshire.

4. There are photographs showing John Sedgwick Billings in 1910 at Southhampton, New York, at both his tennis and golf clubs and at the Bay Head tennis tournament. Others show him at the Metropolitan Tournament at the West Side Tennis Club in 1912. At the time of his death in 1928, he was vice president of the West Side Tennis Club. MP vol. bd., c. 1875–1912. Earliest pictures of John Shaw Billings; Herbert Chase to Mrs. John S. Billings, May 28, 1928, MS vol. bd., 1877–1959. Career data on John Sedgwick Billings, John Shaw Billings Scrapbook Collection, SCL.

5. John Sedgwick Billings had a thriving general practice in New York. In addition, he worked for the New York Department of Health and was a medical officer for the New York Stock Exchange, the New York Public Library, and the New York Telephone Company. Although he earned as much as $20,000 in good years, he was evidently a spendthrift. MP vol. bd., 1862–1913. Billings family tree; MS vol. bd., 1877–1959. Carrer data on John Sedgwick Billings; MS vol. bd., 1855–1908. Autobiographical account of "the early life of John Shaw Billings II"; MS vol. bd., c. 1860–1961. Time Inc. data, ibid.

your help, your sympathy, your love as I have never needed them before. You have been so generous to me always, don't be hard on me now. I am more alone and unhappy than I have ever been before in my life. And oh, so miserably puny and weak. Love me and forgive me.

Your distracted Katharine

KATHARINE H. BILLINGS TO JULIA H. RICHARDS[b]

Cotuit, Mass., July 15, 1912

Dearest Julia:

I worked every minute of yesterday—from seven in the morning till ten last night. Then I slept as I hadn't done the night before. But I have had some things to do today and I took a bath before dinner—so I do believe I am more tired than I was yesterday. Indeed I feel as if I could hardly hold my pen I am weary from my head to the soles of my feet. My work yesterday was for Henry's birthday party. Late the afternoon before, they sent me word I couldn't get any ice cream in Cotuit. Mr. and Mrs. Blake took us ten miles over to Osterville in their car and we ordered some there. It was bed time when we got back I did everything for the party myself—made all of the arrangements and did all the work. At four o'clock—the ice cream hadn't come—but the guests had. They waited quite patiently for nearly an hour. Then I fed them on sandwiches, thinking the ice cream would come at any minute. Quantities of sandwiches were devoured—then they fell too on the cake and candy. I had given up all hope of ever getting the ice cream—the children were playing about the yard and out house—they call Casino, when the ice cream arrived at 6 o'clock. They all had to go into supper then—but when they got through we moved everything out to the Casino—had more cake—and such quantities of ice cream—it was good too! The children ate until they couldn't hold any more—and all the servants on the place had some. The weather is horrid—every now and then little showers of rain but never a real good downpour. Everything is nasty—sticky and damp—and oh, how things smell! It is not cool either, it is close and sultry.

Dr. Billings seems better since he has been here. He has nothing to say to any of us, he lies on the sofa and reads all of the time, going out for an occasional game of tennis—or a swim. There have been long,

long silences between us whenever we have been alone. Last night I screwed up my courage and asked him a few questions about his affairs. They are absorbing him very deeply I suppose. He spoke some of Mrs. [Josephine] West and his past connections with her.[1] He feels Elliot Norton[2] can do him the greatest harm if he turns against him at this time. Yet he feels E.N. is such a blackguard—he can't trust him to handle his case. He has engaged Mr. Moen his great friend, but who never does this sort of work. Dr. Billings naturally does not talk to me with any frankness. Of course he has been horribly upset by it all. Every man in his Dept. read that account in Thursday morning's paper[3]— and an hour or so after he had to go down and face them all. He is perfectly absorbed in his own moritification—I don't believe he has given the boys and myself a thought. Suppose John—who reads some papers pretty faithfully—had happened on the Herald or Times and read that account of his Father! I believe Dr. Billings is still angry with me just because I am I—but I think he has entirely forgotten how he insulted me the last part of May in New York. Julia it will take death itself to wipe out those last three days in New York—and the way Dr. Billings treated me then. His utter cruelty and selfishness I can never forget. I have told him I shall never live at the Great Northern[4]—or in the old way again. I don't think he noticed. He was entirely preoccupied with the idea that the boys and I would spend the month of Sept. with his Mother.[5] Please tell Henry all of this West matter that has come up

1. Although John Sedgwick Billings and Josephine West were no longer seeing each other, it was not until the summer of 1912 that Mrs. West's husband sued for divorce. *New York Herald*, July 11, 1912.

2. Elliot Norton was a lawyer and the brother of Rupert Norton, one of John Sedgwick Billings's closest friends, who had been in residence with Billings at Johns Hopkins Hospital. Rupert was Billings's best man and was Henry Billings's godfather. James Henry Hammond Billings baptismal certificate, April 24, 1902, MS vol. bd., 1908–1912. Resumé of John Sedgwick family history, John Shaw Billings Scrapbook Collection, SCL.

3. Katharine's reference was to the newspaper account of John West's divorce proceedings. John Sedgwick Billings was named correspondent and dates were given of the meetings between Billings and Mrs. West at the Brighton Hotel in Atlantic City from October 8, 1907, to October 27, 1908. *New York Herald*, July 11, 1912.

4. The Great Northern Hotel on West 56th Street became the residence of the Billings family in October 1910. They had moved from their 53rd Street house to save money to pay for their sons' private schools, and to relieve Katharine of the burdens of housekeeping. MP vol. bd., 1862–1913. Billings family tree; MS vol. bd., 1908–1912. Resumé of John Sedgwick family history, John Shaw Billings Scrapbook Collection, SCL.

5. This visit never took place since her mother-in-law died in August 1912 at Sharon, Connecticut. The fourteen-year-old John Shaw Billings said he felt no grief nor sense of loss, for "Grandmother, to me, had always been just a sick old woman in a gray wrapper who sat in an armchair by her bedroom window." MS vol. bd., 1927–n.d. "Myself and Family," ibid.

so unexpectedly. I wrote to Henry a few days ago—you have probably seen the letter. I want Henry to know all of this—but you will tell him for me until I know more what to write to him.

I am so tired! With love to all.

Katharine

P.S.   Henry had lovely beautiful letters from you and Jim today. The money came to him safely. I hope in the course of time he will write to you both. I will tackle this task after his Father's visit is over.

JOHN SEDGWICK BILLINGS TO JULIA H. RICHARDS[b]

New York, January 8, 1916

Dear Julia:

Oh—I am so sorry for you. Not for him—despite your loving care of him, it must have been a lonely world for him. I am so glad the boys saw him last year. This is the first death that has really struck home to them.[1] They were too young at the time of the others. We made all arrangements for Katharine to leave on the Coast Line this morning— but when she learned from your's and Henry's telegram that she would be too late for the funeral, she felt that she could postpone it—and see to getting the boys off to school. We have not received your letter yet, but were relieved to know that he had not suffered much or long. I had a beautiful letter from him only two days ago, as in the case of most of his letters he was thinking of someone else, and wanted information about spinal operations. I had obtained it, and was just about to write him when the news came. He and I were "always the best of friends"— who said that—Joe and Pip in Our Mutual Friend, was it not?[2] And by the time this reaches you he will be lying in his beloved graveyard. You must keep up his flowers there for him.

You and Jim will be lonely in the big old house—you must have more of your parties than ever. And remember your sister and brother

---

1. Harry Hammond died in his sleep on January 7, 1916. He was the last surviving parent of Katharine and John Billings. Emily Hammond had died in 1911; the elder Katharine Billings in 1912; and John Shaw Billings I in 1913.

2. Joe Gargery, the blacksmith, and Pip Pirrip, his orphaned young brother-in-law, are major characters in Dickens's Great Expectations, not his Our Mutual Friend.

in the north, and that we always have the warmest kind of a welcome for you at any and all times. With love and sympathy to all the family—

Yours ever,

John

JOHN SHAW BILLINGS TO KATHARINE H. BILLINGS[b]

Ormond, Georgia, October 6, 1922

Dearest Mother:

Here I am at Uncle Henry's[1] and it is raining for the first time since my arrival. We need it. The roads are oceans of choking dust and the fields stand scorched and brown.

I came up to town yesterday afternoon. They gave me at Redcliffe a horse to drive up, a pitifully lame animal that limped and jerked and slowly swayed. I had to walk the beast over the nine miles along the swamp road—and almost three hours were prodigally wasted by the trip. The purpose of my coming to Augusta was to attend a minstrel show with Henry Cohen,[2] which invitation I had inadvertently accepted earlier in the week. I damned myself for a fool—the idea of coming down here and wasting time in a sweltering theatre to see a third-rate performance! But it would have been unwise to refuse, I guess; everybody has been so good to me that I can't afford to appear carelessly ungrateful of their misdirected efforts to entertain me. . . . But there was a merry dinner at Miss Nora's,[3] where Uncle Henry came. And after the show I was brought out here for the night—

Breakfast is over. Uncle Henry and I ended the meal with an argumentative scrimmage on the standardization of education and now he's

1. John Shaw Billings had been away from South Carolina for six years. He arrived on September 30, 1922, to visit his uncle, Henry C. Hammond, at his home outside of Augusta, and his Aunt Julia at Redcliffe. John Shaw Billings Diary, Jan. 16–Dec. 31, 1922, pp. 225–59, John Shaw Billings Papers, SCL.

2. Henry Cohen, the Augusta judge, and his wife, Nora, had been close friends of Henry C. Hammond since the late 1890s. MS vol. bd., 1927–n.d. "Myself and Family," John Shaw Billings Scrapbook Collection, SCL.

3. Nora Cohen (1864–1950) was one of the few women that Henry Hammond ever loved. Henry and Nora remained steadfast friends for over fifty years. Ibid.; MS vol. bd., c. 1860–1951. Time Inc. data, ibid.

out in the back somewhere at work—busy, always busy; a true Hammond trait.

Aunt Julia is killing a pig today with the intention of giving Uncle Henry and Miss Nora some sort of celebration down by the pond at Redcliffe. I am fearful that this steady rain will put a crimp in her plans and we will have to dine inside— But at least I shall get back to Redcliffe shortly after noon, which is all I desire. I despise Augusta and long to keep away from it. Ormond's great drawback is its proximity to the city—

But let me take up my story from the beginning:

I left Washington a week ago this afternoon—and every mile I travelled therefrom brought peace to my spirit. The trip down was vilely dirty—otherwise uneventful. The passengers in the Pullman thought I was crazy, the way I jumped from side to side of the car and squealed with delight at all the familiar sights along the way from the mill at Kathwood on into Augusta where Jim and Uncle Henry met me Saturday morning. The latter drove me out here at once. He was going out on court to Burke County Monday;[4] therefore he appropriated my company before I could sneak away to Redcliffe. . . . His place here I found rurally charming—but without tradition (what Miss Moore would call "background" or "atmosphere"). The pond with the swans (you should have seen them swimming phantom-like across its dull moon-silvered surface last midnight!—It was something from Kubla Khan.); the pine trees like noisy green beggars always asking alms—and then the very up-to-date comforts of this house. . . . I found Uncle Henry had changed but little: a little greyer, a little more imperious and dogmatic with his opinions, a little more reckless with the cuss words. . . . otherwise the same. We have had two or three good talks, about education this morning, about the strikes and general labor situation, about Tom Watson[5] and politics—and a certain fundamental harmony of thought cements our interest and attention. I don't think I am too great a disappointment to him—though I can't bring myself to work out of doors

4. Henry Hammond was appointed state Superior Court judge on December 24, 1904, to fill a vacancy, and held the position until 1930. He continued to practice law until 1948. Henry C. Hammond Memorial Resolution of the Augusta Bar Association, Jan. 15, 1962, HBC Family Papers, SCL.

5. Thomas Watson of Georgia (1856–1922) was a frustrated Populist who was elected to the U.S. Senate by the Democrats in 1920. In the course of his career he had become the epitome of Southern intolerance, spewing forth attacks against blacks, Catholics, and Jews. C. Vann Woodward, *Tom Watson: Agrarian Rebel* (New York: Macmillan and Company, 1938), pp. 416–30.

with him, in his fig orchard (for breakfast today I ate some of his first fruit from trees planted last January), or in his huge vineyard where he has 2500 scuppernong vines growing. (Oh you home-brew!)

Saturday and Sunday nights we supped at the Cohens'. Mrs. C. is the most delightful lady I know. I love her and her cool serenity and good sense. It is just a simple joy to be with her. I feel very close to her. There is understanding between us and we talk confidentially in the most boldly sensible way about Aunt Julia, the Richards, and Uncle Henry. And she loves you very dearly, Mother; otherwise she would not have been so good to me.

Last Sunday I was taken on a most tiresome picnic by the Smiths. Ugh! It was Annie's birthday (I thought she was ageless, therefore without birthdays). I was 25 years younger than anybody else on the party which consisted of millions of Butts (husband and wife; complete set $1.98), a thick sprinkling of the spinster Smiths (I can't tell one from the other; hence can't discriminate in my dislike)—and then the usual trimmings of unknown and undesirable-to-know. The picnic was out in the woods—and dull as the devil, with all these senilities trying to frisk about like flappers! But I grinned manfully and thanked 'em all abundantly when at sunset the affair broke up. . . . How precious time is when you have only a scant fortnight—and the art of politeness to be compelled to squander it on such affairs as old-age picnics and bad minstrel shows—

—I got out to Redcliffe Monday noon; was there till Thursday; am going back today, with the secret vow not to leave it until I go down to the station Sunday afternoon of next week to take the Coast Line back to Washington. There is happiness at Redcliffe. It is the corporate Present symbolizing the Past—and I don't want to leave it!

Of course I had been carefully warned of the changes of time at the dear old place in the last six years—by you, by Henry, by Nora Cohen. In a way it was a shock—but when I saw the house rising up in all its old-time grandeur, supremely indifferent to the queer little narrow-visioned mortals who lived in it, I felt a catch at my throat, and thanked God that I had such a secure association with the place—

But things aren't so bad. The dining room is again in use—though the stubby little table brings to mind the long, long board of other days, with a dozen feasters on a side! But when I start to eat ochra soup, solid with rice—why, I forget everything. And there has certainly been no deterioration in the quality or quantity of the food served. And Lena [the cook at Redcliffe]—Lord bless her. Incidentally she is the most observing negro I ever saw—with a shrewd sense of human comedy.— And here's another thing; long absence and recollection based on childish impressions have given me an exaggerated sense of the size of Redcliffe. I was disappointed to find the back yard so small—the windmill so near and so on. Younger eyes saw this place as a vast arena for amusement—where we could go chugging about and play train—

Grandfather's room—I don't object to its use as a living room. It has a musty atmosphere of comfort. It is preferable to the sewing room. The upper house is as I expected dark and dirty. I have not yet explored the library, curtained in all the sombre gloom of wisdom. The drawing room is bare—and beautiful. What ghosts haunt the house, what reproachful ghosts! All things considered, I am inclined to commend silently the present occupants of Redcliffe for keeping the place up as well as they have. Nothing has been sold. The landmarks are in each room as of old. I have spent hours walking through them, standing in the shadows—and brooding on things that are never to be again—The first time I stood in the doorway of the top hall and gazed down over the fields and trees, receding to the blue hills of Georgia, I was transfixed. "Well," I thought, "no matter what else decays, the view will always be the same. Human beings can't destroy that"—God—I love the place! If only you could be here with me, dearest mother, to share this strange feeling of devotion and crazy idealization. The whole place strikes a booming chord on the strings of my ego. I forget my realism, my mundane sophistries—and am carried away on a wave of sheer emotionalism by being there, with the ghosts. Why aren't you here? I confess that I think I could love you more deeply more rapturously, more poetically, at Redcliffe than anywhere else under the sun! Lord—I am convinced that Henry and I approach Redcliffe and its significance from quite opposite directions—but then how could it be otherwise, since he was born in Bronxville. He may have the name[6]—but I claim the truer sentiment of the inheritance of tradition.

Aunt Julia—I first saw her in the field watching Sidney pitch hay. She looked very small and round and bent. Her shoulders have rounded down by the years. And she is given to obsessions. She is now preaching

6. Henry, John's younger brother, was baptized James Henry Hammond Billings in honor of his great-grandfather, the builder of Redcliffe.

the gospel of poverty. Also she is reducing everything to a dollars and cents basis. What a change! Her mind can't grapple with facts. You can't have any sort of extended conversation of a serious nature with her. She won't keep up her end. She is constantly breaking off to relate some anecdote or other. . . . . I have done little talking to her. Instead I sit back and listen to her telling her many tales, embroidered by the wildest kind of exaggeration. I tell her a simple fact. I go places with her and hear her repeat that fact to the people she meets. It grows in importance and size with each telling, until the simple truth is lost. . . . And then our philosophies of life are not in accord. She thinks I am burdened with morbid gloom and never see the bright happiness of life. We recite poetry to each other—and our poems are at the extreme poles of thought.—Her poverty complex is a bit trying. She has gone crazy in her fierce economy. She has carried her ideas to the verge of insanity in this matter; and when you try to question her directly about it and ask the why and wherefore, she becomes evasive and uncertain. It is a mania, born of her idolatry for Jim Richards.

And the Richards obsession still obtains. It sickens me at heart to hear Aunt Julia talk about what rare spirits Minnie and Annie[7] are— and about Jim's deep culture and lofty idealism. It is one of the most impossible illusions I have ever encountered. Of course I conceal my opinions behind discreet silence. Jim is good and kind to me and I am very fond of him but—. Aunt Julia has been a dear to me and I thoroughly enjoy being with her. But she has changed far more than Redcliffe. Her perverted ideas, especially about making speeches to school children in Beech Island and Augusta, have carried her into some nasty disagreements—and she has lost friends. Fancy her going to an Aiken school and talking for an hour and a half to some girls about my affair with Marilyn![8] But I think she is now over her public speaking craze.

Henry made such a deep impression when he visited here that my name has been wiped out completely. I am called "Henry" by everybody. At first I laughingly protested and requested my nominal identity—but in vain. So now I pass as my brother! Henry cut a big knick

7. Annie and Minnie Lee were the unmarried sisters of Jim Richards. MP vol. bd., c. 1875–1912. Earliest pictures of John Shaw Billings, John Shaw Billings Scrapbook Collection, SCL.

8. John had a crush on Marilyn Miller, the dancer and actress. Although he dated her a few times, it was a one-sided romance. MS vol. bd., Feb. 1917–Jan. 1918. Chronicle of John Shaw Billings's one-sided love affair with Marilyn Miller, ibid.

in the minds of the local population. Wherever I go I hear endless stories of his doings (duly enlarged by repetition). He is something of a mythical figure in Beech Island, a legend to be reverenced. His cold and courtly manner fluttered many a heart. His art inspired much covert controversy.[9] His charm is a by-word with every yokel wool [hat]. Even his manner of driving his Ford has become a tradition to pass down from father to son. —Your junior son is deserving of great pride from you. He has indelibly impressed his personality upon everybody here—and a dozen times a day I am asked when he will return to gladden the hearts of the multitude. Katherine Cumming, I hear, wants to meet me—because I'm Henry's brother. Frederica Wade[10] sought me out—so she could talk to me about him—But I have resigned myself to my fate of being just Henry's brother—and I am a silent cuss, usually, and won't strive to dispel with fiery words the damp obscurity that hangs over me. I'm here for two weeks. I shall go—and that will be the end of it—

At Redcliffe I have been doing a lot of horseback riding—trotting about alone, and forgetting many things. It means so much to me to be here. I can appraise the value of it all now—Why aren't you here? That would make my enjoyment complete—I am saying little about my reasons for being here—and already Aunt Julia has started wildly romantic rumors flying through the air—I don't want to meet anybody. I want to be alone, to saturate myself with the contentment of the country. It is a real rest. I have pulled down the curtain of my mind and all mental production is now at a standstill. But through the dark in my head there occasionally bursts sharp flashes of—I don't know what. Regret—no,

9. By 1927 Henry was referred to by the New York critics as a promising young artist who should have a "vigorous career." At that time he was painting mainly landscapes and representational figures. By 1931 he was painting murals, "colorful abstractions based on machinery, which are far more suitable for modern buildings than nymphs, satyrs, etc." After World War II he returned to his earlier style. The New Yorker, Nov. 5, 1927, clippings pasted in MS vol. bd., 1926–1936. Letters, snapshots, clippings, programs, invitations; MS vol. bd., c. 1860–1951. Time Inc. data, ibid.

10. John Shaw Billings met Frederica Wade, his future wife, on this visit to Beech Island. On October 4, 1922, he wrote in his diary, "I was taken along for a formal presentation to the beautiful Frederica. In this dinky house was jammed a lot of good city furniture which they had brought from Atlanta when Judge Wade died (He was Chief Justice of the Georgia Court of Appeals). . . . A short wait; footsteps through the thin floors above. Then entered Frederica. She was young—21; she was pretty, except for a large mouth; her eyes were a fine blue and she had the whitest teeth I ever saw. . . . I could see the stamp of the city on her and my heart unconsciously went out to her as one of my own kind." John Shaw Billings Diary, Jan. 16–Dec. 31, 1922, p. 232, John Shaw Billings Papers, SCL.

hardly. But atrophication is not possible—But I won't allow myself to do any retrospective thinking—Sometimes riding along by myself in the late dusk I can almost imagine that there is no such person as Cecil,[11] that the idea of her is something I have conjured up from my inner self to torture myself with—

Thank you so much for your dear letter. My heart is close beside you, loving you more and more with each beat. I was so distressed to hear of your recurrent rheumatism—may it now have ceased to pain you. I wish I could take care of you![12] Mother dearest, you are foolishly good to me. Of course I thank you with all my heart for your check—but you shouldn't have sent it. It will help lots—I have brought Aunt J. some old cast off clothes to give away—we must start for Redcliffe—

With all my love,
John

P.S.   Please let father see this letter. It will save me from writing him a long duplicate of it, repeating my actions and reactions. I shall write him soon. J.

KATHARINE H. BILLINGS TO JOHN SHAW BILLINGS[b]

New York, January 18, 1925

My very dearest John:

I haven't written often of late—but I have thought of you and loved you every minute of the time. I am still so weak and far from well. I can hardly realize how ill I have been for months and months now— indeed it is eight months since I have been able to do anything. Except lie here and dream of you, your future successes and present happiness.

11. Cecil Clark was a sculptor whom John had met in the summer of 1922 at his mother's home in Woodstock, New York. He fell in love with her and seriously considered asking her to marry him, but she said their relationship could not be long-lasting, for she told him "I couldn't say 'I love you.' " Ibid., July 15, 16, 23, 1922, and July 24–Dec. 31, 1922, passim.

12. Katharine Hammond Billings, in poor health since 1907, was intermittently a patient in various sanatoriums. Her physical problems were further compounded by the emotional strain of her husband's infidelity. In 1912 he had been involved with the West divorce suit, which was ultimately dropped. Later he had an affair with his nurse, Mrs. Toering, for whom he purchased expensive presents on the family's department store accounts, making no attempt to conceal them from his wife. HBC Family Papers, 1908–1925, passim; MS vol. bd., 1877–1959. Career data on John Sedgwick Billings; MS vol. bd., c. 1860–1951. Time Inc. data, John Shaw Billings Scrapbook Collection, SCL.

And I have been so glad that you were happy—that your life was so full of joyous youthful love—that the full expectations of your happiness are being realized.[1] Such imagination—idealization—and sentiment as you have are not given to many of us. May it always be yours and keep you as you are now—full of enthusiasm—romance—and feeling. I don't believe you will ever shrivel up and be a hard cold old man—with a heart for nothing but selfish pleasure. If by the cruel laws of inheritance it should come to you, thank God I won't be here to see it. To me you will always be young and beautiful, full of charm and kindliness, with one of the most beautiful minds and highest ideals. You and Henry have had my entire devotion since the moment you were born. And each year I love you more, and am more proud of you, my only reason for existence is to love you two, "and if God choose I shall but love you better after death."

> Your devoted Mother,
> Katharine H. Billings

JOHN SHAW BILLINGS TO HENRY C. HAMMOND[b]

Washington, July 12, 1925

My dear Uncle Henry:

Out of the black mass of my emotions during the past week there comes to the surface today a bright sense of gratitude and appreciation for all you did for us to make things calm and peaceful. Your steady influence was like a guiding star taking us through a dark night and, though our lips were quiet, in our hearts were blessings for you.

Mere words are futile to express to you my own personal acknowledgment of your careful and considerate management of every detail. Your very presence infused the whole home-coming with a certain dignity, a certain decent restraint, that I shall never forget. I know mother rests quietly out there at the edge of the pine thicket, largely because of all you did for her.[1]

1. On April 19, 1924, John and Frederica were married in the Presbyterian Church at Beech Island. John worked for *The Brooklyn Eagle*, and had been its Washington correspondent since October 1921.

---

1. Katharine died of a heart attack at Woodstock on July 5, 1925. *The Augusta Chronicle* noted that she had been "a very brilliant and charming woman, one of rare lovely character, and a delightful companion whose society was eagerly sought by young and old." Her son John commented gloomily, "thus another chapter ends." *The Augusta Chronicle*, July 6, 1925; John Shaw Billings Diary, 1924–1926, July 9, 1925, John Shaw Billings Papers, SCL.

I had hoped to see you again when Frederica and I returned to Redcliffe Wednesday afternoon and was sorry to learn that you had already gone back to town. I wanted to tell you all these things directly and in person—and now to write them makes me feel that they are weak and pale compared with my own inner feelings. From the moment we arrived at the Beech Island station, we felt secure and composed, because we knew your fine hand was on the helm. . . . The whole service was one of beauty, a thing of lingering fragrance that I am sure mother herself would have loved. To have you and Aunt Julia and the others there, all so serene, took the biting edge off the loss. In that great old house there was a warmth of kinship which, I feel, tightened the very bonds of blood.

Father stopped off here for a few hours today with Frederica and myself, before going on to New York at eleven o'clock. Poor fellow, his left elbow was giving him a lot of pain and there seemed little he could do for it. But it was good to see him, if only for so short a while.[2] It was his first glimpse of our little home here—and I think it met with his approval. (If only mother could have seen how snugly my dear wife and I have made our first home!) He speaks of coming down to pay us a real visit later on in the summer.[3] I was particularly interested in hearing of his visit with you, and I only wish that Frederica and I had had sufficient time to remain over and accept your good invitation to drop in for a visit too. I shan't forget the pleasant days I was there with you a year or so ago.

I was pleased that you should be interested in my prospect of going to France for my paper.[4] As yet there are no new developments in that line, except that my managing editor has gone over there himself, with a view to reaching a decision as to the change. I fully appreciate the opportunities that would be mine, should this assignment be given me,

2. John's father suffered from arthritis. In his diary, John commented that his father's brief visit had been unsatisfactory for he made John feel as if he were "rushing on to see somebody—probably that Toering beast. Her putrid shadow already falls darkly across the horizon." John was distressed by the idea that his father might marry her, as, in fact, he did with unseemly haste after Katharine's death. John Shaw Billings Diary, 1924–1926, July 12, 1925, John Shaw Billings Papers, SCL.

3. John's father never visited them in Washington. In early December John received a letter from his father announcing his intention to marry Mrs. Toering on Christmas Eve. Billings's reaction was strong, "God damn him! . . . Mother not dead six months and father goes off and marries the woman who wrecked her life and happiness. Lord, how I hate them—This awful union breaks the last link between father and myself." His father died of "septic arthritis" on April 27, 1928, and no reconciliation had taken place between them. Ibid., Dec. 9, 1925, New York Herald Tribune, April 28, 1928; John Shaw Billings Diary, 1927–1929, April 1928, John Shaw Billings Papers, SCL.

4. There is no record that Billings ever went to France for The Brooklyn Eagle.

and I have every determination to make the most of them. When a decision is reached by my M.E., I shall inform you promptly of the fact.

Tomorrow I shall put my hand to my job here again and I am trusting a great preoccupation will overtake me, at least until I can accustom myself to the idea that mother is gone. And yet I can't realize, somehow, that she is not still at Woodstock, still driving her rattling little car among those beautiful blue mountains she loved so much. You know, she drew strength from those hills and they lent her a certain secret happiness. Spring would come and with it, for her, a great yearning to get back to Woodstock. And yet withal it wasn't home for her, could never be home, in fact. She knew this too well to try to deceive herself. Her home was always where she lies now—across the storm of life her heart turned back to her own dear mother by whose side I know she now lies so contentedly. Oh, Aunt Julia was good and generous to give mother that coveted resting place! . . . Someday I may attempt to tell you just what mother meant to me, someday when the mist of immediate grief clears into the mellow dusk of a quiet sadness. But I can't do it now. . . . This is just a note to tell you how thoroughly satisfied I was with the manner in which the arrangements were executed and how deeply indebted I am to you for all your thoughtful kindness to myself and to Frederica.

Frederica joins me in kindest regards.

Affectionately,

John.

P.S.   I beg you to pardon the use of a typewriter, but by my work I have been robbed of the art of manuscripting. J.

JOHN SHAW BILLINGS TO HENRY C. HAMMOND[j]

New York, March 21, 1935

Dear Uncle Henry:

We got back to New York safely yesterday morning and I returned to work this morning on "that wretched little sheet called TIME." [1] The

---

1. Billings left *The Brooklyn Eagle* in 1929 to work for *Time* magazine. Four years later, Billings became managing editor, a job he held until he became *Life* magazine's first managing editor in 1936.

most exciting thing on our train trip home was killing a woman and seriously injuring a man in Charlotte. Our locomotive hit them at a crossing as their taxi cab tried to beat it over. A ten minute stop to inspect the wreckage and remains by the side of the track—and we had no appetite for our dinner. . . . Frederica has already written you to thank you for the box of candy and both she and I are fairly bursting with gratitude for all you did for us. Your kindness did much to blunt the cutting edge of an otherwise very sad ordeal. . . .[2]

Now to business:

I received your letter this morning with the check for $125 which is hereby acknowledged as payment on Aunt Julia's estate. I forwarded Henry's letter to him promptly.

As to the silver, I suggest that a brief inventory be made of it and submitted to the nieces and nephews. They can then express their preference for this or that item on such a list and return it to you. As for myself, I would then empower you to make the distribution, following the preference lists as far as practicable. I have never inspected the Redcliffe silver and therefore would be quite incapable of starting off the division by expressing a choice.

And now Redcliffe: After due consideration and consultation with Frederica, I have decided to accept your offer to buy it on the following financial terms, as taken from your memorandum:

Price	$15,000	
Credit for my		
⅛ share	1,875	
Total cost	$13,125	
Cash payment		5,625
Notes		7,500
		$13,125

The notes are to bear 4% annual interest, to be paid quarterly to you on such dates as you may specify. They are to run for a period of three years, with the right to anticipate their payment in full at any time or the right to renew them all or in part for another two years, provided

2. Again the Billingses returned to Redcliffe for a sad occasion. This time it was to attend the funeral of Julia Hammond Richards, who died on March 16, 1935. John Billings wrote in his diary that her life had been happy—"The happiest of anyone I know. And life meant nothing to her anymore without Uncle Jim." John Shaw Billings Diary, April 1934–May 29, 1935, March 16, 1935, John Shaw Billings Papers, SCL.

interest has been paid promptly and in full. As owner, I get the farm rent from Simkins.

So much for the money matters, as to which, I think, we are both pretty much agreed. My willingness to purchase, however, depends on three additional provisions:

(1) The purchase price is understood to include the present contents of Redcliffe, with the exception of the silverware, Aunt Julia's personal effects and anything that either belongs to you (i.e. the Cumming tray, the table from your mother) and or that you may want for yourself as a keepsake. Otherwise I am to be given title free and clear to all remaining pictures, books, busts, beds, chairs, sofas, tables, desks, and other furniture; all bric-a-brac and miscellaneous furnishings. (In my talk with you, I failed to mention the china, family and otherwise. Its disposition in whole or in part I leave to your own good judgment.)

(2) It is to be definitely understood by Uncle Kit, Uncle Alf, their wives and children that I am buying Redcliffe because no one else will or can take it and otherwise it might well pass out of the family or be left to rot down. I have a fear that at some future time, perhaps after you are gone, the question may be raised and I may be unfairly charged with having taken off greedily something to which I had no right. I realize that quit claims were obtained from the other heirs at the time you and Aunt Julia came into exclusive possession of Redcliffe and that they are still legally sound. But what I am anxious to avoid at the outset is any possibility of that extra-legal rancor and covetedness which can sometimes divide a large family and make all its members most miserable. Any steps you think necessary to take to prevent such an occurrence will be appreciated by me.

(3) I must be privileged to continue to draw heavily upon your advice and assistance in my future management of Redcliffe. I realize how little I really know about maintaining and operating such an establishment and I would never undertake it if I thought I could not turn to you for counsel, legal and otherwise. Though the title to Redcliffe may pass into my name, the brains and experience behind it will have to remain largely yours. Countless questions will come up which I trust no one but you to answer honestly and fairly and disinterestedly. This, I know, is imposing a large burden on you but I feel I may ask it because of your long association with the same sentiment which prompts me to take this biggest step in my life. About the only help I promise not to seek from you is monetary.

If the foregoing meets with your approval I stand ready to close the deal on short notice. I am prepared to forward you the full cash payment within a week of the receipt of your letter of acceptance as seller. If, however, you have any alterations or counter-proposals to make, I would be glad to receive them.

Assuming that the sale goes through as I have outlined it here, chiefly to keep the record of our conversations straight, I have the following general plans in mind:

(1) To have work started on a new roof for Redcliffe at the earliest possible moment. I think I understood you to say that you had already looked into the prices of this work and had found that a good substantial metal roof could be had for something like $300 or $400. If so, I would like to hear in more detail about the matter so as to be able to give the necessary order to proceed. I feel that it is no extravagance to put about the best metal roof on Redcliffe, to last through the years and preserve the building's fundamental soundness.

(2) To get an estimate on painting the entire outside of Redcliffe. I believe it would be necessary first to go over it with a wire brush to remove the old particles of paint but whether or not the wood needs a priming coat I frankly don't know. Henry Billings suggests that two coats of Atlantic white lead should do the job. I have decided I want to keep the window blinds in place. My idea would be to have them taken off, to have a carpenter repair any broken slats, and then have them painted two coats of medium green and rehung, with new hardware wherever necessary. If you could give me some pointers and start me off in the right direction for this job I would be thankful. The first thing, of course, is to get an estimate on how much it would cost.

(3) To have the broken chimney promptly repaired with good brick by competent labor. This might be done simultaneously with the roofing. But who could do it and for how much?

I think you said these three things could be done for something less than $1500—a price I am ready to pay if necessary.

Today I talked over with Henry Luce the business of my buying Redcliffe. He seemed highly pleased that I was about to take this step, saying that what I needed most for good *Time* work was a vital interest outside my office and that the acquisition and development of an old ancestral home seemed to be just the thing for me.[3] The big problem,

3. Luce agreed with Frederica that Billings's purchase of Redcliffe would provide him with a major interest outside of *Time*. Ibid., March 21, 1935.

professionally, was how and when I could get off to use Redcliffe. We agreed that I should take three or four weeks off in the spring and about the same amount of time in the autumn to go south and enjoy myself. That would put me at Redcliffe during the two most delightful months of the year. Therefore if the sale goes through as scheduled Frederica and I proposed to come down about the middle of May and spend my Spring holiday at Redcliffe, doing a million things that seethe in my brain and having the finest and happiest time in the world. If possible I would like to have the roof, paint and chimney jobs practically done before my arrival. Another idea of mine is to have some carpentry work done on the porch and its steps especially the side ones which are now such a menace.

Immediately after the sale one of my major problems will be some sort of caretaker at Redcliffe. But I have written too much to you already and will take up that matter with you in a later letter.

Again my thanks for all you have done for me in the past and the hope that you won't desert me in the future. [4]

Affectionately yours,

J.S.B.

HENRY C. HAMMOND TO FREDERICA WADE BILLINGS[j]

Augusta, March 25, 1935

My dear Frederica:

Your dear letter so welcome—nonetheless so for being in type, for it lets me go back to you the same way. You all's visit, in spite of the sad occasion, was one of very great delight to me. When only a kid, you sweetly danced with a stiff old man when the others wouldn't and he has never forgotten it, and you have kept in the same kindly way towards him.

Now about John and Redcliffe: Maybe it's not as bad as you and I think. Come to analyze it, rash sentimentality and cool judgment may not be so far apart after all. Redcliffe originally cost the Hammonds $50,000. When dollars were four times as valuable as they are now. It

---

4. After completing this letter to his Uncle Henry, Billings wrote in his diary, "I have never been so happy and excited! I think of nothing but having that wonderful old place for my own. I am about to become a Southern landowner in the grand sense." Ibid.

is down in the deeds as 300 acres—Father said it was nearer 400. I added 2 poor acres from the Wilsons' for which I had to pay $100.00 an acre. 10 acres of Redcliffe land (the school house cut) were sold to the Willises at the same price. I know of no land sale in Beech Island for less than $40.00 an acre. All the land on Redcliffe is good farming land, much of it the best in this section. It has been estimated that there is over $7,500 worth of untouched timber and wood on the place. The house furnished as it is throughout—books, pictures, etc. is certainly of some value. During good times, Julia turned down an offer of $50,000. John's money invested here will probably be as safe as in stocks—certainly as safe and profitable as in automobiles, boats, or a Long Island estate.

But with all this, I am looking to your clear steady head to hold John in leash. You must be his anchor and come down on him like a thousand of brick when he goes plum damn fool. He owns one of the best farms—country estates—ancestral castles, if you please in the South on the rim of a great bowl, nosed out of coastal plain by the Savannah River 7,000,000 years ago by a glacier. But make him go slow. Accept the natural beauty and charm of the place just as it is, doing and spending barely enough to preserve it. He won't have to bother about the land for 2½ years to come. You have played a very wonderful part in John's social, sentimental and romantic life, now you must play an important one in his material affairs.

All the members of the family, I am sure, will welcome and applaud John in this undertaking, and your folks and the neighborhood will welcome him. I am glad he has Henry's support, but Henry is an artist and I count more on you to check his impetuosity.

I did not mean to write so much, but I felt your ears would be open to what I might say.

Love,
Uncle Henry

JOHN SHAW BILLINGS DIARY—1938

[Redcliffe], April 28, 1938

Harry and his men were gathering the Italian rye cut in the backyard. I did odds and ends of work about the place. Later I put Dennis and Jim to waxing and polishing the hall floor for the dance.[1] Lunch. About 3 o'clock there arrived from Savannah Pickens Walker Jr., a young (26) Fitzsimons cousin of mine who was on the Savannah Morning Press. He drove up to discuss his "career." We sat for an hour in the cool of the library and talked and smoked. A nice young fellow— but needlessly concerned about his future. I advised him to stick to his job and learn reporting for a time longer. (F. was meanwhile napping upstairs.) When the boy left, I helped F. give Runzy[2] a bath in her bath tub. Then I bathed and dressed myself. At dusk the floodlight people came out from Augusta to finish their job. They put up a 1000 watt light in the garden, a 1000 watt light at the road Y and two 500's in the shrubs at the side of the house. After supper Harry and Mary Gwynn[3] returned to see the lights. When it was good and dark we turned the floodlights on, drove over to Downer [School] and then back to Redcliffe to see how the illumination looked. It was very beautiful— making the house look like a great white frosted wedding cake or a spectacular movie set.

April 29, 1938

The day of the big dance. I sent William off to Elko early to fetch Ma[1] and Aunt Mary. Harry, Dennis, Jim and I went to work on flower decorations; bowls of magnolias which are just coming into bloom; great boughs of kalmia in the corners of the hall with long-leaf pine at bottom. About 11 Mrs. Cohen and Tracey came out with the punch, cakes, etc. They helped set the dining room table. The Willis girls came in to ask if they could bring house guests. Ma and Aunt Mary arrived about one in the car. Our dinner was served by Mamie in the pantry. Fulcher appeared with his orchestra instruments and made a final test

1. Between March 1935 and April 1938 he and Frederica remodeled and renovated Redcliffe. To celebrate completion of the restoration, they gave a ball on April 29, 1938, for their young cousin Mary Gwynn Hammond and two hundred guests.

2. Runzy was the Billings's wire-haired terrier whose death on June 7, 1945, sent them into mourning. There are ten letters of condolence on Runzy's death pasted in a family scrapbook. MS vol. bd., c. 1860–1951. Time Inc. data, John Shaw Billings Scrapbook Collection, SCL.

3. Mary Gwynn Hammond, the twenty-year-old honoree, was the daughter of Mary Gwynn and Christopher Cashel ("Kit") Fitzsimons Hammond. Billings, Descendants of Hammond, p. 2.

1. "Ma," Frederica Wade Billings's mother, lived with her daughter and son-in-law in New York after 1932. Her death occurred suddenly on May 5, 1938, only a week after the ball at Redcliffe. MS vol. bd., 1809–1962. Genealogical data re the Black, Kirkland, Robison, Reid, Bryan, Lamar, and Peters families, John Shaw Billings Scrapbook Collection, SCL.

of the piano which we had moved into the hall under the Bay of Naples pictures.[2] F. and I lay down for some rest. I got a little nap but F. was too keyed up to sleep.

Everything was in readiness: I went out in the backyard and lay in the warm sun. What a temptation to run away into the woods—and hide there until the dance was over. Final fixings here and there—and about 7:30 Patience served a stand-up scrambled egg supper in the kitchen. (F. in pink house coat ate hers seated in deck chair.) Then the rush to bathe and dress and be ready before the first guests arrived. Mary Gwynn and her family came about 8:30. Miss Brinien, the caterer, arrived and took over the pantry. The orchestra appeared and began tuning up in the hall. Everything went according to schedule. Ma kept Runzy on her leash. At 9. the music started and F. (in blue lace), Mary Gwynn (in pink chiffon) and I (in Palm Beach dinner jacket) took up our places in the parlor to receive our guests. They were slow arriving—dancing started about 9:30. A nice good-looking crowd of youngsters—many from Savannah. William managed traffic outside (70 cars) and the floodlights made the yard bright as day. By 10:30 I released Mary Gwynn from the reception line as most of our 200 guests had arrived. The dancing was going good—and so was the punch, which Mrs. Cohen had made mostly out of corn whiskey. Back in the nursery Harry H. and I began serving highballs—a regular bar at the wash stand. A tedious job which took me away from the fun of the party. Rum-pots gathered in the nursery and drank and drank and I grew disgusted. A crisis developed about the supper: Uncle Henry and Mrs. Cohen began asking for food at 11:15 p.m.—but Mary Gwynn and her Catholic family couldn't eat ham and chicken salad until after midnight. Service began about 11:30—and the Catholics had to wait half an hour. . . . I drank no punch, ate no supper, took no highballs—kept myself empty and well. I danced only with F., Mary Gwynn, Sarah Simkins and Margaretta Black (I forgot to say she and Aunt Nita arrived about 8:30). I complimented Sybil on her handwriting. Later she consulted me on her career—and I distressed her by advising her to take a newspaper

2. On his European trip in 1836–1837, James Henry Hammond had become so entranced with Naples and its bay that he commissioned an artist to paint five water-colors of the area, including one of Vesuvius all asmoke. These pictures were hung on the east side of the main hall. JHH "List of Paintings"; JHH Diary of European Trip, 1836–1837; JHH Traveling Account, May 1836–Nov. 1837, JHH Papers; MS vol. bd., 1887–1939. History of Redcliffe, John Shaw Billings Scrapbook Collection, SCL.

job.—I relieved Ma several times of Runzy, taking her for little walks outside. . . . Six quarts of whiskey were consumed in nursery—and half a dozen drunks remained, terrible fellows, including Red Cohen Jr. I got mad about 12:30 and "closed the bar," serving nothing more. I hate souses who spoil the landscape! Mary Gwynn asked me to let the party run from 1 to 1:30—I agreed. It is better to stop a dance when it is going good than to let it drag out till dawn—I was in the parlor when I heard something in the hall that sounded like the start of Big Apple. I feared this dance lest its vibration shake Redcliffe disastrously. Mad clean through, I dashed into the hall, banged on the piano, stopped the music and broke up the dance. Later Mary Gwynn apologized for starting the Big Apple against my wishes. . . . At 1:30 "Home Sweet Home" was played and by 2 all our guests were gone. F. and I stood in the hall to tell them all good night. Much post--mortem talk—and we got to bed at 3 a.m. The dance, I think, was a success—and worthy of Redcliffe which never looked better.[3]

3. A local columnist wrote that Redcliffe, that evening, was a thing of beauty. "The minute you drove through the avenue of huge magnolia trees and caught a glimpse of the three-story home, resplendent in the bright lights, you felt transported back to the days when the beaus and belles of the fifties gathered there for gay parties. . . . Last night's guests marvelled at the solid silver hinges on the doors, the mantels and bookcases of native woods, the prism crystal chandeliers, the silver one in the downstairs hall, the four poster canopy bed. . . . The last notes of the final dance music came all too soon, and back came the guests to the land of reality after a short sojourn into that of make believe." The *Augusta Herald*, May 1, 1938.

Epilogue

John Shaw Billings became editorial director of all publications of Time, Inc. in July 1944, but he never was happy in that exalted position. In a letter of resignation to Luce he drafted in 1946, he explained his dissatisfaction: "I should quit. I am not doing anything. You have nothing really for me to do." It was a job in which he felt "soggy and stale." So why stay on? "I have no children to keep me to the treadmill for money," nor did he strive for fame. His motivation for accepting the position seems to have been that he had expected to be in regular contact with Henry Luce whom he deeply admired. "But it hasn't worked out that way. I rarely see you—you only grunt at me—you don't talk or listen. So all the stuffing has gone out of me."[1] Never having received the personal praise or attention he craved, he wanted to go to South Carolina and "sit down and read the books that I've meant to read for years."[2] However, he never sent Luce the letter.

In 1948, at age fifty, Billings wrote again in this moody vein. He confided that he had nothing more to look forward to, that he had about all the worldly goods he craved, and that he would never be richer than he was then with "about $150,000 before taxes." Furthermore, he did not want Luce's job, for he got no pleasure out of "boss[ing] people around intellectually." Nor, he confessed, was he any longer "dedicated to my job to make Time-Life-Fortune better." Perhaps, he mused, if he had children, they might have given a focus to

1. "Views on My Job and Henry Luce," Dec. 1946, The Time-Life-Fortune Papers, SCL.
2. Ibid.

his life. For "if you have any children you can live for and through them, their triumphs and successes are vicariously yours. You can enjoy their graduations, their marriages, the coming of their children; you can suffer their tragedies, deaths, divorce. I have none of this. I even have no temptation to be a dissolute rake."[3]

Three years later, on his fifty-third birthday, he wrote gloomily that he felt age enveloping him "like a night fog." He saw himself sometimes "lying in a coffin in the Redcliffe parlor—but I cannot make out my own face and determine my age." As for Redcliffe, he wondered why he worked and worried over it. "I have no heirs; no dynasty will follow me to enjoy its grace and traditions. It is indeed a monument, but not to me."[4] As his disenchantment with all his surroundings deepened he wrote, "I've fallen out of love with Redcliffe and never want to see it again." For Redcliffe he compared to "a woman you have divorced but still pay alimony to. Redcliffe now just means work and worry."[5]

He finally fought off his depression with his announcement to Luce, in April 1954, that since he was no longer happy in his work, was fifty-six years old and feeling "creaky," and had a wife who suffered from hypertension, it was time to quit and get away for good. Luce did not try to persuade him to stay on. Billings registered his disappointment at Luce's farewell after more than twenty-five years: "What a stinking parting! I was deeply depressed at his failure to say one kind friendly word in farewell."[6] Nevertheless, he was "free at last!" on an annual pension of $18,000 to $20,000, and stock holdings in Time that were worth more than a million and a half dollars before his death. Luce did comment on Billings's retirement to Allen Grover, a *Time* and *Fortune* editor, that "John wanted to be Robinson Crusoe, and he seems to be having his wish."[7]

Extremely happy in his retirement at Redcliffe, Billings may have sounded very much like Robinson Crusoe. He wrote a friend, "I refuse to leave Redcliffe for any purpose or any place for profit or for pleasure."[8] Friends and relatives flocked to Redcliffe. Moreover, Bill-

3. "Selected Miscellaneous Written Passages, 1921–1969," John Shaw Billings Miscellaneous Collection, SCL.
4. Ibid., May 11, 1951.
5. John Shaw Billings Diary, Feb. 27, 1953, John Shaw Billings Papers, SCL.
6. Ibid., April 13 and May 3, 1954.
7. Ibid., Feb. 28, 1967; Allen Grover to John Shaw Billings, July 1, 1954, The Time-Life-Fortune Papers, SCL. See also: Henry Luce to John Shaw Billings, July 2, 1954, ibid.
8. John Shaw Billings to Daniel Longwell, July 12, 1955, The Time-Life-Fortune Papers, SCL.

ings for almost two decades collected and put in order the family correspondence and exhaustively searched out obscure family members,
places, and events in an effort to put together the complicated history
of the Hammond-Bryan-Cumming families. That work was still incom-
plete when his health failed. Before then, however, the last of Emily
and Harry Hammond's children died. Uncle Henry went at ninety-two
in 1961, and in May 1962, at the age of eighty-nine, "Uncle Alf Hammond died . . . just stopped breathing, the last of his generation."[9]
Frederica, whose health had never been good, suffered a series of heart
attacks and strokes and lived in a haze of drugs until she died in March
1963. Billings was now very much alone at Redcliffe. A month after
Frederica's death, he wrote that "physically I had long ago learned to
take care of myself in Redcliffe, without any help from her. But spirit-
ually she was a great help and comfort to me in all things. Now that
she is gone I am left in a spiritual solitude—a great silence lacking even
an echo from beyond."[10]

Less than six months after Frederica's death, John Billings, like his
father before him, remarried. The second Mrs. Billings, Elise Lake
Chase, a native of South Carolina, was the widow of James Mitchell
Chase, a lawyer and Congressman from Pennsylvania. Her husband
had died more than eighteen years before. Billings insisted this was no
sudden "youthful" romance on his part, for Elise, five years his senior,
had been Frederica's friend since 1917, and he had known her for over
thirty years.[11] Like Frederica, Elise, a retiring, shy person, preferred the
background to the foreground of Billings's life. With his new wife, Billings felt the "terrible days of loneliness in this big empty house" were
over, and "I can live again."[12]

The next decade at Redcliffe was one of happiness and companionship. Billings, knowing that there was no dynasty to follow him and
Elise at Redcliffe, gave the estate in 1973 to the State of South Carolina
so it could be enjoyed by all South Carolinians—all of them would be
the heirs to his great-grandfather's legacy. Also in 1973, he donated his

9. John Shaw Billings Diary, July 26, 1961, May 2, 1962, John Shaw Billings Papers, SCL.
10. April 1963, John Shaw Billings Miscellaneous Collection, SCL.
11. John Shaw Billings to Aunt Clara [Black], Aug. 5, 1963, Mr. and Mrs. John Shaw Billings Papers, SCL; *Biographical Directory of the American Congress 1774–1949* (Washington: U.S. Government Printing Office, 1950), p. 968.
12. John Shaw Billings to Aunt Clara [Black], Aug. 5, 1963, Mr. and Mrs. John Shaw Billings Papers, SCL.

books, his manuscripts, and his film collections to the University of South Carolina. For his generosity he received an honorary Doctor of Laws degree from his grandfather's and his great grandfather's alma mater. Of that ceremony on May 11, 1974, he wrote, "of course I did not go. I am an old man crippled by arthritis. . . . The day was last Saturday—my 76th birthday. But I would not have gone had I been 20 years younger. It was just tit for tat: I gave a lot of Great Grandfather's books and they gave me an honorary degree." He wrote, "LL.Ds are common as pig tracks—now if it had been a D.C.L. like grandfather Billings."[13]

On his next birthday, his seventy-seventh, he wrote his brother Henry that he was growing very old—"the woes of old age and little or no hope that you get over it."[14] He died three months later on August 25, 1975, and was buried in the cemetery at Redcliffe.

Redcliffe, at John Shaw Billings's death, passed to the state of South Carolina. It was indeed, in the end, to be a monument.

13. LL.D., Doctor of Laws; D.C.L., Doctor of Civil Law; John Shaw Billings to Henry Billings, May 13, 1974, private papers in the possession of Henry Billings, Sag Harbor, New York.
14. Ibid., May 1975.

Bibliography

I. *Manuscripts*

Account Book of Paul F. Hammond and His Son Claude, 1882–1884. Hammond-Bryan-Cumming Family Papers, SCL.

The Adams Family of Augusta. Loose Papers, John Shaw Billings Papers, SCL.

Robert Francis Withers Allston Papers. SCHS.

James Henry Billings Papers. Private Possession of James Henry Billings, Sag Harbor, New York.

John Shaw Billings, comp. "The Adams Family of Augusta [Genealogy]." Loose Papers, John Shaw Billings Papers, SCL.

——————, comp. "Compilation of Silver Bluff, Cowden, and Redcliffe Land Papers." Album C., James Henry Hammond Papers, SCL.

——————, comp. "File on Willy Hammond." Miscellaneous Collection, John Shaw Billings Papers, SCL.

——————, comp. "History of the Hammond, Fox and Spann Families, with special attention to James Henry Hammond and information on Silver Bluff, Cowden, and Redcliffe Plantations." Hammond-Bryan-Cumming Family Papers, SCL.

——————, comp. "The Lamar Family [Genealogy]." Loose Papers, John Shaw Billings Papers, SCL.

——————, comp. "Notes on Charlotte Walker." John Shaw Billings Papers, SCL.

——————, comp. "Notes on Christopher Fitzsimons (1762–1825)." John Shaw Billings Papers, SCL.

——————, comp. "Random Recollections of Henry C. Hammond." Hammond-Bryan-Cumming Family Papers, SCL.

——————, comp. "Red Letter Baby Book." John Shaw Billings Papers, SCL.

——————, comp. "Woolsey Genealogy." John Shaw Billings Papers, SCL.

John Shaw Billings Diaries (77 vols.), 1910–1972. SCL.

John Shaw Billings Loose Papers. SCL.

John Shaw Billings Miscellaneous Collection. SCL.

John Shaw Billings Papers. SCL.

John Shaw Billings Papers. In private possession of Henry Billings, Sag Harbor, New York.

John Shaw Billings Scrapbook Collection. 75 vols., SCL.

John Shaw Billings and Frederica Wade Billings Papers. SCL.

Phillips Brooks Folder. Harvard University Archives, Cambridge.

Clement Claiborne Clay Papers. Duke.

Major Joseph B. Cumming. "A Sketch of Descendants of David Cumming of Inverness, Scotland. . . ." A printed copy in the possession of Joseph B. Cumming, Augusta, Georgia.

Thomas Jones Davies Papers, 1784–1907. SCL.

Thomas Jones Davies Scrapbook, 1849–1903. SCL.

Elizabeth Hammond Eve. "Notes," Arranged by John Shaw Billings. Loose Papers, John Shaw Billings Papers. SCL.

Faculty Minutes. University of Georgia, August 1, 1860. University of Georgia Archives, Athens.

Farmer's Club Records, 1846–1934. Beech Island, Aiken County. 2 vols., SCL.

William Hawkins Ferris Manuscripts. Rare Book and Manuscript Library, CU.

Arthur Gilman Private Records. Radcliffe College Archives, Cambridge.

[South Carolina] Governors' Papers, 1877–1890. SCDAH.

Hammond-Bryan-Cumming Family Papers. SCL.

Hammond-Bryan-Cumming Family Papers. Legal Size. SCL.

Christopher Fitzsimons Hammond Diary, 1888. SCL.

E. Spann Hammond Diary, 1852. E. Spann Hammond Papers, SCL.

E. Spann Hammond Diary 1857–1858. E. Spann Hammond Papers, SCL.

E. Spann Hammond Letterpress Book. E. Spann Hammond Papers, SCL.

E. Spann Hammond Scrapbook. E. Spann Hammond Papers, SCL.

Hammond Family Account Book, 1883–1885. James Henry Hammond Family Collection, SCL.

Harry Hammond Account Books (13), 1865–1914. Hammond-Bryan-Cumming Family Papers, SCL.

Harry Hammond Plantation Journal. Hammond-Bryan-Cumming Family Papers, SCL.

Harry Hammond, Speculative Notes, No. 1, 1873–1900. Hammond-Bryan-Cumming Family Papers, SCL.

James Henry Hammond Business Papers, 1848–1862. James Henry Hammond Papers, SCL.

James Henry Hammond Diary, August 6, 1836–April 7, 1837, with specimens of bills paid while traveling in Europe. James Henry Hammond Papers, SCL.

James Henry Hammond Diary of European Trip 1836–1837. James Henry Hammond Papers, SCL.

James Henry Hammond List of Paintings. James Henry Hammond Papers, SCL.

James Henry Hammond Orchard Diary. James Henry Hammond Papers, SCL.

James Henry Hammond Papers. Duke.

James Henry Hammond Papers. LC.

James Henry Hammond Papers. SCL.

James Henry Hammond Papers. SHC.

James Henry Hammond Plantation Journal. James Henry Hammond Papers, SCL.

James Henry Hammond Plantation Records 1856–1887. James Henry Hammond Papers, SCL.

James Henry Hammond Traveling Account May 1836–November 1837. James Henry Hammond Papers, SCL.

Julia B. Hammond Diary, December 9, 1877–September 1, 1878. Hammond-Bryan-Cumming Family Papers, SCL.

Marcellus C.M. Hammond Folder. SCL.

Marcellus C.M. Hammond Papers. SCL.

Marcellus C.M. Hammond, Volume 1837–1883. Marcellus C.M. Hammond Papers, SCL.

Kathwood Manufacturing Company, Beech Island Papers, 1896–1901, 1904. SCL.

Minutes of the Beech Island Farmer's Club, Beech Island, South Carolina. SCL.

Minutes of the Proceedings of the Board of Trustees of the University of Georgia November 8, 1858–August 1, 1860. University of Georgia Archives, Athens.

New England Women's Club. Club Histories Folder. Manuscripts, Schlesinger Library, Radcliffe College, Cambridge.

New England Women's Club Papers, 1868–1970. Schlesinger Library, Radcliffe College, Cambridge.

Photograph Album, 1741–1955. Hammond-Bryan-Cumming Family Papers, SCL.

Francis Wilkinson Pickens Collection. SCL.

Arthur Ravenel Collection. SCHS.

Silver Bluff Plantation Slave Lists, 1843, 1845, 1853, and 1863. James Henry Hammond Plantation Journal, James Henry Hammond Papers, SCL.

The Time-Life-Fortune Papers of John Shaw Billings. SCL.

II. Newspapers

The Aiken [S.C.] *Journal and Review.*

The Aiken Sentinel.

The Atlanta Constitution.

The Augusta Chronicle.

The Augusta Herald.

The Boston Evening Transcript.

The Boston Globe.

The Cambridge Chronicle.

The Cambridge Transcript.

The Cambridge Tribune.

The Charleston Mercury.

The Charleston News and Courier.

The Greenwood [S.C.] *Index.*

The New York Herald.

The New York Herald Tribune.

The New York Times.

The State [Columbia, S.C.].

The Taunton [Mass.] *Daily Gazette.*

III. Government Documents

Barnwell District Tax Returns, October 1864. SCDAH.

Birth and Death Certificates. Office of Vital Statistics. John W. McCormick Building, Boston.

Compiled Service Records of Confederate Soldiers Who Served in Organizations from the State of South Carolina, Roll 273, Fourteenth Infantry, H-K. Microcopy no. 267. Washington: National Archives Microfilm Publications, 1958.

Edgefield County, South Carolina. Equity Records, Roll 2630. Filmed by the Genea-
logical Society, Salt Lake City, Utah.
Edgefield County, South Carolina. Record of Deeds, 1853–1855. SCDAH.
Edgefield County Wills, 1852–1866. SCDAH.
Edgefield District Inventories, Appraisements and Sales Book 1858–1866. Microfilm
copy in SCDAH.
Edgefield District Tax Returns, October 1864. SCDAH.
Geognastic Map of Abbeville District, South Carolina, 1860.
Richmond County Wills and Inventories. Richmond County Court House, Augusta,
Georgia.
South Carolina State Board of Agriculture. *South Carolina Resources and Population,
Institutions, and Industries.* Charleston: Walker, Evans and Cogswell Printers,
1883.
U.S. Census, 1850, 1860, 1870, 1880, 1900. Washington: Government Printing Of-
fice.
U.S. Congress, Senate. *Congressional Globe,* 1858–1861.
U.S. Department of Agriculture, Office of Experiment Stations. *The Cotton Plant: Its
History, Botany, Chemistry, Culture, Enemies and Uses.* Washington: Govern-
ment Printing Office, 1896.
U.S. Department of Education. *Report of the Commissioner of Education for the Year
1879.* Washington: Government Printing Office, 1881.
—————. *Report of the Commissioner of Education for the Year 1880.* Washington:
Government Printing Office, 1882.
—————. *Report of the Commissioner of Education for the Year 1881.* Washington:
Government Printing Office, 1883.
—————. *Report of the Commissioner of Education for the Year 1882–83.* Washing-
ton: Government Printing Office, 1884.
*War of the Rebellion: A Compilation of the Official Records of the Union and Confed-
erate Armies.* 128 vols. Washington: Government Printing Office, 1880–1901.

IV. *Dissertations and Theses*

Blake, Russell L. "Ties of Intimacy: Social Values and Personal Relationships of Ante-
bellum Slaveholders." Ph.D. dissertation, University of Michigan, 1978.
Corley, Florence. "The Canals and Railroads in the Development of Ante-Bellum Au-
gusta, Georgia." Independent Study Program paper, Agnes Scott College, June
1954.
Dunbar, Arabella Sumter. "The History of the Development of Education in Beech
Island, South Carolina." M.A. thesis, University of South Carolina, 1929.
German, Richard Henry Lee. "The Queen City of the Savannah: Augusta, Georgia
During the Urban Progressive Era 1890–1917." Ph.D. dissertation, University
of Florida, 1971.
Marcus, Ann. "The Letters of Julia Bryan Hammond Written While Studying at the
Harvard Annex in 1881." Independent Study Paper, Colgate University, De-
cember 1976.
Thogersen, Harriet. "Katharine Fitzsimons Hammond, 'The Change That Didn't Hap-
pen.' " Graduate History Paper, University of South Carolina, December 1976.
Tucker, Robert C. "James Henry Hammond, South Carolinian." Ph.D. dissertation,
University of North Carolina, 1958.

Werner, Randolph. "Hegemony and Conflict: The Political Economy of a Southern Region, Augusta, Georgia, 1865–1895." Ph.D. dissertation, University of Virginia, 1977.

Whatley, William. "A History of the Textile Development of Augusta, Georgia 1865–1883." M.A. Thesis, University of South Carolina, 1964.

Williams, William Bates. "John Shaw Billings: The Man Behind the Editor." M.A. thesis, University of South Carolina, 1978.

Williamson, Gustavus. "Cotton Manufacturing in South Carolina, 1865–1892." Ph.D. dissertation, Johns Hopkins University, 1954.

V. *Interviews*

Billings, Henry. Sag Harbor, New York. Interview, June 21, July 19, August 29, 1979, and January 27, 1980.

Cobb, Eugene. South Carolina Department of Parks, Recreation, and Tourism, Redcliffe, Beech Island. Interview, January 6, 1979.

Edmunds, Marion. South Carolina Department of Parks, Recreation, and Tourism, Edgar A. Brown Building, Columbia. Interview, January 6, 1979, August 4, 1980.

Foley, Michael. South Carolina Department of Parks, Recreation, and Tourism, Edgar A. Brown Building, Columbia. Telephone Interview, January 5, 1979, Interview, August 4, 1980.

Helm, Mrs. Leslie. Augusta, Georgia. Interview, July 30, 1979.

Jordan, Margaret. Columbia, South Carolina. Interview, January 20, 1979.

Knowles, Jane. Radcliffe College Archives, Radcliffe College, Cambridge. Interview, December 18, 1978.

Suber, Katharine Hammond. Kathwood Plantation, Jackson, South Carolina. Interview, July 31, 1979.

Wates, Wylma. South Carolina Department of Archives and History, Columbia. Interview, August 8, 1979.

VI. *Gravestones*

Gravestones in Beech Island Cemetery. Beech Island, South Carolina.

Gravestones in Magnolia Cemetery. Augusta, Georgia.

Gravestones in Mt. Zion Cemetery. Sparta, Georgia.

VII. *Articles*

Artz, Curtis P., and Artz, Mary E. "Caroline Hampton Halsted: A Lady Who Broke Traditions." *Sandlapper*, September 1973, pp. 53–58.

"Dr. John Shaw Billings, Director of the New York Public Library, 1896–1913." *The Bulletin of the New York Public Library*, April 1913.

Briggs, Le Baron Russell. "An Experiment in Faith: Radcliffe College." *Atlantic Monthly*, January 1929, pp. 185–89.

Bunce, O.B. "Augusta, Georgia." *Appletons' Journal of Literature, Science and Art*, September 23, 1871, pp. 352–54, reprinted in *Richmond County History*, Summer 1972, pp. 33–36.

————. "The Savannah at Augusta." *Appletons' Journal of Literature, Science and*

Art, November 18, 1871, pp. 575–77, reprinted in *Richmond County History*, Summer 1972, pp. 37–39.

Byerly, W.E. "Arthur Gilman and the Harvard Annex." *Harvard Graduates' Magazine*, March 1910.

Carlton, Mary Gillies. "A Brief Sketch of the Life of Arthur Gilman." Copy in Radcliffe College Archives, Cambridge.

Cashin, Edward J. "Summerville, Retreat of the Old South." *Richmond County History*, Summer 1973, pp. 44–59.

Dickinson, Ellen E. "The Harvard Annex for Women." *Domestic Monthly*, March 1884.

Franz, Caroline Jones. "Johns Hopkins." *American Heritage*, February 1976, pp. 31–33, 98–102.

Hayne, Paul H. "Aiken, South Carolina." *Appletons' Journal*, December 2, 1871, pp. 623–26.

Howard, Mary E. "It Happened Seventy-Five Years Ago." *Radcliffe Quarterly*, November 1954.

"Johns Hopkins: An Informal Picture of Its Institutions, 1876–1976." *Johns Hopkins Magazine*, May 1976, pp. 37–52.

Johnson, Michael P. "Planters and Patriarchy: Charleston, 1800–1860." *The Journal of Southern History*, February 1980, pp. 45–72.

"Life of the Great Divine." *Boston Herald*, n.d., in Phillips Brooks folder, Harvard University Archives, Cambridge.

Scott, Anne Firor. "Women's Perspective on the Patriarchy in the 1850's." *The Journal of American History*, June 1974, pp. 52–64.

Shore, Debra. "John Shaw Billings: Hopkins' Forgotten Soldier." *Johns Hopkins Magazine*, November 1975, pp. 20–34.

——————. "The Launching of a Love Affair: Daniel Coit Gilman and the American University." *Johns Hopkins Magazine*, May 1976, pp. 18–36.

"Surgeon-Bibliophile." *MD*, April 1976, pp. 115–20.

Taylor, Rosser H., ed. "Boyce-Hammond Correspondence." *Journal of Southern History*, August 1937, pp. 348–54.

Thayer, William Roscoe. "Memoir of Lucien Carr." *Massachusetts Historical Society Proceedings*, November 1915.

Werner, Joseph. "Radcliffe College." *Harvard Graduates' Magazine*, 1894.

Wiener, Jonathan M. "Planter Persistence and Social Change: Alabama, 1850–1870." *Journal of Interdisciplinary History*, Autumn 1976, pp. 235–60.

Wiley, Franklin B. "All About the Annex." *The Boston Evening Transcript*, November 14, 1891.

Woodward, Mary V. "Women's Education in the South." *Educational Review*, May 1894, pp. 466–78.

VIII. *Books, Pamphlets, and Published Proceedings*

"Aiken, South Carolina History." Copy in Pamphlet Collection, SCL.

Alvord, Brigadier General Benjamin. "Biographical Sketch from the Life of M.C.M. Hammond." Copy in Pamphlet Collection, SCL.

Ariés, Philippe. *Centuries of Childhood*. Translated by Robert Baldick. New York: Alfred A. Knopf, 1962.

The Arts Committee of the Junior League of Augusta, Georgia, comp. *Augusta Yesterday and Today*, 2nd ed. Augusta, 1951.

Benedict, Michael Les. *A Compromise of Principle: Congressional Republicans and Reconstruction, 1863–1869.* New York: W.W. Norton and Company, 1974.

Billings, John Shaw, comp. *Descendants of James Henry Hammond of South Carolina.* New York: By the Author, 1934.

Biographical Directory of the American Congress, 1774–1961. Washington: Government Printing Office, 1961.

Biographical Souvenir of the States of Georgia and Florida. Chicago: F.A. Battey and Company, 1889.

Blassingame, John W. *The Slave Community: Plantation Life in the Antebellum South* New York: Oxford University Press, 1972.

Boston Almanac and Business Directory. Boston: Sampson and Davenport and Co., 1881.

Brodman, Estelle. *The Development of Medical Biography.* Baltimore: Medical Library Association, 1954.

Brooks, Ulysses Robert. *South Carolina Bench and Bar.* Columbia: The State Company, 1908.

Brown, W. Norman. *Johns Hopkins Half-Century Directory.* Baltimore: Johns Hopkins University, 1926.

Buel, Clarence C., and Johnson, Robert U., eds. *Battles and Leaders of the Civil War.* 4 vols. New York: The Century Company, 1884.

Bulloch, Joseph. *A History and Genealogy of the Habersham Family.* Columbia: The R.L. Bryan Company, 1901

Caldwell, J.F.J. *A Memorial of Christian H. Suber.* Charleston, South Carolina: Walker, Evans and Cogswell Co., Printers, 1892.

——————. *The History of a Brigade of South Carolinians Known First as "Greggs" and Subsequently as "McGowan's Brigade."* Philadelphia: King and Baird Printers, 1866.

Cambridge Directory, 1881

Candler, Allen D., and Evans, Clement A. *Cyclopedia of Georgia.* 3 vols. Atlanta: State Historical Association, 1906.

Cauthen, Charles E., ed. *Family Letters of the Three Wade Hamptons, 1782–1901.* Columbia: University of South Carolina Press, 1953.

The Charleston City Directory, 1892. Charleston: Southern Directory and Publishing Company, 1892.

Chesnut, Mary Boykin. *A Diary from Dixie,* ed. by Ben Ames Williams. Boston: Houghton Mifflin Company, 1949.

Cleveland, Henry, ed. *Alexander H. Stephens in Public and Private With Letters and Speeches Before, During, and Since the War.* Philadelphia: National Publishing Company, 1866.

Coffin, Amory, and Geddings, W.H. *Aiken; or, Climate and Cure.* Charleston: Walker, Evans and Cogswell Printers, 1869.

Coleman, Kenneth, gen. ed. *A History of Georgia.* Athens: University of Georgia Press, 1977.

Converse, Florence. *The Story of Wellesley.* Boston: Little, Brown and Company, 1915.

Cooper, William J., Jr. *The Conservative Regime: South Carolina 1877–1890.* Baltimore: Johns Hopkins University Press, 1968.

——————. *The South and the Politics of Slavery, 1828–1856.* Baton Rouge: Louisiana State University Press, 1978.

Coulter, E. Merton. *College Life in the Old South.* New York: The Macmillan Company, 1928.

Cox, John, and Cox, LaWanda. *Politics, Principle, and Prejudice, 1865–1866: Dilemma of Reconstruction America*. New York: Free Press of Glencoe, 1963.

Cyclopedia of Eminent and Representative Men of the Carolinas of the Nineteenth Century, vol. 1. Madison, Wisconsin: Brant and Fuller, 1892.

Davidson, Chalmers Gaston. *The Last Foray; The South Carolina Planters of 1860: A Sociological Study*. Columbia: University of South Carolina Press, 1971.

DeCaradeuc, A. *Grape Culture and Wine Making in the South*. Augusta: D. Redmond, 1858.

Degler, Carl N. *At Odds: Women and the Family in America from the Revolution to the Present*. New York: Oxford University Press, 1980.

DeHuff, Elizabeth. *The Family of James Dunbar Our First Dunbar Ancestor in South Carolina*. n.p., 1954.

Derry, J.T. *Georgia: A Guide to Its Cities, Towns, Scenery, and Resources*. Philadelphia: J.P. Lippincott and Co., 1878.

Dock, Lavinia. *A Short History of Nursing from Earliest Times to the Present Day*. New York: G. P. Putnam and Sons, 1938.

Donald, David. *Charles Sumner and the Coming of the Civil War*. New York: Alfred A. Knopf, 1960.

Dorland, W.A. Newman. *The American Illustrated Medical Dictionary*. 20th ed. Philadelphia and London: W.B. Saunders Company, 1947.

Douglas, Ann. *The Feminization of American Culture*. New York: Alfred A. Knopf, 1977.

Duberman, Martin. *James Russell Lowell*. Boston: Houghton, Mifflin Company, 1966.

Duffy, John. *A History of Public Health in New York City: 1866–1966*. New York: Russell Sage Foundation, 1974.

Dwight, Timothy. *Memories of Yale Life and Men*. New York: Dodd, Mead and Company, 1903.

Elliott, Maud H. *This Was My Newport*. Cambridge: The Mythology Company, 1944.

Estes, Claud. *List of Field Officers, Regiments and Battalions in the Confederate States Army 1861–1865*. Macon, Georgia: The J.W. Burke Co., 1912.

Evans, General Clement A., ed. *Confederate Military History*, vol. 5. Atlanta: Confederate Publishing Co., 1899.

Faunt, Joan Reynolds; Rector, Robert E.; and Bowden, David K., eds. *Biographical Directory of the South Carolina House of Representatives*. Vol. 1: *Sessions Lists 1692–1973*. Columbia: University of South Carolina Press, 1974.

Faust, Drew Gilpin. *A Sacred Circle: The Dilemma of the Intellectual of the Old South 1840–1860*. Baltimore: Johns Hopkins University Press, 1977.

Federal Writers Project. *Beaufort and the Sea Islands*. Savannah: The Clover Club, 1938.

Fielder, Herbert. *A Sketch of the Life and Times and Speeches of Joseph E. Brown*. Springfield, Massachusetts: Springfield Printing Company, 1883.

Fields, Annie. *Authors and Friends*. Boston: Houghton, Mifflin and Company, 1897.

Fischer, David Hackett. *Growing Old in America*. New York: Oxford University Press, 1977.

Foner, Eric. *Free Soil, Free Labor, Free Men: The Ideology of the Republican Party Before the Civil War*. New York: Oxford University Press, 1970.

Foote, Shelby. *The Civil War: A Narrative*, 3 vols. New York: Random House, 1958–1974.

Franklin, John Hope. *A Southern Odyssey: Travelers in the Antebellum North*. Baton Rouge: Louisiana State University Press, 1976.

"Freedom in Kansas, Speech of William H. Seward in the Senate of the United States, March 3, 1858." Washington: Buell and Blanchard Printers, 1858.

Garlington, J.C. *Men of the Time: Sketches of Living Notables: A Biographical Encyclopedia of Contemporaneous South Carolina Leaders*. Spartanburg: Garlington Publishing Co., 1902.

Garrison, Fielding H. *John Shaw Billings, A Memoir*. New York: G.P. Putnam's Sons, 1915.

Genovese, Eugene. *Roll, Jordan, Roll: The World the Slaves Made*. New York: Pantheon Books, 1974.

Georgia Directory Co.'s Directory of Augusta, Georgia, 1898, vol. 14. Richmond, Virginia: J.L. Hill Printing Company, 1898.

Gilman, Arthur. *Private Collegiate Instruction for Women by Professors and Other Instructors of Harvard College, Second Year Reports of the Treasurer and Secretary, 1881*. Copy in Radcliffe College Archives, Cambridge.

——————. *The Society for the Collegiate Instruction of Women by Professors and Other Instructors of Harvard College, Ninth Year*. November 5, 1888. Copy in Radcliffe College Archives, Cambridge.

——————, ed. *The Cambridge of Eighteen Hundred and Ninety-Six*. Cambridge: Riverside Press, 1896.

Gordon, Michael, comp. *The American Family in Social-Historical Perspective*. New York: St. Martin's Press, 1973.

Grant, Ulysses S. *Personal Memoirs of U.S. Grant*. 2 vols. New York: Charles L. Webster and Company, 1885.

Greven, Philip J., Jr. *Four Generations: Population, Land, and Family in Colonial Andover, Massachusetts*. Ithaca: Cornell University Press, 1970.

——————. *The Protestant Temperament: Patterns of Child-Rearing, Religious Experience and the Self in Early America*. New York: Alfred Knopf, 1977.

Hammond, Harry. "Notes on Wine and Vine Culture in France." Copy in Agricultural Pamphlets, SCL.

——————. "Sketch of James Henry Hammond." Copy in Hammond-Bryan-Cumming Family Papers, SCL.

Hammond, Paul. "Memoirs of James Henry Hammond." Copy in Hammond-Bryan-Cumming Family Papers, SCL.

Hammond, Roland. *A History and Genealogy of the Descendants of William Hammond*. Boston: Clapp and Sons, 1894.

Hareven, Tamara K., ed. *Transitions: The Family and the Life Course in Historical Perspective*. New York: Academic Press, 1978.

Harvard College. *Harvard College Catalogues 1858–59, Lawrence Scientific School*. Cambridge: Harvard University, 1858–59.

——————. *Harvard College Class of 1856, Secretary's Report*, 1899. Cambridge: Riverside Press, 1899.

Harvard University. *Harvard University Directory*. Cambridge: Harvard University, 1910.

Heath, Milton Sydney. *Constructive Liberalism: The Role of the State in Economic Development in Georgia to 1860*. Cambridge: Harvard University Press, 1954.

Herbert, George. *Works in Prose and Verse*, ed. by Robert Aris Wilmott. New York: D. Appleton, 1857.

Historical Register of Harvard University 1636–1936. Cambridge: Harvard University Press, 1963.

Hollis, Daniel W. *University of South Carolina.* Vol. 1: *South Carolina College.* Columbia: University of South Carolina Press, 1951.

Holt, Michael F. *The Political Crisis of the 1850's.* New York: John Wiley and Sons, 1978.

Holt, Thomas. *Black Over White: Negro Political Leadership in South Carolina During Reconstruction.* Urbana: University of Illinois Press, 1977.

Johns, Ethel, and Pfefferkorn, Blanche. *The Johns Hopkins Hospital School of Nursing, 1889–1949.* Baltimore: Johns Hopkins Press, 1954.

Johns Hopkins University. *Daniel Coit Gilman, First President of the Johns Hopkins University, 1876–1901.* Baltimore: Johns Hopkins Press, 1908.

——————. *Reports of the Johns Hopkins Training School* Vol. 1: 1889–1901. Baltimore: Johns Hopkins Press, 1901.

Jones, Charles C., Jr., and Dutcher, Salem. *Memorial History of Augusta, Georgia.* Syracuse: D. Mason and Co., Publishers, 1890; reprint ed., Spartanburg, South Carolina: The Reprint Company, 1966.

Jones, Charles E., Jr. *A Confederate Roster of General Officers.* Richmond: Southern Historical Society, 1876.

Kaufman, Martin. *Homeopathy in America: The Rise and Fall of a Medical Heresy.* Baltimore: The Johns Hopkins Press, 1971.

Kett, Joseph F. *Rites of Passage: Adolescence in America 1790 to the Present.* New York: Basic Books, 1977.

Kirwan, Albert D. *John J. Crittenden: The Struggle for the Union.* Lexington: University of Kentucky Press, 1962.

Knight, Lucian Lamar. *A Standard History of Georgia and Georgians.* 6 vols. Chicago: The Lewis Publishing Company, 1917.

Koenig, Louis. *Bryan: A Political Biography of William Jennings Bryan.* New York: G.P. Putnam's Sons, 1971.

LaBorde, Maximilian. *History of the South Carolina College From Its Incorporation, December 19, 1801 to December 19, 1865.* 2nd ed. Charleston: Walker, Evans and Cogswell, 1874.

Laslett, Peter. *The World We Have Lost.* New York: Charles Scribner's Sons, 1965.

"List of Students at the Annex 1881–82." Radcliffe College Annual Reports, 1879/80–1907/08, Schlesinger Library, Radcliffe College, Cambridge.

Litwack, Leon F. *Been in the Storm So Long: The Aftermath of Slavery.* New York: Alfred A. Knopf, 1979.

MacCallum, W.G. *William Stewart Halsted.* Baltimore: Johns Hopkins Press, 1930.

McCord, David. *An Acre for Education: Being Notes on the History of Radcliffe College.* Rev. ed. Cambridge: Crimson Printing Company, 1958.

MacDowell, Dorothy K. "Beech Island, South Carolina: Four Remarkable Centuries and More." Beech Island: Written Expressly for First National Bank, 1968. Copy in Pamphlet Collection, SCL.

Malloy, Robert. *Charleston, A Gracious Heritage.* New York: D. Appleton and Company, 1947.

Marquis, Nelson, ed. *Who's Who in New England.* Chicago: A.N. Marquis and Co., 1909.

Massachusetts: A Guide to Its Places and People. Boston: Houghton, Mifflin Company, 1937.

Merritt, Elizabeth. *James Henry Hammond 1807–1864.* Baltimore: The Johns Hopkins Press, 1923.

Mitchell, Broadus. *William Gregg: Factory Master of the Old South*. Chapel Hill: University of North Carolina Press, 1928.

Moore, Andrew Charles, comp. *Alumni Records*. 7 vols. Columbia: University of South Carolina, 1905.

Morison, Samuel, ed. *The Development of Harvard University Since the Inauguration of President Eliot, 1869–1929*. Cambridge: Harvard University Press, 1930.

————. *Three Centuries of Harvard 1636–1936*. Cambridge: Harvard University Press, 1936.

Myers, Robert M., ed. *The Children of Pride: A True Story of Georgia and the Civil War*. New Haven: Yale University Press, 1972.

The New England Female Medical College. *14th Annual Catalogue and Report of the New England Female Medical College*. 1862. Copy in Boston University Archives.

Northen, William, ed. *Men of Mark in Georgia*. 7 vols. Atlanta: A.B. Caldwell Publishers, 1907.

Nuermberger, Ruth Ketring. *The Clays of Alabama: A Planter-Lawyer-Politician Family*. Lexington: University of Kentucky Press, 1958.

Nutting, M.A. *A History of Nursing; The Evolution of Nursing System from Earliest Times*. New York: G.P. Putnam and Co., 1907.

Oliphant, Mary C.; Odell, Alfred Taylor; and Eaves, T.C., eds. *The Letters of William Gilmore Simms*. 5 vols. Columbia: University of South Carolina Press, 1952–1956.

Paterson, George. *The Destructive Freshets and Floods of the Savannah River: Their Causes*. Augusta, Georgia: Printed by J.M. Richards, 1889.

Percy, Townsend, comp. *Appleton's Dictionary of New York and Vicinity*. New York: D. Appleton and Company, 1879.

Perkins, Dexter. *The Monroe Doctrine 1826–1867*. Baltimore: The Johns Hopkins Press, 1933; reprint ed., Gloucester, Mass.: Peter Smith, 1965.

Perry, Lewis. *Childhood, Marriage, and Reform: Henry Clarke Wright 1797–1870*. Chicago: University of Chicago Press, 1979.

Pope, Thomas H. *The History of Newberry County, South Carolina*. Vol. 1: 1749–1860. Columbia: University of South Carolina Press, 1973.

Randall, James G., and Donald, David H. *The Civil War and Reconstruction*. 2nd ed. Boston: D.C. Heath, 1961.

Ransom, Roger L., and Sutch, Richard. *One Kind of Freedom: The Economic Consequences of Emancipation*. Cambridge: Cambridge University Press, 1977.

Ravenel, Henry Edmund. *Ravenel Records*. Atlanta: The Franklin Printing and Publishing Co., 1898.

Reynolds, Emily B., and Faunt, Joan Reynolds, eds. *Biographical Directory of the Senate of the State of South Carolina, 1776–1964*. Columbia: South Carolina Archives Department, 1964.

Roark, James L. *Masters Without Slaves: Southern Planters in the Civil War and Reconstruction*. New York: W.W. Norton and Company, 1977.

Rose, Willie Lee. *Rehearsal for Reconstruction: The Port Royal Experiment*. New York: Bobbs-Merrill Company, 1964.

Rothstein, William G. *American Physicians in the Nineteenth Century: From Sects to Science*. Baltimore: The Johns Hopkins University Press, 1972.

Rowland, A. Ray, ed. *Historical Markers of Richmond County, Georgia*. Rev. ed. Augusta: The Richmond County Historical Society, 1971.

Savitt, Todd L. *Medicine and Slavery: The Diseases and Health Care of Blacks in Antebellum Virginia.* Urbana: University of Illinois Press, 1978.

Scarborough, William K. *The Overseer: Plantation Management in the Old South.* Baton Rouge: Louisiana State University Press, 1966.

Schultz, Harold S. *Nationalism and Sectionalism in South Carolina 1852–1860: A Study of the Movement for Southern Independence.* Durham: Duke University Press, 1950.

Scott, Anne F. *The Southern Lady: From Pedestal to Politics, 1830–1930.* Chicago: University of Chicago Press, 1970.

Selections from the Letters and Speeches of the Hon. James H. Hammond of South Carolina. New York: John F. Trow and Co., Printers, 1866; reprint ed., Clyde N. Wilson, comp., Spartanburg, South Carolina: The Reprint Company, 1978.

Sholes' Dictionary of the City of Charleston, 1882. Charleston: Sholes and Co. Publisher, 1882.

Shorter, Edward. *The Making of the Modern Family.* New York: Basic Books, 1975.

Simkins, Francis B. *Pitchfork Ben Tillman.* Baton Rouge: Louisiana State University Press, 1944.

Simkins, Francis B., and Woody, Robert H. *South Carolina During Reconstruction.* Chapel Hill: University of North Carolina Press, 1932.

Simpson, R.W. *History of Old Pendleton District.* Anderson, South Carolina: Oulla Printing and Binding Company, 1913.

Smith, Alfred Glaze, Jr. *Economic Readjustment of an Old Cotton State: South Carolina, 1820–1860.* Columbia: University of South Carolina Press, 1958.

Snowden, Yates. *History of South Carolina.* 2 vols. New York: The Lewis Publishing Company, 1920.

The Society for the Collegiate Instruction of Women Commonly called "The Harvard Annex" The Story of Its Beginnings and Growth, Its Organizations and Present Supporters, The Scholastic and Social Life of Its Students, Etc. Cambridge: W.H. Wheeler, Printer, 1891.

Spiller, Robert E. *et al. Literary History of the United States.* 2 vols. 3rd ed. rev. New York: Macmillan Company, 1963.

Stampp, Kenneth M. *The Era of Reconstruction, 1865–1877.* New York: Alfred A. Knopf, 1965.

——————. *The Peculiar Institution: Slavery in the Ante-Bellum South.* Alfred A. Knopf, 1956.

The Statistical History of the United States from Colonial Times to the Present. Stamford, Connecticut: Fairfield Publishers, Inc., 1965.

Steadman, Joseph Earle. *A History of the Spann Family with Attached Hammond Connections, Compiled by Edward Spann Hammond from the Notes of James H. Hammond.* n.p., 1967.

Sterling, Ada, ed. *A Belle of the Fifties: Memoirs of Mrs. Clay of Alabama, Covering Social and Political Life in Washington and the South 1853–66.* New York: Doubleday, Page and Company, 1904.

Stevens, W. LeConte. *The Admission of Women to Universities.* New York: S.W. Green's Sons, 1883.

Stone, Lawrence. *The Family, Sex and Marriage in England, 1500–1800.* New York: Harper and Row, 1977.

Thompson, William Y. *Robert Toombs of Georgia.* Baton Rouge: Louisiana State University Press, 1966.

Tindall, George Brown. *The Emergence of the New South, 1913–1945.* Baton Rouge: Louisiana State University Press, 1967.

Trumbach, Randolph. *The Rise of the Egalitarian Family: Aristocratic Kinship and Domestic Relations in Eighteenth-Century England.* New York: Academic Press, 1978.

Tuther, T., Jr. *Tuther's Augusta Directory for 1861.* Augusta, Georgia: Steampower Press Chronicle and Sentinel, 1861.

Union Club, New York City. *Officers, Members, Constitution and Rules of the Union Club of the City of New York.* New York: Club House, 1925.

Vinovskis, Maris A., ed. *Studies in American Historical Demography.* New York: Academic Press, 1979.

Wakelyn, Jon L. *Biographical Dictionary of the Confederacy.* Westport: Greenwood Press, 1977.

Walker, Anne Kendrick. *Braxton Bragg Comer His Family Tree From Virginia's Colonial Days.* Richmond: The Dietz Press, Inc., 1947.

Wallace, David Duncan. *The History of South Carolina.* 4 vols. New York: American Historical Society, 1934.

Walsh, William H. *Walsh's Columbia South Carolina City Directory for 1911.* Charleston: The Walsh Directory Company, Inc., 1911.

—————. *Walsh's Directory of the City of Augusta, Georgia for 1902.* Charleston: W.H. Walsh Directory Co., 1902.

Wardlaw, D.L., and Burt, Armistead. "Report of the Committee on the Freedmen of South Carolina, October 25, 1865." Pamphlet Collection, SCL.

Warner, Ezra J. *Generals in Blue, Lives of the Union Commanders.* Baton Rouge: Louisiana State University Press, 1964.

White, George. *Statistics of the State of Georgia.* Savannah: W. Thorne Williams, 1849.

Whitehill, Walter M. *Boston: A Topographical History.* Cambridge: Belknap Press, 1959.

Wiley, Bell Irvin. *Confederate Women.* Westport: Greenwood Press, 1974.

Williamson, Joel. *After Slavery: The Negro in South Carolina During Reconstruction, 1861–1877.* Chapel Hill: The University of North Carolina Press, 1965.

Winsor, Justin, ed. *The Memorial History of Boston Including Suffolk County, Massachusetts.* 4 vols. Boston: James R. Osgood and Company, 1881.

Wood, W. Kirk, ed. *A Northern Daughter and a Southern Wife: The Civil War Reminiscences and Letters of Katharine H. Cumming 1860-1865.* Augusta: Richmond County Historical Society, 1976.

Woodward, C. Vann. *Origins of the New South, 1877–1913.* Baton Rouge: Louisiana State University Press, 1951.

—————, ed. *Mary Chestnut's Civil War.* New Haven: Yale University Press, 1981.

—————. *Tom Watson: Agrarian Rebel.* New York: Macmillan and Company, 1938.

Woodward, K., ed. *The Augusta Directory and City Advertiser For 1841.* Augusta, Georgia: Browne and McCaffey, 1841.

Woody, Thomas, ed. *A History of Women's Education in the United States.* 2 vols. New York: The Science Press, 1929.

Wright, General Marcus J. *General Officers of the Confederate Army.* New York: The Neale Publishing Company, 1911.

Index

Woolsey, John Munro (judge; s. of William W. Woolsey), his *Ulysses* decision, 361

Woolsey, Marie De Hertburn (d. of William W. Woolsey), 360

Woolsey, Theodore Dwight (president of Yale Univ.), 225

Woolsey, William Walton (nephew of preceding), 142, 216, 291, 297, 360; his Breeze Hill plantation, 225; letters from, 226, 232, 234, 286, 301, 323, 346, 360; letters to, 235, 291, 296, 298, 317, 329

Wright, Brig. Gen. A.R., 113

Yale University, 225

Yancey, William Lowndes (politician), 96-97

"Young America," 52, 59, 61, 85

Young, Ernest (student of Henry Adams), 184

Xenophon, 25